A History of the Later Roman Empire

From Arcadius to Irene (395 A.D. to 800 A.D.)

(Volume I)

J. B. Bury

Alpha Editions

This edition published in 2020

ISBN : 9789354010743

Design and Setting By
Alpha Editions
email - alphaedis@gmail.com

As per information held with us this book is in Public Domain.
This book is a reproduction of an important historical work. Alpha Editions uses the best technology to reproduce historical work in the same manner it was first published to preserve its original nature. Any marks or number seen are left intentionally to preserve its true form.

PREFACE

THERE is no period of history which has been so much obscured by incorrect and misleading titles as the period of the later Roman Empire. It is, I believe, more due to improper names than one might at first be disposed to admit, that the import of that period is so constantly misunderstood and its character so often misrepresented. For the first step towards grasping the history of those centuries through which the ancient evolved into the modern world is the comprehension of the fact that the old Roman Empire did not cease to exist until the year 1453. The line of Roman Emperors continued in unbroken succession from Octavius Augustus to Constantine Palaeologus.

Now this essential fact is obscured as far as language is able to obscure it by applying the name "Byzantine" or the name "Greek" to the Empire in its later stages. Historians who use the phrase "Byzantine Empire" are not very consistent or very precise as to the date at which the "Roman Empire" ends and the "Byzantine Empire" begins. Sometimes the line is drawn at the foundation of Constantinople by Constantine the Great, sometimes at the death of Theodosius the Great, sometimes at the reign of Justinian, sometimes (as by Finlay) at the accession of Leo the Isaurian; and the historian who adopts one line of division cannot assert that the historian who adopts a different line is wrong. For all such lines are purely arbitrary. No "Byzantine Empire" ever began to exist; the Roman Empire did not come to an end until 1453.

But, it may be objected, is it not true that the Roman

Empire in the days of Constantine VII, who reigned in the tenth century, was completely different from what it was in the days of Constantine I., who reigned in the fourth century? and having in view this great difference in character, is it not permissible for historians, as a mere matter of convenience, to distinguish the later period by some confessedly appropriate word like " Byzantine " or " Graeco-Roman " ? Such a use may be of course convenient and harmless in conversation among those who are fully aware that it is only a phrase of convenience ; and there is no objection to " Byzantine art " or " Graeco-Roman law." But in writing or lecturing, such expressions as Byzantine, Greek, or Romaic Empire are highly objectionable, because they tend to obscure an important fact and perpetuate a serious error.

It seems especially unfortunate to adopt one of these names as the title of a book, and thus help to stereotype as a separate unity what is really a part of a continuous series. Every century of the Roman Empire differed from the preceding and from the succeeding, but the development was continuous; the Empire was still the Roman Empire, and I am not aware that it is usual to give a man a new name when he enters upon a new decade of life. We designate a man as young and old; and so we may speak of the earlier and later ages of a kingdom or an empire. But *Byzantine* is a proper adjective, and is too apparently precise not to be misleading. Gibbon perhaps is almost the only modern historian who, in treating this subject, has not done injustice to the continuity of history by the title of his work; but unfortunately in reading the later chapters one is apt to forget what that title is.

Moved by these considerations, I have avoided speaking of a Byzantine, a Greek, or a Graeco-Roman Empire, and have carefully restricted myself to the only correct appellation. For the sake of distinction the word " later " has been added on the title-page; and no further distinction is required, at least till the year 800, which marks the termination of my work.

This brings us to another unfortunate use of words, which similarly tends to perpetuate an erroneous impression. A rival Roman Empire was founded in the West by the coronation of Charles the Great in 800 ; and it is evidently very convenient to distinguish the rival Empires by prefixing the adjectives Western and Eastern. And this nomenclature is not only convenient, but quite justifiable; for it suggests no historical error, while it expresses succinctly the European situation.

But unhappily the phrase *Eastern Roman Empire* is not confined to this legitimate use. We hear of an Eastern and a Western Roman Empire in the fifth century; we hear of the Fall of a Western Empire in 476. Such language, though it has the sanction of high names, is both incorrect in itself and leads to a further confusion. In the first place, it is incorrect. The Roman Empire was one and undivided in the fifth century; though there were generally more Emperors than one, there were never two Empires. To speak of two Empires in the fifth century—and if such speech applies to the fifth it applies also to the fourth—is to misrepresent in the grossest manner the theory of the imperial constitution. No one talks about two Roman Empires in the days of Constantius and Constans; yet the relation of Arcadius and Honorius, the relation of Theodosius II and Valentinian III, the relation of Leo I. and Anthemius, were exactly the same as the political relation which existed between the sons of Constantine. However independent one of another, or even hostile, the rulers from time to time may have been, theoretically the unity of the Empire which they ruled was unaffected. No Empire fell in 476; that year only marks a stage, and not even the most important stage, in the process of disintegration which was going on during the whole century. The resignation of Romulus Augustulus did not even shake the Roman Empire, far less did it cause an Empire to fall. It is unfortunate, therefore, that Gibbon spoke of the "Fall of the Western Empire," and that many modern writers have given their sanction to the phrase. Notwithstanding all that Mr. Freeman has said on the matter in sundry places, it will be probably a long time yet before the inveterate error of assigning a wrong importance to the year 476 A.D. has been finally eradicated.

In the second place, this nomenclature leads to a further confusion. For if the erroneous expression *Eastern Roman Empire* be admitted into use for the fifth century, the inevitable tendency is to identify this false abstraction with the Eastern Roman Empire, rightly so called, of later days. And this identification unavoidably leads to the idea that a state called the Eastern Roman Empire came into being after the death of Theodosius the Great, in 395 A.D., and continued until 1453 A.D.

The simplicity of history is thus obscured. Nothing can be easier than to apprehend that the Roman Empire endured, one and undivided, however changed and dismembered, from the first century B.C. to the fifteenth century A.D.; and that from the year 800 forward we distinguish it as *Eastern*, on account of the foundation of a rival Empire, which also called itself Roman, in the West.

I have now explained my title, and I may add that by discarding the word Byzantine an additional advantage has been gained. So many prejudicial associations have grown up round this inauspicious word that it almost involves a *petitio principii*, like the phrase *Bas-Empire* in French. This is due to the unhistorical manner in which many eminent authors have treated the later Roman Empire. These writers knew very little about it, and they regarded it as a safe subject for derision. Voltaire, for instance, speaks of Byzantine history "as a worthless repertory of declamation and miracles, disgraceful to the human mind." "With this remark," says Finlay, "the records of an empire, which witnessed the rise and fall of the Caliphs and Carlovingians, are dismissed by one who exclaimed, 'J'ôterai aux nations le bandeau de l'erreur.'" Gibbon hurried over the history of the Emperors later than the seventh century with contemptuous celerity, and his great authority has much to answer for. The remarks of Hegel in his *Philosophie der Geschichte* amount to much the same as the remark of Voltaire.

The sins of M. Guizot are of omission rather than of commission. His well-known *Histoire de la civilisation en Europe* is open to two criticisms. In the first place, it is not what it professes to be,—a history of European civilisation,—for it only deals with western Europe. But, waiving this, the author entirely ignores one of the most important and essential factors in the development of civilisation in western Europe —the influence of the later Roman Empire and New Rome. On this subject I may refer the reader to the concluding chapter of my second volume; I mention it here because M.

Guizot's extraordinary omission was clearly due to the inveterate prejudice that the "Byzantine Empire," and all things appertaining thereto, may be safely neglected.

In his *History of European Morals* (ii. p. 13) Mr. Lecky writes: "Of that Byzantine Empire the universal verdict of history is that it constitutes, with scarcely an exception, the most thoroughly base and despicable form that civilisation has yet assumed." I am not sure what Mr. Lecky means by "the universal verdict of history"; in recent years, certainly, the Younger Rome has found some staunch and eminent champions. But I am sure that the statement fairly represents the notions generally prevalent on the subject.

All this shows that *Byzantine* is a dangerous word, when it is used in a political sense. It is convenient and harmless to talk about Byzantine art or even "la vie byzantine," but it is dangerous to talk about a Byzantine Empire; for if we do so we run the risk of provoking universal verdicts of history. It might therefore be advisable, even if this were the only ground for doing so, to abandon the name and elude hard sentences by leading the accused forth under a different appellation. But it is not the only or the most important ground; as we have already seen, the name is improper, and it is therefore not only advisable but necessary to discard it.

I have been obliged to dwell at some length on a matter of nomenclature. I must add a few words on the scope of these two volumes, which, I venture to hope, may have some value as a very modest contribution to the study of a period which is too little known. They cover the four centuries during which the transition from the ancient world to the medieval world may be said to have taken place. *Ancient* and *medieval* are vague terms, but, whatever latitude we give them, we can hardly apply the term medieval to the fourth century or the term ancient to the eighth. In the year 395 A.D. the Empire was intact, but with the fifth century its dismemberment began; and 395 A.D. is consequently a convenient date to adopt as a starting-point. I propose to trace briefly the history of its dismemberment by the Germans, then more fully its recovery under Justinian, its decline after Justinian, and its redintegration in the eighth century; making the fall of Irene in 802 A.D. my point of termination, because it happens to be conveniently close in time to the foundation of the rival Roman Empire in 800 A.D. The coronation of Charles the Great marks a new departure in European history, and it therefore forms, as Arnold recognised, a suitable end as well as a suitable beginning. After 800 there are two Roman Empires; and the history of the successors of Irene would naturally occupy a separate book, entitled *A History of the Eastern Roman Empire*.

The history of the fifth century is better known, and has been more thoroughly worked up than that of its successors. I have therefore treated it with comparative brevity, and omitted many of the details, which the reader may find in the works of Gibbon and Mr. Hodgkin. In fact, I originally intended to treat the dismemberment of the Empire by the Germans and the fortunes of the houses of Theodosius and Leo I. as a mere introduction to a history of the subsequent period. But I was carried further than I intended, and the result considerably exceeds the limits of an introduction, while it is something less than a co-ordinate part of the work. The dismemberment of the Empire by the Germans brings us into contact with the nations who dismembered it, and tempts a writer to stray into the domains which have been so fully surveyed by Dahn in his *Könige der Germanen*. I have been careful not to yield to this temptation; I have avoided episodes and digressions; and have not concerned myself with tracing the doubtful antecedents of the various nations who settled in the Roman provinces. In fact, I have tried to trespass as little as possible on the field occupied by Dahn in Germany and by Mr. Hodgkin in England.

Coming to the sixth century, my account of the reconquest of Italy by Belisarius and Narses is compressed; while I have narrated fully the Persian wars on the Euphrates and in Colchis. As far as I am aware, no complete account of the latter has ever been published in an English form, Gibbon's treatment being nothing more than a sketch; while as to the former, after the brilliant fourth volume of Mr. Hodgkin's *Italy and her Invaders*, one could not think of rewriting all the details. But, notwithstanding, a critic may charge me with want of proportion, and ask why I occupy considerable space with the details of wars, which, even for special historians, have been almost buried in oblivion, and at the same time content myself with only a general account of the famous Italian campaigns of Belisarius. My reply is that I am concerned with the history of the Roman Empire, and not with the history of Italy or of the West; and the events on the Persian frontier were of vital consequence for the very existence of the Roman Empire, while the events in Italy were, for it, of only secondary importance. Of course Italy was a part of the Empire; but it was outlying—its loss or recovery affected the *Roman* Republic (strange to say!) in a far less degree than other losses or gains. And just as the historian of modern England may leave the details of Indian affairs to the special historian of India, so a general historian of the Roman Empire may, after the fifth century, leave the details of Italian affairs to the special historian of Italy. It seemed to me that the real want of proportion would have been to reproduce at length the *Gothica* of Procopius and neglect his *Persica*.

On the same principle I have given a detailed narrative (I believe for the first time) of the somewhat tedious wars in the Balkan peninsula at the end of the sixth century, described by Theophylactus. Ranke deplored the want of an essay concerning the invasions of Avars and Slaves in the reign of Maurice; the learned and patient Hopf went hopelessly astray over the curious sentences of an "Attic" euphuist; and these facts induce me to hope that some future historian, repelled equally by an ancient language and an affected style, may applaud a predecessor for having reproduced most of the details in bald English.

The Church was so closely connected with the State that the ecclesiastical element cannot be ignored in histories that are not ecclesiastical; but I have endeavoured to encroach on this ground as little as possible. As time went on, the influence of the Greek Church became stronger, and consequently, with each succeeding century, church affairs claim a larger measure of a historian's attention. Hence in the latter part of this work the reader may expect to find more information on ecclesiastical matters than in the earlier.

The short chapters on life and manners consist of jottings, which could not be conveniently introduced into the narrative, and were too characteristic to be omitted; they do not aim at any standard of completeness.

Both historians and classical scholars are divided on the question of the transliteration of Greek names. To be thoroughly consistent in the "new" spelling, one would have to speak not only of Athênai, but of Kônstantînupolis and Rhodos. Such apparitions on the pages of a book are intolerable to plain readers; and special difficulties arise in the case of Roman names of Greek-speaking individuals. I determined finally to be consistently Roman rather than either consistently or inconsistently Greek, and use, except in a few cases, the Latin forms, which, justified by the custom of many centuries, are more familiar to the eye. In some obvious cases, of course, it would be pedantic not to use forms which are neither Greek nor Latin, such as Constantine, Rhodes, or Rome. I confess that I was at first tempted to adopt the plausible compromise of Mr. Freeman; but an admirable article in the *Fortnightly Review* for January 1888, by Mr. R. Y. Tyrrell, confirmed me in the course which I have pursued. On the other hand, I have adopted Mr. Freeman's way of spelling Slave (for Slav). Speaking of Mr. Freeman, I am impelled to add that his brilliant and stimulating essays first taught me in all its bearings the truth that the Roman Empire is the key to European history.

In conclusion, I have to record my thanks to my wife, who contributes a chapter on "Byzantine Art" (vol. ii. p. 40 *sqq.*), and to Professor Mahaffy for his assistance in revising the proof-sheets and for valuable suggestions and corrections.

J. B. BURY.

24th June 1889.

ERRATA TO VOL. I.

Page 52, line 27 from top, *read* south-western course, and by the Propontis *for* south-eastern course.

,, 55, ,, 34 ,, *read* Augusteum again, will *for* Augusteum, again will.
,, 57, ,, 28 ,, ,, Chrysopolis ,, Chalcedon.
,, 160, ,, 15 ,, ,, Dorystolon ,, Dorostylum.
,, 299, ,, 26 ,, ,, Odessus ,, Odyssus.
,, 323, note 1, ,, du Méril ,, de Méril.
,, 360, line 5 ,, ,, Silverius ,, Sylverius.
,, ,, ,, 9 ,, ,, ,, ,, ,,
,, ,, ,, 12 ,, ,, ,, ,, ,,
,, 386, note, line 2, ,, once— ,, once,
,, 395, line 10 from top, ,, Theudebert ,, Theudibert.
,, ,, ,, 24 ,, ,, ,, ,, ,,
,, 397, ,, 6 ,, ,, ,, ,, ,,
,, ,, ,, 15 ,, ,, ,, ,, ,,
,, ,, ,, 19 ,, ,, ,, ,, ,,
,, ,, ,, 20 ,, ,, Theudebald ,, Theudibald.
,, ,, note 6, ,, Theudebert ,, Theudibert.
,, 412, line 21 ,, ,, nephew ,, son.
,, 414, lines 3-4 ,, ,, Theudebald ,, Theudibald
,, ,, line 6 ,, ,, ,, ,, ,,
,, 444, ,, 13 ,, ,, the Hippis ,, Hippis.
,, 445, ,, 9 ,, ,, at the Hippis ,, at Hippis.
,, 460, ,, 8 ,, ,, at the Neocnus ,, at Neocnus.

TABLE OF THE DIVISIONS OF THE ROMAN EMPIRE AT THE BEGINNING OF THE FIFTH CENTURY

I

PREFECTURE OF THE EAST.
(*Praefectus Praetorio per Orientem.*)

DIOCESIS 1.—Oriens, under the *comes orientis*.

Provincia	I. Palaestina Prima,	under a	*consularis.*
,,	II. Phoenicia Maritima,	,,	*consularis.*
,,	III. Syria Prima,	,,	*consularis.*
,,	IV. Cilicia Prima,	,,	*consularis.*
,,	V. Cyprus,	,,	*consularis.*
,,	VI. Arabia,	,,	*dux.*
,,	VII. Isauria,	,,	*comes rei militaris.*
,,	VIII. Palaestina Salutaris,	,,	*praeses.*
,,	IX. Palaestina Secunda,	,,	*praeses.*
,,	X. Phoenicia Libanesia,	,,	*praeses.*
,,	XI. Euphratesia,	,,	*praeses.*
,,	XII. Syria Salutaris,	,,	*praeses.*
,,	XIII. Osrhoene,	,,	*praeses.*
,,	XIV. Mesopotamia,	,,	*praeses.*
,,	XV. Cilicia Secunda,	,,	*praeses.*

DIOCESIS 2.—Aegyptus, under the *praefectus Augustalis*.

Provincia	I. Libya Superior,	under a	*praeses.*
,,	II. Libya Inferior,	,,	*praeses.*
,,	III. Thebais,	,,	*praeses.*
,,	IV. Aegyptus,	,,	*praeses.*
,,	V. Arcadia,	,,	*praeses.*

DIOCESIS 3.—Asiana, under a *vicarius*.

Provincia	I. Pamphylia,	under a	*consularis.*
,,	II. Hellespontus,	,,	*consularis.*

xvi CHRONOLOGICAL AND GENEALOGICAL TABLES

Provincia	III. Lydia,	under a *consularis*.
,,	IV. Pisidia,	,, *praeses*.
,,	V. Lycaonia,	,, *praeses*.
,,	VI. Phrygia Pacatiana,	,, *praeses*.
,,	VII. Phrygia Salutaris,	,, *praeses*.
,,	VIII. Lycia,	,, *praeses*.
,,	IX. Caria,	,, *praeses*.
,,	X. Insulae,	,, *praeses*.
,,	XI. Asia,[1]	,, *proconsul*.

DIOCESIS 4.—Pontica, under a *vicarius*.

Provincia	I. Galatia,	under a *consularis*.
,,	II. Bithynia,	,, *consularis*.
,,	III. Honorias,	,, *praeses*.
,,	IV. Cappadocia Prima,	,, *praeses*.
,,	V. Cappadocia Secunda,	,, *praeses*.
,,	VI. Pontus Polemoniacus,	,, *praeses*.
,,	VII. Helenopontus,	,, *praeses*.
,,	VIII. Armenia Prima,	,, *praeses*.
,,	IX. Armenia Secunda,	,, *praeses*.
,,	X. Galatia Salutaris,	,, *praeses*.
,,	XI. Paphlagonia,	,, *corrector*.

DIOCESIS 5.—Thracia, under a *vicarius*.

Provincia	I. Europe,	under a *consularis*.
,,	II. Thracia,	,, *consularis*.
,,	III. Haemimontus,	,, *praeses*.
,,	IV. Rhodope,	,, *praeses*.
,,	V. Moesia Secunda,	,, *praeses*.
,,	VI. Scythia,	,, *praeses*.

II

PREFECTURE OF ILLYRICUM.

(*Praefectus Praetorio per Illyricum.*)

DIOCESIS 1.—Macedonia, under a *vicarius*.

Provincia	I. Achaia,[2]	under a *proconsul*.
,,	II. Macedonia Prima,	,, *consularis*.

---

[1] Asia was not under the control of either the *vicarius* of Asiana or the *praefectus praetorio per orientem*; but this is the most suitable place to insert the province.

[2] The proconsul of Achaia, like the proconsul of Asia, was independent of vicar and prefect.

Provincia	III. Creta,	under a *consularis*.
,,	IV. Thessalia,	,, *praeses*.
,,	V. Epirus Vetus,	,, *praeses*.
,,	VI. Epirus Nova,	,, *praeses*.
,,	VII. Macedonia Salutaris,[1]	,, *praeses*.

Diocesis 2.—Dacia.

Provincia	I. Dacia Mediterranea,	under a *consularis*.
,,	II. Dacia Ripensis,	,, *praeses*.
,,	III. Moesia Prima,	,, *praeses*.
,,	IV. Dardania,	,, *praeses*.
,,	V. Praevalitana,	,, *praeses*.

III

PREFECTURE OF ITALY.

(*Praefectus Praetorio Italiae.*)

Diocesis 1.—Italia, under the *vicarius Italiae*.

Provincia	I. Venetia (et Histria),	under a *consularis*.
,,	II. Aemilia,	,, *consularis*.
,,	III. Liguria,	,, *consularis*.
,,	IV. Flaminia et Picenum Annonarium,	,, *consularis*.
,,	V. Tuscia et Umbria,	,, *consularis*.
,,	VI. Picenum Suburbicarium,	,, *consularis*.
,,	VII. Campania,	,, *consularis*.
,,	VIII. Sicilia,	,, *consularis*.
,,	IX. Apulia et Calabria,	,, *corrector*.
,,	X. Lucania et Bruttii,	,, *corrector*.
,,	XI. Alpes Cottiae,	,, *praeses*.
,,	XII. Raetia Prima,	,, *praeses*.
,,	XIII. Raetia Secunda,	,, *praeses*.
,,	XIV. Samnium,	,, *praeses*.
,,	XV. Valeria,	,, *praeses*.
,,	XVI. Sardinia,	,, *praeses*.
,,	XVII. Corsica,	,, *praeses*.

Diocesis 2.—Illyricum.

Provincia	I. Pannonia Secunda,	under a *consularis*.
,,	II. Savia,	,, *corrector*.

---

[1] In the *Notitia Dignitatum*, part of Macedonia Salutaris is in the diocese of Macedonia and subject to the *praeses* of New Epirus, while the other part is in the diocese of Dacia and governed by the *praeses* of Praevalitana.

Provincia	III. Dalmatia,	under a *praeses*.
,,	IV. Pannonia Prima,	,, *praeses*.
,,	V. Noricum Mediterraneum,	,, *praeses*.
,,	VI. Noricum Ripense,	,, *praeses*.

DIOCESIS 3.—Africa, under a *vicarius*.

Provincia	I. Byzacium,	under a *consularis*.
,,	II. Numidia,	,, *consularis*.
,,	III. Mauretania Sitifensis,	,, *praeses*.
,,	IV. Mauretania Caesariensis,	,, *praeses*.
,,	V. Tripolis,	,, *praeses*.
,,	VI. Africa,[1]	,, *proconsul*.

IV

PREFECTURE OF GAUL.

(*Praefectus Praetorio Galliae.*)

DIOCESIS 1.—Hispania, under a *vicarius*.

Provincia	I. Baetica,	under a *consularis*.
,,	II. Lusitania,	,, *consularis*.
,,	III. Gallaecia,	,, *consularis*.
,,	IV. Tarraconensis,	,, *praeses*.
,,	V. Carthaginiensis,	,, *praeses*.
,,	VI. Tingitana,	,, *praeses*.
,,	VII. Insulae Balearum,	,, *praeses*.

DIOCESIS 2.—Septem provinciae, under a *vicarius*.

Provincia	I. Viennensis,	under a *consularis*.
,,	II. Lugdunensis Prima,	,, *consularis*.
,,	III. Germania Prima,	,, *consularis*.
,,	IV. Germania Secunda,	,, *consularis*.
,,	V. Belgica Prima,	,, *consularis*.
,,	VI. Belgica Secunda,	,, *consularis*.
,,	VII. Alpes Maritimae,	,, *praeses*.
,,	VIII. Alpes Penninae et Graiae,	,, *praeses*.
,,	IX. Maxima Sequanorum,	,, *praeses*.
,,	X. Aquitania Prima,	,, *praeses*.
,,	XI. Aquitania Secunda,	,, *praeses*.
,,	XII. Novempopuli,	,, *praeses*.

---

[1] I insert the province of Africa here for the sake of symmetry; but the proconsul, like those of Achaia and Asia, was independent of higher sub-imperial authority.

Provincia	XIII. Narbonensis Prima,	under a	*praeses*.
,,	XIV. Narbonensis Secunda,	,,	*praeses*.
,,	XV. Lugdunensis Secunda,	,,	*praeses*.
,,	XVI. Lugdunensis Tertia,	,,	*praeses*.
,,	XVII. Lugdunensis Senonia,	,,	*praeses*.

DIOCESIS 3.—Britanniae, under a *vicarius*.

Provincia	I. Maxima Caesariensis,	under a	*praeses*.
,,	II. Valentia,	,,	*praeses*.
,,	III. Britannia Prima,	,,	*praeses*.
,,	IV. Britannia Secunda,	,,	*praeses*.
,,	V. Flavia Caesariensis,	,,	*praeses*.

GENEALOGICAL TABLE OF THE HOUSE OF THEODOSIUS

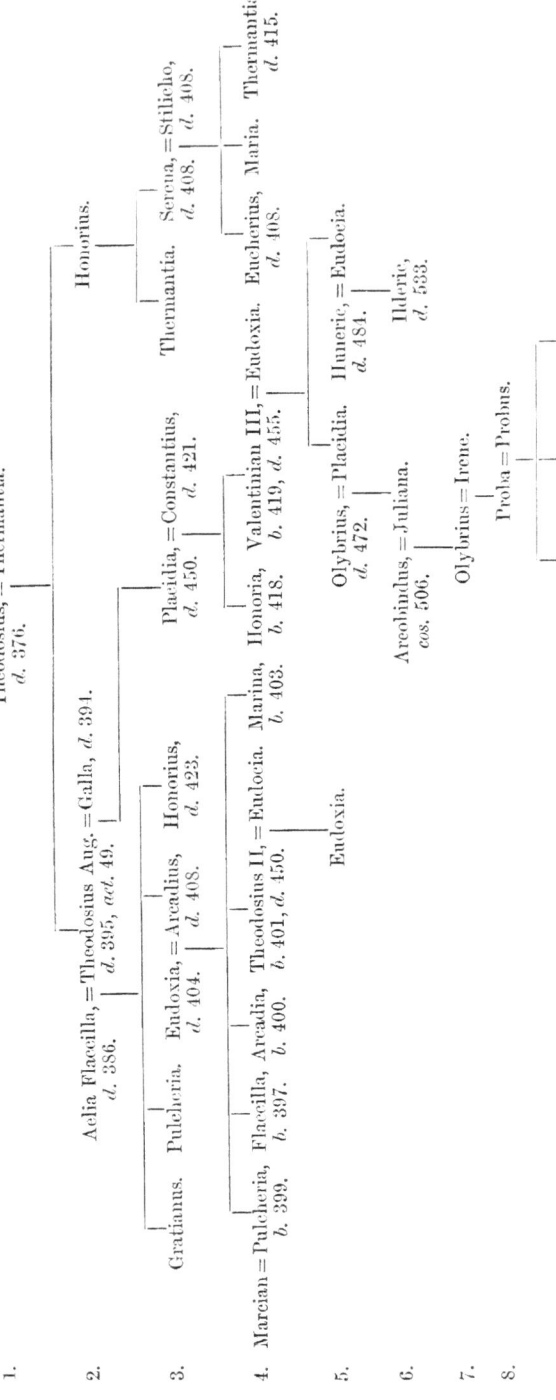

GENEALOGICAL TABLE OF THE HOUSE OF JUSTIN

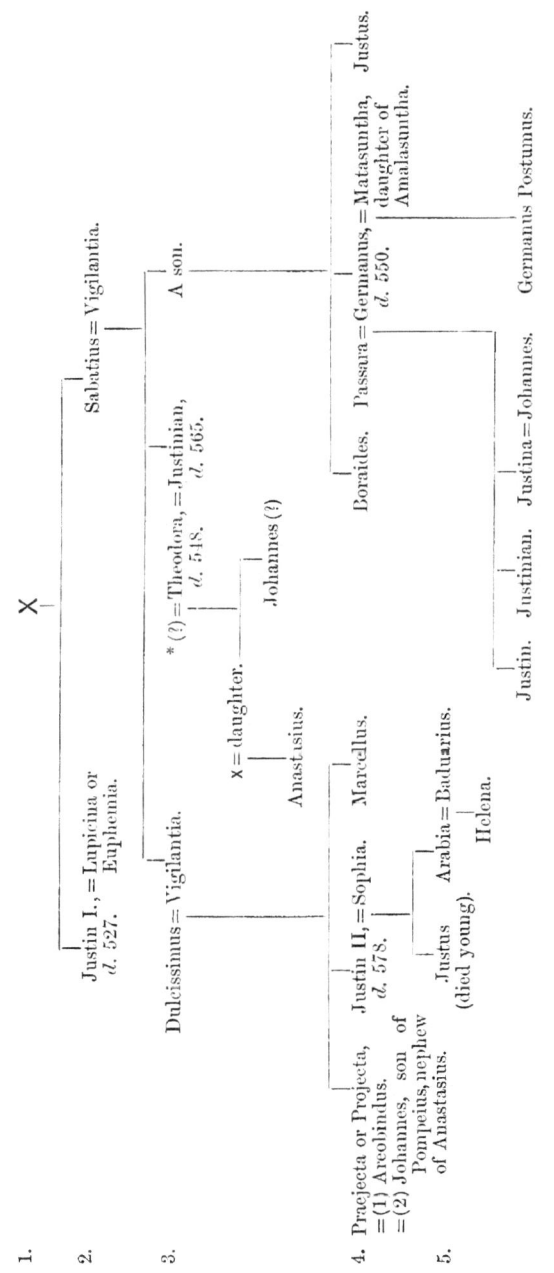

CHRONOLOGICAL TABLE FROM THE ACCESSION OF ARCADIUS, 395, TO THE DEATH OF JUSTINIAN, 565

A.D.	INDICTION.	A.M.	IMPERIAL ACCESSIONS.	EVENTS.
395	8–9	5887–8	Arcadius and Honorius.	
396	9–10	5888–9		Alaric in Greece.
398	11–12	5890–1		Gildo quelled in Africa.
399	12–13	5891–2		Fall of Eutropius.
400	13–14	5892–3		Revolt of Gainas.
402	15–1	5894–5		Battle of Pollentia.
404	2–3	5896–7		Exile of Chrysostom.
405	3–4	5897–8		Invasion of Radagaisus.
406	4–5	5898–9		Vandals, Suevians, etc., enter Gaul.
407	5–6	5899–900		Constantine proclaimed Emperor in Britain.
408	6–7	5900–1	Theodosius II.	Death of Stilicho. Alaric at Rome.
409	7–8	5901–2		Vandals, Suevians, etc., enter Spain. Alaric again at Rome.
410	8–9	5902–3		Alaric occupies Rome. Death of Alaric.
411	9–10	5903–4		Constantine the tyrant quelled in Gaul.
414	12–13	5906–7		Marriage of Athaulf and Placidia.
415	13–14	5907–8		Death of Hypatia at Alexandria.
417	15–1	5909–10		Marriage of Constantine and Placidia.
418	1–2	5910–1		Settlement of Visigoths in Gaul by treaty.
421	4–5	5913–4	Constantius III.	Hostilities with Persia. Theodosius II marries Athenais (Eudocia).
422	5–6	5914–5		Expedition of Castinus against Vandals in Spain.
423	6–7	5915–6		Death of Honorius.
424	7–8	5916–7		John usurps the throne at Ravenna.
425	8–9	5917–8	Valentinian III.	John overthrown.
429	12–13	5921–2		Vandals pass into Africa.
430	13–14	5922–3		Death of St. Augustine.

NOTE.—The indiction and the *annus mundi* (A.M.) are concurrent, both beginning on 1st September and ending 31st August. I have calculated the A.M. on the basis 5493, which was adopted by the chronicler Theophanes, and differs from the more usual (Roman) Era of the Nativity (5509) by sixteen years.

CHRONOLOGICAL AND GENEALOGICAL TABLES xxiii

A.D.	INDICTION.	A.M.	IMPERIAL ACCESSIONS.	EVENTS.
431	14–15	5923–4		Third Ecumenical Council at Ephesus.
432	15–1	5924–5		Civil war in Italy between Aetius and Boniface.
435	3–4	5927–8		Treaty of Empire with Vandals.
438	6–7	5930–1		Publication of *Codex Theodosianus*.
439	7–8	5931–2		Carthage taken by Vandals.
441	9–10	5933–4		Empire at war with Vandals, Huns, and Persians.
447	15–1	5939–40		Peace of Anatolius (with Huns).
448	1–2	5940–1		Embassy of Maximin to Attila.
450	3–4	5942–3	Marcian.	
451	4–5	5943–4		Battle of the Catalaunian Field. Fourth Ecumenical Council at Chalcedon.
452	5–6	5944–5		Aquileia stormed by Huns. Attila in northern Italy.
453	6–7	5945–6		Death of Attila. Death of Pulcheria, Augusta.
454	7–8	5946–7		Death of Aetius.
455	8–9	5947–8	Maximus.	Gaiseric invades Italy and spoils Rome.
457	10–11	5949–50	Avitus. Leo I. Majorian.	
461	14–15	5953–4	Severus.	
464	2–3	5956–7		Death of Aegidius.
465	3–4	5957–8		Great fire at New Rome. Death of Severus.
467	5–6	5959–60	Anthemius.	
468	6–7	5960–1		Great expedition against the Vandals.
471	9–10	5963–4		Execution of Aspar.
472	10–11	5964–5	Olybrius.	Death of Anthemius. Death of Ricimer.
473	11–12	5965–6	Glycerius.	Ostrogoths attack the Empire.
474	12–13	5966–7	Leo II. Zeno. Julius Nepos.	
475	13–14	5967–8	Romulus Augustulus. Basiliscus.	Basiliscus usurps and Zeno flees to Isauria. Orestes drives out Nepos.
476	14–15	5968–9		Romulus Aug. resigns and Odovacar rules in Italy as king.
477	15–1	5969–70		Restoration of Zeno. Death of Gaiseric.
478	1–2	5970–1		Ostrogoths under the two Theodorics in the Balkan peninsula, 478-481.
481	4–5	5973–4		Death of Theodoric, son of Triarius.
483	6–7	5975–6		Henotikon of Zeno.
484	7–8	5976–7		Revolt of Illus. Proclamation of Leontius.
489	12–13	5981–2		Theodoric (the Amal) overcomes Odovacar.
491	14–15	5983–4	Anastasius I.	
496	4–5	5988–9		Chlodwig subdues the Alemanni at Tolbiacum.

A.D.	Indiction.	A.M.	Imperial Accessions.	Events.
499	7–8	5991–2		Bulgarians invade Thrace.
502	10–11	5994–5		Bulgarians invade Thrace. War with Persia.
503	11–12	5995–6		Amida taken.
505	13–14	5997–8		Peace with Persia.
507	15–1	5999–6000		Erection of Anastasius' Long Wall. Chlodwig defeats Visigoths at Poitiers.
511	4–5	6003–4		Death of Chlodwig.
514	7–8	6006–7		Revolt of Vitalian.
518	11–12	6010–1	Justin I.	
526	4–5	6018–9		Death of Theodoric. Great earthquake at Antioch. War with Persia.
527	5–6	6019–20	Justinian I.	
529	7–8	6021–2		Code of Justinian published. Schools at Athens closed.
530	8–9	6022–3		Battle of Daras.
531	9–10	6023–4		Accession of Chosroes to the Persian throne.
532	10–11	6024–5		Nika sedition. Peace with Persia.
533	11–12	6025–6		Expedition against Vandals. Digest (Pandects) of Justinian published.
535	13–14	6027–8		Ostrogothic war begins. Belisarius in Sicily.
536	14–15	6028–9		Naples taken. Witigis elected king of Goths.
537	15–1	6029–30		First siege of Rome. Completion and dedication of St. Sophia.
538	1–2	6030–1		Siege of Ariminum.
539	2–3	6031–2		Capture of Milan, Faesulae, and Auximum by Romans.
540	3–4	6032–3		Ravenna taken. Belisarius' triumph. Ildibad, king of Goths. Chosroes invades Syria.
541	4–5	6033–4		Totila elected king of Goths. Chosroes invades Colchis. Belisarius in Mesopotamia.
542	5–6	6034–5		The Great Plague. Chosroes invades Commagene.
543	6–7	6035–6		The Roman armies invade Persarmenia. Naples surrenders to Totila. Death of St. Benedict.
544	7–8	6036–7		Chosroes invades Mesopotamia. Siege of Edessa. Belisarius arrives in Italy.
545	8–9	6037–8		Peace for five years with Persia. Totila lays siege to Rome.
546	9–10	6038–9		Totila takes Rome (December).
547	10–11	6039–40		Rome reoccupied by the Romans. Pope Vigilius arrives at Constantinople (February).
548	11–12	6040–1		Death of the Empress Theodora. Totila retakes Rome (third siege of Rome during this war). Conspiracy against Justinian.

A.D.	INDIC- TION.	A.M.	IMPERIAL ACCESSIONS.	EVENTS.
549	12-13	6041-2		Lazic war begins.
550	13-14	6042-3		Death of Germanus (nephew of Justinian).
551	14-15	6043-4		Naval battle of Sinigaglia. Sicily lost by the Goths. Capture of Petra by Romans.
552	15-1	6044-5		Narses arrives in Italy. Defeat and death of Totila.
553	1-2	6045-6		Fifth Ecumenical Council at Constantinople. Teias defeated on the Draco. End of Ostrogothic war. Siege of Phasis.
554	2-3	6046-7		Great earthquake at Constantinople.
557	5-6	6049-50		Embassy of Avars to Constantinople.
558	6-7	6050-1		Invasion of Huns under Zabergan (date doubtful).
562	10-11	6054-5		Peace of fifty years with Persia. Verona and Brixia taken by Narses. Conspiracy against Justinian. Invasion of Huns.
565	13-14	6057-8		Death of Justinian (November). Death of Belisarius (March).

TABLE OF CONTENTS

BOOK I

INTRODUCTION

CHAPTER I

CHRISTIANITY AND PAGANISM

Transitional period of history—Greek *destiny* and christian *consolation*—Historical connection of Christianity with the past—Stoicism—Epicureanism—Decay of paganism—Attitude of christians to pagans—Legends of Cyprian and Macarius—Neoplatonism—Proclus . . . Pages 1-16

CHAPTER II

INFLUENCE OF CHRISTIANITY ON SOCIETY

Christianity and the Teutons—Attractions of Christianity—Anchorets and monks—Position of women—Value of human life—Fraternity of mankind—Altruism—Sin 17-24

CHAPTER III

ELEMENTS OF DISINTEGRATION IN THE ROMAN EMPIRE

Depopulation—Slave system—Fiscal and curial systems—Serfdom and colonatus—Reforms of Majorian—Germans in the Empire—*Semibarbari*—Christianity as a disintegrating force—Survey 25-36

CHAPTER IV

THE ADMINISTRATION OF THE EMPIRE

System of Diocletian—The senate and senators—Official titles—Change in nomenclature in the fourth century—Taxes—Grades of society—Praetorian prefects—Other ministers—Civil service—Education—Army . Pages 37-49

CHAPTER V

CONSTANTINOPLE

Choice of Constantine—Description 50-58

BOOK II

THE HOUSE OF THEODOSIUS

CHAPTER I

RUFINUS AND EUTROPIUS

Death of Theodosius I.—Arcadius—Rufinus—Stilicho—The Visigoths—Claudian—Huns in Syria—Eutropius—Revolt of Gildo . . . 61-78

CHAPTER II

THE GERMANS IN THE EAST

Three parties at Constantinople—Aurelian—"Typhos"—Synesius—Revolt of Tribigild—Gainas—Fall of Eutropius—Danger from the Goths . 79-90

CHAPTER III

JOHN CHRYSOSTOM

Court of Eudoxia—Chrysostom and his friends—His visit to Asia Minor—Theophilus—Monks of Nitria—Epiphanius—Synod of the Oak—Conflagration of St. Sophia—Chrysostom banished—St. Nilus—Byzantine Patriarchs—Relations of Old and New Rome—Death of Arcadius . . . 91-106

CHAPTER IV

STILICHO AND ALARIC

Relations of Germans to the Empire—Visigoths in Italy—Battle of Pollentia—
—Radagaisus—Relations of Stilicho and Alaric—Movements in Gaul—Death
of Stilicho—Visigoths again in Italy—Alaric at Rome—Attalus—Death of
Alaric . . . . Pages 107-122

CHAPTER V

THEODOSIUS II AND MARCIAN

Anthemius—Pulcheria—Athenais—Significance of reign of the younger Theodosius
—Cyrus the prefect—University of Constantinople—*Codex Theodosianus*—
Eudocia in Palestine—Her fall—Chrysaphius—Reign of Marcian . 123-136

CHAPTER VI

BEGINNINGS OF THE DISMEMBERMENT OF THE EMPIRE

Barbarians in Gaul—Tyrants in Gaul—Constantine at Arelate—He wins Spain—
Gerontius—Fall of the tyrants—Jovinus and Athaulf—Revolt of Heraclian—
Visigoths in Gaul—Wallia—Constantius—Vandals and Suevians in Spain
—Lands assigned to Visigoths and Burgundians—Local government in
southern Gaul—Death of Constantius III—Placidia—Boniface—Death of
Honorius—John the tyrant suppressed and Valentinian III proclaimed—
Aetius 137-160

CHAPTER VII

INVASIONS OF THE HUNS

Rise of the Hun power—Relations with Vandals—Attila invades the Empire—
Asemus—Peace of Anatolius—The Hun empire . . . 161-166

CHAPTER VIII

THE PATRICIAN AETIUS

Africa—Boniface and Aetius—The Vandals—Burgundians and Alemanni—Theodoric the Visigoth—Aetius—Honoria—Attila—Battle of the Catalaunian
Field—Huns take Aquileia—Death of Attila—Deaths of Aetius and Valentinian 167-183

CHAPTER IX

THE CHURCH IN THE FIFTH CENTURY

Relations of Church and State—Arian controversy—Christological problems—Nestorianism—Monophysitism—Councils of Ephesus and Chalcedon—Henotikon—Great schism—Donatism—Pelagianism—St. Augustine, Pages 184-196

CHAPTER X

LIFE AND MANNERS IN THE FIFTH CENTURY

Luxury of court and higher classes—Amusements—Relation of the visit of Porphyrius of Gaza to Byzantium—Paganism at Gaza—Birth and baptism of Theodosius II—Anthemius, a typical educated Byzantine—Alexandria—Hypatia—Antioch 197-212

CHAPTER XI

A GLIMPSE OF HUN LIFE

Embassy of Maximin to court of Attila, as related by his friend Priscus, 213-223

BOOK III

THE HOUSE OF LEO THE GREAT

CHAPTER I

LEO I

Theory of imperial succession—Aspar—Isaurians in army—Fall of Aspar—Policy and character of Leo—Loss of Jotaba—Great fire in Constantinople—Paganism—Death of Leo 227-233

CHAPTER II

RICIMER THE PATRICIAN

Maximus—Gaiseric in Italy—Avitus—Ricimer—Majorian—Severus—Count Marcellinus—Claims of Gaiseric—Anthemius—Great expedition of Leo against Vandals—Fall of Anthemius—Olybrius—Death of Ricimer . 234-249

CHAPTER III

ZENO

Leo II—Reign of Basiliscus—Restoration of Zeno—Great fire in Constantinople—Character and policy of Zeno—Harmatius—Illus—Verina—Revolt of Leontius and Illus—Pamprepius—Zeno's son—Death of Zeno, Pages 250-260

CHAPTER IV

THE OSTROGOTHS IN ILLYRICUM AND THRACE

Battle of Netad—Theodoric, son of Theodemir—Theodoric, son of Triarius—Alliance of Zeno with son of Theodemir—Alliance of two Theodorics—Alliance of Zeno and son of Triarius—Son of Theodemir in Epirus—Adamantius—Bulgarians 261-273

CHAPTER V

ODOVACAR THE PATRICIAN AND THEODORIC THE PATRICIAN

Glycerius—Julius Nepos—Euric—Orestes—Romulus Augustulus—Odovacar—So-called "Fall of Western Empire"—Odovacar, the successor of Merobaudes—Fall of Odovacar's kingdom and Theodoric in Italy—The Franks—Chlodwig—European geography in 500 A.D.—St. Severinus . . . 274-289

CHAPTER VI

ANASTASIUS I

Anastasius—Isaurian war—Bulgarian invasions—The Long Wall—Recovery of Jotaba—Unpopularity of Anastasius—Revolt of Vitalian—Character of Anastasius—Chrysargyron—Marinus—Death of Anastasius . 290-303

CHAPTER VII

THE PERSIAN WAR

The Sassanid dynasty—Isdigerd I. and Arcadius—War in 420-421 A.D.—Ephthalite Huns (Viddhal)—Perozes—Kobad—Mazdak, the communist—The war breaks out 502 A.D.—Siege of Amida—Amida recovered—Peace—Foundation of Anastasiopolis (Daras) 304-309

CHAPTER VIII

GREEK LITERATURE OF THE FIFTH CENTURY

Decadence of literature—Influence of Christianity—Want of ideas and originality—Julian—Synesius—Proclus—Athens—Alexandria—Hypatia—Nonnus—*Christus Patiens*—Egyptian school of poetry—The romance—*Daphnis and Chloe*—Heliodorus—Achilles Tatius—Xenophon of Ephesus—History—Eunapius—Zosimus—Olympiodorus—Priscus—Malchus—Candidus—Latin literature—Claudian—Sidonius—Christian poetry . . Pages 310-330

BOOK IV

THE HOUSE OF JUSTIN

PART I

THE AGE OF JUSTINIAN

CHAPTER I

THE REIGN OF JUSTIN I.; AND THE EARLIER YEARS OF JUSTINIAN'S REIGN

The sixth century—Reaction against Anastasius—Accession of Justinian—John of Cappadocia—Theodora—The Blues and Greens—Sedition of *Nika*—Fall of John of Cappadocia—Absolutism of Justinian—*Praetores plebis*—*Quaestor*—Imperial style 333-350

CHAPTER II

JUSTINIAN AND THEODORA

Historical position of Justinian; his connection with the past and with the future—His artificial system—The *Secret History*—Johannes Lydus—The Empress Theodora—Character of Justinian 351-358

Appendix on the *Secret History* attributed to Procopius . . 359-364

CHAPTER III

THE LEGAL WORKS OF JUSTINIAN

Codex—Digest—Institutes—Pythagoreanism—Roman law modified by history—Slavery . . . . Pages 365-371

CHAPTER IV

FIRST PERSIAN WAR (528-532 A.D.)

Kobad and Justin—Outbreak of war—Battle of Daras—Battle of Callinicum—The endless peace 372-380

CHAPTER V

THE RECONQUEST OF AFRICA AND ITALY

Ostrogothic kingdom — Theodoric — Amalasuntha — Vandalic war — Events in Africa after the Imperial Restoration—Gothic war—Conquest of Sicily and Dalmatia—Siege of Naples—Siege of Rome by the Goths—Siege and relief of Ariminum—Conquest of Milan and Liguria—Surrender of Faesulae and Auximum—Fall of Ravenna—Attitude of the Franks—St. Benedict, 381-398

CHAPTER VI

THE GREAT PLAGUE

Significance of plagues—The account of Procopius . . . 399-403

CHAPTER VII

THE FINAL CONQUEST OF ITALY AND THE CONQUEST OF SOUTH-EASTERN SPAIN

Ildibad—The logothetes—Totila—Gothic power revives—Belisarius arrives in Italy—John, the nephew of Vitalian—Second siege of Rome—Belisarius at Portus—Policy of Totila—Recall of Belisarius—Third siege of Rome—Germanus—Narses—Defeat of Totila—Teias—Alemanni in Italy—Imperial conquest in south-eastern Spain—Reconquest by Visigoths . 404-417

CHAPTER VIII

SECOND PERSIAN WAR (540-545 A.D.)

Saracens of Hirah and Ghassan—Causes of war and fears of Chosroes—Chosroes invades Syria (540 A.D.)—He invades Colchis (541 A.D.)—Invades Commagene (542 A.D.)—Romans invade Persarmenia—Chosroes invades Mesopotamia—Siege of Edessa—Peace of 545 A.D. . . . Pages 418-440

CHAPTER IX

THE LAZIC WAR (549-556 A.D.)

Gobazes seeks protection of Justinian—Dagisthaeus besieges Petra—Revolt of the Abasgians—Apsilia—Bessas besieges and takes Petra—Persian siege of Archaeopolis—The Island—Assassination of Gobazes—Trial of his assassins—Wiscard—Siege of Phasis—Expedition against the Misimiani—Peace of 562 A.D. 441-468

CHAPTER X

THE LATER YEARS OF JUSTINIAN'S REIGN

Justinian's imperial policy—Homerites—Heruls—Tetraxite Goths—Second period of the reign—Decay of the army—Silkworms brought to Europe—Buildings—Earthquakes—Conspiracy of Artabanes—Cotrigur and Utrigur Huns—Invasion of Zabergan—Last days of Belisarius—Death of Justinian, 469-482

BOOK I

INTRODUCTION

CHAPTER I

CHRISTIANITY AND PAGANISM

IN the fourth and fifth centuries A.D. a great change came over the face of Europe; the political order of things was broken up. This movement ushered in the Middle Ages, and it presents a noteworthy parallel to that other great European movement which ushered out the Middle Ages, the movement of the fifteenth and sixteenth centuries by which the spiritual order of things was broken up. The atmosphere of the age in which the Empire of Rome was dismembered was the christian religion; the atmosphere of the age in which the Church of Rome was ruptured was the Renaissance of culture. The formation of independent Teutonic kingdoms in the earlier period corresponds to the Reformation in the later; in both cases the German spirit produced a mighty revolution, and in both cases the result was a compromise or division between the old and the new. The Roman Empire lived on in south-eastern Europe, even as the Catholic Church lived on, confined to a limited extent of territory; and there was a remarkable revival of strength, or reaction, in the fifth and sixth centuries at Constantinople, which, following out the parallel, we may compare to the Counter-reformation. And this analogy is not a mere superficial or fanciful resemblance; the same historical principle is involved. Christianity and the Renaissance performed the same functions; each meant the transformation of the spirit of the European world, and such a transformation was a necessary precursor of the disintegration of European unity, whether political or ecclesiastical. In the strength of ancient ideas lay the strength of the Roman

Empire; Christianity was the solvent of these ideas, and so dissolved also the political unity of Europe. In the strength of medieval ideas lay the strength of the Roman Church; the spirit of the Renaissance was the solvent of medieval ideas, and therefore it dissolved the ecclesiastical unity of western and northern Europe.

For the philosopher who looks upon the march of ideas over the heads of men the view of history is calm, unlike that of the troubled waters of events below, in which the mystic procession is often but dimly discerned. For him the spirit of old paganism departs before the approach of Christianity as quietly as the sun sinks before the sweeping train of night; and the dark glimmerings of the medieval world yield to the approach of the modern spirit as the stars "touched to death by diviner eyes" pass away before the rising sun. But to the historian who investigates the details of the process a spectacle is presented of contrast, struggle, and confusion; and its contemplation has a peculiar pleasure. For both the great periods, of which we have been speaking, were long seasons of twilight—the evening twilight and the morning twilight,—during which light and darkness mingled, and thus each period may be viewed in two aspects, as the end of an old, or as the beginning of a new, world. Now this doublesidedness produces a variety of contrasts, which lends to the study of such a period a peculiar interest, or we might say an aesthetic pleasure. We see a number of heterogeneous elements struggling to adjust themselves into a new order—ingredients of divers perfumes and colours turning swiftly round and blending in the cup of the disturbed spirit. The grand contrast of the old and the new in the fourth and fifth centuries stands out vividly; old and new nations as well as old and new religions are brought face to face. We see civilised Greeks and Romans, semi-civilised or wholly civilised Germans, Germans uncivilised but possessing potentialities for civilisation, Huns and Alans totally beyond the pale, moving to and fro in contact with one another. In the lives of individuals too we see the multiplicity of colours curiously reflected. St. Helena, the mother of an Emperor, makes a pilgrimage to Jerusalem, since Hadrian's time usually called Aelia Capitolina, and finds the relics of the true cross with a

thrill of overpowering delight, something like the delight that
was felt by Renaissance scholars when an old Roman corpse
was disentombed. Or we see Julian, a pagan philosopher, a
noble man and an enlightened Emperor, trying to dislodge
Christianity from the position it had won, and yet unable to
avoid borrowing hints from it for his own system; just as
in the writings of his friend, the anti-christian professor
Libanius, we occasionally find an unconscious echo of the
new religion. While the pagan Neoplatonist Hypatia is
lecturing in the Museum at Alexandria, her semi-pagan pupil
Synesius is a bishop at Cyrene. At Athens, now a fossilised
provincial town, but still the headquarters of learning, paganism
has its last stronghold; and even from this camp of heathen-
ism the most christian Emperor, Theodosius II, obtains the
daughter of a philosopher as his consort, and she, after her
conversion to Christianity, writes religious poems composed of
scraps of Homeric lines. St. Augustine, the poet Sidonius
Apollinaris, and the poet Nonnus were, like Synesius, remarkable examples of persons who, born and reared pagans, turned
in later life to the new faith; and the writings of these men
illustrate the contrasts of the age.

The christian Church itself, it may be added, was full of
contrasts just then; for the christian doctrine had not yet
sunk, or risen, to the monotony of a formula. There were
still many open questions, even for orthodox Athanasians;
there was still room for the play of individuality. It has
been noticed how heterogeneous in spirit were the writings
of the Greek Church; we have "the zelotic dogmatism of
Epiphanius, the poetic speculation of Synesius, the philosophy
of religion of Aeneas of Gaza and Nemesius, the sobriety of
Theodoret, the mysticism of Pseudodionysios." Basil and Gregory
of Nazianzus had been fellow-students of the pagan Julian
at Athens; Chrysostom was a pupil of Libanius.

Thus the general impression we receive is one of contrast,
and it is in the battle of conflicting elements that the keen-
ness and quickness of life consist. But the conflict was
carried on, and the quick life breathed in a gray, often
murky, atmosphere, different from the brightness that lit
up those other conflicts in Athens during the fifth century
B.C., and in Italy during the fifteenth century A.D. There

was a general feeling of misfortune; the world-sadness pressed on the souls of all; and books were written to account for the woes that had come upon the human race. Nature too seemed to have prepared a dark background for the enactment of the miseries involved in the break-up of society and the incursions of the barbarians; plagues and earthquakes seemed to be signs of the times—like the tempest in *King Lear*, a suitable setting for the tragedy. The pagans of course were fain to attribute the misfortunes of the time to the new religion, and the "pale cast" of the spirit to the victory of the "pale Galilean." But in history what men superficially connect as cause and effect are really both effects of some deeper cause. The world had grown gray independently of Christianity, and if it had not grown gray, Christianity would hardly have been possible—would not have had much meaning; it met the need of the world at the time.

For there are two ways in which we may intuite the world and avoid quarrelling with life. We can regard our experience as *destiny*—fortune and misfortune as alike determined for us by conditions beyond our control. It was in this objective way that the old Greeks regarded their experience, and in this way they were content; for it never occurred to them to exalt subjective wishes of their own in opposition to the course of destiny, and grieve because such wishes remained inachievable.

Otherwise we may feel our own subjective aims more keenly, and be unable to see them sacrificed without experiencing sorrow or even despair. In this case we shall need something in their stead to make us contented with life, we shall require a *consolation*. If circumstances render a man's life joyless and hopeless, it becomes endurable for him through the belief that another existence awaits him; the world is thereby rendered less unintelligible, or there is a hope of understanding it in due time; the heavy and weary weight seems less weary and heavy to bear; his belief is a consolation. The old Greeks needed no repentance and no consolation. The centuries from Alexander the Great to Marcus Aurelius were the time in which the thorns were penetrating. The ancient Greek spirit could indeed exclaim, "Oh, how full of briars is the working-day world!" but they were only burs thrown upon it in holiday foolery, burs upon the coat that could be shaken off. The spirit of the later ages said, "These burs are in my heart." When Anaxagoras was informed that his son had died, he said, "I never supposed him to be immortal"; but a christian hermit, on receiving similar news in regard to his father, rebuked the messenger, "Blaspheme not, my father is immortal." The christian had a compensation for death which the heathen did not require.

Christianity provided the needed consolation.[1] But we must apprehend clearly the fact that the need had at one time not existed, and also the fact that it had come into existence in the regular course of the spiritual development of man. We are hereby reminded that if in one respect Christianity forms a new start in history, from another aspect it stands in close historical connection with the old Greek and Roman worlds; its philosophical doctrines are the logical end of the ancient Greek philosophy and the direct continuation of Stoicism and Epicureanism.

We may then first consider the connection of the new religion with the past, and its points of resemblance and contrast with the last form of pagan philosophy; and then, in another chapter, glance at the new departure made by Christianity and its most obvious influences on society.

The post-Aristotelian individualistic philosophies of Zeno, Epicurus, and the Sceptics were all characterised by the same motive. Their object was, not to understand the universe, but to secure for the individual the *summum bonum*; the end of philosophy was personal, no longer objective. It is from a similar cause that *philosopher* and *philosophical* in colloquial English are used in a degraded sense; we talk of "bearing pain like a philosopher."[2] We may contrast the apathy of Zeno, the freedom from affections which make us dependent on external things, with the metriopathy of Aristotle, who therein reflected the general spirit of the ancient Greeks. Epicurus placed the highest good in a deep haven of rest, where no waves wash and no sound is heard; his ideal too was

---

[1] The word παραψυχή had for the ancient Greeks nothing of the emotional import which Greek Christians placed in the word παράκλητος.

[2] We find φιλοσοφῶ used in this sense in Theophylactus Simocatta; *e.g.* viii. 11, 3, τὸ δυστύχημα. It has also another sense in the same author, *operam dare*.

mainly negative, freedom from bodily pain and mental trouble. These philosophies were over against the world rather than above it; the note of them was dissatisfaction with life and estrangement from the world.

This spirit, which set in as old Greek life was falling asunder, increased and became universal under the cold hand of Roman rule, which assorted well with the cold Stoic idea of $\phi\acute{u}\sigma\iota\varsigma$, nature. It has been said that the early Empire, up to the middle of the second century at least, was a golden age of felicity, and we may admit that in some respects it did approach more than other ages to the ideal of utilitarians; but for thinkers it was not an age of felicity or brightness, heaviness was hanging over the spirit and canker was beginning to gnaw. The heavy cloud soon burst, and after the reign of Marcus Aurelius, Europe was a scene of general misfortune.

The philosophical attitude of the Stoics, whose tenets were more widely spread than those of any other school, could not be final; it naturally led to an absolute philosophy. For it disparaged the world and isolated the soul; but the world thus disparaged was a fact which had to be explained, and reason was constrained to complete its dialectic by advancing to repose itself in the Absolute or the One, just as in the eighteenth century the system of Kant necessitated the absolute philosophies of Fichte, Schelling, and Hegel.

Or, to put it from a religious point of view, the individual's own soul was not found a sufficiently strong refuge. Some stronger and surer resting-place was needed, something above the world and not over against it. And so the spirit endeavoured to grasp itself anew. The new idea was the Logos; the new world was the kingdom of the Son. A need was felt for mediation—for a place or mansion as it were for the soul to be near God. This was the positive idea that animated the age of the Roman Empire and tended to supersede Stoicism; it was common to the system of Philo, to Gnosticism, to Christianity, and to Neoplatonism. And in Christianity, especially, approach to God seemed a sort of refuge, and the negative tendency, derived from the apathy of the Stoics and the unsociability of the Cynics, to flee from the environments of life, was very strong, and found its expression in monastic ideals.

Thus these philosophies of the Infinite were the sphere to

which the Stoic, Epicurean, and Pyrrhonic systems naturally led, by their own inherent defect. But we must now turn to the historical side and see how these late Greek thinkers prepared the way for the reception and spread of Christianity. It may be pointed out in a few words. In the first place, Epicureanism and Scepticism were atheistic and tended to discredit the popular beliefs in the pagan gods. In the second place, Epicureanism discredited devotion to one's country, and so, by uprooting patriotism, made the ground ready for the theory of universal brotherhood. In the third place, Stoicism, by its positive pantheistic theory and the surrender of the individual to the pulse of the universe, made a step towards the dependence of man on God's will or the doctrine of obedience, which is so cardinal in Christianity. And in the fourth place, the Stoic cosmopolitanism, combined with the Stoic theory of the law of nature, supplemented the non-patriotic sentiments of the Epicureans, and thus anticipated the christian embrace of all humanity. The fact that this Stoic theory affected the theory and practice of the Roman lawyers, and transformed the meaning of the phrase *jus gentium*, was an advance of the greatest importance in the same direction.

The resemblance between Christianity and Stoicism, which is in many points so striking, is sometimes unduly dwelt on. For if the Stoic and the Epicurean systems correspond to two different types of human nature, if some men are naturally stoical and others naturally epicurean, Christianity contained elements which attracted men of both these natures; as well as a stoical it had an epicurean side, and the second side should not be lost sight of.

For one of the most important elements in Christianity was the weight it gave to the tender affections, and one of the most attractive incidents in a christian life was the formation of a spiritual friendship or brotherhood. Now friendship and comradeship were regarded as most important elements in life by the Epicureans, beginning with the founder of the sect, who collected around himself a friendly society, while his disciples used to meet solemnly every month, and once a year in commemoration of his birth, in a manner which reminds us of the christian apostles meeting to commemorate their master. Friendship was a feature among the Epicureans as it was among the Christians, but not so in the system of the independent and lonely Stoics.

And then we may say that the joint life of brethren in a monastery, which, in the western lands of the Empire, ultimately acquired in many cases a certain brightness and cheerfulness, corresponded to the Epicurean spirit; while the solitary life of hermits who fled from their fellows and mortified their bodies was derived from the spirit of Stoicism, tinctured with oriental asceticism, and sometimes degenerating into the life of Cynics, who were a sort of caricature of the Stoics.

A noteworthy difference between the two philosophies was that the Stoics looked back, while the Epicureans looked forward. The great poem of Lucretius is permeated with optimism, not indeed with the optimism which holds that there is more pleasure than pain in the world, but with an optimistic belief in human progress. The human race is represented as progressing, gradually freeing itself from the fetters of superstition and opening its eyes to a clearer view of truth. The Stoics, on the other hand, prefer to dwell on the glories and the heroes of the past, and care little to look forward; their pantheism did not lead them to an idea of progress. Now Christianity involved optimism in two ways. It not only involved happiness for believers in another life; it also involved the theory that the course of history had been one of progress, designed and directed by the Deity, and that the revelation of Christ had introduced a new era of advance for the world,[1] just as the teaching of Epicurus was hailed by followers like Lucretius as ushering in a new age. It was believed indeed that at any time the end of the world might come, and that a great change might take place; but, allowing for all differences, we cannot help perceiving that in the idea of the world's progress Christianity approaches more nigh to Epicureanism than to Stoicism.

And, in general, the heroism of the Stoics, even of the later and milder Stoics, was not a christian virtue; and man's dignity, which for Christians depended on his having a soul, was reduced by the feeling of his abasement before God. On the other hand, Christianity exalted the feminine un-Roman side of man's nature, the side that naturally loves pleasure

---

[1] This idea underlies St. Augustine's *de civitate Dei*. Ambrose, in his letters to Valentinian II, speaks of gradual progress, light coming out of darkness.

and shrinks from pain and feels quick sympathy,—in fact, the Epicurean side; and thus Mr. Walter Pater makes Marius, a natural Epicurean, or rather a refined Cyrenaic, turn by the force of that very nature, *anima naturaliter christiana* in Tertullian's words, to the new religion. This is the human, and to most men attractive, side of Christianity [1]; it had another, an inhuman, side, of which I shall have to speak hereafter.

After the victory of Christianity, paganism was dying out, but even in the sixth century it was not yet dead. Towards the end of the fourth century Gratian gave up the title of Pontifex Maximus; the altar of Victory in the Senate House at Rome was removed, though Symmachus and the senators made an affecting appeal to spare it; the Olympic games were abolished, and the oracle of Apollo became silent. The effort of Julian, the last effort of the benighted faith, lured the exiled gods of Greece back for a moment to their ancient habitations. But the verses—εἴπατε τῷ βασιλῆι χαμαὶ πέσε δαίδαλος αὐλά, etc.—in which the Hellenic spirit uttered its latest breath, expressed the consciousness that the old things had passed away,—the laurel, the spring, and the emblems of paganism. "Tell the king, on earth has fallen the glorious dwelling"—the words have a dying fall; and with the song of Greece the gods of Greece also retreated down the vast and dreary edges of the world, which was no longer a meet habitation for the deities of Olympus. But the schools at Athens still flourished in the fifth century, and the pagans who taught there—as Leontius, Plutarch the philosopher, Proclus—were in no danger of suffering the fate of Hypatia at Alexandria. They were quietistic; they did not attempt to oppose the new faith, and the government wisely left them in peace.

The Christians themselves were not quite emancipated from the charm, or, as some thought, the evil glamour, of classical antiquity. The pagan rhetoric, with all its ornaments, was not dispensed with by the most learned christian divines. It was as dear to the heart of Chrysostom as to that of

---

[1] M. Édélestand du Méril says of Christianity: "Non seulement il minait par la base les deux grands empêchements de l'amour dans l'ancien monde, le laisser-aller de l'épicuréisme au plaisir et les orgueilleuses indifférences du stoïcisme; il initiait l'Humanité tout entière à cette vie de l'âme que quelques sages avaient seuls encore soupçonnée." (Introduction to *Floire et Blanceflor*, p. c.)

Libanius, and Eusebius, the historian of Constantine, succeeded by its means in producing some effective passages. Similarly, Latin divines like Augustine and Salvian did not despise the science of style. But the art of the ancients had more than this external influence. Christians who had really a taste for art were, by embracing the new religion, placed in a spiritual difficulty. The new religion created a repugnance to the old fabulous mythology, as a sort of emanation from Tartarean powers, and to the old philosophies and modes of thought. There were not many like Synesius who could be both a Platonist and a Christian. There were not many even like Tertullian, who would admit that the best of the ancients possessed "a soul naturally christian." And yet in spite of themselves they could not put away a hankering after the classical art whose subject-matter was pagan myth and pagan history, now to be replaced by the truths of the Old Testament. St. Augustine felt a thrill, and deemed the thrill wicked, at such lines as—

> infelix simulacrum atque ipsius umbra Creusae.

Jerome could not resist the fascination of Cicero. One Germanus, a friend of Cassian, had to confess with many tears that often, while he was engaged in prayer, the old heroes and heroines would pass into his soul, and the remembrance of the ancient gods disarrange his thoughts of God. Such asceticism as this was more common in the West than among the Greek-speaking Christians. It may be added that pagan symbols and mottoes were used on christian tombs, and pagan ideas adapted in christian art.

There is a legend which made its appearance about the fourth century, remarkable both in itself and as having been versified by the Empress Eudocia, the legend of Cyprian and Justina. It illustrates the thaumaturgy and the asceticism of the age as well as the conflict of Christianity and paganism, and is also interesting as presenting us with a prototype of Faust. Justina was a beautiful christian maiden of Antioch, passionately loved by a pagan youth Aglaides, who, unable to win her affections which were given to Christ, determined to move Acheron. For this purpose he engaged the services of Cyprian, a powerful magician, learned in all the wisdom of the Egyptians and in the magic of the Chaldeans. But the demons of temptation that the wizard's art raised against Justina were repulsed by the sign of the cross. Whereupon Cyprian, moved by the firmness and power of her faith, became enamoured of her, abjured his magic arts, and was baptized a Christian. Both he and Justina suffered martyrdom in the persecution of Diocletian. The vanity of all his arts and lore is described by Cyprian in a manner which reminds us of the opening lines of Faust's soliloquy in Goethe's drama. Pagan learning is associated with magic and powers of evil, and opposed to the light of Christianity. Another point in the contrast is the conception of a purified spiritual love opposed to the love of the carnal man which enlists the powers of darkness.

Regarding the dealings of holy men with demons, a curious tale is told of St. Macarius of Alexandria. He conceived the idea of visiting the garden and sepulchre (*kēpotaphion*) of Jannes and Jambros, magicians who had lived in the time of Pharaoh, that he might meet and make inquiries of the demons who had been lodged there by the art of the magicians. They had planted the garden with all sorts of trees, and surrounded it with a wall of square stones; they had built a tomb in it, wherein they placed rich treasure of gold, and had dug a great well—in hopes that after death they might luxuriate in this paradise. Macarius made his way, like a mariner at sea, by the guidance of the stars, and as he traversed the desert he stuck reeds in the ground at certain intervals to mark the way home. For nine days he crossed the desert, and as it was night when he reached the garden, he lay down and slept. But meanwhile the "wild demon" collected all the reeds, and when the saint awoke he found them lying in a bundle at his head. As he approached the garden seventy demons met him, shouting and gesticulating, leaping, and gnashing with their teeth: flying like crows in his face they asked him, "What want you, Macarius? why have you come to us?" He replied that he merely wished to see the garden and would leave it when he had seen it; whereupon the demons vanished. In the garden there was little to see; a bronze cask hung in the well by an iron chain worn by time, and a few dry pomegranates. Having satisfied his curiosity, Macarius returned to his cell.[1]

As there were two sides to the old Greek religion—the ridiculous side which Lucian brought out so humorously, and

[1] Palladius, Ἱστορία Λαυσιακή, ed. Meursius, 1616, p. 44 *sqq*.

the ideal but human side which made it lovely—there were two sides also to the christian religion. There was the ugly, inhuman side, from which the humanism of the fourteenth and fifteenth century revolted, manifested in extreme and grotesque asceticism, a sort of war with the instincts of humanity; and there was the consolatory side, the hopes which it offered to mankind, at that time almost weary of living. But in spite of the dismalness, as far as the world is concerned, of the Christianity of the time, when men even looked forward to a very speedy end of a universe which seemed a theatre of misery, we can see traces of cheerfulness and traits of human feeling in the Church, which had now outgrown the hopeful freshness that gave it such a charm in the first and second centuries. Christian women with gracious faces move before us, Olympias, Melania, Eudocia, though a lighter atmosphere seems to linger round the pagan ladies, Hypatia, Asclepigeneia, and Athenais.

It might be asked, was no middle course open? could not the attractions of paganism[1] be combined with the attractions of Christianity, and a new theory of life, combining the requisite consolation with the antique grace, be constructed? Neoplatonism might seem at first something of this kind. With a theology generically similar to the christian theology, it taught a high ideal of ethics, the practical aim being to purify the soul from the thraldom of matter by an ascending series of cleansing processes, so that it might finally, by a sort of *henosis* or at-one-ment, become conscious of the Absolute. But it is clear that Neoplatonism involved the same essential opposition which was involved in Christianity, the opposition of soul and body, and therefore must logically lead to the same cast of inhumanity, tinctured with cynicism. Theoretically, indeed, soul and body were two terms in a descending series, but practically they were opposed. And so, although the new philosophers, who studied Plato and Pythagoras and Aristotle and old Orphic mysteries, might invest their doctrine with an antique borrowed charm, they were really as much children of the gray time they lived in as the Christians. But they were recognised opponents; in such a spirit Augustine speaks of Plotinus and Porphyrius, and the

---

[1] At this period the pagan ritual endeavoured to seduce men's senses and maintain itself by brilliant forms of worship (*cf.* Richter, *Das weströmische Reich*, p. 550).

massacre of Hypatia at Alexandria was a manifestation of the antagonism.

Proclus, the last original Greek philosopher, lived at Athens throughout the greater part of the fifth century (410-485). Born in Lycia, he was dedicated by his parents to Apollo, for it behoved (as we are told by his biographer Marinus, whose work is full of interesting incidents and traits) that one who was to lead all sciences should be reared and educated under the god who leads the Muses. He studied rhetoric at Alexandria and philosophy at Athens, where, under the guidance of the old philosopher Plutarchus and his daughter Asclepigeneia, he was initiated in the mysteries of Platonism. We must glance at the system of Proclus, the last term in the history or chain of Greek philosophy. In a general history we cannot go into its difficult details, but we must take note of its leading features; for a historian of any particular state of the world is concerned with the way in which a thinker placed therein approaches metaphysical problems. It might even be said that we must go to the philosophers, as to mystics, in order to understand the real forces that underlie the history of a time, and determine even events like a war or a revolution. The men who act in history, the men who "make history," have only to do with this treasure, or this kingdom, or this woman [1]; the philosopher has not to do with this and that, but has to become a witness of the processes of the spirit in which this and that are nothing more than this and that. So in reading a philosophy we are getting at the secret of the age, and learning the manner in which the spirit contemplated itself at the time.

Proclus understood Plato more thoroughly and worked more in his spirit than his great predecessor Plotinus, on whom he made a marked advance in many respects. If Plotinus is the Schelling of Neoplatonism, Proclus is its Hegel. There was an unreduced surd in Plotinus and a certain cloudiness in his system, a sediment as it were in the bottom of the cup which clouded the liquid to a certain degree. The sediment disappears in Proclus, the wine is strained and clarified; he presents us with a thoroughly articulated system, that bears a distinct resemblance in its method to Hegel's Logic.

[1] *See* Hegel, *Werke*, xv. p. 96.

Proclus, like Plotinus, started with the One or the Absolute, that which cannot be called Being, for it is beyond Being, and cannot be called intelligent, for intelligence is too low a category to assert of it. It is the source of all things, and yet it would be improper to assert cause of it; it is a cause and yet not cause, ἀναιτίως αἴτιον. Now from the One, according to *Plotinus*, emanates an image which, through and in the act of turning towards the One from which it emanates, is Nous or Thought. This is the point at which *Proclus* makes a new departure. The immediate procession of the Nous from the One rests on a confusion, a middle term is required, and Proclus interposed the *henads* between them— a plurality of ones, whereby alone there can be participation in the One. The doctrine of the henads is the philosophical analogue of the famous *filioque* clause in the Latin creed; as the holy Spirit proceeds not from the Father alone, but from the Father and Son, so the Nous or Spirit proceeds not from the One directly, but from the One and the company of henads. The henads he terms Gods. Next to them, and third in the descending line, comes the sphere of Nous, differentiated into numerous categories arranged in triads. It is this triadic arrangement, of which we find the origin in Plato, that reminds us of the Hegelian system. From the intellectual world emanates the fourth term, Soul; and here he repeats his triple division, assuming three kinds of souls, divine, human, and demonic. Fifth and last in the scale comes Matter.[1]

This process of development is one of descent from higher to lower. There is a reverse process, the epistrophe or turning back; and this process is performed by the soul, when in the study of philosophy it turns to the intellect from which it came forth, and in whose nature it shares. Thus it is the aim of the "musical" or cultured soul to retrace the world-process in which it is involved.

In the hymns of Proclus, which he wrote under the inspiration of older Orphic hymns, and in which he celebrated all kinds of strange deities—for he used to say that a philosopher should not confine himself to the religious ideas of one people, but be "a hierophant of the world,"—he emits some of that

---

[1] Hierarchical scales were a feature of the period; they meet us in the military, civil, and ecclesiastical organisations, as well as in Neoplatonism.

mystic emotion with which the philosophical writings of Plotinus are suffused, but of which we can find little in his own severe treatises. For Plotinus, like Empedocles or Spinoza, often seems in a sort of divine intoxication, and the severity which attends undisturbed contemplation was lighted up, shall we say, or shadowed, by his enthusiasm as a combatant against the new religion. In his time, before Christianity attained its dominant position, no thinker with native enthusiasm could fail to be drawn into the vortex of the contending theories of the world. But in the fifth century the only thing left for non-christian philosophers was quietism. Out of the world, "a solitary worker in the vast loneliness of the Absolute," Proclus was able to develop the timeless and spaceless triads, and study the works of Plato with a leisure and severity that Plotinus could hardly realise. Most of his works assume the modest form of commentaries on Plato.

The practical end of the Neoplatonists was, like that of the Stoics, *ataraxia*, freedom from disturbance; and this they thought was obtained by contemplation, herein agreeing with the Aristotelian ideal of the "theoretic life." Thus they differed from both Stoics and Christians. For the Stoic and the Christian, theorising—the study of pure metaphysics—is valuable only as a means to right conduct, a sort of canonic for ethics; but for the Neoplatonist the practice of the ethical virtues is subsidiary to the contemplation of the metaphysical truth which is the end. And thus, although it had an atmosphere of religion about it, Neoplatonism was and could be strictly no more and no less than a philosophy. Stoicism had perhaps a larger number of the elements of a religion, and yet it too was only for the sage.

There is a certain contrast and there is also a certain analogy between the course of development of Christianity and that of Neoplatonism. As Christians had been divided into Athanasians and Arians, so Neoplatonism may be said to have fallen asunder into two divergent schools. There were the soberer and truer followers of Plotinus, among whom Hypatia may be mentioned, and there were the wilder mystical speculators like Iamblichus and the writer on Egyptian Mysteries. Thus the divergency from orthodox Neoplatonism was into the realm of the imagination; the divergency from orthodox Christianity was into the realm of the understanding. Among the new Platonists there were no rationalists like the Arians; and we may be sure that men of a cold logical temper, on whose faith the creed of Nicaea laid too heavy a burden, were more inclined to embrace the modified form of Christianity than any form of the new pagan philosophy.

Again, the minute determination of the nature of Christ in the fifth century, through the Nestorian and Eutychian controversies, was almost[1] the last period in the development of christian doctrine, just as the minute determination of the higher categories by Proclus was the final stage of the development of Neoplatonic thought. The first great inspiration, which in its ardour could not tolerate, or rather did not think of, precise analysis of ideas, had passed away, and men were able to reason things out more calmly and realise the subtler difficulties.

What, it may be asked, was the historical result for mankind of the new philosophy and the new religion? The presence of the Infinite, whether to an individual or a race, is bought at a great cost. Humanity seeks a deliverer; it obtains a deliverer and a tyrant. For the Infinite, having freed the human mind from the bonds of the finite, enslaves it unto itself, like a true tyrant; we may say, and the paradox is only apparent, that the human mind was cabined by the Infinite. Thought was rendered sterile and unproductive for centuries under the withering pressure of an omnipresent and monotonous idea. But through this *selva oscura* lay the path from ancient to modern civilisation, and few will be disposed to assert with Rousseau and Gibbon that the cost was greater than the gain.

---

[1] The monotheletic dispute in the seventh century, set at rest by the sixth Ecumenical Council, was actually the last stage in christological controversy; but it was really only a corollary to the monophysitic question.

CHAPTER II

INFLUENCE OF CHRISTIANITY ON SOCIETY

HAVING seen how closely Christianity was connected with the past ages of civilised Europe, whose beliefs it superseded, we must glance at its other historical aspect, in which it appears as a new departure. It has been said that the function of the German nations was to be the bearers of Christianity. The growth of the new religion was indeed contemporary with the spread of the new races in the Empire, but at this time in the external events of history, so far from being closely attached to the Germans, Christianity is identified with the Roman Empire. It is long afterwards that we see the mission fulfilled. The connection rests on a psychological basis; the German character was essentially subjective. The Teutons were gifted with that susceptibility which we call heart, and it was to the needs of the heart that Christianity possessed endless potentialities of adaptation. From the very first German princesses often embraced Christianity and adorned it, but it required many centuries for those nations to be regenerated by its influence. Yet even in the exclamation of the rude barbarian Chlodwig, when he heard the story of Christ's passion, "If I had been there with my Franks, I would have revenged his injuries!" we feel the presence of this heart, in its wild state, which Christianity was destined to tame. To an old Roman, like Aurelian or Constantine, such an exclamation would have been impossible. Christianity and Teutonism were both solvents of the ancient world, and as the German nations became afterwards entirely christian, we see that they were historically adapted to one another.

This aspect of Christianity as the religion of the future has brought us to consider it as a religion rather than as a theology, in which light its connection with the past naturally exhibited it. As a religion it was a complete novelty, and was bound to displace Stoicism and Neoplatonism. Stoicism was indeed practical, but it could only be accepted by a man of more than average intellect, while Christianity descended to the dull and the uneducated. Stoicism aimed at stifling the emotions and repressing the affections; Christianity cherished the amiable affections, and was particularly suited to be understood and embraced by women and children who, according to Aristotle, are creatures of passion, as opposed to men who are capable of living by reason. We must now point out some of the leading changes which Christianity produced in society, having first considered why Roman society adopted it.

What induced the civilised world to be converted to Christianity is a question that naturally suggests itself. Mr. Lecky tells us that it was not from conviction after careful sifting of evidence that men believed it; it was rather because they wanted to believe something, and Christianity was the best they found. It was consoling; it had an oriental flavour, and yet was not wrapped in such an envelope of mystic theosophy as to preclude it from acceptance by European minds. But it was, above all, I think, the cheerful virtue of the christian life that exercised a fascination on the cultured, and a passage in the *Confessions* of Augustine seems worthy of special remark.[1] Having stated that the christian life attracted him, he says:—

"Aperiebatur enim ab ea parte qua intenderam faciem et quo transire trepidabam, casta dignitas continentiae, *serena et non dissolute hilaris*, honeste blandiens ut venirem neque dubitarem et extendens ad me suscipiendum et amplectendum pias manus plenas gregibus bonorum exemplorum."

"In the direction where I had set my face, and whither I was hastening to cross over, there was exposed to my view a chaste and dignified temper of self-restraint, serene and cheerful but never dissolute, honourably enticing me to come without hesitation, and holding out to embrace and receive me affectionate hands, full of good examples."[2]

---

[1] viii. 11.
[2] It might seem that the Roman Empire might have attained of itself to this gentleness of manners, as it

But beside this ideal of a calm and cheerful social life there was the ideal of the ascetic and unsocial life of the hermit, which exercised a sort of maddening fascination over countless men of high faculties. The object of the hermit was to free himself from temptations to sensuality[1]; and thus the men who embraced such a life were probably, in most cases, men of strongly-developed physical passions, seized with a profound conviction of the deadliness of impurity. They were therefore generally men of robust frame, and this may explain how they could live so long under privations and endurances which seem sufficient to bring the life of an ordinary man to a speedy end. A rage for the spiritual life, far from the world, seized on individuals of all classes. In the sixth century an Ethiopian king, Elesbaa, abdicated his throne to retire to fast and pray in the desert, where he lived as a saint of no ordinary sanctity and power. In the reign of Theodosius the Great, a beautiful young man, who attained to the highest political offices, suddenly bade good-bye to his family and departed to Mount Sinai, stricken with a passion for the desert. But we need not enumerate here the countless disciples of St. Antony and St. Pachomius[2]; they meet us at every page of history.

In the same way among women the horror of unchastity —of desecration of the body, the temple of the soul—which had taken possession of the age with a sort of morbid excess, led to vows of perpetual virginity, and even children were dedicated in their infancy with a cruel kindness to a life of monasticism.[3] When we regard the effects of these habits, we observe, in the first place, that the great value set by the triumphant Church on the unmarried life must have conduced to depopulation; and in the second place, that the refusal of the most spiritually-minded in the community to assist in

advanced in civilisation and enjoyed a long peace; and it did tend in that direction, as we can see by the mild character of later Stoicism. But, as Lecky points out, there were three great checks on such a tendency (*History of European Morals*, i. 287)—(1) the imperial system itself—the cruelty of emperors worshipped as gods; (2) the institution of slavery; (3) the continuance of the gladiatorial shows.

[1] Evagrius describes how certain monks of Palestine succeeded so well in their endeavours to mortify the flesh that they became unconscious of the differences of the sexes (*Hist. Ecc.* i. 21).

[2] The coenobitic monks who lived together in cells in the desert were practically hermits.

[3] I do not propose to illustrate at length this subject, of which long accounts and numerous anecdotes may be found in any ecclesiastical history.

reproduction must have contributed to a decrease in really spiritually-minded persons, on the principle of heredity. If the best refuse to have children, the race must decline. It would be an error, of course, to insist too much on the distant effects of celibacy, but it cannot be overlooked that these were its natural tendencies. When Jerome remarked that in one respect marriage was laudable, because it brought virgins into the world, he did not see that the observation was really a retort upon his own position.

This unsocial passion invaded family life, and must have caused a considerable amount of suffering. Among the most pathetic incidents in the history of the growth of Christianity were those of the great gulf fixed between husbands and wives by the conversion of the latter. And after Christianity had prevailed, parents of average notions have been often filled with despair when a divine longing for the lonely life came upon their children.

The position of women was considerably changed by Christianity. Their possession of immortal souls equalised them with the other sex, and an emancipation began, which has since indeed progressed but slowly, by the recognition that they had functions beyond those of maternity and housewifery. In fact, those Christians who did not approve unreservedly of celibacy considered that the chief end of marriage was not production of children, but rather to be a type of the primitive union of human society.[1] This theory set women and men on an equal footing. St. Chrysostom expressed himself strongly on this subject. In a letter to a Roman lady he said that nature had assigned domestic duties to women and external duties to men, but that the christian life extended woman's sphere, and gave her a part to play in the struggles of the Church.[2] This part was that of the consoler and "ministering angel." And thus, to use a cant phrase of the present day, woman was admitted to have a "mission." Olympias, the friend of Chrysostom, was a lady of the new type.

As in the present day, the admiration of enthusiastic women for saints and priests was unbounded. Jerome had a spiritual circle of women about him in Old Rome, and Chry-

---

[1] *See* Ozanam, *La civilisation au cinquième siècle*, part ii. p. 81.

[2] Tertullian wrote a book on the duties of a christian woman.

sostom was the centre of similar attentions from ladies in New Rome. The name *auriscalpius*, or ear-picker, was given to a priest who was noted for his successes in making such spiritual conquests. The new view of women's position must have tended to make them more independent, just as does nowadays the spread of more liberal theories on women's education; and old-fashioned people probably looked with horror on the life of deaconesses as implying an immodest surrender of female retirement. That many of these religious sisters did become really "fast" in dress and behaviour we know from the letters of Chrysostom.

One of the most far-reaching changes introduced by Christianity into the conduct of life was the idea that human life as such was sacred; an idea distinctly opposed to the actual practice of the pagans, if not quite novel to them. This idea, in the first place, altered the attitude to the gladiatorial shows, and although they were not immediately abolished on the triumph of Christianity, they became gradually discredited and were put down before the end of the fourth century. As these amusements were one of the chief obstacles to the refining and softening influences of Roman advanced civilisation, we can hardly rate too highly the importance of this step.[1] Again, the attitude towards suicide, which the pagans, if they did not recommend it, at least considered venal,[2] was quite changed by the new feeling, and became a heinous crime, which was hardly condoned even to heroic christian maidens, though it were the only means of preserving them from dishonour. Another corollary from the respect for inviolability of life was the uncompromising reprobation of all forms of removing unwelcome children by exposition, infanticide, or even abortion.

Along with this negatively working idea of the sanctity of life was the other idea which succeeded and elevated Stoic cosmopolitanism, the idea that all men are brothers bound by

---

[1] Friedländer, *Sittengeschichte*, ii. p. 279, says of the deleterious effects of the games: "Sie erfüllten die geistige Atmosphäre Roms mit einem Ansteckungsstoff, dessen Einflusse selbst hohe Bildung und bevorzugte Lebensstellung nicht zu brechen vermochten, für die auch das andre Geschlecht nur zu empfänglich war."

[2] Plotinus forbade suicide on the ground that it entailed a disturbance which infected the purity of the soul. Stoics looked upon the possibility of self-destruction as a gauge of their independence.

a common humanity. Besides softening to some extent the relation between the Roman world and the barbarians, this idea had a considerable effect within the Empire itself on the position of slaves, who as men and members of the christian Church were the brothers of their masters and on an equality with them. This both improved the condition of slaves and promoted to some degree a decrease of slavery and an increase in the frequency of emancipation. Beyond this, it penetrated and quickened all the emotions of life and furthered the cultivation of the amiable side of human nature.

Yet we can hardly say that there was much altruism in early christian society, in spite of the altruistic tendencies of Christ's teaching. There were abundant instances of self-sacrifice for others, but they were not dictated by the motive of altruism; they were dictated by the motive of a transfigured selfishness which looked to a reward hereafter, by the desire of ennobling and benefiting one's own soul. The impossible and, as Herbert Spencer has shown, undesirable aim of loving one's neighbour as oneself, in the literal sense of the words, was not attained or even approached by the saints. Many people in modern England come far nearer to the realisation of the idea than they did. Alms, for example, were not given merely out of pure and heartfelt sympathy for the poor: they were given for the benefit of the giver's soul, and to obtain the prayers of the recipients who, just because they happened to be poor, were supposed to be not far from the kingdom of heaven.

The ideas of sin and future punishment, enforced by an elaborate legislature regulating degrees of sin and the corresponding penances, were another great novelty of Christianity, raising as it were the elaborate ritual of pagan ceremonies of purification into the spiritual sphere, where evil thoughts were wellnigh as black as evil acts. The tortures of hell gave a dark tint to the new religion, which to natures of melancholy cast made it a sort of haunting terror; while the claims of Christianity to dominate the most trifling deed and smallest thought, leaving almost no margin for neutral actions, tended to make the dread of sin constant and morbid.

And here we have touched on a side of Christianity which was distinctly unreasonable and would have revolted the clear intellect of a healthy Greek. The idea that God's omniscience takes account of the smallest and meanest details of our lives, and keeps, as it were, a written record of such nugatory sins against us, would have appeared utterly absurd, as well as a degradation of the Deity, to an old Greek possessed of the most elementary culture. It is an idea that cannot well be accepted by the reason of the natural man; and, like that other idea of extreme asceticism which led to a solitary life, equally repugnant to Hellenic reason, it was carried to excess by the Christians. For like all true lovers, the true lovers of God "run into strange capers." And while to many this idea was welcome, as bringing them into close and constant relation with the Deity, as making them feel his presence, to some Christians the divine supervision of trifles must have been felt as an oppressive tyranny. And the Church was able to enforce its moral laws by fear of the ultimate and dreaded penalty of excommunication which made the criminal an outcast from society, avoided and abhorred.

In forming an idea of the christian society and sentiments of the early ages, we must not forget that the believers of those days realised far more vividly than the believers of our days the realities of their religion. While the conceptions of the saints were confined to a smaller sphere of observed facts, their imaginations had a wider range and a greater intensity. The realm of scientific knowledge was limited; and therefore the field of fancy which they inherited, the field of divine or automatous intimations, was all the more spacious. They were ever contending or consorting with the demons or angels of imagination, now uplifted and rejoicing in the radiant raptures of heaven, now labouring and heavyladen in the lurid horrors of hell. This variation between two extreme poles—between a dread of God's wrath and a consciousness of his approval— which produced the opposing virtues of christian pride and christian humility, was alien to the Hellenic instinct which clung to the mean (τὸ μέσον). The "humble man" of the Christians would have been considered a vicious and contemptible person by Aristotle, who put forward the "man of great spirit" (ὁ μεγαλόψυχος) as a man of virtue.

This chapter may be concluded with the remark that a considerable change had come over Christianity itself since its first appearance. It had lost the charm that attended the novelty of the first revelation; the flower of its youth had faded. The christian temperament could not be unaffected by the cold winter waves that washed over the world in the fourth and fifth centuries; and although the religious consolation remained, the early cheerfulness—cheerfulness even under persecution—and the freshness which contrasted pleasantly with the weary pagan society were no longer there.

CHAPTER III

ELEMENTS OF DISINTEGRATION IN THE ROMAN EMPIRE

THE most obvious element of weakness in the Roman Empire was the increasing depopulation. The vitality of a state depends ultimately on the people, and from the time of Augustus, who was obliged to make special laws to encourage reproduction, to the time of Marcus Aurelius the population steadily decreased. In the reign of Aurelius the great plague inflicted a blow which the Empire was never able to recover, as it was involved in a continuous series of evils, the wars of the third century, until the time of Constantine. The original cause of depopulation in Italy was the slave system, which ruined the middle class of small proprietors and created a proletariat. A similar tendency manifested itself in the East under Roman rule, though in a lesser degree; and the financial policy of the later Empire, which maintained oppressive taxation by means of the "curial system," effectually hindered the population from recovering itself. Thus to the social cause which had operated for a long time was added in the fourth century a political cause, and just as the first was an indispensable element of Roman society, the second soon became indispensable to the Roman administration.

Moreover, the only remedy which the government could apply to meet the evil was itself an active element of disintegration. This was the introduction of barbarians as soldiers or agriculturists (coloni) into the Roman provinces.

Thus slavery and oppressive taxation, the causes of depopulation, and the importation of barbarians, the remedy of depopulation, may be looked on as three main elements of disintegration in the Empire. A fourth element was the christian religion which, while it was entirely opposed to the Roman spirit which it was destined to dissolve, nevertheless was not theoretically opposed to the Empire and the imperial administration. We may take these four points in order :

(1) It was a consequence of the slave system that those great estates which, according to an ancient writer, ruined Italy were formed, and swallowed up the small proprietors. It is important to note precisely how this effect took place. In time of war all free proprietors, rich and poor alike, were obliged to take the field; but while the land of the rich, who employed slaves to cultivate it, was not affected by this circumstance, the lands of the small farmers, who had no staff of slaves, remained uncultivated during their absence. This fact, in a time when wars were frequent, tended directly to reduce the petty proprietors to beggary and add to the wealth of the rich capitalists. Another effect of wars, which conduced to the same result, was that the ranks of the small farmers were decimated, while the numbers of the slaves, who did not serve in the army, multiplied. We must also remember that a bad harvest raised prices then to an extent that appears now quite enormous; so that the small farmer was obliged to buy corn at an exorbitant price, and, if the harvest of the following year turned out very successful, prices descended so low that he was unable even to reimburse himself.[1]

Besides destroying the middle class, the slave system facilitated and encouraged the unproductive unions of concubinage, and these to the self-indulgent were more agreeable than marriage, which entails duties as well as pleasures. This convenient system naturally confirmed and increased the spirit of self-indulgence, and also increased its psychological concomitant, cruelty or indifference, which tended to keep up the practice of exposing infants, a direct check on population.

Under the Empire even the number of the slaves decreased. For to purchase slaves in the markets of the East the precious metals were requisite, since the produce of the West did not readily find a sale in the East, and the supply of gold and silver was declining, especially after the time of Caracalla, as is proved

---

[1] I have availed myself here of the acute remarks of *von Jhering* on the *Quellen des Pauperismus* in his *Geist des römischen Rechts*, vol. ii. p. 237 *sqq.*

by the great depreciations of coinage.¹ This diminution in the number of slaves led to the rehabilitation of free labour; but the freemen were soon involved in the meshes of the caste system which reduced them not to slavery, but to serfdom.

(2) It was in the times of Diocletian and Constantine that the municipal institutions of the Empire were impressed with the fiscal stamp which characterised them henceforward. During the three preceding centuries the provinces had gone through much tribulation, of which Juvenal, for example, gives us a picture; but this oppression was at least mitigated by the fact that it was not legal, and it was always open to the provincials to take legal proceedings. Nor was extortion always countenanced by the Emperors; it is recorded that Tiberius found fault with the prefect of Egypt for transmitting to Rome an unduly large amount.²

But at the beginning of the fourth century the old municipal curia or senate was metamorphosed into a machine for grinding down the provincial proprietors by a most unmerciful and injudicious system of taxation. The curia of a town consisted of a certain number of the richest landowners who were responsible to the treasury for a definite sum, which it was their business to collect from all the proprietors in the district. It followed that if one proprietor became bankrupt the load on all the others was increased. The provincials had two alleviations. The first was that a revision of taxes took place every fifteen years, the so-called *indiction*,³ which became a measure of time, and thus there was a prospect that an excessive burden might be reduced. The second consisted in the institution of the *defensores*, persons nominated to watch over the interests of the provincials and interfere in behalf of their rights against illegal oppression.⁴ On the other hand we must remember that, as Finlay noticed, the interests of the *curia* were not

---

¹ Compare Merivale, *History of the Romans under the Empire*, vol. viii. pp. 351, 352. For the drain of specie to Asia, Pliny is cited (*Hist. Nat.* vi. 26; xii. 41).

² Suetonius, *V. Tib.* 32. See Finlay, *History of Greece* (ed. Tozer), vol. i. p. 41.

³ The *indictio* (ἐπινέμησις) was properly the first year of the period of fifteen years. Afterwards it was used of any year of this period. The first indiction began on 1st September 312 A.D.

⁴ The duties of a *defensor civitatis* are enumerated in a rescript of Gratian, Valentinian, and Theodosius (*Cod. Just.* i. 55, 4): *scilicet ut imprimis parentis vicem plebi exhibeas*—he is to act as a parent to the populace, to protect both *rustici* and *urbani* from oppression, to withstand "the insolence of office," to prevent the exaction of anything beyond the amount due, etc. This office of clemency was afterwards closely connected with the christian Church.

identical with those of the municipality, as the *curiales* were only a select number of the most wealthy.

This system tended to reduce the free provincial gentlemen to the state of serfs. They were enclosed in a cage from which there was almost no exit, for laws were passed which forbade them to enlist in the army, to enter the church, or go to the bar. They were not allowed to quit their municipality without permission from the governor, and travelling was in every way discouraged. Moreover, the obligations of the decurionate were hereditary, and exclusion from all other careers rigidly enforced. Thus a caste system was instituted, in which the individual life must have been often a hopeless monotony of misery.

The kindred institutions of serfdom and the *colonatus* gradually arose by a double process of levelling up and levelling down; slaves were elevated and freemen were degraded to the condition of labourers attached to the soil. The slave proprietors were called *ascripticii*; while the free farmers were known as *coloni*. Economic necessities naturally brought about this state of things, and then it was recognised and stereotyped by law. An account of the colonatus which, while it is concise, loses sight of no essential fact, has been given by Dr. Ingram in his essay on "Slavery," from which the following passage may be conveniently quoted: "The class of coloni appears to have been composed partly of tenants by contract who had incurred large arrears of rent and were detained on the estates as debtors (*obaerati*), partly of foreign captives or immigrants who were settled in this condition on the land, and partly of small proprietors and other poor men who voluntarily adopted the status as an improvement in their position. They paid a fixed proportion of the produce (*pars agraria*) to the owner of the estate, and gave a determinate amount of labour (*operae*) on the portion of the domain which he kept in his own hands (*mansus dominicus*). The law for a long time took no notice of these customary tenures, and did not systematically constitute them until the fourth century. It was indeed the requirements of the fiscus and the conscription which impelled the imperial government to regulate the system."[1]

---

[1] Article on "Slavery," by Dr. J. K. Ingram in the *Encyclopædia Britannica*. The best work on the subject of the colonatus is the essay by M. Fustel de Coulanges in his recent volume of *Recherches*. He points out clearly how the *fermiers par contrat* became gradually transformed to colons. "Ce n'est

The caste system was carried out not only in the class of landed proprietors, to secure the land tax, but in all trades and professions whose members were liable to the capitation tax. Two other taxes were introduced at the same period, the *chrysargyron*, a tax on receipts which fell very heavily on poor people, and was afterwards abolished by Anastasius amidst general rejoicings; and a class tax on senators.

The uses to which a large part of the fiscal income was put gave the system an additional sting. The idle populaces of the great cities were supplied with corn—the drones fed on the labours of the bees. But this was only the unavoidable consequence of the economical relations of the ancient world, which led necessarily to pauperism on a tremendous scale. A more real grievance was the system of court ceremonial and aulic splendour, introduced by Aurelian, confirmed by Diocletian, and elaborated by Constantine, which consumed a vast quantity of money, and was ever increasing in luxury and unnecessary extravagance. As Hallam said, in speaking of the oppression under Charles VI of France, "the sting of taxation is wastefulness."

The principle of this system was to transfer to the imperial treasury as much as possible of the wealth circulating in the Empire. Want of capital in the provinces was a necessary result; there were no means to repair the damages of time, fire, or earthquakes save by an application to the central authority, which entailed delay and uncertainty, especially in distant provinces. A decrease in the means of life was soon produced, and thereby a decrease in the population.

The western suffered more than the eastern provinces, a fact which we must attribute primarily to a different economic condition, resulting from a different history. The distribution of property was less uneven in the East, and the social

pas le colonat qui s'est substitué en bloc au fermage; c'est, chaque jour, ici ou là, un colon qui s'est substitué à un fermier. Le fermage et le colonat ont longtemps vécu côte à côte" (p. 24). The class of *ascripticii*, who arose through the practice of *tenures serviles*, are recognised in a law of Alexander Severus, 224 A.D. (*Cod. Just.* viii. 51, 1). The distinction between *ascripticii* and *coloni*, clearly marked in several laws of Justinian (*e.g. Cod.* i. 4, 24; Nov. cvii. ed. Zachariä), was kept up still in the seventh century, but disappeared in the eighth; at least there is no mention of *adscripticii* in the νόμος γεωργικός, see Zach. von Lingenthal, *Griechisch-römisches Recht*, p. 241. M. de Coulanges is wrong in attributing the treatise αἱ ῥοπαί to the eighth century; it was probably composed in the reign of Heraclius; see von Lingenthal, *ib.* p. 9.

character of the people was different. For while the East was under the more genial and enlightened rule of Alexander's successors, the West was held by the cold hand of Rome. After the division of the Empire, 395 A.D., the state of the West seems to have become rapidly worse, while the East gradually revived under a government inclined to reform. Of the misery to which the Occident was reduced by the middle of the fifth century we have a piece of incontestable evidence in the constitutions of the Emperor Majorian, who seems to have been inspired by the example of the government of Constantinople, and desired to alleviate the miseries that were produced by the curial institutions. He was perhaps animated by some faint reflection of the spirit of ancient Rome, if we may judge from the enunciation of his policy in the letter which he addressed to the senate on his accession.[1] His short reign impresses us with a peculiar melancholy, a feeling of ineffectuality, and brings home to us perhaps more than anything else in the fifth century how fruitless it was to struggle against the doom which was implied in the circumstances of the Empire and therefore impended inevitably over it, and how impracticable any reformation was when the decay had advanced so far.

The language used in Majorian's constitutions of the state of the provincial subjects is very strong. Their fortunes are described as "wearied out by the exaction of diverse and manifold taxes." The municipal bodies of decurions, which should be regarded as the "sinews of the republic," have been reduced to such a condition by "the injustice of judges and venality of tax-collectors" that they have taken refuge in obscure hiding-places. Majorian bids them return, guaranteeing that such abuses will be suppressed. It is particularly to be noted that he abolished the arrangement by which the corporation was responsible for the whole amount of the land tax fixed at the last indiction; henceforward the curia was to be responsible only for what it was able to collect from the tax-payers. He further discharged the accumulated arrears and re-established the office of *defensor provinciae*, which was falling into disuse.

---

[1] *Nov. Maj.* 1: "Praesumite justitiam nostris vigere temporibus et sub innocentiae merito proficere posse virtutes. Nemo delationes metuat," etc.

We need not dwell on the extortions and oppressions of the officials—the governors of the provinces, the vicars of the dioceses, the praetorian prefects—which made the cup of misery run over. It is enough to call attention to a flagrant defect in the Roman imperial system—the fact that the administration of justice was in the hands of the government officials; the civil governors were also the judges. By a constitution of Constantine there was no appeal to the Emperor from the sentence of the praetorian prefect. Thus there was no protection against an unjust governor, as the offender was also the judge.[1]

It follows from this that the interests of the government and the governed were in direct opposition; and it is evident that the sad condition of the provinces, depopulated and miserable, was a most serious element of disintegration, the full effects of which were produced in the West, while in the East it was partially cancelled by the operation of other tendencies of an opposite kind.

(3) The introduction of barbarians from Central Europe into the Empire was due to two general causes. They were admitted to replenish the declining population, or they were admitted from the policy that they would be less dangerous as subjects within than as strangers without. Even in the time of the Republic there had been instances of hiring barbarian mercenaries; under the Empire it became a common practice. Marcus Aurelius made settlements of barbarians in Pannonia and Moesia.[2] It is probable that the barbarisation of the army progressed surely and continuously, but this plan of settling barbarians as *coloni* within Roman territory was not carried out on a large scale until the latter half of the third century. Gallienus settled Germans in Pannonia, and Claudius, after his Gothic victory, recruited his troops with the flower of the Gothic youth; but Probus introduced multitudes of Franks, Vandals, Alans, Bastarnae; in fact, the policy of settling barbarians on

---

[1] "Quid aliud," cries Salvian, a divine of the fifth century, "quorundam quos taceo praefectura quam praeda ? . . . ad hoc enim honor, a paucis emitur, ut cunctorum vastatione solvatur . . . unius honor urbis excidium est" (*de Gubernatione Dei*, iv. 21). Salvian is severe on all classes of the community. "The life of all merchants," he says, "is nothing but a tissue of fraud and perjury, the life of the curials is nothing but injustice, that of the administrative officials (*officialium*) is devoted to collusion, while the career of soldiers is a career of rapine" (iii. 50, ed. Pauly).

[2] Cassius Dio, 72, 11.

Roman ground was the most important feature of Probus' reign. Thrace, for example, received 100,000 Bastarnae. Moreover, he compelled the conquered nations to supply the army with 16,000 men, whom he judiciously dispersed in small companies among Roman regiments. The marklands of the Rhine and Danube were systematically settled with Teutons. Constantius Chlorus continued the policy of Probus; his allocations of Franks in the neighbourhood of Troyes and in the neighbourhood of Amiens deserve special notice, for these colonists succeeded in Germanising the north of France, so that they have been called "the pioneers of the German nations." The Carpi [1] (perhaps Slaves), subdued by Diocletian and Galerius, were transported in masses to Pannonia. Constantine is said to have allotted lands to 300,000 Sarmatae, and he seems to have adopted a policy, perhaps received from his father, of treating the barbarians with great consideration. Ammianus says that Julian reproached his memory for having been the first to advance barbarians to the consulate.[2] From the time of Constantine the importance of the Germans in the Empire increased rapidly. It became apparent in the revolt of Magnentius, which Julian regarded as a "sacred war in behalf of the laws and constitution." Magnentius himself was an "unfortunate relic of booty won from the Germans,"[3] and his standard was joined by the Franks and Saxons, "who were most zealous allies on account of kindred race" ($\kappa\alpha\tau\grave{\alpha}\ \tau\grave{o}\ \xi\upsilon\gamma\gamma\epsilon\nu\acute{\epsilon}s$). In the days of Constantius "a multitude of Franks flourished in the palace."[4] When Theodosius I. subdued the Alemanni he sent all the captives to Italy, where they received fruitful farms on the Po as *tributarii*. Valens followed the same principle in 376, when he admitted the fugitive bands of West Goths into Thrace, an act which, owing to the avarice and rapacity of the Roman officials, had such disastrous consequences. The favour shown to Germans, especially to the influential

---

[1] Ammian. Marcel. xxxiii. 1, 5: "Carporum quos antiquis excitos sedibus Diocletianus transtulit in Pannoniam." Maximin, the prefect of Italy in the days of Valentinian, and painted in black colours by Ammianus, was of the stock of the Carpi on his father's side.

[2] *Ib.* xxi. 10, 8: "Eum aperte incusans, quod barbaros omnium primus adusque fasces auxerat et trabeas consulares." But Julian, as Ammianus remarks, did himself what he censured Constantine for doing, and conferred the consulship on Nevitta.

[3] Julian, *Or.* i. p. 42, ed. Hertlein: $\tau\hat{\eta}s\ \dot{\alpha}\pi\grave{o}\ \Gamma\epsilon\rho\mu\alpha\nu\hat{\omega}\nu\ \lambda\epsilon\acute{\iota}\alpha s\ \lambda\epsilon\acute{\iota}\psi\alpha\nu o\nu\ \delta\upsilon\sigma\tau\upsilon\chi\grave{\epsilon}s\ \pi\epsilon\rho\iota\sigma\omega\zeta\acute{o}\mu\epsilon\nu o\nu$.

[4] Ammian. xv. 5, 11. For settlement of the Alemanni, *ib.* xxviii. 5, 15.

Merobaudes, at the court of Gratian, led to the revolt of Maximus, which was a movement of old Roman discontent against the advances which the Germans were making.

The facts instanced are sufficient to show that a new element, the German nationality, was gradually fusing itself in the fourth century throughout the Roman world, especially in the West. It was plainly an element of disintegration. For, by the incorporation of barbarian elements, the wall of partition between the Empire and the external nations was lowered; it made the opposition between Rome and the barbarians somewhat less sharp; in particular, the bonds of a common nationality did not fail to assert themselves between the Germans in Roman service and the independent tribes; the Germans within had a friendly leaning to the Germans without. The rising of Magnentius exhibits this relation; and we shall see it repeated in the fifth century in the careers of Stilicho, Aetius, and Ricimer, of whom the first was a Vandal and the last a Sueve; Aetius was of barbarian descent, and, although a Roman environment for some generations back had served to identify him more thoroughly with Roman interests, he is always quite at home with the barbarians. Throughout the fifth century we can observe, in the dealings of Romans and Teutons in the West, that the line of demarcation is growing less fixed, and the process of assimilation advancing. We may remark the case of the Patrician Syagrius, who reigned as a sort of king in northern Gaul, and spoke German perfectly.

Jerome uses the word *semibarbarus* of Stilicho, and we may conveniently adopt the word semi-barbarian to denote the whole class of Germans in Roman service. The significance of these semi-barbarians is that they smoothed the way, as we have already mentioned, for the invaders who dismembered the Empire; not being attached by hereditary tradition to Roman ideas and the Roman name, but having within them the Teutonic spirit of individual freedom, directly opposed to the Roman spirit of tyrannical universal law, they were not prejudiced sufficiently strongly in favour of the Roman Empire to preserve it, although they admired and partook of its superior civilisation.

(4) Christianity emphasised the privileges, hopes, and fears of the individual; Christ died for each man. It was thus

opposed to the universality of the Roman world, in which the individual and his personal interests were of little account,[1] and had in this respect a point of community with the individualistic instinct of the Germans—the attachment to personal freedom of life, which always struck the Romans as the peculiar German characteristic.[2] In two ways especially the opposition of Christianity to the Roman Empire manifested itself—by the doctrine of a divine law independent of and superior to temporal law, and by the dissociation of spiritual from secular authority. For the spirit of Christianity was really alien to the spirit of Rome, though it appeared to blend with it for a while; and this alien nature was manifested in the position of the Church as an independent, self-constituted body existing within the Empire. But in the process of the dissolution of the Empire in the West the Church supported the falling State against the barbarians, who were Christians, indeed, but tainted with Arian heresy. And when we remember that in the East the Church allied itself closely with the imperial constitution, and that this union survived for many centuries, we must conclude that Christianity did not contribute to produce what is loosely called the Fall of the Western Empire. Its spirit revolutionised the condition of the whole Roman world; the Roman spirit was undergoing a change; but yet, as far as Christianity itself is concerned, there seems no reason why the Roman Empire should not have continued to exist in the West just as it continued to exist in the East. Christianity made the prevailing misery and oppression more tolerable by holding out the hopes of a future world.[3] But thereby it tended to confirm the growing feeling of indifference; the political and social environment seemed an alien, unhomelike world; and this indifference, a natural outcome of the senility of the Empire, was as fatal in its effects as the actual risings of peasants. In

---

[1] The individual soul was considered of more importance than a city, a nation, or an empire. There was also a firm belief in the stability of the Church independently of the State: "The Church is immovable," says John Chrysostom, "and the more the world takes counsel against it, the more it increases; the waves are dissipated, but the rock stands immovable." This standpoint involved a limit on the universality of the Empire.

[2] For the "dominant sentiment of the barbarian state," compare Guizot, *L'histoire de la Civilisation en Europe*, p. 59.

[3] In the present world the christian Church relieved distress, and this fact reacted on the administration, as is shown by the rescript of Honorius in 409 (*Cod. Just.* i. 55, 8), by which the bishop and clergy are to take part in the nomination of the *defensores civitatum*.

a certain direct way, too, Christianity contributed to depopulation in the fourth and fifth centuries, namely, by the high value set on personal chastity and the ascetic spirit of monasticism, which discouraged marriage and caused large numbers to die without progeny.

These four elements undermined the Roman world, partly by weakening it, partly by impairing its Roman character and changing the view of life which determined the atmosphere of Roman society. Other less capital elements of disintegration might be mentioned, such as the depreciation of coinage; and elsewhere we shall have to notice the dislocating effects of geographical separation and national difference on the Empire.

We may close this chapter by considering the political situation of the Empire in the fourth and fifth centuries. We see at the first glance that there coexisted in it three separate organisations, representing the three ideas which were mixing and striving with each other, engaged in the process of producing a new world; and these were therefore the fundamental political forces of the age. The first of these was the civil service which was organised by Diocletian and Constantine in the form of a staircase or hierarchy, descending by successive grades from the highest ministers to the lowest clerks. With it the idea of the Roman Imperium was closely bound up, and it was the depository of the great product of the Roman spirit, the system of Roman law. Secondly, there was the army, which was Roman in its organisation and traditions, but was the chief opening by which the Germans were able to gain influence and political power in the Empire; at this time it really represented the semi-barbarians. It has been often remarked that the old Roman spirit seemed to preserve itself best in the army, a result of observation which at first sight might seem to be curiously at variance with the most obvious fact that the army was recruited with Germans. And yet on looking deeper we see that these facts have a causal connection; it was just the fresh German spirit which was able to give some new life to the old forms and throw some enthusiasm into the task of maintaining the Roman name of which they were really proud. And it was this coalition of Roman and German elements in the army which made the dismemberment of the Empire in the West less violent than it might have been.

The army and the civil service were institutions produced by Rome herself, subject to the Emperor as the supreme head expressing the unity of the State. The third organisation, the christian Church, was in a different position, within the Empire and yet not of it, but in the fourth and fifth centuries closely connected with it.

The manner in which these three forces, the Roman system, the semi-barbarians, and the christian Church, interacted and produced a new world was conditioned by two essential facts: (1) the presence of the German nations outside the Empire pressing on it as its strength declined; and (2) the heterogeneity of the parts of which the Roman world consisted. For the Roman world was a complex of different nations and languages, without a really deep-reaching unity, held together so long by the mere brute strength of tyrannical Roman universality, expressed in one law, one official language, and one Emperor—a merely external union. Naturally it fell into two worlds, the Greek (once the dominion of Alexander) and the Roman; and this natural division finally asserted itself and broke the artificial globe of the Roman universe.

But the globe was not burst asunder suddenly; it cracked, and the crack enlarged by degrees and the pieces fell apart gently. The separation of the eastern and western worlds (*gemini orbes*) took place gradually, and the actual territorial division between the sons of Theodosius did not theoretically constitute two Roman Empires. The remarkable circumstance is that the name and traditions of Rome clung to the Greek more closely than to the Roman part of the Empire; and that the work of fusion wrought there by Alexander and his successors may be said truly to have contributed as much to the long duration of the Roman Imperium as the work of the Caesars themselves.

CHAPTER IV

THE ADMINISTRATION OF THE EMPIRE

THE reader will remember that the new system instituted by Diocletian and developed by Constantine divided the Empire into a number of dioceses, each of which consisted of a group of adjacent provinces. The governor of a province was accordingly under the control of the governor of the diocese to which his province belonged; and in his turn the governor of the diocese was under the control of that praetorian prefect under whose jurisdiction the diocese happened to be. A hierarchy of officials was thus formed. The number of the prefects and the extent of the jurisdiction of each varied during the fourth century with the various partitions that were made by co-regent sovereigns; but from the time of Constantine there was always a prefect of the Gauls, including Spain and Britain, and always a prefect of the East, while Italy and the Balkan lands were sometimes united under one prefect, and sometimes severed under two. But the final partition between the sons of Theodosius in 395 determined that there were to be four praetorian prefects, two in the East and two in the West; so that after that date we may consider the Empire as definitely divided into four prefectures, each prefecture consisting of a certain number of dioceses, and each diocese of a certain number of provinces.

But to understand what the Roman Empire really was, we must penetrate behind these administrative divisions, and find in its origin the secret of its essence. It was mainly an aggregate of cities which were originally independent states, and which still were allowed to retain enough of independence and of their municipal government to stand in their old relation of exclusiveness towards one another. In England a resident of Leeds is at home in Manchester, and has judicially the same position as a citizen of Manchester, whereas in the Roman Empire a citizen of Thessalonica was an alien in Dyrrhachium, a citizen of Corinth was an alien in Patras. Thus the citizens of different provincial towns stood in a double relation to one another; they were all Roman citizens, subject to the same central authority, and herein they were united; but they were also severally citizens of some particular city, and herein they were politically severed from the rest of the Roman world. The Empire has been therefore compared to a federation of Swiss cantons, governed by an emperor and senate.

But there was one important sphere from which this doublesidedness was excluded, namely, the sphere of senatorial rank. When the member of a municipality, for example, became elevated to the senate, he was thereby withdrawn from the duties which devolved on him in his native place to participate in the privileges and obligations of a senator. The senatorial world was thus the undiluted atmosphere of pure Roman imperialism, in which the unity of the Empire is reflected. From this point of view we may regard the Empire as consisting of three parts, the Emperor, the senators, and the mass of Roman citizens. The personages of senatorial position formed a homogeneous society which, in the political structure, may be looked on as a mean between the unity of the imperial person and the heterogeneity of the general body of citizens.

It is of great importance to understand what the senate and the senatorial rank really meant. We must carefully distinguish senators in general from those senators who actually sat in the conclaves which were held in the "senate house of Julian" at Constantinople. To be a senator in the first sense meant merely a distinction of social rank which involved certain taxes and burdens, but implied no political action as a senator. On the other hand, this social distinction was determined by political position, and the aristocracy of the Roman Empire in the fifth century was an aristocracy of officials. This is a fact to be borne in mind, that social rank ultimately depended upon a public career, and to render it intelligible it is necessary to explain the constitution of the senate.[1]

In the time of Constantine only those who had held the highest official rank, consuls, proconsuls, or prefects, were members of the senate. The new forms of court ceremony, which were instituted by Aurelian and Diocletian and elaborated by their successors, gave to such personages precedence over lesser dignitaries, and they were distinguished by the title of *clarissimi*, "most renowned." Social rank depended on precedence at court, and precedence at court depended on official position. Thus, under Constantine and his immediate successors, *clarissimi* and senators denoted the same class of persons, though regarded under different aspects. Officers of lower rank were grouped into two classes, the *perfectissimi* and the *egregii*, who were not members of the senate; these included the governors of dioceses and provinces, dukes, *correctores*, and others.

But in the course of time the senatorial rank was extended beyond these narrower limits and conferred upon the provincial governors and many subordinate officials. This involved the elevation of the *perfectissimi* and *egregii* into the class of the "most renowned." And this elevation necessitated a further change; for it would have been plainly incongruous to give to the governor of Helenopontus or Palestine the same title of honour as to the praetorian prefect of the East. Accordingly, while the class of "the most perfect" and the class of "the excellent" fell away because their members had become "most renowned," two new ranks of higher honour than the "most renowned" were created, namely the *illustres* and the *spectabiles*. Those who had

---

[1] The institution of a senate at New Rome as a twin sister to the senate of Old Rome, and resting on an exactly similar basis, has been generally attributed to Constantine; but in spite of the authority on which this idea rests it is extremely probable that Constantine did not go so far in his imitation of the city of the Tiber, and that the historian Zosimus may be right in ascribing the foundation of the senate of Constantinople to Julian, who certainly built the senate house. *See* Zosimus, iii. 11; Libanius, *Or.* i. 633, 15. Johannes Lydus calls the senate house "that of Julian"; Sozomen, ii. 3, and *Chron. Pasch.* p. 529, attribute it to Constantine. But the fact that no prefect of Constantinople was appointed until 359 (by Constantius) shows that Constantinople was not made in all respects in the image of Rome; and it should be noted especially that there was no prefect of the city to preside over meetings of the senate as in Rome. It seems probable that Constantine granted new privileges to the municipal senate of Byzantium and increased its numbers by noble Roman emigrants; and that as the duties of the Roman senate were gradually becoming less than imperial, those of the Byzantine senate were becoming more than municipal.

been before *clarissimi* or *perfectissimi* were raised to a higher degree.

Thus in the reign of Constantine and at the beginning of the fifth century there were different sets of titles. *Clarissimus*, which was the greatest title at the earlier period, was the least title at the later period. The praetorian prefects, the prefects of Old Rome and New Rome, the masters of foot and horse, the quaestors, the masters of offices, the count of the exchequer and the count of the privy purse, were all addressed as "illustrious"; the vicars of the dioceses and others were known as "respectable," while the provincial governors were "most renowned."[1]

Three important changes, then, took place between the reigns of Constantine and Arcadius. (1) The great mass of the civil and military officials were incorporated in the senatorial aristocracy; (2) as a consequence of this, there were formed three grades of senatorial rank, instead of three grades of official rank of which the highest alone was senatorial; (3) the highest class, the *illustres*, became larger than that of the *clarissimi* used to be, by the elevation of a number of officers to an equality with the prefects and consuls, namely the quaestor, the master of offices, the *comes sacrarum largitionum*, and the *comes rei privatae*.

The extension of the senatorial rank was probably made in the interests of the treasury. We have already remarked that this rank did not imply a seat in the senate house of New Rome or of Old Rome. The majority of the senatorial classes probably lived in the provinces,—not only the provincial governors whose duty compelled them to do so, but also a large number of retired officials, who were known by the name of *honorati*. All, except those who were specially excused in consideration of past services, were obliged by their nobility to heavy burdens and expenses. Like all others, they were liable to the property tax and to the burden of supplying recruits for the army and relays of horses in the imperial service; besides this they had three other sources of expense, a regular tax, an

---

[1] The word *clarissimus* might be still applied in a loose sense to a member of either of the two higher classes, betokening that he was a member of the senate and aristocracy; just in the same way that *illustris* itself had been in earlier times sometimes added in a general sense of honour to the technical title *clarissimus*. On the subject of these titles my chief guide has been Kuhn, *Die Städte und bürgerliche Verfassung des römischen Reichs*.

irregular tax, and an indirect burden. The regular tax was the *follis*[1] or *gleba*, a tax on property, which the Emperor himself, as a senator, paid. The irregular tax was the *aurum oblaticium*,[2] an offering in money, which senators were obliged to present to the Emperor on the fifth, tenth, and such anniversaries of his accession, or on occasion of a victory. The indirect burden consisted in the fact that any senator might be compelled to discharge the functions of a praetor, and expend large sums on the exhibition of games and shows; and thus a man of senatorial standing, living in the provinces, was sometimes compelled to reside temporarily in the capital in order to discharge this unwelcome duty.[3] The praetors in Constantinople were at first two, but gradually reached the number of eight, but as the games and spectacles did not call the fortunes of all into requisition, some of them were compelled to contribute to the erection of public buildings.[4] From this burden it was customary to exempt retired civil servants, and this exemption was called *allectio*.

This explanation of the position of the senators or aristocrats of the later Roman Empire will show how utterly mistaken was a celebrated German historian, when he characterised the aristocracy as resting on the principle of hereditary immunity from taxes.[5] He misinterpreted the word *immunitas*, which is applied to the senators, and means merely *freedom from municipal taxes*. Only a certain number were admitted to the privileges and condoned the obligations of the class, namely the retired civil servants; curials who, having discharged their municipal burdens for many years, were in advanced age raised to senatorial standing; and professional men, such as court physicians and public professors and teachers licensed by the government.[6]

---

[1] Not to be confounded with the coin *follis*.

[2] This must be distinguished from the *aurum coronarium*, a tax which fell only on decurions.

[3] One of the measures that rendered Marcian's reign (450-457) popular was the release of all senators who did not reside in the capital from this burden. The same Emperor abolished the *follis*.

[4] Leo I. reduced the number to three (*Cod. Just.* ii. 1, 39).

[5] Burckhardt, *Constantin*, p. 453.

The error is often repeated, and has been clearly pointed out by Kuhn.

[6] The word count, *comes*, became (1) a title of general application to those nondescript senators who had held no civil or military office, and had thus no special designation; (2) its original use in combination with an office was still retained, as in *comes sacr. largitionum;* (3) it was used as an additional title of honour for persons whose office was regular, and included in the *Notitia Dignitatum*. See Kuhn, *op. cit.* pp. 194, 195.

From all this we may deduce with tolerable clearness the general social relations that existed in the fifth century. Between the Emperor and the mass of the subjects there existed an aristocracy, based on public service and consisting of three grades of nobility, the higher, the middle, and the lower aristocracy. In it were included some who would nowadays belong to the middle classes, statesmen, professors, physicians of distinction, such as in England might be honoured by knighthood, or exceptionally by a peerage. Between the aristocracy and the lower class of artisans and peasants may be reckoned a sort of middle class, including the decurions or provincial magnates who might look forward to elevation to the aristocracy if they lived long enough, and who in social position may be roughly compared to "county people" in England; rich merchants; young lawyers beginning their political career, who might look forward to winning a high position in the aristocracy. Hovering between this middle class and the lower strata were probably the physicians not patronised by the Emperor, and unlicensed teachers and rhetoricians, who depended on the patronage of the rich.

In this conspectus of society nothing has been said of the clergy. They formed a hierarchy by themselves, and their social position would correspond to their place in the hierarchy; although it must not be forgotten that the sanctity attaching to his office gave the humblest monk or deacon in those early days of piety an honourable position such as is hardly enjoyed by a curate of the English Church at present. The Patriarch of Constantinople was a peer of the Emperor, the bishops and archbishops may perhaps be considered peers of the aristocracy, while the mass of the clergy may be reckoned in the middle class.

Turning now from the social to the official side, we may briefly consider the position of the most important officers in the Roman system of administration, confining ourselves to the eastern half of the Empire. Highest in the first class of the aristocracy, "the illustrious," stood the four praetorian prefects, of whom each exercised authority over about a quarter of the Empire. Under the praetorian prefect of the East were all the Asiatic provinces, as well as six European provinces in Thrace. This dominion was divided into five dioceses—Asia, Pontus, the East, Thrace, and Egypt; the governor of Egypt, however, was practically independent of the prefect of the East. Under the prefect of Illyricum, who resided at Thessalonica, were all the lands of the Balkan peninsula, except Thrace and the islands of the Aegean. These lands were divided into two dioceses, Dacia and Macedonia.

The functions of the praetorian prefect embraced a wide sphere; they were administrative, financial, judicial, and even legislative. In the first place, the vicars of the dioceses were responsible to him for their actions, and completely under his control. With him rested their deposition, as well as the deposition of the provincial governors; and it was at his recommendation that the Emperor appointed men to fill these posts. In the second place, he had an exchequer of his own, and the revenue accruing to the treasury from his prefecture passed through his hands; it was through him that the Emperor made known and carried into execution his financial measures, and it rested perhaps more with the prefect than with the Emperor whether the subjects were oppressed by taxation. In the third place, he was, as well as the Emperor himself, a supreme judge of appeal. An appeal from the decision of a vicar or a dux might be addressed either to the praetorian prefect or to the Emperor, but if it were addressed to the former there was no further appeal to the latter. In the fourth place, he was empowered to issue praetorian edicts, but they probably concerned only smaller matters of administration or judicial detail.

The exalted position of these ministers was marked by their purple robe, or *mandye*, which differed from that of the sovereign only in being shorter, reaching to the knees instead of to the feet. His large silver inkstand, his pencase of gold weighing 100 lbs., his lofty chariot, are mentioned as three official symbols of his office. On his entry all military officers were expected to bend the knee, a survival of the fact that his office was originally not civil but military. The importance of this minister is illustrated by Eusebius, who compares the relation of God the Son to God the Father with that of the praetorian prefect to the Emperor, and by the remark of Johannes Lydus that "the office of praetorian prefect is like the ocean, encircling all other offices, and ministering to all their needs."

There was no prefect of the city of Constantinople until the close of the reign of Constantius (359 A.D.), and this fact alone shows that the equalisation of New Rome and Old Rome, with which Constantine is credited, has been often exaggerated. On the illustrious prefect of the city devolved the superintendence of all matters connected with the city, the maintenance of order, the care of the aqueducts, the supervision of the markets, the census, the control of the metropolitan police, the responsibility of supplying the city with provisions. He was the supreme judge in the metropolitan courts.[1]

The grand chamberlain, *praepositus sacri cubiculi*, was a functionary rendered necessary by the oriental tincture given to the imperial surroundings by the policy of Diocletian.[2] He issued commands to all the officers connected with the palace and the Emperor's person, including the count of the wardrobe (*comes sacrae vestis*), the count of the residence (*comes domorum*), the officer of the bedroom (*primicerius cubiculorum*), and also to the officers of the palace bodyguard, called *silentiarii*. His constant attendance on the person of the Emperor gave this minister an opportunity of exercising a vast influence for good or evil, especially if the Emperor happened, like Arcadius, to be of a weak and pliable disposition.

We now come to the ministers of finance, the count of the sacred bounties (*sacrarum largitionum*), and the count of the private estates (*rerum privatarum*).

The count of the sacred bounties was the lord treasurer or chancellor of the exchequer, for the public treasury and the imperial fisc had come to be identical[3]; while the count of the private estates managed the imperial demesnes and the privy purse.[4] Thus in the fifth century the "sacred bounties" corresponded to the *aerarium* of the early Empire, while the *res privatae* represented the fisc.[5]

The duties of the illustrious master of the offices, *magister*

---

[1] Under his control were a large number of officers—the prefect of the watch (*i.e.* the police), the *praefectus annonae*, or prefect of the market, who looked after the supplies of corn from Egypt, etc.

[2] Aurelian originated this system.

[3] The *aerarium* finally disappeared (as a state treasury) in the third century, about the time of Alexander Severus. It became a municipal Roman treasury.

[4] The counts of the private estates had jurisdiction, in Rome and Constantinople, in cases of incest or spoliation of graves—a curious arrangement.

[5] *See* O. Hirschfeld, *Untersuchungen auf dem Gebiete der röm. Verwaltungsgeschichte*, i. (1876).

CHAP. IV   ADMINISTRATION OF THE EMPIRE   45

officiorum, were somewhat nondescript. He had control over the bureaux of imperial correspondence,[1] over messengers despatched on imperial orders, over the soldiers on guard at the palace, over manufactories of arms. He introduced foreign ambassadors to the imperial presence, and arranged for their entertainment. He superintended court ceremonies (*officium ammissionum*). Arcadius transferred to him the control of the imperial post or *cursus publicus*, which had been a function of the praetorian prefects; and if it were the policy of an Emperor to diminish the sphere of the prefects, it was the master of offices who was ready to take upon him new duties.

The second rank of the *spectabiles*, "respectables," embraced all the governors of dioceses, whatever their titles; the count of the East, the augustal prefect of Egypt, the vicars of Asiana, Pontica, the Thraces, and Macedonia. It also included the governors of two provinces who had the privilege of not being subject to any vicar or prefect, the proconsuls of Asia and Achaia. The military counts and dukes were all of "respectable" rank, as well as some high officers in the palace.

To the third degree of the "most renowned" belonged all the governors of provinces who bore the title of *praeses, corrector*, or *consularis*, as well as a large number of subordinate officers in the imperial bureaux.

When we turn from the ministers and governors themselves to their staffs, we find that there was a great difference between the *palatini*, or servants of the higher bureaux, and the *cohortalini*,[2] as the staffs of the provincial governors were called, this name being one of the many survivals of the military origin of the civil service. The chief officials in the bureau of the count of the sacred bounties or of the master of offices regarded the honours of their rank as privileges which they were glad to transmit to their children; and the same remark applies to the subordinates of the praetorian prefect or of the master of soldiers, although they were not palatine. On the other hand,

---

[1] Namely, the *magister memoriae, mag. epistolarum, mag. libellorum, comes dispositionum*. Imperial messengers were called *agentes in rebus*—also *magistriani*.

[2] *Cohortes*, originally used of all *officiales*, became by use restricted to provincial *officia*, while *apparitores* was used of the higher *officia*. ταξεῶται was another general name. *Primipilares* were *cohortalini* who had the rank of a *princeps* in their bureau.

the *cohortalini* considered it a great hardship that they were obliged to follow their fathers' profession.[1] They were not allowed to obtain promotion into the higher civil service.

Promotion was strictly regular; and no one could reach the highest posts until he had filled in order all the inferior grades. This excluded the interference of influential friends to a considerable extent. At the same time every promotion depended on the Emperor, in whose hands all appointments rested[2]; though in the majority of cases he was of course determined by the recommendation of the heads of the bureaux.

In many departments the officials were able to increase the fixed income which they received from the State by fees which were paid them for supplying copies of documents or signing bills.[3] The highest official in a department was a general superintendent or chief, often more than one, under whom came the chiefs of special divisions. Thus, in the office of the praetorian prefect there were three chiefs, the *princeps*,[4] the *cornicularius*, and the *adjutor*, whose duties were of a general character; and in the second grade the *abactis*, who presided over the civil department, the *commentariensis*, who, as a sort of chief of police or under-home-secretary, presided over the criminal jurisdiction, and the *numerarius*, who was a chief accountant. No one could hope for promotion to higher posts who had not the advantage of a good general education, but there were subordinate offices of a mechanical nature which could be filled by persons who had received only a primary education.

The support of higher education by the State deserves to be

---

[1] As to the size of the offices, some idea will be obtained from the following numbers. The *officium* of a governor in Illyricum numbered 100, that of the *comes orientis* 600, that of the *vicarius Asianae* 200. The *comes sacr. larg.* had 224 *statuti* or regular officials, 610 supernumeraries. The regular number of the schola of *agentes in rebus* was 1174 in the time of Theodosius II; in the time of Leo I. it was as high as 1248; but in Justinian's time the number was reduced. For these data I obtained references to the *Cod. Theod.* and *Cod. Just.* from Kuhn, *Die Städte und bürgerliche Verfassung des römischen Reichs*, i. 157.

[2] Except in the case of the *cursus publicus*, whose very nature excluded the possibility of always consulting the Emperor.

[3] For the pay of officials compare the following details (collected by Kuhn). The proconsul of Cappadocia had £900 a year; the praefectus praetorio of Africa (an office instituted in Justinian's reign) £4500; the duke of Libya £4635; the praef. augustalis £1800, in the reign of Justinian.

[4] The *princeps* had a unique position. He seems to have acted as a sort of auditor to oversee the provincial offices.

mentioned here, not only because some of the chief teachers were admitted to the ranks of the aristocracy, but because the schools of the sophists and rhetors were the nurseries of the statesmen. Hadrian had established an academy at Rome, called the Athenaeum, in imitation of the Museum at Alexandria, and Marcus Aurelius founded chairs (political and sophistic) at Athens, endowed with salaries paid by the State. But it was not only in large towns like Rome, Athens, or Alexandria, that there were licensed teachers publicly paid; in all provincial towns of any size there were a certain number of such schoolmasters. In small towns there were three sophists; in towns of medium size (where there were ἀγοραὶ δικῶν, our county court towns) there were four sophists and four grammarians; in capital cities there were five rhetors and five grammarians. It is to be observed that the grammarians were not merely teachers of grammar; they were rather what we call philologists—they read and interpreted ancient authors. A distinction between sophists and rhetors is also to be observed; while both taught the art of style and oratory, the sophists only taught, while the rhetors also practised publicly in law courts. Alexandria and Athens were in many ways privileged; for example, the philosophers (metaphysicians, not to be confounded with sophists) in those cities were exempted from public burdens, while in other towns they did not participate in the privileges of the rhetoricians and philologists. It is to be remarked that during the fifth century the study of rhetoric was probably declining, and that the law schools of Rome and Berytus were far more fully attended than the lecture-rooms of the sophists.[1]

There were two great divisions of the Roman army in the fourth century, corresponding to two different kinds of military service. There were the soldiers who continually kept guard on the frontiers, and the soldiers who were stationed in the interior and were transported to the frontiers in case of a war. (1) The former were called *limitanei*, "borderers," or *riparienses*, "soldiers of the river bank." The latter term, which was originally applied to the men who guarded the Danube or the Rhine, was afterwards used in as general a sense as *limitanei*.

[1] Libanius makes this complaint at the end of the fourth century. The best book to consult on this subject is Sievers, *Das Leben des Libanius*.

(2) The latter were the soldiers of the line (*numeri*), and consisted of *comitatenses* and *palatini*. They correspond to the legionary soldiers of early times, who were drawn altogether from Italy, in contrast with the *auxilia*, who were supplied by the rest of the Empire, until the edict of Caracalla cast down the wall of privilege that encompassed Italy and thereby admitted non-Italian citizens to the legions. The *palatini* were properly those regiments which protected the imperial palace, and were under the command of the illustrious *magister militum in praesenti*[1]; while other regiments were called *comitatenses*, a term derived from the retinue (*comitatus*) of a general. These soldiers were obliged to serve for twenty years, whereas the less favoured border troops were obliged to serve for twenty-four years. The position of the latter in respect to the *comitatenses* and *palatini* may be compared to the position of the *auxilia* in respect to the legions of the early Empire. The troops located in the East were commanded by the *magister militum per orientem*, those in Thrace by the *magister militum per Thracias*, and those in Illyricum by the *magister militum per Illyricum*. In all these armies the barbarian element was large during the fourth century and was continually increasing.

The *limitanei* were not only soldiers; they were tillers of the soil, who were settled on the *limes* or frontier territory, which they were allowed to cultivate for their own support and bound to defend.[2] The warfare against the barbarians chiefly consisted in defending the forts, *castra*, which were built along the *limes*, whence they received the name *castriani*.[3] This sort of life is an anticipation of the Middle Ages. Veteran soldiers used to receive lands, if they chose, on the *limes*; but care was taken that they should really cultivate their farms, as old soldiers were likely to bully their neighbours and levy blackmail if they were not looked after.

The separation of the civil from the military power by Diocletian, and the restriction of the praetorian prefect's func-

---

[1] There were also some *comitatenses* among the soldiers of this commander.

[2] Alexander Severus laid the foundations of this system.

[3] The name *pseudocomitatenses* was also applied to the borderers. We may add here that the number of men in the legion was greatly reduced; and that the new name given to cavalry was *vexillatio*. Recruits were drawn chiefly from the *coloni*, of whom a large number were of Teutonic race, and also directly from the barbarians.

CHAP. IV   *ADMINISTRATION OF THE EMPIRE*   49

tions to civil matters were attended by the disappearance of the praetorian guards, and the substitution of a new body of guards called *scholares*, who were under the supervision of the *magister officiorum*. This fact indicates that the *magister officiorum* corresponds to a considerable degree to the praetorian prefect of the third century; he was commander of the guards, and combined civil with military functions. The number of the scholarians in the fourth and fifth centuries was 3500.[1] They received higher pay than the troops of the line, and had, of course, the prestige that is naturally attached to guardsmen. They were entitled to receive *annonae civicae*, which they could bequeath or sell.

There were also other guardsmen named *domestici*, of whom certain corps were called *protectores*, and these appear to have been superior in rank to the scholarians.

[1] Justinian increased them to 5500 (Procop. *Hist. Arcan.* cap. 24) and afterwards to 10,000 (Lydus, *de Mag.* ii. 24).

CHAPTER V

CONSTANTINOPLE

AT the beginning of the fourth century it would have entered into the dream of no Roman, whether christian or pagan, that the city of Byzantium, which he chiefly associated with the commerce of the Euxine, was in a few years to receive a new name and become the rival of Rome. Still less could one have imagined that the city, which was almost immediately to overshadow Alexandria and Antioch, was soon to overshadow Rome also, and that two centuries and a half thence the city on the Tiber would be desolate and the city on the Bosphorus the mistress of Europe and Asia.

Constantine thought of other sites for his new city before he fixed on the idea of enlarging and enriching Byzantium. Both Antioch and Alexandria were eminently and obviously unsuitable for his purpose. The great objection to both of those cities was that they were not sufficiently central; another grave objection was that the temper of the inhabitants of those once royal capitals would not easily endure the moulding and remodelling which the founder of a new imperial residence must wish to carry out.[1]

The idea seems to have flashed across the mind of Constantine of choosing some Illyrian town, Sardica or his favourite Naissus; but, notwithstanding the prepossessions which as a native he naturally felt for those regions, he could hardly entertain the idea seriously. Their distance from the sea, their situation not readily approachable, even with good roads, put

---

[1] To Antioch there were special objections; it was the victim of constant earthquakes, and was not maritime.

Sardica and Naissus at once away from the number of possible capitals; but it is interesting that there was just a chance that the capital of modern Bulgaria—Sofia is the old Sardica—might have been made the capital of the Roman Empire, and called Constantinople. Other places that might have claimed the honour were Thessalonica and Corinth; the city of the Isthmus especially would have been an excellent centre between East and West.

But Constantine did not desire a centre for the whole Empire; he rather desired a centre for the eastern half. As a centre for the whole Empire, the most suitable city would obviously have been Aquileia. But he did not desire to depress the dignity of Old Rome; his New Rome was to occupy the same position in the East as Old Rome occupied in the West. If the situation of Old Rome had been more central, it is probable that New Rome would never have been founded. This, too, formed a vital objection to Naissus, and even to Sardica; neither they nor Corinth nor Thessalonica were close enough to Asia. The same objection that told against allowing Rome to remain the sole centre of the whole Empire, told equally against choosing any city in Illyricum or Greece as the new capital. If there was any reason for a new capital at all, it must be geographically central for the eastern half of the Empire; in other words, it must be on the borders of the Illyrian peninsula and Asia Minor. Therefore neither Antioch nor Alexandria on the one hand, nor Sardica, Naissus, Thessalonica, or Corinth on the other hand, could become Constantinople.

It remained, then, for Constantine to choose some city close to the Propontis. The first name that would naturally offer itself was Nicomedia, the residence of Diocletian when he administered the eastern provinces. But the idea of Nicomedia could not be entertained long when its situation was compared with the city which dominates the Bosphorus. Constantine, however, seems to have hesitated for a time between Byzantium, Chalcedon, and the site of ancient Ilium. But it is obvious that Chalcedon could never have been a serious rival of the city on the hills which looked down upon it[1]; and in spite of

---

[1] The advantages which Byzantium enjoyed from the nature of the tides of the Bosphorus are dwelt on by Polybius (iv. 44), and compared with the disadvantages of Chalcedon.

Homeric memories, associated with the example of Alexander the Great, the idea of a new Mysian city was soon abandoned for the place which commands the entrance to the Euxine and seems adapted by nature to be the key of Europe and the mistress of Asia Minor. And so it came to pass that the city which looks down upon the Chalcedonian sands became the rival of Rome—

> urbs etiam magnae quae dicitur aemula Romae
> et Chalcedonias contra despectat arenas.

Constantine, in the words of a chronicler,[1] "decorated it, as if it were his native city, with great adornment, and desired that it should be made equal to Rome; and then, having sought citizens for it from all parts, he lavished great riches, so that he exhausted on it almost all the treasures and royal resources. There, too, he established a senate of second rank." In two respects, especially, the new city was not co-ordinate with the old city; the senate had not equal rights, and there was no *praefectus urbis*, but these differences were soon obliterated, the two capitals became politically peers before the death of Julian, though ecclesiastically Old Rome maintained the primacy. It was more, apparently, to have been called the city of St. Peter, than to have been the city of the Caesars.

The shape of Constantinople is triangular; it is bounded on two sides by water and on one side by land. At the east corner and on the south side it is washed by the Bosphorus, which flows at first almost from north to south and then takes a south-eastern course; on the north by the inlet of the Bosphorus, which was called the Golden Horn; and on the west by the wall of Constantine, protecting the enlarged city.[2]

The eastern angle formed by the Golden Horn and the Bosphorus, was dominated by the acropolis, on whose summit were situated the palace of the Emperors, the hippodrome, and the church of St. Sophia. The northern angle, formed by the Golden Horn and the land wall, was marked by the church and gate of Blachernae.[3] In the south-western corner was the

---

[1] *Anonymus Valesii*, 6, 30.

[2] The number of houses in Constantinople in the fifth century was 4388; there were 8 thermae, 153 private baths; 20 public, 120 private bakeries; 14 churches. See *Notitia urbis Constantinopolitanae*. By Greek writers the city is constantly called ἡ βασιλεύουσα, ἡ βασιλίς, or ἡ μεγαλόπολις.

[3] At Blachernae was a great church of the Virgin, still extant. For the word Βλαχέρναι various explanations have

Golden Gate,[1] by which triumphal processions used to enter Constantinople, and hard by was the Julian Harbour. If the relative positions of the Golden Gate, the region of Blachernae, and the imperial palace are remembered, it is easy to find one's way in the topography of Constantinople, as far as it concerns general history. The city was divided into fourteen regions,[2] and, like Rome, was a city of seven hills; but it is unnecessary for us here, as we are not concerned with the topography for its own sake, to take account of these divisions. It is the great square on the acropolis, with the surrounding buildings, which demands our attention, as it was in that region that the political life of Constantinople was carried on.[3]

A traveller coming (let us suppose about 600 A.D.) from Old Rome to New Rome, by Brundusium and Dyrrhachium, would proceed overland along the Via Egnatia, and, passing through the towns of Heraclea and Selymbria on the Propontis, would enter Constantinople by the Golden Gate, which was erected by Theodosius the Great. A long street, with covered colonnades —suggesting an eastern town—on either side, would lead him in a due easterly direction to the great Milion, the milestone from which all distances were measured. For since Constantinople had become the capital all roads tended thither; and the most recent explorers in Asia Minor are struck by the fact that, whereas in the early Empire all the roads led to Ephesus,

---

been given, but a passage in Theophylactus Simocatta (viii. 5, 1) deserves especial attention: εἶτα πρὸς τὸν τῆς Θεομήτορος νεὼν παρεγένοντο ὃν Λακέρνας ἀποκαλοῦσι τιμῶντες Βυζάντιοι. . . . This church is very much revered λέγεται γὰρ περιστόλια τῆς παρθένου Μαρίας . . . ἐν σηκῷ χρυσοπάστῳ ἀποτεθῆναι ἐνταῦθα. Cp. Codinus, Antiq. Constant. p. 95. Krause (die Byzantiner des Mittelalters, p. 21) decides for the derivation from βλάχνα. If the region were originally called βλάχνα, the foundation of a church called from λακέρναι might produce βλαχέρνα, on the natural principle of Lewis Carroll's frumious (from fuming—furious). In the same way the change of an old γουστεῖον into the Φόρον τοῦ Κωνσταντίνου might have led to the place being popularly called Αὐγουστεῖον.

[1] Built by Theodosius I.; cf. Corpus Inscriptionum Latinarum, iii. 1, 735— haec loca Theudosius decorat post fata tyranni; aurea saecla gerit qui portam construit auro.

[2] See the Notitia urbis Constantinopolitanae, published along with the Notitia Dignitatum in Seeck's edition.

[3] This chapter is mainly based on the valuable researches of the Greek scholar M. A. G. Paspatis, who embodied them in a book entitled Τὰ Βυζάντινα Ἀνάκτορα, "Byzantine Palaces." If all his results are not certain, he has discovered new landmarks, which will serve as a basis for new work in Byzantine topography. But it can hardly be hoped that any great discovery will be made until the Turks have left Constantinople. I have also consulted Ducange, Constantinopolis Christiana, and M. Jules Labarte's work, Le palais impérial de Constantinople et ses abords . . . tels qu'ils existaient au dixième siècle (1861).

at the time of Constantine this system was revolutionised and all tended to the new capital.¹ But before he saw the Milion the traveller would be struck by the imposing mass and great dome of St. Sophia, the eternal monument of Justinian and his architect Anthemius. As he stood in front of the west entrance of the great church, the northern side of the hippodrome would be on his right hand.

Then passing on a few steps farther and standing with his back to the south side of St. Sophia, he would see stretching before him southward a long rectangular place, bounded on one side by the eastern wall of the hippodrome and on the other by the western wall of the imperial palace. This place was called the Augusteum or Augustaiôn, that is, "the Place of Augustus" or "the Imperial Place."² It is not clear, however, whether the name was chosen as a sort of renovation of *Gusteôn*,³ "vegetable market," the place having been used for that purpose in old Byzantium; or whether *Gusteôn* was a corruption of *Augusteôn*, and this gave rise to the derivation. The magnificence of Justinian had paved this piazza with marble, and the southern part was distinguished as the "Marble Place,"⁴ while the northern part, near St. Sophia, was called Milion, from the building of that name, which the traveller, looking southward, would see on his right hand, close to the wall of the hippodrome.

The Milion was not a mere pillar; it was a roofed building, open at the sides, supported by seven pillars, and within were to be seen the statues of Constantine the Great and his mother St. Helena, those of Justin the Younger and his wife Sophia, those of Arabia, Justin's daughter, and of another Helena of less renown, a niece of Justin.⁵ The Milion was an important station in the public processions of the Emperors. Walking from

---

¹ *See* Professor Ramsay, "The Tale of Saint Abercius," *Hellenic Journal*, iii. 345. Cf. *Journal of Royal Asiatic Society*, vol. xv. p. 100 *sqq*.

² It was also called the forum of Constantine—probably its official name. Topographers (*e.g.* Labarte, *op. cit.* p. 32) generally distinguish the forum of Constantine from the Augusteum, placing the former farther west, but a passage in Cedrenus is decisive (i. 660, ed. Bonn), when he speaks of the senate house, τὸ σενάτον, as in the forum of Constantine. *See* above, p. 52 note 3. Cf. Paspatis, p. 65.

³ Dances which were celebrated on certain occasions in the Augusteum οἷον ἐν τῷ ὀψοπωλείῳ seem to have kept up an old pre-Constantinopolitan usage. Cf. Suidas, *sub* Αὔγουστος, and Codinus, p. 232. Paspatis, p. 72.

⁴ Τὸ Μαρμαρωτόν or Πλακωτόν, Const. Porphyr. i. 84, ed. Bonn.

⁵ Codinus, p. 28. Paspatis, pp. 102-104.

the south, and still keeping to the west side of the Augusteum, our traveller would have seen the great pillar surmounted by the statue of Justinian, and the other great pillar surmounted by the statue of the Empress Eudoxia, of which the stylobate still exists. Having passed some mansions of private individuals, he reaches the southern limit of the Augusteum and returns along the eastern side, which is occupied with more important edifices. Of these buildings, which are separated from the walls of the palace by a long portico called the "Passage of Achilles,"[1] the most southerly was the baths of Zeuxippus. Originally built by Severus, these baths were enriched with splendid statues,[2] chiefly of great men, Homer and Hesiod, Plato and Aristotle, Demosthenes and Aeschines, Julius Caesar, Virgil. But these valuable works perished in the flames which consumed the whole building in the great Nika revolt of 532. Justinian rebuilt it, but he could not restore the labours of antiquity.

North of the Zeuxippus was the senate house (*Buleuterion*), originally built by Julian and adorned with even more precious monuments of Hellenic sculpture than the baths of Severus. But it too did not escape fire; like St. Sophia it had to be twice rebuilt, first in the reign of Arcadius, on the occasion of Chrysostom's arrest, and afterwards in the Nika sedition,[3] which was fatal to so many public buildings.

After the senate house he comes to the residence of the Patriarch (*Patriarcheion*), which probably faced the Milion on the opposite side. The Patriarch's house contained a splendid hall,[4] called the Thomaites, and also halls of justice for the hearing of ecclesiastical cases. A visitor to Byzantium,[5] at the beginning of the thirteenth century, mentions that an excellent garden was attached to the patriarchal palace, and perhaps it lay between the house itself and the senate house.

Our imaginary traveller, having now reached the north side of the Augusteum, again, will notice a small church between the palace wall and the south-east corner of St.

---

[1] τὰ διαβατικὰ τοῦ Ἀχιλλέως, so called from the Bath of Achilles, which was somewhere close to St. Sophia.

[2] Mentioned by the poet Christodorus, who lived in the reign of Anastasius.

[3] Procopius, *Aed.* iii. 202 : λόγον μὲν τῇ τε πολυτελείᾳ καὶ τῇ κατασκευῇ τῇ πάσῃ κρεῖττον Ἰουστινιανοῦ ἔργον. It probably faced the pillar of Justinian. Paspatis, p. 76.

[4] τρίκλινος.

[5] This visitor was the Russian monk Antonius. *See* Paspatis, p. 83.

Sophia. This is the church of our Lady (ἡ Θεοτόκος) of the Chalkoprateia, so called because originally this region was a quarter of Jewish bronzesmiths.[1] Hard by a gate will be observed in the wall of the palace, the gate of Meletius, from which the Emperor used to issue when he visited St. Sophia; entering the church of the Chalkoprateia, he used to proceed into the great church by a private covered staircase, called the "Wooden Scala," which spanned the distance between the two churches.[2]

North of St. Sophia stood two important buildings, the hospice of Sampson[3] and the church of St. Irene.[4] Both of these were burned down in the Nika revolt, and newly erected.

The hippodrome, constructed by Septimius Severus, improved and adorned by Constantine, was the scene of many important political movements and transactions at Constantinople. Its length from north to south was 639 cubits, its breadth about 158.[5] Its southern end was of crescent shape, like a sigma, the northern end was occupied by a small two-storied palace, and the Emperor beheld the games from a box or *cathisma*, which he entered through the palace by a winding stair (*cochlias*). Under the palace were porticoes (like the Roman *carceres*), in which horses and chariots were kept, called the "Mangana." The same name was applied to the great storehouse of arms at Constantinople. The hippodrome[6] had at least four gates; one on the right of the cathisma, through which the Blue faction was wont to enter; a second corresponding on the left, which was appropriated to the Greens; a third, "the Gate of Decimus," close to the second; a fourth, called the "Dead

---

[1] Codinus, p. 83 : εἰς δὲ τὰ Χαλκοπράτεια ἐπὶ τοῦ Μεγάλου Κωνσταντίνου Ἰουδαῖοι κατῴκουν χρόνους ρλβ' καὶ ἐπίπρασκον τὰ χαλκώματα· ὁ δὲ μικρὸς Θεοδόσιος ἐξέωσεν αὐτοὺς καὶ τὸν τόπον ἀνακαθαρίσας ναὸν τῆς Θεομήτορος ἀνήγειρε.

[2] Paspatis, p. 85 *sq.* σκεπαστὴ σκάλα.

[3] Sampson was a man who had attended Justinian when he was ill. He built, with the Emperor's co-operation, a hospice for the sick and poor. After the fire Justinian erected it with greater splendour. It is conjectured by Paspatis (p. 67) that it was done away with in the thirteenth century to make room for the new wall of Michael Palaiologos.

[4] The second Ecumenical Council was held there. Leo III built the new St. Irene.

[5] According to the measurements of M. Paspatis, which differ from the previous measurements of P. Gylle and Scarlatus Byzantius (*see* p. 43 *sq.*) The hippodrome is now the Atmeidan.

[6] The hippodrome was divided into two parts by three monuments, which have survived to the present day—the Egyptian obelisk, the three-headed serpent, and a square bronze pillar, which stood in a line (lengthways) in the centre.

Gate," through which the corpses of the slain were carried away, in the east wall. There was probably another gate opposite to the Dead Gate in the west wall, for when the Emperors visited the church of Sergius and Bacchus,[1] which lay south-west of the hippodrome, they passed through the hippodrome.

As for the interior of the imperial palace, new light has been thrown upon the intricate details, which puzzle the student of Constantine Porphyrogenitus, by the researches of M. Paspatis, who has discovered new topographical marks for its reconstruction. In the first place, he was able to determine the direction of the old walls of the palace, the building of the Thracian railways having opened up the ground; and in the second place, the identification of the Pharos provided a starting point for tracing the situation of the buildings and chambers of the palace mentioned by historians, with the help of some other data derived from his studies on the spot. Into this reconstruction it is not necessary for us to enter here, for the internal arrangement of the palace concerns the history with which we have now to do very slightly. If we were dealing with the history of the Eastern Empire, and had to tell of the court of Theophilus or the court of Constantine VII, we could not afford to neglect the reconstruction of M. Paspatis; but the historians of the period from 395 A.D. to 800 A.D. seldom trouble us with perplexing details about the palace.

Constantinople had two suburbs over the water, to both of which the word *peratic* might be applied. There was the suburb of Chalcedon, now Scutari, on the other side of the Bosphorus; and there was the suburb of Sycae on the other side of the Golden Horn. Sycae had two regions, Galata and Pera,[2] both of which names are still in use. When we read of the *peratic demes* in Byzantine historians, members of the demes who lived on the north side of the Golden Horn " across the water" seem to have been meant; but when we read of the *peratic themes*, the troops quartered in Asia Minor are meant. Galata, I conjecture, is a very old name, dating from the third century B.C., when it was usual for kings and towns to hire the

---

[1] Now the little St. Sophia. It was erected by Justinian on the old palace of Hormisdas, where he used to live when he was a private person.

[2] So, *e.g.*, the Rhodians called the district on the opposite mainland Peraea.

Celts as mercenaries. The Byzantines probably hired bands of Celts, and, afraid of admitting them into the city, allotted them a Celtic or "Galatian" quarter on the other side of the Golden Horn; and the name Galata clung to the place when the Galatae had been long forgotten.[1]

[1] Compare Professor Mahaffy, *Greek Life and Thought*, pp. 157, 300, 348.

BOOK II

THE HOUSE OF THEODOSIUS

CHAPTER I

RUFINUS AND EUTROPIUS

ONE of the few men in history who have won the title of great, the Emperor Theodosius I.,[1] who had by his policy, at once friendly and firm, pacified the Goths, who had confirmed the triumph of Athanasian over Arian Christianity, who had stamped out the last flames of refractory paganism represented by the tyrant Eugenius, died on the 17th of January 395 A.D. His wishes were that his younger son Honorius, then a boy of ten years, should reign in the West, where he had already installed him,[2] and that his eldest son Arcadius, whom he had left as regent at Constantinople when he set out against Eugenius, should continue to reign in the East. But he was not willing to leave his youthful heirs (Arcadius was only eighteen) without a protector, and the most natural protector was one bound to them by ties of relationship. Accordingly on his deathbed he commended them to the care of the Vandal Stilicho, whom he had raised for his military and other talents to the rank of commander-in-chief, and deeming him worthy of an alliance with his own family, had united to his favourite niece Serena. We can hardly doubt that it was in this capacity, as the husband of his niece and a trusted friend, not as a general, that Stilicho received Theodosius' dying wishes[3]; it was as an elder member of the same family that the husband of their cousin

---

[1] He was called the friend of the Goths. It was, however, as Richter remarks (*Gesch. des weströmischen Reichs*, p. 511), Bauto and Arbogast who really deserved the credit of having pacified the Goths. Theodosius brought their work to completion.
[2] After his victory at Milan.
[3] Ambrosius, *de obitu Theod.* 5, *liberos praesenti commendabat parenti.* Compare Sievers, *Studien zur Gesch. der röm. Kaiser*, p. 338.

could claim to exert an influence over Arcadius and Honorius, of whom, however, the latter, it would appear, was more especially committed to his care, not only as the younger, but because Stilicho, being *magister militum* of the armies of Italy, would come more directly into contact with him than with his brother.

Arcadius, with whom we are especially concerned, was about eighteen at the time of his father's death.[1] He was of short stature, of dark complexion, thin and inactive, and the dulness of his wit was betrayed by his speech, and by his eyes, which always seemed as if they were about to close in sleep. His smallness of intellect and his weakness of character made it inevitable that he should come under the influence, good or bad, of commanding personalities, with which he might be brought in contact. Such a potent personality was the praetorian prefect Rufinus, a native of Aquitaine, who in almost every respect presented a contrast to his sovereign. He was tall and manly, and the restless movements of his keen eyes and the readiness of his speech signified his intellectual powers. He was a strong worldly man, ambitious of power, and sufficiently unprincipled; avaricious, too, like most ministers of the age. He had made many enemies by acts which were perhaps somewhat more than usually unscrupulous, but we cannot justly assume that in the overthrow of certain rivals[2] he was entirely guilty, and they entirely innocent, as is sometimes represented. It is almost certain that he formed the scheme and cherished the hope of becoming joint Emperor with Arcadius.

This ambition of Rufinus placed him at once in an attitude of opposition to Stilicho,[3] who was himself not above the

---

[1] Flavius Arcadius Pius Felix, born about 377; created Augustus, January 16, 384, at Constantinople; consul 386. He was educated first by his mother Aelia Flaccilla, then by a certain deacon Arsenius, finally by the pagan Themistius. For his personal appearance, see Philostorgius, *H. E.* xi. 3.

[2] Promotus (Zosimus, iv. 51), Tatianus, and Proclus (id. 52). Through the influence of Rufinus a law was passed depriving all Lycians of civic rights; see *Cod. Theod.* ix. 38, 9, *macula in Lycios*. Claudian, *in Ruf.* i. 232, *nomen gentis delere laborat*.

[3] Their hostility was of older date. Theodosius, at Rufinus' instance, prevented Stilicho from taking vengeance on the Bastarnae who had slain Promotus, whom Rufinus had caused to be exiled. Claudian, *de laud. Stil.* i. 94-115. In the first chapter of his fifth book Zosimus represents Stilicho and Rufinus as ethically on a level; but his tone towards Stilicho afterwards changes when his source is no longer Eunapius but Olympiodorus. See Eunapius, fr. 62, 63: ἄμφω τὰ πάντα συνήρπαζον ἐν τῷ πλούτῳ τὸ κράτος τιθέμενοι. Power depended on wealth at this time as at a later date, in the fifth century, when we find Marcellinus unable to contend with Ricimer, because he was not so rich.

suspicion of entertaining similar schemes, not however in the interest of his own person, but for his son Eucherius. The position of the Vandal, who was connected by marriage with the imperial family, gave him an advantage over Rufinus, which was strengthened by the generally known fact that Theodosius had given him his last instructions. Stilicho, moreover, was popular with the army, and for the present the great bulk of the forces of the Empire was at his disposal; for the regiments united to suppress Eugenius had not yet been sent back to their various stations. Thus a struggle was imminent between the ambitious minister who had the ear of Arcadius, and the strong general who held the command and enjoyed the favour of the army. Before the end of the year this struggle began and concluded in an extremely curious way; but we must first relate how a certain scheme of Rufinus had been checkmated by an obscurer but wilier rival nearer at hand.

It was the cherished project of Rufinus to unite Arcadius with his only daughter; once the Emperor's father-in-law he might hope to become speedily an Emperor himself. But he imprudently made a journey to Antioch, in order to execute vengeance personally on the count of the East,[1] who had offended him; and during his absence from Byzantium an adversary stole a march on him. This adversary was the eunuch Eutropius, the lord chamberlain (*praepositus sacri cubiculi*), a bald old man, who with oriental craftiness had won his way up from the meanest services and employments. Determining that the future Empress should be bound to himself and not to Rufinus, he chose Eudoxia, a girl of singular beauty, the daughter of a distinguished Frank, but herself of Roman education. Her father Bauto[2] was dead, and she lived in the house of the widow and sons of one of the victims of Rufinus. Eutropius showed a picture of the Frank maiden to the Emperor, and engaged his affections for her; the nuptials were arranged by the time Rufinus returned to Constantinople, and were speedily celebrated (27th April 395).[3] This was a blow to Rufinus, but he was still the most powerful man in the East.

---

[1] Lucian, *comes orientis*, whom he caused to be beaten to death with whips loaded with lead; Zosimus, v. 2.

[2] *Magister mil. per Orientem.* He had a high reputation for probity. Zosimus calls him Baudôn.

[3] *Chron. Pasch. sub anno.*

The event which at length brought him into contact with Stilicho was the rising of the Visigoths, who had been settled by Theodosius in Moesia and Thrace, and were bound in return for their lands to serve in the army as *foederati*. They had accompanied the Emperor to Italy against Eugenius, and had returned to their habitations sooner than the rest of the army. The causes of discontent which led to their revolt are not quite clear; but it seems that Arcadius refused to give them certain grants of money which had been allowed them by his father, and, as has been suggested,[1] they probably expected that favour would wane and influence decrease, now that the "friend of the Goths" was dead, and consequently determined to make themselves heard and felt. To this must be added that their most influential chieftain, Alaric, called Baltha ("the bold"), desired to be made a commander-in-chief, *magister militum*, and was offended that he had been passed over.

However this may be, the historical essence of the matter is, that an immense body of restless uncivilised Germans could not abide permanently in the centre of Roman provinces in a semi-dependent, ill-defined relation to the Roman government: the West Goths had not yet found their permanent home. Under the leadership of Alaric they raised the ensign of revolt, and spread desolation in the fields and homesteads of Macedonia, Moesia, and Thrace, even advancing close to the walls of Constantinople. They carefully spared certain estates outside the city, belonging to the prefect Rufinus; but this policy does not seem to have been adopted with the same motive that caused Archidamus to spare the lands of Pericles. Alaric may have wished not to render Rufinus suspected but to conciliate his friendship and obtain thereby more favourable terms. Rufinus actually went to Alaric's camp, dressed as a Goth,[2] but the interview led to nothing.

It was impossible to take the field against the Goths because there were no forces available, as the eastern armies were still with Stilicho in the West. Arcadius therefore was

---

[1] Güldenpenning, in his *Geschichte des oströmischen Reichs unter den Kaisern Arcadius und Theodosius II*, a work whose carefulness and completeness make it an extremely convenient book of reference.

[2] Claudian, *in Rufin.* ii. 78—
Ipse inter medios ne qua de parte relinquat
barbariem revocat fulvas in pectora pelles.
. . . .
nec pudet Ausonios currus et jura regentem
sumere deformes ritus vestemque Getarum.

obliged to summon Stilicho to send or bring them back immediately, to protect his throne. This summons gave that general the desired opportunity to interfere in the politics of Constantinople; and having, with energetic celerity, arranged matters on the Gallic frontier, he marched overland through Illyricum, and confronted Alaric in Thessaly, whither the Goth had traced his devastating path from the Propontis.

It appears that Stilicho's behaviour is quite as open to the charges of ambition and artfulness as the behaviour of Rufinus, for I do not perceive how we can strictly justify his detention of the forces, which ought to have been sent back to defend the provinces of Arcadius at the very beginning of the year. Stilicho's march to Thessaly can scarcely have taken place before October, and it is hard to interpret this long delay in sending back the troops, over which he had no rightful authority, if it were not dictated by a wish to implicate the government of New Rome in difficulties and render his own intervention necessary. We are told, too, that he selected the best soldiers from the eastern regiments and enrolled them in the western corps.[1] If we adopted the Cassian maxim, *cui bono fuerit*, we should be inclined to accuse Stilicho of having been privy to the revolt of Alaric; such a supposition would at least be far more plausible than the calumny which was circulated charging Rufinus with having stirred up the Visigoths. For such a supposition, too, we might find support in the circumstance that the estates of Rufinus were spared by the soldiers of Alaric; it would be intelligible that Stilicho suggested the plan in order to bring odium upon Rufinus. To such a conjecture, finally, certain other circumstances, soon to be related, point; but it remains nothing more than a suspicion.

It seems that before Stilicho arrived, Alaric had experienced a defeat at the hands of garrison soldiers in Thessaly[2]; at all events he shut himself up in a fortified camp and declined to engage with the Roman general. In the meantime Rufinus induced Arcadius to send a peremptory order to Stilicho to despatch the eastern troops to Constantinople and depart himself whence he had come; the Emperor resented, or pretended to resent, the presence of his cousin as an

---

[1] Zosimus, v. 4: εἴ τι δυνατὸν αὐτοῦ καὶ πολεμικώτατον ἦν τοῦτο κάτεσχε, τὸ δὲ ἀπεσκληκὸς καὶ ἀπόβλητον χωρεῖν ἐπὶ τὴν ἑῴαν ἠφίει.   [2] Socrates, vii. 10.

officious interference. Stilicho yielded so readily that his willingness seems almost suspicious; but we shall probably never know whether he was responsible for the events that followed. He consigned the eastern soldiers to the command of a Gothic captain, Gainas, and himself departed to Salona, allowing Alaric to proceed on his wasting way into the lands of Hellas.

Gainas and his soldiers marched by the Via Egnatia to Constantinople,[1] and it was arranged that, according to a usual custom,[2] the Emperor and his court should come forth from the city to meet the army in the Campus Martius, which extended on the west side of the city near the Golden Gate. We cannot trust the statement of a hostile writer that Rufinus actually expected to be created Augustus on this occasion, and appeared at the Emperor's side prouder and more sumptuously arrayed than ever; we only know that he accompanied Arcadius to meet the army. It is said that, when the Emperor had saluted the troops, Rufinus advanced and displayed a studied affability and solicitude to please towards even individual soldiers. They closed in round him as he smiled and talked, anxious to secure their goodwill for his elevation to the throne, but just as he felt himself very nigh to supreme success, the swords of the nearest were drawn, and his body, pierced with wounds, fell to the ground. His head, carried through the streets, was mocked by the people, and his right hand, severed from the trunk, was presented at the doors of houses with the request "Give to the insatiable!"

We can hardly suppose that the lynching of Rufinus was the fatal inspiration of a moment, but whether it was proposed or approved of by Stilicho,[3] or was a plan hatched among the soldiers on their way to Constantinople, is uncertain. One might even conjecture that the whole affair was the result of a prearrangement between Stilicho and the party in Byzantium, which was adverse to Rufinus, and led by the eunuch Eutropius; but there is no evidence.

---

[1] Claudian, *in Rufin.* ii. 291—
percurritur Hebrus
deseritur Rhodope Thracumque per ardua tendunt
donec ad Herculei perventum nominis urbem.
The city of Herculean name, Heraclea, is the ancient Perinthus.

[2] Zosimus, v. 7, 5: ταύτης γὰρ τῆς τιμῆς ἠξιῶσθαι τοὺς στρατιώτας ἔλεγε σύνηθες εἶναι.

[3] Zosimus attributes the plan to Stilicho and Gainas. *Ib.* 7, 3. On the confiscation of Rufinus' property, cf. Symmachus, *Epist.* vi. 14.

Our knowledge of this scene unfortunately depends on a partial and untrustworthy writer, who, moreover, wrote in verse —the poet Claudian. He enjoyed the patronage of Stilicho, and his poems "Against Rufinus," "Against Eutropius," and "On the Gothic War" are a glorification of his patron's splendid virtues. Stilicho and Rufinus he paints as two opposite forces, the force of good and the force of evil, like the principles of the Manichaeans. Rufinus is the terrible Pytho, the scourge of the world; Stilicho is the radiant Apollo, the deliverer of mankind. Rufinus is a power of darkness, whose tartarean [1] wickedness surpasses even the wickedness of the Furies of hell; Stilicho is an angel of light. In the works of a poet whose leading idea was so extravagant, we can hardly expect to find much fair historical truth; it is, as a rule, only accidental references and allusions that we can accept, unless other authorities confirm his statements. Yet even modern writers, who know well how cautiously Claudian must be used, have been unconsciously prejudiced in favour of Stilicho and against Rufinus.

We must return to the movements of Alaric, who had entered the regions of classical Greece, for which he showed scant respect. Gerontius, the commander of the garrison at Thermopylae, and Antiochus, the proconsul of Achaia, offered no resistance, and the West Goths entered Boeotia, where Thebes alone escaped their devastation. They occupied the Piraeus, but Athens itself was spared,[2] and Alaric was entertained as a guest in the city of Athene. But the great temple of the mystic goddesses Demeter and Persephone, at Eleusis, was burnt down by the irreverent barbarians; Megara, the next place on their southward route, fell; then Corinth, Argos, and Sparta. But when they reached Elis they were confronted by an unexpected opponent. Stilicho had returned from Italy, by way of Salona, which he reached by sea, to stay

---

[1] *Tartareus* is the Latin equivalent of diabolical; cf. Ammianus Marcellinus, xxviii. i. 10.

[2] The walls of Athens had been restored in the time of the Emperor Valerian (Zosimus, i. 29), and the difficulty of the siege made Alaric amenable to terms. The legend was that he saw Athene Promachus standing on the walls and Achilles in front of them; which story Zosimus, the zealous "hellén," relates seriously (v. 6). Philostorgius (xii. 2) says that Alaric "took Athens," εἷλεν 'Αθήνας, but he means the Piraeus. *See* Sievers, *Studien*, p. 347.

the hand of the invader. He blockaded him in the plain of Pholoe, but for some reason, not easily comprehensible, he did not press his advantage, and set free the hordes of the Visigothic land-pirates to resume their career of devastation. He went back to Italy, and Alaric returned, plundering as he went, to Illyricum and Thrace, where he made terms with the government of New Rome, and received the desired title of *magister militum per Illyricum*.[1]

No one will suppose that Stilicho went all the way from Italy to the Peloponnesus, and then, although he had Alaric practically at his mercy, retreated, leaving matters just as they were, without some excellent reason.[2] If he had genuinely wished to deliver the distressed countries and assist the Emperor Arcadius, he would not have acted in this ineffectual manner. And it is difficult to see that his conduct is explained by assuming that he was not willing, by a complete extermination of the Goths, to enable Arcadius to dispense with his help in future. In that case, what did he gain by going to the Peloponnesus at all? Or we might ask, if he wished Arcadius to summon his assistance from year to year, is it likely that he would have adopted the method of rendering no assistance whatever? But, above all, the question occurs, what pleasure would it have been to the general to look forward to being called upon again and again to take the field against the Visigoths?

It seems evident that Stilicho and Alaric made at Pholoe some secret and definite arrangement, which conditioned Stilicho's departure, and that this arrangement was conducive to the interests of Stilicho, who was in the position of advantage, and at the same time not contrary to the interests of Alaric, for otherwise Stilicho could not have been sure that the agreement would be carried out. What this secret compact was can only be a matter of conjecture; but I would suggest that Stilicho had already formed the plan of creating his son Eucherius Emperor, and that he designed the Balkan peninsula to be the dominion over which Eucherius should hold sway. His conduct becomes perfectly explicable if we assume that by a secret agreement he secured Alaric's assistance for

---

[1] See Güldenpenning, *op. cit.* p. 54. The decisive passage is Claudian, *de B. G.* l. 537 *sq.* Cf. Dr. Hodgkin, *Italy and her Invaders*, i. 257.

[2] Zosimus says that at Pholoe Stilicho gave himself up to luxury and the society of prostitutes, and incapacitated himself for vigorous action, v. 7, 2.

the execution of this scheme, which the preponderance of Gothic power in Illyricum and Thrace would facilitate. It is subsequent events, to be related in another chapter, that suggest this theory.

It was not only the European parts of Arcadius' dominions that were ravaged, in 395, by the fire and sword of barbarians. In the same year hordes of trans-Caucasian Huns poured through the Caspian gates (*per Caspia claustra*), and, rushing southwards through the provinces of Mesopotamia, carried desolation into Syria. St. Jerome was in Palestine at this time, and in two of his letters we have the account of an eye-witness. "As I was searching for an abode worthy of such a lady (Fabiola, his friend), behold, suddenly messengers rush hither and thither, and the whole East trembles with the news, that from the far Maeotis, from the land of the ice-bound Don and the savage Massagetae, where the strong works of Alexander on the Caucasian cliffs keep back the wild nations, swarms of Huns had burst forth, and, flying hither and thither, were scattering slaughter and terror everywhere. The Roman army was at that time absent in consequence of the civil wars in Italy. . . . May Jesus protect the Roman world in future from such beasts! They were everywhere, when they were least expected, and their speed outstripped the rumour of their approach; they spared neither religion nor dignity nor age; they showed no pity to the cry of infancy. Babes, who had not yet begun to live, were forced to die; and, ignorant of the evil that was upon them, as they were held in the hands and threatened by the swords of the enemy, there was a smile upon their lips. There was a consistent and universal report that Jerusalem was the goal of the foes, and that on account of their insatiable lust for gold they were hastening to this city. The walls, neglected by the carelessness of peace, were repaired. Antioch was enduring a blockade. Tyre, fain to break off from the dry land, sought its ancient island. Then we too were constrained to provide ships, to stay on the seashore, to take precautions against the arrival of the enemy, and, though the winds were wild, to fear a shipwreck less than the barbarians—making provision not for our own safety so much as for the chastity of our virgins."[1] In another letter, speaking of these "wolves of

[1] *Epist.* lxxvii. 8.

the north," he says: "How many monasteries were captured? the waters of how many rivers were stained with human gore? Antioch was besieged and the other cities, past which the Halys, the Cydnus, the Orontes, the Euphrates flow. Herds of captives were dragged away; Arabia, Phoenicia, Palestine, Egypt were led captive by fear."[1]

The Huns, however, were not the only depredators at whose hands the provinces of Asia Minor and Syria suffered. There were other enemies within, whose ravages were constant, while the expedition of the Huns from without occurred only once. These enemies were the freebooters who dwelled in the Isaurian mountains, wild and untamed in their secure fastnesses. Ammianus Marcellinus describes picturesquely the habits of these sturdy robbers.[2] They used to descend from the difficult mountain slopes like a whirlwind to places on the seashore, where in hidden ways and glens they lurked till the fall of night, and in the light of the crescent moon, watched until the mariners riding at anchor slept; then they boarded the vessels, killed and plundered the crews. Thus the coast of Isauria was like a deadly shore of Sciron; it was avoided by sailors, who made a practice of putting in at the safer ports of Cyprus. The Isaurians did not always confine their land expeditions to the surrounding provinces of Cilicia and Pamphylia; they penetrated in 403 A.D. northwards to Cappadocia and Pontus, or southwards to Syria and Palestine; and the whole range of the Taurus as far as the confines of Syria seems to have been their spacious habitation. An officer named Arbacazius was entrusted by Arcadius with an office similar in object to that which, four and a half centuries ago, had been assigned to Pompeius; but, though he quelled the spirits of the freebooters for a moment, Arbacazius did not succeed in eradicating the lawless element, in the same way as Pompeius had succeeded in exterminating the piracy which in his day infested the same regions. In the years 404 and 405 Cappadocia was overrun by the robber bands.[3]

Meanwhile after the death of Rufinus, the weak Emperor

---

[1] *Epist.* lx. 16. Jerome is dwelling on the miseries of human society (*temporum nostrorum ruinas*), which he also illustrates by the ravages of Alaric in Europe, and the fate of Rufinus, Abundantius, and Timasius. The letter was written in 396.

[2] xiv. 2, 1.

[3] *See* the letters written by Chrysostom in his exile.

Arcadius passed under the influence of the eunuch Eutropius, who in unscrupulous greed of money resembled Rufinus and many other officials of the time, and, like Rufinus, has been painted far blacker than he really was. All the evil things that were said by his enemies of Rufinus were said of Eutropius by his enemies; but in reading of the enormities of the latter we must make great allowance for the general prejudice existing against a person with Eutropius' physical disqualifications.

Eutropius naturally looked on the praetorian prefects, the most powerful men in the administration next to the Emperor, with jealousy and suspicion, as dangerous rivals. It was his interest to reduce their power and to raise the dignity of his own office to an equality with theirs. To his influence, then, we are probably justified in ascribing two innovations which were made by Arcadius. The administration of the *cursus publicus*, or office of postmaster general, was transferred from the praetorian prefects to the master of offices, and the same transference was made in regard to the manufactories of arms. On the other hand, the grand chamberlain, *praepositus sacri cubiculi*, was made an *illustris*, equal in rank to the praetorian prefects. Both these innovations were afterwards altered.[1]

The general historical import of the position of Eutropius, is that the Empire was falling into a danger, by which it had been threatened from the outset, and which it had been ever trying to avoid. We may say that there were two dangers which constantly impended over the Roman Empire from its inauguration by Augustus to its redintegration by Diocletian—a Scylla and Charybdis, between which it had to steer. The one was a cabinet of imperial freedmen, the other was a military despotism. The former danger called forth, and was counteracted by, the creation of a civil service system, to which Hadrian perhaps made the most important contributions, and which was finally elaborated by Diocletian, who at the same time averted the other danger by separating the military and civil administrations. But both dangers revived in a new form. The danger from the army became danger from the Germans, who preponderated in it; and the institution of court ceremonial tended to create a cabinet of chamberlains and imperial dependants.

---

[1] *See* Johannes Lydus, *de Mag.* iii. 40.

This oriental ceremonial, so marked a feature of late "Byzantinism," involved, as one of its principles, difficulty of access to the Emperor, who, living in the retirement of his palace, was tempted to trust less to his eyes than his ears, and saw too little of public affairs. Diocletian appreciated this disadvantage himself, and remarked that the sovereign, shut up in his palace, cannot know the truth, but must rely on what his attendants and officers tell him. We may also remark that absolute monarchy, by its very nature, tends in this direction; for absolute monarchy naturally tends to a dynasty, and a dynasty implies that there must sooner or later come to the throne weak men, inexperienced in public affairs, reared up in an atmosphere of flattery and illusion, easily guided by intriguing chamberlains and eunuchs. Under such conditions, then, aulic cabals and chamber cabinets are sure to become dominant sometimes. Diocletian, whose political insight and ingenuity were remarkable, tried to avoid the dangers of a dynasty by his artificial system, but artifice could not contend with success against nature.

The greatest blot on the ministry of Eutropius (for, as he was the most trusted adviser of the Emperor, we may use the word ministry), was the sale of offices, of which Claudian gives a vivid and exaggerated account.[1] This was a blot, however, that stained other men of those days as well as Eutropius, and we must view it rather as a feature of the times than as a personal enormity. Of course, the eunuch's spies were ubiquitous; of course, informers of all sorts were encouraged and rewarded. All the usual stratagems for grasping and plundering were put into practice. The strong measures that a determined minister was ready to take for the mere sake of vengeance, may be exemplified by the treatment which the whole Lycian province received at the hands of Rufinus. On account of a single individual, Tatian, who had offended that minister, all the provincials were excluded from public offices. After the death of Rufinus, the Lycians were relieved from these disabilities; but the fact that the edict of emancipation expressly enjoins "that no one henceforward venture to wound a Lycian citizen with a name of scorn" shows what a serious misfortune their degradation was.

[1] *In Eutrop.* 1, 197 : *Institor imperii caupo famosus honorum*, etc.

The eunuch won considerable odium in the first year of his power (396) by bringing about the fall of two men of distinction—Abundantius, to whose patronage he owed his rise in the world, and Timasius, who had been the commander-general in the East. An account of the manner in which the ruin of the latter was wrought will illustrate the sort of intrigues that were spun at the Byzantine court.[1]

Timasius had brought with him from Sardis a Syrian sausage-seller, named Bargus, who, with native address, had insinuated himself into his good graces, and obtained a subordinate command in the army. The prying omniscience of Eutropius discovered that, years before, this same Bargus had been forbidden to enter Constantinople for some misdemeanour, and by means of this knowledge he gained an ascendency over the Syrian, and compelled him to accuse his benefactor Timasius of a treasonable conspiracy, supporting the charge by forgeries. The accused was tried,[2] condemned, and banished to the Libyan oasis, a punishment equivalent to death; he was never heard of more. Eutropius, foreseeing that the continued existence of Bargus might at some time compromise himself, suborned his wife to lodge very serious charges against her husband, in consequence of which he was put to death. Whether Eutropius then got rid of the wife we are not informed.

Among the adherents of Eutropius, who were equally numerous and insincere, two were of especial importance—Osius, who had risen from the post of a cook to be count of the sacred largesses, and finally master of the offices, and Leo,[3] a soldier, corpulent and good-humoured, who was known by the sobriquet of Ajax, a man of great body and little mind, fond of boasting, fond of eating, fond of drinking, and fond of women.

On the other hand, Eutropius had many enemies, and enemies in two different quarters. Romans of the stamp of Timasius

---

[1] Zosimus, v. 8.

[2] The general feeling in favour of Timasius, a man of the highest character, was so great that the Emperor gave up his first intention of presiding at the trial, and committed its conduct to Procopius and Saturninus. The letter of Jerome (lx.—quoted above, p. 70), which was written in 396, proves that Abundantius and Timasius were exiled in that year.

[3] Claudian describes Leo in lines almost worthy of Juvenal (*in Eutrop.* ii. 376 *sq.*)

Acer in absentes, linguae jactator, abundans
corporis, exiguusque animi, doctissimus artis
quondam lanificae, etc.

Leo was once employed in the wool trade, and Claudian puts into his mouth, with considerable cleverness, expressions redolent of wool-making.

and Aurelian were naturally opposed to the supremacy of an emasculated chamberlain; while, as we shall see subsequently, the German element in the Empire, represented by Gainas, was also inimical. It seems certain that a serious confederacy was formed in the year 397, aiming at the overthrow of Eutropius. Though this is not stated by any writer, it seems an inevitable conclusion from the law (*Cod. Theod.* ix. 14, 3) which was passed in the autumn of that year, assessing the penalty of death to any one who had conspired " with soldiers or private persons, including barbarians," against the lives " of *illustres* who belong to our consistory or assist at our counsels," or other senators, such a conspiracy being considered equivalent to treason. Intent was to be regarded as equivalent to crime, and not only did the individual concerned incur capital punishment, but his descendants were visited with disfranchisement. It is generally recognised that this law was an express palladium for chamberlains; but surely it must have been suggested by some actually formed conspiracy, of which Eutropius discovered the threads, before it was carried out. The particular mention of *soldiers* and *barbarians* points to a particular danger, and we may suspect that Gainas, who afterwards brought about the fall of Eutropius, had some connection with it.

While the eunuch was sailing in the full current of success at Byzantium, the Vandal Stilicho was enjoying an uninterrupted course of prosperity in the somewhat less stifling air of Italy. The poet Claudian, who acted as a sort of poet-laureate to Honorius, was really an apologist for Stilicho, who patronised and paid him. Almost every public poem he produced is an extravagant panegyric on that general, and we cannot but suspect that many of his utterances were direct manifestoes suggested by his patron. In the panegyric in honour of the third consulate of Honorius (396), which, composed soon after the death of Rufinus, breathes a spirit of concord between East and West, the writer calls upon Stilicho " to protect with his right hand the two brothers " (*geminos dextra tu protege fratres*). Such lines as this are written to put a certain significance on Stilicho's policy. In the panegyric in honour of the fourth consulate of Honorius (398), he gives an absolutely false and misleading account of Stilicho's expedition to Greece two years before, an account which no allowance for poetical exaggeration can defend. At the same time he extols Honorius with the most absurd eulogiums, and overwhelms him with the most extravagant adulations, making out the boy of fourteen to be greater than his father and grandfather. If Claudian were not a poet, we should say that he was a most outrageous liar. We are therefore unable to accord him the smallest credit when he boasts that the subjects in the western provinces are not oppressed by heavy taxes, and that the treasury is not replenished by extortion.[1]

Stilicho and Eutropius had shaken hands over the death of Rufinus, but the good understanding was not destined to last longer than the song of triumph. We cannot justly blame Eutropius for this. No minister of Arcadius could regard with goodwill or indifference the desire of Stilicho to interfere in the affairs of New Rome; for this desire cannot be denied, even if one do not accept the theory that the scheme of detaching Illyricum from Arcadius' dominion was entertained by him at as early a date as 396. His position as master of soldiers in Italy gave him no power in other parts of the Empire; and the attitude which he assumed as an elderly relative, solicitously concerned for the welfare of his wife's young cousin, in obedience to the wishes of that cousin's father, was untenable, when it led him to exceed the acts of a strictly private friendship.

We can then well understand the indignation felt at New Rome, not only by Eutropius, but probably also by men of a quite different faction, when the news arrived that Stilicho purposed to visit Constantinople to set things in order and arrange matters for Arcadius.[2] Such officiousness was intolerable, and it was plain that the strongest protest must be made against it. The senate accordingly passed a resolution declaring Stilicho a public enemy. This action of the senate is very remarkable, and its signification is not generally perceived. If the act had been altogether due to Eutropius, it would surely have taken the form of an imperial decree. Eutropius would not have resorted to the troublesome method of bribing or threatening the whole senate even if he had been

[1] *In Hon. Cons.* 495 *sq.* Claudian is at his finest in his eulogies of Theodosius *avus*, the hero of Africa and Britain, and Theodosius *pater*, the Great.
[2] Zosimus, Bk. v. 11.

able to do so. We must conclude, then, that the general feeling against Stilicho was strong, and we must confess naturally strong.

The situation was now complicated by a revolt in Africa, which eventually proved highly fortunate for the glory and influence of Stilicho.

Eighteen years before, the Moor Firmus had made an attempt to create a kingdom for himself in the African provinces (379 A.D.), and had been quelled by the arms of Theodosius, who received important assistance from Gildo, the brother and enemy of Firmus. Gildo was duly rewarded. He was finally appointed military commander, or count, of Africa, and his daughter Salvina was united in marriage to a nephew of the Empress Aelia Flaccilla.[1] But the faith of the Moors was as the faith of Carthaginians. Gildo refused to send aid to Theodosius in his expedition against Eugenius. After Theodosius' death he prepared to take a more positive attitude, and he engaged numerous African nomad tribes to support him in his revolt. The strained relations between Old and New Rome, which did not escape his notice, suggested to him that his rebellion might assume the form of a transition from the sovereignty of Honorius to the sovereignty of Arcadius. He knew that if he were dependent only on New Rome, he would be practically independent.[2] He entered accordingly into communication with the government of Arcadius, but the negotiations came to nothing. It appears that Gildo demanded that Libya should be consigned to his rule, and he certainly took possession of it. It also appears that embassies on the subject passed between Italy and Constantinople, and that Symmachus the orator was one of the ambassadors. But it is certain that Arcadius did not in any way assist Gildo, and the comparatively slight and moderate references which the hostile Claudian makes to the hesitating attitude of New Rome indicate that the government of Arcadius did not behave very badly after all.

We need not go into the details of the Gildonic war,[3] through which Stilicho won well-deserved laurels, although he did not take the field himself. What made the revolt of the

---

[1] Nebridius. Salvina was afterwards a friend of John Chrysostom.
[2] Orosius, *Historiae adv. Paganos*, vii. 36.
[3] See the *Bellum Gildonicum* of Claudian.

count of Africa of such great moment was the fact that the African provinces were the granary of Old Rome, as Egypt was the granary of New Rome. By stopping the supplies of corn, Gildo might hope to starve out Italy. The prompt action and efficient management of Stilicho, however, prevented any catastrophe; for ships from Gaul and from Spain, laden with corn, appeared in the Tiber, and Rome was supplied during the winter months. Early in 398 a fleet sailed against the tyrant, whose hideous cruelties and oppressions were worthy of his Moorish blood; and it is a curious fact that this fleet was under the command of Mascezel, Gildo's brother, who was now playing the same part towards Gildo that Gildo had played towards his brother Firmus. The undisciplined nomadic army of the rebel was scattered without labour at Ardalio, and Africa was delivered from the Moor's reign of ruin and terror, to which Roman rule, with all its fiscal sternness, was peace and prosperity.[1] This subjugation of the man whom the senate of Old Rome had pronounced a public enemy redounded far and wide to the glory of the man whom the senate of New Rome had proclaimed a public enemy. And in the meantime Stilicho's position had become still more splendid and secure by the marriage of his daughter Maria with the Emperor Honorius (Spring 398), for which an epithalamium was written by Claudian, who, as we might expect, celebrates the father-in-law as expressly as the bridal pair. The Gildonic war also supplied, we need hardly remark, a grateful material for his favourite theme; and the year 400, to which Stilicho gave his name as consul, inspired an enthusiastic effusion.[2]

[1] The complications which resulted in Africa from the despotism of Gildo, and the attempts to right wrongs and restore property, lasted for many years. The large property which Gildo had amassed required a special official to administrate it, entitled *comes Gildoniaci patrimonii.* See *Cod. Theod.* vii. 8, 7, and *Notit. Occ.* xi.

[2] Two inscriptions on marble bases, found at Rome (*C. I. L.* vi. 1730 and 1731), celebrate the career of Stilicho. One of them (1730) is as follows—

FLAVIO STILICHONI INLUSTRISSIMO VIRO MAGISTRO EQUITUM PEDITUMQUE COMITI DOMESTICORUM TRIBUNO PRAETORIANO ET AB INEUNTE AETATE PER GRADUS CLARISSIMAE MILITIAE AD COLUMEN GLORIAE SEMPITERNAE ET REGIAE ADFINITATIS EVECTO PROGENERO DIVI THEODOSI COMITI DIVI THEODOSI AUGUSTI IN OMNIBUS BELLIS ADQUE VICTORIIS ET AB EO IN ADFINITATEM REGIAM COOPTATO ITEMQUE SOCERO D. N. HONORI AUGUSTI AFRICA CONSILIIS EJUS ET PROVISIONE LIBERATA.

Several inscriptions found on Roman gates commemorate the restoration of the "walls, gates, and towers" of the city by Honorius, a work which was undertaken at Stilicho's suggestion, (see *C. I. L.* vi. 1188-1190) before the invasion of Alaric in 402.

It may seem strange that now, almost at the zenith of his fame, the father-in-law of the Emperor and the hero of the Gildonic war did not make some attempt to carry out his favourite project of interference with the government of the eastern provinces. But there are two considerations which may help to explain this. In the first place, Stilicho himself was not the man of indomitable will who forms a project and carries it through; he was a man rather of that ambitious but hesitating character which Mommsen attributes to Pompey. He was half a Roman and half a barbarian; he was half-strong and half-weak; he was half-patriotic and half-selfish. His intentions were unscrupulous, but he was almost afraid of them. Besides this, his wife Serena probably endeavoured to check his policy of discord and maintain unity in the Theodosian house. In the second place, it is sufficiently probable that he was in constant communication with Gainas, the German general of the eastern armies and chief representative of the German interests in the realm of Arcadius, and that Gainas was awaiting his time for an outbreak, by which Stilicho hoped to profit and execute his designs. He had no excuse for interference, and he was willing to wait. His inactive policy of the next few years must not be taken to indicate that he cherished no ambitious projects.

The Germans looked up to Stilicho as the most important German in the Empire, their natural protector and friend, while there was a large Roman faction opposed to him as a foreigner. But as yet this faction was not strong enough to overpower him. It is remarkable that his fall was finally brought about by the influence of a palace official (408 A.D.), while the fall of his rival Eutropius, which occurred far sooner (399 A.D.), was brought about by the compulsion of a German general. These facts indicate that the two dangers to which I already called attention—the preponderating influence of German soldiers and the preponderating influence of chamberlains and eunuchs—were mutually checks on each other. I must reserve for the next chapter an account of the danger from the Germans which threatened New Rome, but was fortunately weathered —a danger whose aversion was of really critical importance for the maintenance of the Roman Empire in the East, and whose gravity has not always been sufficiently accentuated.

CHAPTER II

THE GERMANS IN THE EAST

THERE were at this time three political parties at Constantinople. There was the German party, of which the chief representative was Gainas, the commander of the Eastern army, and which counted not only barbarians but Romans among its members. It is probable that this party was in constant communication with Stilicho in the West, and it is possible that the Frankish Empress Eudoxia may have looked upon it with a certain amount of favour. But I think we must reject the assumption of any very close bond between her and the Goths, because she was an orthodox Catholic and they were Arians. It must never be forgotten that the difference in religion which marked off the German nations was an important element in the situation. Secondly, there was the party of Eutropius, consisting entirely of time-serving hangers-on, bound together by no principle or common purpose—an ephemeral clique, clustering round the eunuch to receive his favours as long as he was in favour himself. These two factions, the faction of Eutropius and the faction of Gainas, were opposed.

There was a third party, opposed to both of these, consisting of those senators and ministers who entertained a Roman abhorrence of the increase of German influence in the Empire, and a strong Roman detestation of the bedchamber administration of eunuchs[1]; men who were equally scandalised by the fact that three commanders-in-chief in the Roman Empire were Germans (Stilicho in Italy, Alaric in Illyricum, and

[1] The Roman sentiment against the power of eunuchs is strongly expressed in Claudian's poem against Eutropius.

Gainas in the East), and by the appointment of Eutropius to the consulship in the year 399, an honour which was soon followed by his elevation to the rank of *Patrician*, which, after the imperial, was the highest title in the State. *Omnia cesserunt eunucho consule monstra.* We may call this party the party of Aurelian, for Aurelian was its most important and respected member. He was the son of a distinguished praetorian prefect named Taurus, and he had himself filled the offices of quaestor and prefect of the city.

I have said that the Germans had friends among the Romans. The most distinguished of their Roman supporters was an enigmatical figure, whose real name we shall probably never know, the brother of Aurelian, but in character diametrically opposed to him. This shadowy person, who played a leading part at this period, is one of the riddles of history, like the Man of the Iron Mask. We derive all that we know about him from a historical sketch, written in the form of an allegory, by Synesius, bishop of Cyrene, entitled *Concerning Providence, or the Egyptians.* Its subject is the contest for the Egyptian kingdom between the two sons of Taurus,[1] Osiris and Typhos. Osiris, by whom is meant Aurelian, is the type of everything that is good and laudable; while Typhos, a sort of nature's byblow, differing from Osiris as Edmund differed from Edgar in *King Lear*, is "left-handed" and perverse, gross and ignorant. It will be most convenient to call this unknown person by his allegorical name.

We are told that Typhos at one time held a financial post,[2] but was soon obliged to abdicate it on account of malversation. He then obtained some other office, and performed its duties equally badly.

He allied himself closely with the German party, who saw in him, as a Roman of good family and position, an important supporter. In private life he is represented as a profligate, and Synesius tells stories to illustrate his indecent and frivolous habits. He mentions, as the climax of indecency, that Typhos used to snore on purpose when awake, and take delight in hearing others producing the same noise, as if it were marvellously

---

[1] γέγραπται μὲν ἐπὶ τοῖς Ταύρου παισὶν (Προθεωρία of the Αἰγύπτιοι). Compare Sievers, *Studien*, p. 387 *sqq.*

[2] ταμίας χρημάτων, Synes. p. 1217, ed. Migne. The expression usually means *comes sacrarum largitionum*.

fine music; and he used to praise and honour him who uttered most tunefully the licentious sound, and evolved the finest and "roundest snort."[1] We must remember that these are the allegations of an opponent, but at the same time it is just to observe that the prose allegory of Synesius has a truer ring than the poetical histories of Claudian.

The sketch which Synesius gives of the wife of Typhos, an ambitious and fashionable lady, is valuable and interesting, even if it be considerably overdrawn, as the picture of a type of contemporary society. She was, in the first place, her own tirewoman,[2] a reproach which seems to imply that she was inordinately attentive to the details of her toilet. She liked to be seen, and constantly showed herself in the market-place and the theatre, thinking that the eyes of all were turned towards her. This desire of notoriety prevented her from being too nice in her choice of society; she liked to have her house and drawing-room filled, and her doors were not closed against professional courtesans. It may be supposed that select Byzantine society refused to know her. Synesius contrasts with her the wife of Aurelian, who never left the house, and asserts the great virtue of a woman to be that neither her body nor her name should ever cross the threshold. Such an extreme idea, however, was almost obsolete; and if Synesius really believed in it he cannot have approved of the behaviour of his friend and teacher Hypatia. But I believe this is a mere rhetorical flourish, in imitation of the celebrated dictum of Thucydides.

The great struggle between the alien and the native element in the East, which was to decide that the eastern provinces were not to be dismembered by the Teutonic nations, began at the end of the year 398. It took the form of a contest between the two brothers, Aurelian and Typhos, for the office of praetorian prefect. The former was successful in obtaining the nomination, which was a great triumph for the anti-German party. Synesius was at this time at Constantinople, and lived on very intimate terms with Aurelian and his friends, so that

---

[1] μουσικὴν τινα θαυμαστὴν τὸ πάθος ἡγούμενος. Dio Chrysostom finds fault with the people of Tarsus for their habit of snoring. We might imagine from this account that Typhos was the leading spirit of a sort of society for the promotion of indecency.

[2] ἑαυτῆς κομμώτρια, θεάτρου καὶ ἀγορᾶς ἄπληστος, κ.τ.λ.

he had an excellent opportunity of observing all that went on. Penetrated with the spirit of old Hellenedom, especially Platonism, and feeling a Hellenic antagonism to barbarians, he sympathised fully with the aspirations and purposes of the Roman party at Byzantium. Aurelian seems to have been a man of culture and learning, and was surrounded with men of letters, such as Troilus the poet and Polyaemon the rhetor.

The success of Aurelian was a great blow to Typhos and his wife and his friends. His wife had been looking forward eagerly to the prefecture for the sake of the social advantages which it would confer. Synesius gives a curious account of the measures which Typhos took to console himself and his friends for their disappointment. He constructed a large pond (κολυμβήθρα), in which he made artificial islands, provided with warm baths; and in these islands he and his friends, in the company of women, used to indulge in licentious pleasures.

But this was only the prologue to the drama proper. It was a movement on the part of Ostrogoths, who had been settled in Phrygia by Theodosius, that brought on the main struggle; and this movement was hardly independent of the German faction in the capital, though we have no distinct evidence to show that it was instigated by Gainas or Typhos.[1] The Count Tribigild, who commanded the troops in Phrygia, bore a personal grudge against Eutropius, and this drove him to excite to revolt the Teutonic *laeti*, or colons, consisting of Ostrogoths and Gruthungi,[2] whom Theodosius, the friend of the Goths, had established in the fertile regions of Phrygia in 386. The revolt broke out in spring, as Arcadius and his court were preparing to start for Ancyra in Galatia, whither the Emperor was fond of resorting in summer on account of its pleasant and salubrious climate. The barbarians, recruited by runaway slaves, spread destruction throughout many provinces, Galatia and Pisidia and Bithynia.

[1] Tribigild was in Constantinople at the beginning of 399, paying his respects to the new consul Eutropius, who on that occasion offended him by neglect. It seems very probable that he arranged the whole plan of campaign with Gainas before he left the capital. That their complicity began only after Gainas had taken the field is hard to believe. On the chronology of these events, see Güldenpenning, p. 99.

[2] Claudian, *in Eutrop.* ii. 153. *Ostrogothis coliturmistisque Gruthungis Phryx ager.* Is the first part of *Gruthungus* the same as Gurth?

At this moment Synesius presented a crown to Arcadius on behalf of his native town, Cyrene, and delivered his celebrated speech, "Concerning the Office of King."¹ This may be regarded, as has been well pointed out,² the anti-German manifesto of the Roman party of Aurelian. It urged the policy of imposing disabilities on barbarians, and thereby eradicating the German element in the State. The argument depends on the by no means christian assumption that the Roman and the barbarian are different in kind, and that therefore their union is unnatural. The soldiers of a state should be like watchdogs, as Plato says, but our armies are full of wolves in the guise of dogs; moreover, our homes are full of German servants. The lawgiver cannot wisely give arms to any who are not born and reared in his laws; the shepherd cannot expect to tame wolves' cubs. The German soldiers are a stone of Tantalus suspended over the State. The only salvation is to remove the alien element—$\dot{\epsilon}\kappa\kappa\rho\hat{\iota}\nu\alpha\iota$ δὲ δεῖ τἀλλότριον. This speech was not calculated to induce Gainas to take energetic measures against his fellow-Germans, whom he was sent to reduce.

For there seem to have been only two generals of any account at this time—Gainas, the Goth, and Leo, the Falstaff of that age. Both were sent with armies against Tribigild. The rebels, seeking to avoid an engagement with Leo, turned their steps to Pisidia and thence proceeded to Pamphylia, where they met with a brave and unexpected resistance.³ While Gainas was purposely inactive, and writing in his letters to Constantinople that Tribigild was very formidable, a land proprietor of the town of Selge, named Valentinus, formed a corps of peasants and slaves and laid an ambush hard by a winding narrow pass in the mountains leading from Pisidia to Pamphylia. The advancing enemy was surprised by showers of stones from the heights above them, and there was no means of escape, as they were hemmed in by a treacherous marsh. After a great loss of life, Tribigild bribed the commander, Florentius, who held the pass, and thus succeeded in effecting his escape. But he had no sooner escaped than he was shut in between two rivers,

---

¹ Compare Sievers, *Studien*, p. 379.
² Güldenpenning has brought out this point.
³ *See* the narrative in Zosimus, v. 16.

the Melas and the Eurymedon, by the warlike inhabitants of those regions, who were well used to warfare from their experience of Isaurian freebooters. Leo meanwhile was advancing, and the insurrection might have been utterly and easily crushed, but that Gainas secretly replenished the forces of Tribigild with detachments from his own army. Thus Leo had really two enemies in the field against him, one in the disguise of a friend. He found Tribigild at the head of a large army, with which he could not attempt to cope; but this was not all. The German regiments in his own army preponderated, and they suddenly attacked the minority of Roman soldiers, and easily overpowered them. Leo lost his life in attempting to escape,[1] so that Gainas and Tribigild were left masters of the situation.

Gainas, who still posed as a loyal general foiled by the superior ability and power of Tribigild, despatched a message to the Emperor, misrepresenting the defeat of Leo, dwelling on the superiority of the rebel, and urging Arcadius to yield to his demands—the chief demand being that Eutropius should be surrendered. The Emperor hesitated, for he was probably attached to his chamberlain, but, in addition to the pressure of the Germans, another influence was brought to bear which secured the fall of the eunuch. The Empress Eudoxia, who had owed her position to the machinations of Eutropius, became jealous of his power with her husband; dissension and antagonism were born between them; and one day Eudoxia appeared in the presence of the Emperor, leading her two little daughters, Flaccilla and Pulcheria, by the hand, and complained bitterly of the eunuch's insulting behaviour.

When Eutropius heard of the demand of Gainas, he did not disguise from himself his extreme peril, but fled to the refuge of the sanctuary of St. Sophia.[2] There he might not only trust in the protection of the holy place, but might expect that the Patriarch of Constantinople, Johannes Chrysostomus, would stand by him in his extremity, when he was abandoned by his noonday friends. For it was through his influence that Johan-

---

[1] Claudian's account of Leo's death is intended to be a little comical—appropriate to the Falstaff of the age. He was killed, according to the poet, by fright—*valuit pro vulnere terror* (*in Eutrop.* ii. 240 *sq.*)

[2] For the fall of Eutropius, *see* Socrates, *H. E.* vi. 5; Sozomen, *H. E.* viii. 7; Philostorgius, *H. E.* xi. 6; Zosimus, v. 18.

nes, a Syrian presbyter of Antioch, had been nominated to the episcopal chair (398 A.D.) And the personal interference of Johannes was actually necessary; he had to stand between the cowering eunuch and those who would have dragged him from beneath the altar. This incident seems to have taken place on Saturday, and on the following day, Sunday, the service must have been curiously impressive, and the feelings of the congregation strange. Hidden under the altar, overwhelmed with fear and shame, lay the old chamberlain, whose will had been almost supreme a few days before, and in the pulpit the eloquent archbishop delivered a sermon " on the fallen eunuch," beginning with the words, " Vanity of vanities, all is vanity."[1] In this discourse he dwelled without mercy on the frivolity and irreligion of the party of Eutropius; but at the same time he sought to excite the sympathy of the audience.

When the church had been again surrounded and entered by soldiers, and Johannes had again personally interposed, Eutropius allowed himself to be taken away, on condition that his life should be spared. He was banished to Cyprus. Gainas, however, was not content with anything less than his death; and availing himself of the quibble that security of life had been granted to him only in Constantinople, Arcadius caused him to be brought back and tried at Chalcedon, where he was condemned on trivial, probably false, charges, and executed (autumn 399 A.D.)

The edict concerning Eutropius which was issued by Arcadius is a curious document, and deserves to be quoted. It will serve also as a specimen of imperial edicts in general.

"The Emperors Arcadius and Honorius, Augusti, to Aurelian, Praetorian Prefect.

"We have added to our treasury all the property of Eutropius, who was formerly the *Praepositus Sacri Cubiculi*, having stripped him of his splendour, and delivered the consulate from the foul stain of his tenure, and from the recollection of his name and the base filth thereof; so that, all his acts having been repealed, all time may be dumb concerning him; and that the blot of our age may not appear by the mention of him; and that those who by their valour and wounds extend the Roman borders or guard the same by equity in the maintenance of law, may not groan over

---

[1] *See* Chrysostom's Works, ed. Montfaucon, vol. iii. ὁμιλία εἰς Εὐτρόπιον εὐνοῦχον πατρίκιον καὶ ὕπατον. We are reminded of Massillon's words in the funeral oration on Louis XIV, "Dieu seul est grand."

the fact that the divine guerdon of consulship has been befouled and defiled by a filthy monster. Let him learn that he has been deprived of the rank of the patriciate and all lower dignities that he stained with the perversity of his character (*morum polluit scaevitate*). That all the statues, all the images —whether of bronze or marble, or painted in colours, or of any other material used in art—we command to be abolished in all cities, towns, private and public places, that they may not, as a brand of infamy on our age, pollute the gaze of beholders. Accordingly under the conduct of faithful guards let him be taken to the island of Cyprus, whither let your sublimity know that he has been banished; so that therein guarded with most watchful diligence he may be unable to work confusion with his mad designs.

"Dated . . .[1] at Constantinople in the Consulship of Theodorus, *vir clarissimus*."

The quaestor in drawing up this document did not spare vigorous language, and it seems strange that Arcadius should have allowed an edict to go forth which reflects so seriously on himself, by provoking immediately the question why the Emperor countenanced the "filth" so long. The weakness of the Emperor was proportional to the force of the language.

It was after the fall of Eutropius that Gainas seems to have declared his real colours openly, and acted no longer as a mediator for Tribigild, but as an adversary, bargaining for terms. He and Tribigild had met at Thyatira and proceeded to the Hellespont, plundering as they went. At Chalcedon, Gainas demanded and obtained an interview with Arcadius, and an agreement was made that Gainas should continue to hold the post of *magister militum per orientem*, and that he and Tribigild might cross over with impunity to Europe. As a security, three hostages were to be handed over to Gainas— namely, Aurelian, the praetorian prefect; Saturninus, one of the chief men of Aurelian's party; and Johannes, the friend (report said the lover) of Eudoxia.

The surrender of Aurelian as a hostage to the German general was a triumph for his brother Typhos, who appears to have succeeded him in the prefecture. Synesius attributes the combination against Aurelian to a drawing-room cabal—a plot brewed for his destruction by the wife of Typhos and the wife of Gainas.[2] It is evident at least that both city and camp were

---

[1] xvi. Kal. Febr. (MSS.) *Febr.* seems to be an error for *Octobr.* or *Novembr.*, though the order of laws in the Codex seems to forbid this. The edict will be found in *Cod. Theod.* ix. 40, 17.

[2] τυρεύεται δὴ τὸ κακὸν ἐν δύο γυναικωνίτεσι. Synes. *Aegypt.* i. 15.

full of intrigues at this time, and that during the first half of the year 400 A.D. Typhos was the most important minister in the Empire. He did not however prevail upon the cautious Gainas to sacrifice his brother Aurelian; the three hostages underwent a sham execution, the sword grazing their necks, and were banished for a short time. We may probably attribute this unexpected clemency partly to the intercession of the Patriarch Johannes, who crossed over to Chalcedon in order to plead for them.

This event took place towards the end of 399 A.D., and soon afterwards Gainas crossed the Bosphorus with his Goths,[1] and took up his quarters in the capital. Of Tribigild we hear no more; his historical importance is that he was a tool in the hands of Gainas. What events took place during the next six months, what were the designs of Gainas, what were the details of the administration of Typhos—all these, and many other questions, history leaves unanswered. Above all, we desire to know what circumstances checked and almost paralysed the action of Gainas and his Goths in Constantinople. It certainly seems that there were somewhere in the vicinity Roman troops (over and above the bodyguard of the Emperor), of which our authorities have left no record; for (1) Fravitta had troops at his command to oppose Gainas when he left the city; and (2) what is the meaning of Gainas' bargain with the Emperor for a safe-conduct to Europe, if he had not some hostile force to fear? (3) All that we hear of the conduct of Gainas in the city demands such a supposition.

One great object of the combination of Typhos and Gainas was to relieve the Arians of their disabilities and establish the full freedom of Arian worship in the city. We might almost conjecture that it was their common religious belief that united originally the interests of Typhos and the Germans. This policy, however, was defeated by the firmness and courage of the Patriarch, who opposed Gainas face to face. The Emperor refused to yield to the demands of the Goths, and here we may suspect that the influence of Eudoxia was also operative.

About midsummer Gainas formed the resolve to leave the city, which he and Typhos together had kept in a ferment for six months. In two clandestine attempts—one to seize the

[1] Güldenpenning (p. 119) reckons their number about 30,000.

imperial palace, the other to sack the bureaux of the money-changers—he had been frustrated; and combining this with his resolution to quit the capital with his large army, we must conclude that some material danger threatened or checked him. We know not what his wishes or designs were,[1] but we can hardly see why he could not have carried them through, if Constantinople was as entirely unprotected by military forces as historians generally represent it to have been.

At length, feeling that his position in the city was not agreeable, Gainas resolved to leave it. Making an excuse of illness, he went to perform devotions in a church of St. John, about seven miles distant, and he ordered the Gothic forces to follow him in relays. The preparations made by the foreigners for departure frightened the citizens, who did not understand their intentions, and the city was in such a state of excitement that any accident might lead to serious consequences. It so happened that a beggar-woman standing at the gate of the city early in the morning to receive alms, and seeing the Goths depart, thought the end of the world was coming, and prayed aloud. Her prayer offended a Goth who had just approached, and as he was about to cut her down, a Roman intervened and slew him. This occurrence brought about a general tumult, in which the citizens proved superior, and gave full vent to their rancour against the barbarians. Many of the Goths fled from the city. Then the gates were closed, and more than seven thousand remained, unable to communicate with their friends without, at the mercy of the infuriated mob. They fled to their church, which was near the imperial palace, but the sanctity of the building was not respected. The Romans obtained permission from the Emperor to resort to extremities, and the Gothic soldiers suffered a fate similar to that which befell the oligarchs at Corcyra during the Peloponnesian war. The roof of the building was removed, and the detested barbarians were crushed under showers of stones and burning brands[2] [12th July 400].

---

[1] Güldenpenning thinks he had none, and we may admit that he had no clearly defined plan.

[2] ξύλα πεπυρωμένα, Zosimus, v. 19, 10. This historian gives a sufficiently full account (taken doubtless from Eunapius) of the revolt of Gainas, but many of the minor details are gathered from the *Egyptians* of Synesius. Cf. also Sozomen, viii. 4; Socrates, vi. 6; Philostorgius, xi. 8.

Soon afterwards the conduct of Typhos was subjected to an investigation, his treasonable collusion with Gainas was abundantly exposed, and he was condemned preliminarily to imprisonment. He was afterwards rescued from the vengeance of the mob by his brother Aurelian, who had returned from banishment: but what further befell him we do not hear. Gainas meanwhile, as a declared enemy, proceeded through Thrace, seeking what he and his Goths might plunder.[1] But his expedition was disappointing, for the inhabitants had in good time retreated into the strong places, and he was unable to take them. No resource remained but to pass over into Asia, and he marched to the Hellespont. But when he arrived at the coast near Abydos, he found that the opposite shore was occupied by an army, ready to dispute his passage, under the loyal pagan Goth Fravitta, who had once rescued Theodosius I. from his own countrymen,[2] and was now, in advanced years, to perform a similar service for Arcadius. Gainas tarried on the shore until his provisions were exhausted, and then, constrained to essay the passage for which he was unprovided with ships, constructed rude rafts, which he committed to the current. Fravitta's ships easily sank these unwieldy contrivances, and Gainas, who remained on shore and saw his troops exterminated before his eyes, hastened northward through Thrace, beyond Mount Haemus, even beyond the Ister, expecting to be pursued by the victor. Fravitta made no attempt to capture him, but he fell into the hands of Uldes, king of the Huns, who cut off his head and sent it as a grateful offering to Arcadius.[3]

The Gothic discomfiter of the Goths enjoyed a triumph for his decisive success, and the christian Emperor granted to the old pagan the only favour he requested—to be allowed to worship God after the fashion of his fathers.[4]

Thus the great danger which was hanging over the Empire was warded off from the eastern provinces at the very beginning of the fifth century, and it was decided that it was not in the east that the Empire was to be dismembered by the Germans.

---

[1] The neutral attitude of Alaric during these events is presumably to be explained by jealousy of Gainas.

[2] Fravitta had also cleared the east, "from Cilicia to Syria and Palestine," of pirates. Zosimus, v. 20, 2.

[3] In February 401 the head arrived at Constantinople. The sea fight took place about 23d December 400.

[4] Fravitta was made consul in 401.

Alaric, indeed, was still commander-in-chief in Illyricum, but his eyes were bent westward, and within a few years the Illyrian lands were to be delivered for ever from the Visigoths. It was indeed an important episode in Roman history, and although modern writers have often treated it more casually than it deserves, it attracted appropriate attention in the fifth century, and was celebrated in two epic poems [1] as well as in the myth of Synesius of Cyrene.

It is worthy of observation that it was this German movement that brought about the fall of the eunuch Eutropius. Eight years later it was the machinations of the palace official Olympius that brought about the fall of the German Stilicho. Thus, as I remarked before, the chamberlains in the palace and the Germans in the camp—the representatives of the Orientalising and Germanising tendencies that were eating into the Roman spirit—were each a check upon the other; and the antagonism between these forces of corrosion was a temporary safeguard for the Roman party. With the Roman party, moreover, the Church was thoroughly in sympathy, for a defeat of the Germans was equivalent to a defeat of Arianism.

---

[1] The *Gainea* of Eusebius (a pupil of Troilus, the friend of Aurelian), and a poem by Ammonius (recited in 437). Güldenpenning is the first historian who has insisted duly on the importance of this German movement, and this perhaps is the most valuable part of his work.

CHAPTER III

JOHN CHRYSOSTOM

THE strange drama of Gainas, which decided the relation of the Empire to its German subjects in the East, was followed by another drama, equally strange, wherein the power of the Patriarch of Constantinople appeared in conflict with the imperial authority. A collision had not taken place before. With the exception of Valens, no Emperor had resided for any length of time in the capital until Arcadius, who never left it except to take a summer holiday at Ancyra. Hitherto the Emperors had been military commanders, who flew from frontier to frontier and city to city to direct campaigns or arrange administrative innovations. Moreover, the see of Constantinople had not attained to the first rank in the eastern half of the Empire until the council of 381. Hence in the reign of Arcadius it was inevitable that a mutual adjustment of the relations between the court and the patriarchal palace should take place. To this adjustment the characters of the persons concerned gave a peculiar complexion. If it had depended solely on Arcadius, who was pious and weak, the struggle perhaps would not have come to pass so soon, but would have been reserved for a stronger Emperor, of the temper of his father. But he had a worldly queen, who exerted great influence over him, and she drew him into collision with the bishop. On the other hand, if the mild old Nectarius had lived ten years longer, there would hardly have been room for discord, and in this case, too, the adjustment would have been reserved for the advent of a more decided and independent hierarch. But he died, and a man thoroughly independent and thoroughly in earnest, of rough and uncourtly ways, one who was not afraid to hear his own voice crying in a wilderness of worldliness, and who, if he did not desire to fight, was perfectly ready for the fray, was appointed to the episcopal throne.

And thus we have a spectacle of more than usual interest, the asceticism of the Church, represented by John Chrysostom,[1] ranged against a superb court led by the Empress Eudoxia, who made herself, as it were, the champion and example of the pride of life and the pomps and vanities of the world. And on the other hand, the course of the conflict brings out the worldliness, the enmities, the unscrupulousness, the abuses that grew rank within the Church itself. Side issues disguised the real import of this war of four years; but though it appeared merely to concern Chrysostom personally, it really decided that in future the Patriarch of Constantinople was to be dependent on the Emperor.

We must first become acquainted with some of the actors in this drama, which began in social circles before it acquired a political significance.[2]

The Empress Eudoxia herself, on whose worldliness and ambition we have dwelt, naturally gave the tone to the ladies of her court, and to the more frivolous portion of the gentlemen. Whether she was guilty of adultery or not, the mere fact of the rumour prevailing that Count John[3] was the father of her son Theodosius is evidence as to the character she bore; and we can imagine what the society was like over which this ambitious and beautiful woman, not above the

---

[1] Johannes, called Chrysostomus ("golden-mouthed") from his eloquent preaching, was born at Antioch in 351 or 352; ordained deacon in 381 and presbyter in 386; succeeded Nectarius as Patriarch of Constantinople 26th February 398. A monograph, which I believe is good, has been written on Chrysostom by F. Ludwig (*Der hl. Joh. Chrys. in seinem Verhältniss zum byzantinischen Hofe*, 1883); Neander has written an elaborate study, but unfortunately with a view to be edifying; there is a book on the *Life and Times of Chrysostom* by Mr. W. R. W. Stephens (1872); there is a monograph (*St. Jean Chrysostome et l'impératrice Eudoxie*) by Amédée Thierry; and there is a full and careful article by Mr. E. Venables in the *Dictionary of Christian Biography*.

[2] For the events connected with Chrysostom's career, the *Dialogue* on his life written by Palladius (the author of the *Historia Lausiaca*), his own letters and sermons, and the accounts given by Socrates and Sozomen, are the most important sources. Zosimus' notice of the fall of Chrysostom is characteristic (Bk. v.)

[3] One of the causes of Eudoxia's dislike to Chrysostom is said to have been that he was reported to have pointed out Count John's hiding-place when he was pursued by a furious mob.

suspicion of criminal intrigues, presided. One curious trait of manners indicates clearly enough the tone of the court. It was the custom of christian ladies to wear veils or bands on their foreheads, so as to conceal their hair. Women of meretricious life were distinguished by the way they wore their hair cut and combed over their brows, just like modern fringes. The ladies of Eudoxia's court were so immodest, and had such bad taste, as to adopt this fashion from the courtesans.[1] The next step probably was that the example of the court influenced respectable christian matrons to wear the obnoxious fringe. In this fast aristocratic society three ladies were prominent—Marsa, the widow of Promotus, a distant relation of the Empress; Castricia, the widow of Saturninus; and Eugraphia, who had also lost her husband. These widows were all rich, and if they were not young in years they made themselves young in appearance. Eugraphia used rouge and white lead to maintain her complexion—a habit which was a serious scandal to pious Christians, and which Chrysostom condemned especially on the ground that it was a waste of money which should be given to the poor.

Such a court was revolting to the austere and earnest spirit of Chrysostom, who was far too sincere to make any compromise with Mammon. He used, as a matter of duty, to pay pastoral visits to these great ladies, and we may be sure that he did not hesitate, through any scruples of politeness, to tell them unpleasant truths and urge them to amend their ways. His unbending austerity and uncompromising candour made him an unwelcome visitor. But his campaign against luxury and worldliness did not cease here. He not only preached publicly on the subject in St. Sophia, but made such open and unmistakable allusions, which he could make the more pointed by turning his eyes towards the Empress and her ladies, who sat in a prominent place in the gallery,[2] that he gave great umbrage, and was hated as the mother of Herodias hated John the Baptist. The climax came when he preached a sermon in which Eudoxia was openly called Jezebel, and it was partly from this allusion that the unfounded tale got abroad that

---

[1] This trait is mentioned by Palladius (cap. 8).
[2] Chrysostom preached from the ambo, not from the apse. Am. Thierry, in his monograph on Chrysostom, brings out this point very well.

Eudoxia had actually robbed a widow of her vineyard, as Ahab robbed Naboth.[1]

The aristocratic ladies, indignant at being insulted and outraged, as they considered it, before the mob, determined to work the ruin of Chrysostom, and formed a league against him, of which the centre was the house of Eugraphia. Although it was evident enough, and all probably knew in their hearts that Chrysostom was a single-hearted man, thoroughly in earnest and austerely moral, yet it was easy to find pretexts against him; and his ascetic mode of life and certain peculiar theories which he held made it all the easier. Moreover, he had a great many enemies within the Church—priests, monks, and nuns, who had revolted against the strict discipline of their Patriarch, and eagerly embraced the opportunity to place themselves at the service of the great persons who wished to undo him. For it was not only against the corruption of the court that the reformer had to contend, but against the corruption of the clergy and monks. Their sensuality, their gluttony, their avarice, were matters of public scandal; and John's austerity was to them, in the words of Palladius, "as a lamp burning before sore eyes." Women were introduced into the monasteries, or shared the houses of priests as spiritual sisters; and this was always a "snare," even if it were often innocent. But still more scandalous was the conduct of the deaconesses, who, if they could not adopt the meretricious apparel that had become the mode, arranged their coarse dresses with an immodest coquetry[2] which made them more piquant than an ordinary courtesan. Another class of religious persons hostile to Chrysostom were the begging tramps, drones whom he had endeavoured to suppress.

But the Patriarch was also the centre of a society of admirers. Of these, the most attached and most distinguished was Olympias,[3] the daughter of a woman who had been be-

---

[1] The tale (*see* Nicephorus Callistus, xiii. 14, xiv. 48) seems to have arisen partly from this and partly from a passage in Marcus' *Life of Porphyrius of Gaza*, where Chrysostom is represented as saying that Eudoxia was angry with him διότι ἐγκάλεσα (ἐνεκάλεσα?) αὐτῇ χάριν κτήματος οὗ ἐπιθυμήσασα ἀφήρπασεν. *See* Güldenpenning, p. 142.

[2] On the other hand, actresses and public prostitutes used to imitate the dress of consecrated virgins, and this abuse had to be suppressed by legislation. *See* the constitution of Theodosius I. i. 394 (*Cod. Just.* i. 4, 4): "Mimae et quae ludibrio corporis sui quaestum faciunt publice habitu earum virginum quae deo dicatae sunt non utantur."

[3] Sozomen, viii. 9.

trothed in her youth to the Emperor Constans, had afterwards married a king of Armenia, and after his death married a Roman noble. Her bounty to the poor, her untiring devotion to Chrysostom in his misfortunes, her delicacy and unselfishness, have earned for her a high place among the "good," as distinguished from the great, women who appear in history. Another friend of Chrysostom was the Moorish princess Salvina, daughter of Gildo, whom Theodosius had taken as a hostage and given in marriage to Nebridius, his wife's nephew. She led a calm life in Constantinople; and in a "letter to a young widow," Chrysostom contrasts this peaceful happiness with the turbulent and unrestful life of her father. The deacon Serapion must also be mentioned here as a person devoted to John, but one whose influence was exerted in the wrong way. He was a man without judgment or moderation, and instead of trying to calm the hot temper of the bishop, he used to incite him to rash acts, with thoroughly honest intentions. It is interesting to note that Cassian, who afterwards founded the monastery of St. Victor at Marseilles, was in Byzantium at this period and a warm friend of Chrysostom.

But the great strength of John's position lay in his popularity. It was not merely that he possessed the christian virtues of charity and sympathy with the poor, or even that he was no respecter of persons; he actually held theories of socialism— a sort of Ebionistic socialism—which might have been very dangerous to the established order of things if he had carried them to any length. He rejected not political but social inequality, in fact he held a sort of social socialism. It might seem that such a theory, if it gained ground, would necessarily lead to a political revolution, an overthrow of the Empire; but there was no danger of such a catastrophe. The idea of the Empire was almost a necessity of thought to the Romans of that time; it would not have been possible for them to conceive the world without the Empire; the end of the Empire would have seemed to them the Deluge. But Chrysostom's spirit attracted the lower classes, and his tirades against the rich delighted the poor. On the occasion of an earthquake he said publicly that "the vices of the rich had caused it, and the prayers of the poor had averted the worst consequences."

It was easy for his enemies to fasten on such utterances as

these, and accuse Chrysostom of "seducing the people." His intimate relations of friendship with Olympias and other women, whom he used to receive alone, perhaps unwisely, supplied matter for another charge. Having a weak digestion, and obliged to restrict himself to the most lenten fare, he made a practice of never dining out[1]; and this anchoretic habit, combined with the reception of women alone in his house, was converted into the charge that he used to celebrate Cyclopean orgies under the cover of unsocial habits.

The expedition which he made in the year 400 to regulate the affairs of the Ephesian and other churches[2] in Asia Minor, where abuses had crept in, not only made many new enemies, but furnished another ground of accusation. He seems to have acted here with more zeal than wariness; he deposed and appointed bishops like an autocrat, not only going beyond his proper jurisdiction, but neglecting to give a fair hearing to the cases. On some occasions, it is said, he had been himself accuser, witness, and judge.

In another way also this visit to Asia Minor was disadvantageous to him. His enemies had time and room to arrange their machinations against him, and the man whom he had left at Byzantium to fill his place, Severian of Gabala, wishing to oust and succeed Chrysostom, flattered the court and joined the league of his enemies. When Chrysostom returned and found his church disorganised by the unbecoming conduct of Severian, of which the deacon Serapion had no few complaints to make, he preached a sermon in which he made allusion to the timeserving relations of Severian to the Empress. Severian, feeling himself sure of support in high quarters, would not yield, and Chrysostom, with the people on his side, excommunicated the ambitious Syrian. He fled to Chalcedon, and the Emperor and Empress begged the Patriarch to allow him to return to the fold. Their intervention prevailed, but the enthusiasm of the populace for their beloved bishop was not satisfied, and in order to quiet them and remove peaceably the ban of excommunication, he had to exert all his powers of

---

[1] Acacius of Beroea, displeased with the entertainment of the patriarchal palace, said "I'll season his soup for him," and joined the party opposed to Chrysostom.

[2] Cf. Sozomen, viii. 6. Eusebius of Valentinopolis accused Antoninus, bishop of Ephesus, of simony, etc., and Chrysostom was appealed to. He deposed and replaced several bishops.

eloquence in a pacific sermon,[1] which ended with the words, "Receive our brother Severian the bishop." The next day Severian preached a sermon, of which the note was likewise peace.

It was crying peace where there was no peace. After a short lull, the storm burst louder than ever over the Patriarch, but came from a new quarter. Theophilus, the Patriarch of Alexandria, was a worldly man, whose ambition and avidity have been painted in the blackest colours. He had hoped, on the death of Nectarius, to place a candidate of his own on the pontifical chair of Constantinople, and he owed Chrysostom a grudge for his disappointment, so that he willingly seized an opportunity to assist in compassing his ruin. His power in Egypt was very great, and he exercised considerable influence in Syria and Palestine. It was he who had excited the people to dismantle the great temple of Serapis in Alexandria, in the days of Theodosius.

Now at Nitria in Upper Egypt there was a monastic settlement over which the four so-called "Tall Brothers" presided.[2] Theophilus desired to gain over the monks to his interests and make them bishops, but they refused positively, and the vengeance of the Patriarch pursued them. He brought against them the charge of Origenism, and obtained troops from the augustal prefect to arrest them. Warned in time, they concealed themselves, but their monastery was sacked, and they made their way slowly and with great difficulty to Constantinople, to place themselves under the protection of John Chrysostom. In their journey through Syria they had no rest for the soles of their feet, as the authority of Theophilus induced the bishops of those parts to refuse them shelter. Chrysostom was rightly wary in his dealings with the suppliants. He would not communicate with them, although he promised them his protection, and he lodged them in the cloisters of the church of Anastasia, where their wants were ministered to by religious women. The astuteness and unscrupulousness of Theophilus made him a dangerous foe, and he wrote to Arcadius in regard to the Tall Brothers, accusing them of

---

[1] This sermon is preserved in a Latin translation, *de recipiendo Severiano*.
[2] Charles Kingsley has given a sketch of life at Nitria in his *Hypatia*. See Socrates, vi. 9, Sozomen, viii. 11, 12, 13, for the following events.

practising magic. The envoys whom he sent to Constantinople spread such calumnious reports about the Tall Brothers that they were unable to stir from their lodgings, and at length in despair they drew up, contrary to the wishes of Chrysostom, a manifesto, accusing Theophilus as well as the envoys, without any reserve, of the grossest iniquities, so that Chrysostom recoiled in horror. This document must have been extremely curious, for Palladius declines to give a full account of its contents, as they would appear quite incredible.

Chrysostom's disavowal was fortunate for the Tall Brothers and unfortunate for himself. A reaction set in in their favour; Eudoxia espoused their cause, and it became a matter for fashionable interest. Theophilus was cited to appear and answer for his conduct.

It was some time before the bishop of Alexandria arrived on the scene himself, but he sent one to prepare the way before him. In the selection of an ally he manifested his craft for intrigue. He wrote to Epiphanius, the aged bishop of Salamis in Cyprus,[1] and, representing to him that the Tall Brothers held the heretical opinions of Origen, and that Chrysostom also shared them, asked him to proceed to Constantinople as the champion of orthodoxy and the accuser of the Patriarch. Theophilus knew how much prestige the high character of the veteran churchman would lend to his cause, and he also knew how to touch his weak side. Epiphanius was an upright and single-hearted old man, but extremely vain of his theological learning. He fancied himself a sort of infallible oracle on questions of doctrine, and thought his own *ipse dixit* of paramount importance. We have examples of old men, in all ages and all departments, trading on a reputation acquired in the prime of their manhood. Theophilus judiciously anointed the old bishop with flattery, and made him harbour the agreeable fancy that a vital crisis in the Church depended on his interference. Epiphanius was like an old war-horse, eager for battle; he sailed to Constantinople, but he soon found himself out of place amid the intrigues, the enmities, the calumnies and violences which filled that city; and he discovered that the questions of doctrine were a mere pretext to cloak unworthy motives. He became acquainted with the Tall Brothers, and

[1] Sozomen, viii. 14.

saw that there was no guile in them. Disgusted and dejected, he set sail for home, but the fatigue and excitement had overtaxed his failing strength and he died on the voyage. There is something melancholy in this visit of Epiphanius to Constantinople before his death, and the somewhat humorous conceit of the old man enhances the pathos.

At length Theophilus appeared, with the unconcealed object of deposing John Chrysostom. The affair of the Tall Brothers was now a secondary consideration to him. In the meantime the relations between Eudoxia and Chrysostom, who did not cease his *ex cathedra* attacks upon her, were as hostile as ever; so that on Theophilus' arrival there were two hostile camps—the camp of aristocrats in the house of Eugraphia, and the camp of the Alexandrian party in the palace of Placidia, where Theophilus had taken up his quarters, refusing to accept of Chrysostom's proffered hospitality. The city was a scene of uproar and excitement. It was divided into two parts, the adherents of Chrysostom and the Alexandrians. So high ran the popular feeling that the opposition party were afraid to hold the council, which was to decide on Chrysostom's conduct, within the precincts of Constantinople; it was held on the other side of the Bosphorus at Chalcedon, and was called the Synod of the Oak (*ad quercum*). Three different points were discussed at this council · (1) the affair of the Tall Brothers; (2) the complaints of Asiatic ecclesiastics against Chrysostom for his proceedings in 400; (3) various charges preferred against Chrysostom, among the rest that of fornication.[1] The Patriarch refused to appear at this synod or to acknowledge it; he and his party held a counter-synod in the reception room (triclinium) of the patriarchal palace. He was condemned in his absence and formally deposed, but so far was he from being intimidated that in the few days which intervened between the condemnation and the execution of the sentence he preached a sermon,[2] in which he played with pointed sarcasm on the name of the Empress, using the word *adoxia*. But the matter could not rest here; the people would not lightly submit to the removal of their idol. At this period of history, one notices, it was in church matters that the spirit of the people revealed itself, it was

---

[1] Mansi, *Concil.* iii. 1152, *sqq.*
[2] ὁμιλία πρὸ τῆς ἐξορίας (in the third volume of Montfaucon's ed.)

for church matters chiefly that they cared. Loud clamours were raised for a general council. The condemnation of a small packed assembly like that of the Oak would not be accepted. The city was in an uproar, distracted with scenes of riot and violence between the small but united body of the Alexandrians, who had come to support their bishop, and the followers of the man of the people. Theophilus fled to Egypt, and there was a revolt in Constantinople. In addition to all this, an earthquake took place,[1] which frightened the Empress, who, if she had few scruples, was, like her husband, very superstitious. Chrysostom, who had gone to Bithynia, was allowed to return and resume the duties of his office. If he had at this time assumed a more conciliatory tone towards the court, or even adopted a policy of quietism and abstained from open attacks on the Empress, he might have continued to hold the episcopal chair till his death. But he was not the man to compromise or to turn back on his way; and if we consider him often obstinate and devoid of ordinary tact, we cannot but yield respect to the unswerving man who chose the difficult road and followed it to the end.

In September 403 a silver statue on a porphyry column was erected to Eudoxia in the Augusteum by Simplicius, the prefect of the city.[2] The erection of public statues usually took place on Sunday, and was accompanied by certain old pagan customs which lingered on, like formulae which have lost their meaning, overlooked and even countenanced in the christian world. The dances and merriment of the festivity, probably innocent enough, were so loud that they interrupted the services of St. Sophia. What course was taken by Chrysostom we cannot say, as we have no reliable testimony,[3] but he must have manifested his disapproval and indignation in some way which outraged the pride of the Empress, for after this event

---

[1] Theodoret, v. 34.

[2] D. N. Aeliae Eudoxiae semper Augustae vir clarissimus Simplicius Prf. U. dedicavit, was on one side of the stylobate; on the other Greek hexameters—
κίονα πορφυρέην καὶ ἀργυρέην βασίλειαν
δέρκεο, ἔνθα πόληι θεμιστεύουσιν ἄνακτες.
οὔνομα δ' εἰ ποθέεις Εὐδόξια· τίς δ' ἀνέθηκεν;
Σιμπλίκιος μεγάλων ὑπάτων γόνος, ἐσθλὸς ὕπαρχος.

The stylobate was discovered in 1848, when the ground was dug up for the erection of the University. See Paspatis, Βυζαντινὰ Ἀνάκτορα, p. 97. For the uproar, see Sozomen, viii. 20, Marcell. Com. ad ann.

[3] I agree with Ludwig, Güldenpenning, and others that the discourse beginning "Herodias is furiously raging again," attributed to Chrysostom, is a malicious forgery. But Socrates and Sozomen quote the words.

the breach became so wide that the mild Emperor Arcadius refused to communicate with the Patriarch.

A new synod was summoned early in 404. Theophilus did not venture to be present, but Chrysostom was again condemned. Arcadius hesitated until Easter to enforce the sentence, which the Patriarch declined to obey; but at length, on the night of Easter Eve, he sent a corps of soldiers into the great church, in which at that moment male and female catechumens of riper years were receiving the rite of baptism. The congregation was scattered by the soldiers, who showed little reverence for the sanctity of the place. On the following day the people would not attend the services in St. Sophia, and, leaving the city, celebrated Easter under trees in the country; it was a sort of church secession, and the seceders were called Johannites. Meanwhile Johannes had not been arrested, and things continued as they were until Whitsuntide,[1] owing to the timorous indecision of the Emperor, who perhaps felt some compunction. But on the 20th of June the final blow was struck, and Chrysostom, submitting to the inevitable, quietly allowed himself to be conducted stealthily to the shore and conveyed in a boat to the Asiatic coast.

On the same night a memorable event took place, the conflagration of St. Sophia. Late in the evening the people had crowded into the church, expecting Chrysostom. He did not come, and as they were leaving it the fire broke out. It began at the episcopal chair, and flaming upwards caught the roof and twined round the building "like a serpent." A short time previously a high wind had arisen, and the flames were blown southwards in the direction of the senate house, which was involved in the conflagration. The destruction of the senate house was a greater misfortune than that of the church, for the former was a museum of the most precious antique works of art. The statues of the nine Muses were burnt, and here the pagan historian Zosimus observes that the conflagration betokened " estrangement from the Muses"; it was some consolation to him, however, as a sign of the providence of the Olympians, that the Zeus of Dodona and the Athene of Lindus escaped.[2]

[1] Attempts were made on Johannes' life by assassins who were tried, but allowed to escape.

[2] On the other hand the Christians rejoiced because the episcopal treasury was found intact in the sacristy.

The cause of this misfortune was made a matter of judicial investigation. Some actually attributed it to Chrysostom himself; others to his followers.[1] The superstitious said it was miraculous; while the bigoted, who had infidelity on the brain, said it was the work of a pagan. A modern writer suggests that some fanatical admirer of Chrysostom wished to light a farewell bonfire in his honour.[2] It was at all events made an excuse for persecuting the friends of John, and we hear of all sorts of cruelties perpetrated; for example, of tortures inflicted on a young lad named Eutropius, "pure as a virgin," who had been a lector of the Patriarch. Olympias was condemned to exile, as well as many others. Among those who anticipated the sentence by flight was an old maid named Nicarete, who deserves mention as a curious figure of the time. She was a philanthropist who devoted her means to works of charity, and always went about with a chest of drugs, which she used to dispense gratis, and which pious rumour said were always effectual. She reminds us of charitable ladies of modern times who distribute tracts, have a craze for homoeopathy, and hang on the lips of some favourite clergyman. Many were exiled for refusing to communicate with Arsacius, the new Patriarch. Partaking of the communion with him was made a sort of test for discovering who was a Johannite.[3]

Meanwhile John was being transported to Cucusus, a place where the mountain chains of Cappadocia and Armenia meet, hardly consoling himself with the reflection that Barabbas was preferred to Christ. We cannot follow out the details of his experiences in that cold climate,[4] of all the hardships he underwent, of the various projects he still entered into with Jerome, of his correspondence with Olympias. Such details are for the biographer or the ecclesiastical historian. But we may note here a refined trait of the spiritual woman in Olympias; she did not mention in her letter to Chrysostom the persecution which she had undergone for his sake. But she was seized by a deep melancholy, that had a flavour of distrust in God, in spite of her own convictions; and all the arguments of Chrysostom to prevent her from feeling scandalised at the

---

[1] Zosimus, v. 24.
[2] Güldenpenning, p. 163.
[3] For the Johannites, *see* Socrates, vi. 18. For Nicarete, *see* Sozomen, viii. 23.
[4] For the Isaurian depredations, *see* above, p. 70.

triumph of the unjust cause seem to have hardly consoled her. A legend was current in later times that her encoffined body had, by her own directions, been cast into the sea at Nicomedia, that it had been carried to Constantinople and thence to Brochthi, where it was placed in the church of St. Thomas. The sea voyages of sainted bodies were a favourite subject of christian legend, and reappear in the legends of the Round Table.

About a year after John's exile earthquakes took place, which terrified the superstitious nature of the Emperor. He sent to consult a certain St. Nilus,[1] who lived on Mount Sinai. Nilus had been once a brilliant figure in the world; a handsome and elegant man at the court of Theodosius, he had attained to the highest political office, the praetorian prefecture of the East; he had contracted a happy marriage with a woman whom he loved, and he had two sons. Quite suddenly he said goodbye to them all, except one of his sons, with whom he departed and took up his abode on Mount Sinai. A sudden desire had come upon him to save his soul, a sudden craving for the spiritual life. He enjoyed a great and widespread reputation for sanctity, and was consulted as a sort of oracle.[2] In answer to Arcadius' queries he replied by blaming him for the exile of John, whom he called "the lamp of truth and the trumpet of God," saying that when he heard of what had happened he was "lightning struck with the fire of grief." But the oracle had no effect; the earthquake ceased, and then Arcadius, like Pharaoh, hardened his heart.

In 407 it was determined to change the place of Chrysostom's exile. At Cucusus he had kept up a large correspondence, and his life, if dreary, was tolerable. His enemies wished that he should be quite out of the world, and Pityus, a desolate place on the south-eastern coast of the Euxine, was fixed on as his future abode. But on the way thither he died from exhaustion (14th September).[3]

Besides the fact that they decided the relation of the patriarchate to the imperial power in Constantinople, the events narrated in this chapter present other points worthy of remark.

[1] *See* Nilus, *Epist.* iii. 279 (Migne, *Patr. Gr.* lxxix.)
[2] It should be noticed that anchorets were in the christian world what oracles had been in the Greek world.
[3] Socrates, vi. 21.

Never after Chrysostom have we the spectacle of a Byzantine Patriarch standing out against the corruption or frivolity of the court, and inveighing against those who are arrayed in purple and fine linen and fare sumptuously every day. We meet many Patriarchs ready to defy the Emperor and endure persecution for a comparatively nugatory tittle of doctrine, but few who threw all their soul into the spirit of the religion, as distinct from the theology of Christianity, and none who would have had the boldness or ill-breeding to criticise the dress or censure the habits of the Empress and her ladies. The Patriarchs after Chrysostom were, if not mere theologians, either austere quietists like John the Faster under Maurice, or ambitious men of the world. It was the distinguishing mark of John Chrysostom, that he cared more for religion and less for theology.[1] It is further interesting to reflect that, at the very beginning of the long period of the queenship of New Rome, where some of the leading traits of Byzantinism, especially the oriental style of the court, had already been fully developed, a great protest was raised against it—the voice of one crying in the midst of it, denouncing the luxury and the pomp. It was as if the spirit of early Christianity, which was now extinct—smothered by its contact with empire and the things of this world—were, through Chrysostom, raising its voice from the grave and protesting against the worldliness, the splendour, and the lusts of the new christian Empire.

The treatment of John Chrysostom led to an estrangement between the courts of Constantinople and Ravenna, or rather to an exacerbation of an estrangement that already existed. Two important elements enter into these transactions—the reference of ecclesiastical affairs in the East to the bishop of Rome as to a court of appeal, and the influence exercised by the bishop of Rome on the Emperor Honorius.

Theophilus, the Patriarch of Alexandria, now triumphant, first apprised Innocent that John had been deposed from his office; letters from John himself and his Byzantine clergy, delivered three days afterwards by four "Johannite" bishops, probably convinced the pontiff that the condemnation of Chrysostom

---

[1] Compare Gass, *Gesch. der christlichen Ethik*, i. 201. The practical tendency of Chrysostom—who, as Gass remarks, was an ethical optimist—contrasts with the idealistic tendency of Gregory of Nyssa.

was unjust; and this conviction was confirmed, when he received a copy of the acts of the synod *ad quercum*, for which his signature was required. He determined that it was necessary to summon a general council, and in the meantime refused to desist from communion with the Patriarch, to whom he indited a letter of consolation. A preliminary synod, held in Italy, declared the condemnation of Chrysostom invalid, and demanded that a general council should be held at Thessalonica.

Meanwhile the Emperor Honorius, under the influence of Innocent, wrote a severe letter of admonition to his elder brother,[1] deploring the tumults and conflagrations that had disgraced and disfigured Constantinople in the recent affair, and censuring the inconvenient haste with which the sentence against the condemned had been carried out, before the decision of the head of the Church had been ascertained.

The important and striking point in this letter of Honorius is that it contains the declaration *by an Emperor* of a principle which had before been asserted *by a Bishop*, that "the interpretation of divine things concerns churchmen, the observation of religion concerns us (the Emperors)"[2]—a principle directly opposed to that tendency of the princes who ruled at New Rome, which was to result in the Caesaropapism of Justinian.

Arcadius vouchsafed not to notice his brother's communications, whose candid censure offended him, and took no steps towards summoning a general council. At length four bishops, including Aemilius of Beneventum, and two priests, were sent from Italy with imperial letters to Arcadius. They had reason to repent of their expedition. Their treatment was such that if it had been practised by an oriental despot, it would have been considered outrageous and exceptional. Escorted by soldiers from Athens to Constantinople, they were not allowed to land in that city, but were thrown into a Thracian fortress, forcibly deprived of the letters which they bore, and then hardly permitted to return to Italy (406 A.D.).

---

[1] Honorius refers in his letter to the criticisms which the imperial honours of Eudoxia had evoked in the West; "quamvis super imagine muliebri novo exemplo per provincias circumlata et diffusa per universum mundum obtrectantium fama litteris aliis commonuerim" (Mansi, iii. 1122). See Güldenpenning (*op. cit.* p. 167), whose account of this affair is very good. Palladius gives the details of these transactions (*de vita Chrys.* caps. 1, 2, 3).

[2] Ad illos enim divinarum rerum interpretatio, ad nos religionis spectat obsequium.

The estrangement which ensued between the two halves of the Empire, in consequence of this imbecile barbarity on the part of the eastern government, continued until the death of Arcadius on 1st May 408,[1] after which event friendly relations were renewed between "the twin worlds" which constituted the Empire.

[1] Socrates, vi. 23 ; Prosper Aquit. *Chron. ad ann.*

CHAPTER IV

STILICHO AND ALARIC

THE fourth century has a dull and murky atmosphere about it, an atmosphere which hangs over the pages of Ammianus; the storm was brewing that was to change the face of Europe. The usurpation of Magnentius, the battle of Hadrianople, the consulate of Merobaudes were foresigns of the storm that was to come, but it did not actually come until after the death of Theodosius the Great. We may perhaps say that it began with Alaric's invasion of Greece.

But we must not exaggerate the storm and conceive it as greater than it really was. The idea of the "wandering of the nations" and unproven speculations as to its connection with tremendous movements in the heart of Asia—an hypothesis which is as superfluous as it is indemonstrable—have led to unhistorical notions as to the nature of the breakup of the Empire. The facts do not warrant us in looking at the German movements in the fourth and fifth centuries as anything more than a continuation of the old war on the frontiers (*limites*).

We must understand clearly the form which the danger from the Germanic nations assumed. Three kinds of Germans must be distinguished—(1) the nations and tribes outside the Empire; (2) those settled within the Empire, such as the Visigoths settled by Theodosius I. in Illyricum and Thrace, and the Ostrogoths settled in Phrygia; (3) the Germans distributed throughout the Empire as soldiers or serfs, half or wholly Romanised, but with German sympathies, whom we already named semi-barbarians. All three classes of Germans contributed to the dislocation of the Empire and the Germanisation of occidental Europe, and there is no greater mistake than to imagine that the Empire was suddenly overwhelmed by foreign hordes. In the third century it had been in imminent danger from the nations who bordered on the Rhine and the Danube, and it was again harassed in the fourth century, especially in the reign of Constantius. At the same time the dangers latent in the position of Germans in the Roman army became apparent in the revolt of Magnentius (350 A.D.) It has been remarked that the battle of Mursa, in which Constantius quelled that revolt, is a sort of anticipation of the battles of the fifth century. The danger arising from the settlements of German *foederati* displayed itself in a manner still more unequivocal by the disaster of Hadrianople in 378. The policy of Theodosius I., who was called the friend of the Goths, maintained the integrity of the Empire during his own reign, but on his death, the dangers which were only averted by his personal ability, immediately appeared. Through these dangers, as we have seen, the eastern half of the Empire was safely steered; on the other hand, the provinces of the western dynasty were dismembered, and developed into German kingdoms. It is not my purpose to go into all the details of this process of dismemberment or of the history of the Emperors who reigned at Ravenna and Rome, but an outline of the chief facts is indispensable. Through all these facts a double process is observable. On the one hand, provinces are cut off from the Empire by Germans from without, who invade and take possession; on the other hand, the Empire is undermined within by the influence of half-Roman Germans or half-German Romans, like Stilicho, Aetius, and Ricimer.

The career of Stilicho and Alaric's invasions of Italy present themselves first to our view. Stilicho was absent in Rhaetia in the latter months of 401 A.D., when Alaric, who occupied the double position—characteristic of this ambiguous epoch—of king of the West Goths and master of the soldiers in Illyricum, suddenly advanced with a large army to the Julian Alps and entered Italy.[1] The causes which led him to

---

[1] By the pass *ad Pyrum* near Hrudschizza (Güldenpenning, p. 133); the date was 18th November 401, for there can be no doubt that von Wietersheim

take this step are sufficiently clear, though they are not categorically asserted. His relations to the government of New Rome, lately elated with having subdued a Germanic revolt, were not of an agreeable kind; to attempt to make himself an independent king of the Balkan peninsula would have been impracticable, for he could not have maintained such a position in the heart of the Roman Empire; and he became weary of a monotonous life, destitute of enterprise, in a land exhausted by plunder. With the Teutonic instinct to turn the face westwards, he determined to invade Italy. There was, however, I believe, another element in the situation—the relation of Alaric to Stilicho. If my conjectures were right respecting an understanding between the two generals at Pholoe in 396 A.D., Alaric was continually expecting Stilicho to carry out the execution of his design,[1] while Stilicho was prevented by the revolt of Gildo and other affairs which demanded his attention. This will explain what may seem surprising, that Alaric waited so long (five years) inactive in Illyricum. At length—willing to wait no longer, and indignant at the delays of Stilicho, who was not sufficiently imbued with the illness that should have attended his ambition, and was probably also influenced by his wife Serena, who did not approve of his projects[2]—he marched into Italy,[3] and thus placed himself in a position of hostility to his confederate. Stilicho hastened to protect the throne and kingdom of Honorius; the legions of Gaul and Britain were summoned to defend Italy. The Emperor, who was at Milan, proceeded, on Alaric's approach, to Asti, and Alaric followed him into Liguria. At Pollentia, on the river Tanarus, a battle was fought on Easter Day (6th April 402), and Alaric, although perhaps he did not experience an absolute defeat, thought it prudent to make a truce and retire.[4] But as he

and others are right in following here the Ravenna Chronicle and rejecting the date of Prosper (400).

[1] This is expressly stated by Zosimus (v. 26) who, however, omits the invasion of 402, and passes from 396 to 405 as though Alaric had stayed all that time quiet in Epirus. His words are: τὸ παρὰ Στελίχωνος ἀνέμενε σύνθημα τοιόνδε πῶς ὄν. The σύνθημα was τῇ Ὀνωρίου βασιλείᾳ τὰ ἐν Ἰλλυρίοις ἔθνη πάντα προσθεῖναι, with the help of Alaric. Of the advantages which Alaric was to gain, we only know that he was to be made *magister utriusque militiae*.

[2] Serena's influence in this direction is expressly stated in respect to a later period (Zosimus, v. 29).

[3] The passage of Alaric into Italy is placed by Anon. Cuspin. in November 401, but Prosper gives the date 400.

[4] O celebranda mihi cunctis Pollentia seclis! writes Claudian (*de Bell. Get.* 635). The words of Prosper are, *vehementer utriusque partis clade pugnatum est*. As far as I understand, it

returned he attempted to surprise Verona, and Stilicho was obliged to attack him again. The army of the Goths was decimated by a noxious disease, and was entirely at Stilicho's mercy, but he acted as he had acted before in the Peloponnesus, making a compact with Alaric and allowing him to withdraw to his Illyric provinces.[1]

It was in the course of the year 402 that Honorius, influenced perhaps by the invasion of Alaric, established his home and court at Ravenna, and discarded the former imperial residences of Rome and Milan. This step was decisive for the history of Ravenna, which, but for the choice of Honorius, would probably never have been the capital of the Ostrogothic sovereigns or the seat of the Exarchs.

The years 403 and 404 passed peacefully enough away, but in 405 Stilicho was called upon to defend Italy against a vast invasion of German hordes, which had combined to plunder the land.[2] The invaders, who were perhaps half a million in number—East Goths, Alans, Vandals, and Quadi—overran northern Italy. After some time they divided into three companies, of which one under Radagaisus besieged Florence. Stilicho seized the favourable moment and enclosed him in an inextricable position at Fiesole, where the Romans were able to massacre the barbarians at their pleasure. It is strange that we are not told what became of the other two companies.

In 407 Stilicho at length made up his mind to strike the blow and occupy Illyricum. The unfriendly feeling which had arisen between the eastern and western courts on the subject of the treatment of John Chrysostom (*see* p. 106) offered a ready pretext for a hostile movement. An edict was issued, at the instance of Stilicho, closing the ports of Italy to the ships of Arcadius' subjects, and breaking off all intercourse between the two halves of the Empire.[3] Stilicho and Alaric formed a plan to seize Illyricum and transfer it from the rule of Arcadius to that of Honorius; but it is hinted that the

---

[1] Claudian apologises for Stilicho was a victory for Stilicho in the same sense that the battle of the Catalaunian Plain was a victory for Aetius. Alaric, like Attila, was not defeated, in the strict sense, but his plans were defeated; he was disabled from proceeding further. (*de Bell. Get.* 104), saying that care of Rome influenced him: *tua cura coegit inclusis aperire fugam ne pejor in arto saeviret rabies venturae nuntia mortis.*

[2] Paulinus, *Vita Ambros.* cap. 50; Augustine, *de civ. Dei*, v. 23; *C. I. L.* vi. 1196.

[3] See *Codex Theodosianus*, vii. 16, 1.

real purpose was to establish a separate dominion under Stilicho's son, Eucherius. Stilicho was at Ravenna making preparations to join Alaric on the other side of the Adriatic, when a letter arrived from Honorius that Constantine, the general of Britain, had crossed over to Gaul and raised the standard of rebellion. A report also spread that Alaric was dead, and Stilicho's design was thwarted when it seemed on the point of fulfilment. He was obliged to desist from the enterprise that had been so long deferred, and to repair to the presence of the Emperor at Rome to consult as to the measures to be taken against the tyrant Constantine.

Of the tyrant Constantine I shall have more to say in another chapter, but we must observe here that this rebellion of the Britannic army signified an opposition to the influence of the foreigner Stilicho, and was specially directed against him, just as the revolt of Maximus had been aimed against Merobaudes. During the year 406 two tyrants had been elevated in Britain, but both, proving incompetent, were slain; Constantine was their successor. What measures in the meantime, one naturally asks, was Stilicho taking against these movements in Britain, which must soon spread to Gaul? They must have been known to him, and their significance apprehended long before the passage of Constantine across the English Channel. The answer seems to be contained in a notice of Orosius and a notice of Prosper Tiro, which state that Stilicho solicited a mixed host of barbarians to cross the Rhine and enter Gaul at the end of the year 406.[1] Both these writers affirm as his motive that he wished to force the Emperor to bestow imperial rank upon his son Eucherius; but that can hardly have been the direct, though it may have been the indirect, cause. It seems probable that Stilicho wished to have his hands free for operations in Illyricum, and that he called the barbarians into Gaul that they might oppose the progress of the Britannic legions. He thought that once the

---

[1] The words of Orosius deserve to be quoted (vii. 38): *gentes Alanorum Suevorum Vandalorum ultro in arma sollicitans, eas interim ripas quatere et pulsare Gallias voluit sperans quod et extorquere imperium genero posset in filium et barbarae gentes tam facile comprimi quam commoveri valerent.* L. von Ranke, I think, has set these transactions in their true light (*Weltgeschichte*, iv. 1, 253, 254). The edict which condemned Stilicho after his death confirms the charge—*opes quibus ille usus est ad omnem ditandam inquietandamque barbariem.*—*Cod. Theod.* ix. 42, 22.

barbarians had accomplished what he wished them to accomplish, he would easily be able to crush them and drive them out, as he had crushed the army of Radagaisus.

But Alaric, who was not dead, was deeply disappointed, and disdained to wait meekly for the convenience of Stilicho. He advanced to the frontiers of Italy at the Julian Alps, and loudly demanded compensation for the time he had wasted by waiting in Epirus and for the expenses of his march. Stilicho's influence induced the Roman senate, which assembled to decide the matter (408 A.D.), to agree to Alaric's demand, and pay compensation money to the amount of £180,000; but many were dissatisfied with Stilicho's Germanising policy, and one senator bolder than the rest exclaimed, "That is not a peace; it is a compact of thraldom." Such, however, was the almost imperial power of the Emperor's father-in-law,[1] and such the awe in which he was held, that the rash speaker after the dissolution of the assembly deemed it prudent to seek refuge in a church.

Stilicho was not destined either to carry out his designs against the Balkan provinces of New Rome or to win the glory of suppressing the new Constantine, the Emperor whom Gaul had accepted. There was a strong though secret opposition to Stilicho in Italy; at any time a favourable moment might be seized to poison the ears or enlighten the eyes of Honorius respecting the designs of his father-in-law, on which an ugly interpretation might be placed. Even among the soldiers Stilicho's popularity was by no means so established as to be secure. From an obscure passage in one of our authorities we can gather this at least, that a forensic friend of Stilicho, even while he and Honorius were yet at Rome in the early months of 408, foresaw the danger that awaited the general, and connected it—rightly as the event proved—with the spirit of the soldiers stationed at Ticinum.[2]

Honorius was at Bononia, on his way from Ravenna to Ticinum, when the news reached him of his brother's death (May 408).[3] He entertained the idea of proceeding himself

---

[1] The marriage of Honorius and Maria had been celebrated in 398. Claudian had written a wanton epithalamium; but the wife is said to have died a virgin. Honorius married her sister Thermantia in 408, who died in 415.

[2] Zosimus, v. 30, 4; the prophet was Justinianus.

[3] *Ib.* 31, 1.

to Constantinople to set in order the affairs of the realm, which now devolved on a child of seven years; and he summoned Stilicho from Ravenna for consultation. Stilicho dissuaded him from this purpose, and undertook to proceed himself to New Rome, while he proposed to employ Alaric against the usurper Constantine, who ruled in Gaul. The death of Arcadius seemed to present to Stilicho an opportunity for accomplishing his purposes without Alaric's aid. But meanwhile a minister named Olympius was winning the ear of Honorius. The Romans who hated Germans and Arians were weaving a web of destruction for the Vandal father-in-law of the Emperor; they accused him of treason; and on 23d August Stilicho was put to death at Ravenna. Many ministers were executed at the same time, as members of his party and privy to his treasonable designs.[1] His son Eucherius was slain soon afterwards, while his wife Serena was spared; but she was destined to be strangled a year later, by order of the Roman senate, for pagan impiety, while Alaric was besieging Rome. Thermantia, the wife of the Emperor, was put away because she was the daughter of Stilicho.[2] It was stated definitely by Stilicho's opponents that he aimed at winning the imperial purple for his son Eucherius,[3] and the poet Claudian had hinted at a possible marriage between the Emperor's half-sister Galla Placidia and the son of Stilicho. I have already stated my opinion that this charge was in the main true, nor does it seem confuted by the mere fact—which may have been actually intended to disarm suspicion—that Eucherius was entrusted with insignificant posts by his father.[4]

The relations between the eastern half and the western half of the Empire had been strained and often positively hostile during the reign of Arcadius; or, I think, we should rather say

[1] Zosimus, v. 32, 4; Limenius, praet. pref. of Gaul; Chariobaudes, master of soldiers in Gaul (both of them had fled to Italy before the tyrant Constantine); Vincentius, *magister equitum praesentalis*. Stilicho himself was *magister utriusque militiae*. See note of Mendelssohn on the cited passage of Zosimus. Vincentius was succeeded by Turpilio, Stilicho by Varanes. Heraclian, who slew Stilicho, was appointed count of Africa.

[2] *Ib.* 35, 3. Eucherius very nearly escaped his fate; for when he was slain Alaric was approaching Rome, and if the executioners had been a little slower he would have fallen into Alaric's hands and been saved (*ib.* 37, 4).

[3] Orosius, *Hist.* vii. 38; Zosimus, v. 32, 1; Sozomen, ix. 4.

[4] Zosimus, v. 34, 7.

during the lifetime of Stilicho. The death of the great general changed the relations of the courts; concord and friendly co-operation succeeded coldness and enmity; and the law which excluded eastern commerce from western ports, passed by the influence of the "public enemy" Stilicho, was rescinded. It is a mistake to attribute this to the death of Arcadius. If Arcadius had lived many years longer, the death of Stilicho would have been followed by the same result. This is evident if we reflect on the elements of the situation. In the realm of Arcadius the Roman spirit had triumphed and won the upper hand by the suppression of Gainas and Tribigild. In the realm of Honorius, on the contrary, the German interest predominated as long as Stilicho lived. Hence the two courts were discordant. But the fall of Stilicho was a triumph for the Roman party in Italy, and a cause of rejoicing for the court of Byzantium; he who was the obstacle to unity, he whose private ambition threatened an integral portion of the provinces ruled from New Rome, was removed, and the Empire was again for a time really as well as nominally one.

After Stilicho's death, the new government, led by Olympius,[1] who was appointed master of offices, had two problems to face. How was Alaric, still threatening in Noricum, to be dealt with? and what measures were to be taken in regard to Constantine, the Emperor or tyrant of Gaul? Alaric promised to withdraw from Noricum to Pannonia if the balance of the sum of money promised by the senate, and as yet only partly paid, were delivered to him. With an unwise audacity the Emperor's new advisers refused the proposal, and at the same time took no measures for defence. It would have been best to pay the money, but if they were determined to defy the Goth they should have taken steps to resist him, and (as a historian of that century suggested)[2] they might have enlisted a Goth named Sarus, an excellent warrior and a rival of Alaric, to oppose the entry of the latter into Italy.

The king of the West Goths invaded Italy for the second

---

[1] Zosimus, v. 35. The chamberlain Deuterius and the scribe Peter, friends of Stilicho, were beaten to death, because they refused to make any revelations about the deceased general.

[2] *Ib.* 36. Zosimus (after Olympiodorus) insists on the desire of Alaric to come to terms. In these transactions the obstinacy of Honorius was a vital element.

time and marched straight to Rome,[1] without turning aside to besiege Ravenna, where Honorius resided sufficiently secure. It is related that a monk warned the invader not to turn his arms against the capital of the world, and that Alaric replied that he was irresistibly led thither, not by his own will but by a divine impulse [2]; and the story is suitable to the solemnity of the moment. The German king laid siege to the eternal city. Reduced to extremities by famine,[3] and even plague, the inhabitants of Rome, where there was still a strong pagan element, essayed the efficacy of heathen sacrifices; but they were at length compelled to make a hard peace with Alaric. Honorius and Olympius, however, still persisted in adopting the strange policy of defying the invader and not resisting him. But Olympius soon fell, through the hostility of a cabal of eunuchs,[4] and the praetorian prefect and Patrician, Jovius, succeeded to his influence.[5] Other changes in the civil service and the military commands were made about the same time; after the death of Stilicho ministers rose and fell in rapid succession.[6] Jovius was anxious to bring about a peace with Alaric, and was ready to make reasonable concessions; and for this purpose he appointed an interview with the Gothic king at Ariminum. Alaric demanded that the provinces of Venetia, Noricum, and Dalmatia [7] should be ceded to himself and his people as a permanent abode, and that a certain annual supply of corn and money should be granted by the Emperor. In his letter to Honorius Jovius suggested that Alaric might relax the severity of these demands, if the rank of *magister*

---

[1] His route by Aquileia, Concordia, Altinum, Cremona (?), Bononia, Ariminum is described by Zosimus, v. 37.

[2] Socrates, vii. 10.

[3] It is mentioned that Laeta, the widow of the Emperor Gratian, and Tisamene her mother, alleviated the want by their distributions (*ib*. 39, 4). The siege took place in the last months of 408.

[4] Olympius fled to Dalmatia (Zosimus, v. 46, 1). He obtained power, however, once more, and was once more disgraced; Constantius, the husband of Placidia, cut off his ears and beat him to death. (Olympiodorus, fr. 8.)

[5] *Ib*. 47. Olympiodorus calls him Jovian.

[6] Varanes, the *magister peditum*, had been deposed some time before, and Turpilio, the *mag. equit.*, had succeeded him, while Vigilantius, the count of the domestics, stepped into the place of Turpilio, and Allobich (or Hellebich) succeeded Vigilantius as *comes domesticorum*. Turpilio was now banished on account of a military sedition, and Valens, the other *comes dom.*, succeeded him, and in the following year (410) was elevated to the rank of *magister utriusque militiae;* Hellebich succeeded Vigilantius, who was a victim of the same sedition as *mag. eq.* See Mendelssohn's note on Zosimus, v. 47, 2.

[7] *Ib*. 48, Βενετίας ἄμφω καὶ Νωρικοὺς καὶ Δελματίαν.

utriusque militiae, which Stilicho had held, were conferred on him. But Honorius could not rise to the idea of granting to the barbarian Visigoth the post which had been held by the semi-barbarian Vandal; he decidedly refused either to confer the title or to grant the lands. It is interesting to note, however, that there was for a moment the possibility that a West Gothic kingdom might have been established to the north-east, instead of to the west of Italy.

Jovius opened the answer of Honorius in the presence of Alaric and read it aloud. The German looked upon the refusal of the military command as a contumely to himself, and " rising up in anger, ordered his barbarians to march to Rome to avenge the insult which was offered to himself and all his kin."

Here we have the Roman exclusiveness, manifested by the son of Theodosius, and the ambition of the German to win a place and recognition in the Empire, as the main elements of the situation; and the remarkable circumstance is that Alaric did not desire war, and that Honorius had no adequate forces to support his resistance.[1]

Once more Alaric attempted to induce the Emperor to accept his proposals, and even offered more moderate terms. The bishop of Rome, which the Goths once more threatened, was, with other bishops,[2] sent as an envoy to Ravenna, if even yet the Emperor might pause ere he exposed the city which had ruled over the world for more than four hundred years to the ravages of barbarians, and allowed the magnificent edifices to be consumed by the fire of the foe. All that Alaric asked now was the province of Noricum on the Danube; he did not ask for Venetia nor yet for Dalmatia. Let Honorius assign the Goths Noricum, and grant them a certain sum of money and supplies of corn annually; Italy would then be delivered from the invader. It is hard to see why Honorius and his ministers declined to accept these terms, which, considering the situation, were moderate; but on this occasion Jovius, instead of advising peace, which he had desired before, advised a firm refusal. It appears that Honorius had taken him to task for his disposition to yield to Alaric at Ariminum, and that, fearing for

---

[1] Zosimus (v. 50) states that Honorius called in 10,000 Huns, and imposed upon the Dalmatians the burden of supplying them with corn, sheep, and oxen. But of these Huns we hear nothing more.

[2] Zosimus uses the plural τοὺς κατὰ πόλιν ἐπισκόπους.

his personal safety, he had rushed to the other extreme, and sworn, and made others swear, by the head of Honorius, to war to the death with Alaric.[1]

Having met with this new refusal, and perceiving that it was a hopeless aim to extort anything from the obstinacy and prejudice of the son of him who "pacified the Goths," Alaric marched to the walls of Rome, and called upon the citizens to side with him against the Emperor. When this invitation was refused, he seized the port and blockaded the eternal city for the second time. The corn stores of the city lay in the harbour, and Alaric threatened that if the Romans did not comply with his demand he would use them for his own army. The senate met, and, with the fear of famine before their eyes, yielded.

Alaric's purpose was to elect a new Emperor who should be more pliable than Honorius. He had selected the prefect of the city, Attalus, to play this somewhat undignified part; and Attalus was invested with the purple and crowned with the diadem. Alaric received the post of master of soldiers, which the legitimate Emperor had disdained to bestow on him; and Athaulf, his brother-in-law, was created count of the domestics.[2]

Nor was it merely to the Goths that a new Emperor was acceptable; he was also welcome to the pagans[3] and the Arians, who were numerous in the city on the Tiber and had suffered from the severe laws of the orthodox Honorius. One might say that the elevation of Attalus involved a twofold reaction against the established order of things; a reaction on the one hand against catholicism, an opposition on the other hand of the Teutonic to the Roman spirit. In fact the coalition of Alaric and Attalus was a repetition in a new form of the coalition of Arbogast and Eugenius. What saved the throne of Honorius was that the two factors of the coalition fell asunder, because they too were divided by the opposition of Roman to Teuton.

It is worthy of remark that the situation in Gaul—which will be described in another chapter—was determined by the same three elements as the situation in Italy, but these elements were

---

[1] *See* Zosimus, v. 51.
[2] Sozomen, ix. 7.
[3] Attalus had been once a pagan himself; Sozomen, ix. 9.

not adjusted in the same relations. In both countries the imperial authority was represented; in both countries there were tyrants or usurpers; and in both countries there were barbarians hostile to the imperial government. But in Gaul it was the tyrant against whom the legitimate Emperor prepared to contend; in Italy it was the Emperor against whom the tyrant prepared to contend. In Gaul the tyrant and the barbarians, Vandals, Suevians, and Alans, had originally been in opposition, and had come to terms, which left them independent of each other; in Italy the tyrant was the creation of the barbarian, and an opposition developed itself afterwards. The watchword of the new Augustus who came from Britain had been opposition to German influence; the watchword of the new Augustus who arose at Rome was opposition to catholic intolerance. Constantine was the successor of Maximus; Attalus was the successor of Eugenius.

Attalus created Lampadius,[1] probably the same senator who had once exclaimed bravely in the senate house against the "compact of servitude" with Alaric, praetorian prefect of Italy, and a certain Marcian prefect of the city; Tertullus was elected as consul for the year 410. We are told that the inhabitants of Rome were in high spirits, because the new officers were well versed in the art of administration; only the rich house of the Anicii was vexed at the new order of things.[2]

The first problem which presented itself to Attalus and Alaric was how they were to act in regard to Africa, which was held by Count Heraclian, an officer loyal to Honorius. They were not safe as long as they did not possess the African provinces, on which Rome depended for her supplies of corn. Alaric advised that troops should be sent to seize the power in Africa by force; but Attalus would not consent, confident that he could win Carthage without fighting a battle. He appointed a certain Constans commander of the soldiers in Libya, and sent him thither with a small company of guards, while he prepared himself to march against Ravenna.

Honorius was overwhelmed with terror at the tidings that a usurper had arisen in Italy, and that Rome had given her adhesion. He made ready ships in Classis, which, if it came to the worst, might bear him to the shelter of New Rome, and

---

[1] Zosimus, vi. 7. Valens, who had been general in Dalmatia, was created *magister militum*. [2] *Ib.* 7, 4.

sent messages to Attalus, proposing a division of the Empire.¹ But Attalus had such high hopes that he would not consent to a compromise; he agreed to allow the legitimate Caesar to retire to an island and end his days as a private individual. So probable did it seem that the tottering throne of Honorius would fall, and so bright the prospects of his rival, that the praetorian prefect Jovius or Jovian, who had sworn eternal enmity to Alaric, went over to the camp or the palace of the usurper. The policy of Jovius was ever, when he adopted a new cause, to carry it to a further extreme than any one else. From wishing to make large concessions to Alaric, he had rebounded to the position of refusing to make even small concessions; and now, when he joined the side of Attalus, he went further than Attalus in hostility to Honorius, and recommended that the Emperor, when he was dethroned, should be deformed by bodily mutilation.² But for this proposal Attalus is said to have chidden him; Attalus knew not then that it was to be his own fate hereafter.

Attalus and his master of soldiers advanced upon Ravenna, and it seemed probable that Honorius would flee. But at this juncture the eastern came to the assistance of the western government, and Anthemius, the praetorian prefect of the East, sent about four thousand soldiers to Ravenna. With these Honorius was able to secure the city of the marshes against the hostile army, and await the result of the operations of Constans, Attalus' emissary in Africa. If Heraclian maintained the province loyally against the usurper, the war might be prosecuted in Italy against Alaric and Attalus; if, on the other hand, Africa accepted a change of rule, Honorius determined to abandon the position.³

The news soon arrived that Constans had been slain. At

---

¹ Several embassies passed between Attalus and Honorius (Olympiodorus, fr. 13). Besides Jovius, Valens *mag. utr. mil.*, Potanius the quaestor, and Julian *primicerius notariorum*, were employed as envoys. Attalus created Jovius patrician (*ib.*); according to the text of Zosimus he created him praet. pref., but that post he had already given to Lampadius. Zosimus drew his facts from Olympiodorus, and here I suspect a slight omission in the text has produced the confusion; the word πατρίκιος has probably fallen out. Read (vi. 8, 1) Ἰόβιος ὁ τῆς αὐλῆς ὕπαρχος [πατρίκιος] παρὰ Ἀττάλου καθεσταμένος. Between the somewhat similar letters παρχος and παρα on either side, it might easily have been omitted.

² So Olympiodorus, followed by Sozomen (ix. 8) and Zosimus. Philostorgius, however (xii. 3), attributes the proposal of *acroteriasm* to Attalus himself.

³ Zosimus, vi. 8.

this point, the latent opposition between the ideas of Attalus and the ideas of Alaric began to assert itself. Alaric wished to send an army to Africa; and Jovius supported the policy in a speech to the Roman senate. But neither the senate nor Attalus were disposed to send an army of barbarians against a Roman province; such a course seemed *indecent*[1]—unworthy of Rome.

Jovius, the shifty Patrician, seems to have decided, on account of the failure in Africa, to desert his allegiance to Attalus, and return to his allegiance to Honorius; and he attempted to turn Alaric away from his league with the Emperor whom he had created. But Alaric would not yet throw off his allegiance. He had said that he was resolved to persist in the blockade of Ravenna until he had taken it, but the new strength which Honorius had obtained from Byzantium seems to have convinced him that it would be futile to continue the siege. He marched through the Aemilia, receiving or extorting from the cities acknowledgment of the Empire of Attalus, and failing to take Bononia, which held out for Honorius, passed on to Liguria, to force that province also to accept the tyrant.

Attalus meanwhile returned to Rome, which he found in a sad plight. Count Heraclian had stopped the transport of corn and oil from the granary of Italy, and Rome was reduced to such extremities of starvation, that some one cried in the circus, *Pretium impone carni humanae,* " Set a price on human flesh."[2] The senate was now desirous to carry out the plan which it had rejected with Roman dignity before, and send an army of barbarians to Africa; but the Princeps again refused to consent to such a step, as he had formerly refused when it was proposed by Alaric.

Accordingly Alaric determined to pull down the tyrant whom he had set up; he had found that in Attalus, as well as in Honorius, the Roman temper was firm, and that he too was keenly conscious that the Visigoths were only barbarians. Near Ariminum Attalus was discrowned and divested of the purple robe with ceremonious solemnity; but Alaric provided for his safety, and retained him in his own camp.[3]

---

[1] Zosimus, vi. 9, ἀφεὶς πρὸς αὐτὴν [the senate] ἀπρεπῆ τινα ῥήματα.
[2] *Ib.* 11.
[3] Along with his son Ampelius (*Ib.* 12).

It now seemed that Alaric might approach Honorius again with better chance of a satisfactory adjustment; and he marched in the direction of Ravenna. At this juncture the Goth Sarus, a brave warrior, appears upon the scene. With three hundred men he had stationed himself in the Picentine territory, and held aloof from the two contending parties. According to one writer,[1] he now attacked the Goths of Alaric or Athaulf, because he wished to prevent the conclusion of peace; according to another writer,[2] he was not the attacker, but the attacked. Whichever of the two accounts be true, his accession to the side of the Emperor seems to have induced Honorius to continue in his implacable hostility to Alaric.[3]

It was in August 410 that Alaric marched upon Rome for the third time, but now he occupied it without resistance. It is not clear how far this occupation was due to an unfriendly attitude on the part of Honorius; events may have intervened between the battle with Sarus and the march on Rome of which we are ignorant. The eternal city was surrendered to the pillage of the soldiers; but it was confessed that respect was shown for churches, and that the "immanity" of the barbarians was softened by the veneration which christian things inspired.[4] Alaric then proceeded to southern Italy with the purpose of crossing to Africa, and relieving Italy from the pressure of famine. If Alaric had succeeded in this enterprise and returned to Italy, that peninsula might have been the seat of a West Gothic kingdom, almost a hundred years before it became the seat of an East Gothic kingdom. But Alaric died in Bruttii,[5] before the year was over, at Consentia, and the Goths laid his body in the bed of the river

---

[1] Sozomen, ix. 9.

[2] Zosimus, vi. 13. Cf. Olympiodorus, fr. 3, τοῦτον ὅτι Ῥωμαῖοι ἡταιρίσαντο δι' ἔχθρας Ἀλαρίχῳ ὄντα ἄσπονδον ἐχθρὸν Ἀλάριχον ἐποιήσαντο.

[3] Philostorgius, xii. 3, says that Alaric's proposals were rejected through the influence of Sarus. Philostorgius, however, makes the wrong statement that Sarus succeeded Stilicho as *magister utriusque militiae* (cf. Mendelssohn's note on Zosimus, vi. 9); and this may lead us to question his other statements about Sarus, when they are unsupported.

[4] St. Augustine, *de civ. Dei*, Lib. i. cap. 7 : "quod autem more novo factum est, quod inusitata rerum facie immanitas barbara tam mitis apparuit, ut amplissimae basilicae explendae populo cui parceretur eligerentur et decernerentur, ubi nemo feriretur, etc. . . . hoc Christi nomini, hoc Christiano tempori tribuendum quisquis non videt caecus" (cf. cap. 1). He comes back to the subject in iii. 29, and contrasts the invasions of the Gauls.

[5] Orosius states that ships of Alaric, when he attempted to cross to Sicily, were wrecked in the Straits (*Hist.* vii. 43).

Bucentus. His work had been accomplished; he had not himself entered in to possess, but he had prepared the way for a Visigothic kingdom, which was to arise, not in Illyricum, where he had sojourned so long, not in Italy, nor yet in Africa, but in a country where Alaric had never trodden. Alaric might be called the Moses of the Visigoths; he guided them on their wanderings until they came in sight of the promised land which he was not destined to enjoy himself.

CHAPTER V

THEODOSIUS II AND MARCIAN

WHEN Arcadius died in 408, his son Theodosius was only eight years old. Anthemius acted as protector of the Empire, and apparently also as guardian of the young prince until 414,[1] and the measures which were passed during these six years exhibit an intelligent and sincere solicitude for the welfare of the people and the correction of abuses. At the same time a better understanding subsisted between the court of New Rome and the court of Ravenna, due partly to the death of Arcadius and partly to that of Stilicho, who was executed in the same year. As a result of the new mode of palatial life, the influence of women as well as the influence of eunuchs made itself felt. The keynote of this new departure was struck by Eudoxia, the first wife of a Roman Emperor who received the title Augusta, a novelty to which the court of Honorius objected; and throughout the whole space of the fifth and sixth centuries we meet remarkable ladies of the imperial house playing a prominent part. The daughters of Eudoxia formed a great contrast to their mother, and the court of Theodosius I. was very different from that of Arcadius. The princesses Pulcheria, Arcadia, and Marina, and the young Emperor, inherited the religious temperament of their father, with which Pulcheria combined her grandfather's strength of character. The court, as a contemporary says, assumed the character of a cloister. The singing of hymns, pious practices, and charitable works were the order of the day, and the Patriarch Atticus

---

[1] Socrates, vii. 1. For the children of Arcadius, see the genealogical table of the house of Theodosius. Theodosius II was born 10th April 401.

acted as a spiritual adviser. But religion was accompanied with culture; Theodosius was a student of natural science, and from his skill in writing received the name of Kalligraphos.

In 414 Pulcheria was created Augusta, and assumed the regency in the name of her brother, who was two years younger than herself. She superintended and assisted in his education; she supported by her countenance the reforming spirit of the senate, and protected her brother from falling under the influence of intriguing court officials, to which his weak character would easily have rendered him a prey. This was the import of Pulcheria's political position. She resolved to remain a virgin, and influenced her sisters to form the same determination, in which they were confirmed by their friend Atticus, who is said to have written a book for them on the subject of virginity.

In 421 a new element was introduced into the monastic court life by the marriage of the Emperor with Athenais. The story of the Athenian girl who became the Empress Eudocia is well known. She was the daughter of Leontius, a philosopher and a pagan, and was by him instructed in all pagan learning. After the death of her father she sought refuge in Constantinople (418) from her brothers, who were less than kind, and the beauty and learning of the girl, dedicated to Athene, won the patronage of Pulcheria, who chose her as a suitable bride for her brother.[1] The marriage was followed by the birth of a daughter, Eudoxia (named after the late Empress), who afterwards became the wife of Valentinian III, and in 423 Eudocia was proclaimed Augusta. She had embraced Christianity before her marriage, and she wrote religious poetry; but she always retained some pagan leanings, and we may be sure that, when her influence began to assert itself, the strict monastic character of the court was considerably modified, and that breaches with Pulcheria were not infrequent, as both ladies had decided characters. The early undivided allegiance of Theodosius to his sister was gone; by degrees it was felt that there were two not necessarily united powers in the

[1] The modern parallel is Sophia of Russia marrying her brother Ivan to a beautiful young Siberian named Soltikof (Voltaire, *Histoire de Russie sous Pierre le Grand*, cap. v.) Gregorovius has made *Athenais* the subject of a historical monograph.

palace; and of this feeling intriguing courtiers or churchmen would not be slow to take advantage. The dissension showed itself clearly in the Nestorian controversy.

When we read the chronicles of the reign of Theodosius II, we at first receive the impression that it was a period of few important events, though set with curious stories. The invasions of Attila and the general council of Ephesus are the only facts which seem to stand out prominently in the chronicles, while they are full of stories and interesting traits which attract the imagination, such as the life of Athenais, the martyrdom of Hypatia, the monastic life of the imperial votaries Pulcheria and her sisters, the story of the waking of the seven sleepers—the young saints who in the reign of Decius had fallen asleep in a cave. But on further study we come to the conclusion that it was a period of capital importance,—a period in which the Empire was passing a vital crisis.

To an unprejudiced observer in the reign of Arcadius it might have seemed that the Empire in its eastern parts was doomed to a speedy decline. One possessed of the insight of Synesius might have thought it impossible that it could last for eight hundred years more when he considered the threatening masses of barbarians who environed it, the corruption and divisions of the imperial court, the oppression of the subjects, and all the evils which Synesius actually pointed out. For with the beginning of the fifth century a critical time approached for the whole Empire. At the end of the same century we find that while the western half had been found wanting in the day of its trial, the eastern half had passed the crisis and all the dangers successfully; we find strong and prudent Emperors ruling at New Rome, disposed to alleviate the burdens of the subjects, and in the court a different atmosphere from that of the days of Arcadius.

Now the significance of the reign of Theodosius II is that it was the transition from the court of Arcadius to the court of the steady reforming Emperors in the latter half of the century, and it partook of both characters. This double-sidedness is its peculiarity. Theodosius was weak, like his father, but he was not so weak, and he seems to have profited more by his education. The senate struggles with effect against irresponsible officialism, and although we hear that there was venality and corruption in the days of Pulcheria,[1] a great improvement is in progress. In the chronicles we do not hear much about the senate, everything is attributed to Pulcheria or Theodosius; but the words of Socrates that the Emperor was much beloved " by the senate and people " are significant, and there is no doubt that the much-lauded wisdom of Pulcheria's regency consisted in the wisdom of the senate which she supported. And although towards the close of the reign eunuchs had power, the ground gained by the senate was not lost; the spirit of its administration and the lines of its policy were followed by the succeeding Emperors, and it guided the State safely through a most momentous period which proved fatal to the integrity of the western provinces.

As has been already stated, the guidance of the State through this critical period following the death of Arcadius devolved upon the praetorian prefect Anthemius,[2] and was successfully performed by him. A new treaty was made which secured peace on the Persian frontier; it was agreed that Roman merchants were not to travel farther east than Artaxata and Nisibis, nor Persian merchants farther west than Callinicum. An invasion of Lower Moesia by Uldes, the king of the Huns who had executed Gainas, seemed at first serious and menacing, but was successfully tided over.[3] In words worthy of his successor Attila, Uldes boasted that he could subdue the whole earth or even the sun. He captured Castra Martis, but as he advanced against Thrace he was deserted by a large multitude of his followers, who joined the Romans in driving their king beyond the Danube. An immense horde of Scyri were in Uldes' host, and so many were taken prisoners that the government had some trouble in disposing of them. They were given to large landowners to be employed as serfs (*coloni*) in Asia, not in Thrace or Illyricum. In order to prevent future invasions of Huns or other barbarians, Anthemius provided for the improvement of the fleet stationed on the Danube; a large number of new ships were built to protect the borders of Moesia and Scythia, and the old crafts were repaired.[4]

[1] Eunapius, fr. 87.
[2] Anthemius was the grandson of Philippus, who was praet. pref. in 346. In 400 he held the office of *comes sacrarum largitionum*, in 404 he was *magister officiorum*, in 405 he was praetorian prefect and consul, in 408 he was made a Patrician. Güldenpenning gives an excellent and detailed account of his administration.
[3] Sozomen, *Hist. Ecc.* ix. 5.
[4] *Cod. Theod.* vii. 1 (28th January

THEODOSIUS II AND MARCIAN

Of the other acts of "the great Anthemius" we may mention that he strengthened the capital, which tended to stretch beyond the wall of Constantine, by a new wall (413),[1] and that he made provision for the more efficient transportation of the corn supplies from Alexandria to Constantinople.[2] He also took measures to revive the prostrate condition of the Illyrian provinces, which through the protracted presence of Alaric and his Visigoths had been reduced to a state of defencelessness and misery.[3]

One of the men who held a distinguished position in this reign, and was highly characteristic of the epoch in many ways, was Cyrus of Panopolis. A poet, like his fellow-townsman Nonnus, a student of art and architecture, a "Greek" in faith, he was penetrated with thoroughly Hellenic instincts; and when it is remarked that the Empire was beginning to assume in the East a Greek complexion in the reign of Theodosius II, "the first Greek Emperor,"[4] it is often forgotten that Cyrus had a great deal to do with this, and was in fact the chief leader of the movement. He was prefect of the city for many years, and he used to issue decrees in Greek, an innovation for which a writer of the following century expressly blames him. His prefecture was very popular and long remembered at Constantinople, for he built or restored many buildings and improved the illumination of the town, so that the people enthusiastically cried on one occasion in the circus, "Constantine built the city but Cyrus renewed it." This popularity made the prefect an object of suspicion, and his fall soon followed, his paganism furnishing a convenient ground for accusation. By a sort of irony he was compelled to take orders and made bishop of Cotyaeum in Phrygia.[5] His first sermon, which his mali-

---

412). The Danube boats were called *lusoriae*. For the Scyri, see *Cod. Theod.* v. 4, 3.

[1] The towers of the *novus murus* are mentioned in *Cod. Theod.* xv. 1, 51 (cf. Socrates, *Hist. Ecc.* vii. 1). It is interesting to find a reference in an inscription (*Corp. Ins. Lat.* iii. 2, 739)—

Portarum valido firmavit omine muros
Pusaeus magno non minor Anthemio.

[2] The responsibility was transferred from the *navicularii*, or naval *collegia*, to the *summates* of the fleets, whose recompense for their trouble was increased by the addition of a *mercedula*.

The island of Carpathus was the halfway station between Alexandria and Byzantium, and thus the care of the corn supplies devolved conjointly on the prefect of the city, the prefect of Egypt, and the *praeses insularum*.

[3] Compare *Cod. Theod.* xii. 1, 177.

[4] Julian might also claim this title, but although a Greek in sympathies, he was in many ways more Roman than Greek.

[5] It strikes one as a very curious thing that an undisguised pagan should be not only compelled to take orders but appointed to a bishopric, as a sort

cious congregation forced him to preach against his will on Christmas Day, is delectable, and shows the readiness of the man :—

"Brethren, let the birth of God, our Saviour, Jesus Christ be honoured by silence, because he was conceived in the holy virgin through hearing only. To the Word itself be glory for ever and ever, Amen."[1]

The two most important acts of Theodosius were the foundation of a university at Constantinople and the compilation of the code called after his name. The inauguration of the university was an important measure for Byzantine life, and indicates the enlightenment of Theodosius' reign. It was intended to supersede the university of Athens, the headquarters of paganism—with which, however, the government preferred not to interfere directly—and thereby to further the cause of Christianity. This negative effect was expected, and did to a certain extent follow. The Latin language was represented by ten grammarians or philologists and three rhetors, the Greek likewise by ten grammarians, but by five rhetors or sophists; one chair of philosophy was endowed and two chairs of jurisprudence. Thus the Greek language had two more chairs than the Latin, and this fact may be cited as marking a stage in the Graecisation of the eastern half of the Roman Empire.

In the year 429 Theodosius determined to form a collection of all the constitutions issued by the "renowned Constantine, the divine Emperors who succeeded him, and ourselves." The new code was to be drawn up on the model of the Gregorian and Hermogenian codes, and the execution of the work was entrusted to a commission of nine persons, among whom was Apelles, professor of law at the new university. In 438 the work was completed and published, but during the intervening years the members of the commission had changed;

---

of punishment ; and that such a measure was not considered an insult to the Church. Gregorovius says that he was perhaps made bishop of Cotyaeum "weil die dortige Christengemeinde in dem Rufe stand vier ihrer Bischöfe umgebracht zu haben" (*Athenais*, p. 198). For laws concerning the pagans, see *Cod. Theod.* xvi. 10. *Lex* 24 of this title is a law of toleration (423 A.D.)

commanding Christians not to dare to attack *Judaeis ac paganis in quiete degentibus—religionis auctoritate abusi*. May we attribute this to Eudocia's influence?

[1] This sermon is preserved by John Malalas. I have corrected the text by a change of punctuation ; παρθένῳ evidently ends a period, and I suspect τῷ should be inserted before λόγῳ.

of the eight who are mentioned in the edict which accompanied the final publication only two, Antiochus and Theodorus, were among the original workers, and a constitution of 435, which conferred full powers on the committee for the consummation of the work, mentions sixteen compilers, *contextores*.

The new codex was issued conjointly by Theodosius and Valentinian, and it impressed a sort of seal on the unity of the Empire (15th February 438). The visit of the younger Emperor to Constantinople on the occasion of his marriage with Eudoxia facilitated this co-operation. On 23d December of the same year, at a meeting of the senate of Old Rome, the code which had been drawn up by the lawyers of New Rome was publicly recognised, and an official account of the proceedings on that occasion—*gesta in senatu Urbis Romae de recipiendo Codice Theodosiano*—may still be read. The praetorian prefect and consul of the year, Anicius Acilius Glabrio Faustus, spoke as follows :—

"The felicity of the eternal Emperors proceeds so far as to adorn with the ornaments of peace those whom it defends by warfare. Last year when we loyally attended the celebration of the most fortunate of all ceremonies, and when the marriage had been happily concluded, the most sacred Prince, our Lord Theodosius, was fain to add this dignity also to his world, and ordered the precepts of the laws to be collected and drawn up in a compendious form of sixteen books, which he wished to be consecrated by his most sacred name. Which thing the eternal Prince, our Lord Valentinian, approved with the loyalty of a colleague and the affection of a son."

And all the senators cried out in the usual form, "Well spoken!" (*nove diserte, vere diserte*). But instead of following the course of the *gesta* in the Roman senate house, it will be more instructive to read the imperial constitution which introduced the great code to the Roman world.

"The Emperors Theodosius and Valentinian, Augusti, to Florentius, Praetorian Prefect of the East.

"Our clemency has often been at a loss to understand the cause of the fact, that, when so many rewards are held out for the maintenance of arts and (liberal) studies, so few are found who are endowed with a full knowledge of the Civil Law, and even they so seldom ; we are astonished that amid so many whose faces have grown pale from late lucubrations hardly one or two have attained to sound and complete learning.

"When we consider the enormous multitude of books, the diverse modes of process and the difficulty of legal cases, and further the huge mass of imperial constitutions, which hidden as it were under a veil [1] of gross mist and darkness precludes men's intellects from gaining a knowledge of them, we feel that we have met a real need of our age, and dispelling the darkness have given light to the laws by a short compendium. We selected noble men of approved faith, lawyers of well-known learning; and clearing the interpretation of all difficulties, we have published the constitutions of our predecessors (*lit.* back Emperors), so that men may no longer have to await formidable Responses from expert lawyers as from an inner shrine, when it is really quite plain what action is to be adopted in suing for an inheritance, or what is to be the weight of a donation. These details, unveiled by the assiduity of the learned, have been brought into open day under the radiant splendour of our name.

"Nor let those to whom we have consigned the divine secrets of our heart imagine that they have obtained a poor reward. For if our mind's eye rightly foresees the future, their names will descend to posterity linked with ours.

"Thus having wiped away the cloud of volumes, on which many wasted their lives and explained nothing in the end, we establish a compendious knowledge of the Imperial constitutions since the time of the divine Constantine, and allow no one after the first day of next January to use any authority in the practice of law except these books which bear our name and are kept in the sacred bureaux. None of the older Emperors however has been deprived of his eternity, the name of no issuer of a constitution has fallen to the ground; nay rather they enjoy a borrowed light in that their august decrees are associated with us. The glory of the originators, duly refined (filed), remains and will remain for ever; nor has any brilliance passed thereby to our name except the light of brevity (*nisi lux sola brevitatis*).

"And though the undertaking of the whole work was due to our auspicious initiation, we nevertheless deemed it more worthy of the imperial majesty (*magis imperatorium*) and more illustrious, to put envy to flight and allow the memory of the authors to survive perennially. It is enough and more than enough to satisfy our consciences, that we have unveiled the laws and redeemed the works of our ancestors from the injury of obscurity.

"To this we add that henceforward no constitution can be passed in the West (*in partibus occidentis*) or in any other place, by the unconquerable Emperor, the son of our clemency, the everlasting Augustus, Valentinian, or possess any validity, except the same by a divine pragmatica be communicated to us.

"The same precaution is to be observed in the acts which are promulgated by us in the East (*per Orientem*); and those are to be condemned as spurious which are not recorded in the Theodosian Code, excepting special documents in the official bureaux.

"It would be a long tale to relate all that has been contributed to the completion of this work by the labours of Antiochus, the all-sublime ex-prefect and consul; by the illustrious Maximin, ex-quaestor of our palace,

---

[1] Sub alto crassae demersa caliginis et obscuritatis *vallo*. I read *velo*, compare below *revelatis legibus*.

eminent in all departments of literature ; by the illustrious Martyrius, count and quaestor, the faithful interpreter of our clemency ; by Sperantius, Apollodorus, and Theodore, all respectable men and counts of our sacred consistory ; by the respectable Epigenes, count and magister memoriae ; by the respectable Procopius, count, formerly magister libellorum. These men may be compared to any of the ancients.

"It remains, O Florentius, most dear and affectionate relation, for your illustrious and magnificent authority, whose delight and constant practice is to please Emperors, to cause the decrees of our August Majesty to come to the knowledge of all peoples and all provinces.

"Date 15 February at Constantinople" (438).

We have already referred to the fact that a marriage was arranged between the young princess Eudoxia and the youthful Emperor, Valentinian III, her second cousin. It was celebrated in 437 at Constantinople, whither the bridegroom came for the occasion. After the departure of her daughter the Empress probably felt lonely, and she undertook, in accordance with her husband's wishes, a pilgrimage to Jerusalem to return thanks to the Deity for the marriage of their daughter. In this decision they seem to have been confirmed by a saintly lady of high reputation, Melana by name, a Roman of noble family, who had been forced into a marriage repugnant to her, and had afterwards, along with her husband, whom she converted to Christianity, taken up her abode at first in the land of Egypt, where she founded monastic houses, and then at Jerusalem. She had visited Constantinople to see her uncle Volusian, whom she converted before his death, and, moving in the most exalted society of the capital, she exercised considerable influence even over the Emperor and his household. The journey of Eudocia to Jerusalem (in spring 438) was marked by her visit to Antioch, where she created a great effect by the elegant Greek oration which she delivered, posing rather as one trained in Greek rhetoric and animated with Hellenic traditions and proud of her Athenian descent, than as a pilgrim to the great christian shrine. Although there was a large element of theological bigotry both in Antioch and in Alexandria, yet in both these cities there was probably more appreciation of Hellenic style and polish than in Constantinople. The last words of Eudocia's oration brought down the house—a quotation from Homer,

$$\dot{v}\mu\epsilon\tau\acute{\epsilon}\rho\eta s\ \gamma\epsilon\nu\acute{\epsilon}\eta s\ \tau\epsilon\ \kappa\alpha\grave{\iota}\ \alpha\H{\iota}\mu\alpha\tau os\ \epsilon\H{v}\chi o\mu\alpha\iota\ \epsilon\H{\iota}\nu\alpha\iota,$$

"I boast that I am of your race and blood." The city that

hated and mocked the Emperor Julian and his pagan Hellenism loved and fêted the Empress Eudocia with her christian Hellenism; a golden statue was erected to her in the curia and one of bronze in the museum. Her interest in Antioch took a practical form, for she induced Theodosius to erect a new basilica, restore the thermae (hot baths), extend the walls, and bestow other marks of favour on the city.

Eudocia's visit to Aelia Capitolina, as Jerusalem was called, brings to the recollection the visit of Constantine's mother Helena, one hundred years before, and, although Christianity had lost some of its freshness in the intervening period, it must have been a strange and impressive experience for one whose youth was spent amid the heathen memories and philosophers' gardens of Athens, and who in New Rome, with its museums of ancient art and its men of many creeds, had not been entirely weaned from the ways and affections of her youth, to visit, with all the solemnity of an exalted christian pilgrim, a city whose memories were typically and diametrically opposed to Hellenism, a city whose monuments were the bones and relics of saints.[1] It was probably only this ideal side that came under Eudocia's notice; for Jerusalem at this period was a strange mixture of idealism with gross realism—it was double in character as it was double in name. The christian reminiscences which affected Eudocia were the rich hangings in a more than homely house; epicurism and lust made it "more like a tavern or a brothel than a graced palace." We are told by an ecclesiastical writer of the age that it was more depraved than Gomorrah; and the fact that it was a garrison town had something to do with this depravity.

The fall of Eudocia took place soon after her return, but although a circumstantial story is told about it, historians are all inclined to treat it as a legend, and the matter seems shrouded in impenetrable obscurity. It is best to relate the story in the words of the earliest chronicler who records it.[2]

---

[1] Of the relics which she received (the bishop of Jerusalem plied a trade in relics), especially remarkable were the chains with which Herod gyved Peter. One of these she gave to her daughter Eudoxia, who founded a church in Rome (called originally after herself, and in later times St. Peter ad vincula), where it is still preserved. Gregorovius brings out very well the psychological element in Eudocia's visit to Aelia.

[2] John Malalas, Bk. xiv. p. 356, ed. Bonn.

"It so happened that as the Emperor Theodosius was proceeding to the church in sanctis theophaniis, the master of offices, Paulinus, being indisposed on account of an ailment in his foot, remained at home and made an excuse. But a certain poor man brought to Theodosius a Phrygiatic apple, of enormously large size, and the Emperor was surprised at it, and all his court (senate). And straightway the Emperor gave 150 nomismata to the man who brought the apple, and sent it to Eudocia Augusta; and the Augusta sent it to Paulinus, the master of offices, as being a friend of the Emperor. But Paulinus, not being aware that the Emperor had sent it to the Empress, took it and sent it to the Emperor Theodosius, even as he entered the Palace. And when the Emperor received it he recognised it and concealed it. And having called Augusta, he questioned her, saying, 'Where is the apple that I sent you?' And she said, 'I ate it.' Then he caused her to swear the truth by his salvation, whether she ate it or sent it to some one; and she sware, 'I sent it unto no man but ate it.' And the Emperor commanded the apple to be brought and showed it to her. And he was indignant against her, suspecting that she was enamoured of Paulinus and sent him the apple, and denied it. And on this account Theodosius put Paulinus to death. And the Empress Eudocia was grieved, and thought herself insulted, for it was known everywhere that Paulinus was slain on account of her, for he was a very handsome young man. And she asked the Emperor that she might go to the holy places to pray; and he allowed her. And she went down from Constantinople to Jerusalem to pray."

Gregorovius remarks that Eudocia's apple of Phrygia eludes criticism as completely as Eve's apple of Eden, but perhaps both may be explicable as having arisen from the language of oriental metaphor.[1] We know on good evidence that the

[1] In regard to the famous story of the apple, whose oriental colour—it has a parallel in the Arabian Nights—makes it seem suspicious, so that it is generally rejected as a legend, it must be remarked that there is nothing intrinsically impossible or even improbable in it, and the fact that it is first related by a writer who at the earliest lived in the seventh century—though it is plainly alluded to by Evagrius—is really no evidence against it, as of fifth century historians only fragments remain to us. The question is, did Evagrius and Malalas derive their knowledge of it from Priscus (or a writer of that time) or from oral tradition? If Priscus related it, we should be bound to accept it: but if Priscus had related it, it is almost certain that Evagrius would not have rejected it as untrue, for Priscus' authority as to the events at Theodosius' court could not be reasonably impugned by him. The probability therefore is, that Priscus did not countenance the story, and that it is not true, but sprang up or was invented at a later period—probably before the end of the fifth century (one might conjecture that it was related by Johannes of Antioch, who flourished in the reigns of Anastasius and Justin, and that both Evagrius and Malalas derived their information from him). I have never seen any suggestion as to the way in which it might possibly have arisen. It seems to me that its germ may have been simply an allegorical mode of expression, in which (perhaps at Antioch) some one covertly told the story of the suspected intrigue. Remembering that the basis of the tale is the amorous intercourse of Paulinus and the Empress, we can conceive one accustomed to oriental allegory saying or writing that Eudocia had given her precious apple to Paulinus, symbolising thereby that she had surrendered her chastity. Like the rose in the "Romaunt

magister officiorum Paulinus was put to death by Theodosius' command [1] in 440; and history seems entitled to draw the conclusion that it was probably a charge, whether true or false, of a criminal attachment to the beautiful Paulinus that led to the disgrace of the Empress and the execution of the minister. It would be unwarrantable to ascribe this affair to machinations of the eunuch Chrysaphius, whose influence began about this time, and who is said to have been in league with Eudocia to bring about the decline of Pulcheria's influence. Pulcheria retired from court to Hebdomon at this period. These court intrigues, scarcely more than hinted at by our authorities, are very slippery ground, and we must beware of that tendency among modern as well as ancient historians to attribute on all occasions unprincipled acts to eunuchs.

For two or three years after the death of Paulinus, the Empress remained at Constantinople; in what relation she stood to the Emperor, whether she was partially reconciled or quite estranged, we know not. It is possible that the affair of Paulinus may have been forgotten, and that her retirement to Jerusalem in 443 [2] was either voluntary or the result of some web of intrigue spun perhaps by the eunuch Chrysaphius. However this may have been, a messenger of Theodosius' displeasure or jealousy, the count of the bodyguard, Saturninus, followed her to Jerusalem, and "slew the priest Severus and the deacon Johannes who served the Empress Eudocia in the town of Aelia." [3] Eudocia avenged this act by permitting the death of Saturninus; the words of the best authority would lead us to suppose that she caused him to be assassinated,[4]

---

of the Rose" the fruit signified chastity or virginity. Out of such a germ, I would suggest, the myth of the apple of Athenais may have grown up, the metaphorical expression being taken literally. One might compare the origin of the tale (already told and explained) that Eudoxia robbed a widow of her vine. *See* p. 94. It may also be remembered that in Hellenistic romances the apple was a conventional love gift, and meant on the part of a woman who bestowed it on a man a declaration of love.

[1] Marcellinus, *Chron. ad annum*. Paulinus was brought up along with Theodosius, and at his marriage acted as παράνυμφος or "groom's man."

[2] Both Cedrenus and Zonaras place Eudocia's visit to Jerusalem in the 42d year of Theodosius; "also 450, was ganz irrig ist," says Gregorovius, p. 187, and himself determines the date between the limits 441 and 444. But Gregorovius is mistaken. We must reckon the 42d year, not from 408, but from 402 (Jan. 10) when he was created Augustus. The 42d year = Jan. 10, 443—Jan. 10, 444. This explanation is confirmed by Malalas' mode of reckoning; he says of Theodosius, ἐβασίλευσε δὲ τὰ πάντα ἔτη ν′ καὶ μῆνας ζ′. Although the figures are not exact, it is plain that he reckoned from the earlier date.

[3] Marcellinus, *Chron. ad* 444.

[4] Besides Marcellinus, Priscus, speak-

but it has been suggested that officious servants or an indignant mob may have too hastily anticipated her supposed wishes. Then, by her husband's command, she was compelled to "disquantity" her train, and she remained at Aelia, where she was destined to die.

When Theodosius died, of a spinal injury caused by a fall from his horse,[1] in 450 (28th July), leaving only one daughter, Eudoxia, the wife of Valentinian III, the difficulty of the succession to the throne was solved by the Empress Pulcheria, who became the nominal wife of Marcian, an able senator and soldier. We read that on his deathbed Theodosius said to Marcian, in the presence of Aspar, the general, and all the senators, "It has been revealed to me that you will reign after me." Thus a capable successor was secured and the Theodosian dynasty formally preserved. The first act of the new reign[2] was the execution of Chrysaphius, the obnoxious eunuch, whose influence with Theodosius had been on the decline for some time before his death. It is significant that Chrysaphius had favoured the green faction of the circus, and that Marcian patronised the Blues, while at the same time the new reign was attended with a religious reaction against the monophysitic heresy, which Theodosius had been inclined to favour.[3]

Marcian belonged to the senatorial party of reform, which at the beginning of Theodosius' reign was led by Anthemius; and we are told that his reign and that of his successor Leo were a period of profound calm, a sort of golden interval, all the more striking when contrasted with the storms which preceded the dismemberment of the Empire in the West. The good policy of these sovereigns consisted in paying regard to the condition of their subjects and alleviating the pressure of taxes as far as Roman fiscal principles would permit, in assisting them from the imperial treasury when unwonted calamities befell, in keeping the expenses of the court within reasonable

ing of the heiress of Saturninus, says, τὸν δὲ Σατορνίλον ἀνῄρήκει Ἀθηναΐς ἡ καὶ Εὐδοκία (Müller, F. H. G. iv. 93). See the discussion of Gregorovius, Athenais, cap. xxiii.

[1] See John Malalas and Paschal Chronicle. The accident happened near the river Leucos, not far from the city. Arcadia had died in 444, Marina in 449.

[2] Marcian was raised to the throne 25th August.

[3] I have reserved the subject of the religious controversies of the reigns of Theodosius and Marcian for the ninth chapter of this Book. As to the green and blue factions the reader will find some information below, Bk. iv. cap. i.

limits. Marcian in particular did away with the *follis*, which pressed heavily on the higher classes; he confined the burdensome office of the *praetura* to residents in the capital, and made its burden lighter by compelling the consuls to share the expenses of building with the praetors.[1] Leo, Zeno, and Anastasius pursued more or less the same policy; for the financial difficulties in which the Empire was involved during the last thirty years of the century were greatly due to the mismanagement of the expensive naval expedition of Leo against the Vandals, as will be explained in due course. At this period of the world heaven was often wroth; earthquakes were frequent and cities were constantly laid in ruins by these divine visitations (*theomenia*). The Emperors always exhibited a laudable solicitude to repair these losses.

One of Marcian's first acts at once reduced the expenses of the treasury, and redounded to the dignity of the Roman name. Attila sent an embassy demanding the tribute which he had been wont to receive, and Marcian refused to pay it. This refusal would have involved a war, if it had been made some years before, but Attila was already preparing to overwhelm the West, and was interfering in the politics of the Franks. Marcian was doubtless well informed of the state of Attila's affairs, and knew he could refuse with impunity.[2]

The only event of striking importance in the East during this reign was the council of Chalcedon (451), which finally decided the orthodox christian doctrine as to the natures of Christ; of this something will be said in another place. Pulcheria died in 453, having earned by her pious and charitable works the eulogies of the Church; Marcian died in the first month of 457,[3] and with him the Theodosian house, of which he may be considered a representative, as being the husband of Pulcheria, ceased to reign at New Rome.

---

[1] *See* above, p. 41. The first Novel of Marcian aims at reforming the bad administration of justice which prevailed in the provinces—due to a lack of "integrity and severity" in local judges. Complaints and complainants had flocked to the Emperor from all sides — *caterras adeuntium infinitas*. In the second Novel he states the ideal of an Emperor's duty: *curae nobis est utilitati humani generis providere*, etc.

[2] *See* below, cap. vii. Chronologically the relations of the Huns to the Empire belong to the present chapter, but it is more convenient to treat of them separately.

[3] Some time between 26th January and 7th February. *See* Clinton, *F. R. ad ann.* 427.

CHAPTER VI

BEGINNINGS OF THE DISMEMBERMENT OF THE EMPIRE

ALARIC'S brother-in-law Athaulf (Adolphus) succeeded him (410), and the Visigoths remained in Italy for two years longer, spoiling the land. In 412 they came to an understanding with Honorius, and Athaulf engaged to suppress the tyrants who had risen up in Gaul.[1] This leads us to record the events which had agitated the Gallic provinces during the preceding six years.

The noteworthy circumstance about the events of these years, which were decisive for the future of Gaul, Spain, and Britain, was that two series of phenomena were going on at the same time, to some extent side by side and without clashing, but mutually conditioning and limiting one another. These two series of events are the rise of usurpers and the invasion of barbarians; and it seems that the same conditions which favoured the dismemberment of the western provinces by the Teutons favoured also the enterprise of illegitimate aspirants to the purple.

Up to the year 406 the Rhine was maintained as the frontier of the Roman Empire against the numerous barbarian races and tribes that swarmed uneasily in central Europe. From the Flavian Emperors until the time of Probus (282), the great military line from Coblenz to Kehlheim on the Danube had been really defended, though often overstepped and always

---

[1] Jordanes says (cap. 31) that Athaulf captured Placidia and married her. *Ut gentes hac societate comperta, quasi adunata Gothis republica* [that is the Empire] *efficacius terrerentur. Honoriumque Augustum quamvis opibus exhaustum tamen quasi cognatum grato animo derelinquens Gallias tendit*, and Orosius, although he wrote in 417, seems also to commit the error of placing the marriage in 411.

a strain on the Romans, and thus a tract of territory (including Baden and Würtemberg) on the east shore of the Upper Rhine, the titheland as it was called, belonged to the Empire. But in the fourth century it was as much as could be done to keep off the Alemanni and Franks who were threatening the provinces of Gaul. The victories of Julian and Valentinian produced only temporary effects. On the last day of December 406 a vast company of Vandals, Suevians, and Alans crossed the Rhine. The frontier was not really defended; a handful of Franks who professed to guard it for the Romans were easily swept aside, and the invaders desolated Gaul at pleasure for the three following years. Such is the bare fact which the chroniclers tell us, but this migration seems to have been preceded by considerable movements on a large scale along the whole Rhine frontier, and these movements may have agitated the inhabitants of Britain, and excited apprehensions there of approaching danger.[1] Three tyrants had been recently elected by the legions in rapid succession; the first two, Marcus and Gratian, were slain, but the third Augustus, who bore the auspicious name of Constantine, was destined to play a considerable part for a year or two on the stage of the western world.[2]

It seems almost certain that these two movements, the passage of the Germans across the Rhine and the rise of the tyrants in Britain, were not without causal connection; and it also seems certain that both events were connected with the general Stilicho. The tyrants were elevated in the course of the year 406, and it was at the end of the same year that the Vandals crossed the Rhine. Now the revolt of the legions in Britain was evidently aimed against Stilicho, as the revolt of Maximus had been aimed against Merobaudes; there was a Roman spirit alive in the northern island, which was jealous of the growth of German influence. There is direct contemporary evidence, to which I have referred in a preceding chapter, that it was by Stilicho's invitation that the barbarians invaded Gaul;

---

[1] *See* the monograph on "Tyrants of Britain, Gaul, and Spain" (*English Historical Review*, Jan. 1886), which has been my guide for the following events. It is written in Mr. Freeman's most attractive style, and lights up the meagre statements of the chroniclers, which form the basis of the history of this period.

[2] Olympiodorus, fr. 12. Zosimus, vi. 2.

he thought that when they had done the work for which he designed them he would find no difficulty in crushing them or otherwise disposing of them.[1] We can hardly avoid supposing that the work which he wished them to perform was to oppose the tyrant of Britain—Constantine, or Gratian, or Marcus, whoever was tyrant then; for it was quite certain that, like Maximus, he would pass into Gaul, where numerous Gallo-Roman adherents would flock to his standards. Stilicho died before Constantine was crushed, and the barbarians whom he had so lightly summoned were still in the land, harrying Gaul, destined soon to harry and occupy Spain and seize Africa. From a Roman point of view Stilicho had much to answer for in the dismemberment of the Empire; from a Teutonic point of view, he contributed largely to preparing the way for the foundation of the German kingdoms.

The first act of the tyrant Constantine was to cross with all his military forces into Gaul, which sorely needed a defender to expel the barbarians who were harrying it, or, failing that, to protect the Rhine frontier against new invaders. He inflicted a severe defeat on the intruders, though he did not expel them; and, according to Zosimus, he guarded the Rhine more securely than it had been guarded since the reign of Julian. The representatives of the rule of Honorius, the praetorian prefect Limenius and the general Chariobaudes, fled into Italy probably soon after the arrival of the usurper from Britain, and Constantine passed into the south-eastern provinces which had escaped the devastations of the barbarians. "For two years," writes Mr. Freeman, "they and he both carry on operations in Gaul, each, it would seem, without any interruption from the other. And when the scene of action is moved from Gaul to Spain, each party carries on its operations there also with as little of mutual let or hindrance. It was most likely only by winking at the presence of the invaders and at their doings that Constantine obtained possession, so far as Roman troops and Roman administration were concerned, of all Gaul from

---

[1] *See* p. 111 note 1, where the passage in Orosius is quoted. Cf. Prosper Tiro, *universarum gentium rabies Gallias dilacerare exorsa, inmissu quam maxime Stilichonis indigna ferentes filio suo regnum negatum.* For the Chronicle of Prosper of Aquitaine, which ends A.D. 455, and its continuation (in the *Codex Havniensis*), which ends A.D. 514, *see* an article by Holder-Egger in *Neues Archiv*, 1876.

the Channel to the Alps. Certain it is that at no very long time after his landing, before the end of the year 407, he was possessed of it. But at that moment no Roman prince could be possessed of much authority in central or western Gaul, where Vandals, Suevians, and Alans were ravaging at pleasure. The dominion of Constantine must have consisted of a long and narrow strip of eastern Gaul, from the Channel to the Mediterranean, which could not have differed very widely from the earliest and most extended of the many uses of the word Lotharingia. He held the imperial city on the Mosel, the home of Valentinian and the earlier Constantine."

When Constantine obtained possession of Arelate, then the most prosperous city of Gaul, it was time for Honorius and his general to rouse themselves. Stilicho formed the design of assigning to Alaric the task of subduing the adventurer from Britain, who had conferred upon his two sons, Constans, a monk, and Julian, the titles of caesar and nobilissimus respectively. But this design was not carried out. A Goth indeed, and a brave Goth, but not Alaric, crossed the Alps to recover the usurped provinces; and Sarus defeated the army which was sent by Constantine to oppose him. But he failed to take Valentia, and was obliged to return to Italy without having accomplished his purpose (408).

The next movement of Constantine was to occupy Spain.[1] It is not necessary for us to follow Mr. Freeman in his account of the difficult and obscure operations which were carried on between the kinsmen of Theodosius and the troops which the Caesar Constans and his lieutenant Gerontius led across the Pyrenees. It is sufficient to notice the main point, which Mr. Freeman has made out, that we are not justified in accepting the version of the story which states that the representatives of the Theodosian house were engaged in defending the northern frontier of the peninsula against the Vandals and their fellow-plunderers before Constantine attempted to occupy it. The defenders of Spain were overcome, and Caesaraugusta (Zaragoza) became the seat of the Roman Caesar. Thus in the realm of Constantine almost all the

---

[1] Zosimus, vi. 4. Terentius was appointed *mag. mil.*, Apollinaris (father of Sidonius the poet) praetorian prefect (*ib.*), and Decimius Rusticus master of offices (Greg. Tur. ii. 9, quoted fr. Renatus Frigeridus).

lands composing the Gallic prefecture were included; he might claim to be the lord of Britain, which he had left masterless; the province of Tingitana, beyond the Straits of Gades, was the only province that had obeyed Limenius and did not in theory obey Constantine.

Constans, however, was soon recalled to Gaul by his father, and elevated to the rank of Augustus. But Constantine himself meanwhile, possessing the power of an Emperor, was not wholly content; he desired also to be acknowledged as a colleague by the son of Theodosius, and become, as it were, legitimised. He sent an embassy for this purpose to Ravenna, and Honorius, hampered at the time by the presence of Alaric, was too weak to refuse the pacific proposals. Thus Constantine was recognised as an Augustus and an imperial brother by the legitimate Emperor; but the fact that the recognition was extorted and soon repudiated, combined with the fact that he was never acknowledged by the other Augustus at New Rome, justifies history in refusing to recognise as the third Constantine the invader from Britain who ruled at Arelate.[1] Some time afterwards another embassy, of whose purpose we are not informed, arrived at Ravenna, and Constantine promised to assist his colleague Honorius against Alaric, who was threatening Rome. Perhaps what Honorius was to do in return for the proffered assistance was to permit the sovereign of Gaul to assume the consulship. In any case it was suspected that Constantine aspired to add Italy to his realm as he had added Spain, and that the subjugation of Alaric was only a pretext for his entering Italy, as it might have been said that the subjugation of the Vandals and their fellow-invaders had been only a pretext for his entering Gaul. A high official, Allobich, master of the horse, was also suspected of favouring the designs of the usurper, and the suspicion, whether true or false, cost him his life; Honorius caused him to be assassinated. When this took place Constantine was already in Italy, and the fact that when the news reached him he immediately recrossed the mountains, strongly suggests that the suspicion was

---

[1] Captives of the Theodosian house, who had been taken in the Spanish expedition, were in the hands of Constantine, and a hope of their release seems to have been one of Honorius' motives in sending the purple robe to the usurper; but before the embassy was sent the captives had already been put to death.

true, and that he depended on the treason of the master of horse for the success of his Italian designs.

Constans had left the general Gerontius in charge of Spain,[1] and the error was committed—it is not clear whether through a want of judgment on the part of Gerontius or of Constans—of substituting barbarian mercenaries for the Spanish legions to defend the Pyrenees. This unwise act produced an insurrection of the legions; the barbarian soldiers indulged in unlawful plunder; and Constans was sent back to Spain to restore order. Blame seems to have been thrown on Gerontius, and the Augusti resolved to supersede him by the appointment of a certain Justus; but Gerontius was not of a spirit to submit tamely. He rose against the usurper whom he had supported, and, though he did not assume the purple himself, raised up a new Emperor—a tyrant against a tyrant—in the person of Maximus, who was perhaps his own son. For a while there were six Emperors, legitimate or illegitimate, ruling over parts of the Roman Empire, even as there had been one hundred years before. Besides Theodosius ruling at New Rome and Honorius at Ravenna, there were Constantine and his son Constans at Arelate; there was Attalus at Old Rome, who had been set up by Alaric; and Maximus at Tarragona, who had been set up by Gerontius.

This act of Gerontius, although both he and the Emperor he made soon vanished from the scene, led to important consequences. In order to hold out against the old usurper, the new usurper adopted the momentous course of inviting the Vandals, Suevians, and Alans, who for three years had been ravaging Gaul,[2] to pass into Spain. This act led to the loss of Spain; it led also to the loss of Africa. And thus we may say that it was the loss or abandonment of Britain in 407 that led to the further loss of Spain and Africa. Africa would not have been conquered by the Vandals if they had not passed into Spain; Spain would not have become the possession of Vandals and Suevians, to be afterwards the realm of the Visigoths, if Gerontius had not revolted and invited them to enter; the revolt of

---

[1] Zos. vi. 5 : φύλακα τῆς ἀπὸ Κελτῶν ἐπὶ τὴν Ἰβηρίαν παρόδου. Zosimus affects to speak of the Keltoi instead of the Galatai.

[2] The misfortunes of Gaul are described by Jerome (ad Ageruchiam, 409 A.D. before October), who mentions that Mainz was taken by the barbarians, and Tolosa only delivered through the bishop Exuperius.

Gerontius and his presence in Spain were a direct consequence of the "tyranny" of Constantine; and the tyranny of Constantine in Gaul and Spain depended upon his abandoning Britain. It is really worthy of notice how the loss of the furthest outlying of the Roman conquests in the West was followed by this curious series of effects; and how when the Roman armies retired from the Britannic borders, the retreat did not cease even at the Pillars of Hercules.

It may be noticed here that Britain was not yet forgotten. We learn that Honorius, when Alaric retired from besieging Ravenna, wrote letters to the cities of Britain, bidding them defend themselves, perhaps against Saxon enemies.[1]

Constans soon fled before Gerontius and his new allies; and while Maximus reigned in state at Tarraco, his maker, if not his father, marched into Gaul against the father and son, who had been once his masters. Constans was speedily captured at Vienna and put to death; and the victor, marching down the Rhone, laid siege to Arelate.

Meanwhile Honorius had sent an army under the command of Constantius and Ulfilas to do what Sarus had failed to do before and win back "the Gauls." Thus Constantine was menaced on the one hand by the general of a usurper and on the other hand by the general of the lawful Emperor. Before the representatives of legitimacy the blockading army fled, and Gerontius returned to Spain, to meet death there at the hands of his own troops. The house in which he took refuge was set on fire; he and his Alan squire fought long and bravely against the besiegers; and at length in despair he slew his squire and his wife Nunechia, at their own request, and then stabbed himself.[2]

Thus besiegers in the interest of Honorius replaced the besiegers in the interest of Maximus at Arelate, where Constantine and his second son Julian held out. For more than three months the siege wore on, and the hopes of the usurper depended upon the arrival of Edobich, his Frankish master of soldiers (it is to be presumed he held this title), who had been sent to engage barbarian reinforcements beyond the Rhine.

---

[1] Zosimus, vi. 10 : 'Ονωρίου δὲ γράμμασι πρὸς τὰς ἐν Βρεταννίᾳ χρησαμένου πόλεις φυλάττεσθαι παραγγέλλουσι. There is no reason to read the conjecture of Godefroy—Βρουττίᾳ.

[2] I reproduce here the short account in Olympiodorus (fr. 16); a romantic narration of the scene will be found in Sozomen, ix. 14.

Edobich at length returned with a formidable army, and a battle was fought near the city, which resulted in a victory for the besiegers. Edobich was slain by the treachery of a friend in whose house he sought shelter, and Constantine, seeing that his crown was irrecoverably lost, thought only of saving his life. "He fled to a sanctuary, where he was ordained priest, and the victors gave a sworn guarantee for his personal safety. Then the gates of the city were thrown open to the besiegers, and Constantine was sent with his son to Honorius. But that Emperor, cherishing resentment towards them for his cousins, whom Constantine had slain, violated the oaths and ordered them to be put to death, thirty miles from Ravenna."[1] (September 411.)

But Constantine and Constans were not the only adventurers who called themselves Emperors in Gaul in the year 411. While the army of Constantine was still blockading Arelate, Jovinus, a Gallo-Roman, was proclaimed at Moguntiacum (Mainz). Like Attalus, he was set up by barbarians, but by barbarians farther from the pale of civilisation than Alaric. Gundicar, the king of the Burgundians—prototype of the Gunther of the Nibelungen—and Goar, a chief of the Alans, were the makers of this Emperor, and his elevation was intimately connected with the occupation of the Middle Rhine by the Burgundians. We know not how it was that Constantius and Ulfilas, the victors of Arles, returned to Italy without striking a blow against the other tyrant who had arisen on the Rhine, ere he had yet gathered strength. But the subjugation of Jovinus was reserved, not for the Roman general, but for his rival in war and love, the Visigothic king.

At the beginning of 412 Athaulf[2] and his Goths abandon Italy and pass into Gaul, just as four years before Alaric had abandoned Illyricum and passed into Italy; the Visigoths were inevitably drawn to the shores of the Atlantic. It is sometimes represented that Athaulf crossed the Alps as the bearer of a commission from Honorius to suppress the tyrant Jovinus, but this was not so. Athaulf had come to no understanding with the court of Ravenna; he carried the captive Placidia with him, against her own will and the will of her brother, and

[1] Olympiodorus, fr. 16.
[2] For the reign of Athaulf, see Dahn, *Könige der Germanen*, v. pp. 55-64.

he was far more disposed to side with Jovinus against Honorius than with Honorius against Jovinus. An accident decided that he was to be the champion of the legitimate Emperor.

Attalus, the ex-Emperor, who was to become a sham Emperor once more, was in the train of the Visigoths, and his persuasions induced Athaulf to march to Mainz, that he might co-operate with the tyrant. But it appears that the arrival of this unexpected help was not so welcome to the Augustus who reigned on the Rhine as the Visigoths might have hoped, and Jovinus blamed Attalus in dark sayings as the cause of the presence of an ungrateful supporter. Why the prince who had been elevated by one Teutonic king disliked the support of another is not clear; but perhaps he had already entered into friendly negotiations with Sarus, that Visigoth whom he saw acting with partial success against Constantine, and who was the mortal enemy of Athaulf as he had been the mortal enemy of Alaric. Sarus certainly arrived on the scene at this juncture with about a score of followers to attach himself to the fortunes of Jovinus; the feeble and prejudiced Honorius, who was unable to retain his best officers, had refused to grant him justice for the murder of a faithful domestic. The feuds of the West Goths proved favourable to the cause of legitimacy; Athaulf was incensed when he heard of the approach of Sarus, and advanced with ten thousand to crush twenty soldiers. Hardly was Sarus, after having performed deeds of marvellous heroism, taken alive; his relentless conqueror put him to death.[1]

A quarrel soon ensued between Athaulf and Jovinus, and the latter defied the desires and injunctions of the former by proclaiming his brother Sebastian Augustus. Then Athaulf decided to war against him whom he had come to assist, and defend the rights of the Emperor whom he had intended to oppose. He sent envoys to Honorius, promising to send him the heads of Jovinus and Sebastian, and he seems to have been so prompt that when the ambassadors returned Sebastian was already crushed.[2]

It is not clear how far the Roman prefect Dardanus, who

---

[1] All this is related by Olympiodorus, fr. 17.

[2] I deduce this from the words of Olympiodorus, combined with those of Orosius; Olymp. fr. 19, ὧν ὑποστρεψάντων καὶ ὅρκων μεσιτευσάντων Σεβαστιανοῦ μὲν πέμπεται τῷ βασιλεῖ ἡ κεφαλή, which sounds as if the head of Sebastian was ready to be sent when the envoys arrived at Athaulf's camp. This is

had resolutely opposed the tyranny of the man who was set up by the Burgundians, influenced Athaulf's change of attitude, but it is clear that once Athaulf had turned against the tyrant he co-operated with Dardanus. Jovinus fled from Mainz on the Rhine to Valence on the Rhone,[1] but soon surrendered to the Visigoths who blockaded him, and was executed by Dardanus at Narbonne (autumn 413).[2] His head, and that of his brother, were exposed at New Carthage in Spain,[3] to assert in that troubled country the might of the Empire and the Theodosian house.

Before following further the actions of Athaulf in Gaul, we must turn for a moment to Africa and notice the revolt of Count Heraclian, whose rebellion, by the express testimony of a contemporary, was influenced by the examples of usurpation which he had observed in Gaul.[4] The man who, three years before, had resisted so staunchly the proposals of Attalus and the threats of Alaric, and stood by the throne of Honorius, was now seized by the infectious disease of tyranny and threatened his sovereign without provocation. With an immense fleet, whose numbers even at the time were grossly exaggerated, he sailed to Italy, but was almost immediately defeated, and fled back to Africa to find its provinces prepared to reject him. He was slain at Carthage about the same time that Jovinus was slain at Narbo.

---

supported by Orosius (vii. 42), *Sebastianus frater ejusdem hoc solum ut tyrannus moreretur elegit. Nam continuo ut est creatus occisus est.* It seems clear that between the presence of Athaulf at Mainz and the blockade of Valentia hostile operations were carried on, battles perhaps fought—totally lost to history—between the Visigoths and the adherents of Jovinus.

[1] Olympiodorus does not name the city. *See* Prosper Tiro (19 Honor.), *Valentia nobilissima Galliarum civitas a Gothis effringitur ad quam se fugiens Jovinus contulerat.* He also mentions the death of Sallustius as one associated with the brother tyrants.

[2] The place of execution is mentioned by Idatius, who wrongly unites the deaths of the two brothers in time and place. The executioner is mentioned by Olympiodorus.

[3] Olympiodorus, 19 : καὶ ἀποτίθενται ἄμφω αἱ κεφαλαὶ Καρθαγένης ἔξωθεν—where, he adds, the heads of Constantine and Julian had been formerly "cut off" (a loose expression for "exposed when cut off"), as also those of the tyrants Maximus and Eugenius who had been subdued by the great Theodosius. Much difficulty has been found in these words, which are always referred to Carthage. Why should the heads have been exposed at Carthage? Mr. Hodgkin would read Milan—but that is arbitrary. Surely, if Olympiodorus meant Carthage, he would have written Καρχηδόνος. Surely he meant Carthagena — Carthago Spartaria in Spain. It seems quite probable that Honorius might have liked to assert the triumphs of his arms in the country of his kin, then so terribly overrun by barbarians.

[4] Philostorgius, xii. 4.

DISMEMBERMENT OF EMPIRE BEGINS

This revolt in Africa was partly influenced by recent events in Gaul, and it also exercised in turn an influence on affairs there. The great aim of Honorius, whose mental horizon was bounded by his family and his poultry-yard, was to recover his sister Placidia from the hands of the Visigoth, and this desire was ardently shared by his influential general Constantius, who aspired to the hand of the princess. Accordingly negotiations were carried on with Athaulf, who demanded that he and his people should be supplied with corn, and, as a consequence thereof, be recognised as dependants of the Roman Empire. To this Honorius and Constantius agreed; but Africa was the corn chamber of Italy, and when Heraclian revolted and inhibited the transport of supplies, it became impossible to fulfil the engagement with Athaulf. He therefore refused to fulfil his part of the treaty, and seized the three most important towns of south-western Gaul, Narbo Martius, Tolosa, and Burdigala (Bordeaux) the city of the poet Ausonius.[1] He also made an attempt to take Massilia, which he hoped might fall by treachery; but it was defended by "the most noble Boniface," who was afterwards to play a more ambiguous and more conspicuous part in Africa, and Athaulf himself was wounded wellnigh to death by a stroke which the Roman dealt him.

The assault on Massilia seems to have taken place in one of the latest months of 413, and almost immediately after it Athaulf determined to give himself a new status by marrying his captive, the Roman princess. Whether he had meditated this design before we are not told; but doubtless its execution at this juncture partly depended on the lady herself. It was celebrated in January 414 at Narbonne, in the house of one Ingenius, a leading citizen; and the pride of Constantius in his first consulship was spoiled for him by the news that the lady whom he loved was the bride of a barbarian. We are told how, arrayed in the dress of a Roman and a royal bride, Placidia sat in the hall of the citizen of Narbo, and how Athaulf sat beside her, he too

---

[1] Rutilius Namatianus, *Itiner.* i. 496. Paulinus of Pella, *Eucharisticon de vita sua* (published in the Appendix of 1579 to de la Bigne's *Bibl. ss. Patr.*), l. 317. *Aspera quaeque omni urbe irrogavere cremata*. This Paulinus (not to be confounded with his namesake of Nola) had joined Attalus, and was created by him *comes privatae largitionis* (a combination of the titles *com. sacr. larg.* and *com. rei priv.*) Prosper Tiro says that Aquitaine in this year was given to the Goths.

dressed as a Roman. With other nuptial gifts the Visigoth gave his queen fifty comely youths, apparelled in silk, each bearing two large chargers in his hands, filled one with gold, the other with priceless gems—the spoils of Rome. They had an ex-Emperor to pronounce an epithalamium, and Attalus was assisted by other Romans. The marriage festivities were celebrated with common hilarity by barbarians and Romans alike.[1]

A contemporary writer[2] has recorded words spoken by Athaulf, which throw light on his attitude to the Empire. "At first," he said, "I ardently desired that the Roman name should be obliterated, and that all Roman soil should be converted into an empire of the Goths; I longed that Romania should become Gothia[3] and Athaulf be what Caesar Augustus was. But I have been taught by much experience that the unbridled licence of the Goths will never admit of their obeying *laws*, and without laws a republic is not a republic. I have therefore chosen the safer course of aspiring to the glory of restoring and increasing the Roman name by Gothic vigour; and I hope to be handed down to posterity as the initiator of a Roman restoration, as it is impossible for me to change the form of the Empire."

The birth of a son, Theodosius, who died in infancy, rendered the sentiments of Athaulf still more Roman; but Honorius and Constantius were disposed to reject his friendly advances. Moved by resentment or policy, Athaulf, who had put down the tyrant Jovinus, set up the tyrant Attalus, the same who had been created Augustus by Alaric in 409, and was always ready to be made or unmade as it suited his Gothic friends. In the following year we find Constantius at Arelate, determined to drive his enemy from Gaul into Spain, and preventing all ships from reaching the coast of Septimania. Athaulf, taking his Emperor Attalus, complied with the wishes of the general and moved

---

[1] Olympiodorus, fr. 24. Philostorgius compares this marriage to the union of iron with pottery, and the Spanish bishop Idatius, who lived in the second half of the fifth century, saw in it the fulfilment of Daniel's prophecy, that the queen of the south should marry a king of the north.

[2] Orosius, *Historiae adv. Pag.* vii. 42.

[3] Romania, *ut vulgariter loquar*. This use of Romania for the territory of the Roman Empire deserves notice. In the sixth century Chosroes II is to use Ῥωμανία of the dominions of Maurice. It is chiefly put in the mouths of persons without the Empire, or used by writers when they are looking at the Empire from an enemy's point of view.

southward along the coast to Barcelona, where it was destined that the death of Sarus should be avenged. Unsuspectingly and unwisely he had received into his service a certain Dubius, one of the followers of Sarus, who avenged his first master by slaying his second master. The king had gone to the stable, as was his custom, to look after his own horses, and the servant, who had long waited for a favourable opportunity, stabbed him (September 415). Perhaps the assassin had been encouraged to commit this deed by Singeric, the brother of Sarus, who immediately seized the royalty, and put to death the children of the dead king, tearing them from the arms of the bishop Sigesar, to whose protection they had fled for refuge. Placidia herself, whose husband had killed and whose brother had offended Sarus, was compelled by the brother of Sarus to walk on foot in the company of captives. But Singeric's reign endured only for seven days; he was slain and succeeded by Wallia.[1]

The new king was not disposed to adopt the policy of Athaulf and assume a pacific attitude towards Rome. The historian, who wrote two years later, informs us that "he was elected by the Goths just for the purpose of breaking the peace, while God ordained him for the purpose of confirming it."[2] His first act, apparently at the beginning of 416, was to organise an expedition against Africa; but it was not destined that the Visigoths should set foot there. Alaric had essayed the sea just before his death and could not reach Sicily; even so the ships of Wallia were shattered in the Straits of Gades. The object of Wallia was probably the same as the object of Alaric—he was pressed by want of supplies of corn. This ill-success had the fortunate effect of changing his policy. "Alarmed at the loss of a large body of Goths, who had perished last year by the storm in the straits, attempting to cross into Africa, he concluded a treaty with Honorius and honourably restored Placidia, engaging to undertake for the Romans the war against the barbarians in Spain. So far we are told that the Alani,

---

[1] Olympiodorus, fr. 26. Theodosius, the son of Placidia and Athaulf, died at Barcelona, and was buried in a church there in a silver coffin. The other children were perhaps the offspring of that Sarmatian wife whom Athaulf seems to have divorced in order to marry Placidia (Philostorgius, xii. 4). The news of Athaulf's death arrived at Byzantium on 24th September 415.

[2] Orosius, vii. 43.

the Vandals, and the Suevi are destroying one another, and it is said that Wallia is very anxious to bring about a peace." [1]

The conditions of this peace of 416 were that the Romans on their part should supply Wallia with corn; [2] that Wallia on his part should restore Placidia, should give up the tyrant Attalus, and should fight in Spain against the barbarians who had occupied it. During the lifetime of Athaulf such a treaty could not have been concluded, the narrow-minded Honorius, who held fast by the Roman pride of family, would never have recognised a king of the Visigoths as his brother-in-law, and rivalry in love placed a barrier between the husband and the suitor of Placidia. Placidia might now be restored without detriment to Gothic honour.

Attalus escaped in a ship, and tried to elude the vigilance of the Romans, but he was captured and delivered alive to Constantius.[3] In the eleventh consulship of Honorius and the second of Constantius, the Emperor entered Rome in triumph, with Attalus at the wheels of his chariot. He punished the inveterate and harmless tyrant by maiming him of a finger and thumb, and condemning him to the same fate that he had wished to inflict upon himself. Honorius had doubtless not forgotten how Attalus demanded, with an air of patronising clemency, that the son of Theodosius should retire to some small island, and he now banished his prisoner to Lipara. If the consulate of Honorius was sweetened by the triumph over Attalus, the second consulate of Constantius was sweetened for him by attainment to the object of his hopes, the hand of Placidia, even as his first consulate, three years ago, had been embittered by her marriage with Athaulf. On the first day of January she married him [4] against her own will, by the constraint of her brother. The marriage was followed by the

---

[1] Orosius, vii. 43. He wrote his History against the Pagans in the following year, 417.

[2] Olympiodorus, fr. 31; Philostorgius, xii. 4: καὶ τὸν Ἄτταλον τῷ βασιλεῖ παρατίθενται αὐτοὶ σιτήσεσι τε δεξιωθέντες καὶ μοῖραν τινὰ τῆς τῶν Γαλατῶν χώρας εἰς γεωργίαν ἀποκληρωσάμενοι; the last clause seems due to a confusion with the compact of 418.

[3] The news reached Constantinople on 28th June 416. Prosper wrongly places the capture of Attalus in the tenth consulate of Honorius, but rightly places his punishment in the eleventh. As to the capture, he says, *a Gothis ad Hispanias migrantibus neglectus et praesidio carens capitur*; cf. Orosius (viii. 42) *unde discedens navi incerta moliens in mari captus et ad Constantium comitem deductus*, etc. Philostorgius also mentions his punishment.

[4] Placidia was escorted to Italy by the magistrianus Euplutius (Olymp. fr. 31).

birth of two children, Honoria in 418 and Valentinian III in 419 (3d July).

A personal description of the Count and Patrician Constantius, now the most influential minister of Honorius, the brother-in-law of the Emperor, and destined to be an Emperor himself, has come down to us from the pen of a contemporary writer. "When he walked in public," says Olympiodorus, "his eyes were downcast, and he looked askance; he had large eyes and a large neck and a flat head; when he rode, his whole body inclined over the neck of his steed, and he used to cast his eyes obliquely hither and thither; all deemed his appearance that of one who might aim at empire. At feasts and carouses he was amenable and sociable, descending even to vie with the mountebanks who performed for the guests." We can understand that Placidia was not attracted by this rough Roman. In 420 he entered upon his third consulate, and early in the following year was co-opted by Honorius and proclaimed Augustus, Placidia at the same time receiving the title Augusta, against whose assumption by his sister-in-law Eudoxia Honorius had protested more than twenty years ago.

We must now return to Spain, which we left in 409 when the barbarian, at the invitation of Gerontius, entered that fair land, rich in corn and crops, rich in mines of gold and precious stones. The four nations, the Vandal Asdings and the Vandal Silings, the Suevians and the Alans, divided the land between them. The Suevians and the Asdings together occupied the north-western province of Gallaecia, the regions north of the Douro; the Alans took up their abode in Lusitania, the modern Portugal; and the Silingi obtained the southern lands of the Baetis, whose name was changed by the Saracen occupation, and is now called Guadalquiver. The eastern coast of the peninsula was not occupied by the invaders, and throughout the whole country the Spaniards were able to defend themselves in the cities; but the bloody harryings and devastations of the Germans soon forced the inhabitants to make a compromise, by which the natives retained the cities and the invaders possessed the open country.[1]

[1] Idatius, xvii. Honorii. Cf. Orosius, vii. 40. The Vandals belong to the Gothic group of Teutonic nations. Cf. Dahn, *Kön. der Germanen*, i. 140. They were conquered by Marcus Aurelius 171-173 A.D. (Capitolinus, *V. M. A.*

Wallia's treaty with the Empire had been made before the month of June in 416. He marched against the barbarians of Spain before the year was over, and fought successfully against the conquerors of Lusitania and Baetica.[1] The chief of the Silingian Vandals was sent to Honorius. In the following year, still fighting "for the Roman name," *Romani nominis causa*, he inflicted great slaughter upon the barbarians, and in 418 the Silingians were totally extinct through the valour of the Visigoth. Hispalis, Corduba, and Gades were at length delivered from the presence of a menacing foe. The Alans were not so completely exterminated, but their king Atax was killed, and the remnant of them who escaped the sword of Wallia fled to Gallaecia and submitted to Gunderic, the king of the Asdingian Vandals.[2]

Thus Wallia the chief, who had been elected for the express purpose of reversing the policy of Athaulf and warring with the Romans, is by the stress of events found fighting for the Roman name, and carrying out the ideal which Athaulf professed to have set before himself—the ideal of restoring the Roman power by Gothic arms. He received his reward. He was not obnoxious to Constantius and Honorius, as the rival and brother-in-law had been; and they were ready to recompense him for his services in Spain, as they were unwilling to recompense Athaulf for his similar services in Gaul. It was apparently in the consulship of Monaxius and Plintha (419) that the compact was made[3] by which the Empire granted to the Visigoths a permanent home in south-western Gaul. The whole province of Aquitania Secunda, the northern part of the province of Narbonensis and part of Novempopulania, formed the nucleus of the Visigothic kingdom, which was afterwards to include a larger portion of Gaul. Thus the two great cities that are built on the banks of the Garonne, Burdigala at its mouth, now Bordeaux, and Tolosa, were ruled over by Wallia and his successors; but Narbo Martius, on the Mediterranean coast,

---

17). The Asdings were a royal family among them; Dahn would connect *asd* with High-Dutch *art* = genus (nobile), p. 186. [1] See the notices in Idatius.
[2] Idatius, xxiv. Honorii. Gunderic succeeded his father Godigisel *in Spain* in 409 or 411 (Dahn, *Kön. der Germanen*, i. 143).

[3] Compare Prosper: *Constantius pacem firmat cum Wallia data ei ad habitandum Aquitania et quibusdam civitatibus confinium provinciarum.* Idatius places this and Wallia's death in the twenty-fourth year of Honorius = 418.

was reserved by the prudence of Constantius, who was the author of this compact. This final settlement of the Visigoths —who had been able to find no home in Illyricum, nor yet in Italy—after many wanderings, was a momentous event; it was the beginning of that compromise between the Empire and the Teutons to which everything had been tending for many years. Constantius was herein the successor of Theodosius the Great and Stilicho; he carried out that in which they had failed. About the same time the same policy was adopted in regard to the Burgundians who had settled on the Middle Rhine; a definite territory was marked out for them, and they were recognised as dependent on the Empire.

It has been justly pointed out that this arrangement in regard to the Visigoths must have been acceptable to the Gallo-Roman inhabitants of those regions.[1] In the year 418 an edict of Honorius—the work of Constantius—conferred local government on the inhabitants of the Seven Provinces [2]; a representative council was to be held every year at Arelate; and we may assume that the government, solicitous for the welfare of those provinces, would not have imposed the Visigoths upon any one of them against the will of the inhabitants. In fact, is it not legitimate to assume that the settlement of the Goths and the measure which instituted a provincial assembly were closely connected? The imperial government seems to have been deeply concerned for the state of southern Gaul, which had lately endured so much at the hands of tyrants and barbarians, and Constantius conceived the idea of combining a remedy with the solution of another problem. It was evident that the Visigoths must be allowed to occupy the lands which they had conquered for the Empire in Spain, or else receive an allotment of territory elsewhere. In any case the Roman Emperor would probably have hesitated to concede Spain, the land of gold mines, the land of Theodosius, to a German people; but perhaps the choice of south-western Gaul was influenced by the idea that the presence of the Visigoths might invigorate a declining region. The Roman inhabitants of the provinces where the strangers settled would naturally be in a

---

[1] By von Ranke, *Weltgeschichte*, iv. i. pp. 271, 272.
[2] The Maritime Alps, Narbonensis Prima, Narbonensis Secunda, Novempopulania, Aquitania Prima, Aquitania Secunda Viennensis.

looser relation to the Empire; but it was important that the relation should not cease to exist. We can hardly then avoid seeing in the edict of Honorius of April 418 a very ingenious idea, intended not only to give new life to southern Gaul, but to enable the Empire to retain a hold on the lands which it was determined to surrender to the Goths. The idea consisted in relaxing the strict bonds of administration which connected all the Seven Provinces with the central government, by removing the imperial governors and allowing the inhabitants, as a dependent federation, to conduct their own affairs, for which purpose representatives of all the towns were to meet every year in Arles. Thus the Gallo-Romans of those provinces and towns, which were to pass into the hands of the Goths, would, without clashing with their masters, belong to a Roman political body, which was under imperial control. It seems hardly possible to set aside the notion (although, as far as I know, it has never been put forward) that the rescript was drawn up with full consciousness on the part of Constantius that the Visigoths were to be settled in Gaul. That settlement cannot have been made on the spur of the moment; it must have received long and serious consideration, for it is represented by the consent of all our authorities as coming spontaneously from the Patrician.

The scheme of representative government for the Seven Provinces, intended to multiply social relations, to increase commerce and healthy life, was not taken up with enthusiasm by the municipalities. If the idea had taken root the history of southern Gaul might have been different. "The city of Constantine," the little Rome of Gaul, where all the famous products of the rich Orient, of perfumed Arabia and of delicate Assyria, of fertile Africa, of fair Spain and of brave Gaul, abounded so profusely that one might have thought the various marvels of all the world were indigenous in its soil—Arelate,[1] built at the union of the Rhone with the Tuscan sea, provided with all the facilities of trade, might have been the centre of a federation, able to have maintained a distinct Gallo-Roman life for many centuries, to have accelerated the civilisation of the Franks,

---

[1] Of the fourteen *nobiles urbes* sung by Ausonius Arelate comes eighth—

Gallula Roma Arelas, quam Narbo Martius et quam
accolit Alpinis opulenta Vienna colonis.

In the fifth century Arelate was close to the sea.

and to have prevented the Asiatic stranger from ever crossing the Pyrenees.

After the Visigoths left Spain there was war between Gunderic, king of the Vandals, and Hermeric, king of the Suevians.[1] The latter were blockaded in the Nervasian mountains; but suddenly Asterius, count of the Spains, appears upon the scene, and in consequence of his operations the Vandals abandoned their blockade of the Suevians. At Bracara a large number were slain by the Romans, and then they left Gallaecia and passed into the southern provinces of Baetica (420), which Wallia had cleared of their kinsmen two years before. Vigorous measures were now demanded if the Roman Emperor desired to save Spain, if the work of the Visigoths was not to be undone. The elevation of Constantius in February 421[2] seemed of good augury for the interests of the Roman republic[3]; but the third Constantius was not destined to wear the purple long. It is characteristic that he is said to have found the restraints attending imperial power intolerably irksome; he was not free to go and come as he used, when he was still a private individual. We shall see how this trait came out in his daughter Honoria. And his elevation was not without a bitter element. The announcement of his co-option was sent to Constantinople, but Theodosius refused to recognise him; and the new Augustus, indignant at the insult, prepared to force recognition by the sword. We are in the dark as to the motive of the hesitation of the ruler of New Rome to acquiesce in the choice of his uncle; it has been conjectured[4] that he looked forward to the death of Honorius without heirs and the devolution of the western provinces upon himself. The warlike intentions of Constantius were fortunately not to be realised. After a reign of seven months he died of pleurisy (2d September).[5] We know not whether it was at his suggestion that an expedition was undertaken in the following year (422) against the Vandals in Spain. Castinus commanded this

---

[1] See the notices in Idatius' Chronicle.

[2] Theophanes, 5913 A.M.

[3] He is said, after his marriage with Placidia, to have lapsed into the vice of avarice, and after his death Ravenna was deluged by the claims of persons by whom he had dealt unjustly. Olymp. fr. 39. Honorius was unwilling to grant him the imperial title. (Ib.)

[4] By Güldenpenning, p. 240.

[5] Olymp. fr. 34.

expedition; but all the expeditions which were sent at various times against the Vandals were destined to fail, until the days when the great Belisarius overcame Gelimer. The general Castinus fled before the enemy to Tarraco.

After the death of Constantius the relations between Honorius and his step-sister became close and tender, and slanderous tongues whispered that their kisses and endearments portended a criminal intimacy. But the sweetness was soon turned into gall. A cabal was formed, in which Leonteus, the steward of Placidia, and two of her women, Spadusa and Elpidia, played a prominent part in fostering suspicion and unkindness. There were frays in the streets of Ravenna, and the barbarians who had come with the widow of Athaulf from Barcelona struck blows for the name and the fame of their mistress. The breach widened, and at length the Augusta, with her two children, was banished from the city which Honorius loved, and sought refuge with her kindred in New Rome (423), even as her mother had once fled from the usurper Maximus.

It is probable that in the court intrigue more powerful personages were involved than the subordinates, such as the nurse Elpidia, who are mentioned as sowing the seeds of discord. We can hardly help conjecturing that the general Castinus and the Count Boniface were concerned in it. The celebrated Boniface now appears on the stage of history, and he was at this time probably count of Africa (422).

The circumstances, however, which attended his presence in Africa are veiled in obscurity.[1] In 422 he was ordered to accompany Castinus on the expedition against the Vandals in Spain, but he quarrelled with the commander and proceeded to Africa. It is hard to decide whether this was more than an act of disobedience,—whether he seized the African government without imperial warrant,[2] or, having been already governor in that province and having been summoned specially to Italy to organise the expedition, he returned in pique to the sphere of his administration. It may be observed that there is no hint that at this time Boniface really quarrelled with the court of Ravenna, and there is no mention of any commander in Africa whom Boniface ousted from his office; we may there-

---

[1] *See* Mr. Freeman's article on "Aetius and Boniface," *Eng. Histor. Review*, July 1887.   [2] Idatius, *Chron.*

fore best suppose that the intention was to combine the forces of Italy and the forces of Africa against the invaders of Spain, and that a quarrel between the two commanders thwarted its execution.

This act of Boniface, whatever character it bore, was, according to a chronicler, "the beginning of many labours to the republic." His administration was highly lauded by a contemporary, and he is not represented as having defied, at this period, the court of Ravenna. On the contrary, we shall find him espousing the cause of legitimacy against the usurper John in 424, when that very Castinus with whom he had quarrelled "connived" at the usurpation.[1] If we combine with this the fact that Boniface strongly upheld the cause of Placidia in her quarrel with Honorius in so far as he supported her with money in her exile at Constantinople, and remember that the quarrel between the brother and sister must have begun much upon the same time as the ambiguous departure of Boniface for Africa (422) took place, we shall be disposed to conjecture that the two events had some links of connection. If, when the Augustus and Augusta were in conflict, the latter were supported by Boniface and opposed by Castinus, not only would the conduct of Boniface be explained, but the uncertain language of the chroniclers in regard to his "seizure" of Africa would be accounted for. If he "deserted the palace" and proceeded to Africa, the seat of his administration, against the will and consent of Honorius, his act might be regarded as disobedient and illegitimate; while the same act, if it were approved of and supported by the Augusta Placidia, might be regarded as lawful.

Honorius, who, weak though he was, had by his mere existence held things together, died of dropsy on 15th August 423. When the news arrived at Constantinople, the first care of the government was to occupy the port of Salona in the province of Dalmatia, which belonged to the prefecture of Italy. The event was then made public [2]; for seven days the hippodrome of Constantinople was closed, and the city mourned for the deceased Emperor. The intervention of Theodosius at this

---

[1] Prosper: "conniventi ut putatur Castino." [2] Cf. "Socrates, vii. 23. Theoph. 5915 A.M."

crisis was evidently indispensable, and two courses were open. He might overlook the claims of Valentinian, the son of the Augustus whom he had refused to recognise, he might aspire to rule the whole Empire himself, as his grandfather and namesake had ruled it, without dividing the power; or else he might recognise his child step-cousin as his colleague and act provisionally as his regent and protector. In either case there was fighting to be done in the West, for a usurper, whose name was John, had arisen at Ravenna, and the general Castinus did not disapprove of the usurpation. Theodosius and Pulcheria decided to take the second course, and to support the rights of their kinsman Valentinian and their kinswoman Placidia. The ambassadors of John, who soon arrived to demand his recognition by the sovereign of New Rome, were banished to different places on the Propontis[1]; if Theodosius had disdained Constantius as a colleague, how much more would he have disdained John, the *primicerius notariorum?*

When Constantius had been proclaimed Augustus, Placidia had also been proclaimed Augusta, and the child Valentinian had received the title of *nobilissimus*; but the court of Constantinople had as little vouchsafed to recognise the nobilissimus or even the Augusta, as to recognise the Augustus. And so now Placidia and Valentinian received those titles anew,[2] and then set forth with a large army to recover their inheritance. The army was commanded by Ardaburius, who was supported by his son Aspar, and by Candidian, who had probably accompanied Placidia in her exile. At Thessalonica, which by this time had recovered from the terrible vengeance of the great Theodosius, the grandson of Theodosius was raised to the rank of Caesar. It was destined that he should once more see its churches, and look forth over Grecian waters, when he returned, not from a sort of exile, but from marriage festivities, accompanied by his bride Eudoxia.

The infantry were commanded by Ardaburius and the cavalry by Aspar, and when they arrived at Salona, the city of Diocletian's palace, the troops of Ardaburius embarked in the ships which were stationed there and sailed across to the coast of Italy, while the troops of Aspar proceeded by land to

---

[1] Philostorgius, xii. 11.
[2] ἐπαναλαμβάνει is the word of Olympiodorus, fr. 46.

CHAP. VI   *DISMEMBERMENT OF EMPIRE BEGINS*   159

Sirmium, and thence over the Julian Alps to the great city of the Venetian march, Aquileia.

The fleet of Ardaburius was unfortunate; it was caught in a storm and scattered. The general himself, driven ashore near Ravenna, was captured by the soldiers of John. If the usurper had immediately proceeded to operate against Aspar, he might have thwarted the expedition. But he waited and gave the enemy time. He relied on the arrival of an army of Huns, who were advancing to support him under the command of Aetius.

Ardaburius employed the time of his captivity in forming connections with the officers and ministers of the tyrant, and shaking the fidelity of his adherents in Ravenna. He then succeeded in sending a message to his son, who waited uneasily and expectantly at Aquileia, bidding him advance against Ravenna with all haste. Guided by a shepherd through the morasses which secured that city, the soldiers of Aspar entered without opposition; some thought that the shepherd was an angel of God in disguise. John was captured and conducted to Aquileia, where Placidia doomed him to death. His right hand was cut off; and, mounted on an ass, he was driven through the circus before he was executed.

Aetius now arrived on the scene with 6000 Huns; but John was no longer there to employ their aid. Aetius himself was pardoned and reconciled with Placidia; and his influence with the Huns was so great that he was able by a donation of money to induce that large army to retire to their homes.[1] The general Castinus, who had connived at the tyranny of John, was banished; and when all things had been peacefully arranged Valentinian was proclaimed Augustus at Rome on 23d October (425).

It is strange that the first appearance of Count Aetius, who was destined to be the great support of the Theodosian house, the right hand of Valentinian as was afterwards said,

---

[1] It is conjectured by Güldenpenning (p. 264) that a statement of Socrates (vii. 43) to the effect that the Huns whom Aetius had collected to aid John ravaged Roman territory on their return, should be brought into connection with Marcellinus' notice that Pannonia was recovered in 427: *Pannoniae quae per quinquaginta annos ab Hunnis retinebantur a Romanis receptae sunt.* He holds that the troops of Theodosius, in repelling the Huns who had invaded parts of his own provinces, followed them into their haunts in Pannonia and recovered the province for the realm of Valentinian.

should have been as the champion of a usurper; it may seem strange too that the first sight we have of him who was to be the great deliverer of Europe from the Huns is as the leader of an army of Huns, with whom he is on the best terms. But it has been well pointed out by Mr. Freeman that there was nothing remarkable—nothing recreant, we may say—at this period for a Roman to use Huns in contending against Romans [1]; every general used Hun and Alan, as well as German, mercenaries in civil as well as in other wars. This employment of Huns on the part of Aetius did not mean that he Hunnised in an opprobrious sense. The circumstances of his youth had brought about his familiarity with the barbarians. He was the son of an Italian mother and of Gaudentius, who had fought with Theodosius against the tyrant Eugenius; and he was born at the town of Dorostylum or Dorostena (now Dristra or Silistria) in Lower Moesia. He had been, as a child, a hostage with Alaric, and had afterwards been sent as a hostage to Rugila, king of the Huns; his sojourn in Hunland made him familiar with Scythian ways. In later years too he was on friendly terms with Attila, until Attila threatened Europe.

[1] "Aetius and Boniface" (*English Historical Review*, July 1887).

CHAPTER VII

INVASIONS OF THE HUNS

IN 441 A.D. the realm of Theodosius was in danger from a powerful combination. It was involved in war with three powers, the Huns, Vandals, and Persians,[1] at the same time, and at least two of them, the Huns and Vandals, were in league.

The rise of the great Hunnic power, which threatened European civilisation in the fifth century, was as sudden and rapid as its fall. The Huns had gradually advanced from their Caucasian abodes, pressing westward the Goths who lined the north shores of the Black Sea, and had now become a great power. Attila, their king, ruled over a European empire stretching from the Don to Pannonia, and including many barbarian kingdoms. In 395 Asia Minor and Syria had been ravaged by Huns entering by the north-east passes, but in 400 we find Uldes, a king of other Huns, hovering on the shores of the Danube and putting Gainas to death. At the beginning of Theodosius' reign the Romans gained a victory over this Uldes, and followed up the success by defensive precautions. The strong cities in Illyricum were fortified, and new walls were built to protect Byzantium; the fleet on the Danube was increased and improved. But a payment of money was a more effectual barrier against the barbarians than walls, and about 424 Theodosius consented to pay 350 lbs. of gold to Rugila or Rua, king of the Huns, who had established himself in the land which is now Hungary, and to whom, about 433, the western government conceded a part of

[1] The relations of the Persian kingdom to the Empire during the fifth century may be more conveniently resumed in another place. With two short interruptions in the reign of Theodosius, an unbroken peace prevailed until the reign of Anastasius. (*See* below, Bk. iii. cap. vii.)

Pannonia. It was to Rugila probably, that Aetius, afterwards to be the terror of Huns, was sent as a hostage; and it was he who supplied Aetius with the auxiliaries for the support of the tyrant John.[1] When Rugila died in 434 his nephews Attila and Bleda,[2] the sons of Mundiuch, succeeded him, and a new treaty was contracted by which the payment was doubled.[3]

Attila cherished friendly relations with Aetius, the general of Valentinian, and entered into an alliance with Gaiseric, king of the Vandals, who had passed from Spain into Africa in 429 and established themselves there, as will be related in another chapter. The movements of Attila from 434 to 441 are lost to us, but at the latter date we find him ruler over an enormous barbaric empire in central Europe, which stretched to the Caucasian mountains on the east, threatening the provinces of Theodosius. At the same time the forces of the East were required against the Vandals and the Persians; and it has been suspected that the hostilities of the latter were not uninfluenced by the Huns, as the hostilities of Attila were certainly influenced by the movements of Gaiseric.

The Vandals were unique among the German nations by the fact that they maintained a fleet, so that they were able to afflict the eastern as well as the western lands of the Mediterranean, and to make piratical raids on the coasts of Greece; it was even thought advisable to fortify the shore and harbours of Constantinople against a possible Vandal expedition. The security of traders and commercial interests demanded that an attempt should be made to suppress this evil, and a large armament, whose numbers have perhaps been exaggerated, was fitted out by Theodosius, and placed under the command of Areobindus.[4] It was despatched to Sicily to operate against Gaiseric, who had taken Lilybaeum and was besieging Pan-

---

[1] Priscus, fr. 1. On all matters relating to the Huns and their relations with the Empire Priscus is our chief and best-informed authority. 350 lbs. = £15,750, or rather more.

[2] There is a difficulty as to which was the elder. It seems more probable that Bleda was older than Attila; cf. Prosper Tiro (eleventh year of Theodosius). *Rugila rex Chunnorum, cum quo pax firmata, moritur cui Bleda successit.* He at least thought that Bleda succeeded Rugila, and Attila Bleda. The spelling *Bdella* in Theophanes perhaps preserves an unkind Greek pun.

[3] Priscus, fr. 1, where the meeting of the Roman ambassadors with the Huns at Margus-Constantia is described.

[4] Theophanes, 5941 A.M. Other generals were Anaxilla, Arintheus, Germanus, and Inobind. The number of ships, which included private vessels and corn transports, is given by Theophanes as 1100, which has a suspicious resemblance to the number of Leo's great armada in 468 A.D.

ormus; but tidings of some dark danger which threatened him in Africa induced the friend of pirates to make a truce with the Roman general and hurry back to his kingdom. The danger came from a son-in-law of Boniface, the famous Sebastian, who died as a martyr and became a favourite subject with Italian painters; but how his passage into Mauretania, of which Prosper tells us, menaced Gaiseric is not clear. From a fragment, attributed to John of Antioch and preserved by Suidas,[1] it would seem that he was the commander of a pirate crew which served the Emperor Theodosius; and so we might suspect that his invasion of Mauretania was closely connected with the Sicilian expedition.

Most of the military forces which had not accompanied Areobindus to the West accompanied Anatolius and Aspar to the East. What happened there is not recorded clearly, but the hostilities were of short duration and slight importance.[2]

At this moment Attila determined to invade the Empire. It was destined that he, like Alaric the Visigoth at an earlier, and Theodoric the Ostrogoth at a later time, should desolate the provinces of the East before he turned to the West. He condescended to allege a cause for his invasion; he complained of the irregular payment of tribute, and that deserters had not been restored; but the government at Constantinople disregarded his embassy.[3] Then Attila, who had advanced towards the Danube from his home, which was somewhere on the Theiss, laid siege to the city of Ratiaria, an important town on the Ister in Dacia ripensis. Here ambassadors arrived from New Rome to remonstrate with the Huns for breaking the peace, and the invader replied to their complaints by alleging that the bishop of Margus had entered Hunnic territory and robbed treasures from the tombs of their kings; the surrender of these treasures and of deserters was demanded as the condition of peace. The negotiations were futile, and, having

[1] Fr. 194, ed. Müller. The Mediterranean at this time was infested by pirates, who seem to have been encouraged by Gaiseric. In 438 a pirate chief, Coteadis, was caught and executed (Marcellinus *ad ann.*) In 440, it may be noticed here, an ancestor of Cassiodorus won glory by opposing Gaiseric in Sicily (Variae, i. 4).

[2] The cause of the war was the invasion of Roman territory by the Persians with Saracen and Tzanic auxiliaries (Marcellinus).

[3] I have followed Güldenpenning in his transposition of the second and third frag. of Priscus, which seems very reasonable; and he is evidently right in placing the capture of Naissus (fr. 1b) after the capture of Viminacium, etc. (fr. 2).

captured Ratiaria, the Hunnic horsemen rode up the course of the Ister and took the great towns which are situated on its banks. Viminacium and Singidunum, in Upper Moesia, were overwhelmed in the onslaught of the "Scythian shepherds," and it seems that the friendship of Attila with Aetius did not preserve the town of Sirmium in Lower Pannonia from being stormed. The town of Margus, which faces Constantia on the opposite side of the river, fell by treachery; the same bishop whom Attila accused of robbing tombs incurred the eternal disgrace of betraying a Roman town and its christian inhabitants to the greed and cruelty of the heathen destroyer. The invaders advanced up the valley of the Margus, now called the Morawa, and halted before the walls of Naissus, now called Nisch, in the province of Dardania—the city which had been strengthened and improved by the affection of the great Constantine, and which had recently given to the Empire a Third Constantius. The inhabitants made a brave defence, but the place fell before the machines of Attila and the missiles of a countless host. Then the victors passed south-eastward through narrow defiles into Thrace and penetrated to the neighbourhood of Constantinople. Attila was not to lay siege to New Rome, just as ten years later when he invaded Italy he was not to lay siege to Old Rome; but he took Philippopolis and Arcadiopolis, and a fort named Athyras, not far from the Bosphorus.[1]

If the nameless bishop of Margus is branded with infamy for his recreant Hunnism, the name of the strong fortress of Asemus in Lower Moesia deserves to be handed down by history in golden letters for its brave and successful resistance to the Hun, even as the town of Plataea earned an eternal fame by its noble action in the Persian war. While the great towns like Naissus and Singidunum yielded to the violence of the whirlwind, Asemus did not bend. A division of the Huns, different from that which marched to Thrace, but of countless multitude, invaded Lower Moesia and laid siege to Asemus. The garrison not only defied the foes, but so effectually harassed them by sallying forth that they retreated. The Asemuntians were not satisfied with a successful defence. Their scouts discovered the opportune times, when plundering bodies of the Hunnic army were returning to the camp with spoils, and these

---

[1] Theophanes, 5942. *See* Güldenpenning, p. 344.

moments were eagerly seized by the adventurous citizens; the pillagers were unexpectedly attacked; many Scythians were slain, and many Roman prisoners, destined to languish in the wilds of Hungary, were rescued from captivity.[1]

Meanwhile the Roman armies were returning from their campaigns in the East and in the West, but it is not clear whether the troops were actually employed against Attila, or whether Areobindus, who had commanded against Gaiseric, or Aspar, who had commanded against Isdigerd (Yezdegerd), the Persian king, accomplished anything of note against the Huns. A battle was certainly fought in the Thracian Chersonese, and Attila won the victory; but we know not who was his opponent.[2] Nor do we know what the master of soldiers in Thrace, Theodulus by name,[3] was doing at Odessus.[4] After this battle a peace was concluded between Theodosius and Attila. As it was Anatolius who was the negotiator, it was generally known as the "Peace of Anatolius" (443 A.D.)[5] The terms were that the former payment of 700 lbs. of gold, made by the Romans to the Huns, was to be trebled; besides this 6000 lbs. of gold were to be paid at once; all Hunnic deserters were to be restored, while Roman deserters were only to be given up for a payment of 10 solidi a head.

For four years after this the Illyrian and Balkan lands were not laid waste by the harryings of the great enemy, but in 447 Scythia and Lower Moesia, which had suffered less in the former invasion, felt the presence of the Hun again.[6] Marcianopolis was taken, and the Roman general Arnegisclus fell in a battle fought on the banks of the river Utus. At the same time another multitude descended the valley of the Vardar and advanced southward—though some doubt the record—as far as Thermopylae.[7]

Meanwhile embassies passed to and fro between the court of Attila and the court of Theodosius; and of the embassy

---

[1] Priscus, fr. 5.
[2] *Ib. ad init.*
[3] *Ib.*
[4] *Id.* fr. 4.
[5] The date is rightly determined by Güldenpenning (p. 346) to 443, who points out that the *expeditio Asiana* (Marcellinus, cf. *Chron. Pasch.*) would not have been undertaken by Theodosius until after the conclusion of the peace.

For these negotiations, *see* Priscus, fr. 5. Güldenpenning notices that the small success of the Huns in Lower Moesia proves the efficiency of the measures taken by Anthemius, the prefect, for the defence of the Danube east of the Cebrus (p. 346).
[6] *See* Marcellinus *ad ann.*; *Chron. Pasch.* (whose author used Priscus).
[7] Marcellinus.

of Maximin the historian Priscus, who accompanied the ambassador, has left us copious and interesting details, which give us a glimpse of Hun life, and will be reproduced in another chapter.

Until the end of the reign of Theodosius the oppressive Hun-money was paid to Attila; but when Marcian came to the throne he refused to pay the stipulated tribute. It seemed that the Illyrian peninsula would be again trampled under the horse-hoofs of Hunnic cavalry; but complications in the West averted the course of the destroyer in that direction, and the realm of Valentinian, not the realm of Marcian, was to resist the storm.

The Hunnic empire had assumed a really formidable size and power under the ambitious warrior Attila, who, we are told, in spite of his hideous features and complexion, had the unmistakable aspect of a ruler of men. Gepids and Ostrogoths, with many other German tribes, acknowledged the overlordship of the king of the Huns, who, as Jordanes says, " possessed Scythian and German kingdoms "—*Scythica et Germanica regna possedit*—though the extent of his domination is often exaggerated. Before 440 the Huns had attempted an invasion of Persia, and Roman officers talked of the chances of the overthrow of the Persian power by Attila and the possible consequences of such an event for the Roman world. But it was not destined that Attila should attempt to confront the great power of Asia; he was to shatter his strength in a contest with the forces of Europe on one of the great battlefields of the world's history.

CHAPTER VIII

THE PATRICIAN AETIUS

WE have seen how Spain was lost to the Empire and occupied by the Teutonic Vandals and Suevians, and the probably not Aryan Alans,[1] whom the rebel Gerontius invited south of the Pyrenees. We have seen too how the Visigoths, who crossed the Alps to put down the usurpers in Gaul, formed a dependent kingdom in Aquitaine—the kingdom of Tolosa, as it is called by Dahn. Stilicho and Alaric, Constantius and Athaulf, who played such prominent parts in the first scene of the dismemberment of the Empire, have passed from the stage; new figures, Bonifacius and Aetius, Theodoric and Gaiseric, will now come to the front; we shall see what became of Africa and what became of Spain, and follow further the fortunes of Gaul, where so many peoples ruled and so many kingdoms fell; we shall see, finally, how the shadow of the Hun fell upon Teutons and Romans, invaders and invaded alike, and how they successfully united to drive away the horror of darkness and desolation which menaced them.

Africa, so far away from the Rhine and the Danube, where the Teutonic foes were pressing on the Empire, had not as yet suffered from their invasion; but the occupation of Spain by the hordes of Vandals and Suevians was now bringing them into closer proximity. But the Roman legions in the Afric provinces had work enough to occupy them in defending the southern frontier against another persistent enemy, the Moors,

---

[1] For the various opinions as to the ethnical position of the Alans, *see* Dahn's note, *Die Könige der Germanen*, i. 261. In favour of a German origin, Amm. Marc. 31, 2 (combined with Procopius, *B. G.* i. 1) is appealed to. After 406 Alans seem to have dwelt on the Loire (Dahn, *ib.* 263).

who at this time seem to have been carrying on active operations. At least we find the heroic Boniface[1] shortly after, if not before, the year 422, delivering Africa from many barbarous nations.[2]

We have seen how Boniface supported the claims of the sister and nephew of Honorius, and refused to acknowledge the claims of John. After the restoration of the legitimate dynasty, he may have been rewarded by the title "Count of Africa," though it seems more likely that he held that title before; but it appears that he began to degenerate,[3] and complaints were made that he no longer repelled the incursions of the Afric barbarians with his pristine energy. In 427 he was summoned to Ravenna to answer the charges and account for his conduct, Placidia acting here by the advice of Felix, the master of soldiers who had succeeded Castinus. By refusing to obey the order, Boniface placed himself in the position of an "enemy of the republic," and an army was sent against him under three commanders,[4] all of whom were slain.

Thus there was civil war in Africa, but its events are merged in obscurity. Of the following facts alone can we be certain. The Goth Sigisvult was sent to Africa against Boniface, after the death of the three commanders (probably in 428)[5]; the Vandals, under Gaiseric (who succeeded Gunderic in 427), arrived in Africa in May 429, having perhaps been summoned thither by Boniface or by his opponents, or by both; there were operations at Hippo, which was besieged by the Vandals, and an army was sent from the East under Aspar against the invaders. But the relations between the recalcitrant general, the general who was sent to crush him, and the alien nation cannot be recovered; it seems most likely that the two former combined

---

[1] Olympiodorus, fr. 42 (p. 67, *F. H. G.*) Βονηφάτιος ἀνὴρ ἦν ἡρωϊκὸς καὶ κατὰ πολλῶν πολλάκις βαρβάρων ἠρίστευσεν.

[2] πολλῶν βαρβάρων καὶ διαφόρων ἐθνῶν ἀπήλλαξε τὴν Ἀφρικήν (*ib.*) In this chapter I have made full use of Mr. Freeman's elaborate and convincing article on "Aetius and Boniface," in the *English Historical Review*, July 1887.

[3] See Mr. Freeman, *Aetius and Boniface*, p. 434, and the reproofs of St. Augustine, who was a correspondent of Boniface, letter 220. Boniface "had vowed chastity after the death of his wife, but he was now not only married to a rich lady named Pelagia, but he had allowed his child to receive Arian baptism, and he was further suspected of living with mistresses," cf. p. 436.

[4] Mavortius, Galbio, and Sinox.

[5] Prosper mentions the appointment of Sigisvult after the mention of the summoning of nations, *quae navibus uti nesciebant*, and places both events in 427. But the Vandals came in 429.

against the common enemy.[1] However this may have been, the Vandals conquered Africa; both the rebel and the suppressor of rebellion seem to have soon retired; and in the year 432 Boniface appears in Italy restored to favour and holding the office of master of soldiers. His rival Felix had been slain in a military tumult in 430,[2] but now he has a new opponent in Aetius, the hero who had been lately distinguishing himself in Gaul, and was destined to win yet greater distinction when it devolved upon him to resist the Hun.

For some unknown cause Placidia decided to depose Aetius from his office as general; and Aetius, as Boniface before, refused to submit. Boniface was now called upon to play the opposite part to that which he had recently played, and, like Sigisvult, to force a self-willed general to submission. There was civil war in Italy. A battle was fought near Ariminum and Aetius was defeated, but he proved superior to his opponent in strategy, and Boniface died shortly afterwards of disease—it is said produced by chagrin—and his opponent obtained possession of his property and his wife.[3] Curious legends have grown up round this battle which was fought at Ariminum; Boniface and Aetius were afterwards represented as rivals of ancient date, who decided their feud by single combat, and the story has only recently been finally exploded by our greatest living English historian.

We saw the Vandals in Africa besieging Hippo, which, however, they did not take. But they extended their dominion rapidly over Africa; they defeated the army which was sent from the East under Aspar; and soon they held all the strong cities except Cirta, Hippo, and Carthage herself. This expeditious conquest is to be explained not only by the fact that in

---

[1] Von Ranke (*Weltgeschichte*, iv. 1, 279) rightly doubted the story that Boniface invited the Vandals. It rests on Procopius (*B. V.* i. 3), who is not a reliable authority on history before his own time.

[2] *Aetius and Boniface*, p. 445.

[3] See John of Antioch, *F. H. G.* iv. fr. 201 (p. 614), who in recounting the deeds of Aetius, enumerates among them that . . . τὸν δὲ Βονηφάτιον σὺν πολλῇ διαβάντα χειρὶ ἀπὸ τῆς Λιβύης κατεστρατήγησεν ὥστε ἐκεῖνον μὲν ὑπὸ φροντίδων νόσῳ τελευτῆσαι, αὐτὸν δὲ τῆς αὐτοῦ γαμετῆς καὶ τῆς περιουσίας κύριον γενέσθαι. This important notice, which I have no doubt rests on the history of Priscus, has been overlooked by Mr. Freeman. Observe that (1) it confirms Mr. Freeman's rejection of the legend of a single combat, and points plainly to civil war; (2) it indicates that the battle of Ariminum was not decisive, the victor *in the war* was not Boniface but Aetius, who outgeneralled his opponent; (3) as the victor in a war, Aetius seized the property and wife of Boniface, whence the legend that Boniface before his death counselled her to marry Aetius.

Italy Africa was forgotten for the more immediate struggle between Aetius and Boniface, but by the state of Africa itself, where a large portion of the population were heretics and prepared to welcome a change of rule. The oppression of the Donatists, and their consequent opposition to the imperial government, gave an excellent opening for an invader, and if any invitation was sent to Gaiseric, who was known not to be a Catholic—he had lapsed from Catholicism to Arianism—it probably came from these heretics. The bands of Circumcellions, who went about the country preaching and practising socialism, sworn foes of existing circumstances and closely identified with the followers of Donatus, also prepared the way for a conqueror.

In spite of his wonderfully rapid career of success, Gaiseric was glad to make a compact with the Empire in 435 (11th February, at Hippo), of a similar nature with the compacts which had been made with the Burgundians and the West Goths. The province of Africa—except the city of Carthage—the province of Byzacena, and a part of Numidia, were handed over to the Vandals, who bound themselves to pay a tribute, perhaps of corn and oil, for their lands. Thus the Vandals were in the same position as the Burgundians and Visigoths, the position of dependants allowed to live in Roman territory. Aetius, who was now the right hand of Placidia and Valentinian, had pursued the policy of Constantius, and might be called the friend of the Vandals with more justice than Boniface, who, if he had lived, might have taken steps to expel the invader.

But this compact could only be provisional, and Gaiseric did not intend to stop short of the total conquest of Africa. In less than five years Carthage was taken (October 439), and Africa had become a Vandalic kingdom. A large part of the land was reserved as a royal domain, another portion was distributed among the Vandal warriors in lots (*sortes Vandalorum*); probably the poorest territory was left to the Roman provincials.

It is to be observed that the Vandals now held a position of vantage in regard to the Empire that none of the other Teutonic nations ever occupied. In relation to the foreign peoples of northern Europe, the front of the Roman Empire was the Rhine and the Danube. And so we may say that the Vandals had come round to the back of the Empire and were able to attack it behind. Another peculiar feature was that, in the language of a chronicler, the sea was made pervious to them; they created a naval power and attacked the Empire by sea, as no other Teutonic people had done in the Mediterranean, though the Saxons and other men of the north used ships to harry it in the northern ocean. Sicily was soon the object of their attacks; Panormus was besieged, but not taken; and Corsica and Sardinia became for a time parts of the Vandalic kingdom.

The dependent kingdom of the Burgundians in the districts of Mainz and Worms (Gesoriacum) was not of long endurance, for in 437 Aetius almost exterminated the nation, and the small remnant which escaped the punishment of disloyalty moved south-westward, and received from the Romans territory in Sapaudia (Savoy), about Lake Leman, which may be called the second Burgundian kingdom.

This change made way for the Alemanni. They had been driven from Roman ground by the arms of Julian, but at the beginning of the fifth century, amid the general confusion of migration, they came back to their old haunts and settled on the Upper Rhine. Thus before 437 there were three nations, two at least nominally under Roman supremacy, from the mouth of the Rhine to its source, the Franks, the Burgundians, and the Alemanni. When the Burgundian kingdom was overthrown, the Alemanni profited by the event, and extended their dominion northwards. Before the end of the century their extended kingdom was incorporated in Francia by the battle of Tolbiacum (496).

It was not only against the Burgundians that Aetius was active in Gaul to maintain the respect due to the Roman name, and prevent the nations from trespassing on soil which was not opened to them. He warred successfully against the Franks, who had invaded the regions between the Somme and the Rhine,[1] and he kept the ambition of Visigothic Theodoric, Wallia's successor, in check. For Theodoric tried to do what Gaiseric actually did in Africa, to enlarge the land which he held with Roman consent by acquiring new lands without Roman consent. Aetius prevented him from realising his aims, as Boniface,

[1] The leader of the Franks was Chlojo, 431 A.D. *See* Idatius, *Chron.*

if he had lived, might have prevented Gaiseric; and the Visigoths were beaten back from Arelate. We need not follow these hostilities, but it may be noticed that Aetius employed Alan and Hunnic auxiliaries against the Teutons. In 439 an event occurred which paved the way for friendly relations between the great general and the great king. When Aetius was absent in Italy the Roman captain Litorius, whom he had left in charge of the army, hoping to accomplish a success which would throw the deeds of his commander in the shade, attacked Tolosa, and was repulsed by Theodoric. The opposition between Christianity and paganism was emphasised here, and the fact that the Visigoths were believers in Christ and the Huns infidels. Litorius gratified the Hunnic soldiers by the performance of pagan rites and the consultation of auspices; and this rendered conspicuous the christian attitude of Theodoric; it showed how much nearer he was to Aetius than were Aetius' soldiers.[1]

It is time for us to speak more particularly of Aetius himself, the great figure of the West. So far we see in him only the successor of Stilicho and Constantius, with the former of whom he presents many points of resemblance. It was the function of both Stilicho and Aetius to keep the Teutonic barbarians in check, and yet both, coming of barbarian stock themselves, had considerable sympathy with the barbarian. In this neither of them was like Constantius, who was a Roman of the Romans; but nevertheless, in regard of the Visigoths and Gaul, Aetius carried on the work which Constantius had begun. But he never fully won the confidence of Placidia, or even of Valentinian, as Stilicho had won the confidence of Honorius; and his disgrace in 432, a strange reward for his services in Gaul, indicates clearly this distrust. When the war with Boniface was over, Aetius, after several adventures, withdrew to Pannonia, and obtained the assistance of the Huns, whose help he had obtained nine years before to support John. They did not fail him in his need; by their means, by a menacing embassy, perhaps, or even by a hostile demonstration, the court of Ravenna received the general again into favour, and conferred on him the title of Patrician (433) and the office of *magister*

[1] Prosper Aquit. *ad* 439.

utriusque militiae.[1] This transaction is significant of Aetius' position throughout his career; he forced Placidia and Valentinian to have him against their will. Conscious, perhaps, that he was the one man who could guide the Empire through this critical stage, and arrange the delicate relations into which it was thrown with the Teutonic nations, by both yielding and refusing to yield at the right time, he pressed himself on the court, and made it follow his leadership. A panegyrical description of the man has been preserved to us, written by Renatus Frigeridus. He was " of middle height, of manly condition, well shaped, so that his body was neither too weak nor too weighty, active in mind, vigorous in limb, a most dexterous horseman, skilled in shooting the arrow, and brave in using the spear; he was an excellent warrior and famous in the arts of peace; free from avarice and greed, endowed with mental virtues, one who never deviated at the instance of evil instigators from his own purpose, most patient of wrongs, a lover of work, dauntless in perils, able to endure the hardships of hunger, thirst, and sleeplessness."[2]

But the successful accomplishment of the gigantic task which now awaited Aetius has made him justly famous as no panegyrics could have done.

Hitherto he has appeared to us greater indeed than Constantius, but not as great as Stilicho; we shall now see him as the man who had most to do with the happy decision of a crisis which concerned wider interests than those of the Roman Empire. The exigency of a common interest—the opposition to a common foe—was now to set a seal on the relations which had been recently established between the Empire and many of the Teutonic nations; and the germ of a new idea, the idea of Europe as the habitation of Teutons and Romans—Romans in the widest sense,—was to be sown on the Catalaunian Fields.

The rise of the Hunnic empire under Attila, and the devastation suffered by the Illyrian and Thracian provinces, have been related. At the time of the embassy of Maximin it had seemed that there was little likelihood of serious hostility against western Europe on the part of the Huns; for,

[1] Idatius *ad* 433.
[2] Gregory of Tours, ii. 8. A panegyrical poem on Aetius by Merobaudes is extant.

though small points of difference arose, Aetius had kept up very friendly relations with Attila. The factors which operated in bringing about Attila's invasion of Gaul seem to have been three, but one of these was more important than the others.

Here we are brought to speak of the strange story of the princess Honoria, daughter of Placidia and Constantius. At the age of sixteen she had condescended to the embraces of a chamberlain named Eugenius,[1] and when the signs of pregnancy revealed the degradation of a princess, the indignation of her mother and her brother [2] banished her to Constantinople, where she lived for fifteen years or more in the prim and irksome society of her religious step-cousins. She was betrothed against her will to a respectable consular named Herculanus, and at length, with a wildness which she had perhaps inherited from her father's Illyrian ancestors, she took the adventurous course of offering her hand to the great enemy of the Empire; the daughter of the lady who shrank from union with christian Athaulf was willing to unite herself to heathen Attila, the husband of innumerable wives. Attila was not slow to take advantage of her impetuous act. Adopting the principle that all children, male and female, inherit equal portions from their father, he sent the ring of betrothal which he had received from Hyacinthus, the secret messenger of Honoria, to her brother Valentinian, and demanded that the share of the Empire, whereof that sovereign had unrighteously deprived his sister, should be instantly restored.[3]

---

[1] 434 A.D. Marcellinus places the cohabitation with Eugenius and the appeal to Attila in the same year; but the latter event must have taken place at least fifteen years later. Jordanes tells the story of Honoria.

[2] At this time Valentinian was only fifteen years old. The punishment of Honoria must have been willed by Placidia, but afterwards Valentinian seems to have nourished resentment against his sister. He had some of that quality which was weak obstinacy in his uncle Honorius and a more gentle firmness in his cousin Theodosius. Like Honorius, he had perhaps a disproportionate reverence for the conventional laws of respectability, and was as unwilling to pardon a disgrace wrought to the Theodosian house by one of its members as to forgive an insult or injury offered to it by a stranger. If the subject of the princess Honoria were chosen for a historical romance, one might take a hint for its treatment from a story of George Eliot, and represent the brother and sister as a Tom and Maggy Tulliver of the fifth century. From a political point of view, it was only natural that a princess who dared to consult her caprice or her affections should be strictly dealt with. The ultimate fate of Honoria is buried in a defective fragment of John of Antioch. Valentinian gave her as a gift to his mother; Placidia blamed her daughter much; and thus Honoria . . .

[3] For this part of the story we have

The act of Honoria gave Attila an excellent pretext against the Empire, but he might not have taken advantage of it so soon save for another event which arose, not from a quarrel at the court of Ravenna, but from the relations between the Teutonic courts of Carthage and Tolosa. Theodoric had two daughters, of whom one was married to the king of the Suevians in Spain, and the other to Huneric, the son of Gaiseric the Vandal. The Suevic son-in-law was on good terms with the Visigoths—we hear of his paying his father-in-law a visit at Tolosa; but for the daughter who was sent across the seas to Carthage misfortunes were reserved by fate. Gaiseric suspected her of plotting against himself, and with a cruelty which even Attila might hardly have practised, he mutilated her ears and nose, and sent her back to her father. The bitter hatred which followed upon this outrage influenced the attitude of the Huns. Theodoric was the friend and ally of Aetius; Gaiseric sought the friendship and alliance of Attila, and stirred him up to make war upon the Romans and their allies. Priscus, who is our best contemporary authority, and especially credible in all that relates to Hunnic politics, states expressly that Attila made war "to oblige Gaiseric."[1]

But the quarrel in the imperial court itself and the quarrel between the barbarians within the Roman pale were not the only factors which operated in bringing about Attila's invasion; a quarrel among barbarians outside the pale also operated. In a struggle for the succession between two Frank princes the rivals appealed to Attila, and he against whom Attila decided appealed for help to Aetius. Here was another circumstance which forced the Huns and the Romans to measure swords.

Thus when Attila invaded Gaul in 451, he came to wrest from Valentinian half of his dominion, in the name of Honoria, and he came equally to make war on the Visigoths for the sake of the Vandals. As against the Empire he could claim to be the champion of a recreant imperial princess; as against the Teutons he could claim to be the ally of a recreant Teutonic nation. But the question at stake was not a quarrel between

the unimpeachable authority of the contemporary Priscus, whose intimacy with important ministers afforded him every opportunity of knowledge of the political transactions and court intrigues of the day.
[1] Priscus, fr. 15. The story of Theodoric's daughter is told by Jordanes.

Valentinian and Honoria, nor a feud between two German peoples, nor a disputed succession of the Franks; it was the perpetual question of history, the struggle told long ago by Herodotus, told recently by Trikoupis, the struggle between Europe and Asia, the struggle between cosmos and chaos—the struggle between Aetius and Attila. For Aetius was the man who now stood in the breach, and sounded the Roman trumpet to call the nations to do battle for the hopes of humanity, and defend the cause of reason against champions of brute force. The menace of that monstrous host, which was preparing to pass the Rhine, was to exterminate the civilisation that had grown up for centuries, to spread desolation in Gaul and Italy, to undo the work of Plataea and the Metaurus, and to paralyse the beginnings of Teutonic life. If Attila had not been repelled, western Europe might have been converted into a spiritual waste, unspeakably more lost and degraded than Turkey at the present day.

But the interests of the Teutons were more vitally concerned at this crisis than the interests of the Empire. We can imagine that if Attila had been the victor on the great day, and had hurled Valentinian from his throne, and had reigned at Rome or Ravenna, cities which were happily never to be called the seats of an Asiatic sovereign, or at Arelate, which was once to pine for a short space under the rule of the Saracen, even then the Empire might have held out in the East, and Marcian and Leo and Aspar might have beaten back the Hun. But the doom of the Visigoths and the Burgundians and the Franks would have been inevitable; their nascent civilisation would have been crushed under the yoke of that servitude which crushes and blights, and they would not have been able to learn longer at the feet of Rome the arts of peace and culture.

The work of Aetius, then, was as much for the future of the Teutonic nations as it was for the Roman Empire. Theodoric the Visigoth did not realise the danger. But Avitus, the emissary of Aetius, explained the situation, and persuaded him to join the Romans against the invader. This decision was momentous; the Roman and the Teuton were to make common cause against the Hun. Neither knew—that was the secret of history—that there was a latent affinity between them, and that in the remote past their ancestors had spoken the same language; they knew not that they were kindred nations fighting against a true enemy. Burgundians and Franks joined their ranks, and all the inhabitants of Brittany and Armorica. The Ostrogoths and the Gepids and the Thuringians, some Burgundians and Franks and Suevians, fought in the ranks of Attila, but these were yet wild peoples without the pale, mostly Attila's subjects and possessing no choice in the matter.

Attila, having taken Metz and other towns, laid siege to Aureliani (Orleans), but the city was relieved by the arrival of Aetius (June 451), and the great battle took place in the wide district known as the Catalaunian Fields. Neither the day of this event nor the exact place are known; the month was perhaps July, and the *locus Mauriacus* was probably either Méry-sur-Seine or Moirey,[1] in the neighbourhood of Troyes.

The chief feature of this battle is that Attila was rendered unable to advance; herein lay the great success of the Romans and their allies. Strictly speaking, the battle was drawn; the Huns and the Visigoths fought long and hard without any result, except slaughter on both sides. But the Hunnic forces were innumerable, while the soldiers of Aetius and Theodoric were comparatively few, as were the Greek soldiers at Plataea or the Greek sailors at Salamis, against the overwhelming numbers of the foe. The fact, then, that the small army hewed down the ranks of the immense host, and withstood, though it did not rout, the Huns, was a tremendous victory. The king of the Visigoths, Theodoric,—whose name deserves to be handed down to fame, no less than that of his more celebrated Ostrogothic namesake, whose father and uncles fought with Attila,—was killed in the fray, and his son Thorismond was proclaimed king on the field of battle. As for the part played by the Roman general himself in the engagement, we hear that at the onslaught of Attila the "prudence of the Patrician Aetius, was such that by hastily collecting around him a band of warriors from all sides he was able to oppose the multitude of the enemy on an

---

[1] Arendt, the editor of the *M. G. H.* ed. of Gregory of Tours, decides for Moirey (p. 69). The question is discussed in the second volume of Mr. Hodgkin's *Italy and her Invaders;* he accepts Méry-sur-Seine as the most probable place (p. 163). Most writers have given up the old theory of Durocatalaunum, Châlons-on-Marne. The discovery (in 1842) of bones, rusted arms, and gold ornaments—of which Mr. Hodgkin gives an account—near Méry-sur-Seine, does not help to decide the question. It cannot be proved that they are relics of Theodoric.

equality" (*non impar*).[1] The union of a certain clearness with a certain obscurity as to the events of this great day of deliverance lends the tale of the battle of the Catalaunian Fields a peculiar charm, preparing us for those legends which afterwards grew up that the spirits of the fallen warriors continued the battle in the air.

Thus the cause of the Romans and the Teutons, the cause of Europe, prevailed; the cause even of those Teutons who fought for the invader. The Ostrogoths were in his ranks, and the Thuringians, who out-Hunned the Huns by deeds of unutterable cruelty; but both Thuringians and Ostrogoths were as yet without the pale, as were all the other Germans who warred for Attila. We cannot forget that the only Teutons within the Roman pale, who, though they did not take part in the conflict, not only hoped for the victory of the Hun, but had even provoked him to war, were the settlers in Africa; we cannot forget that when Aetius and Theodoric did battle for the common cause of cosmos and civilisation, the Vandals alone sided with chaos and barbarism; even as the Greeks could not forget that the Thebans had chosen the side of the Persian invader and refused to fight for the freedom of all the Greeks. But the Vandals had no Epaminondas, no Pindar, no Plutarch to redeem their name. It seemed that, when they entered Africa, a part of the mantle of the Phoenicians had fallen upon them, though they came by another way, from the West and not from the East, and though they were Christians; it seemed that something in their nature drove them to espouse the cause which had been before represented by the Carthaginians, and was afterwards to be represented by the Saracens on the northern coast of Africa. But their power passed away quickly, even as the power of the Huns passed away, and their name has only been commemorated in an opprobrious word expressing the barbarous spirit which defaces the exterior graces of civilisation.

---

[1] Gregory of Tours (ii. 7) tells how "the sound came to Rome — *Romam sonus adiit*—that Aetius was labouring in the greatest peril amid the phalanxes of the enemy, whereupon his wife, anxious and sad, constantly visited the basilicas of the holy apostles, and prayed that she might receive her husband safe from this way" (*de hac via*). Sidonius represents this lady, whose name is not recorded, as the descendant of Gothic chieftains. *See* Panegyric on Majorian, 203. Her father's name was Carpilio, after whom one of her two sons was called; the other, who plays a passive part in history afterwards, was Gaudentius.

After the great check, Attila, "having lost confidence in fighting," returned to his own land, and then with renewed strength invaded Italy.[1] Aquileia, the city of the Venetian march, the city which two hundred years before had endured with bravery and constancy the terrible siege of the barbarian tyrant Maximin, now fell before the Huns, and was razed to the ground, never to rise again; in the next century hardly a trace of it could be seen. Verona and Vicentia did not share this fate, but they were exposed to the violence of the Scythian, while Ticinum and Mediolanum were compelled to buy from the invader exemption from fire and sword.

But the Hun was suddenly induced to retreat; the lands south of the Po, and Rome herself, were spared the humiliating sight of the presence of the Scythian shepherds. According to the generally received account, the thanks of Italy were on this occasion owed not to the general Aetius but to the bishop of Rome. Aetius, now unaided by his Visigoths and other German allies, is said to have dreamed of departing with Valentinian to Byzantium; but Leo I. with two noble Romans, Avienus and Trigetius, visited the camp of Attila, perhaps near the south shore of Lake Garda, and the majesty of the Church persuaded the barbarian to withdraw. The story is surrounded with a legendary halo; the apostles Peter and Paul are said to have appeared to Attila, and by their threats terrified him into leaving Italian soil.[2]

The fact of the embassy cannot be doubted; but that it was the sole cause which brought about the departure of the Huns cannot be admitted. It is not in itself probable that heathen Attila, the enemy of Christendom, would have cared for the thunders or the persuasions of the Church; and a trustworthy authority hands down another account, which does not conflict with the circumstance of the embassy, but gives a rational and evidently correct explanation of the true reasons which induced Attila to receive the embassy favourably. "The Huns," says Idatius, "are stricken by strokes from heaven,

---

[1] In 450 Italy suffered from a severe famine; see Novel xxxii. of Valentinian III (ed. Haenel), 31st January 451, obscoenissimam famem per totam Italiam desaevisse.

[2] "The safety of Rome might deserve the interposition of celestial beings; and some indulgence is due to a fable which has been represented by the pencil of Raphael and the chisel of Algardi." (Gibbon.)

partly by famine and partly by disease; moreover, they are slain by auxiliary troops, which were sent by the Emperor Marcian, under the leadership of Aetius. . . . And being thus subdued, having made peace with the Romans, they all returned to their own abodes."[1]

Thus the position of the Huns was untenable in northern Italy; famine and pestilence thinned their ranks, and the troops of Aetius, which had been sent from Marcian, harassed them. Thus Aetius was not skulking or preparing to flee; with a force too small to venture an open battle, he was vexing the host of the destroyers. Attila was glad to make peace, he had obtained sufficient booty to satisfy him, and he yielded graciously to the arguments or entreaties of Leo and Avienus.

Attila survived this Italian expedition only one year. He died of the bursting of an artery, and in the morning his attendants found the bride whom he had married the night before sitting beside his bed in tears. Some said that he was "stabbed by the hand and knife of a woman."[2]

"It is a saying," writes Gibbon, "worthy of the ferocious pride of Attila, that the grass never grew on the spot where his horse had trod. Yet the savage destroyer undesignedly laid the foundation of a republic, which revived, in the feudal state of Europe, the art and spirit of commercial industry." But there was another benefit as well as the doubtful foundation of the city of St. Mark that Attila conferred undesignedly on Europe,—a spiritual benefit. It was the need of opposition to him that first awoke the idea of a Roman and Teutonic Europe in the West; it was under the dread of his unshapely shadow that it first dawned upon Romans and Teutons that they had a common cause. Greece alone fought at Salamis; republican Rome alone fought at Metaurus and Zama; imperial Rome alone held the Euphrates against the Persian Sassanid; but both Romans and Teutons, both Romania and Germania (not Gothia alone), fought side by side on the Mauriac Plain.

As the death of Attila followed hard upon his defeat, the death of Aetius followed hard upon his victory. His reward

---

[1] Do the words *pariterque in sedibus suis et caelestibus plagis et per Marciani subiguntur exercitum* imply that the troops of Marcian invaded Hunland?

[2] Marcellinus: 454 A.D.

for supporting Valentinian's Empire was, that he should fall by Valentinian's hand; his fate was like that of Stilicho, and due to a similar cause, the cabal of certain persons who were jealous of his power and had influence at court.[1]

Maximus, a noble and powerful man, who had been twice consul, entertained enmity against Aetius, the master of soldiers in Italy. He discovered that Heraclius, a eunuch who had very great influence with the Emperor, was also an enemy of Aetius, and wished, like himself, to oust the general from power; accordingly, he conspired with him, and they persuaded the Emperor that he would perish at the hands of Aetius, unless he hastened to slay him first.

"It was fated that Valentinian should pull down the bulwark of his own government; so he admitted the representation of Maximus, and devised death against Aetius." Even when the general was in the palace, laying his account before the Emperor and reckoning up the moneys that had been collected by taxation, Valentinian suddenly leaped from the throne and accused him of treason, perhaps of seeking the Empire for his son Gaudentius. Not allowing him time to defend himself, he drew his sword, and rushed upon the defenceless officer, who was at the same moment attacked by the chamberlain Heraclius. Thus perished the patrician and consul Aetius[2]— *Aetium Placidus mactavit semivir amens*[3]; and some one afterwards aptly remarked, it is said, to the Emperor, "You have cut off your right hand with your left." Who was now to oppose the Vandals?[4]

The assassination of Aetius led directly to the assassination

---

[1] I follow the account of John of Antioch (fr. 201, 1, 2), because I hold that he followed Priscus. That Maximus played a part in the fall of Aetius is confirmed by Marcellinus: *Valentinianus dolo Maximi patricii cujus etiam fraude Aetius perierat*, etc. The story of Valentinian's adultery with the wife of Maximus cannot be accepted as historical. The Salmasian fragment, attributed by Müller to John of Antioch (fr. 200), in which the story is related, is not genuine, and probably comes from lost parts of the history of John Malalas. Prosper mentions that Aetius and Valentinian had agreed about the marriage of their children—that is of a son of Aetius, probably Gaudentius, with one of the Emperor's daughters. He attributes the *fomes odiorum* to the eunuch Heraclius.

[2] 21st Sept. 454. Boethius, the praetorian prefect, was slain at the same time, even as Heraclius afterwards shared the fate of Valentinian (Prosper). Idatius mentions the "jugulation" of *aliqui honorati*.

[3] Sidonius Apollinaris, *Pan. Avit.* 359. Placidus means Valentinian—an allusion to his mother's name.

[4] See the spurious frag. of John of Antioch (200 ed. Müller); also Procop. *Bell. Vand.* i. 4.

of Valentinian, of which the most authentic account has been preserved by the historian John of Antioch. It will be best to narrate it in his own words.

"And after the murder of Aetius, Valentinian slew also Boethius, the prefect, who was a very dear friend of Aetius. And having exposed their bodies unburied in the forum, he immediately summoned the senate, and brought many charges against the men : this was a precaution against a revolt on account of the fate of Aetius. And Maximus, after the death of Aetius, went to Valentinian, seeking to be promoted to the consulship ; and failing it he desired to obtain the rank of patrician, but in this too was foiled by Heraclius, who countervailed the aims of Maximus and persuaded Valentinian that being well rid of the oppressive influence of Aetius he ought not to transfer his power to Maximus. Thwarted in both his wishes, Maximus was wroth, and he sent for two Scythians (Huns), brave in war, named Optila and Thraustila, who had fought campaigns with Aetius, and were intimate with Valentinian.[1] When he met them pledges were exchanged, and he accused the Emperor of the murder of Aetius and advised them to take vengeance on him, suggesting that they would win very great advantages by justly avenging the victim.

"A few days later, it seemed good to Valentinian to ride in the Campus Martius with a few guards, accompanied by Optila and Thraustila and their attendants.[2] And when he dismounted and proceeded to practise archery, Optila and those with him attacked him.[3] Optila struck Valentinian on the temple, and when the prince turned to see who struck him, dealt him a second blow on the face and felled him. And Thraustila slew Heraclius. And the two assassins taking the imperial diadem and the horse hastened to Maximus. . . . They escaped all punishment for their deed. But a strange marvel happened to the corpse of Valentinian. A swarm of bees lit upon it, and drained and wiped away all the blood that flowed from it to the ground. Thus died Valentinian, having lived thirty-seven years."[4]

The death of Aetius and the death of Valentinian, which were causally in close connection, were grave misfortunes for the West. The strong man who might have opposed the imminent danger from the Vandals, and the weak man whose mere existence maintained the Imperium, were removed ; there was no general to succeed Aetius as there was no member of the Theodosian house to succeed Valentinian. Marcellinus speaks

---

[1] Prosper notices that Valentinian was imprudent enough to cultivate intimacy with the friends of Aetius—*ut interfecti Aetii amicos armigerosque ejus sibimet consociaret.* Gregory of Tours calls Optila *Occila bucellarius Actii,* "guardsman of Aetius."

[2] Idatius notices that the army stood round—*exercitu circumstante.*

[3] The place of the deed was called the Two Laurels : μέσον δύο δαφνῶν (*Chron. Pasch.*), *ad duas lauros* (Prosper). He had left the "Laurel Palace" (Lauretum) of Ravenna to be slain between the laurel trees in the Campus.

[4] 16th March 455 (Prosper).

of the Patrician Aetius as "the great safety of the western republic" (*magna occidentalis reipublicae salus*), the terror of King Attila; "and with him the Hesperian realm fell, and up to the present day has not been able to raise its head." We cannot disagree with this judgment; the death of Aetius marked a distinct stage in the dismemberment of the western provinces. But we must not leave out of sight the importance of the death of his master Valentinian without male offspring. A legitimate heir of the Theodosian house might have prevented some of the troubles which befell Italy in the days of Count Ricimer and the array of Emperors whom he pulled down or set up.

CHAPTER IX

THE CHURCH IN THE FIFTH CENTURY

In the fourth century the Church had to solve two problems; one was political and the other theological. The political problem was to determine the relation of the Church to the Imperium; the theological problem was to determine the relation of the Son to the Father. At the end of the fourth century both these questions had received general solutions; and these very solutions gave birth to new problems which agitated the fifth century.

I. Whether Constantine the Great was personally a Christian is a point that is open to dispute. The evidence seems to show that his religion was a syncretistic monotheism, he was content to see the Deity in the Sun, or in Mithras, or in the God of the Hebrews. The important point, however, is that he did not break with the old Roman ritual; although, as Constantine, he may possibly have been a Christian before he died, as Emperor he was a pagan. He extended special favour to the new religion, but the general line of his policy was toleration.

Constantius conceived a political idea which was a distinct advance on his father's system, the idea of a close union between the Imperium and the christian Church, but of such a kind that the Church should be entirely dependent on the Emperor. Herein he anticipated the policy of Justinian; he wished to concentrate all things in imperial absolutism. Ammianus speaks of him as wearing on all occasions the cothurnus of imperial power (*imperatoriae auctoritatis cothurnum ubique custodiens*). In order to realise his idea it was desirable to produce a unity in the Church itself, which was rent asunder by the schism of Arius; and Constantius' interference took the form of adopting the formula that the Son was of *like* essence (*homoiousios*) with the Father—a compromise between the *homo-ousios* (of *same* essence) of Athanasius and the *heterousios* (of *other* essence) of Arius. This intermediate formula of Sirmium could not stand; it was merely a way of avoiding the difficulty; but Constantius carried it at the time, in spite of much opposition, by his personal influence. His policy is further characterised by his persecution of Athanasius, whose stability and power in the Church stood most in the way of the designed unification.

The depression of the Church under the pagan Julian, whose reign was the last glimmer of the ancient faiths, only strengthened it. And just as Julian's championship of the dying cause furthered the victorious creed, so the patronage which the Emperor Valens bestowed on the less deep doctrine of the Godhead, the doctrine of Arius, went far to strengthen the deeper, less easily comprehensible homo-ousian belief of Athanasius, which prevailed in the West.

Gratian and Theodosius the Great completed the union of the Church with the Imperium. Their edict in 380 officially adopted Athanasianism, the creed of Damasus, bishop of Rome; and the councils of 381 (at Constantinople and Aquileia) defined one creed for the universal Church. But the union of State and Church could not be looked on as complete, as long as the official religion of the Empire, as distinguished from the personal religion of the Emperor, was not christian. Gratian had abdicated and abolished the office of Pontifex Maximus; but an act of the pagan party in Rome in 384 brought the question to a crisis. The restoration of the altar of Victory in the senate house, which Constans had removed, was requested by the senate. Symmachus, prefect of the city, addressed a petition of this purport to Valentinian II; it was rejected through the influence of Ambrosius, bishop of Milan. But the decision of the young Valentinian was not so important as the attitude of Theodosius, Emperor in the East. The revolt of Eugenius, which was directly connected with the pagan party in Rome, and aimed at restoring the religious customs of the old Imperium, rendered a declaration on the part of Theodosius necessary; he took the side of Ambrose and Valentinian. The defeat of Eugenius combined the Church and State closer than ever, and the penance of Theodosius at Milan indicated that if the Church was not to be first, at least it was not to be second. At the same time the State entered upon a path of intolerance, and heretics were esteemed as guilty and as dangerous as pagans; it may be said that the last spark of religious freedom was contained in the law of Valentinian II in favour of Arians, passed in 386. Almost at the same time we have the earliest example of a State inquisition in the prosecution of Priscillian by Maximus (385).

Thus at the end of the fourth century the Roman Imperium was christian, and at the same epoch the Church had asserted her independence. The bishop of Rome, as the successor of St. Peter, was the head of the Church, and the weakness of the Empire in the West increased his power and confirmed his independence, while from Constantinopolitan interference he was quite free. But the geographical distance from Constantinople had also another effect; it contributed to rendering the Patriarch of Constantinople and the eastern churches independent of the bishop of Rome.[1] The oriental and occidental churches had a tendency to separate along with the political systems to which they belonged; and consistent with this tendency was the desire of the Patriarch of Constantinople, which in the fifth century became the most important city in the world, to free himself from the jurisdiction of Rome. In order to do so he naturally leaned on the power of the Emperor, whose ecclesiastical authority was further increased by the fact that his capital was the Patriarch's residence, whereas the independence of the bishop of Rome was aided by the fact that the Emperors resided at Milan or Ravenna.

The result was that in the West the ecclesiastical hierarchy was independent in spiritual matters, and afterwards attained secular power, but in the East the Church and the Imperium were closely allied, the Church being dependent on the Emperor.[2] This was a leading feature in the Byzantine world. The

---

[1] Note that at first the rivalry was between Alexandria and Rome, afterwards between New Rome and Old Rome.

[2] The Emperor was regarded in the East as endowed with a semi-pontifical character. He was considered (like the bishop of Rome in the West) the successor of St. Peter. Gasquet has some good remarks on this subject in his recent work, *L'empire byzantin et la monarchie franque*, pp. 23-33.

Emperor was the head of the three hierarchies, the Church, the army, and the civil service; and his position depended on the allegiance of all three. The consent of the Church was officially recognised as a condition of elevation to the throne by the introduction of the ceremony of coronation. Leo I. was the first Emperor crowned by the Patriarch.

The career of John Chrysostom illustrates the power and the weakness of the Patriarchs,[1] and it was his defeat in a long struggle with the court that mainly determined the subsequent relations between the imperial and the patriarchal palaces. In one respect the Patriarchs obtained a new hold on the sovereigns during the fifth century, when the custom of coronation became indispensable, and Euphemius made use of this power to extort a confession of faith from Anastasius; but Anastasius' treatment of the same hierarch some years later shows how subordinate the representative of spiritual was to the holder of temporal power. The opposition of Chrysostom to Eudoxia naturally suggests the opposition which Ambrose of Milan presented to the Empress Justina. In both cases the populace sided with the bishop; but Ambrose defied the Empress with impunity and carried the day, while the Patriarch of Constantinople was not strong enough even to avoid punishment.

II. The great controversy between Arius[2] and Athanasius concerned the relation of Christ to the Father. Arius adopted the rationalistic and easier doctrine that their essence was not the same; the Son had a beginning. Athanasius held that their essence was the same; the Logos was God, co-eternal with God the Father.

The question might be raised whether this controversy was really of importance for the future of mankind, whether its interest is more than merely ecclesiastical, or is only of historical note in so far as it affected the immediate politics of the fourth century; whether in fine, if Arianism had survived, the spirit of the world would have been much altered. I conceive that its importance is world-historical, and that the victory of Athanasianism, representing the triumph of a distinct

---

[1] A special cause which in the fifth and sixth centuries tended to weaken the position of the Patriarchs, but in the later Empire no longer existed, was the opposition and jealousy of the powerful sees of Alexandria and Antioch.

[2] The subject of Arianism has been treated in an admirable and elaborate work by Mr. H. M. Gwatkin.

idea, is of just as great consequence to the general historian as to the ecclesiastical specialist. The very essence of Christianity was at stake. For the special power of Christianity depended on the idea of Christ, and the doctrine of Arius tended to depress Christ, as less than God, a tendency which, if it had prevailed, would have ultimately banished Christ prematurely from the world. For the whole significance of Christ, or the Logos, was contained in his Divinity.

Soon after the final decision of the Church (381) that the Son was co-essential with the Father, the political divergence of the East and West began. The western and eastern Churches henceforward underwent each a different development, and the controversies which distracted them were of a different kind. The western Church held fast by the Athanasian doctrine, and was not concerned to probe it further; its divines turned from the rare air of the sphere of the Absolute to anthropological questions concerning original sin, faith, and works. The tendency of eastern theologians was always metaphysical. They could not rest content with the general symbolum that the Son was "of one substance with the Father"; they must determine the exact mode of this coincident identity and difference.

And thus in the fifth century the eastern Church embarked in a series of christological controversies [1] as bitter as the Arian.

How were the two natures, the human and the divine, combined in Christ—this was the problem of Christology. We can see from the mere statement of the question that two opposite views would necessarily arise according as the human or the divine nature were emphasised.

Early authorities had contented themselves with vague phrases to express the union of the natures, such as *mixture*, *inweaving*, *envelope*. But such phrases were unsatisfactory, because they were vague. The problem was to find a category which could express the union and avoid the confusion of the two natures—" an unconfounded nature-union," ἀσύγχυτος φυσικὴ ἕνωσις, as Athanasius said.

The two opposite schools of the fifth century which swerved

---

[1] It may be noticed that simultaneously with these controversies there were virulent disputes over the writings of the great Origen, but the Origenistic question is of purely ecclesiastical interest.

from the rigid mean line of orthodoxy on either side were the schools of Nestorius and Eutyches. But the spiritual fathers of Nestorianism and Eutychianism were Theodoros of Mopsuestia and Apollinaris of Laodicea, men who did not, like the eponymous propagators of the heresies, take an active part in party contention.

Apollinaris explained the nature of Christ on this wise. The nature of a human individual, he said, consists of body, soul, and spirit ($\pi\nu\epsilon\hat{u}\mu a$); the nature of the Divine man consists of body, soul, and logos,—logos, not spirit, for spirit implies free will, and thereby the possibility of change.

In opposition to this theory, which did not ascribe complete humanity to Christ, Theodore of Mopsuestia founded a new christological theory, which ascribed to Christ the fulness of humanity, including a free will, but a will higher than mere choice. To explain the union of the two natures he adopted the category of *inhabitation*, $\dot{\epsilon}\nu o\iota\kappa\eta\sigma\iota\varsigma$; the category of *becoming* ("the Word became flesh") he judged rightly to be inadequate for philosophical purposes. But the main point is that he assumed two persons, whom in their union he esteemed one person, illustrating this junction by man and woman being one flesh; whereas Apollinaris blended two natures—the human clipt of certain elements, namely the pneumatic—in one person.

The theory of Theodore was taken up by Nestorius,[1] bishop of Constantinople, and the controversy turned especially upon what was really an incidental corollary of the main doctrine, namely, whether Mary should be called Mother of God, or, as Nestorius held, only Mother of Christ; and thus the word Theotokos (Mother of God) became the catchword of the controversy. The Nestorian heresy was crushed at the council of Ephesus in 431, chiefly through the energy of Cyril of Alexandria, the most influential opponent of Nestorius.[2]

[1] Sisinnius succeeded the mild and courtly Atticus, whose soul cared for other things than controversy, in 426, and was succeeded by Nestorius in 427. Nestorius, like Chrysostom, was a presbyter of Antioch. He was a man of surprising energy; we may call it fanaticism. He was only five days Patriarch when he burned down the church in which the Arians used to hold clandestine services; and he promised to present Theodosius with the kingdom of heaven on condition that he purified the Church of heretics.

[2] Both Cyril and Nestorius appealed to Celestine the bishop of Rome; but while Cyril adroitly deferred to his superior knowledge and dignity, Nestorius assumed the attitude of an equal. It was Celestine's duty and pleasure to

One of the most vehement anti-Nestorians was Eutyches; his zeal against the heresy of the two persons made him rebound into the opposite extreme and promulgate the doctrine that there was only one nature in Christ, the doctrine of monophysitism. He did not clearly see that the tenet of two natures does not imply the tenet of two persons; he did not understand the category of hypostasis; being, as Pope Leo I. wrote in his celebrated Dogmatic Epistle to Flavian, "very imprudent and exceedingly unskilled."

This Dogmatic Epistle was the basis of the symbolum of orthodox doctrine, the *unio hypostatica*, or unity of person in both natures, laid down at the ecumenical council of Chalcedon (451). That council, at which the Emperor Marcian presided, condemned monophysitism, of which the real originator was Apollinaris. The value of this doctrine turns evidently on the category of *hypostasis*, which seems to have received a new shade of meaning since it was used by Athanasius. Athanasius rejected hypostatic union, for he understood thereby merely *substantial* union, which seemed to confound the substances. The hypostasis of Chalcedon is not substance; it is a category higher than substance, but is not yet the subject of modern philosophy; we may perhaps render it approximately by *personal substrate*.

We must make a remark on the attitude of Theodosius II. Both he and his father were religious men, and took a great interest in ecclesiastical affairs. But it cannot be said that Theodosius was consistent either in orthodoxy or heterodoxy. Before the synod of 431 he was a partisan of Nestorius, and wrote rather sharply in answer to the appeals of Cyril; afterwards he completely deserted to the opposite side.[1] In the

side with the deferential and orthodox Patriarch of Alexandria; and Nestorius was condemned by a synod of Italian bishops held in Rome (430). At Ephesus more than 200 bishops deposed the Patriarch of Constantinople, with whom Johannes the Patriarch of Antioch sided, and whom the Emperor Theodosius was long disposed to favour. After many intrigues and indecent scenes, Theodosius recognised the acts of the synod and the condemnation of Nestorius; and in 433 Johannes was reconciled with Cyril. Pulcheria was throughout opposed to Nestorianism, but Eudocia seems to have been inclined to it. Cyril left no stone unturned to win the favour of the court, sending presents to Pulcheria, to influential ministers, and to court ladies.

[1] From a letter of Theodosius to Cyril it is clear that there was rivalry and disunion at the court between Eudocia and Pulcheria, and that the ecclesiastical parties endeavoured to take advantage of this: ἤ τίνα εἶχε λόγον ἕτερα μὲν πρὸς ἡμᾶς καὶ τὴν εὐσεβεστάτην Αὐγούσταν Εὐδοκίαν τὴν ἐμὴν σύμβιον ἐπιστέλλειν, ἕτερα δὲ πρὸς τὴν ἐμὴν ἀδελφὴν τὴν εὐσ. Αὐγ. Πουλ-

CHAP. IX   THE CHURCH IN THE FIFTH CENTURY   191

Eutychian strife, which was not decided until the reign of his successor Marcian, he was a partisan of Eutyches, who held diametrically opposite views to the Nestorians. In this he was probably influenced by the favourite eunuch Chrysaphius, who patronised Eutyches, as Eutropius had patronised Chrysostom.[1]

Dyophysitism became, by the council of 451, the recognised doctrine of the whole christian Church, but the heresies lingered on, Nestorianism especially in the far east, Eutychianism in Alexandria, Palestine, and Armenia. In the reigns of Leo and Zeno the scandalous acts of violence committed by both the orthodox and the monophysites in Alexandria under Timothy the Weasel (monophysite), who was deposed by Leo, and Timothy *Salophakialos*, who succeeded him, and in Antioch, under Peter the Fuller, became so serious that a new attempt at union was demanded. In the struggle of Basiliscus and Zeno the religious question played an important part, and the restoration of Zeno was a triumph for orthodoxy. Zeno and the Patriarch Acacius, in order to effect the desired union, manufactured the Henotikon, a symbolum which was intended to reconcile both parties by veiling the point at issue. It was expressly stated that Christ was both God and man, in accordance with the doctrine of Chalcedon; but the word "nature" was diligently avoided, and an indirectly slighting allusion to the council of Chalcedon was inserted to win the monophysites. This half measure (which reminds us in its spirit of the homoiousian doctrine of the preceding century) not only failed to satisfy either party, but was a live coal blown

χερίαν εἰ μὴ διχονοεῖν ἡμᾶς ᾠήθης ἢ διχονοήσειν ἤλπισας ἐκ τῶν τῆς σῆς θεοσεβείας γραμμάτων; (Harduin, *Concilia*, i. 1341). Compare Güldenpenning, *Das oströmische Reich*, p. 294 sq.

[1] I must refer the reader to an ecclesiastical history for an account of the events of 449 — the Robber-Synod of Ephesus, at which Flavian (Patriarch of Constantinople) was condemned, the violence of Dioscorus, who out-Cyriled Cyril, the edifying spectacle of bishops compelled to write their names on a paper which was to be filled in afterwards. The Eutychianism of Theodosius caused an unpleasant difference of opinion between himself and his son-in-law Valentinian III, whose opinions were guided by Leo, the bishop of Rome. Those who are interested in the monophysitic struggles may consult the Memoirs of the Patriarch Dioscorus, written in Coptic and translated by E. Révillout (*Revue Égyptol.* 1880, 1882, 1883), the Ethiopian Chronicle of Johannes of Nikiou, written about 700 A.D., and published by Zotenberg in *Journal Asiatique*, seventh series, vol. x. xii., and the *Eccl. History* (in Syriac) of Zacharias of Mitylene (died before 553), published by Land in twelve books (of which Three to Seven are genuine), as well as the *Breviarium* of Liberatus. See the monograph of G. Krüger, *Monophysitische Streitigkeiten in Zusammenhange mit der Reichspolitik* (Jena, 1884).

between the eastern and western Churches, unquenched for thirty years. In this schism the rivalry of the see of Rome and the see of Constantinople comes to a climax, and represents the opposition of the East and West. During the first half of the fifth century the western Church had, as it were, come of age; it was no longer dependent on the Greeks for its theology. Jerome's translation of the Scriptures and Augustine's new theological system had set occidental Christendom on an independent path of development —had, we may say, founded Latin Christianity.

Simplicius was Pope when the Henotikon of Zeno was published (482). A special circumstance tended to widen the breach which was caused by the opposition of Simplicius to Acacius. In the same year Timothy *Salophakialos*,[1] Patriarch of Alexandria, died, and two rivals for the vacancy appeared, John Talaias, who was actually consecrated bishop, and Peter the Stammerer, who was favoured by Zeno. The rejected Talaias repaired to Rome and laid his case before Simplicius, who took his part. Soon after this Simplicius died, and Felix II, his successor, prosecuted the opposition to Constantinople with vehement energy. The legates whom he sent thither were induced, by imprisonment and threats, to recognise the appointment of Peter, whereupon Felix, informed of the circumstance by the "sleepless" monks, who were strong pillars of orthodox Chalcedonism in Byzantium, held a council at Rome (484), at which he deposed the apostate legates from their bishoprics, and excommunicated Acacius. It would have been dangerous for any one to deliver the sentence of excommunication openly to the Patriarch, and a secret stratagem was adopted. It was pinned to the back of Acacius as he was officiating in St. Sophia, and a few moments afterwards he retorted the sentence on Felix, thus placing his power on a par with that of the bishop of Rome.

The schism[2] continued after the deaths of Felix and Acacius, during the reign of Anastasius, who, though not unquestionably

---

[1] According to Ducange, this word means "with a white bandage or turban (φακίαλος=*fasciola*, and σαλος, a fictitious word for *white*). This does not seem likely. I propose to read Salakophialos, and to translate "coxcomb-sleek" (φιαλος, from φιαρός, ρ becoming λ on account of the preceding λ).

[2] The most recent work on this schism is G. Schnürer's essay (in Grauert's *Historisches Jahrbuch*, ix. 251 *sqq.* 1888), *Die politische Stellung des Papsttums zur Zeit Theoderichs des Grossen.*

orthodox like Zeno, adopted Zeno's Henotikon. At this time the Ostrogoths ruled in Italy, and the Popes were thus independent of the Emperor, and able to resist his authority. Felix was succeeded by Gelasius, who emphatically insisted on the precedence of the Roman see as the highest spiritual authority on earth; we may refer especially to his letter to the bishops of Dardania. His successor, Pope Anastasius, was a milder man, like his namesake the Emperor, and more conciliatory, but the bitterness broke out again in the episcopate of Hormisdas, and was not finally allayed until 519, the year after Anastasius' death, when the new Emperor Justin inaugurated an orthodox reaction. This pacification was a victory for Rome; the names of Acacius and Peter the Stammerer were erased from the diptychs of Constantinople.

DONATISM AND PELAGIANISM.—It has already been noticed that the foundations of Latin Christianity, or western Catholicism, as well as the foundations of the German kingdoms, were laid in the first half of the fifth century. It is not our business here to go into the work of Augustine and Jerome, whose varied activity chiefly contributed to the creation of an independent western Church with a Latin theology. But we must briefly notice the suppression of the schisms of Donatus and Pelagius, against both of which the bishop of Hippo was a leading combatant.

Britain was said to have been fertile in tyrants; Africa may be said to have been fertile in schisms; at least there was no part of the Empire which was more rent and riven by the divisions and the furies of religious sects. In the fourth century the followers of Donatus had been men of strict and pure morals, and presented an edifying contrast to the demoralisation that infected the orthodox Church[1]; but pride in their own sanctity led to a holy contempt for all who were not of themselves, and ultimately to a fanatical hatred which doomed Catholics and other sects to the flames of hell. They were highly objectionable to the civil power, nor was the saying of Donatus forgotten, "What has the Emperor to do with the Church?" But in Africa they had force on their side. The

[1] Donatism, as Ziegler says (*Gesch. der Christlichen Ethik*, ii. 189), was "ein Protest gegen die Verweltlichung der Kirche." Donatus was not a heretic; he disagreed with the Church only on questions of discipline.

rich proprietors lived in constant fear of bands of men, who were called *circumcellions* and threatened their possessions and their lives. These men were socialists, infected with religious fanaticism. Having suffered from the stress of the times, they desired to introduce into society an equality, by which they could profit, and regarded themselves as the instruments of divine vengeance. They posed as the protectors of slaves, and used clubs in their deeds of violence, because Christ had said to Peter, "Put up thy sword." In 348, when the Donatists were threatened by the military power, they enlisted the circumcellions to fight in their cause. Julian favoured the Donatists, perhaps because Constantius had oppressed them; but Gratian deprived them of the right of holding services (377). In 405 severe laws were passed against them, and in 411 the great public controversy took place, in which the dialectic of Augustine won the victory — according to the judgment of the tribune Marcellinus, who was appointed to arbitrate — over the Donatist Petilian.[1] After this judgment, which Honorius confirmed, severe penalties were enforced; the Donatists were persecuted, but they continued to exist as an unquiet factor, and probably assisted in the conquest of Africa by the Vandals.

But in the last twenty years of St. Augustine's life (410-430) the great question of the day was the problem of predestination and free will. Pelagius, born of a Roman family in Britain, propounded, and his friend Celestius supported, the doctrine that man's will is free; that God has given us the capacity for good, but that the will and the performance are our own. The doctrine was opposed by Orosius and Augustine; it was condemned by synods in Africa; it was condemned by Innocent, bishop of Rome; it was condemned by his successor Zosimus, who had at first exonerated Pelagius and his views from blame. In 418 an imperial rescript ordained that all Pelagians should be banished, and their theory was afterwards rejected at the general council of Ephesus. Thus the wisdom of the Church condemned the deadly doctrine of free

---

[1] Augustine wrote controversial works against Donatism, and also an alphabetical psalm (*Abecedarius*) giving a history of the schism (see Ebert, *Allg. Gesch. der Literatur des Mittel-* *alters im Abendlande*, i. p. 242); but perhaps the most important work on the subject is the *de Schismate Donatistarum* of Optatus, bishop of Milevis (about 370 A.D.)

will, and the most learned and earnest theologians did not shrink from the possible consequence of the denial of moral responsibility.

On consideration it can hardly be denied that the view of Pelagius was fraught with peril to Christianity. If man is born as sinless as Adam was before the fall, and if his will is free, there is no inconsistency in assuming that many may pass their lives utterly devoid of sin; and thus there may be righteous men in the world who need no redemption, men who can dispense with the work of Christ and the consolation of Christianity. Such a position was extremely dangerous, and Augustine naturally adopted the more consistent and simple doctrine of christian fatalism, which in later ages assumed the form of Calvinism.

But in this controversy the question was argued on the platform of the understanding; and the view of Augustine won, not because his metaphysical armoury was better, but because he and those who embraced his view had more authority.[1] As each party embraced one horn of the antinomy and rejected the other, the question itself could not be rationally decided, any more than a controversy between men who regard space as finite and men who regard it as infinite. Reason knows that both the doctrine of free will and the doctrine of necessity are defective and therefore false; and that true freedom does not conflict with necessity, but that necessity is only a moment in it. But in the fifth century the

---

[1] As I have not studied the controversial writings of St. Augustine, I cannot decide whether he had any rational glimpse of the higher freedom. It is always hard for a layman to feel quite certain that he has comprehended the technicalities of theological phraseology or penetrated the inmost mazes of theological mystery, but as far as I can gather from the disquisitions of Hefele, Milman, and Robertson, Augustine and the Church—however much they may have been inwardly filled with a religious consciousness of it— had no philosophical idea of true freedom. W. Gass, in his *Geschichte der christlichen Ethik* (1881), i. has a good account of the controversy. Of Augustine's own theory he says (p. 159): "Genauer angesehen versetzt die Lehre Augustin's die ganze Schwere des Unheils in den ersten Act des Ungehorsams, diesen steigert sie sammt seinen unermesslichen Folgen zu einem *Mysterium des Abfalls* (ineffabilis apostasia), um dann zweitens die Erbsünde als eine mit der Fortpflanzung gegebene Verdorbenheit in die Natur selber zu verlegen. Dieser plötzliche Sturz aus der Thätlichkeit in die Erblichkeit und Verdammlichkeit ist der dunkle und *noch niemals aufgehellte Punkt seines Systems*, von welchem alles Weitere abhängt." See also Ziegler, *Gesch. der christl. Ethik* (1886), ii. p. 212 *sqq.*, and Jodl, *Gesch. der Ethik in der neueren Philosophie*, p. 57 *sqq.* Jodl remarks that Augustine gave up the Pauline dualism of the sensual and spiritual nature of man.

opponents did not rise to the point of view of reason; and when Cassian of Massilia[1] tried to compromise between the two views by mixing a little of one with a little of the other— semi-pelagianism—it was really as if one tried to solve the antinomy of Zeno by blending an element of the finite nature of space with an element of its infinity, though the former mixture might not have been on the face of it so absurd.

[1] On Cassian, see Ziegler, op. cit. ii. 208. In his twelve books, de coenobiorum institutis, and in his twenty-four books, entitled Collationes, he attempts to systematise the monastic morality of his time.

CHAPTER X

LIFE AND MANNERS IN THE FIFTH CENTURY

THE life of the higher classes at Constantinople was distinguished by its oriental richness and luxury.[1] To some small extent this oriental colouring may have been due to direct eastern influences affecting Byzantium during the fourth century, but in the main it was merely the splendour of Old Rome translated to the palaces of New Rome. To begin with the Emperor, a rich purple dress enveloped his whole body, wrought dragons shone on his silken robes, and a golden diadem set with precious gems adorned his head. His golden chariot was drawn by white mules, whose harness glittered with the same metal, and when he drove out men gazed in wonder at the sheen of the purple and the gold, the whiteness of the mules, and the revolving plates of gold which gleamed in the sun as the car to which they were attached moved along. The caparisons of his horse were of gold, and as he rode, seated on a saddle white as snow, through the city or the neighbouring country, he was accompanied by imperial guards who carried spears with golden tips and shields with golden centres encircled by golden eyes. And it was not only the Emperor whose appointments were enriched with the most precious of the metals; his courtiers and attendants and all men of opulence used it in ornamenting their saddles and bridles, their belts and their boots; their garments were of gold-threaded

---

[1] *See* the evidences on this subject collected from the works of Chrysostom by his editor Montfaucon (vol. xix.) To be precise, I should have added the words, "in the eastern provinces of the Empire" to the title of the present chapter, which makes no pretension to be exhaustive, and may be supplemented by the details to be found in Bk. i. cap. 2, and in Bk. ii. caps. 2 and 3.

silk, their carriages were covered with gold or silver, their servants were tricked out with golden ornaments. Many rich nobles possessed ten or twenty mansions and as many private baths; a thousand, if not wellnigh two thousand, slaves called them lord, and their halls were thronged with eunuchs, parasites, and retainers. In their gorgeous houses the doors were of ivory, the ceilings lined with gold, the floors inlaid with mosaics or strewn with rich carpets; the walls of the halls and bedrooms were of marble, and wherever commoner stone was used the surface was beautified with gold plate. Spacious verandahs and baths adjoined the houses. The beds were made of ivory or solid silver, or, if on a less expensive scale, of wood plated with silver or gold. Chairs and stools were usually of ivory, and the most homely vessels were often of the most costly metal; the semicircular tables or sigmas, made of gold or silver, were so heavy that two youths could hardly lift one. Oriental cooks were employed; and at banquets the atmosphere was heavy with all the perfumes of the East, while the harps and pipes of musicians delighted the ears of the feasters.

These are some of the details which may be gleaned from the writings of Chrysostom respecting the luxurious life of the great and opulent men of his time, which was so revolting to him that it drove him in the direction of social communism. In the preceding chapters many things have been related in the course of the narrative which illustrate the manners and morals of the age, and they need not be repeated here. It is hardly necessary to say that Christianity had not been able to do very much towards refining the character of theatrical representations[1] or improving the morality of green-rooms. Chrysostom complained of the lewdness prevalent in theatres and the obscenity of the songs that delighted the audiences; he was specially scandalised by the exhibition of women swimming. We must, however, remember that Chrysostom was unusually austere. It surprises us somewhat to learn that the habit was kept up in

---

[1] M. Sathas considers that in the days of Theodosius II the first foundations were laid for the conciliation of the Church and the theatre. Malalas mentions that Theodosius erected theatres; Dioscorus, Patriarch of Alexandria, left money for theatres. See Sathas, Ἱστορικὸν δοκίμιον περὶ τοῦ θεάτρου καὶ τῆς μουσικῆς τῶν Βυζαντίνων (Venice, 1878), p. 289. The heretic Arius conceived the idea of creating a theatre in his church, writing the dramas himself; hence ὁ θυμελικός was used in the sense of heretic, ib. p. 7.

christian society of permitting courtesans to exhilarate or contaminate weddings with their presence. As to the amusements of the Emperor and the nobles, we know that they used to hunt in the neighbourhood of Byzantium. Theodosius II was passionately fond of riding, and it was probably in his reign that the game of *tzukan* or polo was introduced at Constantinople, if we may trust the evidence of a very late writer,[1] who states that he laid out a *tzukanisterion*, or polo-ground, in the precincts of the palace. The game was perhaps derived from the Huns, who were accomplished riders.

The oriental court life which was developed at Byzantium with an elaboration which, perhaps more than anything else, gave that city its peculiar flavour, was stigmatised by the Neoplatonic bishop Synesius, in the speech he delivered before the Emperor Arcadius, as one of the evils that endangered the weal and safety of the Empire. The concern of the Emperors for their dignity, he said, and their fear lest they should become ordinary mortals if their subjects beheld them often, lead to the result that they see and hear as little as they well can of those things by which the wisdom of life is acquired; they live in a sort of sensual retirement, and their soul is a mist. He compares this life to the life of oysters, or of lizards which peep out occasionally on a hot day; and likens the small and stupid men by whom the monarch is surrounded to peacocks flaunting their colours. The motive of this retirement, he insists, is the wish to appear more than man.

As nothing, perhaps, is more effective in conveying an idea of the ways and manners of an age than the actual words of a contemporary narrator describing the unimportant details of a journey or an enterprise, I have thought it well to give a tolerably literal translation of the narrative of Marcus the deacon, recounting what befell Porphyrius, bishop of Gaza, when he and

---

[1] Codinus, p. 81. Basil, the Macedonian, improved and enlarged the ground. σφαιρίζω as well as τζυκανίζω was used of playing *tzukan*, thus we read of Romanus (Theoph. Contin. 472) καὶ τῇ δείλῃ ἐν τζυκανιστηρίῳ σφαιρίσας μετὰ τῶν δοκίμων καὶ ἐμπείρων καὶ πολλάκις τούτους νικήσας. If Hammer is right in his conjecture that tzukan (= *tschewkan*) is a Persian word, the conjecture that the Romans borrowed the game directly from the Huns falls to the ground, but the Persians themselves may have borrowed it from Tartaric races.

others visited Constantinople, including an account of the baptism of Theodosius II.[1]

The bishops set sail from Caesarea and reached Rhodes in ten days, where they visited a holy hermit named Procopius, who was gifted with second sight, and told them all that would befall them when they should arrive at Byzantium. The voyage to Byzantium occupied likewise ten days. Having secured lodgings, they visited the Patriarch John Chrysostom on the morrow of their arrival. "And he received us with great honour and courtesy, and asked us why we undertook the fatigue of the journey, and we told him; and when he learned the reason he recollected that on a former occasion we made this petition by letter, and recognising me [Marcus] greeted me kindly. And he bade us not to despond but to have hope in the mercies of God, and said, 'I cannot speak to the Emperor, for the Empress excited his indignation against me because I charged her with a thing which she coveted and robbed. And I am not concerned about his anger, for it is themselves they hurt and not me, and even if they hurt my body they do the more good to my soul. . . . To-morrow I shall send for the eunuch Amantius, the *castrensis* (chamberlain) of the Empress, who has great influence with her and is really a servant of God, and I shall commit the matter to him, and if God consents all will go well (πάνυ ἔχει σπουδάσαι).' Having received these injunctions and a recommendation to God, we proceeded to our inn. And on the next day we went to the bishop and found in his house the chamberlain Amantius, for the bishop had attended to our affair and had sent for him and explained it to him. And when we came in, and Amantius was told that we were the persons of whom he had heard, he stood up and did obeisance to the most holy bishops, inclining his face to the ground, and they, when they were told who he was, embraced him and kissed him. And the most holy archbishop John bade them explain orally their affair to the chamberlain. And the most holy Porphyrius explained to him all the concernment of the idolaters, how licentiously they perform the unlawful rites and oppress the

---

[1] This narrative, which is but little known, is contained in Marcus' *Life of Porphyrius*, which was printed by Haupt in the *Abhandlungen* of the Berlin Academy for 1879.

Christians. And Amantius, when he heard this, wept and was filled with zeal for God, and said to them, 'Be not despondent, fathers, for Christ can shield His religion. Do ye therefore pray, and I will speak to the Augusta. And I trust in the God of the Universe that He will show His mercy according to his wont.' With these injunctions he departed, and we having conversed on many spiritual topics with the archbishop John, and having received his blessing, withdrew.

"The next day the chamberlain Amantius sent two deacons to bid us come to the Palace, and we arose and proceeded with all expedition. And we found him awaiting us, and he took the two bishops and introduced them to the Empress Eudoxia. And when she saw them she saluted them first and said, 'Give me your blessing, fathers,' and they did obeisance to her. Now she was sitting on a golden sofa. And she says to them, 'Excuse me, priests of Christ, on account of my situation, for I was anxious to meet your sanctity in the antechamber. But pray God on my behalf that I may be delivered happily of the child which is in my womb.' And the bishops, wondering at her condescension, said, 'May He who blessed the wombs of Sarah and Rebecca and Elizabeth, bless and quicken the child in thine.' After further edifying conversation, she said to them, 'I know why ye came (ἐσκύλητε), as the castrensis Amantius explained it to me. But if you are fain to instruct me, fathers, I am at your service' (κελεύσατε). Thus bidden, they told her all about the idolaters, and the impious rites which they fearlessly practised, and their oppression[1] of the Christians, whom they did not allow to perform a public duty (μετελθεῖν ὀφφίκιον πολιτικόν) nor to till their lands 'from whose produce they pay the dues to your imperial sovereignty.' And the Empress said, 'Do not despond; for I trust in the Lord Christ, the Son of God, that I shall persuade the king to do those things that are due to your saintly faith and to dismiss you hence well treated. Depart, then, to your privacy, for you are fatigued, and pray God to co-operate with my request.' She then commanded money to be brought, and gave three darics apiece to the most holy bishops, saying, 'In the meantime take this for your expenses.' And the bishops took the money and blessed her abundantly and departed. And

---

[1] καταδυναστεύουσιν.

when they went out they gave the greater part of the money to the deacons who were standing at the door, reserving little for themselves.

"And when the Emperor came into the apartment of the Empress, she told him all touching the bishops, and requested him that the heathen temples of Gaza should be thrown down. But the Emperor was put out when he heard it, and said, 'I know that city is devoted to idols, but it is loyally disposed in the matter of taxation and pays a large sum to the revenue. If then we overwhelm them with terror of a sudden, they will betake themselves to flight and we shall lose so much of the revenue. But if it must be, let us afflict them partially, depriving idolaters of their dignities and other public offices, and bid their temples be shut up and be used no longer. For when they are afflicted and straitened on all sides they will recognise the truth; but an extreme measure coming suddenly is hard on subjects.' The Empress was very much vexed at this reply, for she was ardent in matters of faith, but she merely said, 'The Lord can assist his servants the Christians, whether we consent or decline.'

"We learned these details from the chamberlain Amantius. On the morrow the Augusta sent for us, and having first saluted the holy bishops according to her custom, she bade them sit down. And after a long spiritual talk, she said, 'I spoke to the Emperor, and he was rather put out. But do not despond, for, God willing, I cannot cease until ye be satisfied and depart, having succeeded in your holy purpose.' And the bishops made obeisance. Then the sainted Porphyrius, pricked by the spirit,[1] and recollecting the word of the thrice blessed anchoret Procopius, said to the Empress: 'Exert yourself for the sake of Christ, and in recompense for your exertions He can bestow on you a son whose life and reign you will see and enjoy for many years.' At these words the Empress was filled with joy, and her face flushed, and new beauty beyond that which she already had passed into her face; for the appearance shows what passes within. And she said, 'Pray, fathers, that according to your word, with the will of God, I may bear a male child, and if it so befall, I promise you to do all that ye ask. And another thing, for which ye

[1] κατανυγείς.

ask not, I intend to do with the consent of Christ; I will found a church at Gaza in the centre of the city. Depart then in peace, and rest quiet, praying constantly for my happy delivery; for the time of my confinement is near.' The bishops commended her to God and left the Palace. And prayer was made that she should bear a male child; for we believed in the words of Saint Procopius the anchoret.

"And every day we used to proceed to the most holy Johannes, the archbishop, and had the fruition of his holy words,[1] sweeter than honey and the honey comb. And Amantius the chamberlain used to come to us, sometimes bearing messages from the Empress, at other times merely to pay a visit. And after a few days the Empress brought forth a male child, and he was called Theodosius after his grandfather Theodosius, the Spaniard, who reigned along with Gratian. And the child Theodosius was born in the purple ($\dot{\epsilon}\nu$ $\tau\hat{\eta}$ $\pi o \rho \phi \acute{u} \rho \alpha$), wherefore he was proclaimed Emperor at his birth. And there was great joy in the city, and men were sent to the cities of the Empire, bearing the good news, with gifts and bounties ($\chi \alpha \rho \acute{\iota} \sigma \mu \alpha \tau \alpha$).

"But the Empress, who had only just been delivered and arisen from her chair of confinement, sent Amantius to us with this message: 'I thank Christ that God bestowed on me a son, on account of your holy prayers. Pray, then, fathers, for his life and for my lowly self, in order that I may fulfil those things which I promised you, Christ himself again consenting, through your holy prayers.' And when the seven days of her confinement were fulfilled, she sent for us and met us at the door of the chamber, carrying in her arms the infant in the purple robe. And she inclined her head and said, 'Draw nigh, fathers, unto me and the child which the Lord granted to me through your holy prayers.' And she gave them the child that they might seal it (with God's signet). And the holy bishops sealed both her and the child with the seal of the cross, and, offering a prayer, sat down. And when they had spoken many words full of heart-pricking ($\kappa \alpha \tau \acute{a} \nu \nu \xi \iota \varsigma$), the lady says to them, 'Do ye know, fathers, what I resolved to do in regard to your affair?' [Here Porphyrius related a dream which he had dreamed the night before; then Eudoxia resumed:] 'If Christ permit, the

[1] $\lambda o \gamma \acute{\iota} \omega \nu$.

child will be privileged to receive the holy baptism in a few days. Do ye then depart and compose a petition and insert in it all the requests ye wish to make. And when the child comes forth from the holy baptismal rite, give the petition to him who holds the child in his arms; but I shall instruct him what to do, and I trust in the Son of God that He can arrange the whole matter according to the will of His loving kindness.' Having received these directions we blessed her and the infant and went out. Then we composed the petition, inserting many things in the document, not only as to the overthrow of the idols but also that privileges and revenue should be granted to the holy Church and the Christians; for the holy Church was poor.

"The days ran by, and the day on which the young Emperor Theodosius was to be illuminated ($\phi\omega\tau\acute{\iota}\zeta\epsilon\sigma\theta\alpha\iota$, i.e. baptized)[1] arrived. And all the city was crowned with garlands and decked out in garments entirely made of silk ($\acute{o}\lambda o\sigma\eta\rho\iota\kappa\hat{\omega}\nu$) and gold jewels and all kind of ornaments, so that no one could describe the adornment of the city. One might behold the inhabitants, multitudinous as the waves, arrayed in all manner of various dresses ($\pi a\nu\tau o\acute{\iota}a\varsigma\ \acute{\iota}\delta\acute{\epsilon}a\varsigma\ \acute{\iota}\mu a\tau\acute{\iota}\omega\nu\ \acute{\epsilon}\nu a\lambda\lambda\acute{a}\tau\tau o\nu\tau a$). But it is beyond my power to describe the brilliance of that pomp; it is a task for those who are practised writers, and I shall proceed to my present true history. When the young Theodosius was baptized and came forth from the church to the Palace, you might behold the excellence of the multitude of the magnates ($\pi\rho o\eta\gamma o\upsilon\mu\acute{\epsilon}\nu\omega\nu$) and their dazzling raiment, for all were dressed in white,[2] and you would have thought the multitude was covered with snow. The patricians headed the procession ($\pi\rho o\eta\gamma o\hat{\upsilon}\nu\tau o$), with the *illustres* and all the other ranks, and the military contingents, all carrying wax candles, so that the stars seemed to shine on earth. And close to the infant, which was carried in arms, was the Emperor Arcadius himself, his face cheerful and more radiant than the purple robe he was wearing, and one of the magnates carried the infant in brilliant apparel ($\acute{\epsilon}\nu\ \lambda a\mu\pi\rho\hat{a}\ \acute{\epsilon}\sigma\theta\hat{\eta}\tau\iota$). And we marvelled, beholding such glory.

---

[1] Used especially of the inner spiritual grace of baptism. $\phi\omega\tau\iota\sigma\tau\acute{\eta}\rho\iota o\nu$ meant a baptistery.

[2] The martyrs, represented in mosaics on the south wall of the nave of S. Apollinare Nuovo in Ravenna as walking in procession from the palace, are all arrayed in white.

" Then the holy Porphyrius says to us : ' If the things which soon vanish possess such glory, how much more glorious are the things celestial, prepared for the elect, which neither eye hath beheld nor ear heard, nor hath it come into the heart of man to consider.'

" And we stood at the portal of the church, with the document of our petition, and when he came forth from the baptism we called aloud, saying, 'We petition your Piety,' and held out the paper. And he who carried the child seeing this, and knowing our concernment, for the Empress had instructed him, bade the paper be showed to him, and when he received it halted. And he commanded silence, and having unrolled a part he read it, and folding it up, placed his hand under the head of the child and cried out, ' His majesty has ordered the requests contained in the petition to be ratified.' And all having seen marvelled and did obeisance to the Emperor, congratulating him that he had the privilege of seeing his son an emperor in his lifetime; and he rejoiced thereat. And that which had happened for the sake of her son was announced to the Empress, and she rejoiced and thanked God on her knees. And when the child entered the Palace, she met it and received it and kissed it, and holding it in her arms greeted the Emperor, saying, ' You are blessed, my lord, for the things which your eyes have beheld in your lifetime.' And the king rejoiced thereat. And the Empress, seeing him in good humour, said, ' Please let us learn what the petition contains that its contents may be fulfilled.' And the Emperor ordered the paper to be read, and when it was read, said, ' The request is hard, but to refuse is harder, since it is the first mandate of our son.' "

The petition was granted, and Eudoxia arranged a meeting between the quaestor, one of whose offices was to draft the imperial rescripts, and the bishops, that all the wishes of the latter might be incorporated in the edict. The execution of it, which was invidious and required a strong hand and will, was intrusted to Cynegius, and the bishops returned to Palestine, having received considerable sums of money from the Empress and Emperor, as well as the funds which the Empress had promised for the erection of a church at Gaza.

This narrative is extremely interesting. It gives us a concrete idea of the manner in which things were done, and of the kind of little dramas that probably lay behind the greater number of the formal decrees and rescripts contained in the Codices of Theodosius and Justinian. The wonder of the provincial bishops at the splendid apparel of the great of the earth, their edifying spiritual conversations with the Empress, with the eunuch, and with the archbishop, the ruse of Eudoxia to compass the success of the petition, all such details help us in attempting to realise the life of the time; while the hesitation of the pious Arcadius to root out the heathen "abominations" because the heathen were respectable taxpayers shows that even he, when the ghostly and worldly policies of the Empire clashed, was more inclined to be the Emperor than the churchman.

As a favourable example of an educated Byzantine of noble position we may take Anthemius, who became Emperor in the West as the colleague of Leo I., and who was the grandson of that prefect Anthemius who guided the State through the critical period following the death of Arcadius. He knew Latin as well as Greek, and a knowledge of Latin was very necessary for a politician, as it was still the official language throughout all the Empire. Yet acquaintance with the imperial language was beginning already to decline in the eastern provinces, and the fact that Pulcheria knew it was considered deserving of especial remark. Sallust, Livy, Tacitus, Plautus, and Virgil were among the books that Anthemius studied, so that he was quite at home in the society of the cultivated senators of Old Rome, when he resided there as Emperor. But if he had studied the Latin language and delighted in the Roman literature, he had not put away from himself the Greek love of speculation and mysticism. He dabbled in theosophy and magic, and this propensity gave him a bad name in Rome. He loved to surround himself with sorcerers, and with men who held strange opinions; pagans and heretics were more welcome guests than orthodox Christians. One of his best friends was Severus, a pagan magician who had lived at Alexandria and made his house the resort of spiritualists, brahmans, and theosophists; and it was said that Severus was wont to ride on a fiery horse which emitted sparks as it galloped. Another of his friends, Philotheus, was an adherent of the sublime or impious doctrine of Macedonius, which held that the Holy Ghost was not a person but a thing spread generally through nature—somewhat like the Earth-spirit in Goethe's *Faust*. The bishop of Rome felt himself obliged to interfere with the meetings which Philotheus held in that city to propagate his doctrine.

Let us now turn to the city of the Ptolemies, Alexandria-on-Nile, where life was as busy, as various, and as interesting as ever. Here Ptolemy Soter had established his "brilliant palace and court, with festivals which were the wonder of the world." "The city," writes Mr. Mahaffy, "was adequate by the largeness and splendour of its external experience. We have it described in later times as astonishing the beholder not only with its vastness—to wander through its streets, says Achilles Tatius, is an ἔνδημος ἐπιδημία, taking a tour without leaving home—but with the splendour of the colonnades which lined the streets for miles and kept the ways cool for passengers; with the din and bustle of the thoroughfares, of which the principal were horse and carriage ways, contrary to the usual Greek practice; with the number and richness of its public buildings; and with the holiday and happy air of its vast population, who rested not day and night, but had their streets so well lighted that the author just named says 'the sun did not set, but was distributed in small change—ἥλιος κατακερματίζων—to illumine the gay night.' The palaces and other royal buildings and parks were walled off, like the palace at Pekin [and that at Constantinople], and had their own port and seashore; but all the rest of the town had water near it and ship traffic in all directions. Every costume and language must have been met in its streets and quays. It had its fashionable suburbs, too, and its bathing resorts to the east—Canopus, Eleusis, and Nicopolis; to the west its Necropolis. But of all this splendour no eyewitness has left us in detail, what we are reduced to infer by conjecture." [1]

The Romans found no city in the Empire so difficult to govern as that of the quick-witted and quick-tempered Alexandrians; the streets were continually the scene of tumults between citizens and soldiers, and revolts against the augustal

[1] *Greek Life and Thought*, p. 197.

prefects. "While in Antioch, as a rule, the matter did not go beyond sarcasm, the Alexandrian rabble took on the slightest pretext to stones and cudgels. In street uproar, says an authority, himself Alexandrian, the Egyptians are before all others; the smallest spark suffices here to kindle a tumult. On account of neglected visits, on account of the confiscation of spoiled provisions, on account of exclusion from a bathing establishment, on account of a dispute between the slave of an Alexandrian of rank and the Roman footsoldier as to the value or non-value of their respective slippers, the legions were under the necessity of charging among the citizens of Alexandria."[1]

Instead of healing the discords and calming the intractable temper of this turbulent metropolis by diffusing a spirit of amity and long-suffering, the introduction of Christianity only gave the citizens new things to quarrel about, new causes for tumult, new formulae and catchwords which they could use as pretexts for violence and rioting. It was only in Alexandria that such acts as the destruction of the Serapeum or the cruel death of Hypatia could take place.

An account of the latter event falls within the limits of our period, and I have reserved it for this chapter, as it illustrates the nature of the Alexandrian atmosphere.

Hypatia was the daughter of Theon, the great mathematician,[2] who was a professor at the Museum or university of Alexandria. Trained in mathematics by her father, she left that pure air for the deeper and more agitating study of metaphysics, and probably became acquainted with the older Neoplatonism of Plotinus[3] which, in the Alexandrian Museum, had been transmitted untainted by the later developments of Porphyrius and Iamblichus. When she had completed her education she was appointed to the chair of philosophy, and her

---

[1] Mommsen's *History of Rome*, vol. v. *Provinces under the Empire* (ii. p. 264, English translation).

[2] His *scholia* on Euclid are extant. He used to lecture on the writings of Hermes Trismegistus and Orpheus, and was probably a mystic as well as a mathematician.

[3] Plotinus and his master Ammonius Sakas belonged to the university, while the later Neoplatonists were not connected with it. This point—Hypatia's affiliation to Plotinus—is due to W. A. Meyer, whose careful little tract, "Hypatia von Alexandria" (1886), has thrown much light on the subject, though Hypatia has been the subject of many tracts. I have followed his conclusions, which seem based on a just view of the fragmentary evidence that remains. Hoche (*Philologus*, xv. 1860) showed that the supposed journey of Hypatia to Athens is based on a mistranslation of Suidas. The date of her birth was about 370.

extraordinary talents, combined with her beauty, made her a centre of interest in the cultured and aristocratic circles at Alexandria, and drew to her lecture-room crowds of admirers. Her free and unembarrassed intercourse with educated men and the publicity of her life must have given rise to many scandals and backbitings, and her own sex doubtless looked upon her with suspicion, and called her masculine and immodest. She used to walk in the streets in her academical gown (τρίβων, the philosopher's cloak) and explain to any person who wished to learn, difficulties in Plato or Aristotle.[1] Of the influence of her personality on her pupils we have still a record in the letters of Synesius of Cyrene, who, although his studies under her auspices did not hinder him from going over to Christianity, always remained at heart a semi-pagan, and was devotedly attached to his instructress. That some of her pupils fell in love with her is not surprising,[2] but Hypatia never married, though a later tradition made her the wife of a heathen philosopher, Isidorus.

The real cause of her tragic fate, which befell her in March 415, is veiled in obscurity. We know that she was an intimate friend of the pagan Orestes, the prefect augustalis of Egypt; and we could be sure, even if we had not the testimony of Suidas, that she was an object of hatred to Cyrillus, the Patriarch of Alexandria, both because she was an enthusiastic preacher of pagan doctrines and because she was Orestes' friend. Moreover, she was murdered just after the great conflict between Orestes and Cyril, in which the Jews played an important part.

The Alexandrian bishop was already very powerful, and Cyril, who succeeded to the chair in 412, aimed at attaining the supreme power in the city and reducing the authority of the imperial prefect to a minimum. The opposition of the

---

[1] I follow Meyer's translation of a passage in Suidas.

[2] One of her pupils is said to have declared his passion for her, and the tale went that she exorcised his desire by disarranging her dress and displaying τὸ σύμβολον τῆς ἀκαθάρτου γεννήσεως: "This, young man," she said, "is what you are in love with, and nothing beautiful." This story, recorded by Suidas, was without doubt a contemporary scandal, and indicates what exaggerated stories were circulated about the independence and perhaps the freespokenness of Hypatia. One cannot help acknowledging, however, that the anecdote is *ben trovato*, for such cynicism or cynism would be the logical consequence of an extremely consistent Neoplatonism, with its contempt for matter and the human body.

Jews[1] to the bishop brought matters to a crisis, for when, on one occasion, they saw a notorious creature of Cyril present in an assembly, they cried out that the spy should be arrested, and Orestes gratified them by inflicting public chastisement on him. The menaces which Cyril, enraged by this act, fulminated against the Jews led to a bloody vengeance on the christian population. A report was spread at night that the great church was on fire, and when the Christians flocked to the spot the Jews surrounded and massacred them. Cyril replied to this horror by banishing all Hebrews from the city, and allowing the Christians to plunder their property, a proceeding which was quite beyond the Patriarch's rights, and was a direct and insulting interference with the authority of Orestes, who immediately wrote a complaint to Constantinople. At this juncture 500 monks of Nitria, sniffing the savour of blood and bigotry from afar, hastened to the scene. These fanatics insulted Orestes publicly, one of them hitting him with a stone; in fact the governor ran a serious risk of his life. The culprit who hurled the missile was executed, and Cyril treated his body as the remains of a martyr.

It was then that Hypatia seems to have fallen a victim in the midst of these infuriated passions. As she was returning home one day she was seized by a band of men, led by a certain Peter, who dragged her to a church and, tearing off her garments, hewed her in pieces and burned the fragments of her body. The reason alleged in public for this act of barbarity was that she hindered a reconciliation between Orestes and Cyrillus; but this, of course, was only a pretext, and the real reason, as Socrates tells us, was envy. Whether the motive of Cyrillus in instigating this murder—for that he was the instigator may be considered almost certain—was a grudge against Hypatia herself, or whether, as has been suggested,[2] he intended by her assassination to wound another person (Orestes or Synesius) we cannot determine.

In my opinion we shall do most wisely to consider that the conflict of Orestes with Cyril was exacerbated by the fact that Orestes was really, though not openly, a heathen, and that

---

[1] Güldenpenning (*Gesch. des oströmischen Reichs*, p. 225) reckons the number of Jews at Alexandria at this period about 200,000.

[2] By W. A. Meyer, *op. cit.* For the death of Hypatia, *see* Socrates, vii. 14.

Cyril wished it to appear that the struggle was not merely the collision of rival authorities or conditioned by his own ambition, but rather a strife of the christian Church with the "Hellenic" society of Alexandria. Hence Hypatia, as a prominent pagan teacher and as the intimate friend of Orestes, was sacrificed in order to lend this aspect to the conflict; and the sacrifice was all the more grateful to the bishop as it was a personal blow to his enemy.

Such was Alexandria at the end of the fourth and the beginning of the fifth century, when Christianity was in conflict with paganism; in the latter half of the fifth century it was as turbulent as ever, but the conflict was then among Christians themselves—various sects of monophysites and orthodox Chalcedonians.

Let us now glance for a moment at Antioch-on-Orontes, the famous capital of another great successor of Alexander, and in christian times a city of note as the seat of one of the great Patriarchs of Christendom. "In no city of antiquity," says Mommsen, "was the enjoyment of life so much the main thing and its duties so incidental as in 'Antioch-upon-Daphne,' as the city was significantly called, somewhat as if we should say 'Vienna-upon-Prater.' For Daphne was a pleasure-garden about five miles from the city, ten miles in circumference, famous for its laurel trees, after which it was named, for its old cypresses, which even the christian Emperors ordered to be spared, for its flowing and gushing waters, for its shining temple of Apollo, and its magnificent much-frequented festival of the 10th August." Its chief street, nearly four and a half miles long, stretched straight along the river, and a covered colonnade afforded shade from sun or rain. Its streets were brilliantly lighted at night, and the supply of water, it has been remarked, was so good that there was no fighting at the public baths. Mommsen, comparing it with Alexandria, observes that "for enjoyment of life, dramatic spectacles, dining, pleasures of love, Antioch had more to offer than the city in which 'no one went idle.'" It was a gay and corrupt place. Julian had abhorred it for its corruption and Christianity, and it had abhorred Julian for his paganism and austerity.[1] Syria was the home of actors, singers, ballet-dancers, and

[1] See Julian's *Misopogon*.

circus clowns, as well as of eloquent theologians; and the heart of Chrysostom was distressed in vain for the depravity of the Antiochian amusements.[1] When riots occurred the causes were generally connected with the circus; and though the men of Antioch, like the men of Alexandria, had sharp tongues, they were generally content with using them, and did not proceed to anything more violent. In Antioch, as well as in Alexandria, it may be observed the Jews formed an important element of the population, which, not counting slaves and children, numbered about 200,000.

The situation of Antioch, however, was not so fortunate as that of its rival. It was fourteen miles from the coast, and thus had not the advantage of being a seaport; and it was liable to be shaken by frequent and violent earthquakes, which ultimately proved its ruin.

Antioch does not seem to have been a resort of pagans.[2] In the fourth century, indeed, Libanius may be mentioned as a pagan of Antioch, but in the fifth century probably very few non-Christians of a serious type were to be found there. If a writer of Antioch were named, we might guess with considerable certainty that he was a Christian, just as we might guess that a writer of Athens was a pagan. An Alexandrian author, except he were a theologian, would more probably be a pagan than a Christian; a Byzantine author would more probably be a Christian than a pagan. As for a native of Asia Minor, the chances in regard to his faith would be about equal.

As a contrast to the highly civilised life of the Roman Empire, it will be well to take a glimpse at the primitive manners of the Huns, as they impressed a contemporary Roman, whose account of an embassy to Attila in the year 448 has been preserved. As the narrative, which I have translated freely, with some omissions, is of considerable length, a separate chapter may be devoted to it.

---

[1] A good deal can be gleaned from Chrysostom's homilies about the manners of Antioch. Pickpockets ("cutpurses") used to frequent the churches. Superstition was rife, and the place was full of jugglers and sorcerers, who practised incantations and studied genethlialogy. In his *Studien aus dem classischen Alterthum* (1881), A. Hug has an interesting essay on Antioch, in special reference to the revolt of 387 A.D.

[2] In the sixth century it was deemed worthy of being re-christened Theupolis, "the city of God."

CHAPTER XI

A GLIMPSE OF HUN LIFE

THE historian Priscus accompanied his friend Maximin on an embassy to Scythia or Hunland in the year 448, and wrote a full account of what befell them. Of this account, which has been fortunately preserved, the following is a free translation [1] :—

"We set out with the barbarians, and arrived at Sardica, which is thirteen days for a fast traveller from Constantinople. Halting there we considered it advisable to invite Edecon and the barbarians with him to dinner. The inhabitants of the place sold us sheep and oxen, which we butchered, and prepared a meal. In the course of the feast, as the barbarians lauded Attila and we lauded the Emperor, Bigilas remarked that it was not fair to compare a man and a god, meaning Attila by the man and Theodosius by the god. The Huns grew excited and hot at this remark. But we turned the conversation in another direction, and soothed their wounded feelings; and after dinner, when we separated, Maximin presented Edecon and Orestes with silk garments and Indian gems. . . .

"When we arrived at Naissus we found the city deserted, as though it had been sacked; only a few sick persons lay in the churches. We halted at a short distance from the river, in an open space, for all the ground adjacent to the bank was full of the bones of men slain in war. On the morrow we came to the station of Agintheus, the commander-in-chief of the Illyrian armies (*magister militum per Illyricum*), who was posted not far from Naissus, to announce to him the imperial commands, and to receive five of those seventeen deserters, about whom Attila had written to the Emperor.[2] We had an interview with him, and having

---

[1] I have used the text of Priscus in Müller's *Frag. Hist. Graec.* vol. iv. It may be well to warn readers that the Latin translation appended cannot be implicitly trusted.
[2] περὶ ὧν 'Αττήλᾳ ἐγέγραπτο (p. 78).

In Müller's Latin translation under the text these words are mistranslated *de quibus ad Attilam scripserat*. τὰ παρὰ 'Αττήλα γράμματα (fr. 7, p. 76) is referred to.

treated the deserters with kindness, he committed them to us. The next day we proceeded from the district of Naissus[1] towards the Danube, we entered a covered valley with many bends and windings and circuitous paths. We thought we were travelling due west, but when the day dawned the sun rose in front ; and some of us unacquainted with the topography cried out that the sun was going the wrong way, and portending unusual events. The fact was that that part of the road faced the east, owing to the irregularity of the ground. Having passed these rough places we arrived at a plain which was also well wooded. At the river we were received by barbarian ferrymen, who rowed us across the river in boats made by themselves out of single trees hewn and hollowed. These preparations had not been made for our sake, but to convey across a company of Huns ; for Attila pretended that he wished to hunt in Roman territory, but his intent was really hostile, because all the deserters had not been given up to him. Having crossed the Danube, and proceeded with the barbarians about seventy stadia, we were compelled to wait in a certain plain, that Edecon and his party might go on in front and inform Attila of our arrival. As we were dining in the evening we heard the sound of horses approaching, and two Scythians arrived with directions that we were to set out to Attila. We asked them first to partake of our meal, and they dismounted and made good cheer. On the next day, under their guidance, we arrived at the tents of Attila, which were numerous, about three o'clock, and when we wished to pitch our tent on a hill the barbarians who met us prevented us, because the tent of Attila was on low ground, so we halted where the Scythians desired. . . . (Then a message is received from Attila, who was aware of the nature of their embassy, saying that if they had nothing further to communicate to him he would not receive them, so they reluctantly prepared to return.) When the baggage had been packed on the beasts of burden, and we were perforce preparing to start in the night time, messengers came from Attila bidding us wait on account of the late hour. Then men arrived with an ox and river fish, sent to us by Attila, and when we had dined we retired to sleep. When it was day we expected a gentle and courteous message from the barbarian, but he again bade us depart if we had no further mandates beyond what he already knew. We made no reply, and prepared to set out, though Bigilas insisted that we should feign to have some other communication to make. When I saw that Maximin was very dejected, I went to Scottas (one of the Hun nobles, brother of Onegesius), taking with me Rusticius, who understood the Hun language. He had come with us to Scythia, not as a member of the embassy, but on business with Constantius, an Italian whom Aetius had sent to Attila to be that monarch's private secretary. I informed Scottas, Rusticius acting as interpreter, that Maximin will give him many presents if he would procure him an interview with Attila ; and, moreover, that the embassy will not only conduce to the public interests of the two powers, but to the private interest of

---

[1] Here is another mistranslation in Müller's Latin version, ἀπὸ τῶν ὁρίων Ναισσοῦ, a montibus Naissi (!). I mention these instances to show that the translation must be used with caution.

Onegesius, for the Emperor desired that he should be sent as an ambassador to Byzantium, to arrange the disputes of the Huns and Romans, and that there he would receive splendid gifts. As Onegesius was not present it was for Scottas, I said, to help us, or rather help his brother, and at the same time prove that the report was true which ascribed to him an influence with Attila equal to that possessed by his brother. Scottas mounted his horse and rode to Attila's tent, while I returned to Maximin, and found him in a state of perplexity and anxiety, lying on the grass with Bigilas. I described my interview with Scottas, and bade him make preparations for an audience of Attila. They both jumped up, approving of what I had done, and recalled the men who had started with the beasts of burden. As we were considering what to say to Attila, and how to present the Emperor's gifts, Scottas came to fetch us, and we entered Attila's tent, which was surrounded by a multitude of barbarians. We found Attila sitting on a wooden chair. We stood at a little distance and Maximin advanced and saluted the barbarian, to whom he gave the Emperor's letter, saying that the Emperor prayed for the safety of him and his. The king replied, 'It shall be unto the Romans as they wish it to be unto me,' and immediately addressed Bigilas, calling him a shameless beast, and asking him why he ventured to come when all the deserters had not been given up.[1] . . .

"After the departure of Bigilas, who returned to the Empire (nominally to find the deserters whose restoration Attila demanded, but really to get the money for his fellow-conspirator Edecon), we remained one day in that place, and then set out with Attila for the northern parts of the country. We accompanied the barbarian for a time, but when we reached a certain point took another route by the command of the Scythians who conducted us, as Attila was proceeding to a village where he intended to marry the daughter of Eskam, though he had many other wives, for the Scythians practised polygamy. We proceeded along a level road in a plain and met with navigable rivers—of which the greatest, next to the Danube, are the Drecon, Tigas, and Tiphesas—which we crossed in the monoxyles, boats made of one piece, used by the dwellers on the banks: the smaller rivers we traversed on rafts which the barbarians carry about with them on carts, for the purpose of crossing morasses. In the villages we were supplied with food—millet instead of corn, and mead ($μέδος$), as the natives call it, instead of wine. The attendants who followed us received millet, and a drink made of barley, which the barbarians call *kam*. Late in the evening, having travelled a long distance, we pitched our tents on the banks of a fresh-water lake, used for water by the inhabitants of the neighbouring village. But a wind and storm, accompanied by thunder and lightning and heavy rain, arose, and almost threw down our tents; all our utensils were rolled into the waters of the lake. Terrified by the mishap and the atmospherical disturbance, we left the place and lost one another in the dark and the rain, each following the road that seemed most easy. But we all reached the village by different ways, and raised an

---

[1] Edecon had betrayed to Attila the design which he and Bigilas had formed against Attila's life. This was the real reason of Attila's roughness towards the latter.

alarm to obtain what we lacked. The Scythians of the village sprang out of their huts at the noise, and, lighting the reeds which they use for kindling fires, asked what we wanted. Our conductors replied that the storm had alarmed us ; so they invited us to their huts and provided warmth for us by lighting large fires of reeds. The lady who governed the village—she had been one of Bleda's wives—sent us provisions and good-looking girls to console us (this is a Scythian compliment). We treated the young women to a share in the eatables, but declined to take any further advantage of their presence. We remained in the huts till day dawned and then went to look for our lost utensils, which we found partly in the place where we had pitched the tent, partly on the bank of the lake, and partly in the water. We spent that day in the village drying our things ; for the storm had ceased and the sun was bright. Having looked after our horses and cattle, we directed our steps to the princess, to whom we paid our respects and presented gifts in return for her courtesy. The gifts consisted of things which are esteemed by the barbarians as not produced in the country — three silver *phialai*, red skins, Indian pepper, palm fruit, and other delicacies.

"Having advanced a distance of ten days further, we halted at a village ; for as the rest of the route was the same for us and Attila, it behoved us to wait, so that he might go in front. Here we met with some of the 'western Romans,'[1] who had also come on an embassy to Attila—the Count Romulus, Promotus governor of Noricum, and Romanus a military captain. With them was Constantius whom Aetius had sent to Attila to be his secretary, and Tatulus, the father of Orestes ; these two were not connected with the embassy, but were friends of the ambassadors. Constantius had known them of old in the Italies,[2] and Tatulus' son Orestes had married the daughter of Romulus.[3]

"The object of the embassy was to soften the soul of Attila, who demanded the surrender of one Silvanus, a silversmith (or banker) in Rome, because he had received golden vessels from a certain Constantius. This Constantius, a native of Gaul,[4] had preceded his namesake in the office of secretary to Attila. When Sirmium in Pannonia was besieged by the

---

[1] It is worth observing how the Greek-speaking Romans spoke of their Latin-speaking fellow-subjects. Valentinian is described as ὁ βασιλεύων τῶν ἑσπερίων Ῥωμαίων. This, it need scarcely be remarked, does not imply that there was any idea afloat at the time of a western Roman Empire. Priscus calls the Latin language τὴν Αὐσονίων "the tongue of the Ausonians" (p. 86), as opposed to "the tongue of the Hellenes." To speak Greek is ἑλληνίζω.

[2] ἐν ταῖς Ἰταλίαις—that is, Italy with its appendages Sicily, Sardinia, Corsica ; just as "the Gauls" meant Gaul and Spain. This use of the plural is parallel to the dual *Mitran* in the Rig-Veda, which does not mean "the two Mitras," but "Mitra and Varuna," because these gods generally went together (like Castor and Pollux). It is possible also that in a passage in the *Iliad* Αἴαντε does not mean the two Ajaxes, but Ajax Telamonius and his brother Teucer, as a writer in Kuhn's *Zeitschrift* suggested.

[3] Romulus and his daughter were of Patavio in Noricum. Orestes' son was called after his grandfather Romulus, and was the same as the famous and insignificant Emperor Romulus Augustulus who resigned in favour of Zeno in 476.

[4] The way in which a Greek Roman spoke of Gaul deserves to be remarked : Gaul for him was "western Galatia :" ἐκ Γαλατῶν μὲν τῶν ἐν τῇ ἑσπέρᾳ (Priscus, p. 84).

Scythians, the bishop of the place consigned the vessels to his (Constantius') care, that if the city were taken and he survived they might be used to ransom him ; and in case he were slain, to ransom the citizens who were led into captivity. But when the city was enslaved, Constantius violated his engagement, and, as he happened to be at Rome on business, pawned the vessels to Silvanus for a sum of money, on condition that if he gave back the money within a prescribed period the dishes should be returned, but otherwise should become Silvanus' property. Constantius, suspected of treachery, was crucified by Attila and Bleda ; and afterwards, when the affair of the vessels became known to Attila, he demanded the surrender of Silvanus on the ground that he had stolen his property. Accordingly Aetius and the Emperor of the Western Romans sent to explain that Silvanus was Constantius' creditor, the vessels having been pawned and not stolen, and that he had sold them to priests and others for sacred purposes. If, however, Attila refused to desist from his demand, he, the Emperor, would send him the value of the vessels, but would not surrender the innocent Silvanus.

"Having waited for some time until Attila advanced in front of us, we proceeded, and having crossed some rivers we arrived at a large village, where Attila's house was said to be more splendid than his residences in other places. It was made of polished boards, and surrounded with a wooden enclosure, designed, not for protection, but for appearance. The house of Onegesius was second to the king's[1] in splendour, and was also encircled with a wooden enclosure, but it was not adorned with towers like that of the king. Not far from the enclosure was a large bath which Onegesius—who was the second in power among the Scythians—built, having transported the stones from Pannonia ; for the barbarians in this district had no stones or trees, but used imported material. The builder of the bath was a captive from Sirmium, who expected to win his freedom as payment for making the bath. But he was disappointed, and greater trouble befell him than mere captivity among the Scythians, for Onegesius appointed him bathman, and he used to minister to him and his family when they bathed.

"When Attila entered the village he was met by girls advancing in rows, under thin white canopies of linen, which were held up by the outside women who stood under them, and were so large that seven or more girls walked beneath each. There were many lines of damsels thus canopied, and they sang Scythian songs. When he came near the house of Onegesius, which lay on his way, the wife of Onegesius issued from the door, with a number of servants, bearing meat and wine, and saluted him and begged him to partake of her hospitality. This is the highest honour that can be shown among the Scythians. To gratify the wife of his friend, he ate, just as he sat on his horse, his attendants raising the tray to his saddlebow ; and having tasted the wine, he went on to the palace,

---

[1] Occasionally Priscus speaks of Attila as ὁ βασιλεύς, a word which in the ordinary spoken language of the time was reserved for the Emperor, while the Latin ῥήξ might be used for a king. Priscus, however, writes in a conventional prose, which avoids the expressions of the spoken tongue. βασιλεύς, however, was still legitimately used of the Persian monarch.

which was higher than the other houses and built on an elevated site. But we remained in the house of Onegesius, at his invitation, for he had returned from his expedition with Attila's son. His wife and kinsfolk entertained us to dinner, for he had no leisure himself, as he had to relate to Attila the result of his expedition, and explain the accident which had happened to the young prince, who had slipped and broken his right hand. After dinner we left the house of Onegesius, and took up our quarters nearer the palace, so that Maximin might be at a convenient distance for visiting Attila or holding intercourse with his court. The next morning, at dawn of day, Maximin sent me to Onegesius, with presents offered by himself as well as those which the Emperor had sent, and I was to find out whether he would have an interview with Maximin and at what time. When I arrived at the house, along with the attendants who carried the gifts, I found the doors closed, and had to wait until some one should come out and announce our arrival. As I waited and walked up and down in front of the enclosure which surrounded the house, a man, whom from his Scythian dress I took for a barbarian, came up and addressed me in Greek, with the word Χαῖρε, 'Hail!' I was surprised at a Scythian speaking Greek. For the subjects of the Huns, swept together from various lands, speak, beside their own barbarous tongue, either Hunnic or Gothic,[1] or—as many as have commercial dealings with the western Romans—Latin; but none of them easily speak Greek, except captives from the Thracian or Illyrian sea-coast; and these last are easily known to any stranger by their torn garments and the squalor of their head, as men who have met with a reverse. This man, on the contrary, resembled a well-to-do Scythian, being well dressed, and having his hair cut in a circle after Scythian fashion. Having returned his salutation, I asked him who he was and whence he had come into a foreign land and adopted Scythian life. When he asked me why I wanted to know, I told him that his Hellenic speech had prompted my curiosity. Then he smiled and said that he was born a Greek[2] and had gone as a merchant to Viminacium, on the Danube, where he had stayed a long time, and married a very rich wife. But the city fell a prey to the barbarians, and he was stript of his prosperity, and on account of his riches was allotted to Onegesius in the division of the spoil, as it was the custom among the Scythians for the chiefs to reserve for themselves the rich prisoners. Having fought bravely against the Romans and the Acatiri, he had paid the spoils he won to his master, and so obtained freedom. He then married a barbarian wife and had children, and had the privilege of partaking at the table of Onegesius.

"He considered his new life among the Scythians better than his old life among the Romans, and the reasons he urged were as follows: 'After war the Scythians live in inactivity, enjoying what they have got, and not at all, or very little, harassed. The Romans, on the other hand, are

---

[1] That is, Hunnic or Gothic were the recognised languages of the Hun empire, in which of course many barbarous Tataric tongues were spoken.

[2] ἔφη Γραικὸς μὲν εἶναι τὸ γένος (p. 86), Γραικός, not Ἕλλην, a *Greek*, not a *Hellene*, which would mean a pagan. Ἑλληνικός and ἑλληνίζειν were still used in their old sense; and we even meet τὴν Ἑλλήνων φωνήν.

in the first place very liable to perish in war, as they have to rest their hopes of safety on others, and are not allowed, on account of their *tyrants*, to use arms. And those who use them are injured by the cowardice of their generals, who cannot support the conduct of war. But the condition of the subjects in time of peace is far more grievous than the evils of war, for the exaction of the taxes is very severe, and unprincipled men inflict injuries on others, because the laws are practically not valid against all classes. A transgressor who belongs to the wealthy classes is not punished for his injustice, while a poor man, who does not understand business, undergoes the legal penalty, that is if he does not depart this life before the trial, so long is the course of lawsuits protracted, and so much money is expended on them. The climax of the misery is to have to pay in order to obtain justice. For no one will give a court to the injured man except he pay a sum of money to the judge and the judge's clerks.'

"In reply to this attack on the Empire, I asked him to be good enough to listen with patience to the other side of the question. 'The creators of the Roman republic,' I said, 'who were wise and good men, in order to prevent things from being done at haphazard, made one class of men guardians of the laws, and appointed another class to the profession of arms, who were to have no other object than to be always ready for battle, and to go forth to war without dread, as though to their ordinary exercise, having by practice exhausted all their fear beforehand. Others again were assigned to attend to the cultivation of the ground, to support both themselves and those who fight in their defence, by contributing the military corn-supply. . . . To those who protect the interests of the litigants a sum of money is paid by the latter, just as a payment is made by the farmers to the soldiers. Is it not fair to support him who assists and requite him for his kindness? The support of the horse benefits the horseman. . . . Those who spend money on a suit and lose it in the end cannot fairly put it down to anything but the injustice of their case. And as to the long time spent on lawsuits, that is due to concern for justice, that judges may not fail in passing accurate judgments, by having to give sentence offhand; it is better that they should reflect, and conclude the case more tardily, than that by judging in a hurry they should both injure man and transgress against the Deity, the institutor of justice. . . . The Romans treat their servants better than the king of the Scythians treats his subjects. They deal with them as fathers or teachers, admonishing them to abstain from evil and follow the lines of conduct which they have esteemed honourable; they reprove them for their errors like their own children. They are not allowed, like the Scythians, to inflict death on them. They have numerous ways of conferring freedom; they can manumit not only during life, but also by their wills, and the testamentary wishes of a Roman in regard to his property are law.'[1]

"My interlocutor shed tears, and confessed that the laws and constitution of the Romans were fair, but deplored that the governors, not possessing the spirit of former generations, were ruining the State.

---

[1] This passage is interesting as an illustration of the attitude of the higher classes in the Empire to slavery in the fifth century.

"As we were engaged in this discussion a servant came out and opened the door of the enclosure. I hurried up, and inquired how Onegesius was engaged, for I desired to give him a message from the Roman ambassador. He replied that I should meet him if I waited a little, as he was about to go forth. And after a short time I saw him coming out, and addressed him, saying, 'The Roman ambassador salutes you, and I have come with gifts from him, and with the gold which the Emperor sent you. The ambassador is anxious to meet you, and begs you to appoint a time and place.' Onegesius bade his servants receive the gold and the gifts, and told me to announce to Maximin that he would go to him immediately. I delivered the message, and Onegesius appeared in the tent without delay. He expressed his thanks to Maximin and the Emperor for the presents, and asked why he sent for him. Maximin said that the time had come for Onegesius to have greater renown among men, if he would go to the Emperor, and by his wisdom arrange the objects of dispute between the Romans and Huns, and establish concord between them ; and thereby he will also procure many advantages for his own family, as he and his children will be always friends of the Emperor and the imperial race.[1] Then Onegesius inquired what measures would gratify the Emperor, and how he could arrange the disputes. Maximin replied : ' If you cross into the lands of the Roman Empire you will lay the Emperor under an obligation, and you will arrange the matters at issue by investigating their causes and deciding them on the basis of the peace. Onegesius said he would inform the Emperor and his ministers of Attila's wishes, but the Romans need not think they could ever prevail with him to betray his master or neglect his Scythian training and his wives and children, or to prefer wealth among the Romans to bondage with Attila. He added that he would be of more service to the Romans by remaining in his own land and softening the anger of his master, if he were indignant for aught with the Romans, than by visiting them and subjecting himself to blame if he made arrangements that Attila did not approve of. He then retired, having consented that I should act as intermediate in conveying messages from Maximin to himself, for it would not have been consistent with Maximin's dignity as ambassador to visit him constantly.

"The next day I entered the enclosure of Attila's palace, bearing gifts to his wife, whose name was Kreka. She had three sons, of whom the eldest governed the Acatiri and the other nations who dwell in Pontic Scythia. Within the enclosure were numerous buildings, some of carved boards beautifully fitted together, others of straight planed beams, without carving, fastened on round wooden blocks which rose to a moderate height from the ground. Attila's wife lived here, and, having been admitted by the barbarians at the door, I found her reclining on a soft couch. The floor of the room was covered with woollen mats for walking on. A number

---

[1] It is worth while noticing this expression $\tau \hat{\varphi}$ ἐκείνου γένει, which unintentionally expresses the general idea that the Roman Empire was hereditary. Theoretically it was not hereditary (*see* p. 227), but it would have been treasonable to hint that any one but a relative (a son, if there were sons) of the reigning Emperor might succeed him.

of servants stood round her, and maids sitting on the floor in front of her embroidered with colours linen cloths intended to be placed over the Scythian dress for ornament. Having approached, saluted her, and presented the gifts, I went out, and walked to the other houses, where Attila was, and waited for Onegesius, who, as I knew, was with Attila. I stood in the middle of a great crowd—the guards of Attila and his attendants knew me, and so no one hindered me. I saw a number of people advancing, and a great commotion and noise, Attila's egress being expected. And he came forth from the house with a dignified strut, looking round on this side and on that. He was accompanied by Onegesius, and stood in front of the house ; and many persons who had lawsuits with one another came up and received his judgment. Then he returned into the house, and received ambassadors of barbarous peoples.

"As I was waiting for Onegesius, I was accosted by Romulus and Promotus and Romanus, the ambassadors who had come from Italy about the golden vessels ; they were accompanied by Rusticius and by Constantiolus, a man from the Pannonian territory, which was subjected to Attila. They asked me whether we had been dismissed or are constrained to remain, and I replied that it was just to learn this from Onegesius that I was waiting outside the palace. When I inquired in my turn whether Attila had vouchsafed them a kind reply, they told me that his decision could not be moved, and that he threatened war unless either Silvanus or the drinking vessels should be given up. . . .

"As we were talking about the state of the world, Onegesius came out : we went up to him and asked him about our concerns. Having first spoken with some barbarians, he bade me inquire of Maximin what consular the Romans are sending as an ambassador to Attila. When I came to our tent I delivered the message to Maximin, and deliberated with him what answer we should make to the question of the barbarian. Returning to Onegesius, I said that the Romans desired him to come to them and adjust the matters of dispute, otherwise the Emperor will send whatever ambassador he chooses. He then bade me fetch Maximin, whom he conducted to the presence of Attila. Soon after Maximin came out, and told me that the barbarian wished Nomos or Anatolius or Senator to be the ambassador, and that he would not receive any other than one of these three ; when he (Maximin) replied that it was not meet to mention men by name and so render them suspected in the eyes of the Emperor, Attila said that if they do not choose to comply with his wishes the differences will be adjusted by arms.

"When we returned to our tent the father of Orestes came with an invitation from Attila for both of us to a banquet at three o'clock. When the hour arrived we went to the palace, along with the embassy from the western Romans, and stood on the threshold of the hall in the presence of Attila. The cup-bearers gave us a cup, according to the national custom, that we might pray before we sat down. Having tasted the cup, we proceeded to take our seats ; all the chairs were ranged along the walls of the room on either side. Attila sat in the middle on a couch ; a second couch was set behind him, and from it steps led up to his bed, which was covered with linen sheets and wrought coverlets for ornament, such as

Greeks [1] and Romans use to deck bridal beds. The places on the right of Attila were held chief in honour, those on the left, where we sat, were only second. Berichus, a noble among the Scythians, sat on our side, but had the precedence of us. Onegesius sat on a chair on the right of Attila's couch, and over against Onegesius on a chair sat two of Attila's sons; his eldest son sat on his couch, not near him, but at the extreme end, with his eyes fixed on the ground, in shy respect for his father. When all were arranged, a cupbearer came and handed Attila a wooden cup of wine. He took it, and saluted the first in precedence, who, honoured by the salutation, stood up, and might not sit down until the king, having tasted or drained the wine, returned the cup to the attendant. All the guests then honoured Attila in the same way, saluting him, and then tasting the cups; but he did not stand up. Each of us had a special cupbearer, who would come forward in order to present the wine, when the cupbearer of Attila retired. When the second in precedence and those next to him had been honoured in like manner, Attila toasted us in the same way according to the order of the seats. When this ceremony was over the cupbearers retired, and tables, large enough for three or four, or even more, to sit at, were placed next the table of Attila, so that each could take of the food on the dishes without leaving his seat. The attendant of Attila first entered with a dish full of meat, and behind him came the other attendants with bread and viands, which they laid on the tables. A luxurious meal, served on silver plate, had been made ready for us and the barbarian guests, but Attila ate nothing but meat on a wooden trencher. In everything else, too, he showed himself temperate; his cup was of wood, while to the guests were given goblets of gold and silver. His dress, too, was quite simple, affecting only to be clean. The sword he carried at his side, the latchets of his Scythian shoes, the bridle of his horse were not adorned, like those of the other Scythians, with gold or gems or anything costly. When the viands of the first course had been consumed we all stood up, and did not resume our seats until each one, in the order before observed, drank to the health of Attila in the goblet of wine presented to him. We then sat down, and a second dish was placed on each table with eatables of another kind. After this course the same ceremony was observed as after the first. When evening fell torches were lit, and two barbarians coming forward in front of Attila sang songs they had composed, celebrating his victories and deeds of valour in war. And of the guests, as they looked at the singers, some were pleased with the verses, others reminded of wars were excited in their souls, while yet others, whose bodies were feeble with age and their spirits compelled to rest, shed tears. After the songs a Scythian, whose mind was deranged, appeared, and by uttering outlandish and senseless words forced the company to laugh. After him Zerkon, the Moorish dwarf, entered. He had been sent by Attila as a gift to Aetius, and Edecon had persuaded him to come to Attila in order to recover his wife, whom he had left behind him in Scythia; the lady was a Scythian whom he had obtained in marriage

---

[1] Ἕλληνές τε καὶ Ῥωμαῖοι. In using this expression Priscus had ancient times in his mind—times when the Greeks were not Romans, but Ἕλληνες, and when Ἕλλην was not opposed to Χριστιανός.

through the influence of his patron Bleda. He did not succeed in recovering her, for Attila was angry with him for returning. On the occasion of the banquet he made his appearance, and threw all except Attila into fits of unquenchable laughter by his appearance, his dress, his voice, and his words, which were a confused jumble of Latin, Hunnic, and Gothic. Attila, however, remained immovable and of unchanging countenance, nor by word or act did he betray anything approaching to a smile of merriment except at the entry of Ernas, his youngest son, whom he pulled by the cheek, and gazed on with a calm look of satisfaction. I was surprised that he made so much of this son, and neglected his other children; but a barbarian who sat beside me and knew Latin, bidding me not reveal what he told, gave me to understand that prophets had forewarned Attila that his race would fall, but would be restored by this boy. When the night had advanced we retired from the banquet, not wishing to assist further at the potations."

It will be noticed that in the foregoing narrative the word Scythian and the word Hun seem at first sight to be used indifferently. A certain distinction between them can, however, be perceived, and therefore, though they are most often practically synonymous, I have reproduced both words in the translation just as they occur in the original. Scythian is not merely an ancient term applied to a new people, in the same way as the Goths and the Slaves were often called Getae by pedantic historians; Scythian was a generic term for all nomadic nations, and as a great many different nomadic nations were united under the sovereignty of Attila, it was a very convenient and natural name to apply to his subjects. The Huns, Attila's own nation, were Scythians, but all Scythians were not Huns. And thus, to use a more modern distinction, we might say that Attila was king of the Huns and emperor of the Scythians.

BOOK III

THE HOUSE OF LEO THE GREAT

CHAPTER I

LEO I

THE Roman Empire never recognised explicitly the principle of hereditary succession; the title of Imperator or Augustus was always conferred by the army, with which the office had been originally so closely connected. At the same time a natural instinct led Emperors to wish that their sons or members of their own house should succeed them; and by adopting the plan of nominating a successor in their lifetime, and securing his recognition by the army as a Caesar or Augustus, Emperors could found a dynasty without violating the theory that the elevation to the throne was elective. Accordingly the Empire tended to become practically hereditary while it was theoretically elective; and the constant examples of claims to the crown founded on relationship prove that there was a feeling that heredity involved a right.[1]

It was always a critical moment when a dynasty ended without a designated successor, or a member of the family who cared to claim the crown. Theodosius I. had created his son Arcadius Augustus; Arcadius had given that title to his infant son Theodosius II; Theodosius had designated Marcian as his successor before his death, Marcian's title being sealed by his marriage with the Empress Pulcheria. On Marcian's death the Theodosian dynasty had come to an end, and the choice of a new Emperor rested with the army, whose consent was

---

[1] Diocletian saw the danger of this tendency, and his system of two Augusti and two Caesars was designed to guard against it; but Constantine undid his work in this respect. The great danger was the devolution of the Empire on princes who were weak or afflicted, like Commodus, with *Kaiserwahnsinn*.

in every case necessary. The man of most authority in the army was the general Aspar (*magister militum per orientem*), an Alan by descent, who with his father Ardaburius had distinguished himself thirty-five years before in suppressing the usurper John and helping Valentinian III to his legitimate succession. Aspar's position in the East resembled that of Ricimer in the West. He and his three sons, being Arians and foreigners, could not hope to sit on the imperial throne; and thus the only course open to Aspar was to secure the elevation of one on whose pliancy he might count. He chose Leo, a native of Dacia and an orthodox Christian, who was steward of his own household. Thus Aspar, like Ricimer, was a kingmaker. But when Leo assumed the purple (7th February)—on which occasion the ceremony of coronation by the Patriarch of Constantinople (then Anatolius), was first introduced—he did not prove as amenable to influence as Aspar had hoped; on the contrary, he took measures to reduce the resources of Aspar's family, which by its close relations with the army had considerable power, and was the centre of a large faction of Arians and barbarians. In fact Aspar, though an Alan and not a German, was the representative of German influence in the Empire, and the danger which had threatened the Empire in the reign of Arcadius through the power of Gainas was now repeated. Leo however firmly resisted the aggressiveness of this influence, and in order to neutralise the great fact which worked in Aspar's favour, namely that the bulk and flower of the army consisted of Germans, he formed the plan of recruiting the line from native subjects. For this purpose he chose the hardy race of Isaurian mountaineers, who lived almost like an independent people, little touched by the influence of Hellenism, in the wild regions of Mount Taurus. This is Leo's great original work, for which he deserves the title "Great," more than for his orthodoxy,[1] for which he probably received it. He conceived an idea, whose execution, begun by himself and carried out by his successor, counteracted that danger of German preponderance which threatened the State throughout the fifth century.

---

[1] Leo was popular with the Church. He received high eulogies from his namesake, the bishop of Rome, and from the bishops of the East. *See* the citations of Tillemont, *Hist. des Emp.* vi. p. 364.

Aspar appears to have possessed all the characteristics of an untutored barbarian. Brave and active in war, he was idle and frivolous in peace. During the reign of Marcian, and doubtless also in the reign of Leo, while the Empire enjoyed rest, "he betook himself to relaxation and womanly ease. His pleasures consisted in actors and jugglers and all stage amusements, and spending his time on these ill-famed occupations he lost all count of the things that make for glory."[1] But if he was no longer active as a warrior, he won repute in the humbler part of an energetic citizen or a competent policeman, for in the great fire which laid waste a large part of Constantinople in 465 it is recorded that Aspar exerted himself unsparingly for the public interest.

Leo had made a promise, apparently at the time of his elevation, to raise one of Aspar's sons to the rank of Caesar, and thereby designate him as his successor, in spite of the fact that he was a barbarian. When he delayed to perform this promise, Aspar is said to have seized him by his purple robe and said, "Emperor, it is not meet that he who wears this robe should speak falsely;" to which Leo replied, "Nor yet is it meet that he should be constrained and driven like a slave." This story, which may be true, shows the relations which existed between the king and the kingmaker—the firmness of Leo, the persistence of Aspar. On this occasion, however, Leo yielded, and created one of Aspar's sons Caesar; but the concession was displeasing to the senate and to the orthodox population of Byzantium, as it was a direct encouragement to the Arian party. It appears that a deputation of orthodox clergy and laymen waited on the Emperor, imploring him to appoint a Caesar who did not hold heretical views, and that there were riots and seditions in the city, a protest against the new Caesar.[2] We may say that the chief political feature of the reign was a sort of duel between the Emperor and the general for power and popularity. When Leo undertook the great naval expedition, which but for the incapacity of the commander would have exterminated the kingdom of the Vandals and made his reign really glorious, Aspar was jealous of the fame that Leo might probably gain, and seems to have wished to thwart its success by obtaining the nomination of

[1] Priscus, p. 20.   [2] Zonaras, vol. iii. p. 251 (ed. Dindorf).

Basiliscus, an incompetent commander, who was perhaps disloyal and certainly avaricious.

The struggle came to a critical point in some matter connected with two unknown persons (Tatian and Vivian),[1] and it was then that Leo decided to have recourse to the Isaurians. In this project he was supported by the Isaurian Zeno, who became his son-in-law.[2] Thereupon Ardaburius, the son of Aspar, attempted to gain over the Isaurians to his father's faction, but these intrigues were betrayed to Zeno. Leo then resorted to the abrupt measure of putting to death Aspar and his son Ardaburius (471 A.D.)[3] In consequence of this act, which was probably unwise, the Emperor received the name of "Butcher" (*makelles*). An attempt was also made to kill Patricius, the son of Aspar who had been created Caesar, but he recovered from his wounds; while a third son, Ermenaric, escaped, happening to be absent. It has been said that Leo's motive in removing Aspar and his sons was to secure the succession of his own infant grandson Leo; he may have feared that he would be unable to hold his own against the powerful barbarian family. But the whole drama has a deeper significance as a repetition of that struggle between Roman and barbarian elements in the Empire, which in the days of Arcadius was decided in favour of the former.

The most striking event of Leo's reign was the enormous "Armada," already referred to, which he organised against the kingdom of Gaiseric the Vandal, who had become a formidable foe of the Empire in the Mediterranean waters, but of this it will be more convenient to speak in the following chapter.

Leo was a man of no education, but of natural good sense. He pursued, as we already remarked, the policy of Anthemius and Marcian, and placed a limit on fiscal oppression. Malchus, the historian, who detested Leo and condemned his civil policy as ruinously rapacious, says that he was a sewer of all wicked-

---

[1] Candidus, p. 135 (*F. H. G.* iv.)

[2] Zeno married Ariadne in 458 or 459; Theoph. 5951 A.M. Five years later he became *mag. mil. per or.* At the end of 469 or early in 470 (*ib.* 5962) an attempt was made on his life in Thrace by the wiles of Aspar; but he escaped to Sardica. "Hence Aspar becomes suspected by the Emperor Leo," according to the chronicler. It should be noted that Zeno is said to have aided the escape of Aspar's son Ermenaric (*ib.* 5964).

[3] After the death of Aspar there was an unimportant Gothic rising led by Ostrys, Aspar's squire, whence the Byzantine proverb, "No one is a friend of the dead except Ostrys."

ness, but admits that his subjects, as well as foreigners, considered him "most fortunate," and we may conclude that his reign was on the whole prosperous, though his military operations were unsuccessful.[1] In regard to Malchus' accusations we must remember, on the one hand, that he hated Leo for his religious bigotry, and, on the other hand, that in spite of all alleviations the mode of collecting taxes, combined with the fatal growth of centralisation, gradually wore away the resources of the provinces and affected disastrously their social and moral life. We must judge of an Emperor's civil policy relatively, not absolutely.

Like Marcian, Leo was solicitous to relieve provincial towns that had suffered disasters,[2] and his clemency was celebrated by his admirers. He is reported to have said that a king should distribute pity to those on whom he looks, as the sun distributes heat to those on whom it shines.

A curious detail has survived regarding the manner in which petitioners addressed themselves to him.[3] His unmarried sister resided in a house in the south-west corner of the Augusteum, close to the hippodrome. The Emperor used to pay her a visit with affectionate regularity every week, "because she was modest and a virgin." She erected a statue to him beside her house, and there seems to have been some contrivance in the pillar like a modern letter-box, in which petitioners used to place their memorials ($\pi\iota\tau\tau\acute{a}\kappa\iota a$), and every week one of the imperial staff used to collect them.

Towards the end of his reign the commerce of the Empire met with a serious blow by the loss of Jotaba, an important depôt on the Red Sea. This leads us to give an account of the Persian (Nocalian) adventurer Amorkesos, who "whether he thought that he was not treated with due consideration in Persia, or for some other reason preferred Roman territory, migrated thence to the adjacent province of Arabia." There he supported himself as a brigand, making raids, not on the Romans, but on the Scenite Saracens. His power gradually increased, and he seized the island of Jotaba, which belonged to the Romans, and, driving out the Greek custom-

---

[1] In the acts of the councils there are dark allusions to a great victory obtained by Leo's arms in Pontus. Tillemont, *op. cit.* vi. 367.

[2] Antioch was laid in ruins by an earthquake in 458. The public edifices were rebuilt by the Emperor (Evagr. ii. 12).

[3] Codinus, p. 36.

officers, he instituted himself master of it, and soon became wealthy by receiving the dues from traders. He made himself ruler of some other communes in the neighbourhood, and conceived the desire of becoming a phylarch or satrap of the Saracens of Arabia Petraea, who were nominally dependent on the Roman Emperor. He sent an ecclesiastic to Leo to negotiate the matter, and Leo graciously signified his wish to have a personal interview with Amorkesos. When the latter arrived, he shared the imperial table, was admitted to the meetings of the senate, and even honoured with precedence over the patricians. The Byzantines, it appears, were much scandalised at these privileges accorded to a Persian fire-worshipper, and Leo seems to have been obliged to pretend that his guest intended to become a Christian. On his departure Leo gave him a valuable picture in mosaic,[1] and compelled the members of the senate to present him with other gifts; and, what was more important, he transferred to him the permanent possession of Jotaba, and added more villages to those which he already governed, granting him also the coveted title of phylarch. Malchus finds fault with Leo severely for the invitation of Amorkesos to his court, on the principle that what is distant is most dazzling; and says that it was impolitic to allow the foreigner to see the towns, through which he had to travel, unarmed and defenceless.

One of the great conflagrations which so often destroyed the buildings of Constantinople broke out in 465. The fire ran both from east to west and from north to south, laying waste a wide area, and lasting for four days. The splendid senate house, which had been erected after the destruction of Julian's senate house by fire in the reign of Arcadius, was burnt down, and also the Nymphaeum, directly opposite to it, a building in which those who had not houses of their own used to celebrate their weddings. Countless magnificent residences of private persons were destroyed. It is said that Aspar ran about the streets with a pail of water on his shoulders, urging the people to follow his example, and offering each a silver nummus (*nomisma*) as pay for his activity. There is no hint of the existence of a fire brigade at Constantinople.

---

[1] εἰκόνα τινά χρυσῆν καὶ κατάλιθον—mosaic work on a gold ground. *See* Malchus, fr. 1.

There were still many pagans in the days of Leo, and we must not omit to notice the case of Isocasius, a native of Aegae in Cilicia and a citizen of Antioch, who was accused and tried on the charge of paganism. His case was to be judged by the governor of Bithynia, but Jacobus,[1] the court physician, a remarkable man of that time, who was so much beloved by the higher classes that the senate erected a statue to him in the baths of Zeuxippus, and who, as well as a physician, was an excellent rhetor and philosopher, interfered in his behalf, and obtained Leo's consent that he should be tried in Byzantium by the praetorian prefect Pusaeus. "Do you see in what position you stand," asked the prefect. "I see, and am not surprised," was the reply, "for I am human, and human misfortunes have befallen me. But do you judge me with impartial justice, as you used to judge along with me."[2] Then Isocasius was led away to the church of St. Sophia and baptized.

Leo died on the 3d of February 474, having previously nominated as his successor his grandson Leo, a young child. His wife, Verina, was an ambitious woman who played a considerable part in the Byzantine world after his death. He had two daughters, Ariadne, who married Zeno the Isaurian, and Leontia, the wife of Marcian, son of Anthemius.

[1] Jacobus, although a pagan, was employed by Leo. Cf. Marcellinus, *Chron. ad ann.* 462. The notices in Photius and Suidas are presumably derived from the lost histories of Priscus and Malchus.

[2] Pusaeus and Isocasius had once been colleagues (Theophanes, 5960 A.M.)

CHAPTER II

RICIMER THE PATRICIAN

It was a critical moment in Italy after the death of Valentinian III (455), as there was no male heir of the house of Theodosius. There had been similar situations before, as in 68, when the Julian-Claudian house came to an end; as in 190, when Commodus had died without issue; as in 363, after the death of Julian. Military riots were inevitable, a civil war was possible; and we read in a trustworthy historian[1]: "After this Rome was in a state of disturbance and confusion, and the military forces were divided into two factions, one wishing to elevate Maximus, the other supporting Maximian, a certain Egyptian merchant, who had been successful in Italy and become the steward of Aetius." A third possible candidate was Majorian, the brother-at-arms of Aetius, with whom he had fought against the Franks, and he had the good wishes of Eudoxia, the widowed Empress. Maximus' command of money[2] decided the event in his favour, even as Pertinax had won the Imperium in 190 by bribing the praetorian guards.

He endeavoured to secure himself on the throne by forcing Eudoxia to marry him, and if she had consented, it is just possible that his subjects might have rallied round him and that he might have reigned not brilliantly but securely like Honorius or Valentinian. But Petronius Maximus, though he was a member of the noble Anician house, was not like Marcian; he was not one whom an Augusta would condescend

---

[1] John of Antioch, fr. 201, 206. His account deserves credit because he drew his information from the contemporary Priscus; it is, moreover, internally probable.

[2] In a letter to Serranus, a friend of Maximus, Sidonius Apollinaris notes the wealth of Maximus (*Ep.* ii. 13).

to marry, even for cogent political reasons. If he was really related to British Maximus, who had been subdued by Theodosius, the great-granddaughter of Theodosius had perhaps not forgotten it; but the widow of Valentinian must have known or suspected the instigator of her lord's murder. In any case, the new Augustus was a paltry person, and Eudoxia hated or despised him so much that she is said to have taken the bold and fatal step of summoning Gaiseric the Vandal to overthrow the tyrant,—an act almost worthy of her sister-in-law Honoria. But in this crude shape we can hardly accept the story; John of Antioch mentions it in language which implies that he did not consider it well attested; it was "told by some."[1] The true account seems to be that Gaiseric came of his own accord, seeing that it was a good opportunity for attacking Italy, and considering that the death of Aetius and Valentinian released him from the treaty of 435, which he regarded as a contract made with them personally, not with the Roman republic. The story of the invitation of Eudoxia will then reduce itself to the probability that, vexed by the importunities and threats of Petronius Maximus, she welcomed Gaiseric on his arrival in Italy as a deliverer from an abhorred oppressor.

On the approach of Gaiseric, Maximus, deserted by his supporters, determined to flee from Rome. His departure was attended with riots, and the tyrant was killed by a stone which a soldier cast at him as he was riding from the gates.[2]

Three days later—it was in the first week of June 455—Gaiseric and his Vandals entered Rome. For fourteen days they abode in the city and plundered, but the intervention of Pope Leo and the Church, although it did not protect the city against pillage, violence, and vandalism,[3] seems at least to have preserved it from the evils of massacre and conflagration.

The monarch of the Vandals ravaged Campania, and loaded his ships with the precious things of Rome. He carried with him the Empress Eudoxia and her two daughters, Eudocia and Placidia. Gaiseric had conceived the idea of an alliance with

---

[1] οἱ δέ φασι (John of Antioch, fr. 201, 206).

[2] Ib. Jordanes (Get. 45) notices that Maximus was afraid of the foederati.

[3] Compare Prosper of Aquitaine, nec ab ecclesiarum despoliatione abstinens quas et sacris vasibus exinanitis et sacerdotum administratione privatas non jam divini cultus loca sed suorum jussit esse habitacula in universum captivi populi ordinem sacrus sed praecipue nobilitati et religioni infensus ut non discerneretur hominibus magis an Deo bellum intulisset.

the Theodosian house. It was no new idea; Athaulf the Visigoth had married Placidia, and Attila had perhaps wished to marry Honoria. It was not strange that a marriage should be determined on between Huneric and Eudocia.

The question was, who was to be Emperor? At Rome things had come to a deadlock, but on this occasion Gaul intervened. Marcus Maecilius Avitus, the man who had fought by the side of Aetius, and had, in the great crisis of Europe, decided by his persuasions the king of Tolosa to march with the Romans against the Scythians, was proclaimed Emperor, first at Tolosa and then at Arelate (9th July 455). It is important to observe that it was by the united voices of the Visigoths and the Gallo-Romans[1] that he was called to fill the vacant throne as the successor of Maximus, from whom he had received the appointment of master of soldiers. Of his short reign we hear little, though his son-in-law, Sidonius Apollinaris the poet, has recorded many personal details about the man himself. We know, however, that it was marked by successes against German enemies, and here again it is important to notice that the Visigoths identified themselves with the Empire.

The Suevian general, Count Ricimer, who now makes his entry on the stage, was sent by Avitus to Sicily to operate against the fleet of the Vandals. Marcian, who did not hesitate to recognise Avitus, had already sent an embassy to Gaiseric to remonstrate with him on his Italian expedition and on the captivity of the imperial ladies. The arms or skill of Count Ricimer now administered a blow to the Vandalic navy, according to one account in Sicilian waters, according to another statement in the neighbourhood of Corsica (456).[2]

While Suevian Ricimer protected one part of the Empire against the Vandals, Theodoric II, king of the Visigoths, was protecting another part of the Empire against the Suevians. In conjunction with the Burgundians, and at the instance of Avitus, he invaded Spain[3]; he defeated the dwellers in Gallaecia, who harried Roman territory, in the great battle of Urbicus (near

---

[1] His friends told Avitus that on his elevation depended the safety of the world — *tibi pareat orbis ni pereat* (Sidon. Apoll. *Carm.* vii. 517).

[2] *See* the *Chronicle* of Idatius.

[3] Jordanes, *Get.* 44; Idatius, *Chron.*

Astorga)[1]; he took the town of Bracara, where the Roman Count Asterius had in former days slaughtered the Vandals of Gunderic; and he put to death the Suevian king Rechiar. This was a mortal blow to Suevic power, and paved the way for Visigothic Hispania.

Avitus meanwhile had crossed the Alps. It seems to have been hardly a prudent step; it seems to have been hardly necessary. At all events it made his position untenable. We may well ask why he did not decide to add Arelate to the number of imperial capitals—the city where he had many friends, the city which had received him first, and which was not too far from friendly Tolosa. But Arelate, the capital of the illegitimate Constantine, did not seem a suitable residence to legitimate Avitus. He abandoned the city of the Rhone to take up his abode in the city of the Tiber. But there he was not welcome; he was looked upon as a sort of interloper, of insufficiently defined position. He was acceptable neither to the army nor to the senate, and his behaviour does not appear to have tended to make him popular. The circumstances of his fall are thus related by a historian, who, we are justified in supposing, derived his facts from the contemporary writer Priscus [2]:—

"When Avitus reigned at Rome there was famine in the city, and the people blaming Avitus compelled him to remove from the city of the Romans the allies from Gaul who had entered it along with him (that so there might be fewer mouths to feed). He also dismissed the Goths whom he had brought for the protection of Rome, having distributed among them money which he obtained by selling to merchants bronze stripped from public works, for there was no gold in the imperial treasury. This excited the Romans to revolt when they saw their city stripped of its adornments.

"But Majorian and Ricimer, no longer held in fear of the Goths, openly rebelled, so that Avitus was constrained—terrified on the one hand by the prospect of internal troubles, on the other hand by the hostilities of the Vandals—to withdraw from Rome and set out for Gaul. But Majorian and Ricimer attacked him on the road and forced him to flee into a sanctuary, where he abdicated the throne and put off his imperial apparel. But Majorian's soldiers did not cease to blockade him, until he died of starvation, after a reign of eight months; others say that he was strangled."

---

[1] 5th October 456 (Idatius). The successes of the expedition were almost synchronous with the fall of their initiator Avitus.

[2] John of Antioch, fr. 202. This notice is our sole authority for the vandalism of Avitus, which, I have no doubt, was the direct cause of Majorian's law for the preservation of public buildings.

According to another account Avitus reached Gaul safely, and there collected an army with which he crossed the Alps once more to assert his contemned authority, but Count Ricimer routed him at Placentia ; he was deposed from the throne and made bishop of the city which witnessed his discomfiture (October 456).

The deposition of Avitus caused a new crisis. It is quite conceivable that at this juncture, or at the death of Valentinian in the year before, the western line of Emperors might have ceased to exist, as it ceased to exist twenty years later. In 476 the presence of the barbarian Odovacar was an essential element in the situation, but in 455 or in 456 the only barbarian whom we can conceive as acting the part of Odovacar was the Vandal Gaiseric. A temporary cessation of a separate imperial rule in the West did, however, take place on several occasions before the deposition of Romulus Augustulus. One of these temporary cessations followed on the overthrow of Avitus. These intervals are often called interregnums; it is natural to say that from October 456 to April 457 there was an interregnum in the West. And the expression really represents the actual situation; but we must not forget that, from a theoretical point of view, the expression is not correct. Legally, Marcian was the sole head of the Empire from the fall of Avitus to his own death at the end of January 457, and Leo was the sole head of the Empire from the death of Marcian to the elevation of Majorian.

It has often been remarked that at the beginning of 457 the situation in Italy was similar to the situation in Constantinople.[1] In both cases the solution of the difficulty depended on the action of a military leader of barbarian birth; Aspar held a similar position to that of Ricimer. Both were the makers of Emperors; neither aspired to be an Emperor himself.

The elevation of Julius Valerius Majorian, the man who had fought with Aetius, the man who had been the chosen

---

[1] Von Ranke has expressed this very well in the following sentence: "Vergegenwärtigt man sich die Situation die damit eintrat, so besteht ihr Wesen vornehmlich darin, dass nun in den beiden Reichstheilen der Gegensatz der effectiven Macht zu der bisherigen Ordnung der Dinge in volle Evidenz gelangte." The supports of Theodosius and Valentinian had been hidden, as it were, by a curtain; the curtain was removed (456-457) and the German supporters stood revealed.

candidate of Eudoxia after the death of Valentinian, and who had combined with Ricimer to suppress Avitus, took place on the 1st April.[1] This elevation rested on a very different combination from that which had crowned Avitus; it was initiated by the proposal of the Emperor Leo, and obtained the consent of Ricimer. It was also acceptable to the Roman senate, for Majorian was a thorough Roman. The laws which he passed during his reign for the preservation of the buildings of Rome were a direct reflection on his predecessor Avitus.[2]

There were two tasks to be accomplished by the new Augustus, both necessary for the security of his seat on the throne. He must, in the first place, quell the Gallo-Roman and Visigothic opposition, and subdue or conciliate the provincials who had been roused to wrath by the death of Avitus. It was the reverse problem, the conciliation of Roman and Italian goodwill, that the Gallic Avitus had been called upon to solve, and it was because he failed therein that he had fallen. It is evident that at this period the enmity between the Romans and the Gallic provincials had an important influence on public affairs. Majorian entered Gaul with an army, and found the Burgundians—the friends of Avitus—in league with the citizens of Lugdunensis Prima against himself.[3] A conciliation, however, was effected with the help of Avitus' son-in-law Sidonius, and Majorian advanced to the relief of Arelate, which the Visigoths were besieging. As Aetius had driven Theodoric back thirty years before, so Aegidius, Majorian's general, drove back a new Theodoric from the walls; and most firm compacts of peace were made between the Augustus Majorian and the King Theodoric.[4]

Majorian had accomplished the first task, but the other was harder. It was absolutely indispensable that an Emperor, whose reign was to be permanent, should win universal confidence

---

[1] In February he had been made *magister militum*.

[2] The address of Majorian to the senate (Novella i. *de ortu imperii divi Majoriani*) is a manifesto which announces the inauguration of a new era (*see* above, p. 30). Ricimer is thus mentioned: *Erit apud nos cum parente patricioque nostro Ricimere rei militaris pervigil cura*. His diligence in relieving the oppression of the curial system has been noticed elsewhere. His first Novel, *de aedificiis publicis* (dated Ravenna, 11th July 458), provides for the preservation of the public buildings, and checks the "discolouring of the face of the venerable city." He also endeavoured to check the political evil of celibacy (Nov. vii.)

[3] Prosp. Contin. 457 A.D.

[4] Idatius, *Chronicle* (spring 459).

by proving himself equal to the great emergency of the time; he must "preserve the state of the Roman world."[1] And just at this moment the great emergency was the hostility of the Vandals, who in their ships harried the Roman provinces and infested the Mediterranean waters. It might have seemed that Avitus, under whose auspices Count Ricimer worsted the fleet of the foe at Corsica or at Sicily, had in some sense met the difficulty. But the blow was not decisive; it did not paralyse the hostilities of the Vandals. The words of an historian indicate that Avitus felt the necessity of facing this problem, and also his inability to grapple with it: "he was afraid of the wars with the Vandals."[2]

Majorian prepared an expedition against Africa on a grand scale; his fleet numbered 300 ships, and was collected in a Spanish port, probably New Carthage. The hopes of the West were awakened, and their eyes were fixed on the preparations of Majorian. But a curious fatality attended all expeditions undertaken against the Vandals, whether they proceeded from Old Rome or from New Rome, or from both together. The expedition of Castinus had collapsed in 422, that of Aspar had failed in 430, the armament of Ardaburius had not even reached its destination in 441, and now the preparations of Majorian fell through in 460. Gaiseric ravaged the coasts of Spain, and incapacitated the Roman ships before they left the port.[3] Yet another expedition, and one on a far larger scale, was to meet with discomfiture; and more than seventy years were to elapse until the rise of the great Justinian, when the numerous failures were to be blotted out by the success of Belisarius.

This misfortune led to the fall of Majorian; he had forfeited confidence; it appeared that he was not able to "preserve the state of the Roman world." He returned from Spain to Gaul, and after a sojourn in Arles[4] passed into Italy, without an army. At Tortona the officers of Count Ricimer, who had judged him unworthy of empire, seized him, stripped him of

---

[1] Nov. i. Maj. *Romani orbis statum . . . propitia divinitate servemus.*

[2] See Priscus, fr. 27, who is almost verbally followed by John of Antioch, fr. 203.

[3] Majorian made a "disgraceful treaty" with Gaiseric (John of Antioch, *ib.*)

[4] He celebrated games at Arles, at which Sidonius Apollinaris was present (*Ep.* i. 11).

the imperial purple, and beheaded him (7th August 461). It is natural enough that only two alternatives could be entertained by the Suevian count, who had the army at his back; he could tolerate a strong Emperor, capable of defending the Empire, or he could tolerate a puppet-Emperor, who depended absolutely on his own will. But an Emperor who was just strong enough to assume an independent position, and was not strong enough to contend with the enemies of the State—such an one was naturally not acceptable to the count. Ricimer himself seemed determined not to leave Italy, probably judging that its security against the Vandals depended on the constant presence of an able general with a strong army; and he did actually defend it in the north against the Ostrogoths of Pannonia and against the Alemanni of the Upper Rhine. He was determined to hold Italy at all costs; he associated himself with the foreign foederati, being himself a Sueve; and he cherished a bitter hatred against the Vandals;—these were the chief elements in his position. His hatred against the Vandals was due to a family feud. He was the nephew of Wallia, and Wallia had fought against the Vandals in Spain; wherefore Gaiseric hated him, and he reciprocated the hatred.

The death of Majorian was followed in less than four months by the election of Libius Severus, a Lucanian. He was elected by the senate with the consent of Ricimer and proclaimed at Ravenna (19th November 461); and though he reigned four years—four months less than Majorian—he did nothing; he was only a figure-head; Ricimer was the true sovereign. Stilicho had guided the councils of Honorius, Aetius had guided the councils of Valentinian; but the personalities of Honorius and Valentinian, weak though they both were, influenced affairs to a certain extent; it would be going too far to say that either Aetius or even Stilicho was a virtual Emperor. Ricimer was the first German who had become a virtual king of Italy[1]; he is the link between Stilicho and Odovacar.

It might seem that at this juncture Italy might have

---

[1] His monogram appears on the reverse of the coins of Severus. Severus died 18 Kal. Sept. (15th August) at Rome (*Anon. Cuspiniani*), 465. According to the Chronicle of Cassiodorus, *ut dicitur Ricimeris fraude Severus Romae in Palatio veneno peremptus est.* If this is true, Ricimer had a hand in the death of no less than four Emperors.

received another Augustus from Gaul, and that Aegidius, the general and friend of Majorian, might have crossed the Alps to avenge Majorian's death. But Aegidius was occupied with the task of defending southern Gaul against the Visigoths, who, shaking themselves loose after the death of Avitus from the bond which attached them to the Empire, were attempting to extend their power in the province of Narbonensis. We find him in 463 winning a great battle at Orleans,[1] and in the following year he died.

Another opponent of Ricimer in another quarter was the Count Marcellinus. We see him in Sicily in the year 461 in command of an army chiefly consisting of Hunnic auxiliaries (Scythians); he had been probably posted there by Majorian to protect the island against the Vandals. But Ricimer operated upon the cupidity of the Huns by bribes to induce them to leave the service of Marcellinus and enter his own.[2] Then Marcellinus, fearing danger and conscious that he could not vie with Ricimer in riches, abandoned Sicily and returned to Dalmatia, where a few years later we find him ruling as if he were the king thereof, even as Ricimer ruled in Italy and as Aegidius and Syagrius ruled in Gaul. At this time Gaul, Italy, and Dalmatia were practically independent kingdoms. On the departure of Marcellinus, who seems to have defended the island ably, Gaiseric sent his Vandals and auxiliary Moors to ravage the island. A pacific embassy from Ricimer did not avail, but another embassy sent at the same time by the Emperor Leo induced Gaiseric to come to terms at last in regard to the ladies of the Theodosian house, whom he still retained at Carthage. He carried out his determination of uniting Eudocia in marriage with his son Huneric, but he sent her mother Eudoxia and her sister Placidia to Constantinople; in return he received a certain share of the property of Valentinian III as the dowry of Eudocia.

But now Gaiseric posed as the protector and champion of the Theodosian house against the upstart Emperors in Italy. Olybrius, a member of the noble Anician gens, had married Placidia, and Gaiseric demanded that he should be acknowledged as Emperor. The situation in 463 is described by Priscus[3] as

---

[1] Cf. Idatius, xlv. *Aegidius comes utriusque militiae in Armoricana provincia* defeated Frederic the brother of Theodoric.
[2] *See* Priscus, fr. 29.   [3] Fr. 30.

follows: "The western Romans were afraid concerning Marcellinus, lest, his power increasing, he should wage war against them; for they were involved in diverse difficulties on other sides; they were threatened by the Vandals, and they were threatened by Aegidius, a man of the western Galatians [we are reminded of Celtic reminiscences in the East], who had fought campaigns with Majorian and had a very large power around him, and was indignant on account of the slaying of the Emperor (Majorian). Hitherto dissensions with the Goths in Gaul withheld him from war against the Italiots. For he fought valiantly against them, contending for border-territory, and performed in that war the greatest deeds of prowess."

We see from this account that the cause of western Rome, the cause of Italy, and the cause of Ricimer were all closely bound together, and that the Italiots looked on Ricimer as their protector. "On these accounts the western Romans sent ambassadors to the eastern Romans, asking them to bring about a reconciliation with Marcellinus and with the Vandals. To Marcellinus was sent Phylarchus, who prevailed on him not to wage war against the Romans; but then having crossed over to the Vandals, he retired ineffectual." Gaiseric claimed all the inheritance left by Valentinian in Italy and also the inheritance of Aetius, whose son Gaudentius he retained in captivity. He led a great expedition against Italy and Sicily, ravaged the unprotected parts of the country, and took undefended towns. There was no efficient navy in Italy to operate against him; and as he was at peace with New Rome, Leo could send no ships to the assistance of Italy. It will be remembered how in the days of Valentinian III Attila was at peace with Ravenna and at war with Constantinople; now in regard to Gaiseric the position was reversed. Priscus makes the remark that the division of the Empire greatly injured "the affairs of the Romans in the West"; it was apparent that their great chance of safety lay in the support of the East.

Accordingly Ricimer, the foe of Gaiseric, begins to enter into closer relations with the Emperor Leo. For a year and six months after the death of Severus, in November 465, no successor was appointed, but at length Leo deigned to select Anthemius as his colleague, and Ricimer's acceptance of an Emperor nominated by Leo indicated a close alliance of interests. The common interest was war against the Vandals; not only Italy and Sicily were threatened, but the entire commerce of the Mediterranean; Africa was now what Illyria had been in the third century B.C., or what Cilicia had been in the first.

Anthemius had married the daughter of Marcian; and thus he might be considered in some sort connected with the house of Theodosius, and his pretensions might be set against those of Gaiseric's candidate, the husband of Placidia. He was the grandson of that Anthemius who guided the Empire during the childhood of Pulcheria and Theodosius. The alliance between Ricimer and the new Emperor was sealed by a marriage of the Patrician with Anthemius' daughter. The elder Placidia had married Athaulf, her granddaughter Eudocia had married Huneric, both indeed under a certain compulsion; yet Anthemius afterwards professed to regard it as a great condescension to have surrendered his daughter to the barbarian count.

The expedition, which was organised to overthrow the monarchy of the Vandals, was on a grand and impressive scale, but it ended in a miserable failure. Its success was paralysed by lukewarmness and even treachery both in the East and in the West.

The number of vessels that set sail from Constantinople is said to have been 1113, and the total number of men who embarked was calculated as exceeding 100,000. But unfortunately Leo, under the influence of his wife Verina and his friend Aspar, appointed as general a man who was both incompetent and untrustworthy, his wife's brother Basiliscus. Aspar, it appears, was not over-anxious that Leo's position should be strengthened by such an exploit as the subversion of the Vandal kingdom; he schemed therefore to procure the election of a general whose success was extremely improbable.[1]

The western armament of Anthemius obeyed a more efficient commander. The pagan Marcellinus, who, in defiance of Emperors, ruled in Dalmatia as an independent prince,[2] was

---

[1] Compare Idatius, xlv. *Asparem degradatum ad privatam vitam filiumque ejus occisum, adversus Romanum imperium, sicut detectique sunt, Wandalis consulentes.*

[2] Marcellinus, *Chron. Marcellinus occidentis Patricius idemque paganus.*

reconciled with Leo, and he left the palace of Diocletian and the city of the tepid Jader[1] to take the command of the Italian fleet. A Roman was now going forth from Illyria to subdue the pirates of Africa; seven hundred years before, the Romans, before their great conflict with the African power, had gone forth to subdue the pirates of Illyria. But here too lay a disturbing element. The participation of Marcellinus in the project alienated Ricimer, who was his enemy; and just as Aspar regarded the project with disfavour, Ricimer, who, as has been already remarked, held in the West a somewhat similar position to that of Aspar in the East, also stood aloof.

The plan of operations was that the eastern forces should be divided into two parts, and that thus the Vandals should be attacked at three points at the same time. Basiliscus himself was to sail directly against Carthage. Heraclius, another general, having taken up the forces of Egypt on his way, was to disembark at Tripolis, and having occupied that town was to march to Carthage by land. Marcellinus, with the Italian forces, was to surprise the Vandals in Sardinia, and sail thence to join the eastern armies at Carthage.

If the commander-in-chief had not been Basiliscus, and if the opponent had not been Gaiseric, the expedition would have easily succeeded. But Gaiseric, though physically the least, was mentally the greatest of the barbarians of his time. He was small in stature, ugly in countenance, but in cunning he was without an equal. He veiled the machinations of his thoughts under a silence that was rarely broken, and he despised luxury, although he was avaricious as well as ambitious. Even as it was, though Basiliscus had such a foe to cope with, success was within the grasp of his hand. The invaders were welcome to the Catholics of Africa, who were sorely persecuted by their Arian lords.[2] Marcellinus accomplished his work in Sardinia without difficulty; Heraclius met no obstacle in executing his part of the project; and the galleys of Basiliscus scattered the fleet of the Vandals in the neighbourhood of Sicily. On hearing of this disaster, Gaiseric gave up all for

---

[1] *Tepidum* is the adjective which Lucan applies to the Jader, the river which "runs out" near "long Salonae."

[2] An account of the persecutions of Africa will be found in the five books of Victor Vitensis, *Historia persecutionis provinciae Africanae*, written about 486. See Ebert, *op. cit.* i. 433 *sqq*. There is a new edition by Petschenig.

lost; the Roman general had only to strike a decisive blow and Carthage would not have resisted. But he let the opportunity slip, and, taking up his station in a haven at some distance from Carthage, he granted to the humble prayers of his wily opponent a respite of five days, of which Gaiseric made good use. He prepared a new fleet and a number of fireships. The winds favoured his designs, and he suddenly bore down on the Roman armament, which, under the combined stress of surprise, adverse wind, and the destructive ships of fire, was routed and at least half destroyed. Basiliscus fled with the remnant to Sicily, to join Marcellinus, whose energy and resources might have possibly retrieved the disaster; but the hand of an assassin, inspired perhaps by Ricimer, rendered this hope futile.[1] Heraclius, who had not reached Carthage when he heard of the defeat of the fleet, retraced his steps, and Basiliscus returned to Constantinople, where amid popular odium [2] he led a life of retirement at Heraclea on the Propontis, until he appeared on the scene of public life again after Leo's death.

The failure of this expedition, organised on such a grand scale that it might have seemed invincible, must have produced a very great moral effect, somewhat like the moral effect produced in Europe by the collapse of the Spanish Armada. The Roman Empire had put forth all its strength and had signally failed, not against the combined powers of the barbarians, but against one barbaric nation. This must have not only raised the pretensions and arrogance of the Vandals themselves, but increased the contempt of other German nations for the Roman power; it was felt to be a humiliating disaster by the government at Constantinople, while the government in Italy was too habituated to defeat to be gravely affected. Immense sums of money had been laid out on equipping the armament, and its failure produced a state of bankruptcy in the imperial treasury, which lasted for about thirty years.

The idea was abroad that the arrival in Italy of Anthemius, the political son of Leo, if I may venture to use the

---

[1] Anon. Cusp. gives August 467 as the date of Marcellinus' death, but the Chronicle of Cassiodorus and that of Count Marcellinus give 468 (second consulate of Anthemius). The words of the latter chronicle are: "dum Romanis contra Wandalos apud Carthaginem pugnantibus opem auxiliumque fert ab iisdem dolo confoditur pro quibus palam venerat pugnaturus."

[2] He was obliged to seek refuge in the sanctuary of St. Sophia.

expression, was the inauguration of a return to unity; and this formed the theme of the panegyric of Sidonius Apollinaris on the Emperor Anthemius. He hails Constantinople thus—

> salve sceptrorum columen, regina orientis,
> orbis Roma tui,

and describes the education of Anthemius in terms of the highest eulogy. Anthemius was suspiciously inclined to paganism, and the pagan character of the poem written by the future bishop of Clermont did not offend him; his predecessor Severus is described as having increased the number of the gods. Ricimer is introduced as

> invictus Ricimer quem publica fata respiciunt.

The poet was made prefect of Rome.

But in Italy the Greek Anthemius was not popular. He was too fond of philosophy or thaumaturgy; he loved strange doctrines; he was inclined to be "Hellenic," in the bad sense of the word. And in spite of his high standard of justice and honest attempts to administer the laws—in one of his own laws he states a fair ideal of equity—he does not seem to have been looked on with favour by the Italians. Soon his relations to Ricimer changed from friendliness or mutual tolerance to distrust and hostility; the father-in-law regretted that he had married his daughter Alypia to a *barbarian;* the son-in-law retorted with the contemptuous epithets Galatian and Greekling (*Graeculus*). And in this contest, in spite of the unpopularity of Anthemius, the senate and the people espoused his cause against the Suevian.

Thus it came to pass that in the year 472 Italy was practically divided into two kingdoms, the Emperor reigning at Rome, the Patrician ruling at Milan. Epiphanius, the bishop of Pavia, was employed to bring about a reconciliation—a characteristic instance of the position of the Church at this period—but the army of Ricimer soon besieged Rome. Leo had overcome the power of Aspar in the East; was his "son" Anthemius to overcome the power of Ricimer in the West? For the two problems were similar; and there is a dark notice in a chronicle which suggests that the opposition of Aspar and his sons to Leo may have had hidden links of connection with the opposition of Ricimer to Anthemius.[1]

The hostilities at Rome lasted for five months, the senate and people siding with the Emperor,[2] while Ricimer headed the multitude of his own barbarians. Along with the besieger was the Scyrian Odovacar, the son of Edecon, destined soon to become famous. Ricimer guarded the Tiber and cut off the supplies; the Romans were soon pressed by hunger and resolved to fight. An army under Billimer had come from Gaul to assist them. The engagement resulted in heavy losses on the imperial side, and the victor subdued the rest by treachery.[3]

Gaiseric, it will be remembered, had wished to have a voice in the election of an Emperor and to elevate Olybrius, the husband of the younger Placidia. At this time Olybrius was at Constantinople, and his Vandal connections made him a suspicious person in the eyes of Leo, who planned a curious stratagem. Hearing of the dangers of his colleague Anthemius at Rome, he employed Olybrius on a mission thither to compass the reconciliation of the two opponents. At the same time he sent a private messenger to Anthemius with a letter instructing him to put Olybrius to death. The artifice was frustrated, as Ricimer intercepted the letter.[4]

This circumstance led to the consummation which Leo least wished. After the success gained in the battle, Ricimer invested Olybrius with the purple; and the new Emperor might claim with some fairness to be a member of the Theodosian house. As for Anthemius, when his adherents had surrendered to "the barbarians" and left him "naked," he disguised himself and mingled with the mendicants who begged in the church of St. Chrysogonus. There he was beheaded by Gundobad, Ricimer's nephew (4th July 472).[5]

---

[1] *Cassiodori Chronicon*, under the year 469 (consulate of Marcian and Zeno). *Ardaburius imperium tentans jussu Anthemii exilio deportatur.* Is it necessary to consider that *Ardaburius* is a mistake for *Arvandus*, prefect of Gaul? May not the son of Aspar have aspired to become an Augustus in the West, supported perhaps by Ricimer?

The conspiracy of Romanus against Anthemius is mentioned by John of Antioch, fr. 207.

[2] *Ib.* fr. 209 : Ἀνθεμίῳ μὲν συνεμάχουν οἵ τε ἐν τέλει καὶ ὁ δῆμος.

[3] *Ib.*

[4] This curious transaction is related by John Malalas, and is quite credible, though historians seem never to have observed it. Compare my note on "The Emperor Olybrius," *English Historical Review*, July 1886.

[5] John of Antioch, fr. 209, says, "Gundobad, Ricimer's brother," and afterwards speaks of Gundibalos as his

The position of affairs was now the reverse of what it had been in the days of Honorius and Stilicho, or in the days of Valentinian and Aetius. When dissensions arose in 408 between the father-in-law and the son-in-law, the son-in-law had the upper hand; and when there was war in 472 between the father-in-law and the son-in-law, the son-in-law also had the upper hand. But in the earlier case the son-in-law was the Emperor, in the later case the son-in-law was the foreign general.

Ricimer did not survive his victim long; he died in less than six weeks[1]; and the new Emperor whom he had created survived him by only two months.[2]

The death of Ricimer, notwithstanding his anomalous position, was a blow to Italy of the same kind as the deaths of Stilicho and Aetius. While Stilicho lived, there was an able general to protect the peninsula against Alaric; when he died, Alaric entered and laid waste. While Aetius lived, there was a general formidable to Gaiseric; when he died, Gaiseric sailed over and plundered. While Ricimer lived, the barbarians did not venture to enter Italy; but four years after his death, they not only entered but they occupied. If Olybrius had lived longer and been a stronger man—he has no personality in history—his Theodosian connection might have aided him to stay the approach of the day when Italy would be ruled by a German king.

nephew. The fact is, that a sister of Ricimer married Gundiok, king of the Burgundians, and their son was Gundobad. From 470 to 490 Gundobad was "tetrarch" of the Burgundians, from 490 to 501 "ex besse dominus," from 501 to 516 sole king. See F. Bluhme's preface to the *Leges Burgundionum*, M. G. H. *Leges*, vol. iii.

[1] 18th August 472. He died, like Attila, from vomiting blood (John of Antioch, fr. 292, 2).

[2] 23d October 472. He died of dropsy (*ib.*)

CHAPTER III

ZENO

ZENO[1] the Isaurian had succeeded to the power and influence of Aspar and Ardaburius at Leo's court, and he was marked out by his marriage with Ariadne, the Emperor's daughter, as a probable successor. He was hardly less rude than Aspar, for the Isaurians were semi-barbarous freebooters, but he had the advantage of not being a German. When Leo I. died in 474 his grandson Leo, the infant son of Zeno and Ariadne, was proclaimed Emperor, in accordance with his grandfather's wishes. The child conferred the imperial dignity on his father and died in the same year, leaving to Zeno nominally as well as actually the sole power.

Zeno was unpopular, and there was a strong spirit of public hatred against the Isaurians, who formed a portion of the army, and by their violence often irritated the inhabitants of Constantinople. Moreover, the elevation of Zeno was not pleasing to the Empress-mother Verina, a woman of great energy and capacity for intrigue. Her brother Basiliscus, who

---

[1] Zeno's original name is variously stated as (1) Tarasikodissa (by Candidus, who, being an Isaurian, should have known); (2) Arikmesos (by Eustathius of Epiphania); (3) Trasalikaios (by Theophanes). He adopted the name Zeno from a distinguished Isaurian. His mother's name was Lallis, his father's Rusumbladeotus, his brother's Longinus—apparently a common name in Isauria. He was married to Arcadia before he married Ariadne, and by her had a son, Zeno, of whom something more will be said. Zeno was a very fast runner, according to the Anonymus Valesii, who seems to have known something about him, and had a marked liking for him. His speed of foot was attributed to a physical peculiarity— *perhibent de eo quod patellas in genucula non habuisset sed mobiles fuissent ut etiam cursu velocissimo ultra modum hominum haberetur* (*Anon. Val.* 9, 40.) Fast running was an Isaurian characteristic; compare the marvellous speed of Indacus, who took part in the revolt of Illus (Suidas, *sub* Ἰνδακός, John Ant. p. 617).

had lived in retirement since his conduct of the Vandalic expedition, aspired to the throne, and he was supported in his designs by the general Illus, a man of considerable influence and ability. The result was that Zeno's position was so insecure that, in the face of a formidable conspiracy, he was obliged to flee to Isauria, with his wife Ariadne and his mother Lallis, at the end of the year 475 (November). Verina was scheming to place her paramour Patricius on the throne, but her endeavours turned to the profit of her brother Basiliscus, whom the ministers and senators elected to the purple after Zeno's flight. This change of power was an opportunity for the Byzantines to settle accounts of old standing with the obnoxious countrymen of Zeno, and a colossal massacre (ἀμύθητος σφαγή) of Isaurians took place in the capital. War was carried on in Isauria against Zeno by Illus and his brother Trocundus, but they soon deserted the cause of Basiliscus, who had already made himself odious by his extortions, and went over to his rival. His nephew Harmatius, a young fop of whom I shall give some account hereafter, was then created *magister militum per Thracias*, and sent with an army against the forces of Zeno and Illus, which were advancing against Constantinople. Illus induced him also to desert the usurper, and this desertion decided the fall of Basiliscus and the restoration of Zeno (July 477). Theodoric, the son of Theodemir, and his Ostrogoths, who had been settled in Lower Moesia, had embraced the cause of Zeno.[1]

In his reign of twenty months Basiliscus had made himself very unpopular. He favoured the heresy of monophysitism, he exacted money from bishops, and was only prevented by a crowd of monks from doing violence to Acacius the Patriarch of Constantinople. His fiscal rapacity was so great that he did not spare from severe taxation even the humblest mechanic, and it was said that the world was full of tears at his exactions. Yet we also hear that he contributed 50 lbs. of gold to restore Gabala in Syria, which suffered from an earthquake

---

[1] See *Anon. Val.* 9, 42 : *Zeno confortans Isauros intra provinciam deinde misit ad civitatem Novam (Novi), ubi erat Theodericus dux Gothorum, filius Walameris* [Walamir was really his uncle, but the Anonymus Val. shared the mistake of the Greek historians], *et eum invitavit in solacium* [= assistance] *sibi adversus Basiliscum, objectans militem, post biennium veniens, obsidens civitatem Constantinopolim.*

in his reign. He and his family were banished by Zeno to a fortress in Cappadocia, where they were mured up and allowed to perish of hunger.[1]

A public misfortune of a most deplorable nature, which has probably had manifold indirect results of a negative character, occurred in the reign of Basiliscus, and helped, as accidents in superstitious ages always help, to render his government unpopular. This was an immense conflagration, which, beginning in the bazaar of the bronzesmiths, spread far and wide, reducing to ashes the colonnades of the public square, with the adjoining houses. But more serious than this was the destruction of the Basilike, the library founded by Julian, which contained no fewer than 120,000 books. Among these rolls, the intestine of a serpent, 120 feet long, on which the *Iliad* and *Odyssey* were written in golden characters, is specially mentioned. A still greater disaster was the destruction of the palace of Lausus, which contained among its splendours some of the most beautiful works of Greek plastic art, the Cnidian Aphrodite, the Lindian Athene, and the Samian Here. But for this fire these precious works might possibly have been still in existence, and it reminds us that the chief cause of the loss of works of art was not christian vandalism, but rather the love of art, which collected monuments from their original scattered homes and exposed them in a mass to increased dangers of destruction in a large town. How far the loss of the library influenced the condition of culture in the succeeding centuries, it would be hard to determine.

Zeno has never been a favourite with historians, and Finlay perhaps was the first who was ready to say a good word for him. "The great work of his reign," writes Finlay, "was the formation of an army of native troops to serve as a counterpoise to the barbarian mercenaries"; and he goes on to remark that the man who successfully resisted the schemes and forces

---

[1] Basiliscus had created his son Marcus Emperor. The fate of him and his family is thus described by *Anon. Val.* (9, 43): "Basiliscus fleeing to the church, enters the baptistery with his wife and sons. Zeno gives him the security of an oath that his blood will not be shed (*securum esse de sanguine*); so, leaving the church, he was shut up with his wife and sons in a dry cistern, where they perished of cold." *See* also the *Paschal Chronicle*. The ghost of Basiliscus appears in a Cretan tragedy (published by M. Sathas in his Κρητικόν θέατρον) entitled Ζήνων. Longinus, Anastasius, Sebastian, Harmatius, and other leading men are introduced.

of the great Theodoric cannot have been contemptible.[1] Yet even from the pages of Malchus we can see that he was not so bad as he was painted, Malchus himself confessing that he was in some respects superior to Leo, especially less greedy. He was not popular, for his religious policy of conciliation did not find general favour; he was not personally brave; and he was an Isaurian. But he was inclined to be mild; he desired to abstain from employing capital punishment. In fiscal administration he was perhaps less successful than his predecessors and his successor Anastasius. Malchus states that Zeno wasted all that Leo left in the treasury by donatives to his friends[2] and inaccuracy in checking his accounts. In 477 the funds were very low, hardly sufficient to supply pay for the army. But the blame of this may rather rest with Basiliscus, who, reigning precariously for twenty months, must have been obliged to incur large expenses, to supply which he was driven to extortion, and in the following years the Ostrogoths were an incubus on the exchequer; while we must further remember that since the enormous outlay incurred by Leo's naval expedition the treasury had been in financial difficulties, which only a ruler of strict economy and business habits, like the succeeding Emperor Anastasius, could have remedied. Zeno was not a man of business, he was indolent and in many respects weak. But in defending him we need not go further than the admission of Malchus (who throughout seems to censure in Zeno weakness rather than evil inclination), that his reign would have been a good one but for the influence of one Sebastian, who was like Eutropius or Chrysaphius, and introduced a system of venality. From an adverse witness this is an important admission. Of Sebastian[3] we hear very little, and we may suppose that his influence was not permanent.

---

[1] *History of Greece*, vol. i. p. 180.
[2] The Anonymus Valesii, whom some have wished to identify with Maximian, the bishop of Ravenna who stands beside Justinian in the mosaics of St. Vitalis, has a great liking for Zeno, and represents him as very popular: *Zeno recordatus est amore senatus et populi, munificus omnibus se ostendit, ita ut omnes ei gratias agerent. Senatu Romano et populo tuitus est ut etiam ei imagines per diversa loca in urbe Roma levarentur. Cujus tempora pacifica fuerunt* (9, 44). One would think that the writer was an Isaurian. Compare also 9, 40: *In republica omnino providentissimus, favens gentis suae.*
[3] It is said that Sebastian used to buy for a small amount an office which Zeno bestowed on a friend, and then sell it to some one else for a much higher price, Zeno receiving the profit. He was prefect in December 477 (*Cod. Just.* viii. 7, 9), and if the date of a certain constitution (*ib.* v. 27, 5), x. Kal. Mart. 477, be correct, he acted as

Malchus further states that Zeno had nothing of Leo's coarse nature, and that his wrath was not wont to be relentless. His attempt to unify the Church by his famous Henotikon, which raised up against him deadly ecclesiastical odium, has been spoken of in a former chapter, and we must remember this when we read the charges, preferred against him by ecclesiastical writers, of undisguised and almost obtrusive immorality. The favour shown by him to his countrymen the Isaurians, whom the Byzantines regarded as brutish clowns, was an additional cause of unpopularity; while the court intrigues and jealousies, which led to constant conspiracies and frequent bloodshed, throw another shadow over his rather obscure reign. The presence of the Ostrogothic pillagers in the Balkan provinces might be used by the Emperor's enemies to complete the gloomy picture.

I must give an account of some of the personages who played a part at the court of Zeno and were objects of interest in the streets of Byzantium. Harmatius, the nephew of Basiliscus, who has already been mentioned, was a young man of fashion, to whose name doubtless many scandals were attached. The most celebrated was his intrigue with Zenonis, his uncle's wife; their love is described by a historian in a passage worthy of a romance.[1]

"Basiliscus permitted Harmatius, inasmuch as he was a kinsman, to associate freely with the Empress Zenonis. Their intercourse became intimate, and as they were both persons of no ordinary beauty they became extravagantly enamoured of each other. They used to exchange glances of the eyes, they used constantly to turn their faces and smile at each other; and the passion which they were obliged to conceal was the cause of dule and teen. They confided their trouble to Daniel a eunuch and to Maria a midwife, who hardly healed their malady by the remedy of bringing them together. Then Zenonis coaxed Basiliscus to grant her lover the highest office in the city."

The preferment which he received from his uncle elated him beyond measure. He was naturally effeminate and cruel. Theodoric, the son of Triarius, despised him as a dandy who

prefect to Zeno before his restoration, but I suspect the date. Erythrius had been praetorian prefect before Sebastian, and was very popular (Malchus, fr. 6). The decline of the scholarian guards is attributed by Agathias (v. 15) to Zeno, who bestowed appointments on Isaurian relations of no valour.

[1] The passage is in Suidas, but probably comes from Malchus. The name is spelt both Harmatus and Harmatius.

only cared for his toilet and the care of his body ; and it was said that in the days of Leo he had punished a number of Thracian rebels by cutting off their hands. When he was exalted by his mistress's husband, he conceived the idea that he was a man of valour, and he manifested this idea by dressing himself as Achilles, in which guise he used to ride about and astonish or amuse the people in the hippodrome. The populace nicknamed him Pyrrhus, on account of his pink cheeks, but he took it as a compliment to his valour, and became still more inflated with vanity. "He did not," says the historian, "slay heroes like Pyrrhus, but he was a chamberer and a wanton like Paris."

Harmatius did not long survive the return of Zeno, and his death may be considered an instance of double ingratitude. Zeno, who owed his recovery of the crown to Harmatius, kept the promise he had made to appoint him *magister militum in praesenti*, and to proclaim his son Basiliscus Caesar. But Zeno did not trust the fidelity of the new *magister*, and he engaged a man, who had risen to high rank by the patronage of Harmatius,[1] to assassinate his patron.

Illus the Isaurian was the most important minister in the Empire after Zeno's return, but his position was surrounded by pitfalls on all sides. Not only was he the object of Verina's enmity and machinations, but Zeno seems to have viewed him with fear and suspicion, and wished to rid himself of him. Only a month or two after his reinstallation on the throne, he was suspected of having suborned a servant to assassinate Illus. In 478 Illus was made consul, and the rebuilding of an imperial *stoa* devolved upon him. One day, while he was attending to matters connected with this work, an Alan, one of the scholarii under the master of offices, was found with a sword, which he plainly intended to use against Illus. He confessed under torture that the prefect Epinicus[2] had suborned him. Zeno immediately deposed the prefect, confiscated his goods, and handed his person over to Illus, who despatched him to a place of safety in Isauria. Soon afterwards, Illus invented

---

[1] This man was Onoulf, brother of Odovacar, his rank was στρατηγὸς Ἰλλυριῶν, *mag. mil. per Illyr.*

[2] Epinicus was a Phrygian who passed from the service of the *praepos. sac. cub.*, Urbicius, to fill successively the offices of count of the privy purse and count of the sacred largesses, and finally prefect of the city (476).

a pretext to leave the capital himself,[1] and visiting the prison of Epinicus, induced him to confess that he had acted in concert with Verina, the Empress-mother. Zeno and the court met him on his return in the neighbourhood of Chalcedon, and Illus induced the Emperor to consign to him that dangerous woman, while Epinicus might be allowed to return to Byzantium. Verina was then placed in confinement in an Isaurian castle, named Dalisandon, having previously taken the vows of a nun at Tarsus. At this period Isauria and Cappadocia were the recognised places for the banishment of political prisoners, and Illus, being a native of Isauria, had considerable influence there. Another captive, whom he kept immured in an Isaurian stronghold, was Longinus the Emperor's brother, —for what reason we know not. But it is evident that the influence and power of Illus in those regions made him formidable to Zeno.

It appears that in 483, Illus, whose life had been recently attempted, this time by the Empress Ariadne,[2] withdrew to Asia Minor, on a plea of wishing for change of air, perhaps really feeling that his life was not safe in Constantinople. In the meantime a certain Leontius had raised the flag of revolt in Syria, with the

---

[1] According to John of Antioch, his brother Aspalius was dead; according to Theophanes, he put forward the plea of requiring change of air.

[2] I have not attempted to reconstruct the details of the revolt from our fragmentary evidence. But it appears to me that the procedure of Zeno against Illus, mentioned by John of Antioch (p. 620), took place after Illus had left the city, though before he had actually revolted, and not *immediately* after his departure. For Zeno appointed him general of the East—in which post he was succeeded by John the Goth, who conducted the siege of the Papirian castle—apparently to operate against Leontius, who, I think, we may assume revolted first on his own account, as Liberatus testifies and as Tillemont considered probable. The conduct that roused Zeno's suspicions or anger against Illus, and induced the latter to join Leontius, seems to have been connected with the Emperor's brother Longinus, whose supposed imprisonment of ten years (stated by Marcellinus) is extremely obscure. *See* John of Antioch, p. 620. Mr. Hodgkin, who gives an account of the revolt (iii. 63, *seq.*), speaks as if Illus had left Constantinople in consequence of Zeno's measures against him. This is certainly not correct. Moreover, he passes over the fact that Illus, when he had resigned the post of master of offices, was made general of the East, and speaks as if John the Goth succeeded Illus in this post ("military command," referring to the scholarians?) I would suggest that Illus left Constantinople in 482, after the affair of Ariadne, and lived in Asia Minor (Nicaea?); that while he was there, Leontius revolted, and Zeno gave him supreme military command to operate against Leontius; that Illus then quarrelled with Longinus, who was also in command against the tyrant, and took the summary measure of imprisoning him in a castle; that this was the cause of Zeno's anger. In this case the "ten years" of Marcellinus must be a mistake, as Tillemont already conjectured. There is evidence that Longinus commanded against Leontius.

intention, it was said, of reviving the forlorn cause of paganism. It seems that Illus was then appointed commander-in-chief of the eastern armies, and was sent against Leontius. But for some unknown reason he incurred Zeno's suspicions, and attached himself to the cause of the rebel. Zeno had delivered an oration against him as a public enemy, sold his property, and made a present of the proceeds to the cities of the Isaurians. The object of the last measure was, we may suspect, to bid for their adherence against Illus.

Illus and Leontius made use of the Empress Verina, who was living as a prisoner in the Isaurian castle, to give a semblance of legitimacy to their cause. She crowned Leontius at Tarsus, and issued in his interests a letter which was sent to various cities. Illus, moreover, put himself in communication with Odovacar, the king of Italy, who, however, was unable to give active help, as well as with the Persians and the Armenians. Leontius entered Antioch on 27th June 484 and established there an imperial court. Theodoric the Ostrogoth, who afterwards conquered Italy, was sent to put down the revolt, and it was practically crushed very soon,[1] although the two leaders held out for four years in the Isaurian castle of Papirius, where Verina died during the siege. The fortress was taken by the treachery of Illus' sister-in-law, the wife of Trocundus, and Illus and Leontius were slain.

The most noteworthy circumstance about the revolt of Illus is that he was an Isaurian rebelling against an Isaurian Emperor. It is impossible to unravel the skein of events and see the motives of the two chief actors, Illus and Zeno, as our sources are mere fragments, but it is hardly justifiable to apprehend its chief significance as an attempt to revive paganism. It is possible that this conception may have guided Leontius, though he seems to have been an insignificant and incapable person, and was finally a mere figure-head, but it was the intimacy of Illus with a very remarkable philosopher named Pamprepius that gave the movement a pagan character. It need hardly be observed that such an idea as the revival of pagan religion had as little real danger for Christianity in the reign of Zeno, as the scheme of Pomponius Laetus for a similar revival in the fifteenth century.

[1] *See* above, p. 256 note 2.

Illus was a man with a taste for letters, as well as a good military captain, and he spent the long hours of the siege in the Isauric fort in study. At Constantinople he perhaps affected to be a patron of letters, but at all events he discovered Pamprepius of Panopolis in Upper Egypt, who became his friend, confidant, and spiritual adviser. The career of Pamprepius is worthy of record, as it illustrates life in the fifth century. He went in his youth from Egypt to the university of Athens, where he studied under the Neoplatonist Proclus, and was appointed professor of grammar (*i.e.* of philology); but he was not only a grammarian and a philosopher, he was also a poet, doubtless of the school of Nonnus, who was born in the same city. Obliged to leave Athens, in consequence of a quarrel with a magistrate, he sought his fortune in the capital, and won the patronage of Illus by a poem which he recited. The influential statesman procured him a professorship, and increased his stipend by a grant of his own. As a man of the highest intellectual ability, as the intimate friend of Illus, and as a pagan who gave bold and undisguised utterance to his unacceptable opinions in a city so religious as Byzantium, he was one of the observed and the dangerous, feared and disliked. In the eyes of the ordinary Christian a "Greek" or heathen was a nefarious individual who was probably a magician; and the mysticism of a Neoplatonist would naturally present many opportunities for charges of sorcery. During the absence of Illus (478) he was banished, but Illus brought his favourite back in triumph and procured him a seat in the senate and the quaestorship, a post which was especially appropriate to a learned man who could write in a good style.[1] The philosopher accompanied Illus in his revolt, and perished with him.

The revolt of Illus was not the only trouble that tended to make Zeno feel insecure. Another rising took place at an earlier period in his reign which was very nearly successful, although Illus supported the throne. Anthemius, the Emperor of the West, had two sons, Marcian and Procopius. Marcian married Leontia, the second daughter of Leo, who could boast of the fact that she was born in the purple as a ground of superiority to her sister the Empress Ariadne.

---

[1] So Cassiodorus was appointed quaestor by Theodoric on account of his Panegyric.

They conspired at the end of 479 to dethrone Zeno on account of the banishment of Verina, and they enlisted a number of citizens as well as barbarians in their cause. One of the brothers surprised the imperial guard in the palace, while everything was quiet in the mid-day heat, and the Emperor was only saved by escaping from the building. But time was wasted, and at night Illus conveyed Isaurian soldiers from Chalcedon in market boats, as Marcian had seized the ferries. On the following day the rebels were overpowered; Marcian was compelled to take orders and banished to Cappadocia; while Procopius found a refuge in the camp of the Ostrogoth Theodoric, the son of Triarius, who had approached the city with hostile intent.

Zeno had one son,[1] of the same name, whose brief and strangely disreputable career must have been one of the chief scandals at the court. His father desired that he should be carefully trained in manly exercises, but unscrupulous young courtiers, who wished to profit by the abundant supplies of money which the boy could command, instructed him in all the vulgar excesses of luxury and voluptuousness. They introduced him to boys of his own age, who did not refuse to satisfy his desires, while their adulation flattered his vanity to such a degree that he treated all who came in contact with him as if they were servants. His excesses brought on an internal disease, and he died, still a boy, after lying for many days in a senseless condition.

In the declining years of Zeno his brother Longinus began to gain influence; he filled high official posts, and looked forward to succeeding his brother. Zeno, however, consulted a certain Maurianos, skilled in occult learning, who informed him that a silentiarius[2] would be the next Emperor. This prophecy was unfortunate for a distinguished patrician of high fame named Pelagius, who had once belonged to the silentiarii, for Zeno, seized with alarm and suspicion, put him to death.[3] The Emperor in his last days seems to have been a prey to

---

[1] By Arcadia, his first wife (Suidas).
[2] The *silentiarii* were palace guards whose duty was to secure that the rest of the Emperor should not be interrupted.
[3] Arcadius, praetorian prefect, expressed such indignation at this that Zeno sought to slay him, but Arcadius fled in time.

suspicions, as was indeed not unnatural, seeing that so many rebellions had vexed his reign; and his unhappiness was increased by his bad health. An attack of epilepsy carried him off in April 491.

One act of Zeno's latter years deserves special notice, the suppression of the school of Edessa in 489. Edessa was a literary centre in western Mesopotamia, and exercised a vast influence in diffusing Hellenism in those regions. The teachers of Edessa, however, were Nestorians, and it is to this fact that we must ascribe Zeno's narrow-minded act, which was clearly designed to please the monophysites and Chalcedonians.

CHAPTER IV

THE OSTROGOTHS IN ILLYRICUM AND THRACE

WE saw how in the reign of Arcadius the Visigoths of Alaric abode in the Illyrian peninsula, and almost formed a kingdom there, before they invaded Italy and established themselves in the West; we shall now see how in the reign of Zeno the same phenomenon was repeated in the case of the Ostrogoths of Theodoric, how they almost formed a kingdom in the land of Mount Haemus, before they went westward and founded a realm in Italy.[1]

After the death of Attila in 453, the subject nations immediately threw off the yoke of the Huns, and asserted their independence on the field of Netad (454).[2] Of these nations the chief was the Ostrogoths, over whom three brothers ruled jointly, Walamir, Theodemir, and Widemir. These brothers made an arrangement with the Emperor Valentinian, by which, probably as *foederati*, they were allowed to occupy Pannonia.[3] After some years, during which they repulsed

---

[1] The chief sources for the events related in this chapter are the fragments of Malchus and the Gothic history of Jordanes.

[2] The foundation of the Gepid kingdom on the Theiss was another consequence of the field of Netad. The original seat of the Gepids was near the mouth of the Vistula. Their king, Ardaric, fought for Attila at the *locus Mauriacus*, but threw off the yoke at Netad, a battle which Dahn considers equal in importance to "Châlons," Poitiers, or Waterloo (*Kön. der Germ.* ii. 15-27): "Die grosse Bedeutung des Königthums Ardarich's zeigt sich in der Rücksicht welche noch das Burgundenrecht auf seine Münzen nimmt, woraus sich eine ziemlich geordnete Herrschgewalt des Königs und ein ansehnlicher Flor seines Reiches folgern lässt."

[3] Their Pannonian territory extended from Sirmium to Vindobona — the "false Vienna." Jordanes attempts to tell us how it was apportioned among the three brothers. The Ostrogoths made war on the peoples around them, *cupientes ostentare virtutem* (Jord. *Get.* 52). Gasquet (*L'empire byz.* p. 57) points out very well that "what the barbarians hated most cordially were [not Romans but] other barbarians."

an attack of the remnant of the Huns, they came into collision with the Emperor Leo, on account of an unpaid allowance of gold (*strenae*), and ravished the Roman provinces; but peace was made in 461, in consequence of which Theodoric, the son of Theodemir, was sent as a hostage to Constantinople, where he remained for ten years, and had the advantage of a Roman training.[1] This training, however, did not perhaps include letters, for it is said that he was never able to write.[2] During these ten years his nation was engaged in wars with the Suevi and King Hunimund,[3] in which Walamir, his uncle, whom contemporary Greek historians wrongly called the father of Theodoric, was killed. In 471 (or 472) Theodoric returned to his people. He distinguished himself by a campaign against the Sarmatians,[4] and a year or two later joined his father in an invasion of Illyricum, while Widemir attacked the Romans of Italy. The father and son marched, capturing cities as they went,[5] as far as Thessalonica, and there the old treaty between the Romans and Goths was renewed, and certain towns (Pella, Methone, Pydna, Beroea) in the neighbourhood of the Thermaic Gulf were assigned to the Goths. But for some unrecorded reason they were soon transferred to Lower Moesia and Scythia, where we find them stationed during the usurpation of Basiliscus.[6]

About the same time Theodoric (Strabo, "Squinter"), the son of Triarius, the chief of another tribe of Ostrogoths that was supported by the bounty of the Empire, comes into prominence. He could not boast the noble descent of his namesake Theodoric, the son of Theodemir the Amal, from whom

---

[1] Theodoric was probably born in 454, for he was eight years old when he was sent to Byzantium. His mother, whose name was Erelieva, seems to have been a concubine treated with the honours of a wife. She accompanied her son on his Thracian and Illyrian marches. Her name in *Anon. Val.* (12, 58, ed. Gardthausen) is Ereriliva; and we learn that she was a Catholic and her christian name was Eusebia.

[2] I am disposed to believe this statement of *Anon. Val.*, which Mr. Hodgkin discredits, suspecting that the story was transferred from Justin to Theodoric. The author of the *Anecdota* relates it of Justin, and I am inclined to reverse Mr. Hodgkin's suspicion, and believe that it was transferred from Theodoric to Justin.

[3] The Suevi, or Suavi, lived with the Alemanni to the east of the Burgundians and to the west of the Bavarians. Suavia must not be confounded with the Roman province of Savia. See Mr. Hodgkin's *Italy and her Invaders*, iii. 21-22.

[4] The Sarmatians had attacked the Empire and taken Singidunum.

[5] Naissus, Stobi, Heraclea. This indicates the line of their march—up the valley of the Margus (Morava) and down the valley of the Axius (Vardar).

[6] *Anon. Val.* 9, 42.

he must be carefully distinguished.[1] War broke out between the Ostrogoths and Scyrians in 467, and both peoples applied to Leo for assistance. The general Aspar counselled the Emperor to remain neutral, but Leo determined to listen to the prayers of the Scyri. Aspar was on friendly terms with the Goths, and it was because he knew that there was no chance of Leo's aiding them that he advised him to reject both requests. In 468 Leo rejected overtures of the sons of Attila, and in the following year the remnant of the Huns combined with the Goths against the Empire, but the campaign was unsuccessful, because they quarrelled among themselves.

The Ostrogothic chief Theodoric, son of Triarius, aspired to succeed to the position of Aspar, and in 473 he sent an embassy to that effect to Constantinople. When Leo refused his demands, Theodoric, having divided his forces in two parts, with one division ravaged the territory of Philippi and with the other reduced Arcadiopolis by starvation. These energetic proceedings extorted concessions from Leo; he agreed to pay a yearly stipend of 2000 lbs. of gold to the Goths, to allot them a district in Thrace, to create Theodoric *magister eq. et ped. praes. mil.* Theodoric, on his part, was to fight for the Emperor against all enemies except the Vandals. He was, moreover, to be recognised as king of the Goths.[2]

In the troubles that followed Leo's decease, the son of Triarius took the part of Basiliscus, while the son of Theodemir supported Zeno. The relations which existed between Zeno and the two Theodorics during the three years succeeding Zeno's restoration (477-479) may be divided into three stages. In the first stage Zeno and the son of Theodemir are combined against the son of Triarius; in the second stage the two Gothic chieftains join forces against the Emperor; in the third stage the son of Triarius and Zeno are allied against the son of Theodemir.

In 477 Zeno received an embassy from the son of Triarius and his federate Goths who were desirous to make a treaty with the successful Emperor. The ambassadors reminded

[1] According to John of Antioch, fr. 214, 3, the son of Theodemir was the ἀνεψιός, cousin of Recitach, who was son of Theodoric, the son of Triarius.

[2] His wish to be recognised as king by the Emperor shows that he was not of royal descent (Dahn, *Könige der Germanen*, ii. 69).

Zeno of the injuries which the son of Theodemir had inflicted on the Empire, though he was called a Roman "general" and a friend. It appears that Theodoric the Amal, who was now stationed in Lower Moesia, had received the title of general in reward for his opposition to Basiliscus. Zeno called the senate, and it was concluded to be impossible to support the two generals and their armies, for the public resources were hardly sufficient to pay the Roman troops. The exchequer, it must not be forgotten, had not yet recovered from the failure of the Vandal expedition of 468. As the son of Triarius had always shown himself hostile at heart, was unpopular on account of his cruelty,[1] and had assisted Basiliscus "the tyrant," it was determined to reject his offer. Yet, as Zeno for a time withheld a reply, three friends of Theodoric in Constantinople, Anthimus, a physician, and two others, wrote him an account of the course which matters were taking; but the letters were discovered, the affair was examined by a senatorial commission of three persons, in the presence of the *magister officiorum*, and the three friends of the Goths were punished by flogging and exile. It is not quite certain, but it is probable, that after the rejection of his request the son of Triarius harried Thrace up to the walls of the capital.[2]

Soon after this, probably in 478, the Emperor, perceiving that while the son of Triarius was becoming stronger and consolidating forces, the son of Theodemir was becoming weaker, deemed it wise to come to terms with the former. He therefore sent an embassy proposing that the son of the chief should be sent to Byzantium as a hostage, and that Theodoric himself should pass the life of a private individual in Thrace, retaining what he had already secured by plunder, but binding himself to plunder no more. Theodoric refused, representing that it was impossible for him, having collected tribes together and formed an expedition, to withdraw now. Accordingly Zeno decided on war; troops were summoned from the dioceses of Pontus, Asia, and the East, and it was expected that Illus would assume the

---

[1] He and Harmatius had made a practice of cutting off the hands of prisoners: χεῖράς τε ἀποτέμνων ἅμα τῷ Ἁρματίῳ. The Greek is hardly ambiguous, and Mr. Hodgkin is perfectly justified in rejecting the interpretation in Smith's edition of Gibbon, "cutting *off the hands of Harmatius.*"

[2] Compare Evagrius (that is, Eustathius of Epiphania) iii. 25, and Theophanes *ad ann.;* also Müller's note in *Frag. Hist. Graec.* iv. p. 120 (and Malchus, fr. 11).

CHAP. IV OSTROGOTHS IN ILLYRICUM AND THRACE 265

command. It seems, however, that Illus did not take the field, for we find Martinianus, his brother-in-law, conducting a campaign against the son of Triarius in the same year, and proving himself incompetent to maintain discipline in his own army. Then Zeno sent an embassy to the other Theodoric, whose headquarters were at Marcianopolis in Lower Moesia, calling upon him to fulfil the duties of a Roman general and advance against the enemy. He replied that the Emperor and senate must first swear that they will never make terms with the son of Triarius. The senators took an oath that they would not do so unless the Emperor wished it, and the Emperor swore that he would not break the contract if it were not first violated by Theodoric himself.

The son of Theodemir then moved southwards. The master of soldiers of Thrace was to meet him with two thousand cavalry and ten thousand hoplites at the passes of Mount Haemus; when he had crossed into Thrace another force was to join him at Hadrianople, consisting of twenty thousand foot and six thousand horse; and, if necessary, Heraclea[1] and the cities in the neighbourhood were prepared to send additional troops. But the master of soldiers was not at the gates of Haemus, and when the Ostrogoths arrived on the banks of the Hebrus no troops met them there. At Mount Sondis they fell in with the army of the other Theodoric, and the antagonists plundered one another's flocks and horses. Then the son of Triarius, approaching his rival's tent, reviled him as a traitor to desert his own countrymen, and as a fool not to see through the plan of the Romans, who wished to rid themselves of the Goths, without trouble on their own part, by instigating them to mutual destruction, and were quite indifferent which party won. These arguments took effect, and the two Theodorics made peace. This is the second stage of alliance, which we noted above.

The reconciled Ostrogothic chieftains then sent ambassadors to Byzantium (in the beginning of 479). The son of Theodemir, upbraiding Zeno for having deceived him with false promises, demanded the concession of territory to his people, a

[1] Heraclea, on the Propontis, formerly called Perinthus. Mr. Hodgkin strangely confounds it with the Heraclea in Macedonia, near the Pelagonian plain, and now Monastir (p. 92).

supply of corn to support his army till harvest time, and also that the *domestics*, who collected the revenue, should be sent at once to give an account of what they had received; and he urged that, if these demands were not satisfied, he would be unable to restrain his soldiers from plundering, in order to support themselves. The son of Triarius demanded that the arrangements he had made with Leo (in 473) should be carried out, that the payment he had been accustomed to receive in former years should be continued, and that certain kinsmen of his, who had been committed to the care of Illus and the Isaurians, should be restored. We are not informed what answer Zeno made to the elder Theodoric, or whether he made any; to the son of Theodemir he replied, that if he consented to break with his namesake and make war upon him he would give him 2000 lbs. of gold and 10,000 lbs. of silver immediately, besides a yearly revenue of 10,000 aurei and an alliance with the daughter of Olybrius or some other noble lady. But his promises did not avail, and Zeno prepared for war, notifying his intention to accompany the army in person. This intention created great enthusiasm in the army, but at the last moment Zeno drew back, and the murmurs of the soldiers threatened a revolt, to prevent which the army was broken up and the regiments sent to their winter quarters.

When the army was disbanded, Zeno's only resort was to make peace on any terms with the son of Triarius. In the meantime Theodoric, the son of Theodemir, was engaged in ravaging the fairest parts of Thrace in the neighbourhood of Mount Rhodope, which divides Thrace from Macedonia; he not only ruined the crops, but extorted from the farmers or slew them. The son of Triarius, when he received Zeno's message,—remarking that he was sorry that the innocent husbandmen, for whose welfare Zeno[1] did not care in the least, suffered from the ravages of his rival—concluded a peace on the conditions that Zeno was to supply a yearly payment sufficient to support thirteen thousand men selected by himself (Theodoric); that he was to be appointed to the command of two scholae and to the post of a master of soldiers *in praesenti*, and receive all the dignities which Basiliscus had

---

[1] "Zeno *or Verina*" (Malchus, fr. 17). This seems to show that Verina had a preponderant influence at this time.

bestowed upon him; that his kinsmen were to inhabit a city assigned by Zeno. The Emperor did not delay to execute this agreement; Theodoric, son of Theodemir, was deposed from the office of master of soldiers, and Theodoric, son of Triarius, appointed in his stead. This marks the third stage in these changeful relations.

In the meantime the son of Theodemir laid waste Macedonia, including Stobi, its chief city. He even threatened Thessalonica, and the inhabitants felt so little confidence in Zeno that they actually believed that the Emperor wished to hand their city over to the barbarians. A sedition broke out which ended in the transference of the keys of the city from the praetorian prefect to the archbishop, a remarkable evidence of the fact that the people looked on the ministers of the Church as defenders against imperial oppression. These suspicions of the Emperor's intentions seem, however, in this case to have been unjust, and Zeno sent Artemidorus and Phocas to Theodoric, who was persuaded by their representations to stay his army and send an embassy to Byzantium. Theodoric demanded that a plenipotentiary envoy should be sent to treat with him. Zeno sent Adamantius, directing him to offer the Goths land in Pautalia, a district of Macedonia, on the borders of Thrace,[1] and 200 lbs. of gold to supply food for that year, as no corn had been sown in the designated region. The motive of Zeno in choosing Pautalia was that if the Goths accepted it they would occupy a position between the Illyrian and Thracian armies, and so might be more easily controlled.

Meanwhile Theodoric had proceeded by the Egnatian way to Heraclea in Macedonia, and sent a message to Epirus to one Sidimund,[2] an Ostrogoth who had been in the service of Leo and had inherited an estate near Dyrrhachium, where he was living peaceably. Theodoric induced him to make an attempt to take possession of that important city of New Epirus, and for this purpose Sidimund employed an ingenious device. He visited the citizens individually, informing each that the Ostrogoths were coming with Zeno's consent to take possession of the city, and advising him to move his property with all haste

[1] Malchus, fr. 18: ἐν Παυταλίᾳ ἢ τῆς μὲν Ἰλλυρικῆς μοίρας ἐστὶν ἐπαρχία. We cannot avoid seeing in his name the Gothic analogue of the English Edwin (Eadwin).
[2] He was cousin of Aidoing, a friend of Verina and *magister domesticorum*.

to some other secure town or to one of the coast islands. The fact that his representations were listened to and that he managed to dispose of a garrison of two thousand men proves that he must have possessed considerable influence. Theodoric was at Heraclea[1] when the messenger of Sidimund[2] arrived with the news that the plan had been successfully carried out; and the Amal chief, having burnt a large portion of the town because its inhabitants could not supply him with provisions, set out for Epirus. This collusion of Sidimund, the Ostrogothic subject of the Empire, with Theodoric, the Ostrogothic despoiler of the Empire, is an example of the manner in which the Germans within helped the Germans without, or more strictly, those who were half foes and half dependants, for Theodoric had been a Roman general, was still a Roman patrician, and had been educated at New Rome.

When he left Heraclea—the city now called Monastir,[3] situated in that plain of Pelagonia which became famous on one occasion in the later history of the Roman Empire—the Gothic invader proceeded along the Egnatian way, crossing the range of the Scardus mountains, and arrived at Lychnidus, which is probably identical with Ochrida. Built in a strong situation on the shore of Lake Ochrida, and well provided with water and victuals, Lychnidus defied the assault of the barbarians, who, unwilling to delay, hastened onwards, and having seized Scampa, the most important town between Lychnidus and Dyrrhachium, arrived at the goal of their journey.

It may be wondered whether at Dyrrhachium (the Calais of the south Adriatic passage if Brundusium was the Dover) it entered the mind of Theodoric to ship his people across to the western peninsula and attack the Italian kingdom of Odovacar in the south, as in old time the power of Rome and the Latin name was attacked by the Epeirot Pyrrhus. Adamantius, the ambassador who had been sent by Zeno to treat with him, seems to have thought it more likely that the Ostrogoths would employ vessels for the purpose of plundering the Epeirot or Dalmatian coasts, for he sent a post messenger to Dyrrhachium,

---

[1] It is worth noticing that Theodoric's sister, as well as his mother and brother, accompanied him on his march; she died at Heraclea and was buried there.

[2] Mr. Hodgkin calls him Sigismund, but Malchus has Σιδιμοῖνδος, according to Müller's text, *F. H. G.* iv. 126.

[3] *See* Mr. Tozer's *Researches in the Highlands of Turkey*, ii. 368.

to blame Theodoric for his hostile advance while negotiations were pending, and to exhort him to remain quiet and not to seize ships until he arrived himself.

Starting from Thessalonica, and passing Pella on the Via Egnatia, Adamantius came to Edessa, the modern Vodena, where he found the captain Sabinianus, and informed him that he had been appointed master of soldiers in Illyricum. The messenger, who had been sent to Dyrrhachium, returned in the company of a priest, to assure Adamantius that he might proceed confidently to the camp of Theodoric; and having issued a mandate to collect all the soldiers available, the general and the ambassador moved forward to Lychnidus. Here Sabinianus[1] made difficulties about binding himself by oath to restore the hostages whom Theodoric was willing to deliver as a gage for the personal safety of Adamantius. This produced a deadlock; Theodoric naturally refused to give the hostages. Adamantius naturally refused to visit Theodoric.

Adamantius invented a simple solution of the difficulty, which led to a strange and striking scene. Taking with him a body of two hundred soldiers he climbed by an obscure and narrow path, where horses had never set hoof before, and reached by a circuitous route an impregnable fort, built on a high cliff, close to the city of Dyrrhachium. At the foot of the cliff yawned a deep ravine, through which a river flowed. A messenger was sent to inform Theodoric that the Roman ambassador awaited him, and, attended by a few horse-soldiers, the son of Theodemir rode to the bank of the river. The physical features, the cliff, the chasm, and the river, are sufficiently simple and definite to enable us to call up vividly this strange scene. The attendants of both Adamantius and Theodoric had retired beyond range of earshot; and "they twain, like a king with his fellow,"—the representative of the Emperor standing on the edge of the cliff, and the Ostrogothic chieftain, whose name was in later years to become so great, on the opposite side of the ravine,—held " converse of desolate speech."

"I elected to live," complained Theodoric, " beyond the

---

[1] Sabinianus was a great disciplinarian, see Marcellinus *ad ann.* 479: *disciplinae praeterea militaris ita optimus institutor coercitorque fuit ut priscis Romanorum ductoribus comparctur.*

borders of Thrace, far away Scythia-ward, deeming that if I abode there I should trouble no man, and should be able to obey all the behests of the Emperor. But ye summoned me as to war against Theodoric, and promised, firstly, that the master of soldiers in Thrace would meet me with his army, yet he never appeared; secondly, ye promised that Claudius, the steward of the Gothic contingent, would come with the pay for foreign troops (ξενικῷ), yet I never saw him; thirdly, ye gave me guides who, leaving the better roads that would have taken me to the quarters of the foe,[1] led me by steep and precipitous rocky paths, where I wellnigh perished with all my train, advancing as I was with cavalry, waggons, and all the furniture of camp, and exposed to the attacks of the enemy. I was therefore constrained to come to terms with them, and owe them a debt of gratitude that they did not annihilate me, betrayed as I was by you and in their power."

"The Emperor," replied Adamantius, "bestowed upon you the title of Patrician, and created you a master of soldiers. These are the highest honours that crown the labours of the most deserving Roman officers, and nothing should induce you to cherish towards their bestower other than filial sentiments." Having endeavoured to defend or extenuate the treatment of which Theodoric complained, the envoy proceeded thus: "You are acting intolerably in seizing Roman cities, while you are expecting an embassy; and remember that the Romans held you at their mercy, a prisoner, surrounded by their armies, amid the mountains and rivers of Thrace, whence you could never have extricated yourself, if they had not permitted you to withdraw, not even were your forces tenfold as great as they are. Allow me to counsel you to assume a more moderate attitude towards the Emperor, for you cannot in the end overcome the Romans when they press on you from all sides. Leave Epirus and the cities of this region—we cannot allow such great cities to be occupied by you and their inhabitants to be expelled—and go to Dardania, where there is an extensive territory of rich soil, uninhabited, and sufficient to support your host in plenty."

---

[1] In Müller's *F. H. G.* the Latin version mistranslates the Greek: οἳ τὰς εὐπορωτέρας τῶν ὁδῶν ἐάσαντες τὰς εἰς τοὺς πολεμίους φερούσας ἀπήγαγον δι' ὀρθίας ἀτραποῦ, κ.τ.λ. is rendered by *qui, tutis et expeditis omissis, per cas quae ad hostem ferebant, per praerupta et praecipitia loca me deduxerunt,* of which words the most obvious meaning is not that of the Greek.

To this proposal Theodoric replied that he would readily consent, but that his followers, who had recently endured many hardships, would be unwilling to leave their quarters in Epirus, where they had fully expected to pass the winter. He proposed a compromise, and engaged that if he were permitted to winter at Dyrrhachium he would migrate to Dardania in the ensuing spring. He added that he was quite ready to leave the unwarlike mass of his Ostrogoths in any city named by Zeno, and giving up his mother and sister as hostages, to take the field against the son of Triarius with six thousand of his most martial followers, in company with the Illyrian army; when he had conquered his rival he expected to succeed to the post of master of soldiers and to be received in New Rome as a Roman.[1] He also observed that he was prepared, if the Emperor wished, "to go to Dalmatia and restore Julius Nepos." Adamantius was unable to promise that the wishes of the Goth would be acceded to; it was necessary to send a messenger to Byzantium to consult the Emperor. And thus the interview terminated.

Meanwhile the military forces, stationed in the Illyrian cities, had assembled at Lychnidus, around the standard of Sabinianus. It was announced to the general that a band of the Ostrogoths led by Theudimund, the brother of Theodoric, was descending in secure negligence from Mount Candaira, which separates the valley of the Genusus from that of the Drilo. This band had formed the rear of the Ostrogoths' line of march, and had not yet reached Dyrrhachium. Sabinianus sent a few infantry soldiers by a circuitous mountain route, with minute directions as to the hour and place at which they were to appear; and himself with the rest of the army proceeded thither, after the evening meal, by a more direct way. Marching during the night he assailed the company of Theudimund at dawn of day. Theudimund and his mother, who was with him, fled with all speed into the plain, and, having crossed a deep gully, destroyed the bridge which spanned it to cut off pursuit. This act, while it saved them, sacrificed their followers, who turned at bay upon the Romans. Two thousand waggons and more than five thousand captives were taken, and a great booty.[2]

[1] τὸν Ῥωμαικὸν πολιτεύσοντα τρόπον. For Julius Nepos, see below, p. 278.

[2] Marcellinus *ad ann.* 479: *Theodoricum idem Sabinianus regem apud*

After this the Emperor received two messages, one from Adamantius announcing the proposals of Theodoric, the other from Sabinianus exaggerating his victory, and dissuading from the conclusion of peace. War seemed more honourable to Zeno, and the pacific offers were rejected; Sabinianus was permitted or commanded to continue the war,[1] which seems to have been protracted in these regions for more than two years longer. But the able general was murdered by an ungrateful master; and we hear that John the Scythian and Moschianus were sent to succeed him.

Of the events of the following years our notices are meagre. We find the son of Triarius assisting Illus in the suppression of the revolt of Marcian in the same year in which the campaign of Epirus took place. Soon afterwards we hear that he operated successfully against "Huns,"[2] and we may be sure that these Huns were identical with the Bulgarians, who were now for the first time roused up by Zeno to make war against both the Theodorics.[3] From another source we learn that Theodoric, the son of Theodemir, defeated an army of Bulgarians.[4] Hence we may conclude that, in the year 480, the two Ostrogothic chieftains combined against the Empire, and that Zeno sought the alliance of the Bulgarians, who, in the movements that had ensued upon the dissolution of Attila's power, had migrated westward from their homes near the Caspian and hovered on the lower Danube. Moreover, both the Theodorics gained victories over the Bulgarian forces.

In the following year (481) "the son of Triarius advanced against Constantinople itself, and he would easily have reduced it if Illus had not guarded the gates in time. Thence he passed to the so-called Sycae (a suburb), where he again failed in an attempt on the city. It remained for him to proceed to the place named *Pros Hestiais* and the so-called Losthenion, and endeavour to cross the straits to Bithynia. But he was defeated in a sea-fight, and departed to Thrace. Thence he set

---

Graeciam debacchantem ingenio magis quam virtute deterruit. Notice that Graecia is used of New Epirus.

[1] The fate of Sabinianus is stated by John of Antioch, fr. 213. According to Marcellinus he died in 481, therefore I conclude that the war continued in Epirus until that year.

[2] John of Antioch, 211, 5.

[3] *Ib.* 211, 4: καὶ ἡ τῶν Θεοδερίχων συζυγία (the pair of the Theodorics) κ.τ.λ. ὡς ἀναγκασθῆναι τὸν Ζήνωνα τότε πρῶτον τοὺς καλουμένους Βουλγάρους εἰς συμμαχίαν προτρέψασθαι.

[4] Ennodius, Panegyric of Theodoric (ed. Vogel in *M. G. H.* series, p. 205, 27).

forth for Greece (Hellas) with his son Recitach and his two brothers and his wife and about 30,000 Goths (Scythians). And when he was at the Stable of Diomede[1] he was killed. Having mounted his horse in the morning he was thrown by it on a spear which was standing erect beside the wall of the tent. Others asserted that the blow was inflicted on him by his son Recitach because he had whipped him. His wife Sigilda buried him by night. Recitach succeeded to his authority over the people, his father's brothers sharing in the power.[2] But he slew them afterwards, and reigned alone over the land of the Thracians, performing more outrageous acts than his father had performed." Recitach was soon afterwards slain by Theodoric, the son of Theodemir, whom Zeno instigated to the deed[3] (483 or 484).

In 482 we find Theodoric—the name is no longer ambiguous—ravaging both the Macedonias and Thessaly and capturing the town of Larissa. For the ensuing six years (until 488) he continues to be a thorn in the side of the Roman Emperor, and a burden and menace to the lands of the Haemus, though, for the most part, he is not openly hostile, having been conciliated by honours and benefits. Parts of Moesia and Dacia were conceded to him (483), and he was appointed master of soldiers.[4] In 484 he enjoyed the great dignity of giving his name to the year as consul, and he assisted Zeno against the rebel Illus. But three years later (487) he marched on Constantinople, laying waste the country as he went; Melantias was taken,[5] and the capital was once more threatened by the Ostrogoths. But in 488 the land was delivered from their presence, and the Ostrogoths, like the Visigoths eighty years before, left Illyricum to seek a new home in the West.

[1] τὸν Διομήδους καλούμενον στάβλον (on the Egnatian Road). I translate the short account of John of Antioch. A more elaborate account will be found in the third fragment of Eustathius (*apud Evagrium*, iii. 25).

[2] παρεδυνάστευον, a word used in later Roman history of influential ministers of the Emperor.

[3] Theodoric was a cousin of Recitach (John of Antioch, 214, 3).

[4] *Magister militiae praesentalis* (Marcellinus *ad ann.* 483).

[5] Marcellinus, 487.

CHAPTER V

ODOVACAR THE PATRICIAN AND THEODORIC THE PATRICIAN

For more than four months after the death of Olybrius, Leo was the sole Roman Emperor, and during that time the power in Italy seems to have rested with the senate and Gundobad, the nephew of Ricimer. On 5th March 473 Glycerius, count of the domestics, was proclaimed Emperor at Ravenna, "by the advice of Gundobad,"[1] even as Severus had been proclaimed Emperor at the same place by the advice of Ricimer. But Gundobad the Burgundian was not like Ricimer, and he soon disappears from the scene of Italian politics. One important public act is recorded of the Emperor Glycerius. Italy was threatened by an invasion of Ostrogoths, who were moving from Pannonia under the leadership of Widemir; Glycerius' diplomacy averted the storm, so that it fell on Gaul.

The eastern Augustus did not approve of the new election, which was made without his consent; and he selected another as the successor of Anthemius.[2] His candidate was the husband of his niece, Julius Nepos,[3] the nephew of Marcellinus, who had ruled independently in Dalmatia. And the career of Julius Nepos partakes of two characters; at one moment we think of him as the successor of Anthemius, at another moment as the successor of Marcellinus.

Glycerius was easily deposed, he did not fight; and in

---

[1] Cassiodori Chron. *Gundibato hortante Glycerius Ravennae sumpsit imperium*. Marcellini Chron. *Glycerius apud Ravennam plus praesumptione quam electione Caesar factus est*—this was the view of New Rome. John of Antioch, fr. 209 : τὴν δὲ τοῦ Ρεκίμερος ὑπεισελθὼν Γουνδουβάλης, ἀνεψιὸς ὢν αὐτοῦ, Γλυκέριον τὴν τοῦ κόμητος τῶν δομεστίκων ἀξίαν ἔχοντα ἐπὶ τὴν βασιλείαν ἄγει. For date, see Anon. Cusp.

[2] John of Antioch, *ib.*

[3] Son of Nepotianus and Marcellinus' sister.

Portus, *Portus Augusti et Trajani*, the town at the mouth of the Tiber, he was ordained as bishop of Salona.[1] It is not quite clear whether he ever reached the city of his episcopate, and lived in the vicinity of the palace, which another ex-Emperor, far different from him, had built for himself at the mouth of the Jader. He was ordained and he died—that is all we know. Nepos was proclaimed Emperor and ruled at Rome (24th June 474).

Once more an Augustus at Old Rome and an Augustus at New Rome reigned in unison. At this juncture Epiphanius, the old bishop of Pavia, who was adored in the land of Liguria, appears on the scene, and negotiates a peace between Nepos and Euric, the Visigothic king, as he had before negotiated a peace between Anthemius and Ricimer.[2] Euric had taken advantage of the recent confusion to extend his dominions, and had attacked Auvergne, which was bravely defended by Ecdicius, the son of Avitus. Sidonius, his brother-in-law, celebrates the enthusiasm of his grateful fellow-citizens—"How they gazed at you from the walls of Arverni."[3] But by the peace of Epiphanius, Arverni was ceded to Euric, in order to save Italy from invasion, and Sidonius breaks out into bitter complaints of this abandonment.[4] What made the yoke of the Visigoths at this time especially intolerable, was the fact that King Euric, who had acceded in 466, was a fanatical Arian. He oppressed the Catholics in his realm; he refused to allow Catholic bishops to be elected at Burdigala, Lemovici (Limoges), and other cities; and Sidonius hesitated whether he should regard him as the leader of an Arian party or as the king of the Goths.[5] Ennodius says that he ruled the "Getae" with an iron sway.

But it was not with Euric, nor yet with Gundobad, that Nepos had to measure swords; a general named Orestes,

[1] Some doubts have been felt as to the appointment of Glycerius to the see of Salona; but John of Antioch, who is trustworthy, is express (fr. 209). Anon. Val. says merely *factus est episcopus*. Marcellini Chron. *in portu urbis Romae ex Caesare episcopus ordinatus est et obiit*: the form of expression suggests a doubt whether Glycerius ever reached Salona.

[2] Liguria seems to have played a considerable part in these negotiations. See Ennodius' *Life of Epiphanius*, ed. Vogel, 94, 15. A provincial council of the Ligurians selected Epiphanius as the emissary to Euric.

[3] Sidon. Apoll. *Ep.* iii. 3. Ennodius, *op. cit.* 94, 6.

[4] Id. *Ep.* vii. 7: *Arvernorum, pro dolor, servitus*.

[5] Id. *Ep.* vii. 6 (ed. *M. G. H.* p. 109, 23). This letter is used by Gregory of Tours, ii. 25.

of patrician rank, was to be his adversary. This was that Orestes who had been the secretary of Attila, and had married the daughter of a certain Count Romulus. He was, perhaps, employed as a general in Gaul by Julius Nepos; certain it is that he was in Italy in 475, and he disdained to submit to the rule of him whom the sovereign of New Rome had sent. He determined to do what Stilicho probably desired to do, what Aetius probably desired to do, what Gerontius probably did; he determined to elevate his son to the imperial throne, and thereby possess the supreme power himself.

We are told that Nepos went to Ravenna, and the Patrician Orestes pursued him with an army. And Nepos, fearing the coming of Orestes, embarked in a ship and fled to Salona. This was on the 28th of August 475; the same year that saw the flight of Zeno from Constantinople saw the flight of Nepos from Ravenna; but while in less than two years Zeno returned, the return of Nepos was not to be. He lived for five years at Salona, the third ex-Emperor who had bent his course thither; and if Glycerius really survived, he had the satisfaction of seeing the man who overthrew him overthrown in turn.

The Caesar Julius was succeeded by the Caesar Augustulus; for so young Romulus was nicknamed,[1] whom his father invested with the imperial insignia (31st October 475). These names, Julius, Augustulus, Romulus, in the pages of the late chroniclers, meet us like ghosts re-arisen from past days of Roman history.[2]

We now come to an event which is often presented in a wrong light, the resignation of Romulus Augustulus on 22d August 476. The immediate cause which led to the fall of Orestes was a mutiny of the foederati, as Gibbon clearly saw; Orestes' own conduct in heading a mutiny against Nepos was "retorted against himself." The foreign soldiers in the army, consisting of Heruls, Rugians, Scyrians, and other obscure nationalities, demanded a third part of Italy for themselves; Orestes boldly refused the demand, and his shield-bearer, Odo-

---

[1] The origin of the name, "the little Augustus," is not recorded.

[2] M. Am. Thierry, "Les derniers temps de l'empire d' occident," makes a similar remark. He adds, "Ces rapprochements fortuits présentaient dans leur bizarrerie je ne sais quoi de surnaturel qui justifiait la crédulité et troublait jusqu'aux plus fermes esprits: on baissa la tête et on se tut" (p. 258).

vacar,[1] headed the mutineers. Pavia, to which Orestes retired, was easily taken, and the Patrician was slain at Placentia; his brother Paul was put to death in the pine-woods of Classis. "Entering Ravenna, Odovacar deposed Augustulus, but granted him his life, pitying his infancy, and because he was comely; and he gave him an income of six thousand solidi, and sent him to live in Campania with his relations."

These words of a chronicler[2] represent what practically took place. Italy was now to be divided among the followers of Odovacar, as south-western Gaul more than fifty years ago had been divided among the followers of Wallia. But as Athaulf and Wallia did not break with the Empire, so Odovacar did not desire to break with the Empire; he aspired to govern Italy as a Patrician, nominally dependent on the Emperor, while he was king of his own Germans. For this purpose he made the deposition of Romulus Augustulus take the form of an abdication; he induced the Roman senate to endorse formally the permanent institution of a state of things which had often actually existed in the days of Ricimer; and ambassadors were sent to the Augustus of New Rome to signify the new order of things. In 477, when Zeno had been restored to the throne of which Basiliscus had robbed him, the messengers of the Roman senate appeared in Constantinople, and informed Zeno that they did not require a separate Emperor to govern them, but that his sole supremacy would be sufficient both for East and West; at the same time they had selected Odovacar as a person capable of protecting their interests, being both a warrior and a man endowed with political intelligence; and they now asked Zeno to confer upon him the rank of Patrician and entrust him with the administration of Italy.[3]

At the same moment, messengers arrived from Nepos, to congratulate Zeno on his restoration, and to ask for his sympathy with one who had suffered the same misfortune, and for his aid in men and money to recover the imperial power. This

---

[1] The nationality of Odovacar is not clear; he is sometimes called a Scyrian, sometimes a Rugian. It is very likely he was a Scyrian; it is certain he was not a Rugian; he afterwards overthrew the Rugian kingdom in Noricum. It is said he was the son of Edecon; but it is not certain whether this Edecon was identical with him whom we met at the court of Attila.

[2] *Anon. Val.* 8, 38.

[3] These details are preserved in a valuable fragment of Malchus (10).

message affected Zeno's reply to the envoys from Italy. To the representatives of the senate he said, that of the two Emperors whom they had received from the East, they had slain one, Anthemius, and banished the other, Nepos; let them now take Nepos back. To Odovacar, who had also sent envoys, he replied that he would do well if he accepted the rank of the Patriciate at the hands of Nepos; he praised the respect for Rome and the observance of order which had marked his conduct; and bade him crown his goodness by acknowledging the rights of the exiled Emperor. The fact that Verina was a kinswoman of the wife of Nepos was a determining element in the situation. But Odovacar did not acknowledge the claim of Nepos, and Zeno was not in a position to do more than give him advice.

The unfortunate phrase "Fall of the Western Empire" has given a false importance to the affair of 476: it is generally thought that the date marks a great era of the world. But no Empire fell in 476; there was no western Empire to fall. There was only one Roman Empire, which sometimes was governed by two or more Augusti. If, on the death of Honorius in 423, there had been no Valentinian to succeed him, and if Theodosius II had assumed the reins of government over the western provinces, and if, as is quite conceivable, no second Augustus had arisen again before the western provinces had all passed under the sway of Teutonic rulers, no one would surely have spoken of the "Fall of the Western Empire." And yet this hypothetical case is formally the same as the actual event of 476. The fact that the union of East and West under Zeno's name was accompanied by the rule of the Teuton in Italy, has disguised the true aspect. And in any case it might be said that Julius Nepos was still Emperor; he was acknowledged by Zeno, he was acknowledged in southern Gaul[1]; so that one might just as legitimately place "the Fall of the Western Empire" in 480, the year of his death. The Italian provinces were now, like Africa, like Spain, like the greater part of Gaul, practically an independent kingdom, but theoretically

---

[1] Candidus, fr. 1 (p. 136, ed. Müller), relates that after the death of Nepos the Gallo-Romans (τῶν δυσμικῶν Γαλατῶν) rejected the rule of Odovacar and sent an embassy to Zeno; but Zeno rather inclined to Odovacar.

the Roman Empire was once more as it had been in the days of Theodosius the Great or in the days of Julian.

When the Count Marcellinus in his Chronicle wrote that on the death of Aetius "the Hesperian realm fell," he could justify his statement better than those who place 476 among the critical dates of the world's history. It is more profitable to recognise the continuity of history than to impose upon it arbitrary divisions; it is more profitable to grasp that Odovacar was the successor of Merobaudes, than to dwell with solemnity on the imaginary fall of an empire. Merobaudes, the German against whose influence in the western court the Britannic legions made a Roman manifestation, was succeeded by the semi-barbarian Stilicho, who at once encouraged and kept in check the barbarians, at once undermined and protected the Empire. After a short Roman reaction under Constantius, who, however, was constrained to do what Stilicho never did, and assign to the Goths lands within the Empire, arose the great Aetius, of German descent on his father's side and reared among barbarians, who now warred with the Teutons and now led them to battle. If Stilicho was a semi-barbarian, Aetius might be called a semi-Roman. His successor was the Suevian Ricimer; with him the opposition between the German element and the principles of the Roman Imperium appears; he will only have an Emperor whom he likes; the Emperor depends upon the Patrician, not the Patrician upon the Emperor. The next step is Odovacar the Patrician, not without an Emperor —for that would have been an absurdity in theory—but subject to an Emperor ruling, not at Ravenna or Rome, but at Constantinople, and therefore practically independent. Odovacar is likewise king of his own nation, and though he is not "King of Italy," Italy is virtually a Teutonic kingdom, like Spain and Africa. The administration of Odovacar therefore does not come within my scope. The significance of his reign is that it prepared for the kingdom of the Ostrogoths. The death of Gaiseric (477) was followed by the decline of the Vandalic power, and Odovacar had less difficulty than his predecessors in providing on that side for the safety of Italy. He annexed Dalmatia to his dominion in 481, after the death of Julius Nepos, and acted in every regard as an independent prince. It is noteworthy that the one extant coin, which may be probably attributed to Odovacar, has no reference to the Emperor.[1]

We may pass on to the circumstances which led to the overthrow of the Scyrian monarch and the establishment of the Ostrogothic kingdom of Theodoric in the Italian peninsula. The words of a chronicle, in which the events are clearly and simply related, may be quoted.[2]

"And so Zeno recompensed Theodoric with benefits; he made him a Patrician and consul, gave him much and sent him to Italy. And Theodoric made a compact with him, that, in case Odovacar were conquered, he should, as a reward for his labours, rule in place of Odovacar, until Zeno came himself.[3] Accordingly Theodoric the Patrician *supervened* from the city of Novae with his Gothic people, being sent by the Emperor Zeno from the east to win and keep Italy for him.

"When he came he was met by Odovacar at the river Sontius (Isonzo), and fighting there was conquered and fled. But Odovacar departed to Verona and fixed his camp in the Lesser Veronese plain on the 27th of September [489]. And Theodoric followed him there, and a battle was fought and people fell on both sides; but Odovacar being overcome fled to Ravenna on the last day of September.

"And Theodoric the Patrician marched on to Mediolanum, and the greater part of Odovacar's army surrendered to him; especially Tufa, the Master of Soldiers, whom Odovacar with his chief men [a German Folcmote] had ordained on the 1st April. In that year Tufa, the Master of Soldiers, was sent by Theodoric to Ravenna against Odovacar.

"Tufa, coming to Faventia, blockaded Odovacar with the army with which he had been sent; and Odovacar left Ravenna and came to Faventia. And Tufa delivered to Odovacar the "comrades" (*comites*) of the Patrician Theodoric, and they were put in irons and led to Ravenna.

"In the consulate of Faustus and Longinus [490], King Odovacar left Cremona and proceeded to Mediolanum. Then the Visigoths came to the assistance of Theodoric,[4] and a battle was fought on the river

---

[1] An account of "Odovacar's Deed of Gift to Pierius," preserved on two separate fragments of papyrus (one in the Imperial Library at Vienna, the other the Theatine Monastery of St. Paul at Naples) will be found in Mr. Hodgkin's third volume, note B, p. 165.

[2] Anonymus Valesii, who drew his facts from the lost annals of Ravenna. Ennodius' Panegyric of Theodoric, written in very obscure language, is important for these years, and has been thoroughly utilised by Mr. Hodgkin for the sixth chapter of his third volume.

[3] Mr. Hodgkin (iii. 130) finds a difficulty in this passage, whose translation seems to me sufficiently evident. The Latin is *cui Theodericus pactuatus est ut si victus fuisset Odoachar pro merito laborum suorum loco ejus dum adveniret tantum praeregnaret*. Zeno is the subject of *adveniret*, and *tantum* means "only"; Theodoric's government in Italy was to be only temporary. As for *praeregnaret*, *prae* seems to be redundant—prefixed on the analogy of *praesideo*, *praesum*, etc.—or else it is a mistake for *proregnaret*. The Latin is so bad that it is difficult.

[4] The Burgundians, on the other hand, under Gundobad, assisted Odovacar by invading Liguria with a great army (*Hist. Miscell.* xv. 16).

Addua, and people fell on both sides. Pierius, the Count of Domestics, was slain on the 11th August, and Odovacar fled to Ravenna. Then the Patrician Theodoric followed him and came to the Pinewoods (*Pineta*) and pitched his camp. And he blockaded Odovacar, keeping him shut up in Ravenna for three years. And a bushel of corn reached the price of six solidi.[1] And Theodoric sent Faustus, the head of the senate, to the Emperor Zeno, hoping to receive at his hands and wear the royal apparel.

"In the consulate of Olybrius, *vir clarissimus*, [491] King Odovacar departed from Ravenna by night and entered the Pinewoods along with the Heruls and came to the camp of the Patrician Theodoric. And soldiers fell on both sides; and Levila, Odovacar's Master of Soldiers, fleeing was killed in the river Bedens.[2] And Odovacar being vanquished fled to Ravenna on the 15th of July.[3]

. . . . . .

"Then [493] Odovacar, being constrained, gave his son Thelane as a hostage to Theodoric, having his pledge that his life would be spared. Thus Theodoric entered in (to Ravenna). And some days after, Odovacar was discovered to be plotting against him,[4] but his design was anticipated; for Theodoric with his own hand slew him with a sword in the palace of Lauretum. On the same day all his soldiers were slain, wherever they could be found, and all his kin."

Thus Theodoric "supervened"[5] and succeeded Odovacar, as Odovacar had supervened and succeeded Orestes. Both for one and for the other it had been a political necessity to slay his rival; it would have been dangerous to accord him his freedom; and it was not the habit of German warriors to immure fallen adversaries in dungeons. The only possible compromise would have been to divide Italy; but Theodoric had come from the East to recover the whole land. The death of Odovacar was the most natural and simple alternative; confinement in an island was not a method likely to be adopted by a German king. The statement that Odovacar was found plotting against Theodoric has been doubted, though it is quite credible; and whether it is true or not, Theodoric could hardly escape the necessity of putting him to death.

---

[1] That is, £3 : 12s. a peck.

[2] The Ronco. Cf. Hodgkin, iii. 228.

[3] During the year 492 no hostilities took place. The *Anonymus Valesii* proceeds as if no interval took place between the defeat of Odovacar in the Pinewoods and the compact of 493 (27th February, *Anon. Cuspin.*)

[4] *Dum ei Odoachar insidiaretur;* the other sources which depend on the Ravennate Annals (*Anon. Cuspin.*, *Continuatio Prosperi Havn.*, and *Agnellus*) do not mention this moment in the transaction, but it is supported by the Chronicle of Cassiodorus (*Odoacrem molientem sibi insidias*) and Procopius, B. G. i. 1 (ἐπιβουλῇ ἐς αὐτὸν χρώμενον). Cassiodorus is perhaps a prejudiced witness, and was likely to adopt a view favourable to Theodoric.

[5] *Supervenio* is the *vox propria* in the *Anon. Vales.*

But Zeno, who had given the commission of recovering Italy to Theodoric the Patrician, had meanwhile been succeeded by Anastasius; and the new Emperor had adopted an attitude of reaction against his Isaurian predecessor. Theodoric therefore could not be sure of imperial recognition. "He had sent Faustus Niger as an ambassador to Zeno. But having learned of his death before the embassy returned, the Goths confirmed Theodoric as their king, when he entered Ravenna and slew Odovacar, and did not wait for the order of the new Emperor."[1] It was not till five years later that he made peace with Anastasius (498) and "received all the ornaments of the palace which Odovacar had sent to Constantinople."[2] The Roman Emperor tardily recognised him, but looked upon Italy as the territory of an enemy rather than of a Patrician, and even sent ships to make a raid on the coast of Apulia (508).[3]

Theodoric adopted Ravenna, the city of Honorius and Placidia and Valentinian, as his capital. The Emperors who reigned in the days of Ricimer had seldom resided in the palace of the Laurelwood, but Odovacar had adopted it as his home. Theodoric built a new palace in another part of the city, close to the church of St. Martin, in which his Arian Goths worshipped. This church, which is still extant, was afterwards dedicated to St. Apollinaris, and is now known as San Apollinare Nuovo. Of the Ostrogothic palace perhaps some relics still remain; but of the Lauretum, where Odovacar was slain, no trace is left.

While Italy was being ruled by the German Patricians Ricimer, Odovacar, and Theodoric, a new power was consolidating itself in Gaul. Aegidius was the successor of Aetius in the work of maintaining Roman authority and resisting Teutonic advance in Gaul; he opposed Frankish Childeric as Aetius had opposed Frankish Chlojo. It was Childeric who really founded the kingdom of the Franks[4]; he acquired the cities of Köln and Imperial Trier; and at Tournai his tomb and corpse with his armour were found in the seven-

---

[1] *An. Val.* 57.
[2] *Ib.* 63. The negotiator was Festus. It is not clear what the *ornamenta palatii* exactly were.
[3] Marcell. Com. *ad annum*.
[4] The story of Childeric's deposition, Aegidius' elevation, and Childeric's restoration, by the Franks in Gregory of Tours, ii. 12, is rightly rejected as legendary by von Ranke, *Weltgeschichte*, iv. 1, 421. [Cf., however, Gasquet, *L'empire byzantin*, pp. 117, 118.] Childeric was accused *filias eorum* (the Franks) *stuprose detrahere*.

teenth century. If Childeric founded, his son Chlodwig reared and extended, the new kingdom, and achieved for it an important position in the political system of Europe. As the Patrician Aegidius was the adversary of Childeric, the Patrician Syagrius, his son, was the adversary of Chlodwig. Syagrius ruled at Augusta Suessionum (Soissons) as independently of the Empire as Odovacar ruled at Ravenna, yet as the representative of the Roman name. But Syagrius had no allies; his forces were not a match for the might of Chlodwig; and in the year 486 he fled vanquished from a field of battle. The Visigoths, with whom he sought refuge, did not dare to save him; he was delivered to the victor and put to death. This battle decided the predominance of the Franks in Gaul.

Among the German nations who settled in the Roman Empire the Franks had a peculiar position. In the first place, they were less imbued with Roman ideas, they were more opposed to the Roman spirit, they represented more purely the primitive German man,[1] with his customs and ways, than the Ostrogoths, the Visigoths, or the Burgundians. In the second place, they had never served as *foederati* under a Roman Emperor, like the Visigoths under Alaric or the Ostrogoths under Theodoric; neither Chlojo nor Childeric had ever been Roman Patricians or masters of soldiers, nor had they received grants of territory from an Augustus[2]; they won their kingdom by force, without the semblance of right. In the third place, while the Burgundians, Visigoths, Ostrogoths, and Vandals formed their kingdoms in countries where people of their races had never settled before, the kingdom of Childeric arose in lands where Franks had been settled for more than a hundred years.[3] Yet another mark distinguished them from the neighbouring Teutonic kingdoms, when Chlodwig was converted to Christianity by the influence of his Burgundian wife Clotilda and embraced the Catholic creed (496 A.D.), whereas the other German kings and peoples had either been originally baptized or afterwards lapsed into the Arian doctrine. This

---

[1] This is clear from the Salic laws. The Salian Franks derived their name from Sala, the old name of the Yssel.

[2] Since I wrote this sentence, I have read the discussion of M. Gasquet (*op. cit.* p. 122 *sqq.*), and am disposed to think it probable that Childeric held the rank of *magister militum*.

[3] Constantius called them in at the time of the revolt of Magnentius; Libanius, Ἐπιτάφιος on Julian (ed. Reiske, i. 533, 7); von Ranke, *op. cit.* iv. 416.

act smoothed the relations between the Gallo-Roman subjects and their Frankish rulers, and was of vital consequence for the history of western Europe.

Chlodwig subdued the Alemanni in a great battle (about 492 A.D.), and rendered them tributary; he defeated the Arian Burgundians, and compelled them, too, to pay tribute; and he won a decisive victory over the Arian Visigoths on the Campus Vocladensis,[1] where King Alaric the Second fell. But against the great Theodoric he could not contend as he had contended against Alaric and Gundobad; he besieged Arelate, but the forces of the Ostrogoths inflicted a terrible defeat on the Franks and Burgundians outside the walls of the Roman city.[2] Provincia was incorporated in the Ostrogothic kingdom, and ruled by a vicar. Before the death of Theodoric its limits were increased to westward and northward, at the expense of Visigoths and Burgundians, and it was ruled by a praetorian prefect.

Chlodwig, meanwhile, who stood as the Catholic power of the West over against the Arian kings, was recognised as an ally by Anastasius. The Roman Emperor conferred upon the king of the Franks the dignity of the consulate.[3] The geographical positions of the Empire and the kingdom of Chlodwig rendered the alliance natural, as their borders did not touch. The bestowal, however, of the consulship on Chlodwig implies the theory that, as his territory once belonged to the Empire, he was in a certain way still connected with, if not dependent on, the Emperor. Anastasius would hardly have thought of bestowing the consular rank on a German prince who lived in a district of central Europe which had never been an imperial province. Chlodwig was hereby recognised by the Emperor as his successor or vicegerent in Gaul.

Of the political administration of Theodoric something will be said in a future chapter. We may point out here that in relation to the Vandals he followed the policy of Odovacar, and allowed them to retain a small corner of Sicily, including the fortress of Lilybaeum, which had in old days belonged to the

---

[1] Greg. of Tours, ii. 37: *in campo Vogladense;* Vouillé, in Department Vienne.
[2] Jordanes, *Get.* c. 58.
[3] Gregory of Tours, ii. 38: *igitur ab Anastasio imperatore codccillos de consolato accepit et in basilica beati Martini tunica blattea indutus et clamide imponens vertice diadema.*

Carthaginians. Thus at the beginning of the sixth century the political geography of Europe was very different from its simple character at the beginning of the fifth, when civilised Europe and the Roman Empire were conterminous. Beside his possessions in Asia and Egypt, the Emperor exercised direct authority over Thrace and Illyricum, that is the prefecture of Illyricum; but the diocese of Illyricum or Western Illyricum, as it is sometimes called, including Rhaetia, Noricum, Pannonia, and Dalmatia, belonged to the Ostrogothic kingdom of Italy.[1] As the Ostrogothic king was a Roman Patrician, it might be said that the Emperor still ruled nominally over Italy. The rest of the old prefecture of Italy, that is, Africa, Sardinia, and Corsica, with a small part of Sicily, was held by the Vandals, whose kings accentuated their independence of the Empire by wearing the diadem on their coins. The old prefecture of the Gauls had been converted into four Teutonic kingdoms: (1) the small realm of the Suevians in north-western Spain; (2) the large realm of the Visigoths, which extended from the Loire to the Straits of Gades; (3) the kingdom of the Burgundians, on the Rhone; (4) the kingdom of the Franks, which comprised all northern Gaul, and extended east of the Rhine. In these kingdoms two corners are not included, the north-western corner, which was inhabited by Celtic Britons, and the south-eastern corner, Provincia, which passed into the hands of Theodoric when he protected it against the Franks. As for Britain, it was at this time experiencing the invasions of the Saxons and the Angles, and passing out of the remembrance of the Roman Empire.

SAINT SEVERINUS.—Before I conclude this chapter I must give some account of one of the strangest episodes in the history of the dismemberment of the Empire in the West—the condition of the provinces of Noricum and Rhaetia under the dominion of a saint. These provinces formed a Roman island in the midst of a barbarian sea, for German nations had pene-

---

[1] Theodoric won Sirmium from the Gepids in 504. The Gepids were assisted by the Bulgarians. Cf. the Chronicle of Cassiodorus (*ad annum*): *victis Bulgaribus Syrmium recepit Italia*. When Theodoric was engaged in the expedition he assisted the Hun Mundo against the imperial general Sabinian, who had Bulgarian allies. The Ostrogoths were successful (505 A.D. Marcellinus Com.)

trated westward along the Julian Alps and formed a wedge dividing Noricum from Italy. They were exposed to constant invasions from the barbarians who encompassed them—the Ostrogoths, who, after the break-up of the Hun empire, had settled in the lands of the Save,[1] the Thuringians in the north-west, the Alemanni and Suevi in the south-west, the Rugians to the north and north-east, with their dependants, the Turcilingi and Heruls. The Rugians proposed to protect these Roman provinces against the other barbarians, but such a protectorate was a pretext for oppression. The Rhaetian and Noric lands fell into a state of complete disorganisation, political, military, and moral. The imperial officers abandoned their dangerous posts in this inhospitable country and departed to Italy, leaving the maintenance of order to the municipal magistrates. The soldiers quartered as garrisons in the strong towns had no means of maintaining communication, and as their pay became irregular, and finally ceased, owing to the interruption of direct relations with Italy, they were more ready to quarrel with the provincials than to fight with the enemy. They reinforced the bands of brigands or scamars,[2] who began to infest the wild mountainous regions and plunder the plains. The moral chaos is represented as appalling. While the distinction of right and wrong vanished, while prudence and pity were forgotten, the grossest superstitions prevailed. Human beings were actually sacrificed in a town of Noricum to appease some deity or fiend, to whom the miserable condition of the country was attributed. In Noricum and Rhaetia the pain which attended the great travail of the fifth century reached its highest degree, the darkness assumed its blackest hue.

Here, if anywhere, there was need of some divine intervention, of a prophet at least who believed himself divinely inspired. A new social organisation was required to render possible an adequate defence against the barbarians, and as joint action requires a certain minimum of unselfishness, some moral regeneration was a condition of success. Such a prophet, "the apostle of Noricum," came from the East.

---

[1] Theodemir, in the neighbourhood of Vienna; Walamir, on the Save; Widemir, between the two.

[2] This name first occurs in Eugippius, whose *Vita Severini* (recently edited by H. Sauppe in the *Mon. Germ. Hist.*) is our authority for these events. *See* X, 2, *scameras*. Afterwards it often occurs as the name of the robbers in the Balkan peninsula.

It was in the year after Attila's death that Saint Severinus appeared in Pannonia. His past history was a secret that went to the grave with himself. It was only known that he was by birth an Italian, and that "he had set out to a solitude in the East, through a burning desire of the more perfect life" (fervore perfectioris vitae), and that he had travelled much in oriental countries. He learned there the austerities of a monk. His life in the lands of the upper Danube makes us imagine him as a sort of mystic theosophist with strong practical energy.

He united the mission of John the Baptist with the mission of Christ; he preached repentance and lovingkindness. The first city to which he came was Astura, an important commercial centre in Pannonia. He bade the people repent and change their ways, prophesying that otherwise destruction would speedily come upon their city — a safe prophecy; but the people were froward, and looked upon the prophet as a common beggar. Having made only one convert, the porter of the city gate who had taken him in, he proceeded to another town, Comagenae.[1] Soon afterwards Astura was surprised by barbarians, and the fulfilment of the prediction of Severinus, which was noised abroad by the porter, who escaped from the sack of the town, changed his position from that of an obtrusive mendicant impostor to that of a prophet and a saint. It was suddenly discovered that he was the one man capable of saving the imperilled countries, which God seemed to have abandoned.

And for this work Severinus proved well adapted. He was not merely an enthusiast capable of exciting enthusiasm in others, but he had a genius for organisation and command. He was skilful in judging an actual situation, in planning a mode of defence or a sally, in dealing with individual men. He soon had an opportunity of displaying his talents at Faviana (now Mauer), where he was summoned on account of an impending famine, owing to the scarcity of corn, which, as the Inn was frozen, could not be obtained in the usual quantity. The disorganisation and immoral tone in the town prevented its fair distribution, but Severinus restored order, and superintended the apportionment with complete effectiveness. In this town, on the borders

---

[1] Now Tulln, near Mount Cettius (Mommsen, *Corp. Insc. Lat.* iii. 683). Astura is perhaps Klosterneuburg (*ib.*) near Mount Cettius.

of Rhaetia and Noricum, he took up his abode, and made it, as it were, the centre of his administration. Having led the people into the path of repentance, he proceeded to teach them charity. He imposed on all a tax of one-tenth of provisions and one-tenth of raiment for the benefit of the poor, who had always been the chief objects of his solicitude. This tax was enforced by his own moral influence. It is to be particularly observed that his charity was extended to barbarians and brigands as well as others. Misery was a sufficient recommendation.

But his practical activity had not subdued his passion for solitude and the life of the hermit. Suddenly he disappeared from Faviana, and made a cell for himself in a valley of Mount Cettius. And so he passed his life, meditating alternately in his mountain cell and in the monastery which he founded at Faviana.[1]

The history of the intimacy of Severinus with Flaccitheus, king of the Rugians, whose territories reached the left bank of the Danube at Faviana; of his relations with that king's two sons, the feeble Feva and the crafty Frederick, and with Ghisa, Feva's wife, whose nature was deadly and pestilential, *feralis et noxia*,[2] might form the framework of a romance. It is a matter of interest that Odovacar visited the saint's cell as he journeyed southward in search of a career, and that the saint prophesied his greatness; and further, that when he had attained the royal power in Italy, the saint predicted his downfall.

Severinus' government in Noricum and Rhaetia lasted about thirty years (453-482). His task was hardest at the beginning and at the end. At the beginning he had to regenerate the inhabitants; at the end the barbarians pressed harder on the provinces. The Ostrogoths were indirectly the cause of this; for their movement from Pannonia into the Illyrian lands left a place for other nations to press in, and disturbed the existing equilibrium. We may attribute the peace that existed during the reign of Flaccitheus between the Rugians and the provincials of Noricum to the constant warfare that was waged between the Rugians and the Ostrogoths. We hear how the saint made the king of the Alemanni tremble in every limb under his glance; but he was obliged first to

---

[1] He founded two monasteries, one at Faviana, called "the great," and one at Passau (Batavis), called "the small."
[2] Eugippius, *Vit. S. Ser.* viii. 1.

abandon Passau and retreat to Lauriacum (Lorch), and afterwards to yield to the determination of Feva that the provincials should be transported into the land of Lauriacum. The saint did not long survive this; he died in 482, the Rugian royal family standing at his bedside. His dying injunctions and menaces had little effect; Frederick pillaged his monasteries as soon as his eyes were closed.

Odovacar avenged the saint. He determined to win back the provinces of Noricum from the Rugians, with whom, though some said he was a Rugian himself, he had nothing in common. He set out for Italy in 487, and exterminated the Rugian nation. After adorning his triumph, Feva was put to death and Ghisa thrown into a dungeon. The provincials were transported to Italy, and the remains of St. Severinus were conveyed to a monastery at the villa of Lucullus, at the request of a Neapolitan lady.

CHAPTER VI

ANASTASIUS I

AFTER the death of Zeno, Flavius Anastasius of Dyrrhachium was proclaimed Emperor (11th April 491) through the influence of the widowed Empress Ariadne, who married him about six weeks later. Anastasius, who held the not very distinguished post of a *silentiarius* or guardsman, was nevertheless a remarkable and well-known figure in Constantinople. He held unorthodox opinions, partly due, perhaps, to an Arian mother and a Manichaean uncle, and he was possessed by a sort of religious craze, which led him to attempt to convert others to his own opinions. He did this in a curiously public manner. Having placed a chair in the church of St. Sophia, he used to attend the services with unfailing regularity and give private heterodox instruction to a select audience from his cathedra.[1] By this conduct he offended the Patriarch Euphemius, who by Zeno's permission expelled him from the church and pulled down his chair of instruction; but he gained golden opinions from the general public by his piety and liberality. It even appears that he may have at one time dreamt of an ecclesiastical career, for he was proposed for the vacant chair of Antioch.[2] Euphemius, unpleasantly surprised at the choice of the Empress, who was supported by the eunuch Urbicius,[3] refused to crown Anastasius until he had signed a written declaration of ortho-

---

[1] *See* Theophanes, 5982 A.M.
[2] In 488, when Palladius was elected. Compare A. Rose, *Kaiser Anastasius I.* (p. 13), who translates συνεψηφίσθη in Theophanes rightly.
[3] Cedrenus (ed. Bonn), i. 626.

doxy, which, in spite of his heretical tendencies, he did not hesitate to do.[1]

The accession of Anastasius must have seemed to Byzantium a great and a welcome change. Instead of a man like Zeno, who in spite of considerable ability was very unpopular on account of the unfair favour shown to the Isaurians, and who scandalised propriety by his loose life, while he could not attract men by an imposing or agreeable exterior, a man of the highest respectability occupied the throne, a man with a strong religious turn, of slender stature and remarkable for his fine eyes, which differed in hue, a man to whom the people called out when he was proclaimed Emperor, "Reign as you have lived," and to whom a bishop of Rome[2] wrote, "I know that in private life you always strove after piety." He is characterised in general[3] as a man of intelligence and good education, gentle and yet energetic, able to command his temper and generous in bestowing gifts, but with one weak point, a tendency to be unduly parsimonious.

But the accession of the new Emperor was not undisputed. Zeno's brother Longinus, who was president of the senate, conceived that he had a claim to the crown, and he had actually a strong support in his countrymen the Isaurians, who saw that their privileges were endangered. Zeno, who knew his brother well, had with real patriotism refused to designate him as his successor, feeling that his elevation would be a disaster to the Empire; somewhat as Antipater the Macedonian refused to transmit his protectorate to his son Cassander. Longinus, supported by a *magister militum* of the same name, played much the same part against Anastasius that Basiliscus, the brother-in-law of Leo, had played against Zeno. He organised the numerous Isaurians who resided in the capital, and the year of Anastasius' elevation was marked for Constantinople by bloodshed and fatal street battles, in the course of which a large part of the town, including the hippodrome, was destroyed by a conflagration. Anastasius, however, succeeded in removing his rival to Alexandria, where he became a priest by compulsion, early in 492. Longinus, the master of soldiers, was

[1] The document was lodged in the church archives under the charge of the skeuophylax.
[2] Gelasius (Mansi, *Concilia*, xiii. 30).
[3] By Johannes Lydus, *de Mag.* i. 47.

deposed from his office and returned with many other Isaurians to his mountainous home in Asia Minor.

The tedious Isaurian war, of which this was the first scene, lasted for five years, 491-496.[1] The events of the first years are often obscured by failing to understand clearly that hostilities were carried on in Constantinople and Isauria simultaneously; the war had begun in Isauria before the Isaurians were expelled from Constantinople. Longinus and his friends, who arrived, filled with indignation, in the regions of Mount Taurus, roused their excitable countrymen to revolt; and an understanding evidently existed between the rebels in Asia Minor and the rebels in Byzantium. Among the generals who led the Isaurians in conjunction with Longinus was Conon, the archbishop of Apamea.[2] Their forces marched in a northwesterly direction towards the Propontis, but at Cotyaeum in Phrygia they were met by a small army which Anastasius had sent against them under the command of many experienced officers. The masses of the rebels were utterly routed and fled back to their mountains, while the imperial soldiers followed leisurely and took up winter quarters at the foot of the Taurus range.

In what relations the various generals in command of Anastasius' small army stood to one another we do not know; but it would be unfair to suppose that Anastasius was adopting the policy of dividing the command from motives of jealousy or suspicion. The number of commanders is quite accounted for by the nature of the warfare to be expected in the defiles of Taurus, where it was necessary for small divisions to act in many places, and a large regiment under a single leader would have been of little use.

The news of Cotyaeum was followed by an edict (issued in the capital in 493) unfavourable to the Isaurians, who thereupon filled the streets with all the horrors of fire and sword, and hauled along with ropes the bronze statues of the Emperor.

---

[1] Marcellinus is probably wrong in placing the latest events of the war in 497. See Rose, *op. cit.* p. 19.

[2] Other commanders were Silingis (Ninilingis?), a bastard brother of Illus; Athenodorus, noted for his wealth (but al. ἀπλούστατος, Theoph. p. 138, ed. de Boor). The forces numbered about 100,000, John of Antioch, 214ᵇ (*F. H. G.* iv.) The generals of Anastasius were Johannes the Scythian, who had conquered Illus; Johannes, the hunchback; Diogenes, a relation of Ariadne; Justin, who was afterwards Emperor; Apsikal, a barbarian.

These scenes of indecent violence were with difficulty suppressed,[1] and then a summary edict was issued banishing all Isaurians from the city, among the rest the family of Zeno,[2] while the Isaurica or annual grant of 1000 lbs. of gold (which Zeno had instituted) was withdrawn.

The banished members of the obnoxious nationality, burning for revenge, reinforced their countrymen in the castles and hiding-places of the Taurus mountains, and for the next three years (493-496) a somewhat desultory but anxious war was carried on round the strong places of the country. Claudiopolis, a very important position, was taken in 493, and in 494 a considerable victory was won near the same city in a battle which was fatal to archbishop Conon. The following year saw the capture and execution (at Byzantium) of Longinus, one of the chiefs, not to be confounded with the ex-magister[3]; and in 496 the last two surviving leaders, Longinus and Athenodorus, were taken, and the war was at an end.

It is important to note that the Isaurians were then removed from their Asiatic home and transported to Thrace,[4] but it is hard to believe that this measure can have been carried out with any degree of completeness. The whole history of the Isaurian war indicates what an isolated position, from their sentiments, habits, and mode of life, the Isaurians held in the Empire, as we have already described. It was as natural for them to take up arms when an Isaurian did not succeed Zeno as it would have been for the Ostrogoths if by some extraordinary concurrence of circumstances Theodoric had become a Roman Emperor and on his death an Ostrogoth did not replace him.

Besides its disastrous effects on agriculture and industry in the south of Asia Minor, this long war led indirectly to other harmful consequences. It was a very unsuitable and unfortunate preparation for the serious Persian war which broke out in 502, and was only temporarily terminated by the

---

[1] By Anastasius' brother-in-law, Secundinus, husband of his sister Caesaria.

[2] Lalis, his mother; Valeria, the wife of Longinus; Longina, her daughter, who married one Zeno, son of Anthemius and Herais. All the property of Zeno and the Isaurians was confiscated; the imperial robes of Zeno were sold.

[3] Thus three persons named Longinus were connected with this Isaurian war—(1) the brother of Zeno, who disappears at the very beginning; (2) the ex-magister; (3) a leader executed in 495, called the Selinuntian.

[4] Procopius of Gaza, *Panegyr.* c. 10.

peace of 505. An account of this three years' war will be given in the next chapter, but it may be here observed that the Isaurian warfare, which required operations in small divisions and introduced the practice of numerous independent commands, was a bad drill for the war in Mesopotamia, which demanded the united action of large bodies under one supreme general.

In the meantime the Balkan lands were becoming acquainted with new foes, who were destined to play a great part in the subsequent history of the Roman Empire. The departure of Theodoric the Ostrogoth to Italy left Thrace and Illyricum free for the Slaves, who dwelt beyond the Danube in the countries which are now called Siebenbürgen and Moldavia, to invade and plunder. The first invasion of which we have record[1] took place in 493, on which occasion they severely defeated Julianus, the master of soldiers, and devastated Thrace. The next invasion that we hear of was in 517, when they penetrated into Macedonia and Thessaly; but it is highly probable that in the intervening years they were not idle, though we have no record. But other enemies had also laid waste the provinces and defeated the legions. These were the Bulgarians, a people of the Ural-Altaic or Ugro-Finnic race, who must not be confounded with the Slaves. They are first mentioned as having been employed by Zeno against Theodoric, by whom they were defeated. In 499 they crossed the Danube, and returned gorged with plunder, and crowned with the glory of a victory over a Roman army; and in 502 they repeated their successful expedition.[2]

It seems clear to me that there must have been invasions, whether of Slaves or Bulgarians, between the years 502 and 512, which our scanty and brief notices have not recorded. For, in the first place, they had met with no repulse; invasion was easy and inviting; nothing except hostilities among the

---

[1] In the Chronicle of Marcellinus they are called Getae, because they lived in the homes of the old Getae. For the Slaves, *see* below, Bk. iv. pt. i. cap. xii.

[2] I may conjecture, though there is no evidence on the subject, that Anastasius formed the settlements of Isaurians in Thrace in order to replenish a population decimated by the incursion of the barbarians. The presence of the Ostrogoths must have in the first instance reduced it; the expedition of the Slaves in 493 did further mischief; and it may have been after 499 that the settlement took place. The Isaurians were a stout race, accustomed to self-help, and would be suitable settlers in a land constantly exposed to the raids of barbarians.

barbarians themselves could have hindered them. In the second place, Anastasius built the Long Wall for protection against their hostilities in 512, and it is hardly conceivable that he would have built it then if, during the ten preceding years, the provinces had been exempted from the devastations of the heathen. It rather seems probable that in 510 or 511 a really dangerous invasion took place, and that this was the immediate cause of the erection of the wall. This wall, of which traces are still visible, stretched from the Sea of Marmora at Selymbria to the Black Sea. Its length was 420 stadia, its distance from the city was 280 stadia, and its effect was to insulate Constantinople.[1]

Thus the arms of Anastasius were so unsuccessful in Europe that at last no serious attempt was made to protect Thrace; he confined himself to saving the capital by a massive fortification. This wall was really efficacious, and it is meaningless rhetoric to call it a "monument of cowardice," an expression which might be applied to all fortifications. On the other hand, in Asia some useful successes were gained in 498 against the Bedouin or Scenite Arabs, who had begun to invade Syria and Palestine. They were thoroughly defeated in two battles.[2] But a success of still greater consequence was the recovery of the island of Jotaba, from which the Romans had been expelled in the reign of Leo. Jotaba was the centre of an important Red Sea trade; all the ships with cargoes from India put in there, and custom-house duties were collected by imperial officers. Its possession was thus extremely important for the Empire.[3]

Anastasius' reign was signalised by many riots and disturbances in Constantinople. These often took the form of conflicts between the Blues and Greens, the latter of whom were favoured by Anastasius, as they identified themselves with the unorthodox monophysitic party. The religious disputes and the schism with Rome were noticed in a previous chapter; here I shall only call attention to the strained relations, already referred to, between the Emperor and the Patriarch Euphemius.

[1] Evagrius, iii. 38.
[2] Eugenius defeated one party at Bithapsus, Romanus routed Agarus at Gamalus.
[3] Theoph. 5990 A.M. Cf. Rose, *op. cit.* p. 28.

It happened that in 495 Anastasius informed the Patriarch that he was sick of the Isaurian war, and would willingly make easy conditions with the rebels, if he could thereby conclude it. Euphemius was treacherous enough to repeat these words to Johannes, a son-in-law of Athenodorus, one of the Isaurian leaders. We cannot determine to what extent Euphemius entertained a traitorous design; but Anastasius, when Johannes made him aware of the Patriarch's communication, looked upon him, or chose to look upon him, as a traitor and accomplice of the rebels. He was banished, or fled, soon afterwards from Byzantium.

There was a strong party of opposition whose hostile machinations must have often made the Emperor feel insecure. How this party, which represented the orthodox faith, acted in regard to the Isaurian revolt we do not hear; but the incident of Euphemius, just related, might incline us to suspect their loyalty during those years. The measures adopted by Anastasius for the reform of abuses created much discontent among those who profited by them; he put down informers (*delatores*) with a firm hand. His conscientious scruples did not permit him to indulge the corrupt populace in the dissolute and barbarous amusements to which they were accustomed. He forbade the practice of contests with wild beasts, a relic of heathen Rome which was an anachronism in the christian world. We cannot be surprised at its survival so long when we remember that gladiatorial shows lasted for fifty years after Rome had become christian; and we must also recollect that the christian doctrine that animals have no souls hindered any strong sentiment on the subject. He also refused to allow the celebration of nocturnal feasts, which were the occasions of licentious orgies. The May feast of Bruta[1] was on two occasions the scene of scandalous riots, resulting in the sacrifice of life, and the Emperor forbade its celebration for the future, thereby (says a contemporary) "depriving the city of the most beautiful dances." Thus his staid and frugal court, which his enemies might call shabby, his strict censorship of morals, which seemed, as we should say, puritanical, and his heretical opinions in theo-

---

[1] John of Antioch, fr. 214c (*F. H. G.* iv.) It was also called feast of Majumas. It was a Roman festival, and the custom was that grave officials (οἱ ἐν τοῖς τέλεσι) should duck one another in sea water.

logy, exposed Anastasius to constant odium, which culminated (511 A.D.) when he sanctioned the adoption of a monophysitic addition to the hymn called Trisagios ("thrice holy").[1] To quell the sedition Anastasius adopted a theatrical artifice, which was successful. He appeared before the people without a crown, and offered to resign the sovereignty in favour of another. The respect which his uniform conscientiousness had inspired in all predominated for the moment, and the multitude cried to him that he should resume the diadem. But discontent continued to prevail, and the opposition was so strong that it seemed a good opportunity for an ambitious man who had soldiers at his command to attempt to dethrone the Emperor.

In 514 such an attempt was made. The commissariat which had been supplied by the State to the corps of foreign foederati, who were stationed to defend Thrace and Scythia, had been withdrawn, and the discontent which ensued afforded a new pretext against the existing government. Vitalian, the son of a man[2] who had been himself count of the foederati, fostered the ill-feeling. He was a man small in stature, and afflicted with a stammer, but he had associated constantly with Huns and Bulgarians, and could count on their co-operation. The brunt of the unpopularity of the government with the soldiers was borne by Hypatius, the Emperor's nephew, who was the master of soldiers in Thrace, and it was against him in the first instance that Vitalian directed his attack. By stratagem he compassed the death of the chief officers of his staff, he corrupted the governor of Lower Moesia, and then capturing Carinus, Hypatius' trusted confidant, he granted him his life on the conditions that he should co-operate in the capture of Odessus and recognise himself as general. Hypatius seems to have escaped to Constantinople.

The rebel, or "tyrant," as he was called, then advanced on the capital with 50,000 soldiers, consisting partly of the foederati and partly of rustics, some of whom were perhaps Slaves settled in Moesia and Scythia. It was not merely as spokesman of the grievances of the army, and as protesting against the administration of Hypatius, that Vitalian posed; he also

---

[1] ὁ σταυρωθεὶς δι' ἡμᾶς was inserted after ἀθάνατος in the following words: ἅγιος ὁ θεός, ἅγιος ἰσχυρός, ἅγιος ἀθάνατος ἐλέησον ἡμᾶς. The orthodox, on the other hand, inserted ἁγία τριάς.

[2] A native of Zaldaba, in Lower Moesia.

professed to be the champion of orthodoxy, indignant at the treatment of certain bishops whom Anastasius had banished. He took care to insist on this pretext; and we may confidently assume that he had established intimate relations with the disaffected party in the city.[1]

"The Emperor, inclined to be timorous on account of his recent experiences (that is, the revolt of 511), and vexed by the unexpectedness of these occurrences as well as by the fact that the adversaries who were advancing made a similar pretence of blaming his religion (as the rebels had done on the former occasion), commanded bronze crosses to be set up over the gates of the walls, setting forth in writing the real cause of the rebellion. He also reduced by one-quarter the tax on animals for the inhabitants of Bithynia and Asia, depositing the bill to that effect on the altar of the First Church (St. Sophia). He employed the officers and ministers as a garrison for the city.

"But when Vitalian attacked the suburbs and marched round the walls, the Master of Soldiers, Patricius, was sent to him. Such missions devolved upon him in virtue of his office; moreover, he was distinguished by honour and dignities, and had considerably helped Vitalian himself in his successful career. He took Vitalian sharply to task, availing himself of the liberty permitted to a benefactor; and in reply Vitalian, as was to be expected, dwelled on many acts passed by the Emperor, and pointed out that the present object of himself and his party was (1) to rectify the injustices committed by the magister militum per Thracias (Hypatius), and (2) to obtain the recognition and sanction of the orthodox theological creed.

"Next day the chief officers of Vitalian's camp came, on the Emperor's invitation, without Vitalian, for he could not be persuaded to enter the city; and an interview was held in which the Emperor, having charged them and proved to them that they were not disdained or passed over, won them by presents and by promises that they would receive their dues, and undertook that the church of Old Rome would be allowed to arrange the religious questions at stake. When they had declared with oaths their future loyalty to him, he dismissed them. Having returned to Vitalian, they departed with him and the army."[2]

Thus the first essay of Vitalian was frustrated by the desertion of his officers, whose confidence Anastasius won. Anastasius followed up his promises by appointing Cyrillus to the

---

[1] So the revolution which overthrew Maurice in 602 rested on a combination of a general (Phocas) without and an opposition party within Byzantium. The parallel is increased by the analogy between the unpopularity of the General Hypatius, Anastasius' nephew, and that of the General Peter, Maurice's brother. Rose, who perhaps passes too lightly over the religious aspect of the revolt, does not seem to have grasped this combination.

[2] John of Antioch, fr. 214e (*F. H. G.* vol. v.) Marcellinus, ill-disposed to Anastasius, describes his diplomacy in this matter, which he does not give in detail, as "pretences and perjuries."

post of *magister militum* instead of his nephew, who was so unpopular with the army. Cyrillus proceeded to Lower Moesia, where he knew that he would find Vitalian actively engaged in new schemes. Vitalian was even more on the alert than he thought, and as the general was enjoying the society of his concubines a Hunnish assassin slew him. This act made it clear that the rebel was irreconcilable, and a decree of the senate was passed in old Roman style—the use of this formality is noteworthy — that Vitalian was an enemy of the republic (ἀλλότριον τῆς πολιτείας).

A large army of 80,000 was collected, and while Alathar, a Hun, was appointed to succeed Cyrillus, the supreme command of the army was assigned to the unpopular Hypatius, who was accompanied by Theodorus, "steward of the sacred treasures." Vitalian's new army consisted of Huns, Bulgarians, and perhaps Slaves, recruited probably as before from rustics of the Haemus provinces. We have no hint that his former adherents, the officers whom Anastasius' adroitness had won over, or their soldiers, fell back again from their allegiance, and we may assume that they joined the imperial army. The Emperor's forces gained an inconsiderable victory, which was soon followed by serious reverses. Julian, a *magister memoriae*, was taken alive by the rebels, and carried about in a cage, as Bajazet was carried about by Timour, but was afterwards ransomed. Hypatius then fortified himself behind a rampart of waggons at Acris, on the Black Sea, near Odyssus. In this entrenchment the barbarians attacked him, and, assisted by a sudden darkness, which a superstitious historian attributed to magic arts, gained a signal victory. The Romans, driven over precipices and into ravines, lost about 60,000 men. Hypatius himself ran into the sea, if perchance he might conceal himself in the waves, but his head betrayed him, for he was unable to practise the cunning trick of the Slaves, who were accustomed thus to elude the pursuit of their enemies, breathing under water through a long hollow reed, one end of which was held in their mouth while the other was just above the surface. Vitalian preserved him alive as a valuable hostage. This victory enabled him to pay his barbarian allies richly, and placed him in possession of all the cities and fortresses in Moesia and Scythia, which he ruled as an emperor. The ambassadors whom Anastasius sent with 10,000 lbs. of gold to ransom his nephew were captured in an ambush at Sozopolis.

In the meantime a tumult, attended with loss of life, took place in Constantinople because the Emperor forbade the celebration of a festival on account of disorders in the circus which had occurred on the same day; among others the prefect of the watch was slain. This disturbance, along with the captivity of his nephew and the threatened siege, may have perhaps contributed to induce Anastasius to make a compromise with Vitalian. The conditions were that Vitalian should be made *magister militum per Thracias*, that he should receive 15,000 lbs. of gold, that the proclamation of the orthodox faith should be renewed, and that Hypatius should be liberated.

The following year (515) was troubled not only by the ravages of a horde of Sabir Huns, who entered Asia Minor through Armenia, and laid waste Cappadocia and the provinces of Pontus, penetrating as far as Lycaonia, whence they returned gorged with booty and laden with captives, but also by a fresh demonstration of hostility on the part of Vitalian. He marched on Constantinople, and took up his quarters at Sycae. He then embarked in a fleet which he had prepared, and was completely defeated off Scutari by Marinus the Lycian, some say with the help of chemicals prepared by a man of science named Proclus, an Archimedes of that day. This naval victory decided the war. Vitalian withdrew, probably to the neighbourhood of the Danube, and we hear that a Hunnish leader named Tarrach was captured and burned at Chalcedon, and that many other prominent rebels were punished.

Although Anastasius did not accomplish anything that can be called brilliant, his reign was prosperous. His mild character and his beneficial reforms partially blotted out, in the eyes of contemporaries and of historians, the deadly taint of heterodoxy, and he appeared in a still more favourable light as he was directly contrasted with his unpopular Isaurian predecessor. Mildness is a trait on which his panegyrist Priscian more than once insists,[1] comparing him to Nerva—

et mitem Nervam lenissima pectora vincunt,

---

[1] This trait is confirmed by Lydus, τῷ πάντων βασιλέων ἡμερωτάτῳ.

and another eulogist[1] represents him as a *deus ex machina* setting right the wrongs and lightening the burdens of the Empire. A member of the civil service, who began his career in this reign, asserts that Anastasius' careful financial policy, and his strictness in supervising personally the details of the budget, really saved the State, which had first become financially involved by the money that was expended on Leo's unsuccessful armament against the Vandals, and had been kept in a depressed condition by the shortsighted and "miserable" policy of Zeno.[2]

The act which earned for him most glory and popularity was the abolition of the Chrysargyron,[3] a tax on all receipts, to which the humblest labourer and the poorest prostitute were liable. It had been instituted by Constantine, and Anastasius abolished it in 498. The chief fault that the Church had to find with this tax was that it recognised vices forbidden by nature and the laws.[4] Another abuse which the Emperor remedied was the unfairness of officers in paying rations to their soldiers, in order to make a private profit; this is not mentioned by any writer, but the facts are preserved in an inscription at Ptolemais in the Pentapolis.[5] His donations to soldiers are perhaps another indication of his interest in the army. He was indefatigable in restoring "prostrate cities," and, besides the Great Wall, he executed an important public work which deserves mention, the construction of a canal connecting Lake Sophon with the Gulf of Astacus.[6]

But the men of Dyrrhachium had the reputation of being avaricious, and even favourable writers say that Anastasius was no exception. Elegiac verses were posted up in the hippodrome by his foes, addressing him as "bane of the world" (κοσμοφθόρε). His love of money, it was said, induced him to listen

[1] Procopius of Gaza.
[2] Johannes Lydus, iii. c. 43 *sqq.*
[3] Anastasius burned all the documents relating to the collection of this tax, so that it could not be renewed. So the Emperor Gratian had caused the lists of arrears of taxes to be burnt in every town throughout the provinces which he ruled over.
[4] Evagrius, iii. 39. Anastasius' abolition of the tax is said (Cedrenus, i. 627, Bonn) to have been due to a play on the subject composed by an actor of Gaza named Timotheus. Anastasius favoured the theatre, and in his reign Choricius of Gaza wrote an essay ὑπὲρ τῶν ἐν Διονύσου τὸν βίον εἰκονιζόντων (*Revue de Philol.* 1877, pp. 212-247).
[5] Zachariä von Lingenthal, *Abhandlungen der Berl. Acad.* 1879; Wetzstein, *ib.* 1863.
[6] "A work which Pliny had proposed to Trajan, and which was restored by the Byzantine Emperor Alexius I." (Finlay, i. 182). *See* Pliny, *Ep.* x. 50.

to the counsels of Marinus, a Syrian scriniarius, who wormed himself into his confidence by promising to raise large sums. It is very probable, however, that our authority, Johannes Lydus, had strong prejudices against the successful Syrian, and misrepresents his policy. There seem to have been a Marinus faction and an anti-Marinus faction in official circles.[1]

The great innovation of Marinus was the abolition of the old curial system, by which the curiae or municipal corporation collected the moneys due to the State. A new farming system was introduced. Officers, named *vindices*, were appointed to collect the revenue, which on the old system was often cheated through the collusion of the provincial magnates with the governors of the provinces and the tax-collectors (*canonicarii*). The enemies of Marinus said that the *vindices* treated the cities like foes, because the appointments were given by auction to those who promised most.[2] The nature of the new system evidently involved this evil, but it is only fair to assume that Anastasius, whose mildness was so remarkable, took care to arrange a mode of checking this by increasing the influence of the *defensores*, and his panegyrist Priscian represents the measure as healing a flagrant abuse.[3] It must be noted that this change involved an increase of centralisation, which seems to have been an object of Anastasius' policy. Henceforward even minute matters were referred to the Emperor, so that few steps could be taken in the provinces "without a divine command."

Anastasius is said to have never sent petitioners empty away, whether they represented a city, a fort, or a harbour. He was above giving offices by favour, and when his wife Ariadne requested him to appoint Anthemius to the praetorian prefecture, he refused to make an exception to his principle that only men of forensic training (λογικοί) were entitled to it. His saving policy necessarily involved a great reduc-

---

[1] I infer this from Lydus' expression οἱ Μαρινιῶντες, who, he says, were enriched by Marinus' policy, as well as Marinus himself and Anastasius (iii. c. 49).

[2] Lydus says the general result was to impoverish the provinces, and thus decrease the business done in the bureaux of the praetorian prefect. This meant a diminution of his own fees. Evagrius, who is hostilely inclined to Anastasius, as heterodox, says of the measure (iii. 42): ὅθεν κατὰ πολὺ οἵ τε φόροι διερρύησαν τά τε ἄνθη τῶν πόλεων διέπεσεν.

[3] Agricolas miserans dispendia saeva relaxas;
curia perversis nam cessat moribus omnis
nec licet injustis solito contemnere leges.

tion of the court expenditure, and he was probably on that account unpopular with the frivolous nobles and the court ladies, accustomed to the pageants and pleasures of Byzantine festivals. But the staid Anastasius did not care for pomp, and the result of his fiscal economy was that he not only righted the financial depression of the Empire, but that at his death 320,000 lbs. of gold were found in the treasury.

Anastasius died in July 518, more than eighty years old.

CHAPTER VII

THE PERSIAN WAR

THE restored Persian empire under the sovereignty of the Sassanid dynasty rose on the ruins of the Parthian Arsacids in the reign of Alexander Severus (226 A.D.) During the third and fourth centuries, the eastern frontier was the scene of fatal wars, in the course of which two Roman Emperors, Valerian and Julian, perished. In 363 a treaty was concluded, by which Jovian ceded five provinces beyond the Euphrates, including Arzanene and Corduene, and the towns of Nisibis and Singara to Sapor, and this cession was followed by an emigration of the Greeks from those lands, because Sapor and the Magi afflicted the Christians with persecutions.

During the fifth century the relations of the Empire with Persia varied, but there were no protracted or considerable hostilities, although Armenia, the perpetual source of annoyance, was in a state of ferment, and a serious war seemed ever on the point of breaking out. This was in a great measure due to the circumstance that the Persian monarchs were fully occupied with dangerous and savage enemies on the north-east frontier of their kingdom—the Ephthalite Huns; while the Roman Emperors had enough to do in weathering the storms that were convulsing Europe.

When our period begins, in the reign of Arcadius, Varahran was on the throne, but was succeeded in 399 by Isdigerd, who was as much an object of veneration to Greek historians as he was an object of detestation to the chroniclers of his own kingdom. He did not take advantage of the childhood of Theodosius II to vex the Empire; and I do not see that there is sufficient reason to follow modern writers in rejecting the statement of Procopius, that Arcadius in his testament made Isdigerd the guardian of his son. There is nothing incredible in this, provided we regard it in the proper light, and recognise that it was only a way of paying a compliment to a royal brother. The guardianship was merely nominal; and Arcadius' act of courtesy is not without a parallel in later Roman history.[1] The fact that Procopius mentions it with no expression of amazement shows that it did not strike all men, who breathed in the atmosphere of the time, with surprise; and it is therefore arbitrary in modern writers to follow Agathias in pronouncing it improbable.

Isdigerd's successor, Varahran II, was sufficiently amenable to the influence of the Magi to persecute the christian residents in Persia. A cruel system of proselytising was carried on in Persarmenia, and some outrages were committed on Roman merchants. The consequence was a war, which lasted for two years (420-421); the Persians held Nisibis against the siege of the Roman general Ardaburius (father of Aspar), and the Romans on their side defended Theodosiopolis against the attacks of the Persians. It is narrated that the war was decided by a sort of medieval single combat between a Persian, Ardazanes, and a Goth, Areobindus, in which the latter was victorious; but the tale should perhaps be relegated to the region of myth. A peace, however, was concluded for one hundred years. An interesting incident of this war, which deserves to be recorded, was the humanity of Acacius, the bishop of Amida, who ransomed 7000 *Persian* captives at his own and the Church's costs.

Varahran appointed a Parthian governor in Armenia in 422, but this governor's personal character made him so unpopular that the Armenian nobles begged in 428 for a Persian satrap, and their petition was granted.

At this time began the struggles of Persia with the Haithal nation, known in Roman history as the Ephthalite or Nephthalite Huns,[2] whose abode was beyond the Oxus. They invaded

[1] Heraclius, when he started for the Persian war, placed his son under the guardianship of the chagan of the Avars. The weightiest objection against the statement of Procopius is the scepticism of Agathias (iv. 26).

[2] They do not seem to have been really Huns, from the physiographical description given by Procopius (*Bell. Pers.* i. 3); *see* Rawlinson, *Seventh Oriental Monarchy*, p. 295.

Persia, but Varahran defeated them. Under Varahran Persia flourished. He was succeeded (440) by Isdigerd "the clement," who straightway declared war against the Empire, but circumstances, on which historians are silent, led to an almost immediate conclusion of peace. Isdigerd was soon engaged in a war with the Ephthalites, which lasted for nine years. He made energetic endeavours to convert Armenia to the religion of Zoroaster, but the Armenians were so tenacious of their Christianity that his efforts were expended in vain. The noble family of the Mamigonians was noted as singularly staunch in supporting the national faith.

Perozes succeeded Isdigerd II (453), having overthrown his rival Hormisdas with the assistance of the Ephthalites, who were the inveterate enemies of the Persian kingdom, but might be the temporary friends of a Persian aspirant. His reign was occupied in quelling serious revolts, which agitated Armenia, and in making war on the khan of the Ephthalites, by whose cunning stratagem of covered ditches he was defeated and slain in 483. Balas (Valâkhesh), perhaps his brother, followed him, and enjoyed a shorter but more peaceable reign. He made a treaty with the Huns, consenting to pay them a tribute for two years. He pacified Armenia by granting unreserved freedom of religion, and ordaining that in future it should be governed directly by a king and not by a deputy. Soon afterward internal conspiracies forced him to make yet further concessions; Vahan the Mamigonian was appointed governor of Armenia, and Christianity was fully reinstated. Balas died in 487.

The reign of his successor Kobad (Cabades), the son of Perozes, is remarkable for the rise of the communistic reformer Mazdak.[1] The first principle of this teacher was that all men are naturally equal. It followed that the present state of society is contrary to nature and unjustifiable, and thence that the acts which society considers to be crimes are, as merely tending to overthrow an unjustifiable institution, themselves blameless. Community of property and wives was another deduction that naturally followed. The remarkable thing is that King Kobad himself embraced and actively helped to promulgate these doctrines, which the Persian lords and the

---

[1] *See* Rawlinson, *op. cit.* 342 *sqq.* Tabari; Agathias, iv. 27; and Procop. Our authorities are Mirkhond and *B. P.* i. 5.

orthodox Zoroastrians viewed with utter repugnance and contempt. Impatient of such a recreant monarch, the nobles immured him in the castle of Lethe, and proclaimed Zamasp king (498-501); while Mazdak was imprisoned, but forcibly released by his disciples. In the space of two or three years Kobad found means to escape, and with the help of the Huns was reinstated on the throne. In his attitude to Mazdakism and Zoroastrianism during his restored reign he adopted a compromise; as a king he was a fire-worshipper, as a man he was a follower of Mazdak.

It was at this point that hostilities were renewed between Persia and New Rome. In 442 it had been agreed that the Roman government was to contribute a certain sum to enable Persia to provide for the defence of the Caucasian pass of Derbend, close to the Caspian Sea, against trans-Caucasian tribes. Demands had been twice made of the Emperor Leo to fulfil the engagement, but he had refused. It is generally stated that Kobad pressed Anastasius for this payment; but it is more probable that the cause of the outbreak of the war was somewhat different.[1] For their assistance in restoring him to his throne the Persian king owed the Ephthalites a large sum of money which he had promised them, and, finding difficulty in raising it, he applied to Anastasius. The Emperor, however, had no intention of lending it to him, and his refusal took the form of a demand for a written acknowledgment or *cautio*, as he knew well that to Kobad, unfamiliar with the usages of Roman law, such a mercantile transaction would appear contemptible and intolerable. Kobad replied by a hostile demonstration in Armenia, and thus the "hundred years'" peace was broken, after a duration of exactly eighty (502 A.D.)

Martyropolis, Theodosiopolis, and Amida, the strong places of the great marchland, fell into the hands of the Sassanid monarch one after another. Martyropolis surrendered, Theodosiopolis was betrayed, and Amida, after a long and laborious winter siege, was surprised during a festival early in the year 503, a Persian soldier having chanced to discover the

---

[1] J. Lydus attributes the war to a demand for the costs of maintaining the castle of Birparach. Rawlinson follows this account, but I follow Theodorus Lector (ii. 52), cf. Theophanes, 5996 A.M.; and so Rose, *op. cit.* p. 33.

issue of a mine.[1] The besiegers had been so long baffled that the garrison and inhabitants ultimately yielded to the negligence of security, and they used to mock the Persians from the walls. A massacre commenced, but was stayed, perhaps by the persuasions of a priest, and Amida was left with a garrison of 1000 men. Thus in the course of a year the three most important frontier fastnesses of the Romans had been lost— Amida in Mesopotamia, Martyropolis and Theodosiopolis on the borders of Armenia.

Anastasius arrayed an army of 15,000 men to take the field, but, still influenced by the traditions of the Isaurian warfare, which had been waged some years before, he committed the grave mistake of dividing the command among several generals. First among these must be named Areobindus, the great-grandson of Aspar (on the mother's side) and husband of the daughter of the Emperor Olybrius; he was a man who seems to have loved dancing and flute-playing better than the serious things of life, and he exhibited slowness and slackness in his conduct of the war. Hypatius, a nephew of Anastasius, also received a general's commission, a post which his military inexperience did not deserve. Other commanders of less importance but more ability or energy were Justin, who afterwards became Emperor; Patriciolus, the father of Vitalian; Romanus.[2]

The campaign of 503 opened with a success for the combined divisions of Areobindus and Romanus in the neighbourhood of Nisibis; but the enemy soon mustered a stronger army and forced Areobindus from the position which he had occupied at Constantina in Arzanene. The jealousy of Hypatius induced him to keep back the assistance which the most moderate standard of duty and patriotism required him to send to Areobindus, and the latter, left unsupported, had almost decided to return to Constantinople. In the meantime, while the Roman generals were quarrelling, the Persians occupied Nisibis, and soon afterwards fell unexpectedly upon the troops of Hypatius

---

[1] Eustathius of Epiphania wrote a special work on this siege of Amida (Evagr. iii. 37), and it is described in the Syriac ecclesiastical history of Zacharias of Mitylene, edited by Land. The chapters relating to Amida were published, with a Latin translation, in Mai's *Script. Vet. Collect.* vol. x. (1838), which I have consulted. A curious wine, in the form of a powder, was found in Amida, but the secret of its production was lost (p. 370).

[2] Phylarch of Euphratesia.

and Patricius (a Phrygian commander) and destroyed a large number of their men.

At this juncture an event happened which changed the tide of fortune, but from which the Romans, had they been led by one able general, might have drawn far greater profit. The Huns invaded Persia, and numerous forces were demanded in the north-east of the kingdom; Kobad therefore desired to make peace. But he thought he could have peace and war simultaneously, and while he treated he devastated. Areobindus, however, defeated him near Edessa, and then he withdrew. The campaigns of 504 were advantageous to the Empire. Hypatius had been recalled, and a valiant Illyrian named Celer, the master of offices, was appointed as a new general. He invaded and devastated Arzanene, and his achievements were followed by successes which the other generals gained elsewhere. Nisibis was wellnigh recovered, and Amida was blockaded. The Roman siege, like the Persian siege two years before, lasted throughout the winter (504-505), and the garrison finally consented to surrender, but on very favourable terms. This advantage was followed by the conclusion of a peace for seven years, by which Amida was left in possession of the Romans, who, however, on the whole had lost, while the Persians on the whole had gained, by this three years' war.

Some years later, probably in 507,[1] Anastasius converted the little village of Daras in Mesopotamia into a splendid fortified town, provided richly with churches, corn magazines, and cisterns, and boasting two public baths. He named it after himself, Anastasiopolis, and it was henceforward one of the centres of frontier warfare. Kobad protested against the work, but, hampered as he was by hostile neighbours in the northeast, he was ready to yield to the diplomacy and accept the bribes of Anastasius, who at the same time strengthened the city of Theodosiopolis on the Armenian borders.

---

[1] Theoph. 6000 A.M. *See* Zacharias of Mitylene, cap. xi. *de urbe Dara condita*. The objects of its foundation were (1) to be *exercitui perfugium et statio*, (2) to be an *armorum officina*, (3) to be *regionis Arabicae praesidium adversus Persas latrones atque Ismaelitas*.

CHAPTER VIII

GREEK LITERATURE OF THE FIFTH CENTURY

AN able critic of the first or second century A.D.[1] describes a discussion which he had with a literary friend as to the causes of the decline of Greek letters; why, they asked, are literary works of supreme excellence, works in the grand style, no longer produced. His friend attributed it to the Empire of Rome, which kept the spirits of men in bondage; he considered that grandeur of thought, and consequently grandeur of style, were largely conditioned by political freedom. The critic himself, on the other hand, was inclined to defend the "peace of the world" against this impeachment, and to attribute the decadence of letters and the lack of inspiration to the decline of human character, to the growing love of money, the growing love of luxury, and, above all, the growing feeling of indifference ($ῥᾳθυμία$).

A modern critic, accustomed to take account of the reciprocal influences of character on environment and of environment on character, would reconcile the disputants by observing that the discrepant opinions were only superficially discordant, and that each gave one aspect of the truth.

Now, while the decadence, so plain in the time of Longinus, could with little justice be called an effect of the Roman Empire, no better could the still lowlier condition which literature reached in the fourth and fifth centuries be called an effect of Christianity. But at the same time, just as the spirit of the Roman sway—the chill of imperial Rome—was a most favourable atmosphere for the rapid decay that had set in, just

[1] The author of the treatise $περὶ ὕψους$, supposed to be Longinus.

as it exercised a freezing influence on the wells of inspiration, so also the spirit of early Christianity was a most favourable atmosphere for the stifling of humane literature; and as christian theology became current, and christian ideas penetrated the minds of men, little breathing space was left for the faint life of that humane literature which had already travelled so far from its former heights. It continued to support in nooks and byways a flickering artificial existence; but the gods of Greece had gone into exile, and inspiration had departed with them.

Although Christianity looked upon pagan literature as full of demonic snares, just as she looked upon the heathen gods as demons, she did not disdain to learn the tricks and ornaments of pagan rhetoric, she did not hesitate to plume her arrow with the eagle's feather. Chrysostom, as a christian priest, could not forget what he had learned in his youth from Libanius; Salvian's treatise *On the Government of God* exhibits careful attention to the effects of rhetorical style. It was not till the sixth century that culture had declined so much that Gregory, the bishop of Rome, could warn his clergy against superfluous concern for grammar. Augustine, in his *Confessions*, only went so far as to marvel that men care to peruse the rules of grammar and not to obey the divine precepts. Both Augustine and Jerome were rhetoricians and stylists, Prudentius wrote christian hymns in Horatian metres, Licentius even spoke of Christ as " our Apollo." Just in the same way pagan art influenced christian art, notwithstanding all christian zeal against it. The habitations of the Greek gods were imitated in the christian churches. Theodosius, who permitted the destruction of temples, who abolished the Olympic games, permitted his victories to be represented as the labours of Hercules. Representations taken from pagan mythology were constantly used in allegorical sense on christian tombs.

It should be borne in mind that while zeal for the house of God exhibited itself prominently as zeal against the houses of the gods, those divinities had still a corner in men's hearts, the charm of paganism still lingered. For, once paganism had lost all power, the works of the ancients lost also their dangerous qualities, and then they were neglected. But in the fifth century the Christians themselves felt the glamour of antique perfection. We see Jerome shrinking in fear from his love of Cicero, we see Augustine shrinking in fear from his love of Virgil. The classics were, for many of the early saints, like beautiful horrors, possessing a double potency, to attract and to repel. Augustine calls Homer *dulcissime vanus;* and even Orosius confessed of his great contemporary Claudian that though he was a "most pervicacious pagan" he was an excellent poet. The children of light felt that they could not approach the children of this world in the finite perfections of genius. " Infelix simulacrum atque ipsius umbra Creusae "—no Christian of his day could approach that, and Augustine knew it.

In western Europe, among the Latin-speaking Romans, paganism held out longest, and offered most resistance to the new faith, and at the same time it is among Latin divines that we find the strongest abhorrence of pagan literature. On the other hand, in eastern Europe, where Christianity had spread rapidly, among Greek-speaking Romans, paganism clung less obstinately to life, and the feeling in regard to pagan literature was more moderate and indulgent,—less saintly, we might say, and more rational. This difference of feeling may be considered as in some degree the beginning of that difference of culture which distinguished the East from the West in later centuries, when in the West indifference to letters prevailed, while in the East learning and the study of ancient writers never fell into disuse.

It may be wondered why no works of great literary value were produced in the fourth and fifth centuries under the inspiration of the great christian idea which was changing the face of the world. Perhaps some one will contest the statement, and cite St. Augustine's *City of God.* But that work is not a work of great literary value; it is a work of great religious and theological value. The idea itself—the idea of the city of God in the world and not of the world—has, potentially at least, literary value, but the work itself possesses very little. The incomparably less important work of Sir Thomas More on an imaginary state has more worth in this respect than the *City of God.* Other christian works of the time, remarkable in many respects, deserve this criticism in a higher degree, for example Salvian's book *On the Government of God.* We go to Chrysostom or Cyril for history or doctrine, but no one would go to either for general ideas.

The fact is that there was a very small stock of new ideas current at the time, and there was no literary instinct. It may seem perverse to say that there was a small stock of new ideas in the face of the fact that the general view of the world was so thoroughly transformed. But the theories current were of a homogeneous kind; they were imbued with that theological tinge which renders thought unfruitful and unfits it for literary handling. The new spirit tended to stereotype itself in technical theology, and also to express itself in a particular phraseology; and thus the thoughts of the time lost their elasticity and their freedom in the bonds of dogma. Men's minds wandered through eternity, but they wandered on a beaten highroad. That is partly the reason why the writings of the stoic philosophers have much more literary flavour than the writings of christian theologians, although Stoicism was so much less effective than Christianity. On the speculations of the Stoics no trammels were imposed from without; the Stoics had no church, no ecumenical councils, no popes. And that too is partly the reason why the New Testament writers were far more fertile in original ideas, expressed with effect, than doctors of the Church in subsequent ages.

To note the want of literary instinct is merely to note the other side of the same fact—the subjective side of it. Literary instinct implies a certain elasticity and freedom of mind, because it implies the faculty of selection; it is not easily compatible with formalism or with dogma. The christian divines had not this sort of elasticity, and they would not have cared to have it; just as they had not originality, and would not have cared to have it. That freedom of mind on which a doctrine or creed sits lightly would have seemed licence to those who delighted in thraldom to a formulated system, just as originality would have seemed undesirable, or at least unnecessary, to those who considered that all things needful had been revealed. The want of literary taste among christian divines may be illustrated by the case of Jerome, who did not care for and could not feel any charm in the *style* of the old Hebrew scriptures, in spite of the prepossession for them that his beliefs would naturally produce.[1]

---

[1] In this Jerome may be contrasted with the old pagan Longinus, who quotes with admiration the opening verses of Genesis as an example of the sublime. Jerome's knowledge of Hebrew is said to have been defective. He boasted of being "trilinguis."

The same want of taste is displayed in his frigid and degrading comparison of the love of Christ to the love of woman, a comparison which is characteristic enough of the man and of the time.

It cannot be denied that there were pagans of some literary ability in the fourth century. Historians of literature deal very hardly with Ammianus Marcellinus, a Greek writing in Latin; yet do we not feel that there is a unique literary quality in his curious style, as though the perfume of the fourth century had passed into his pages? And of Greek writers Julian had considerable literary talent. *The Misopogon*, which deserves attention as an attempt to express the most scathing satire with ironical urbanity, and *The Banquet of the Emperors*, are works that one reads without feeling an inclination to skip a line. He allows his own cultured personality to penetrate his writings in a way that no divine could do, and his writings therefore have a human interest.

But Julian and Libanius and Themistius had no successors. The only essayist of the fifth century who deserves to be mentioned was Synesius, the bishop of Cyrene.[1] He was the pupil and friend of the unfortunate Hypatia; he was superficially imbued with philosophy; he appears for a moment on the stage of public affairs; he was fond of literary composition; he used to indulge in the pleasures of the chase in the vicinity of Cyrene. All these details remind us of Xenophon, who had the same stamp of respectability, a man fond of philosophy, not a philosopher. And we might add that as Xenophon represents the type of transition from the Athenian of the fourth century to the cosmopolitan of the age of Alexander and his successors, so Synesius, dividing his worship between Plato and Christ, is the type of the transition from the pagan to the christian gentleman. If he had been brought up in the atmosphere of Constantinople he would not have been a Platonist, he would have been an unexceptionably orthodox Christian; if he had been brought up in the atmosphere of Athens he would have been a thorough-going pagan and refused to bow the knee to Baal; but brought up

---

[1] The standard work on Synesius is the monograph of R. Volkmann, "Synesius von Cyrene." There is an elaborate article "Synesius" in the *Dictionary of Christian Biography* (ed. Wace), by the late Mr. Halcomb, in which English translations of some of Synesius' verses will be found.

as he was in the atmosphere of Alexandria, which was at this time divided between pagan philosophy and Christianity, his pliable nature adapted itself to both influences and he became a platonic bishop. His works consist of rhetorical compositions, political essays and letters, which possess considerable interest. When he stayed at Constantinople he mixed in a circle of literary mediocrities, who enjoyed ephemeral notoriety, and he is himself a typical member of such a society.

Perhaps the most interesting and attractive feature in Synesius is his love of the pure intellect and his supreme disdain for mere ethical virtue. In this, although a christian bishop, he was more unchristian than the heathen Neoplatonists; in this too he was more platonic than they. Plato did not set store by what we call "goodness"; he almost disdained the demotic virtues. It is curious to see the aristocratic spirit of the pure intellect in the fifth century A.D., and it is only to be regretted that Synesius was not a stronger man.

Far the most important pagan Greek writer of the fifth century was the philosopher Proclus, of whose system I have already spoken. I have dwelt on the dearth of ideas of literary value in that age. Now Proclus has the credit of having expressed a thought that was well worth expressing in a form that deserves to be remembered—in a form that possesses literary value. He said that the true philosopher would never consent to confine himself to any one set of religious ideas; "a philosopher," he said, "is the hierophant of the whole world." Perhaps that is one of the few remarks made in the fifth century that deserves to be remembered in the words in which it was originally expressed. It contains moreover a thought which had long been in the air and had constantly inspired others than philosophers; it idealises in the form of a philosophical maxim that cosmopolitan eclecticism which was practised by such different persons as Alexander Severus and Constantine. Both a great philosopher like Proclus and a great statesman like Constantine can feel themselves above the world and the things, including the religions, that are therein; the eclecticism of Alexander Severus was merely that of a serious dilettante.

The poetical remains of Proclus are a few hymns, conceived in the same style as the famous hymn of Cleanthes to Zeus, and exhibiting the influence of the mystical Orphic poems. The gods are addressed as mythical beings; their attributes have second imports; and the reader feels that he does not possess the key to a chamber of theosophic significances. But they are not lifeless like formulated chants of a sorcerer or a vulgar theosophist; there is in them perceptible the breath of an "immortal longing," the same longing that was felt by Plato and by Plotinus. Proclus was ever pressing to the "way sublime," πρὸς ὑψιφόρητον ἀταρπόν, and he prays to the sun, to Athene, to the Muses for pure light, the kindly light that leads upwards (φῶς ἀναγώγιον), the means of attaining thereto being the study of books that awaken the soul.[1]

Athens, where Proclus studied and afterwards lectured, had preserved its fame as a university town since the days of Cicero, though it had not any political importance. It was the headquarters of the pagans, the "Hellenes," who, suffered by the christian Emperors to live quiet lives in unobtrusive retirement, still practised secretly the old customary sacrifices, still worshipped Athene, Artemis, and Asklepios. They formed here a small cultured society, on which the "urbane" society of the residence might look down as provincial, and which the Christians held in abhorrence as profane. At the same time Athens was regarded with a peculiar respect; it was fashionable to go thither, and it was considered by some a mark of inferiority, almost of philistinism, not to have visited it.

The storm of the Visigoths of Alaric, which laid in ruins the temple of Eleusis, passed by the city of the philosophers without harming it much. But after the foundation of the university in Constantinople Athens gradually declined; it seemed as if the departure of Athenais had led to a cessation of the patronage of the goddess whose name she bore. Even when Synesius visited Athens (about 416 A.D.) he was not favourably impressed with it[2]; in the description of his visit he does not say a word of the beauties of the place, the works of art or

---

[1] The expression in regard to the natural state of men's earth-bound souls, ὑλογράφεσσι περὶ κληροῖσι μανεῖσαι, is worthy of notice.

[2] Synesius, ed. Migne, p. 1524 (*Ep.* cxxxv., to his brother), ὡς οὐδὲν ἔχουσιν αἱ νῦν Ἀθῆναι σεμνὸν ἀλλ' ἢ τὰ κλεινὰ τῶν χωρίων ὀνόματα. "In our time," he goes on to say, "Egypt nourishes the seeds of wisdom which she received from Hypatia; but Athens — long ago she was a home of philosophers, now she is worshipped only by bee-keepers."

the flavour of antiquity. Desolateness and dilapidation overwhelmed for him all other impressions.

But while Athens was the home of the most profound philosophers, Alexandria was the centre of the widest culture, just as was the case in the days of Alexander's successors, when Stoics and Epicureans taught at Athens, while the schools of poetry and learning flourished in the great capital where they came into contact with the general movement of the world. In the fourth and fifth centuries all the Greek poets of any distinction wrote at Alexandria, and most of them were born in Egypt; there too pagan philosophy and christian theology lived side by side.

We are told by Damascius, a pupil of Isidorus, that his master was superior to Hypatia not only as a man to a woman, but as a philosopher to a mathematician. This remark gives us an insight into the character of Hypatia's philosophy. In contrast with those mystical and misty speculators, Iamblichus and the "Egyptian writer on Mysteries," she laid stress on philosophical method, divisions, and definitions, as recommended by Plato, and followed rather the intellectual than the mystical side of Neoplatonism. The germs of both developments, the intellectual and the super-intellectual, were contained in the philosophy of Plotinus. The sober and rational character of this lady's metaphysics may also be deduced from the teaching of her pupil Hierocles, who succeeded her after her death in 415.[1] She was not only a philosopher and a mathematician; she also studied physics, a science which was then generally combined with mathematics. Her pupil Synesius mentions that he had constructed an astrolabe with the assistance of his "respected" instructress,[2] and in another place he asks her to superintend the construction of a hydroscope.[3]

There was one remarkable poet in the fifth century, and only one, who had a sufficiently original manner to found a school of inferior imitators. This was Nonnus of Panopolis. It is particularly interesting to note that having been

[1] This is well brought out by W. A. Meyer in his tract on Hypatia.
[2] πρὸς Παιόνιον ὑπὲρ τοῦ δώρου ἀστρολαβίου λόγος. Migne, LX. p. 1584.
[3] *Ep.* xv. It was perhaps the manner of Hypatia's death (already described) that secured her a place among the stars, as it gave her name a romantic interest.

a pagan in his youth, when he wrote his *Dionysiaca*, he became a Christian in later years, and composed a paraphrase of St. John's Gospel in hexameter verse. He thus presents a parallel in Greek literature to Sidonius Apollinaris or Paulinus of Burdigala.

It is easy to say that Nonnus is artificial, that his long poem in forty-eight books lacks unity, and that he falls into prolix digressive descriptions. It is only in the ninth book that he begins the proper subject of his poem.[1] But living, as he did, in a self-conscious age, how could he be other than artificial? To aim at simplicity when simplicity is not in the air is an affectation which can hardly fail to produce the ridiculous. Recognising that he is always artificial and often tedious, we nevertheless feel in reading his verses that he had a really poetical mind, that he

"ran beside the naked swift-footed
And bound his forehead with Proserpine's hair."

There are few pages on which we do not find some thought or phrase that pleases, if it is nothing more than the picture of Ganymede raising aloft a goblet in his *scratched* hand.[2] We may quote two of the opening lines as a fair example of the general style, which Callimachus did not excel—

ἄξατε μοι νάρθηκα, τινάξατε κύμβαλα, Μοῦσαι,
καὶ παλάμῃ δότε θύρσον ἀειδομένου Διονύσου.

The twelfth book is one of the best. Hôrê wanders in search of the dead Ampelos, and having learned the *symbols* of prophecy from Hyperion, finds wherever she goes prophecies in writing relating to the death and resurrection of the youth. This introduction of writing into mythological history is characteristic.[3] The effect produced on nature by the death of Ampelos is very charmingly portrayed, and the description of

---

[1] The first eight books are occupied with the mythical history of the Cadmean house of Dionysus' mother Semele. The most recent edition is that of A. Koechly, 1858.

[2] γραπτῇ χειρὶ κύπελλον ἀερτάζει Γανυμήδης (xii. 40).

[3] In one place she finds these words (which I quote in illustration of Nonnus' style, as to the general classical reader he is a poet completely unknown)—

Φοίβῳ Ζεὺς ἐπένευσεν ἔχειν μαντώδεα δάφνην
καὶ ῥόδα φοινίσσοντα ῥοδόχροϊ Κυπρογενείῃ,
γλαῦκον Ἀθηναίῃ γλαυκώπιδι θαλλὸν ἐλαίης,
καὶ στάχυας Δήμητρι καὶ ἡμερίδας Διονύσῳ.
τοῖα μὲν ἐν γραφίδεσσι φιλεύιος ἔδρακε κούρη.

Pactolus restraining the flow of his water, wan with grief, and having the aspect of a dejected man, deserves to be noted for its subjectivity. Even when he wrote the *Dionysiaca*, in his pagan youth, Nonnus could not escape from the atmosphere of Christianity. A line, for example, like this,

Βάκχος ἄναξ δάκρυσε, βροτῶν ἵνα δάκρυα λύσῃ,
Lord Bacchus wept, that mortals might not weep,

could hardly have been written before the air was permeated with christian sentiment. But while a trait of this kind occasionally appears, the note of the poem is untrammelled fancy, and thus it has some points in common with the romantic poetry of the nineteenth century. The learning displayed in the composition is prodigious, yet Nonnus wields his lore lightly, and he is as far from the obscure dulness of Lycophron as day from night.

The poets whose influence chiefly affected his style seem to have been Homer and Euripides, the latter of whom was far more read under the Roman Empire than his great elder compeers, because he had a premature tincture of that profound individualism and subjectivity which began to penetrate life in the fourth century B.C. Both Homer and Euripides were favourites with Christians of culture, as may be gathered from the fashion of writing Homero-centra on christian subjects, and from the *Christus Patiens*,[1] an extant Greek drama which has been attributed to Gregory of Nazianzus, and which is practically a cento of Euripidean verses. Whether Gregory was the author or not, it is probably a product of this age, and it possesses some interest as a specimen of a class of dramas to which the medieval mystery plays partly owe their origin.

The paraphrase of St. John's Gospel which Nonnus wrote when he embraced Christianity is a curious composition, far superior to the ordinary christian poem.[2] We cannot read

---

[1] The Χριστός Πάσχων forms the first volume of Ellissen's *Analekten*.

[2] It has been recently edited by A. Scheindler. It is so little known that a specimen may be interesting. "The wind bloweth where it listeth," etc., is thus rendered—

πνεῦμα παλινδίνητον ἀθηήτῳ τινὶ παλμῷ
οἶδε περιπνείειν ὅθι βούλεται. ἀγχιφανῇ δὲ

φωνῆς ἠερίης θεοδινέα βόμβον ἀκούεις
οἴασιν ὑμετέροις πεφορημένον. ἀλλὰ δαῆναι
οὐ δύνασαι βλεφάροις πόθεν ἔρχεται ἢ πόσε βαίνει.
οὕτω παντὸς ἔφυ τύπος ἀνέρος ἐκ πυρὸς ὑγροῦ
πνεύματι τικτομένοιο καὶ οὐ στροφάλιγγι κονίης.

a line without seeing that it is the work of an adept, and although the simplicity of the original is lost, a very readable poem, with many interesting touches, is produced. " I am the vine, ye are the branches," is rendered thus—

> ἄμπελος αὐδήεσσα πέλω καὶ ὁμόζυγες ὑμεῖς
> κλήματα φωνήεντα σοφῷ βεβριθότα καρπῷ.

It was really in its way a triumphant achievement, implying no ordinary poetical skill and command of language, to translate a christian gospel into hexameters that have always a pleasing flow, and into words which, however they expand the original, never offend the taste.

We need not say much of the versifiers who imitated Nonnus and formed an Egyptian school of poetry. Tryphiodorus' *Capture of Ilion* and Koluthos' *Rape of Helen*[1] may still be read, but they possess little interest. The *Hero and Leander* of Musaeus, who probably lived about 500 or a little later, has obtained a reputation which it hardly deserves. It has the merit of brevity and the merit of possessing unity, two advantages which Nonnus lacks, but in all other respects it seems to me inferior. Pamprepius of Panopolis, the friend of Illus, was a poet as well as philosopher, but we have no means of knowing whether he can in any sense be ranked as one of the school of Nonnus.[2] The Athenian Empress Eudocia did not write secular poetry, or if she did no fragment has survived. The most striking of her compositions that remain is the versification of the legend of Cyprian and Justina, which has been mentioned in a preceding chapter.

One species of literature, which had sprung up when the Greek spirit was already declining, reached its best bloom at this period, the romance.[3] Between the world of the new

---

[1] Koluthos flourished under Anastasius.

[2] Other verse-writers of the fifth century were Cyrus, the prefect of Constantinople, some of whose epigrams are extant; Troilus, who wrote an account of the revolt of Gainas; Claudian, who wrote a gigantomachy, and metrical histories of towns—not to be confounded with the great Latin poet Claudian, who was a native of Alexandria, and also wrote a gigantomachy, of which a fragment is extant; Christodorus (flourished in the reign of Anastasius) wrote a description of the statues in the gymnasium of Constantinople. Both Christodorus and Panolbius wrote *Isaurica*.

[3] Several books have been written on the Greek romance: Nicolai, *Ueber Entstehung und Wesen des gr. Romans*, 1867; Chassang, *Histoire du roman dans l'antiquité*, 1862; and more recently and fully, E. Rhode, *Der griech. Roman und seine Vorläufer*, 1876.

Greek comedy and Roman *fabulae palliatae*,—full of amorous gallants, lost maidens, angry fathers, and smart slaves moving in an atmosphere of loose morality—and the world of Boccaccio's *Decamerone* and Shakespeare's comedies—a gay Italian world, equally frivolous but more refined, in which the lights and shades of morality are not unattended to,—there are two intermediate worlds. The first is that of Longus and Heliodorus and the story-writers of the fourth and fifth centuries; the second is that of Floire and Blanceflor, Imberius and Margarona, and the other romances which circulated first in the countries of the Mediterranean and thence found their way to northern Europe in the later Middle Ages. The outward influences that partly determined the evolution of the former were the opening up of eastern lands by Alexander the Great, the spirit of adventure that then set in, and the cosmopolitan life of Alexandria and Antioch; while the evolution of the latter was affected in somewhat the same way by the Saracen element that had penetrated southern Europe. The romance-world of the fifth century is also one of amorous gallants, of barbarous brigands and cruel pirates, of lovers disparted, of children lost in infancy, reared by shepherds and recognised by tokens, of faithful servants; but while it is marked by an unlifelike refinement and an absence of that naked dissoluteness which was a feature of ancient comedy, it has characteristics of Greek life, fibres connecting it with the antique intuitions, and these separate it not only from Boccaccio but from the cycle of medieval tales that was formed a few centuries later. It is a world in the air, which with the help of oriental material was built on the ruins of Greek life, partly to replace it, and which sought in foreign adventure the interest that city life no longer afforded. And we can detect, behind the artificial form, the sentiment of pagans, who, feeling in the christianised Empire that "not here, O Apollo, are haunts meet for thee," sought to revive their weary spirits on a Helicon of fancy, as Theocritus had sought in the sphere of his Sicilian idylls to escape from the close and stifling air of Alexandrian reality. It may be said that the romance succeeded the old drama and fulfilled in some respects the same functions, just as in modern times the novel-writer may be considered to have taken the torch from the composer of plays. In these romances love and adventure were interwoven; the spirit of adventure and travel in strange lands having come in with Alexander the Great, around whose name wonderful legends had soon entwined themselves, while fictitious love-stories may be traced back to Callimachus, perhaps even to Stesichorus.

Unfortunately we know nothing or little of the authors of three remarkable romances that were written at this period. Longus, the author of *Daphnis and Chloe*, is a mere name, and even the name is doubtful; Achilles Tatius, who wrote *Leucippe and Cleitophon*, is little better; of Heliodorus, whose *Ethiopica* became famous, we know only that he was a bishop.

All these stories have great similarity; we could easily believe that they were written by the same person. A diligent concern for elegance of style, for the choice of phrases and the order of words, characterises them all; and quotations, or echoes, sometimes graceful, of old classical writers abound. An unfailing feature is the love of elaborate description of scenes of nature, in which, however, there is no feeling for nature in the modern sense. It is a purely sensual love of nature—the soft grass (ποὰ μαλθακή) and the clear springs and the cool caves of the nymphs,—just as in that idyllic passage at the beginning of Plato's *Phaedrus*, the great charm of the spot is that the grassy sward is so inclined that Socrates and his friend can comfortably lie down. Nature is a picture-frame for lovers; "the spot," says Achilles Tatius of an agreeable place, " is pleasant in every way, and suitable for romances of love." Flowers and fruit have an erotic import. The association of flowers, especially roses, with love and young maidens is natural and ancient; we find it in the fragments of Sappho. Flower-names are often chosen for heroines, Antheia, for example, and Rodane [1]; the song in praise of the rose that was sung by the maiden Leucippe deserves special mention [2]; and if there was

---

[1] So Florizel, Floire, Blanceflor, in medieval romances.

[2] Choricius of Gaza, who lived in the time of Anastasius, wrote a short essay (μελέτη) " On the Rose," which is extant (Mai, *Spicil. Rom.* v. 410). As Aphrodite sought for Adonis she came on a white rose; the thorn bled her naked foot, and her blood made the rose red. He also wrote an "Occasional Essay " on roses in spring (No. 8 *apud* Mai), wherein he describes himself taking a walk outside the city in early spring. Wandering among groves he bethought himself of Socrates (as described in the *Phaedrus*) on the banks of the Ilissus bathing his feet in its cool waters: καὶ ἐπὶ πόα τινὶ μαλθακῇ κατακλίνεται καὶ ψυχάζει. On such scenes these writers loved to dwell. Another essay of Choricius is on a *horologium*.

not a "Language of Fruit," love at least could be declared by the gift of an apple.

In the same way the descriptions of the persons of youths and maidens are long and minute; and we have a consciousness throughout that the writers are thinking of their diction more than of their matter. They have not the art of concealing their art.

The best of these romances and the most popular in recent times is that of *Daphnis and Chloe*, a shepherd and shepherdess of Mytilene, each a child of noble parents, exposed in infancy and found by shepherds.[1] The chief motive of the story turns on the innocence of the boy and girl, who fall in love and are ignorant of their own desires.[2] There is an idyllic realism in the description of Daphnis' initiation that reminds us of a certain idyll of Theocritus, but it is not bolder than the narrative of Alcibiades in Plato's *Banquet*. The maidenhood of Chloe is stainless until her marriage, and it is worthy of remark that in all these romances the chastity of women is considered to have a sort of preternatural value, and heroines pass through the most dangerous situations unharmed. This idea is one of the symptoms of a new spirit in the world, and contrasts with the old Greek feelings on the subject, which were not romantic. As an element that entered into the spirit of chivalry and thence into the notions of modern society the appearance of the new idea deserves special notice.[3] In the sixth century we shall see it in operation on the occasion of the capture of Rome by Totila, the king of the Ostrogoths.

Daphnis and Chloe has perhaps more peculiarities than any of the other romances; the idyllic life of Mytilene, an island which, like Sicily, corresponded to the Arcadia of the Renaissance, invests it with a unique atmosphere. The far longer novel of Heliodorus, the *Ethiopica*, is more typical of the genus, and has had a greater effect on the development of romance-writing. The magic gem Pantarbe, the conceal-

---

[1] "Longus a cru, comme l'auteur de Floire et Blanceflor, légitimer encore leur affection par les ressemblances matérielles de leur destinée" (M. du Méril, Introduction to *Floire et Blanceflor*, p. cii.)

[2] *Daphnis and Chloe* has been often called the *Paul et Virginie* of antiquity.

[3] See Mahaffy, *Greek Life and Thought*, p. 240. The author informs me that he now regards this new idea as an importation from the East to Alexandria in the days of the Diadochi.

ment in tombs, and fancied death, all the wild and varied adventures by sea and land, formed a large repertory from which subsequent writers borrowed motives and incidents.

Descriptions of pictures and works of art, resembling the descriptions of Philostratus, are constantly introduced by these writers, and have often considerable merit, reminding us of word-pictures by Gautier. The romance of Achilles Tatius, *Cleitophon and Leucippe*, opens with a minute account of a picture of the rape of Europa. Love, as a little boy, is leading the bull in the midst of a landscape in which such details as a peasant stooping over a ditch at his work are portrayed. And in another part of the same story a picture of the rape of Philomela by Tereus is graphically described. The accounts which the same writer gives of the crocodile and the hippopotamus remind us of Herodotus, and had at that time a sensational value. The stage sword, that shut up like a telescope and proved the safety of Leucippe, is worthy of a modern "dreadful."

The story of *Abrocomas and Antheia* is the story of the adventures and misfortunes of a pair of married lovers. The name of the author is Xenophon of Ephesus, but it occurs to one that Xenophon may be a pseudonym, and that the author may have adapted the names of his hero and heroine, Antheia and Abrocomas, from Pantheia and Abradates, of whom a touching story is told in the *Cyropaedeia* of Xenophon the Athenian.

History and romance stand in a relation of kinship to one another. We may say that they have a common mother, mythology, and this common origin seems to cause a certain association between them in later times; we have the romantic history of Herodotus, and we have the historical romance of pseudo-Callisthenes. Moreover, in the history and fiction of a period we generally see common characteristics. The affected artificiality of style which we tolerate in the rhetoric of Libanius, which attracts us in the romance of Achilles Tatius, repels us a little in the history of Eunapius; yet we cannot say that the style of historians was inordinately affected and far-fetched until Theophylactus wrote on the reign of Maurice. The love of travel, adventure, and things outlandish, which had developed since the days of Alexander, is reflected in the histories of the fifth and sixth centuries as well as in the fiction. Priscus gives us an account of his personal experiences in Hunland, Nonnosus describes his adventures among the Ethiopians, and Cosmas relates his visit to the Indian Ocean.

The secular Greek historians [1] of the fifth century were chiefly pagans. Olympiodorus, Eunapius, and Priscus flourished in the first half of the century, Malchus, Candidus, and Zosimus in the second half. Of these, only Candidus was an indisputably orthodox Christian; Eunapius and Zosimus were militant pagans; Olympiodorus and Priscus were quiescent pagans; Malchus seems to have been neither for God nor for God's enemies.

Eunapius of Sardis [2] wrote two books, of which only fragments have survived. One was a history of the Roman Empire from Claudius Gothicus (270 A.D., the point at which Dexippus' history ended) to the tenth year of Arcadius (404); the other was a collection of lives of philosophers and sophists. His style bears the impress of a training in rhetoric, which did not teach him taste, though a good critic thought he wrote prettily [3]; he talks of a "rivery tear" ($\pi o \tau a \mu \hat{\omega} \delta \epsilon s$ $\delta \acute{a} \kappa \rho v o v$). His spirit is that of an ardent pagan into whose soul the iron has entered, one to whom the new order of things seems "a world without any order," an œcumenical mistake. Like all ardent pagans of the time he lavishes the most touching hero-worship upon the Emperor Julian (the last who combined the true belief with the power to enforce it), and crowns him with a halo of celestial light. "By virtue of the power of his nature and the greatness, not less than divine, that was in him, he constrained the inherent tendency that drags down-

---

[1] Four writers of ecclesiastical history flourished at the beginning of the fifth century—Socrates, whose history embraces the period from 306 to 439; Sozomen, who dedicated his history in 439 to Theodosius II, and treats almost the same period, 324-415; Theodoret, a disciple of Chrysostom, who wrote in the last years of Theodosius II, and beginning at the same point as Sozomen, carried down his narrative fifteen years later; Philostorgius, who wrote from an Arian point of view a history of almost the same period as that covered by Theodoret. These histories are preserved, except that of Philostorgius, from whose work, however, the diligence of Photius has preserved valuable excerpts. The history of an Arian was less likely to survive than those of orthodox Athanasians. In the following century Theodorus the Reader (Anagnostes) wrote a history of the Church from Constantine to Justinian.

[2] Born about 347. Studied under Proaeresius at Athens.

[3] Photius.

ward, and, rising above all the waves of life, he saw heaven and knew the beautiful things that are in heaven, in commune with the bodiless beings, being himself still in the body." The last pagan Emperor, the last hero of the forlorn cause, who had died when Eunapius was a boy of sixteen, had entered into his "study of imagination" and appeared to him half a god. There was a further bond of attraction in their common mysticism. Eunapius was a thaumaturge, and had been initiated in supernatural mysteries.

The christian Emperors, on the other hand, are for him impersonations of all that is malignant and irrational, and Eunapius' history is written from the point of view that the time is out of joint, and that the course of history is exactly what it should not have been. It is probably the first history ever written in Greek from this point of view.[1] It was followed some years later by the history of Zosimus,[2] whose work, as far as he completed it, has come down to us, and is one of our chief sources for fourth-century history. His political and religious opinions were the same as those of Eunapius, whose work was one of his main sources; but while the opposition of Eunapius to the new order of things was altogether inspired by his religious conviction, the opposition of Zosimus was partly affected by his experiences as an officer in the civil service.

Zosimus states expressly that he looked upon Polybius as his master and model in the art of history. He studied his style with diligence, as Demosthenes studied Thucydides, and he adopted, or adapted from him, rules of hiatus to which he makes the structure of his sentences conform.[3] And Zosimus too, like his master, wrote a history dominated by a pervading idea, but an idea exactly the reverse of the idea of Polybius. Polybius' history was written to prove the *right* of Roman conquest and the merits of Roman conquerors; Zosimus' history was written to show the *unright* of christian

---

[1] Eunapius has a lordly contempt for dates (for which Dexippus was very careful and troubled); he relegates them to the stewards of rich households as something banausic.

[2] A good edition of Zosimus has at length appeared, the editor being L. Mendelssohn (1887). He shows in the preface that the limits of date for the composition of the history are 450 and 501. The text is accompanied with some valuable historical as well as full critical notes.

[3] *See* Mendelssohn, Preface, p. xxviii. *sqq*.

dominion and the demerits of christian Emperors. Polybius justified history, Zosimus impugned it.

Of the nexus of cause and effect the notions of Zosimus are as infelicitous as those of contemporary christian writers. He attributes the decline of the Empire in the West to the fact that the old pagan sacrifices were discontinued in Rome. His superstition is such that he wonders that no oracle foretold the greatness of Constantinople. Of positive historical errors which he employs to justify his political tendency, we may notice that he blames Constantine for having withdrawn all the frontier troops, whereas Constantine removed only the comitatenses from the defence of the marks, which were still protected by the pseudocomitatenses.[1]

Of Olympiodorus, who was also a pagan, but apparently not bigoted, there is little to say. His history was rather a collection of materials for history, a *silva* (ὕλη) or miscellany, as he called it himself, than a history in the usual sense; its style is so simple and uncared for as to be almost vulgar, thus to some extent anticipating the style of late chroniclers like Theophanes, but the substance is extremely valuable and trustworthy.[2] Priscus, whose description of his journey and adventures in the land of the Huns has come down to us, was also a pagan. His style was very good, and we are impressed with the wisdom and the credibility of the writer.[3] The discussion which took place in the Hun town concerning the comparative merits of the freedom of barbaric life and the trammelled existence of the civilised world is of especial interest. Priscus was not only a scholar or "sophist"; he was a man who, moving in the midmost circle of the political world, had a near view of the most stirring events of the time. His history was continued by Malchus of Philadelphia (in Palestine), who wrote in the reign of Anastasius. It is in the pages of Malchus that we read the somewhat puzzling narrative of the marches and countermarches of the two Theodorics in the Balkan provinces. Malchus' style is clear and unaffected,

---

[1] *See* the essay of von Ranke on Zosimus (*Weltgeschichte*, iv. 2).

[2] It embraced eighteen years (407-425, and dealt with western history. It was utilised by Zosimus and Sozomen. As for the style, Olympiodorus does not hesitate to employ words like ῥήξ, δισιγνάτος, etc., without explanation or so much as a ὁ καλούμενος.

[3] Priscus' history probably began between 430 and 440, and ended at 474.

though he was a scholar and a rhetorician; and he has a good reputation as a trustworthy narrator. In regard to his religion I should be inclined to suppose that he was a Laodicean; he is said to have been "not outside" the pale.[1]

The only undoubted Christian who wrote secular history in the fifth century was Candidus the Isaurian.[2] His style was frigid and in bad taste, abounding in poetical phrases inappropriately introduced; "in the suave," says Photius, "he had no part or lot," although it was just the suave that he attempted to achieve. He was orthodox of the orthodox, an admirer of the council of Chalcedon. The tone of the age rather than that of his own mind is illustrated by his derivation of *Isauria*, the land of rough and doubtless hairy mountaineers, from Esau, the brother of Jacob.

On the Latin literature of the fifth century it is not my purpose to dwell at length. The most prominent prose-writers were christian theologians, and the most prominent verse-writers, with two exceptions, were either converts to Christianity when they wrote, or became converts afterwards. Of the two exceptions, the most famous is Claudian, "a most obstinate pagan, but an excellent poet," who towers above the heads of all his contemporaries. Most will agree with Teuffel, that he is far superior to Statius, who had the distinction of being a contemporary of Martial and Tacitus, in fertility, richness of fancy, and many-sidedness. We have already become sufficiently acquainted with the subjects of his historical poems, which throw a mixed light on the history of Arcadius' reign; we need only add that his mythological poem "The Rape of Proserpine" shows him at his best. An inscription on a statue erected in his honour at Naples contains an ancient parallel to Dryden's quatrain on Milton, an elegiac distich expressing that Claudian was Homer and Virgil in one.[3] The other uncompromisingly pagan poet was Rutilius Namatianus, in whose eyes the Christians were "a sect more fell than Circe's poisons,"[4] as he said in his picturesque poem *de reditu suo*, describing his return to Italy from Gaul.

---

[1] οὐκ ἔξω τοῦ χριστιανικοῦ θιάσου (Photius).

[2] His history embraced the reigns of Leo and Zeno, 457-491.

[3] εἰν ἑνὶ Βιργιλίοιο νόον καὶ μοῦσαν Ὁμήρου
Κλανδιανὸν Ῥώμη καὶ βασιλῆς ἔθεσαν.
This inscription was found in 1493.

[4] *Deterior circaeis secta venenis.*

Of converts to Christianity, whose writings are partly or wholly pagan, may be mentioned Macrobius, Licentius, and Sidonius Apollinaris. Paulinus of Burdigala,[1] who afterwards became bishop of Nola, was converted in time to write a panegyric on Theodosius I. in celebration of his victory over Eugenius; and two lines written in his christian period deserve to be remembered as an expression of the general experience of the age—

> plurima quaesivi, per singula quaeque cucurri,
> sed nihil inveni melius quam credere Christo.

The poems of Sidonius Apollinaris, the son-in-law of the Emperor Avitus, possess the peculiar charm of transporting us into a circle of old Roman culture amid the alien surroundings of the fifth century. His pagan poetry is Roman, but decadent, infected with something not Roman; it is the poetry of one who might become a Christian. He is at home in Rome, amid the monuments of the pagan Emperors and the memorials of the pagan republic; but he is by no means at home in Ravenna, the capital of christian Emperors, where all the buildings are of brick, the waterless city of marshes, "where the living thirst and the dead swim," *qua vivi sitiunt natant sepulti*. In the consulate of his friend and father-in-law the Emperor Avitus he spent pleasant days at Rome; he wrote and recited a panegyric on the Emperor[2]; and it was decreed by the senate that a bronze statue should be erected to him in the Forum of Trajan, between the Latin and Greek libraries—

> cum meis poni statuam perennem
> Nerva Trajanus titulis videret
> inter auctores utriusque fixam
> bibliothecae.

---

[1] 353-431 A.D., converted about 390; bishop of Nola 409. His *Epithalamium Juliani et Julianae* is a protest in its spirit against pagan epithalamia, and exhorts to chastity. As to Paulinus of Pella, see above, p. 147. On a curious anonymous poem, *de providentia*, see Ebert, *op. cit.* i. 305; on the African Dracontius, *ib.* 367.

[2] *Panegyricus Avito socero dictus.* The education of Avitus is described; his services to Aetius on the eve of the battle of the Catalaunian Field; and the circumstances of Maximus' elevation. In 458 Sidonius addressed a Panegyricus to Majorian on the occasion of his consulate, and gives in it a remarkable description of the hostility which Majorian experienced from the nameless wife of Aetius. In 467 Sidonius attended the marriage of Ricimer with Alypia, the daughter of Anthemius, and in 468 addressed and read a poem to the Emperor—*Panegyricus quem Romae dixit Anthemio bis consuli*, in which there is an interesting account (see above, p. 206) of the education of Anthemius, the ideal Byzantine. The best edition of Sidonius is that recently published in the *M. G. H.* by C. Luetjohann.

Thus the poet of Avitus was set up in bronze beside the poet of Stilicho and the poet of Aetius.[1] Twelve years later he was to become the bishop of Clermont.

Of christian poetry, beside the hymns of St. Ambrose, the writings of Prudentius[2] won popularity; they blended Horatian love-poetry with Christianity, as it were warm wine with cool water, and the mixture suited the taste of the day. The asclepiads of Severus Endelechius "on the deaths of cattle" exhibit the same christianising tendency as the writings of Paulinus. Two swains are introduced, complaining of the loss of their cattle by the plague, and as they talk, Tityrus, a Christian, enters driving along a herd of cattle which the pestilence had not injured. The animals had escaped, as Tityrus explains, because the sign of the cross, "signum quod perhibent esse crucis Dei," was branded on their foreheads.

Into the characteristics of the ecclesiastical and religious writers, Augustine and Jerome, Salvian and Cassian, I cannot attempt to enter here; I can only repeat what has been said before, that they retained the form of pagan style and employed the arts of pagan rhetoric, while they contended against the pagan spirit. Besides Jerome's translation of the Bible, his enlarged translation of Eusebius' Chronicle was very important and served as a model for Latin chroniclers. Orosius' *History against the Pagans*, written as a sort of supplement to Augustine's *City of God*, attained less celebrity, and is now read more for its historical statements than its arguments.[3] All these writers contributed in a greater or less degree to the establishment of a school of Latin theology, though Augustine and Jerome tower so far above the others that they may be considered its founders.

---

[1] Flavius Merobaudes' *Panegyric on Aetius* has been referred to (above, p. 173). The inscription on the statue erected to him in 435 (on account of his military services and his Panegyric) is extant (*C. I. L.* vi. 1, 1724). A few fragments of other poems remain, and have been published by Bekker in the Bonn *Corpus Hist. Byz.*

[2] Ebert (243 *sqq.*) remarks that his *Psychomachia* has "ein sehr bedeutendes literarhistorisches Interesse," because it is the first christian poem in the West in which the allegorical style is thoroughly worked out; "es gehörte so zu sagen zu den *standard works* des Mittelalters."

[3] It is practically, as Ebert remarks (p. 324), a christian *Weltgeschichte*.

BOOK IV

THE HOUSE OF JUSTIN

PART I

THE AGE OF JUSTINIAN

CHAPTER I

THE REIGN OF JUSTIN I.; AND THE EARLIER YEARS OF JUSTINIAN'S REIGN

IN order to understand the European history of the sixth century and the reign of Justinian, we must grasp the fact that it is a direct continuation of the history of the fifth century, but that there is one great difference in the situation. It is a continuation of the struggle between the Romans and the Germans, but their relation has altered. In the fifth century the Germans were conquering lands from the Romans, in the sixth century the Romans are reconquering lands from the Germans. Europe is now divided between them. North-western Europe is irrevocably lost to the Empire and secured to Teutonic peoples, south-eastern Europe is still Roman in the wide sense of the word. Italy is the intermediate land between these extremes, and consequently becomes the scene of the last combat, which results in the overthrow of the Ostrogoths, and leads to the division of the peninsula between the Romans and the Lombards.

Justinian is the great figure of the time. His enterprising spirit carried out the idea of regaining a footing in western Europe. He set in order a system of law for the world. Politically he was absolute, as against the aristocracy; ecclesiastically he was absolute, as against Pope or Patriarch. His buildings in number and splendour were the marvel of his age; and in St. Sophia he bequeathed to posterity an imposing monument of his greatness.

The reign of Justin I. is chiefly important as preliminary to the reign of his nephew Justinian I.

Justin is said to have been originally an Illyrian peasant who came to Constantinople with his two brothers in the reign of Leo.[1] We have already met him as a trusted officer of Anastasius, assisting in quelling the Isaurians, and he was afterwards advanced to the post of commander of the guards (*comes excubitorum*). At the time of Anastasius' death (1st July 518) the eunuch Amantius formed a plot to invest a friend or creature of his own with the purple. To attain this end it was absolutely necessary to gain over the guards, and he consequently enlisted Justin in his service and supplied him with money to bribe the soldiers. But Justin was more wily and more ambitious than Amantius calculated; he took the treasure and secured the interests of the soldiers for himself; the senate consented, and the people acclaimed.[2]

Observe the position of affairs. The government of Anastasius in his later years had been most unpopular in two ways, financially and ecclesiastically. He hoarded the income of the State instead of expending part of it as productive capital, and he increased his hoard by oppressive exactions; he was, moreover, a pronounced monophysite. The opposition to his government was expressed in the revolt of Vitalian, who professed to represent the cause of orthodoxy. Vitalian had indeed been repressed, but he was still in Thrace, his attitude was hostile, and he was doubtless in relation with a faction in the city which shared his disaffection.

Anastasius, though childless, had near relations, especially two nephews, Hypatius and Pompeius, who might urge a claim to the throne, and were secure of the support of the monophysite party and the green faction, which their uncle favoured.

But Justin ousted both Vitalian and the nephews of the late Emperor. Justin's religion was orthodox, and his accession to the throne rested on the facts that he attached to himself the orthodox anti-Anastasian party, including the blue faction, and that he was, by his military reputation and his position

---

[1] On the Slavonic legend, which makes Justin a Slavonic peasant, see the article of Mr. Bryce on Theophilus' *Vita Justiniani* (a work which had been lost since the days of Alemannus and was discovered by Mr. Bryce) in the *English Historical Review*, October 1887. As to the identification of Justinian's birthplace, Justiniana Prima, see note, vol. ii. p. 7.

[2] Compare Justin's letter to Hormisdas, bishop of Rome (Mansi, viii. 434): "primum inseparabilis trinitatis favore, deinde amplissimorum procerum nostri sacri palatii et sanctissimi senatus, nec non electione firmissimi exercitus ad imperium nos electos fuisse."

as commander of the guards, so formidable that Vitalian could not continue hostilities, especially as the causes for dissatisfaction, which had led to them, were now removed. Vitalian was consoled with a consulship and the office of master of soldiers; and the great schism (which had lasted since Zeno's Henotikon) between the Roman and Byzantine Churches came to an end, as the Emperor recognised the dogmatic symbolum of Pope Leo I. But Vitalian enjoyed his new honours for only a few months; he was assassinated, and his assassination was generally attributed to the jealousy of Justinian.

Justin was an able soldier, but was already wellnigh seventy years old. He had not much aptitude for civil affairs,[1] and he was illiterate. The enemies of the new dynasty afterwards said that he was an imbecile old man, who did neither good nor evil to the Empire, because he was unable to do anything. Such a slight is of no value in regard of the fact. He was a man of ambition and strong will who, notwithstanding his advanced age, steered the Empire into a new era and guided a thoroughgoing reaction.

To make up for his own deficiencies in culture and knowledge of civil government he had the assistance of his nephew Justinian,[2] who was destined to succeed him. Justinian assumed the consulate in 521 A.D., and exhibited games and spectacles of magnificent costliness. This munificence was a contrast to the careful frugality of Anastasius, and indicated to the people the reactionary policy of the new dynasty.[3] In April 527 Justinian was created Augustus, and in August, on the death of his uncle, became sole monarch.

The financial difficulties in which the Empire was involved in the latter part of the fifth century had been solved by the care of Anastasius, and the new Emperor found a large sum of money in the treasury. But before the accession of Justinian this sum is said to have been considerably reduced, for the frugality of Anastasius had been followed by a more liberal expenditure,

---

[1] John Lydus, iii. 51, says he was ἀπράγμων, and understood nothing save military matters. In the *Secret History* a contrivance, which he is said to have used for signing his name, is described. When he came to the throne he was about sixty-six years old.

[2] Justinian was born about 483.

[3] Justin, in a constitution of 519, speaks of Anastasius' frugality as the " parca posterioris subtilitas principis" (*Cod. Just.* ii. vii. 25).

and the exactions for which he had been blamed were not continued.[1] Justinian's ideas soared higher than to the mere maintenance of a brilliant court, and he required money to carry them out. The harmless administration of Justin was incompatible with the achievement of public glories—and there is so much truth in the unkind remark that Justin did no good or evil to the State. The great works by which Justinian's name is remembered, the works on Roman law, the conquest of Italy and Africa, and the public edifices are connected with the names of three men, Tribonian, Belisarius, and Anthemius. The abilities of these men were worthy of the large conceptions of their sovereign. But the great works could never have been executed but for another human instrument, whose name has been handed down to infamy, and not, like theirs, to fame. This was John the Cappadocian, who was appointed praetorian prefect,[2] and supplied the treasury by oppressing the subjects. The most authentic account of him is that of John Lydus, who was a civil servant at the time, and has left us a narrative of his enormities.

It was the duty of the prefect to supply money for needful expenses. John not only supplied it but became immensely wealthy himself, and led a life of gluttony and debauchery. "He did not fear God or regard man."[3] The provinces of Lydia and Cilicia especially suffered from his extortions; he let a company of his creatures loose upon Lydia, and they devastated it for the space of a year, leaving (according to John of Lydia) not a virgin or a youth undeflowered, nor a vessel in a house. He was regarded as a demon, attended by a band of demons, too ready to do his bidding,[4] and such names as Cyclops, Cerberus, Sardanapalus were lavished on him. Of his special acts we may notice the partial abolition, or rather modification, of the State post, *cursus publicus*,[5] the result of

---

[1] John Lydus, iii. 51.

[2] *Ib.* 57. He was at first a logothete. Since the time of Theodosius I. the office of praefectus praetorio had been decreasing in power, and by the end of Justinian's reign the civil service was in a very poor condition. Lydus lays this result partly to the charge of John the Cappadocian, who helped to ruin the subjects.

[3] Procopius, *B. P.* i. 24.

[4] One of his worst creatures was John Maxilloplumacius (Flabby-cheek), who oppressed Philadelphia. According to the *Secret History* (cap. 21) the moneys collected by the praetorian prefect in excess of the regular tribute amounted to 3000 lbs. of gold annually, and were called the *Aerikon*.

[5] The post which connected Byzantium with the Persian frontier was not abolished, as the author of the *Secret*

which measure was economically disastrous. Directly, certain expenses were saved to the treasury, but the unfortunate provincials were obliged to undergo the labour of transporting their produce themselves to the ports for transference to Constantinople, and large quantities of corn rotted in the granaries. The impoverished provincials flocked to the capital; a large number of new taxes were invented to extort money, and justice is said to have been so abused that men would not go into court, and the business of advocates declined. The prefect instituted the use of hideous and painful fetters, he had dark dungeons under the praetorium for punishing his subordinate officials, and none were exempted from the indignity of torture.

The remarkable point is that, according to John Lydus, Justinian was ignorant of the excesses of the prefect. Lydus is continually inserting a parenthesis to warn us that the Emperor knew nothing of this or that unjust transaction. That Justinian was prepared to enforce rigorously the collection of all established dues we know from his laws; but he may not have been aware of, and, we may be sure, did not inquire too curiously into, all the details of his minister's actions. We can easily understand the value he laid upon a prefect who never failed to supply him with the funds requisite for the achievement of his schemes.

Justinian shared his throne with a remarkable woman, the Empress Theodora. She was originally a ballet-dancer; her beauty and intellectual ability attracted the love of Justinian, before he became Emperor, and he married her. A contemporary said it was impossible for mere man to describe her comeliness in words or to imitate it by art [1]; we cannot judge how far this remark was due to the enthusiasm of adulation, but if we were entitled to form an idea of her features from the mosaic picture in San Vitale at Ravenna, we should infer that Procopius, in speaking of her beauty, uses the language of a courtier. Nevertheless I think we may conclude that Theodora was a beautiful woman, not from the praise of Procopius, but from the admissions of the *Secret History*, whose author would doubtless, if he could, have disparaged her

History admits (cap. 30). In the other parts of the East the change for the worse consisted in the substitution of a few asses for a large number of horses.

[1] Procopius, *de Aed.* i. 11. Compare *Anecdota*, cap. 10.

charms. The only blemishes which he can find in her are that she was rather short in stature and had a somewhat pale complexion, but the pallor, which he assures us was not sickly, he seems to admire rather than censure.

In order to understand her political position we must direct our attention to the factions of the circus, which were of considerable historical importance throughout, especially at the beginning of, the sixth century. The origin of the four parties of the circus,[1] symbolised by the colours white, red, green, and blue, is veiled in obscurity. The masters or leaders of these parties (*domini factionum*) are first mentioned in the reign of Nero. Caligula favoured the green, Nero the blue colour, and the rivalry of the parties continued to a late period of the Empire, the Emperor himself generally patronising either blue or green, in which white and red had been respectively absorbed. It was not merely in Rome that these factions existed; they cheered and fought throughout the capitals of the provinces; they had existed in Byzantium since (at latest) the time of Septimius Severus. At Constantinople in the fifth century they seem to have assumed greater political importance, and we can hardly avoid connecting this with the religious differences which agitated the East. For the parties of the circus became soon identified with the parties of the Church; the eunuch Chrysaphius, who was inclined to the heresy of Eutyches, supported the Greens, Marcian, the orthodox Emperor, supported the Blues; and at the end of the fifth century the monophysite Anastasius favoured the Greens. In the year 501 a battle took place between the two parties in the hippodrome. It must be observed that these parties did not consist merely of the participators in the games; any citizen might belong to them. They were maintained on an organised system, recognised by the government, with regular officers. They were a machine by which the opinion or will of the people could be expressed; and the Greek name of a "party" was δῆμος, a deme, or "people."[2]

---

[1] On this subject I have consulted with advantage the article of Wilken in the *Abhandlungen* of the Berlin Academy, 1827, entitled "Ueber die Partheyen der Rennbahn." Much information is to be found in the *de Caerimoniis* of Constantine Porphyrogenitus.

[2] It should be noticed that the distinction of Blues (*Veneti*) and Greens (*Prasini*) prevailed throughout the larger provincial towns — Antioch, Caesarea, Apamea, Tarsus, etc. — and there was doubtless a sort of freemasonry throughout the Empire between members of the same party. At

The support of the Blues was one of the elements on which the new dynasty rested; the hostility of the monophysitic Greens was one of the lurking dangers against which it had to guard. It was natural for Justin and Justinian to favour the blue party, as Anastasius had favoured the green.

Now Theodora, in the days of her life as a public dancer, was identified with the green faction. Her father is said to have been employed in its service; and she held monophysitic opinions. When she married Justinian, she transferred her sympathies to the Blues, but did not change her creed. It is characteristic that the opposition writer, who afterwards treated her with scurrilous virulence in the *Secret History*, ascribed this change of colour to personal pique.

Many looked upon the interest taken by Justinian in the blue faction as a mania. He is said to have allowed it to commit the most outrageous acts of petulance and violence with impunity, and even to have heavily chastised governors who ventured to punish members of that faction for their misdemeanours. The Greens, on the other hand, were harshly treated, exposed to the malevolence of their opponents and unable to retaliate. We must not forget that the factions were mixed companies; and among the Blues there was clearly a select fellowship of unprincipled adventurers and debauchees, who, under the cover of orthodoxy and loyalty, threw off the restraints of society. About this time they adopted the fashion of wearing beards like the Persians; and shaving the crown of the head to the temples, they wore their hair long behind like Huns. But it would be an error to suppose that all the members of the factions were like these obtrusive individuals.

We can perceive that the licence permitted to the favoured party was in a manner a political necessity. Even in the most despotic state, public opinion is more or less a check on the acts of the sovereign, for he feels that there is a limit somewhere at which human endurance will rebel. Now Justinian's financial exigencies forced him to try the endurance of his subjects; his vigorous policy and his rapacious ministers

all events the affairs of the factions in the provinces interested and influenced the factions in the capital, as we can infer from a notice in the *Secret History*, cap. 29. The δῆμοι were organised bodies, over which demarchs (or προστάται) presided.

naturally excited much discontent. The populace were dissatisfied on account of the reduction which was made in the distributions of corn; the conservatism of the patricians and senators revolted against the Emperor's ideas of innovation; and no favour was shown to the professional classes. Besides this the monophysites were hostile to his government, and there were many adherents of the family of Anastasius. Public opinion was a force which he could not ignore, especially as it had made itself heard in the reign of Anastasius. Now the circus was the place in which public opinion could express itself; the demes of the circus were organised parties capable of political combination and action. It was consequently Justinian's policy to enlist in his service one party as a sort of government organ, and his party was naturally the blue, which had been the party of opposition under Anastasius. He could thus paralyse resistance on the part of the people by keeping them divided, and favouring one division. As long as the two parties were opposed, John the Cappadocian and the other unpopular ministers were safe.

But it is evident that such a policy could not be permanent; Justinian could not be content, while his position depended on a party. In 532 A.D. a turning-point came, the sedition of "Nika," which shook the throne. The import of this event was that Justinian attempted to render himself independent even of the blue faction, which had grown intolerably turbulent. The blue faction consequently coalesced with the green; and the Emperor quelled the rebellion by the soldiers. The affair was further complicated by the fact that the disaffection was taken advantage of by the party of the Anastasian dynasty, an element of danger which the Emperor finally extinguished.

On the 13th of January[1] the Greens complained to the Emperor in the hippodrome of the grievous oppression which they suffered, especially from Calapodius, a guardsman, who had been a Green in the days of Anastasius and had become

---

[1] As the conversation which took place between the Emperor and the Greens (recorded verbatim by Theophanes) is not really closely connected with the sedition which followed, I have preferred to reserve it for the chapter on manners, etc., of the age of Justinian. It takes up so much space that the reader receives the impression that it was an important scene of the sedition, whereas it was only an accident that the sedition followed at this moment.

a Blue under the new dynasty. The Blues supported the Emperor, and the streets were soon the scene of sanguinary conflicts. But a circumstance occurred which determined the union of the hostile parties in a common insurrection against the oppressive administration. Seven individuals had been condemned to death, and five of them were executed without difficulty. But in the case of two, a Blue and a Green, the hangman blundered,[1] and twice the bodies fell, still alive, to the ground. Then the monks of St. Conon interfered and carried the two criminals to the adjacent monastery. As some of the criminals were Blues, and as the hitch in the execution tended to make the incident more impressive than usual, the Blues and Greens united in a determination to avenge themselves on the civil authorities, and they chose the watchword *Nika*, "conquer," from which the sedition has received its name.[2]

The most obnoxious ministers were John of Cappadocia the praetorian prefect, Tribonian the quaestor,[3] and Eudemius the prefect of the city, who was especially associated with the executions which had taken place. During five days, from 14th to 18th January, the city was a scene of conflagrations and witnessed all the horrors of street warfare. The troops present in the capital were not numerous. The guards of the palace, who used formerly to be recruited by hardy Armenians or Isaurians, consisted of 3500 men; but as Justinian had made a practice of selling sinecure commissions for large sums, the corps was not very efficient. Belisarius,[4] who had lately returned from the Persian war, had a force of cataphracti—cavalry completely mailed—who were lodged in the precincts of the palace; and it happened that the Gepid leader Mundus, who had done good service on the Danube

---

[1] Procopius, who gives an account of the sedition in his *de Bello Persico*, i. 24, does not mention that three of the prisoners were to be hanged. The other four were to be beheaded. Beside Procopius, the *Paschal Chronicle*, Malalas, and Theophanes are our chief authorities; but there is a short notice in the Chronicle of the contemporary Marcellinus.

[2] Another street cry, designating the coalition of the parties, was "To the friendly Greens and Blues long life!"

[3] Tribonian's love of money ($\phi\iota\lambda o\chi\rho\eta\mu\alpha\tau\iota\alpha$) was notorious (Procopius). He died in 545.

[4] From Procopius (*B. V.* i. 11) we learn that Belisarius was born in a district called *Germania*, between Illyricum and Thrace, a name which points to German colonists. At this time the great general was about twenty-seven years of age. I conjecture that he was of a Slavonic family, and that his name means White Dawn; for Βελι- = Slav. *bel* or *biel* (Russ. *biely*), cf. Βελοχρωβάτοι.

frontier against Bulgarian invaders, was also present in the city with a corps of Heruls. Besides these there were some regiments of municipal guards.

On the 14th (Wednesday) Justinian yielded so far to the public wishes as to depose the three obnoxious ministers and replace them by Phocas,[1] Basilides, and Tryphon. This measure could hardly have been expected to satisfy the Greens, but it might have been fairly expected that it would succeed in dissolving their coalition with the Blues and so paralyse the revolt. But the excitement that prevailed was fomented by the secret machinations and bribes of the partisans of Anastasius' nephews. The people seemed resolved to overthrow the dynasty of Justin. But Hypatius and Pompeius, the nephews of Anastasius, were in attendance on Justinian in the palace, and Probus, their brother, had escaped to Asia,[2] so that the insurgents had no one whom they could proclaim Augustus.

In the afternoon Belisarius issued from the gate of Chalke at the head of his Goths and harassed the rioters until eventide. When he retreated they set fire to the Chalke porch[3]; the flames enveloped the senate house and spread along the Diabatika of Achilles[4] to St. Sophia. On the same evening the offices of the prefect of the city were probably burnt, but we do not know in what locality they were situated. On the 15th (Thursday) the conflagration continued, and a part of the hippodrome on the side of the Augusteum was consumed; on the 16th (Friday) the offices of the praetorian prefect were fired. Meanwhile the ruins of St. Sophia were smouldering, and either from them or from the praetorium (which may have been in that region), a wind blew flames northward, which wrought the destruction of the hospital of Samson and the church of St. Irene. The palace of Lausus, rebuilt after the

---

[1] An account of the good Phocas, his philanthropy and popularity, will be found in John Lydus, *de Mag.* iii. 72 *seq.* Justinian persuaded him with difficulty to accept the office of praetorian prefect. When he drove forth he received an ovation, and during his prefecture money was plentiful and life was secure. 4000 lbs. of gold were spent on the new church without wronging any.

[2] The house of Probus was burnt down when the insurgents sought him and could not find him.

[3] For the order in which the events took place and the buildings were burnt, one must combine Malalas with the *Paschal Chronicle*. Theophanes merely gives a list of the edifices which were destroyed. Malalas makes the initial mistake of placing the affair of the rescue of the condemned men on the third day before the Ides.

[4] Malalas calls it the ἔμβολος. For the topography I may refer the reader to Bk. i. cap. v.

fire in 465, the baths of Alexander, and many private houses perished in the course of the conflagration. On Friday evening some ships arrived with troops from neighbouring cities [1]; and, encouraged by this increase of his forces, the Emperor arranged an attack on the insurgents, who on the following day (17th, Saturday) assembled in the Augusteum, intending perhaps to make a decisive assault on the palace. The conflict ended with the siege of a building in the Augusteum called the Octagon, where the rebels entrenched themselves; the soldiers, unable to expel them, set fire to it.

On Sunday morning Justinian ventured to appear in the cathisma of the hippodrome with a copy of the Gospels (the holy μεγαλεῖον, as a chronicler calls it) in his hands. It was proclaimed that the Emperor would converse in person with the people, and large crowds assembled, but with no purpose of pacification. Justinian sware that he would grant an unreserved amnesty, forget the past, and comply with the demands of his subjects. A sovereign could hardly say more than this; but all he heard in reply was, "You lie!" in conjunction with some abusive vocative [2]; and "As you kept your oath to Vitalian, even so would you keep this oath to us." Justinian, when he returned to the palace, ordered all the senators who were present to leave it, among the rest Hypatius and Pompeius; perhaps he thought that his two rivals would be less dangerous outside. They professed to be devoted to the Emperor, and it is not clear whether their devotion was a mask or not. The insurgents were elated when they learned that Hypatius had left the palace; they met him and constrained him to take the decisive step.[3] On Monday morning (19th January) he was crowned in the Forum of Constantine with a golden chain wreathed like a diadem, and soon afterwards he sat in the cathisma of the hippodrome, while a multitudinous

---

[1] From Hebdomon, Rhegium, etc.

[2] *Chr. Pasch.* i. 624, ἐπιορκεῖς, σγαύδαρι. ἐπιορκεῖς, γαύδαρι has been proposed, the final sigma of the first word producing the initial of the second. γαύδαρι is explained as equivalent to γάδαρε, "ass," for which an almost incredible derivation from ἀειδαρος = "ever flayed" or "beaten" has been proposed. *See* Ducange, *Gloss. Med. et Inf. Graec.*

[3] It is recorded that Hypatius' wife, Maria, tried to prevent this consummation. Marcellinus represents the Nika revolt as an agitation entirely got up by the partisans of Anastasius' nephews. His words are: "Jam plerisque nobilium conjuratis omnique seditiosorum turba armis donisque ministratis illecta dolis invadere tentaverunt (imperium)." This theory of the revolt was doubtless encouraged by Justinian.

assembly below called out, "Hypatie Auguste, tu vincas." They had come to the hippodrome in order to organise an attack on the adjacent palace, contrary to the judicious advice of the senator Origen, who recommended that they should first seize one of the other palaces in the city. Meanwhile Justinian strengthened the fortifications of the palace, and called a council of his ministers. This was the really decisive moment.

John of Cappadocia recommended flight to Heraclea, and Belisarius agreed with his view; but their weighty opinions were outbalanced by the short speech of the Empress Theodora[1]:—

"The present occasion is, I think, too grave to take regard of the principle that it is not meet for a woman to speak among men. Those whose dearest interests are in the presence of extreme danger are justified in thinking only of the wisest course of action. Now in my opinion, on the present occasion, if ever, nature is an unprofitable tutor, even if her guidance bring us safety. It is impossible for a man, when he has come into the world, not to die; but for one who has reigned it is intolerable to be an exile. May I never exist without this purple robe and may I never live to see the day on which those who meet me shall not address me as 'Queen.'[2] If you wish, O Emperor, to save yourself, there is no difficulty; we have ample funds. Yonder is the sea, and there are the ships. Yet reflect whether, when you have once escaped to a place of security, you will not prefer death to safety. I agree with an old saying that 'Empire is a fair winding-sheet.'"[3]

From the mere words of this speech we can understand what effect it might have produced; but we can hardly realise how that effect was magnified when it proceeded from the lips of the Empress—" cette diablesse de génie attachée à l'existence de Justinien."

In the meantime it was believed in the hippodrome that the Emperor and his court had fled. For Hypatius, not yet sure of success, had sent a messenger to Justinian, bidding him attack the people assembled in the hippodrome. Ephraem, the messenger, could not himself reach the imperial presence, but

---

[1] Recorded by Procopius. I have no doubt that these words were actually spoken by Theodora, and that Procopius, if he was not present himself, heard them from Belisarius.

[2] δέσποινα, "mistress," the usual mode of address. The Emperor was addressed as δέσποτα. Compare *Secret History*, cap. 30: ἦν δέ τις τούτων ὁποτέρῳ ἐς λόγους συμμίξας βασιλέως ἢ βασιλίδος ἐπιμνησθείη, ἀλλ' οὐ δεσπότην τε ἀποκαλοίη καὶ δέσποιναν . . . οὗτος δὴ ἀμαθὴς καὶ τὴν γλῶσσαν ἀκόλαστος ἐδόκει εἶναι.

[3] ὡς καλὸν ἐντάφιον ἡ βασιλεία ἐστί. It should be noticed that Procopius does not say that Justinian himself was afraid.

he gave the message to one of the secretaries, Thomas, who was a pagan. Thomas, ignorantly or designedly,[1] gave him the false information that Justinian had fled, and Ephraem proclaimed the tidings in the hippodrome. It now seemed to the rebels and the perhaps unwilling usurper that they had only to take possession of the palace.

When Theodora's resolution had conquered the prudence or pusillanimity of the court, the eunuch Narses was sent forth with a well-filled purse to regain the allegiance of the Blues; and at the same time Belisarius led out his troops with the purpose of cutting the revolutionists to pieces in the crowded enclosure. Belisarius first attempted to reach Hypatius himself by the spiral stair which led up to the cathisma, but the door was kept fast by the guard on the inner side. Failing here, he entered the hippodrome by the general entrance to the west of the cathisma, and at the same moment another force under Mundus appeared at the Dead Gate on the east side. Narses' distribution of bribes meanwhile had succeeded in producing dissension between "the friendly Greens and Blues,"[2] and this favoured the attack of the soldiers. An unsparing massacre took place, and it is said that about 35,000 persons perished in the sedition of Nika. Hypatius and Pompeius were executed.

Those who draw a line between "Roman" and "Byzantine" history might well look on this striking sedition as the last scene in "Roman history," for it resulted in an imperial victory which established the form of absolutism by which "Byzantine history" is generally characterised—a result perhaps partly implied in the remark of Procopius that the revolt was fatal in its consequences to both senate and people. M. Marrast[3] describes it as "the last convulsion which marks the passage from Graeco-Roman antiquity to the Middle Age."

The blue and green factions made themselves conspicuous on several subsequent occasions during the reign of Justinian, but they did not again shake the foundations of the throne as in the Nika revolt. Their rivalry outlived their short union, and as long

---

[1] The fact that Thomas was a pagan has given rise to the suspicion that he may have been at heart disloyal to Justinian.

[2] See *Chron. Pasch. ad ann.* For gates of hippodrome, *see* above, Bk. i. cap. v.

[3] *La Vie Byzantine*, p. 180.

as they were hostile there was no danger for Justinian; and in spite of the occasional storms that broke out their importance was really decreasing. It is recorded that a faction fight took place in 549, and there was a more serious demonstration in 556, during a great dearth at Constantinople, when common suffering seems again to have united the foes. The people cried, "Provide supplies for the city," and they pulled down the house of the prefect of the city. The factions clamoured against Justinian in the circus, and as Persian ambassadors happened to be present, the Emperor felt especially indignant and mortified. In 561 a conflict of the Blues and Greens took place in the hippodrome before the Emperor arrived, but his appearance quelled it; and in 563 the Greens, who were undoubtedly connected with the conspiracy which was at that time formed against Justinian, reviled and stoned the new urban prefect Andreas, and their behaviour led to a battle with the Blues. I shall have to speak of "the colours" once or twice again in the reigns of Maurice and Phocas, but they are then far on their way to political insignificance.

The conflagration of so many important public buildings would have entailed a heavy outlay for their mere restoration, but they were rebuilt by the ambition of Justinian on a more splendid scale. We must postpone to another place some account of the new St. Sophia, and the architectural works of Anthemius, whose skill raised the city from its ashes fairer than ever. Notwithstanding these expenses, which were incurred simultaneously with the costly wars in Africa and Italy, the condition of the subjects seems to have somewhat improved, owing partly to the milder though short administration of Phocas, the new and popular praetorian prefect of the East. But in the course of little more than a year John the Cappadocian returned to office and oppression.[1] We can hardly doubt that the Emperor, for the fulfilment of whose schemes enormous

---

[1] John is praet. pref. in December 533 (Novel ii.), and we can trace him every year in the imperial constitutions as the holder of this office up to September 540. In 541 constitutions are addressed to Bassus, the vicarius of John, praetorian prefect of the East. On 1st June 541 Theodotus is *P. P. orientis*, and he is succeeded by Petrus, to whom laws are addressed in 543, 544, 545, 546. Theodotus perhaps held the office again in 546 and 547, but Bassus seems to have been the prefect during the latter part of 548 (Nov. clvii. clviii.) We find Addaeus praetorian prefect in 551, Areobindus in 553, Petrus in 555 (?), 556 (?), and 559.

funds were necessary, found that his treasury was not so full since the degradation of this unscrupulous minister, and concluded that the only way out of his difficulties was the reappointment of John.

The enemies of Justinian might appeal to this reappointment as their best proof that the Emperor was utterly unscrupulous as to the means employed to carry out his ideas.

The overthrow of John of Cappadocia was due to the hatred of the Empress Theodora. She ruined him by a curious stratagem, contrived by her friend Antonina, the wife of the general Belisarius, who is described by Procopius, her husband's secretary, as a woman "more capable than any one to manage the impracticable."[1] Antonina cultivated the acquaintance of John's daughter Euphemia, and gave her to understand that Belisarius was highly discontented with the reigning powers, who had shown ingratitude for all his services, but that he could make no attempt to throw off the intolerable yoke without aid from some influential person in the ranks of the civil ministers. Euphemia communicated this news to her father, who was not without ambition and eagerly embraced the chance of ascending the throne with the help of the army. He arranged a secret interview with Antonina at Rufinianum, a country house of Belisarius,[2] and the Empress took care that officials[3] with soldiers should lurk near to overhear the implicating words and arrest the unsuspecting conspirator. It is said that Justinian, aware of the plot, sent to John a secret warning against the trap; but notwithstanding, John went, conspired, and fell. He was sent to Cyzicus (541 A.D.), disgraced but wealthy, where he lived for some time as a priest; but the relentless indignation of Theodora still pursued him, and he was scourged and stripped of his goods for slaying a bishop. He ended his days as a presbyter at Constantinople, whither he returned after the death of Theodora in 548.

[1] Proc. *B. P.* i. 25.
[2] Rufinianum had belonged originally to Rufinus, the praetorian prefect in time of Theodosius I. and Arcadius.
[3] The officials were Narses, the eunuch, and Marcellus, captain of the palace guard. Marcellus still held this office in 548, and as he had a very high reputation for uncompromising probity, it appears that, in spite of the *Secret History*, probity was not unrecognised. According to the *Secret History*, the successor of John in the office of prefect, Peter Barsames, was little better than John. Peter was said to have been a favourite of Theodora on account of his skill in magic.

The absolutism of Justinian provoked a strong and bitter opposition, all the bitterer because it was so unsparingly suppressed. He was accused of discouraging all liberal professions, of not only suppressing philosophers and sophists, but of depriving physicians of their allowances, and prohibiting the pay which lawyers (rhetors) had been accustomed to receive. The merchants were harassed by customs and monopolies, the soldiers were ill treated by *logothetae*, who cheated them of their pay, retarded their promotion, and gave them deficient rations. Taxation, pitilessly imposed, weighed heavier than ever on the landed proprietors and farmers, and no arrears were remitted. Such is the general tenor of the charges made by the dissatisfied member of the party of opposition, who has painted the agony of the Empire under "the demon Justinian" in the *Secret History*. On this subject something will be said in the next chapter, but we may remark here that, although the general tone of Justinian's rule was *Tel est notre plaisir*, he always condescends in his constitutions to give reasons, often elaborate reasons, for his acts, and that many of his laws seem really, as well as professedly, to have aimed at the wellbeing of his subjects, and not merely at the external prestige of the Empire or the replenishing of the treasury.

Two new offices instituted by Justinian seem to have been unpopular at Byzantium, that of the *praetores plebis* (πραίτωρες δήμων) and the new quaestorship. In 535 Justinian superseded the prefect of the watch (*praefectus vigilum*), who was in Greek called νυκτέπαρχος, "night prefect," a name which the imperial constitution derides as absurd, and appointed the *praetor plebis*, whose office was to keep order in the city both by night and by day.[1] In 539 he appointed a quaestor, whose chief function was to prevent idlers and strangers who had no special business from sojourning in Constantinople[2]; and in the constitution by which this office was instituted the legislator dwells with complacency on the fact that the institution of the *praetor plebis* had been found by

---

[1] Novel xxxviii. (ed. Zachariä), τῇ μὲν ἡμετέρᾳ φωνῇ *praetores plebis* προσαγορευέσθωσαν, τῇ δὲ Ἑλλάδι ταύτῃ καὶ κοινῇ πραίτωρες δήμων. Justinian always seems to be proud that his native language was Latin.

[2] Novel xcix. (9th March 539). The Justinianean quaestor must be distinguished from the old quaestors of the fifth century, whose duty was to draft imperial rescripts, etc. (*see* above, p. 205).

experience "very advantageous to the inhabitants of this our imperial city," and states that the success of that office suggested the introduction of a new one. Tribonian,[1] the great lawyer, was the first quaestor under the new system, and he is said to have been a lover of gain, and very unpopular. Both these innovations are mentioned in the *Secret History* as organs of Justinianean oppression.

The imperial style adopted by Justinian in his constitutions was pompous and imposing. The preface to the second edition of the Codex (534), couched in the form of a constitution, begins thus[2]:—

"In nomine Domini nostri Jesu Christi Imperator Caesar Flavius Justinianus Alamannicus Gothicus Francicus Germanicus Anticus Alanicus Vvandalicus Africanus pius felix inclitus victor ac triumphator semper Augustus senatui urbis Constantinopolitanae S."

In a law concerning imperial constitutions and edicts, which was read aloud "in the new consistory of Justinian's palace" in 529,[3] the Emperor exclaims: "What is greater, what more sacred than the imperial majesty? who is puffed up with such haughty conceit as to disdain the royal judgment (*regalem sensum*), when even the founders of the old law lay down clearly and distinctly that the constitutions, which have gone forth by imperial decree, are valid as law?" And, he goes on to say, the sole promulgator of the laws is the sole worthy interpreter of them likewise.

The imperial pride is always flavoured with the religious spirit of the time, and Justinian does not weary of boasting of the divine favour which has been vouchsafed to him. For example, the opening sentences of the constitution on the Digest (533), known as *Tanta*,[4] run thus:—

"So great in our regard is the providence of the divine humanity, that it always deigns to sustain us with eternal generosities. For after the Parthian (*Parthica*, meaning Persian) wars had been lulled to sleep by an

---

[1] Tribonian died 545, and was succeeded in the quaestorship by Junilus (*Anecdota*, cap. 20). This institution of Justinian possessed vitality; in the eighth century we shall find that the quaestor existed and exercised the same functions as the Novel of 539 assigned to him.

[2] In Nov. lx. (ed. Zachariä) this heading will be found in Greek. *Triumphator* is rendered by τροπαιοῦχος and *semper Augustus* by ἀεισέβαστος αὔγουστος.

[3] *Cod. Just.* i. xiv. 12.

[4] *Ib.* xvii. 2.

Everlasting Peace and the Vandal nation had been overthrown and Carthage, nay all Libya, had been united again with the Roman Empire, it has enabled the ancient laws, heavy-laden with old age, to assume a new form of beauty in the shape of an abridgment of moderate size, by means of our watchful care—an achievement, which no one, before our reign, ever hoped for or even deemed possible for human intellect."

CHAPTER II

JUSTINIAN AND THEODORA

THE sixth century may be called the age of Justinian. But of the man himself, whose works changed the history of the world, it is hard to win a distinct idea; we have only a vague glimpse of the features of that form which dominated Europe. His elusive personality hides behind meagre statements, uninstructive panegyrics, or malevolent pasquinades, and perplexes the historian. And even those who do not care for the analytical dissection of motives, who see the greatness of Justinian revealed in his works—" by their fruits ye shall know them " —feel nevertheless tantalised at the elusiveness of his individuality.

Beside him stands Theodora, another baffling problem, and indissolubly associated with Justinian for those who have visited San Vitale in Ravenna, as well as for those who have read the *Secret History*, a book of ill fame which has thrown a doubtful light or shadow on the imperial court.

We may first resume briefly Justinian's historical position. He may be likened to a colossal Janus bestriding the way of passage between the ancient and medieval worlds.

On the one side his face was turned towards the past. His ideal, we are told, was to restore the proud aspect of the old Roman Empire,[1] and this was chiefly realised by his conquests in Italy, Africa, and Spain. The great juristic works executed at the beginning of his reign breathe to some degree the spirit of ancient Rome. Moreover he represents the last

---

[1] Johannes Lydus speaks of Justinian as ὅλην τὴν ὀφρῦν τῆς ἀρχαίας ὄψεως ἀνακαλούμενος (ii. 28), and this is the tone of his constitutions. He loved the revival of old names (praetor, etc.)

stage in the evolution of the Roman Imperium; in him was fulfilled its ultimate absolutism. From Augustus to Diocletian there was a dualism, the "dyarchy" of the Emperor and the Senate which was abolished in the monarchy of Diocletian; and from Constantine to Justinian there was another dualism between the Church and the Imperium, which passed into Justinian's absolutism. This second dualism reached in the latter part of the period an antagonism which was conditioned by the falling asunder of eastern and western Europe; and it was by reuniting the West that Justinian was able to overcome the dualism and assert his ecclesiastical authority. The historian Agathias expresses Justinian's absolute government by saying, "Of those who reigned at Byzantium he was the first absolute sovereign (αὐτοκράτωρ) in deed as well as in name."[1]

On the other hand, he was a great innovator and a destroyer of old things[2]; and this was made a ground of complaint by the disaffected. The consulate was abolished, the philosophical schools of Athens were closed, and these two events may be considered symbolic of the death of the Roman and the death of the Greek spirit. The Graeco-Roman, Romaic, or Byzantine spirit is installed in their place. He tampered with and partly changed the administrative system of Diocletian; he allowed the Greek tongue to supplant Latin in official documents; the authority of the Twelve Tables, long in disuse, was at length formally abolished; and fundamental conceptions peculiar to the Roman civil law were set aside. Justinian was thoroughly penetrated with the spirit of the christian world; he spent his nights in theological studies; and in the erection of the great church of St. Sophia, which still remains to commemorate him, it was Solomon and not Pericles that he desired to imitate and surpass.

In four departments Justinian has won an immortal name: in warfare, in law, in architecture, and in church history. Standing on the shore of the medieval or modern period, he cast into the waters of the future great stones which created immense circles. His military achievements decided the course of the history of Italy, and affected the development of western Europe;

---

[1] Agathias, v. 14.
[2] Thus Agathias makes the Colchian *ficta persona* Aietes speak of the Emperor as ταῖς μεταβολαῖς τῶν ἀεὶ παρόντων ἡδόμενον (iii. 9).

his legal works are inextricably woven into the web of European civilisation; his St. Sophia is one of the greatest monuments of the world, one of the visible signs of the continuity of history, a standing protest against the usurpation of the Turk; and his ecclesiastical authority influenced the distant future of Christendom.

But the means by which he accomplished these things rendered him unpopular. He accomplished them by an artificial system, which could be only temporary, and broke down on his death. It consisted of two parts, (1) a very severe taxation, and (2) a system of ingenious diplomatic relations with those barbarian peoples who hung on the northern frontiers of the Empire. He was not able to keep these nations, Huns, Slaves, and Germans, altogether in check; they were continually devastating the Balkan provinces, and he was obliged to oppose them with armies destined for Italy; but he succeeded, partly by money payments, partly by turning them against one another, in paralysing their hostilities sufficiently to prevent them from foiling the prosecution of his projects in the West. Frequent and large money payments were necessary, and in so far the second part of his system depended on the first. There was one limit on his activities, which could not be entirely dealt with by this system, the power of Persia under the great king Chosroes Nushirvan. Money payments were often useful and necessary, but the defence of the Asiatic frontier was a constant and considerable check on the Italian campaigns. This is evident from the increased activity in the West which always succeeded a peace with Persia.

As to the oppressive taxation, we have no option but to conclude that for the bulk of Justinian's subjects his reign was not a blessing. Limited as he was by the circumstances of the time, the execution of his designs was inconsistent with the present prosperity of the people.[1] But history justifies him by the event as she justifies all her true children.

There are the two sides here as elsewhere, the universal and the individual, the historical and the biographical; and on the

---

[1] In spite of all the misery, all the dark shades that we perceive when we look closely at the details of the picture, Justinian's reign will give many the pleasant impression that it gave to Bekker, the impression of a fortunate island in the midst of a raging sea—"quod tamquam insula fortunata in mari infesto eniteat" (Preface to ed. of John Lydus).

principle of good coming out of evil, many condemn the great man, while they are forced to praise his works, both in themselves and in their historical results. History or providence, it may be said, fully justifies present evils by their effects in the future; those effects may be considered equivalent to the historical *motive*; but this avails not the individual at whose door those evils lie; the instrument of history is condemned.

But this theory is cancelled by a rejoinder, which is at least equally valid. Instead of attributing the good results to "providence" and blaming Justinian for the present evils, one might reply, should we not credit Justinian with elevated and far-seeing purposes, and ascribe the miseries of his subjects to the defective economical conditions of the age?

Perhaps the only value of either of these views is to cancel the other; the antinomy teaches us to refrain from introducing the biographical point of view into history, from taking the individual out of his environment and passing irrelevant moral judgments. The motives of all the actions of individuals are more or less personal, and those of prominent men are generally more or less tinged with the desire of fame. This feeling doubtless gave animation to the activity of Justinian, and it would be an anachronism to judge him by the canons of modern philanthropy. To praise Justinian's absolutism in the sixth century is not to praise absolutism. Dante, looking upon the desire of fame as a celestial quality, attributed it to Justinian, and placed him as a revolving light in the planet of Mercury. "Fui Cesare e sono Giustiniano," he says to Dante—words which we might apply in a different sense to signify that the imperial administration and its evils were transient things, now dead, a sort of accident not really appertaining to the glorified Justinian.

There was naturally a strong and virulent party of opposition to the Emperor's government, consisting of monophysites, the green faction, and others who felt the touch of his stern hand. They were interested in putting the most unfavourable construction on all imperial acts, in representing the court as a hotbed of corruption, in aspersing the ministers of the crown. The essence of this virulence has survived in the *Secret History* attributed to the historian Procopius, the secretary of Belisarius.[1]

[1] *See* the Appendix to this chapter.

There are two distinct questions connected with this curious book: (1) Was Procopius of Caesarea the author? (2) Are its statements trustworthy, wholly or partially, or not at all?

We cannot, I think, answer either of these questions with a simple yes or no. The details of both problems are reserved for an appendix; but conclusions may be stated here. In regard to the first, I agree in the main with the opinion of Ranke, that Procopius is not the author, but that the work was nevertheless founded on a diary or ephemeris of that historian; that a member of the opposition, probably of the green faction, having obtained possession of the diary or a copy of it, worked it up into the form of the *Secret History*, incorporating all the calumnies which were afloat about the Emperor and the Empress.

In regard to the second question, it seems plain that, on the one hand, a historian is not entitled to make use of any particular statement resting on the unconfirmed authority of this document; but that, on the other hand, there was method in the author's madness, and there were underlying facts which gave relevancy to the inventions. We can hardly doubt that Theodora before her marriage appeared on the stage, for the author's picture of her career would otherwise have no point; and there is some method apparent in the circumstance that he does not charge her with licentiousness after her marriage.

But setting aside these vexed questions, on which we can but barely touch here, and for the present rejecting the evidence of the *Secret History* on matters of fact, we must observe that the work has a considerable value not only as a product of the age, in which regard it will be spoken of in another place, but also as expressing the feelings of bitterness which the government of Justinian excited.

This book of pain and horror leaves upon the mind the impression that the enlightened spirit of Justinian, his notable projects, his high thoughts, lived in the shadow of some malignant presence; that cowering by the throne of the Emperor, lurking in the gallery of the palace where he walked in meditation at night, ever attending his steps, moved some inhuman horror, some unutterable "Dweller by the Threshold," through whose fatal power the destinies of himself and Theodora, Belisarius and Antonina, John the Cappadocian, and many other victims, were entangled in an inextricable mesh of hates and lusts and bloodshed.

That pasquinades and scandalous stories were in circulation about himself and his wife cannot have escaped the knowledge of the watchful Emperor; and, if I may make a conjecture, he caused a sort of apology to be written before he died, of which a portion is still extant. The treatise on the civil service of John the Lydian bears many traces of having been written with the purpose of defending Justinian; and the introduction of such apologies by the way would make it far more weighty and effectual than a formal panegyric. That Justinian might have employed John the Lydian in the matter may be concluded from the fact that he did at an earlier date employ him to write a panegyric of himself and a history of the Persian war. The circumstance that John was a disappointed civil servant and makes no concealment of the degeneration of the service, may be appealed to in support of the theory that he had some special inducement to speak diligently on every opportunity of Justinian's personal blamelessness.

The Empress Theodora has become, chiefly through Gibbon's reproduction of the portrait in the *Secret History*, a typical example of those fascinating and voluptuous women, who in their own day exercise a baleful influence in the world, and in after times allure the imagination. When we turn from the *Secret History*, to which this effect is due, and read what trustworthy authorities tell us of the Empress, we do not meet a tigress or a malicious demon in woman's form, but a bold and able woman with enough of the *diablesse* in her to explain how she might be traduced. The bold effective speech which she made on the occasion of the Nika sedition is one of the most engaging episodes in history; she was ready to stake everything for empire; and she won.

Her intervention on that occasion, her scheme to overthrow the oppressor John the Cappadocian, her interference for the wife of Artabanes, her active interest in supporting the monophysites and their doctrines, her solicitude for reclaiming abandoned women, her charity and almsgiving, are the only facts of importance that we really know about the Empress. Of these, the fact that damned her most in the eyes of Baronius and Alemannus,[1] and made them ready to believe of her any enormity, her religious faith that Christ's nature was not dual, will certainly in the present day do her memory little harm. Had she believed in the two natures, she might have been more extravagant in lusts even than she is said to have been, and no member of the orthodox Church would have cast a stone. Her enthusiasm for religion when she was an Empress is put on a level with her alleged profligacy as a girl. She is said to have fed the geese of the devil when she was on the stage, she fed the sheep of Christ when she sat on the throne; and in the eyes of orthodox Chalcedonians the second pasture was far more offensive than the first.

John the Lydian speaks of her in high terms, when he describes how she informed her husband of the misdeeds of John the Cappadocian; a woman, he calls her, "superior in intelligence, and in sympathy for the oppressed always awake"; and the remark of Procopius, the historian, that she could not withstand the supplications of the unhappy accords with this; and the two remarks together establish the fact that she was a sympathetic and compassionate lady.

Gibbon's remark that Justinian "was never young" aptly conveys the sort of impression he gives us. There is a cold atmosphere about him—the atmosphere of inexorable Roman logic, afraid of no consequences—which is tinged also with a certain mysticism. His mode of life was severely abstemious and ascetic, his days and nights laborious. He was a man of wide education, learned in philosophy, theology, jurisprudence, music, and architecture, and a friend of his said that the time despaired of by Plato had come, when a philosopher should reign and a king philosophise. The remark suggests the reflection, how different he was from the Emperor Marcus Aurelius, of whom the same had been said before.

But if Justinian were never young, it cannot be said that he did not grow old. There is an unmistakable difference between the first part and the last part of his reign, unequally divided

---

[1] Liberatus and Victor are severe on Theodora for her heresy. Zonaras says that she was avaricious; yet we know from earlier sources that she was charitable.

by the Great Plague. His great ideas were accomplished or undertaken in the earlier period, when he was, if not young, vigorous and hopeful. The plague not only injures the body but paralyses the spirit; a man or a nation that lives through such a visitation is not the same after it. We can hardly, I think, lay too much stress on its moral as well as physical effects. It was after the Plague that Justinian devoted all his energies to theological points of subordinate importance, sat without guards at the dead of night, deep in discussions with very ancient priests, and almost lost his interest in the conquest of Italy. We may say, I think, that he was touched with dispiritedness, or with the malady of the Middle Ages.

His ascetic mode of life and nocturnal studies seemed to lend the Emperor an almost inhuman character; which, combined with his cold Roman spirit, prepared to carry out his plans at all costs, suggested to his enemies the theory that he was really an incarnate demon who took a delight in death and ruin for their own sake.[1] This notion, it may be observed, is a curious, and perhaps one of the earliest, instances of the idea of *Schadenfreude*, delight in mischief for its own mere sake.

The conception of Justinian as a malicious demon, or the conception of him and Theodora as a pair of vampires sucking the blood of the Empire or fiends feasting on the misery of men, may be taken as the outcry of a sacrificed generation—sacrificed without being consulted to the realisation of an idea. But such outcries do not affect the position which Justinian must always hold. The epithet "great" was not indeed permanently bestowed upon him by posterity[2]; but then it was not bestowed on Julius Caesar nor on Augustus, and it was bestowed on Leo I. As of that Caesar who fulminated at the deep Euphrates, so it may be said of the Caesar who reconquered Italy and Africa,

> per populos dat jura viamque affectat Olympo.

---

[1] The *Secret History* is full of tales of this kind. Vigilantia, Justinian's mother, is said to have confessed that his father was a demon, and the Emperor was seen walking in his palace without his head.

[2] Greek writers, however, often speak of ὁ μέγας Ἰουστινιανός.

APPENDIX

ON THE "SECRET HISTORY" ATTRIBUTED TO PROCOPIUS

One of the most interesting and difficult problems in history is the *Arcana Historia*, also called the *Anecdota*, attributed to Procopius. It was discovered in the Vatican by Alemannus, who edited it with a learned commentary. Gibbon, and most historians, including F. Dahn the author of *Procopius von Cäsarea*, follow Alemannus in accepting the statements of the *chronique scandaleuse*, in their general tenor, if not in detail. M. Debidour, in his *L'Impératrice Théodora* (1885), discredits the veracity of the anecdotes, and is followed by Mr. Mallet in his clever essay on "The Empress Theodora" in the *English Historical Review*, January 1887. But neither M. Debidour nor Mr. Mallet call the authorship of the document in question, nor do they refer to the suggestive essay of Leopold von Ranke on Procopius,[1] where the problem is discussed. It is convenient to deal with the two questions, the credibility and the authorship, separately.

(1.) In the first place, the *Secret History* is not consistent in two of its allegations with statements of Procopius in his *Gothic War*, and in one case its statement is intrinsically less credible. According to the *Gothic War*, Theodahad murdered Amalasuntha on his own account, and he had an intelligible motive to do so; according to the *Anecdota*, Theodora devised the murder, and suborned the ambassador Peter to compass its perpetration. But Peter did not arrive in Italy till after the deed was done; nor does an obscure passage in a fragment of a letter from Gundelina to Theodora, preserved in the *Var. Epist.* of Cassiodorus (x. 20), afford even the shadow of a foundation for suspecting the Empress. The only motive assigned for the alleged design of Theodora is jealousy. The other case is that of the death of Constantinus, who, according to the *Gothic War* (ii. 8), tried to stab Belisarius, and was executed on that account. The execution is said by Procopius to be due to "the

---

[1] *Weltgeschichte*, iv. 2, p. 300 *seq.*

envy of Tyche." In the *Secret History* Constantinus is said to have been killed by Belisarius, at the instigation of Antonina, for a private grudge.

To these two cases of divergence as to facts from public history we may doubtfully add that of Pope Silverius, whose death is perhaps ascribed by the *Anecdota* (cap. 1) to Antonina; whereas, according to Liberatus, he was banished to the island of Palms, and perished there of hunger (*qui in Palmariam insulam adductus sub eorum custodia defecit inedia*, cap. 22). Procopius states that Silverius was deposed for suspected intrigues with the Goths. This case, however, is not clear, for the words of the *Anecdota* need not necessarily imply that Silverius was murdered or his death caused by Antonina— ᾧ δὴ καὶ τὸ ἐς Σιλβέριον εἴργασται μίασμα.

The statement that the 320,000 lbs. of gold saved by Anastasius were spent by Justinian in the lifetime of Justin (cap. 19) is at variance with a passage in the *Ecclesiastical History* of John of Ephesus, where it is stated that, after Justinian's death, the fund of Anastasius was still extant. As far as I know, critics have not called attention to this contradiction.

If these inconsistencies of the *Secret History* with public accredited history were the only objections which could be brought against the credibility of the suspected book, they might be sufficient to raise a presumption against it, they would induce us to infuse the judicious *granum salis*, but they would not go very far towards condemning it, whether its authorship by Procopius were proved or disproved. Secret history must know many things to which public history must close its eyes. The inconsistencies that really shake our faith and damage the book irretrievably are the internal inconsistencies. Throughout the work Justinian is spoken of as deceased, as a king of a past age; in the last words of the last chapter his death is referred to as an event in the future. Again, in the preface, the author, whether Procopius himself or another *sub persona Procopii*, says that his treatise is intended to supplement the eight books of the public history, in which he was obliged to leave out many details, because the actors were still alive. The dilemma, which Ranke pointed out, is obvious. The treatise was written either before or after the death of Justinian. If it was written before his death, then the same reason which prevented Procopius from publishing the scandals in his earlier works would have operated still and prevented him from publishing the *Secret History;* and Belisarius, Antonina, and many minor personages survived Justinian, so that the Emperor himself would not have been the only individual to be feared. If it was written after his death, it is in open contradiction with the last words of cap. 30 : ὁπηνίκα οὖν ἢ ἄνθρωπος ὢν Ἰουστινιανὸς ἀπέλθῃ τοῦ βίου ἢ ἅτε τῶν δαιμόνων ἄρχων ἀπολύσει τὸν βίον, ὅσοι τηνικάδε περιόντες τύχωσι τἀληθὲς εἴσονται.

It will be observed that this inconsistency tells both against the credibility of the *Anecdota* and against its ascription to Procopius. Another contradiction has been noticed by Ranke, which has also this double bearing. In cap. 16 we are told by the ἐγώ, professing to be Procopius, that he did not tell the full truth in his earlier work "for fear of the Empress" Theodora. But Theodora died in 548, and the history was not published before 550.

Other inconsistencies within the *Secret History* have been pointed out by Mr. Mallet in the article already mentioned (p. 7):—

"In one place Justinian is described as a wonderfully silly man, and yet, as Alemannus observes, Procopius elsewhere remarks on his keen intellect and constant attendance to business. In another place Theodora is blamed for sleeping all day till nightfall, and all night till daybreak ; and yet the author of the *Anecdotes* is constantly reproaching her for thrusting herself into every department of public affairs. Again we are told that the opposition in the imperial family to Justinian's marriage was so strong that, while the empress Euphemia lived, Justinian could never prevail on his uncle to consent. And yet he had sufficient influence to induce his uncle to confer on this abandoned woman, whom the emperor entirely refused to countenance, the lofty title of patrician. But the most striking inconsistency of all is to be found in the account of Theodora's elevation. If the judgment of the *Anecdotes* is to count for anything, we must believe that, at the time of her marriage to Justinian, Theodora was, by common consent, the most profligate woman of her age. The *Anecdotes* inform us that Justinian was equally remarkable for the self-restraint and austerity of his life. The time of his marriage was a time when he was bent upon conciliating all parties, so as to secure the succession to the throne. He had reached an age when he might well be supposed to have outgrown the passions of his youth. His ambitious calculating temperament would be the least likely to imperil substantial advantages by an act of the grossest imprudence. And yet Procopius tells us that he chose this time to deliberately select for his bride the most infamous woman in Constantinople."

Another feature of the *Secret History*, which decidedly damages its testimony, is the really serious exaggeration in its language concerning the Emperor and the Empress. The description of them as demons of murder, preying upon humanity, demons in no figurative sense of the word, indicates either a malignity or a fatuity on the part of the writer, which discredits his statements, as far as their historical truth is concerned.

It may not be amiss to remind the reader of what is often forgotten. Even if these inconsistencies and childish exaggerations did not appear in the suspected document, it would be incumbent on the student of history to look on every statement contained in it with antecedent suspicion, just because it is a book written with a pronounced tendency strongly antagonistic to the imperial government. The principle is that the admissions and not the pleas of an advocate are to be received when we have no corroborative testimony.

Having seen that the *Secret History* cannot be accepted as a whole, we are met with the question whether it must be entirely rejected and ignored by the historian, or admits of a sifting process.

The principle of Gibbon was as follows: "Of these strange anecdotes a part may be true because probable, and a part true because improbable. Procopius must have known the former, and the latter he could scarcely invent." This is plainly untenable, and has been rightly censured by Mr. Mallet. There is no reason why the author should not have invented; and deliberate invention on the part of *one* man is not the only alternative to the truth of the charges.

But Mr. Mallet's own principle—"That these scandals must be either substantially true or wholly false"—seems to me to be equally untenable. He is indeed right in condemning with Gibbon the pernicious maxim "that where much is alleged something must be true"; but there is another quite different reason for admitting the necessity—necessity is hardly too strong a word—of drawing certain inferences from the statements in the *Anecdota*.

The author of the book, whoever he was, was a contemporary of Justinian; the venomous animosity of his tone is too sincere to admit of the supposition that he did not feel strongly against the object of his maledictions, and wish to poison men's minds against him; it is impossible to suppose that he was a writer in subsequent ages who invented for the sake of invention and got his stories from the air. Even those who may question the correctness of the attribution of the *Anecdota* to Procopius will hardly refuse to admit that it was written by a contemporary of Justinian. This being granted, it will be also admitted that if the writer wished to slander and prejudice men against the Emperor and the Empress he would invent calumnies which were *prima facie* probable, and not calumnies which were evidently improbable. In other words, his statements would have no point except they had some foundation in fact; and they would be improbable if they contradicted some fact generally known about the person traduced. If Theodora had been the daughter of a Teutonic king, a writer who wished to calumniate her and connect scandalous stories with her name would not be likely to choose stories which implied that she was the daughter of a Greek peasant. If her youth had been spent in a monastery in Italy he would hardly represent her as an actress in a theatre at Antioch. We may therefore be sure that, unless the writer, who was evidently a man of brains, intended to discredit his own inventions by making them *prima facie* improbable, and so to stultify his work, the scandals which he records of Theodora must have been consistent, not necessarily with her character, but with some circumstances of her external life before she wedded Justinian. It seems to me that all the anecdotes which the author relates of her early career would have been pointless if she had not at one time been an actress, *scenica* [1]; and the author was far too clever to write pointless stories. The details given concerning the oppression and extortion practised by Justinian and his ministers in taxation, etc., are sufficiently consistent with the actual state of things, as we know it from other writers, to have carried a very sharp sting. The low origin of Justin's family in Dardania gives point to the things that are said about Justinian's uncle ; if he had been one of the Anician family of the Olybrii such things would not have been stated.

While I reject, then, the damaging scandals themselves as incredible, or at least improbable, and as insufficiently vouched for by an enemy who discredits himself, I hold that they rested on some basis of fact which prevented them from falling to the ground as *prima facie* absurd.

(2.) As to the authorship of the *Secret History*, both Professor Dahn, who accepts its statements, and Mr. Mallet, who rejects them, unhesitatingly attribute it to Procopius. Ranke considers it not to be genuine, and I believe he is right.

The inconsistencies already mentioned as affecting its credibility tell equally against Procopian authorship. But the very first words of the treatise are alone sufficient to condemn that hypothesis. They are almost identical with the opening words of the fourth book of the *Gothic War*, to which they formed a suitable introduction ; but as an introduction to the *Secret History* they are quite irrelevant.

ὅσα μὲν οὖν Ῥωμαίων τῷ γένει ἔν τε πολέμοις ἄχρι δεῦρο ξυνηνέχθη γενέσθαι, τῇδέ μοι δεδιήγηται, ᾗπερ δυνατὸν ἐγεγόνει τῶν πράξεων τὰς δηλώσεις ἁπάσας ἐπὶ [καιρῶν τε καὶ] χωρίων ἐπιτηδείων ἁρμοσαμένῳ· τὰ δὲ δὴ ἐνθάδε οὐκ ἔτι μοι τρόπῳ τῷ εἰρημένῳ ξυγκείσεται· ἐπεὶ ἐνταῦθα γεγράψεται πάντα, ὁπόσα δὴ τετύχηκε γενέσθαι πανταχόθι τῆς Ῥωμαίων ἀρχῆς. The words in brackets are added in the *Anecdota* and do not occur in the eighth book of the Ἱστορίαι.

In the eighth book Procopius deserted his system of geographical division and included in it narrations both of events in Italy and events in the East, and this introduction is an apology for changing his plan. But in the *Secret History*, where there is no question of geographical division, the introduction is quite inappropriate. And, asks Ranke, " wie hätte es überhaupt einem Autor einfallen sollen zwei verschiedene Werke mit denselben Worten einzuführen ? "

Again, the preface awakens expectations which the work does not

---

[1] It is worth noticing that Komito, who is mentioned as one of Theodora's sisters in the *Secret History*, is also mentioned by John Malalas and Theophanes (6020 A.M.), who record that she married Sittas, the general of Armenia. This is a confirmation of my position ; it proves that the author built on facts ; he did not invent the name Komito. The other sister was Anastasia.

fulfil. "I have been compelled," says the writer, "to conceal the cause of many things which I recorded in my former books. It will therefore be my duty in this work to publish both facts hitherto suppressed, and the causes of occurrences already recounted." Now the *Anecdota* supply new stories, but do not explain the causes of events related in the public history.

It is, further, almost impossible to believe that Procopius, the author of the Ἱστορίαι, would have ever used the exaggerated language in which the writer of the *Secret History* pours out the vials of his wrath upon Justinian.

Combining the inappropriate character of the preface with the abruptness with which the first chapter commences, Ranke holds that the *Secret History* is to some extent a compilation rather than an independent work. He holds that a member of the opposition party got possession of a manuscript of fragmentary jottings written by the true Procopius, that he worked up these into the form of the *Secret History*, adding and interweaving figments which reveal the most acrid venom and the grossest superstition. "Nach meinem Dafürhalten sind die Anekdota eine Verquickung ächter procopischer Nachrichten mit den oppositionellen Manifestationen einer Partei, welche bei der Thronbesteigung Justinians durch die Besiegung der Nika niedergeworfen, aber keineswegs vollständig unterdrückt worden war." The history of Antonina's adultery, for example, is singled out by Ranke as an "ächte procopische Nachricht" (p. 303).

CHAPTER III

THE LEGAL WORKS OF JUSTINIAN

EVERY government, whether democratical, oligarchical, or monarchical, has two duties to perform; and it must up to a certain point perform them, if it is to exist. It may perform them very badly, but its existence ultimately depends upon their performance. These duties are to protect the community against other communities without, and to protect it against its own individual members within; and the means by which such protection is secured are arms and laws. The efficacy of each of these two instruments depends upon the other; the maintenance of the laws depends on arms, and successful warfare on the maintenance of the laws.

With this general reflection Justinian introduced to the world the first of the great legal monuments, which have immortalised his name and contributed to the welfare and progress of mankind. He states that he has kept both duties clearly before his eyes; that he has provided for the improvement both of the military defences and legal securities of the Empire,—of the latter by preserving old and passing new laws, but chiefly by his collection of the imperial constitutions into a code, called after the fortunate name of Justinian.

Written law was of two kinds, the imperial constitutions or *placita*, and the opinions or answers of recognised—we may say licensed—lawyers, *responsa prudentium*.

(1.) As the Emperor stepped into the place of the sovereign people of the republic, it was logical that the *leges* passed by the people in the *comitia* should be superseded by imperial constitutions. This process of supersession took place in the first century of the Empire; the last *lex* we hear of was an agrarian law of Nerva. There were collections of the constitutions before the time of Justinian; his code was not a novelty. The Gregorian and Hermogenian codes of the fourth century were supplemented by the Theodosian code published in 438, which contained all the constitutions from the time of Constantine. There were two causes which rendered a new code desirable in the reign of Justinian. In the first place, owing to lack of copies, the bulky Theodosian collection could not be always consulted in courts, and therefore the actual practice often failed to conform to the written law; in the second place, a very large number of constitutions had been issued subsequently to the Theodosian code, both by Theodosius II and by his successors, which were not collected in a convenient form, and often seriously modified the law as stated in that code.

A new collection of the constitutions, edited up to date, with the contradictions carefully eliminated, the obsolete laws expunged, superfluous preambles or explanations omitted, words altered, erased, or added for the sake of clearness, was determined on by Justinian (13th February 528), and a commission of ten men, including Tribonian and Theophilus, was appointed to execute it. Clearness, completeness, and brevity were aimed at, and we may say attained, in the Justinianean Code which was published on the 7th April 529.

(2.) Justinian's next undertaking was more difficult, more ambitious, and more novel than the code. No one had ever arranged in an official and accessible volume the *responsa prudentium*, or answers given by lawyers recognised as authorities, in regard to special cases and legal points, which served as precedents for future decisions. These answers were scattered about in many treatises, and not a few difficulties arose in their application, to meet which some attempts had been already made. On many points antagonists might produce two opposite opinions, and on almost any the judge was sure to be perplexed by a large number of inconsistent citations. Hadrian left the choice to the judges' own discretion, and a feeling that certain writers were entitled to precedence in authority gradually established itself without special enactment, to which feeling the choice of authors in the course of jurisprudence for law

CHAP. III *THE LEGAL WORKS OF JUSTINIAN* 367

students considerably contributed. Gaius, and the commentaries of Ulpian and Paulus on the perpetual Edict, Papinian and Modestinus, obtained paramount authority. This inconvenience led Constantine to discredit the notes of Paulus and Ulpian on Papinian, as they frequently differed from the opinions they annotated; but this only lessened, it did not abolish, the evil. Theodosius II passed a very important measure—which may be considered the precursor of the Digest just as his Codex was the precursor of the *Codex Justinianeus*—called the Law of Citations, which ordained that the majority of opinions should determine the decision, and that in cases where the opinions were equally divided that of Papinian should prevail.

There was such a mass of legal responses that the field seemed limitless and beyond all human capacity. But it was not too great for the enterprise of Justinian, who conceived the idea of "enucleating the old law."

On the 15th December 530 he appointed a new commission, under the direction of Tribonian the quaestor, who had assisted in compiling the code, for the purpose of reading the books pertaining to Roman law, written by those lawyers who had been licensed by imperial authority to "interpret" the law. They were to eliminate all contradictions and omit all repetitions,[1] and when they had thus won the nucleus of the vast material, they were to arrange it in one fair work, as it were, a holy temple of justice, which was to be divided into 50 books, containing all the law of 1300 years, purged of superfluities. The undertaking was so immense that it seemed almost impossible, but the commission of seventeen specialists worked so diligently that they completed it in exactly three years.[2] The entire work was called the Digest or Pandects, and henceforward it only was to be consulted. According to Roby's computation, a law library of 106 volumes was compressed to $5\frac{1}{3}$.

(3.) Justinian's third, slightest, and best known work, was a manual of the principles of Roman law, intended for students,

---

[1] Dante makes Justinian say (*Parad.* canto vi.), D'entro alle leggi trassi il troppo e vano. The constitution *Deo auctore* (Cod. i. 17, 1) is well worth reading. The constitution *Tanta* (i. 17, 2) accompanied the publication of the Digest (16th December 533), and contains an account of the arrangement of the material.

[2] Tribonian divided his committee into three parts, and the material to be digested likewise into three parts—the Sabinian school, the commentaries on the Edict, and the works of Papinian.

in 4 books,—the Institutions. It is really a reproduction, with numerous additions, omissions, and changes, of the commentaries of Gaius.[1] At the same time the Emperor made alterations in the course of legal studies to be pursued at the schools of Constantinople and Berytus.

The Digest was a more satisfactory as well as a more stupendous work than the Code, because it could be looked upon as final. The licensed lawyers, *prudentes*, who created the mass of case-law, had long ago ceased to exist, and thus their answers were a given quantity, which no new opinions would supersede. For Constantine had abolished the practice of the *prudentes* and arrogated to the Emperor alone the right of deciding between the letter of the law and the dictates of equity. The Emperor's decisions were constitutions, not responses. The Code, on the other hand, could not be final, as was patent; it must be continually re-edited up to date, and five years after its first publication, Justinian issued a new edition, containing the constitutions passed in the interval; and it is this second edition that has come down to us. But nothing could be more absurd than to insinuate that Justinian spoiled his Code by passing a large number of laws after its publication. A final code in a defective and changing world would be really undesirable; a code in its very nature cannot be final, it can only be "up to date"; and Justinian was not so unpractical as not to apprehend this patent fact. If a code were to prevent all future legislation it would be the reverse of beneficial.

It is a point of special interest, as indicating the spirit of the time, that the Pythagorean theories of number were applied to the arrangement of the Digest, which was determined on *a priori* principles, independently of the nature of the material.[2] In the constitution of 530 A.D. (17th December), which appointed the commission, it is decreed that the work shall consist of 50 books. These were divided into 7 parts, and the divisions were defined by mystic principles: $50 = 7 \times 7 + 1$. The first part[3] consists of 4 books in imitation of the Pytha-

---

[1] Gaius and the Institutes can be most conveniently compared in the parallel-column edition of R. Gneist.

[2] This discovery was made by Friedrich Bluhme in 1820. *See* Preface to Roby's "Introd. to the Digest." Jerome and Cassiodorus in the same way attached importance to numbers.

[3] The remaining six parts fall into two groups, each of which consists of twenty-three books.

gorean tetractys, which also determined the number of books in the Institutions. Students[1] were instructed in 36 of the 50 books, "in order that by reading 36 books they should become perfect youths." The charm of perfection in the number 36 consists in the fact that it is the sum of the first 8, that is, of the first 4 odd and the first 4 even, numbers. The remaining 14 books (2 × 7) they could study afterwards by themselves.

Whether this application of Pythagorean canons to fix the dimensions of the "most holy temple of Justice" was suggested by Justinian himself or by his quaestor Tribonian, we do not know; but it seems more natural to attribute it to the latter, who was a pagan, and doubtless imbued with Greek philosophy.[2] It is characteristic that the orthodox Emperor should have adopted the mystic numbers of the heathen philosopher. And it is characteristic of the Graeco-Roman time that a thorough mastery of the hard science of Roman jurisprudence should be combined with, or set in a frame of, Greek mysticism. Roman law, taken in doses determined by a Greek philosophy, was to make "most perfect youths."

The course of history modified Roman law considerably. Roman law consisted of two portions, the *jus civile*, which rested on the Twelve Tables, and the *jus gentium*. The latter was formed by the sentences of the *praetor peregrinus* in disputes between Roman citizens and foreigners or subject peoples not governed by the *jus civile*, and consisted of the "perpetual Edict," to which Hadrian gave the shape of an unalterable code. As Rome passed from the humble position of a town in Italy to that of mistress of the world, the importance of the second constituent, "the law of nations," increased. It attained greater dignity—the dignity of priority and universality— through the spread of the Stoic philosophy, which at the end of the second century B.C. began to influence Rome. The Stoic law of nature was identified with the *jus gentium*. As

---

[1] First-year students were called Dupondii, and studied the Institutes and first four books of Digest. Second-year students were Edictales; third-year students Papinianistae, fourth-year students Λύται, and fifth-year students Προλύται. *See* the constitution *Omnem* (16th December 533), in which the new course of law for the universities of Constantinople and Berytus is defined. The name for professors was *antecessores*.

[2] Hesychius' notice of Tribonian is curious; he remarks that he was Ἕλλην καὶ ἄθεος.

the Roman spirit became cosmopolitan, Roman law tended to become cosmopolitan too; and in the third century A.D. the Edict of Caracalla, which made all free subjects of the Empire Roman citizens, and consequently rendered the civil law universally applicable, tended not only to widen the range of the old civil law and its peculiar distinctions, but to modify it. For example's sake, *cives, peregrini,* and *Latini* ceased to be a serious distinction. But when the Empire was divided, and a separate seat of rule existed at Constantinople, it was natural that in the eastern provinces, the natural and universal law, the *jus gentium*, should almost completely set aside the old civil law of the Romans. Such forms as *mancipatio* and *in jure cessio* were superseded. But the Twelve Tables continued to enjoy a formal authority until Justinian finally abolished it; and this among other things indicates that his reign marks the furthest limit of the old Roman world, and therefore would be a most suitable point from which to date the so-called Byzantine period. Again, among the distinctions of Roman law, one of the most venerable and fundamental was that of *res mancipi* and *res nec mancipi*; this also Justinian set aside.

As well as by the centralisation of the Roman Empire in lands not Roman, the law was influenced by the spirit of the new religion. Offences before considered only moral came to be considered legal also; and on the other hand the harshness of the cold *jura Romana* was modified by considerations of humanity and equity. Christian influences might easily be, and often are, exaggerated. The disuse of the slave system is often attributed to it; but while we cannot deny that Christianity tended to discourage slavery, and to lessen the evils of slavery by humanising the relations with masters, it is certain that the economical conditions which changed the slave system into the colonate and serf system were the chief cause. Beliefs and sentiments generally adapt themselves to facts, and facts are in turn modified by beliefs. It would be a mistake to say that the religious sentiment adapted itself to circumstances; it would be equally a mistake to say that the circumstances adapted themselves to the sentiment. The course of things is generally a simultaneous and reciprocal process of adaptation of fact to sentiment and sentiment to fact.

We can perceive that between the age of Gaius and the

age of Justinian the feeling that man is naturally free has become stronger, and this feeling was in the spirit of Christianity. Florentinus said that liberty was a natural faculty, whereas servitude was a constitution contrary to nature ; and this view is adopted by Justinian in his Institutes.[1] The ways in which a slave might be manumitted were increased in number by the Emperor[2]; and he speaks of himself as the protector of liberty.[3]

It is interesting to observe the criticism which has been made on the legal work of Justinian by one of the greatest German writers on Roman law, Rudolf von Jhering, in his *Geist des römischen Rechts*.[4] Until Justinian's time, he says, Roman legislation cannot be reproached with invading the dominion of theoretical science ; but Justinian's work is altogether conditioned by the principle of blending theory with practical legislation. The Digest and the Institutions are intended to be at once compendia and lawbooks. The disastrous result of such a proceeding is that science is influenced by authority ; Justinian's authority tended to cow the theorist. "The example of the schoolmaster on the throne, or the legislator on the cathedra, which Justinian set, has been only too readily imitated in modern legislation. Science should leave to Caesar the things that are the Caesar's, but he should leave to science the things that are hers."

---

[1] *See* Ulpian, quoted by Gneist on *Inst.* i. v. (p. 11).

[2] *Inst.* i. v. 2.

[3] "Pro libertate quam et fovere et tueri Romanis legibus et praecipue nostro numini peculiare est." Slavery, however, was still recognised by the laws, and punishments were inflicted in the case of unions between freewomen and slaves, and between freemen and the *servae* of others.

[4] *See* Theil ii., Abtheilung, 2, p. 372. As an example of what he calls *legal constructions*, Jhering mentions a law of Zeno, in which he puts forward the dependent character of emphyteuticaric contract. See *Cod. Just.* iv. 66.

CHAPTER IV

FIRST PERSIAN WAR (528-532 A.D.)

THE Emperor Justin adopted the policy of conciliating minor peoples who, dwelling on the borders of the Roman and Persian realms, were ready to sell or change their friendship or allegiance. Among others the Lazic prince Tzath, who had been the vassal of Persia, visited Constantinople, and became the vassal of New Rome. But Kobad was old, and he did not immediately declare war against the successor of Anastasius. On the contrary, he made the strange proposal—which recalls Arcadius' relations with Isdigerd—that Justin should adopt his son Chosroes. The request was refused, through the influence of the minister Proclus, who pointed out that by Roman law the adopted son would have a legal right to the father's inheritance, and that Persia might claim the Roman Empire. This literal deduction may strike us as amusingly far-fetched, but it is an instance of the ancient habit of pushing things to their extreme logical consequences. The refusal was resented by Kobad, but hostilities did not begin in Justin's lifetime, as a conspiracy of the Mazdakites, which led to their massacre, and an Iberian war occupied Kobad's attention.

When Justinian came to the throne he determined to found a new fortress close to Nisibis, and gave Belisarius, commandant in Daras,[1] directions to that effect. As the building operations were progressing, a Persian army, 30,000 strong, under the command of Prince Xerxes, invaded Mesopotamia. The

---

[1] Belisarius was appointed to this post in the last year of Justin, as successor to Licelarius of Thrace, who had shown his incompetence by an unsuccessful invasion of the territory of Nisibis. Procopius was at the same time chosen by Belisarius as his secretary.

Romans, under several commanders who had joined forces, advanced against them, and were defeated in a disastrous battle. Tapharas, the commander of the Saracen auxiliaries, and Proclianus, duke of Phoenicia, were slain; Sebastian, the general of the Isaurian troops, Kutzis, the duke of Damascus, and the Count Basilius, were taken prisoners.[1] Belisarius escaped, and the beginnings of the new fortress were left in the hands of the enemy. The victors had themselves experienced grievous losses, and soon retreated into their own territory; while Justinian, undismayed, sent garrisons and new captains to the fortresses of Amida, Constantina, Edessa, Suron, and Berrhoea. A new army was formed, consisting of Illyrians and Thracians, Scythians and Isaurians, and entrusted to Pompeius, perhaps the nephew of Anastasius. But nothing more occurred in the year 528, which closed with a severe winter.

The hostilities of 529 began in March with a plundering expedition of Persian and Saracen forces combined, under the guidance of the Saracen king Alamundar, who penetrated into Syria, almost to the walls of Antioch, and retreated so swiftly that the Romans could not reach him and force him to disgorge his booty. The only thing that was left for them to do was to make reprisals, and in the following month a corps of Phrygians plundered in the territories of the Persians and their Saracen allies.[2] Belisarius was appointed at this time master of soldiers in the East[3] (instead of Hypatius), but the rest of the year was drawn out in ineffectual negotiations.

The following year (530) was a year of glory for the Roman name, and for the general Belisarius, who, at the early age of twenty-five, won his first laurels by a victory at Daras. There was much talk of peace, but the great king did not really desire it, and the ambassador Rufinus waited in vain at Hierapolis. Belisarius, with the help of Hermogenes,[4] who

[1] For these events we must combine the slight account of Procopius with the more detailed narrative of Malalas. Procopius exhibits a tendency throughout to colour events or curtail them, so as to reflect favourably on Belisarius. Malalas renders their dues to other commanders. The accounts of the two historians are carefully compared by G. Sotiriadis in his important critical essay on *Johannes von Antiochia* (1887), pp. 114 *sq.*

[2] The hostilities of 529 are altogether omitted by Procopius.

[3] ἔξαρχος Ῥωμαίων (Malalas), στρατηγὸν τῆς ἕω (Procopius). Gibbon was misled by Procopius' conventional term for *mag. mil. per or.* into supposing that Justinian introduced a new title, "general of the East."

[4] Hermogenes had held the post of a *magister*, and was one of the supporters of Vitalian in his revolt.

acted as a sort of informal coadjutor, collected at Daras an army of 25,000 mixed and undisciplined troops, largely consisting of Huns and Heruls; while Perozes, who had been appointed the *mirran*, or sole commander of the Persian army, arrived at Nisibis in June[1] at the head of 40,000 soldiers, confident of victory. They advanced within twenty stadia of Daras, and the mirran sent to Belisarius a message redolent of oriental insolence—that, as he intended to bathe in the city on the morrow, a bath should be prepared for his pleasure.

The Romans did not intend to submit to the indignity or tediousness of a siege; they made preparations for battle, just outside the walls of the town. The Persians arrived punctually as their general signified, and stood for a whole day in line of battle without venturing to attack the Romans, who were drawn up in carefully arranged positions. In the evening they retired to their camp,[2] but returned next morning, resolved not to let another day pass without a decisive action, and found their enemy occupying the same positions as on the preceding day. For the apprehension of the details of the battle, the dispositions which the inventive genius of Belisarius had adopted must be explained.

About a stone's throw from the gate of Daras that looks toward Nisibis a deep trench was dug, interrupted by frequent ways for crossing. This trench, however, was not in a continuous right line; in fact, we may say that it consisted of five separate trenches. At either end of the central trench, which was parallel to the opposite wall of the city, a trench ran outwards almost at right angles; and where each of these perpendicular trenches or "horns" terminated, two other trenches were dug in opposite directions at right angles, and consequently almost parallel to the first trench.[3] Between the central trench and the town Belisarius and Hermogenes were posted with the main body of their troops. On the left, behind the main ditch and near the left "horn," a regiment of cavalry under Buzes, and 300 Heruls under their leader Pharas, were stationed close to a rising ground, which the

---

[1] Theophanes supplies the date.
[2] During the afternoon the armies were diverted by two single combats, in which a Byzantine professor of gymnastics, who had accompanied the army unofficially, slew two Persian champions.
[3] Such, it appears to me, is the evident meaning of the description of Procopius, and thus I believe it was

Heruls occupied in the morning, at the suggestion of Pharas and with the approval of Belisarius. Outside the angle made by the outermost ditch and the horn were placed 600 Hunnic cavalry, under the Huns Sunicas and Aigan. The disposition on the right wing was exactly symmetrical. Troops under John (the son of Nicetas), Cyril, and Marcellus occupied the position corresponding to that occupied by Buzes on the left, while other squadrons of Hunnic cavalry, led by Simas and Askan, were posted on the extreme right.

Half of the Persian forces stood in a long line opposite to the Roman dispositions, the other half was kept in reserve at some distance in the rear, to replace the soldiers in front when they felt weary. Two generals, subordinate to the mirran, commanded the Persians, Baresmanas on the left wing and Pityazes on the right. The corps of Immortals, the flower of the army, was reserved for a supreme occasion. The details of the battle have been described so lucidly by a competent eye-witness that I cannot do better than reproduce the account of the secretary of Belisarius in a loose translation:—

"Neither began the battle till mid-day. As soon as noon was past the barbarians began the action. They had reserved the engagement for this hour of the day because they were themselves in the habit of eating only in the evening, while the Romans ate at noontide, so that they counted

interpreted by Gibbon. I cannot agree with the construction put upon Procopius by Mr. Hodgkin, who has given a far fuller account of the battle than Gibbon, and illustrated it by a diagram; his explanation hardly does justice to ὀρθαί κεραῖαι.

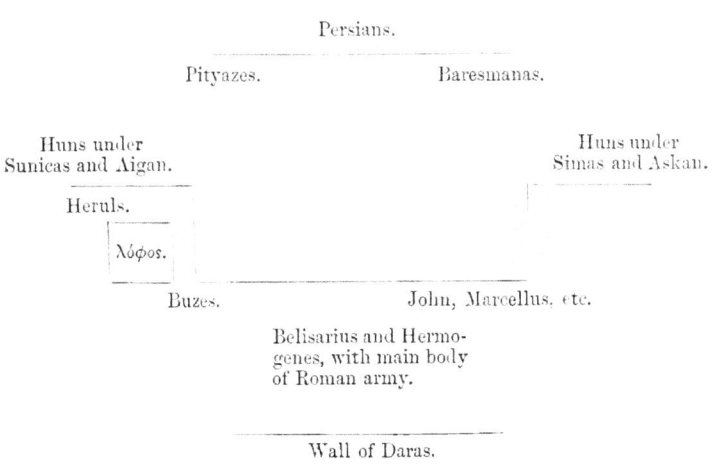

on their offering a less vigorous resistance if they were attacked fasting. At first each side discharged volleys of arrows and the air was obscured with them; the barbarians shot more darts, but a great number of soldiers fell on both sides. Fresh relays of the barbarians were always coming up to the front, unperceived by their adversaries; yet the Romans had by no means the worst of it. For a wind blew in the faces of the Persians and hindered to a considerable degree their missiles from operating with effect. When both sides had expended all their arrows, they used their spears, hand to hand. The left wing of the Romans was pressed most hardly. For the Cadisenes, who fought on the Persian right with Pityazes, had advanced suddenly in large numbers, and having routed their opponents, pressed on them valiantly as they fled, and slew many. When Sunicas and Aigan with their Huns saw this they rushed on the Cadisenes at full gallop. But Pharas and his Heruls, who were posted on the hill, were before them (the Huns) in falling on the rear of the enemy and performing marvellous exploits against the Cadisenes and the other troops. But when the Cadisenes saw the cavalry of Sunicas also coming against them from the side, they turned and fled. When the rout was conspicuous the Romans joined together and inflicted a great slaughter on the enemy.

"The mirran [meanwhile] secretly sent the Immortals with other regiments to the left wing. When Belisarius and Hermogenes saw them, they commanded Sunicas, Aigan, and their Huns, to go to the angle on the right where Simas and Askan were stationed, and placed behind them many of the troops that were under Belisarius' special command. Then the left wing of the Persians, led by Baresmanas, along with the Immortals, attacked the Roman right wing at full speed. And the Romans, unable to withstand the onset, fled. Then those who were stationed in the angle (the Huns, etc.) attacked the pursuers with great ardour. And coming athwart the side of the Persians they cleft their line in two unequal portions, the larger number on the right and a few on the left. Among the latter was the standard-bearer of Baresmanas, whom Sunicas killed with his lance. The foremost of the Persian pursuers, apprehending their danger, turned from their pursuit of the fugitives to oppose the attackers. But this movement placed them between enemies on both sides, for the fugitive party perceived what was occurring and rallied. Then the other Persians and the corps of the Immortals, seeing their standard lowered and on the ground, rushed with Baresmanas against the Romans in that quarter. The Romans met them, and Sunicas slew Baresmanas, hurling him to earth from his horse. Hence the barbarians fell into great panic, and forgot their valour, and fled in utter disorder. And the Romans closed them in and slew about five thousand. And thus both armies were entirely set in motion; that of the Persians for retreat and that of the Romans for pursuit. All the infantry of the defeated army threw away their shields, and were caught and slain pell-mell. Yet the Romans pursued only for a short distance, for Belisarius and Hermogenes would not permit them to go further, lest the Persians, compelled by necessity, should turn and rout them if they followed rashly; and they deemed it sufficient to keep the victory untarnished, this being the first defeat experienced by the Persians for a long time past."

About the same time the Roman arms were also successful in Persarmenia, where a victory was gained over an army of Persarmenians and Huns, which, if it had not been overshadowed by the success of Daras, would have probably been made more of by Byzantine historians.[1]

After the conspicuous defeat which his army had experienced, Kobad was not disinclined to negotiate a peace, and embassies passed between the Persian and Roman courts[2]; but at the last moment the persuasions and promises of fifty thousand Samaritans induced him to break off the negotiations on a trifling pretext. The Samaritans had revolted in 529, and the fifty thousand, who had escaped the massacre which attended the suppression of the rebellion, actuated by the desire of revenge, engaged to betray Jerusalem and Palestine to the foe of the Empire. Accordingly, in the year 531 hostilities were resumed, and at the suggestion of the Saracen Alamundar[3] fifteen thousand Persian cavalry under Azareth, instead of invading Mesopotamia, crossed the Euphrates at Circesium, with a view to invading Syria. They proceeded along the banks of the river in a north-westerly direction to Callinicum, and, pitching their camp near Gabbulon, harried the surrounding districts.

Meanwhile Belisarius arrived from Daras with eight thousand men and took up his position at Chalcis, but did not attempt to hinder the devastations of the enemy. One of his captains, the Hun Sunicas, ventured to evade the general's orders, and attacking a party of Persians, not only defeated them, but learned from the prisoners whom he took the Persian plan of campaign, and the intention of the foe to strike a blow at Antioch itself. Yet the success of Sunicas did not in the eyes of Belisarius atone for his disobedience, and Hermogenes, who arrived at this moment on the scene of action from Constantinople,

---

[1] At this time Dorotheus, a brave and judicious man, was acting general in Armenia. The nominal command of the Armenian army was invested in Sittas, the *magister militum* of Armenia, a new office created by Justinian; see Theophanes, *Chron.* 6020 A.M., προεβάλετο δὲ ὁ βασιλεὺς στρατηλάτην Ἀρμενίας Τζίταν . . . ; he adds that before this Armenia had counts and dukes. Cf. Malalas, p. 429, ed. Bonn. στρατηλάτης is the technical Greek term for *mag. mil.*

[2] *See* Malalas, p. 454, ed. Bonn. Sotiriadis (*op. cit.* p. 119) points out the difficulties in the text and gives a probable solution.

[3] The plot of the Samaritans had been discovered and forestalled, so that it was not the prospect of their cooperation that determined the invasion of Syria.

arranged with difficulty the quarrel between the general and the captain. At length Belisarius ordered an advance against the enemy, who had meanwhile taken the fortress of Gabbulon and other places in the neighbourhood. Laden with booty, the Persians retreated and reached the point of the right Euphrates bank opposite to the city of Callinicum, where they were overtaken by the Romans. A battle was unavoidable, and on the 19th of April the armies engaged. What really took place on this unfortunate day was a matter of doubt even for contemporaries; some cast the blame on Belisarius, others accused the subordinate commanders of cowardice.[1]

At Callinicum the course of the Euphrates is from west to east. The battle took place on the bank of the river, and as the Persians were stationed to the east of the Romans, their right wing and the Roman left were on the river. Belisarius and his cavalry occupied the centre; on the left were the infantry and the Hunnic cavalry under Sunicas and Simas; on the right were Phrygians and Isaurians and the Saracen auxiliaries under their king Arethas.[2] The Persians began the action by a feigned retreat, which had the effect of drawing from their position the Hunnic cavalry on the left wing; they then attacked the Roman infantry, left unprotected, and tried to ride them down and press them into the river. But they were not as successful as they hoped, and on this side the battle was drawn. On the right Roman wing the fall of Apskal, the captain of the Phrygian troops, was followed by the flight of his soldiers; a panic ensued, and the Saracens acted like the Phrygians; then the Isaurians made for the river and swam over to an opposite island. How Belisarius acted, and what the Hun leaders Sunicas and Simas were doing in the meantime, we cannot determine. It was said, on the one hand, that

---

[1] Compare the conflicting accounts of Procopius, the secretary and partisan of Belisarius, and J. Malalas. We have no means of determining the source of the latter, but in many cases he furnishes a number of details omitted by the former, and his narrative has a more genuine ring.

[2] I cannot agree with the plan of the battle implied in Sotiriadis' interpretation of Malalas (p. 123), which would place the Persians *west* of the Romans. I adopt the reverse position, and thus bring the statements of Malalas into accordance with those of Procopius. In the mere fact of the position of troops there is no reason why the two accounts should differ. According to Sotiriadis, "the northern part" (τὸ ἀρκτῷον μέρος) of the Roman army was the right wing; according to my explanation, it was the left.

Belisarius dismounted from his horse, rallied his soldiers, and made for a long time a brave stand against the charges of the Persian cavalry. On the other hand, this valiant behaviour was attributed to Sunicas and Simas, and the general himself was accused of fleeing with the cowards and crossing to Callinicum. There is no sure evidence to make it probable that the defeat was due to Belisarius; it was hardly possible for him to cope against vastly greater numbers in a field where he had no natural or artificial defences to support the bravery of his soldiers or his own skill; and perhaps an over-confident spirit in his army prevailed on him to risk a battle against his better judgment. But the rights and wrongs of the case are enveloped in obscurity, because the facts are known to us from writers whom we cannot acquit of the opposite tendencies to exonerate and inculpate Belisarius; yet it must be confessed that the adverse witness seems the more credible and is generally the more trustworthy of the two.

The Persians retreated, and the remnant of the Roman army was conveyed across the river to Callinicum. Hermogenes[1] sent the news of the defeat to Justinian without delay, and the Emperor despatched Constantiolus to investigate the details of the battle and discover on whom the blame, if any, rested. The conclusions at which Constantiolus arrived resulted in the recall of Belisarius and the appointment of Mundus to the command of the eastern armies.[2] During the interval of delay, Sittas, the general who was commanding in Armenia, provisionally commanded in Mesopotamia.

The arms of Mundus were attended with success. Two attempts of the Persians to take Martyropolis were thwarted, and they experienced a considerable defeat. But the death of the old king Kobad and the accession of his son Chosroes

---

[1] It may be suspected that Hermogenes presented the behaviour of Belisarius in a suspicious light.

[2] We cannot, I think, infer from the recall of Belisarius that the result of Constantiolus' investigation was adverse to him; on the contrary, if it had been adverse to him, the historian who furnished Malalas with his narrative, and who was evidently antagonistic to Belisarius, would have certainly stated the fact in distinct terms. I conjecture that the reason of Belisarius' recall was the circumstance that a bad feeling prevailed between him and the subordinate commanders; and Justinian saw that this feeling was a sure obstacle to success. The investigation of Constantiolus must necessarily have brought out these jealousies and quarrels in the clearest light.

(September 531) led to the conclusion of "the endless peace," which was finally ratified in spring 532. The provisions were that New Rome should pay 11,000 lbs. of gold for the defence of the Caucasian passes; that the Roman headquarters were no longer to be at Daras but at Constantina, and that certain places were to be restored.

CHAPTER V

THE RECONQUEST OF AFRICA AND ITALY

JUSTINIAN'S ideal, we are told by a contemporary, was to restore the grandeur of the old Roman Empire, and accordingly he formed the project of reconquering the western lands, Africa and Italy, which had passed into the hands of German kings; a reconquest of Gaul can hardly have been thought of. The kingdom of Africa and the kingdom of Italy did not bear by any means the same relation to the Empire. The former was openly hostile, and connected by no tie, while the latter was nominally dependent. Before we give a brief account of the campaigns in which the Emperor's generals recovered Africa and made Italy really as well as nominally part of the Empire, we must take a glance at the condition of the Ostrogothic kingdom.

The whole policy of Theodoric was marked by a peculiar deference to things Roman; he combined the independence of a German king with a love of Roman civilisation, and we can see this twofold spirit reflected in the letters written by his secretary Cassiodorus. He said in so many words to Anastasius that his kingdom was an imitation of the Roman polity,[1] and his treatment of the Italians was a strong contrast to the conduct of the Vandals in Africa; it was a contrast even to that of the Visigoths in Spain. The Vandals took possession of all the land, the Visigoths seized two-thirds, the Ostrogoths reserved only one-third. Theodoric published an Edict (like the Breviarium of Alaric II), which

---

[1] *Regnum nostrum imitatio vestri* (Cassiodorus, *Var.* i. 1).

was to determine the legal affairs of Roman subjects.[1] His attitude to the Church was in the highest degree conciliatory. He did not, like Odovacar, attempt to interfere in ecclesiastical matters, but left to the Church the things of the Church. The schism that existed during the greater part of his reign between the bishops of Rome and the patriarchs of Constantinople rendered this policy successful; the Arian Theodoric's abstention from interference contrasted with the ecclesiastical dictation of the Emperors, and the western Church was well contented with Ostrogothic rule. Here again Italy differed from Africa, where conflicts raged between the Catholics and their Arian conquerors. Theodoric's league with the Church favoured both those tendencies, which we pointed out as characterising his policy; it brought him into friendly relation with the most enlightened and "civil" portions of his community, and it promoted the security and independence of his German kingdom. During his reign Italy enjoyed peace. He executed works for the material good of the country, repaired the Via Appia, drained the Pontine Marshes, and restored the walls of Rome.

His position really assumed a European importance. He not only conceived the idea of a Romano-German civilisation in an independent Italy, but he conceived the idea of a system of German states in the West.[2] He was connected by marriage with the royal houses of the Vandals, the Visigoths, the Burgundians, the Thuringians, and the Franks[3]; he watched diligently the course of their mutual relations, and made it his object to preserve a balance of power. His judgment carried great weight at all the Teutonic courts, and he used to intervene to prevent the encroachments of the aggressive Franks. "He was an excellent observer of justice," says Procopius, "and asserted the authority of the laws. He secured his provinces

[1] For this edict, see Mr. Hodgkin's *Italy and her Invaders*, iii. 342. Dahn's researches show that it is based on the *Codex Theodosianus* and the *Sententiae* of Paulus. No historical connection can be proved between the Breviarium of Alaric and the Edict of Theodoric.

[2] This has been often noticed. See Ranke, *Weltgeschichte*, iv. i. 443-445, and cf. Hodgkin, iii. 355.

[3] He was brother-in-law of Thrasamund, king of the Vandals (who married his sister Amalafrida). He married Augofleda, the daughter of Chlodwig, king of the Franks. Alaric, king of the Visigoths, and Sigismund, who became king of the Burgundians (524), were his sons-in-law. Hermanfrid, king of the Thuringians, married his niece Amalaberga. His own daughter by Augofleda, the queen Amalasuntha, was the wife of Eutharic, an Ostrogoth.

from the attacks of neighbouring barbarians, and achieved the culmination not only of prudence, but of bravery. He inflicted no injury on his subjects himself, and allowed no other to do so with impunity. In name Theodoric was a tyrant, in reality a true Emperor, second to none who shone in that position since the beginning of the Empire. Italians and Goths alike had the greatest affection for him."[1]

But everything depended on the personal ascendency of Theodoric, not only peace with foreign powers, but harmonious unity within the limits of Italy. The Roman and Gothic spirits were, as we have seen, united in the king himself, and his study was to impress this unity on his kingdom, to blend Gothic vigour with Roman culture, combining, in Platonic phrase, the gymnastical and musical elements which the two nations represented. But this process of amalgamation would have required a longer time than Theodoric could expect to live, and while it was yet in its initial stage an external force was necessary to prevent the yet unharmonised elements from violently conflicting. The will of Theodoric was such a force. But after his death, in 526, there was no adequate successor. His daughter Amalasuntha assumed the government as regent for her son Athalaric, and we soon behold the discordant elements flying asunder.

Amalasuntha, a woman of remarkable vigour and intelligence, was thoroughly Roman in her ideas and sympathies, and she displayed these tendencies both in political administration and in the education of the young prince, whom she caused to be carefully trained in mental studies.[2] On the other hand, the Gothic nobles were exceedingly discontented; they wished their future king to be a true Goth like themselves, one who would not constrain them to act with over-punctilious justice towards their Roman fellow-subjects, and they despised the effeminate education chosen by his mother for Athalaric. They regarded gymnastic and music as inconsistent, freedom and civilisation as discordant, and were able to appeal to the fact that Theodoric himself had never been educated. Amalasuntha was obliged to yield

[1] Procopius, i. 1.
[2] Cassiodorus compares her education of Athalaric with Placidia's education of Valentinian III, unfavourably to Placidia.

to their clamour, and Athalaric, glad to be freed from the restraints of school discipline, soon became devoted to the pleasures of sensuality. The position of Amalasuntha was critical, and although she steered her course through the perils that beset her with great dexterity, she was soon obliged to beg the Emperor Justinian to grant her a refuge at Constantinople, in case it should become necessary for her safety to leave Italy (533 A.D.)

From the position of affairs in 527 A.D. it might have seemed that no occasion would have been likely to arise for the serious interference of the Emperor in the affairs of the West, for Hilderic, a Catholic Christian and a friend of Justinian, with the blood of the Theodosian family in his veins, sat on the throne of Africa, and Amalasuntha governed Italy with marked favour to her Roman subjects. But this was only the external and momentary aspect of affairs. In Africa the Arian Vandals were not content with their king, and in Italy the barbarian nobles were not content with their queen. The Catholics in Africa, who had long suffered from the persecution of their Arian conquerors, would have been ready to embrace with open arms the protection of eastern Rome; and in Italy the conclusion of the schism between the Churches of the East and the West, which was brought about by the accession of the orthodox Justin, created a new element of danger to the Ostrogothic kingdom, as Theodoric soon became aware. This schism had been a sort of security that the Roman Church and the Italian subjects would not incline to desert their allegiance to Ostrogothic sovereigns and place themselves again under the Roman Emperor. Justin subjected to persecutions the Arian community in the East, which had strong Gothic proclivities, and Theodoric sent Pope John to Constantinople on a mission of threatening remonstrance. The embassy proved unsuccessful, and the Pope, when he returned to Ravenna, was cast into prison.

There was another element in the situation which must not be forgotten,—an element which is a more efficient cause in producing wars than any superficial dispute. The Empire was not the same as it had been in the days of Zeno. Then it was involved in financial difficulties, which were increased by the ravages of the Ostrogoths; but through the prudent policy of the wise Anastasius it had recovered wealth, the sinews of power in a large empire. It was now in a position to assert in the West those rights which it had been obliged to waive in 476, and at the same time a sovereign acceded with the courage and ability to make the attempt.

All things instinctively tended to bring about the restoration of the Empire in the western Mediterranean. Justinian was to do for the German nations what the German nations had done for the Roman Empire; he was to abolish those who were least fitted to survive, the Vandals and Ostrogoths, just as the Germans had reduced the extent of the Empire to those countries where it was best fitted to survive.

VANDALIC WAR.[1]—The crisis which led to Justinian's first westward step occurred in 531 A.D., when the throne of the unwarlike Hilderic[2] was usurped by the warrior Gelimer, and Hilderic himself cast into prison. The Emperor addressed to Gelimer a letter of remonstrance on this act, appealing to the testament of Gaiseric, but Gelimer returned an insulting reply. Justinian was at this time engaged in a war with Persia, but peace was made before the end of the year, and the general Belisarius was recalled from Mesopotamia for the purpose of leading an expedition against the Vandals. The opposition of ministers, who enlarged on the dangers of the design,—they had not forgotten the disastrous enterprise of Leo I.,—delayed the undertaking, and it was not until June 533 A.D. that a fleet of five hundred ships set sail for Africa. The army consisted of 10,000 foot-soldiers and 5000 horse-soldiers, of whom many were federate barbarians. Belisarius was accompanied by his wife Antonina; and Procopius, his secretary, who kept a diary of his experiences, commemorates her foresight in storing a large number of jars of water, covered with sand, in the hold of the general's ship, and tells how this provision stood them in good stead in the long voyage from Zacynthus to Catania.[3]

---

[1] The source is the *Bellum Vandalicum*, in Two Books, of Procopius. The most recent account is that of Mr. Hodgkin, *Italy and her Invaders*, vol. iii.

[2] *Gaiseric* had three sons—Huneric, Genzo, and Theodoric. *Huneric*, who married the daughter of Valentinian III, succeeded his father (477-484), and was succeeded by his nephew *Gunthamund*, the son of Genzo. Gunthamund was succeeded (496) by his brother *Thrasamund*, the husband of Amalafrida. Thrasamund had no children, and the succession went to the family of Huneric, whose son *Hilderic* succeeded in 523. *Gelimer*, who usurped the throne, was a nephew of Gunthamund and Thrasamund, being the son of a brother named Gelaris.

[3] The progress of the fleet was impeded by a disagreeable delay at Methone. John of Cappadocia, for the sake of economy, by which he doubtless

The Vandalic war was brief, and can be briefly related. It was decided by two battles, both of which were fought before the end of the year. Amalasuntha assisted the expedition by granting harbourage in Sicily to the fleet on its outward journey. Tripolis revolted on the arrival of the Romans, and Gelimer was completely unprepared for the attack. The power of the Vandals had waned since the days of Gaiseric, and they possessed no naval forces to annihilate the armament of Justinian, as they had once destroyed the doubly great fleet of Leo. Belisarius having landed at Caputvada, advanced slowly by land to Carthage, without opposition, taking care to maintain the strictest discipline in his army, while Gelimer, as soon as he heard of the proximity of the enemy, hastened to put Hilderic to death. The first battle was fought at ten miles from Carthage (Ad Decimum) in September, and it might have proved a defeat for the invaders but for the amiable imprudence of the Vandal king. Ammatas, the brother of Gelimer, was slain, and Gelimer's affectionate grief made him forget the duties of a commander while he lamented and buried his brother. Belisarius took advantage of the delay, and the Vandals were put to rout. Two days later he entered Carthage, and his prudent discipline so strictly prohibited all pillage and violence that the city presented the same appearance as on an ordinary day.

Another brother of Gelimer, named Tzazo, had been sent some time previously to Sardinia, which had revolted from the Vandals. Gelimer, who had retreated to Bulla Regia, west of Carthage, now recalled him, and the letter of the king shows the despondent mood into which he had fallen: "All the old valour of the Vandals seems to have vanished, and all our old luck therewith. . . . Our only hope is you. . . . It will be some consolation at least in our misfortunes to feel that we endure them together." The brothers marched towards Carthage together, and at Tricamaron, not far from the city, the decisive battle was fought. Gelimer lost a second brother, and the Vandals were utterly defeated. The king fled to the Numidian highlands and found refuge in a cave among the filthy Moors, where he remained with sorry cheer for a while,[1] but soon

profited himself, had supplied the army with bread only once, and that ill-baked. Five hundred soldiers fell victims to a disease caused by the indigestible dough.

[1] The story of Gelimer's request for

surrendered at discretion and adorned the triumph of Belisarius at Constantinople. When he beheld the splendour of the imperial court he merely said, "Vanity of vanities, all is vanity," a remark which, as Ranke notices, had a sort of historical signification. For along with Gelimer, Belisarius brought to Constantinople those vessels of gold of which Gaiseric had robbed Rome, and of which Titus had despoiled Jerusalem. They were part of the riches of the king to whom the words "Vanity of vanities" are traditionally attributed.

EVENTS IN AFRICA AFTER THE IMPERIAL RESTORATION.—It will be convenient to add here a short account of the troubles which agitated Africa after the re-establishment of Roman rule.[2] The eunuch Solomon, who had been left as general by Belisarius to keep the Moors in check, was embarrassed not only by these troublesome invaders, whom he defeated in the battles of Mammas and Burgam, but by the mutinous behaviour of the Roman soldiers, who, dissatisfied with their condition in the newly conquered provinces where they had married the widows and daughters of the Vandals, and intolerant of the burdens of taxation which Justinian imposed upon them, conspired to murder Solomon. The plot failed, but the mutiny continued, and Solomon was obliged to flee to Sicily and seek the assistance of Belisarius, who had just completed the conquest of that island (March 536).[3]

When Belisarius arrived at Carthage it was beleaguered by the rebels, who were led by Stutzas, and numbered 9000 in all, 1000 of these being Vandals. A few hundred Vandals seem to have escaped the sword and chains of the Romans in the year of the conquest; and four hundred, who were being shipped to Syria for military duty there, succeeded in obtaining possession of a ship at Lesbos and returned to Africa, where they found circumstances in a favourable con-

---

three things, a lyre (to accompany a poem he had composed on his misfortunes), a loaf (the Moorish fare was so intolerable), and a sponge (to wipe away his tears), is well known. Tzetzes describes it in the following lines—

κινύραν, Βελισάριε, στεῖλόν μοι σπόγγον, ἄρτον,
τὴν μὲν ὡς τραγῳδήσαιμι τὸ βαρυσύμφορόν μου,

σπόγγον δ' ὡς ἀπομόργνυμι τὰς πλημμύρας,
ἄρτον δ' ὡς ἂν κατίδοιμι κἂν μόνην τούτου θέαν.

(*Chiliads*, 3, 85.)

[2] The regulations for the administration of Africa will be noticed in chapter xiii. below.

[3] Procopius, the secretary of Belisarius, was in Africa at the time, and sailed with Solomon to Syracuse.

dition for adventurers. The arrival of Belisarius struck terror into the besiegers. They retired from the walls, and were pursued by the Roman general, who overtook them beyond the river Bagradas. A battle was fought in which the rebels were utterly defeated, and Belisarius, deeming his presence no longer necessary, returned to Sicily. But the rebellion was not extinguished, and soon after his departure five Roman generals were treacherously murdered by Stutzas. It was reserved for Germanus, the nephew of Justinian, to quell the revolt by the decisive victory of Scalae Veteres. From this time until the death of Solomon[1] in 543, the African provinces, delivered from the presence of the Moors, who during the insurrection had taken up their abode in the land, were tolerably prosperous. During the prefecture of Sergius, who succeeded Solomon, the extinct rebellion came to life again under the old leader Stutzas, and was supported by the Moors; and this revival seems to have been chiefly due to the incompetence of the prefect. Areobindus, the husband of Promota, Justinian's niece, and John, the son of Sisinniolus, commanded the imperial army, and the rebels were routed at Sicca Venerea, Stutzas himself being slain by John (545). In the same year Areobindus succeeded Sergius as prefect, and was slain by Gontharis, the Roman duke of Numidia, who made himself tyrant of Africa. The death of Areobindus was avenged by the Armenian Artabanes, who was then appointed governor, but soon returned to Constantinople, with the hope of marrying Promota, his predecessor's widow, as will be related in another place.

GOTHIC WAR.[2]—In countenancing and assisting the overthrow of the Vandals, Amalasuntha was really smoothing the way for the conquest of Sicily and Italy. Africa was the natural basis of operations for an Italian war, and the troubled course of events in Italy soon gave Justinian a good opportunity of beginning it. Amalasuntha had a cousin Theo-

---

[1] Solomon resumed the government in 539. He seems to have held the office of praetorian prefect with military powers. The original intention was to keep the military and civil powers separate, but the disturbed state of the prefecture seems to have led to their union.

[2] The *Bellum Goticum* of Procopius in Four Books is our source for both the first and the second Italian wars of Justinian. I have not given full details, which will be found in the elaborate and picturesque history of Mr. Hodgkin, vol. iv. *The Imperial Restoration*; a less full relation will be found in Gibbon. I have aimed at giving a succinct account of the chief moments of the war.

dahad, a man of liberal education but of avaricious character, who owned large estates in Etruria and regarded his neighbours' possession of land as a personal injury to himself. He hated Queen Amalasuntha for keeping his greed within limits, and she entertained no high opinion of him, but a circumstance soon occurred which induced her to adopt the course of sharing with him the royal prerogative. This circumstance was the death of her son Athalaric. Such a division of power, which in the language of Cassiodorus was to be "a perfect harmony," meant conflict and could not endure; in April 535 the queen was imprisoned by her colleague in an island of Lake Bolsena and soon afterwards murdered. As she was the friend and ally of Justinian, the moment for decisive action seemed to have come, and the Emperor's envoy Peter declared against Theodahad a war without truce.

In the summer of 535 A.D. an army of 7500 men, under the command of Belisarius, sole consul for the year, to whom the fullest powers were committed, set sail from Constantinople for Sicily. Of this army three thousand, that is two-fifths, were Isaurians. The towns in Sicily, to the great chagrin of the Goths, joyfully opened their gates to the imperialists, with the exception of Palermo, which was besieged and taken, so that by the end of the year the island was entirely in the hands of the Romaioi the Romans, or, as their enemies called them, the Greeks. Theodahad was so impressed with these successes that he opened negotiations with Justinian, which were conducted by the ambassador Peter, who was still at the court of Ravenna. The king undertook to abdicate the crown if landed property, producing a certain annual revenue, were secured to him, and this offer, we need hardly say, Justinian gladly accepted. In these negotiations Theodahad adopted the part of a philosopher who deemed royalty of little worth, and who desired to avoid the loss of human life which a war would involve, while Justinian assumed the attitude of an emperor claiming his own. But the negotiations came to nothing, for while the envoys were at Constantinople, the Roman general Mundus, who had occupied Dalmatia and taken Salona, was defeated and slain[1] in a disastrous battle with an invading army of

---

[1] Maurice, Mundus' son, also perished. Hence an old Sibylline oracle of terrifying import was supposed to have found its fulfilment. The scribe of our text

Goths, who retook the city of the Jader. This success renewed the confidence and changed the plans of Theodahad. When the envoys arrived in Ravenna, the king, supported by his Gothic nobles, drew back from his engagements, and the war began in earnest (536 A.D.) As for Dalmatia, its position was soon reversed again; Salona, the city of Diocletian, which had passed from the Romans in the days of Odovacar, was recovered by them, and the province became permanently part of the Empire.

Belisarius took Rhegium and marched on Naples. When that city refused to surrender, he might have been tempted to leave it for a time in order to advance to Rome, but an Isaurian discovered an unguarded ingress through an aqueduct, which rendered it possible to surprise the garrison by night. This success was of the utmost importance, and has even been considered by some historians to have decided the result of the whole undertaking. Belisarius was now master of southern Italy.

Having placed a garrison in Naples, he proceeded without delay to Rome, which he entered unopposed in December; though the inhabitants were too content with the Gothic rule, under which they had suffered little or no religious persecution, to give the newcomers a very enthusiastic welcome.

Theodahad had shown no activity, he had made no attempt to save Neapolis, so that the Goths were highly discontented with him; and when Witigis, whom he had appointed general, joined the army, the soldiers insisted that their leader should be also their king. Witigis was not unwilling. He was proclaimed *thiudans*, and his first act was to put Theodahad to death. In this election the principle of heredity, which the incapacity of Theodahad seemed to discredit, was disregarded by the soldiers, who declared that Theodoric's true kinsman

---

of Procopius transliterated some of the Latin words of the oracle into Greek, and expressed the others in curiously contorted characters. If we reflect that a Greek would take Latin F for E, P for Ro, C for Σ, the first words AFRICA CAPTA (αεριcαs αρτα) present no difficulty. Of the strange characters the third suggests D, the fifth is clearly S, the sixth probably C, the ninth plainly N. The first is the same as the eighth, and suggests a half-inverted M. The second, fourth, and seventh are the same letter, which we may assume to be U; the tenth letter suggests A. Thus we obtain MUDUS CUM NA. The remaining Greek letters (τξεριστασι; but *apud* Joan. Opsopoeum, *Sib. or.* τξρεριστασι) seem partially corrupt. τξ may represent *tis*, and in the rest some part of *perire* may be contained. *Africa capta mundus cum natis peribit* (or *perit statim ?*) is identical with Procopius' Greek explanation.

was he who could imitate his deeds; but Witigis took the precaution of confirming his position by coercing Matasuntha, the daughter of Amalasuntha, to marry him, thereby connecting himself with the royal family. The new king was an elderly man, and would have made a good sergeant; but he was destitute of originality, destitute of genius. As the historian of *Italy and her Invaders* has well remarked, his election was due to the error of supposing "that respectability will serve instead of genius."[1]

At this time (the beginning of the war) the position of the Goths was complicated by the attitude of the Franks, who threatened to invade the northern provinces of the peninsula; and the presence of a part of the Gothic army was required to defend Provincia. Witigis made up his mind to avert the danger in the north first, and then devote all his resources to the war with the Roman invaders. Leaving Leudaris with 4000 soldiers to hold Rome, he marched with the main body of the army to Ravenna. There he married Matasuntha, he sent to Justinian an embassy treating for peace, and he arranged matters with the Franks by ceding the Ostrogothic possessions in southern Gaul (Provence and Dauphiné) and paying the sum of £80,000. It was evident that the new king was guilty of a most imprudent surrender of opportunity by his expedition to Ravenna. This movement involved the loss of Rome, and we cannot perceive what compensatory advantage he gained thereby. It was not necessary for the army, or even for Witigis himself, to be present at Ravenna, either for the settlement with the Franks, or for the embassy to New Rome, or for his marriage.[2] As far as we can judge of the situation, the thing that Witigis ought to have done was to make the defences of Rome sure.

Belisarius entered the city on the Tiber by one gate (porta Asinaria) on the 10th December, as the Goths of Leudaris went out by another (porta Flaminia); Leudaris himself remained and was taken prisoner. The evacuation by the Goths, without opposition to the Roman occupation, was due to two causes: the prestige which Belisarius had won by his former successes, and the fact that the Pope Silverius had invited him to Rome.

---

[1] *Italy and her Invaders*, iv. 79.
[2] Mr. Hodgkin's remarks on this subject are fully justified.

The second cause depended on the first, for it was not with any warm enthusiasm that the "Romans" (*Romani*), who had never suffered religious persecution from the Goths, welcomed the "Greeks" (Ῥωμαῖοι), but rather from fear. In spite of their veneration for the Roman Emperor, they looked upon his subjects rather as Greeks than as Romans, and the Goths were careful to speak of them as "Greeks." The "Greeks," on the other hand, called the Romans of Italy "Italians."

Belisarius garrisoned three towns to the north of Rome, Narnia, Spoletium, and Perusia, and prepared Rome herself to sustain a siege. In this siege, which began in March 537 and lasted for a year and nine days, two circumstances stood him in good stead,—the strength of the Aurelian wall and his command of Sicily, the granary of Italy. The garrison amounted to five thousand men; the army of Witigis numbered fifteen thousand, and was divided in seven camps around the city. The first act of the besiegers was to cut off the city's supply of water by destroying all the aqueducts, eleven (according to Procopius, fourteen) in number. This was one of the greatest disasters that the Ostrogothic war brought upon Rome, which from having been one of the best supplied cities in the world, became one of the worst supplied, until, in the sixteenth century, Sixtus V provided for the convenience and health of Rome by renewing the aqueducts.

When the aqueducts were cut, there was no water to turn the corn mills which supplied the garrison with food. The inventive brain of Belisarius devised a curious and effective expedient. Close to a bridge (probably the Pons Aelius [1]) through whose arch the stream bore down with considerable force, he stretched across the river tense ropes to which he attached two boats, separated by a space of two feet. Two mills were placed on each boat, and between the skiffs was suspended the water-wheel, which the current easily turned. A line of such boats was formed and a series of water-mills in the bed of the Tiber ground all the corn that was required. The endeavours of the Goths to disconcert this ingenious device and break the machines by throwing trees and corpses

---

[1] Cp. Hodgkin, iv. 182. The account of the water-mills will be found in Procopius, *B. G.* i. 19. As to the line of mills, I cannot agree with Mr. Hodgkin (p. 183) that the language of Procopius is deficient in clearness.

into the river were easily thwarted by Belisarius; he stretched across the stream chains of iron which formed an impassable barrier to all dangerous obstacles that might harm his boats or wheels.

In their first assaults the Goths were defeated with great loss,[1] and in April a reinforcement of 1600 Slaves and Huns, who arrived from Constantinople, encouraged the defenders to organise a series of sallies. But after some successes they experienced a signal defeat, and acted thenceforth chiefly on the defensive. During the long blockade that followed, the Romans suffered from famine, and both parties from pestilence. The siege was varied by a truce of three months, and the inexplicable negligence of the Goths enabled the garrison to introduce provisions into the city.

At length, in March 538, the Goths raised the siege, and as they departed were pursued by the soldiers of Belisarius and utterly defeated at the Milvian bridge. The cause of the departure of the Goths was the capture of Rimini by John, the nephew of Vitalian, who had arrived four months before with troops from Byzantium, and had succeeded in entering Rome. During the truce Belisarius despatched him to Alba in the Apennines, whence, if the truce were broken, he was ordered to ravage the land and assault the cities of Picenum. The Goths violated the truce by forming two unsuccessful schemes to capture the city. The light of their torches as they attempted to penetrate the Aqua Virgo was observed by a watchful sentinel, and a Roman whom they hired to drug the sentries at the Flaminian Gate with a sleeping potion revealed the treachery to Belisarius. The operations of John in Picenum were a reply to this Gothic perfidy. It is interesting to note that, when he took Rimini, Matasuntha, the wife of Witigis, opened treasonable communications with him. Her sympathies, like her mother's, were more with the Romans than with the Goths; they were least of all with her husband, who, although he had slain Theodahad, represented his policy.

The siege and relief of Ariminum (Rimini) may be con-

---

[1] Mounted archers (ἱπποτοξόται) were a feature of Belisarius' army, and the general himself ascribed to them the superiority of the Romans to the Goths (Proc. B. G. i. 27).

sidered the third scene of the war, the sieges of Naples and Rome being the first and second. Belisarius sent two officers[1] to John bearing the mandate that he was to withdraw with his band of two thousand Isaurians from Ariminum, and leave in it a nominal garrison taken from Ancona. John refused to obey, and Witigis soon afterwards appeared before the walls.

At this juncture a new element, of which John's insubordinate refusal had been a sign, was introduced into the situation. Fresh troops arrived from Constantinople under the command of Narses the eunuch, a person of great ability and large influence at the Byzantine court. His instructions were to obey Belisarius in all things, so far as seemed consistent with the public weal. The exception, though it might read as a mere formality, was practically as comprehensive as an exception could be, and was an undisguised expression of doubt or mistrust in Belisarius' conduct of the war. The meaning of Narses' appointment was that the Emperor desired to have in Italy a check on Belisarius; the accrediting formula of Narses' papers was an ingenious but patent way of putting it; the eunuch was really independent.

The affair of Ariminum offered to Narses an occasion to assert himself. Owing to want of provisions, John must soon surrender to the besiegers, and the question for Belisarius was whether he should relieve the place or not. An immediate march to Ariminum, while Auximum (Osimo) was still in the hands of the Goths, was a hazardous enterprise, and John's insubordination was not calculated to hasten the steps of the general. Belisarius and Narses met at Firmum, where Narses convinced the council of officers that circumstances demanded the relief of Ariminum, his chief argument being that the reduction of that important town would have a vast effect on the temper of the Goths, who were now thoroughly dispirited.

Belisarius, by adroit movements, succeeded in dispersing the Gothic beleaguerers and saving the city; but the affair had

[1] One of Mr. Hodgkin's most interesting chapters describes the ride of Ildiger and Martin from Rome to Rimini along the Flaminian way (vol. iv. cap. 10). At this juncture the Goths held the following places between Ravenna and Rome: Cesena, Monte- Feltro, Urbino, Chiusi, Todi, Orvieto (Urbs Vetus); while the Romans held Rimini, Pesaro, Fano, Sinigaglia, Ancona, Nuceria, Foligno (Fulginium), Spoleto, Narnia, Firmo. Todi and Chiusi surrendered to Belisarius in 538.

RECONQUEST OF AFRICA AND ITALY

a prejudicial effect on the imperialists themselves. John said pointedly to Belisarius that he thanked Narses for the deliverance—an expression of the discord that divided the camp.

The result of this discord was the loss of Milan and the massacre of its inhabitants by the Goths. At the request of Datius, bishop of Mediolanum, who visited Rome during the last month of the siege, Belisarius had sent Mundilas to Liguria, and that officer had occupied Mediolanum and other cities with small garrisons. The Goths and a large body of Burgundians, sent by Theudebert, king of the Franks of Austrasia, invested Milan. Belisarius ordered John to relieve it, but John refused to move without the order of Narses, and Narses gave the order too late. Milan and Liguria were lost to the Goths in the early months of 539 A.D.

Justinian was wise enough to see the disadvantages that were involved in the independent and antagonistic position of Narses, and to apprehend that the conquest of Italy depended on his placing implicit confidence in Belisarius. He remedied the mistake that he had committed, and recalled Narses; we may say that this step decided the result of the undertaking.

The latter part of the year 539 was marked by the sieges of Faesulae (Fiesolé) and Auximum, and by the sanguinary invasion of the Franks, who were supposed to be at peace with both parties, but now, under King Theudebert, inflicted terrible slaughter on the Goths, and put the Romans to rout. A disease broke out in their army, and this, joined with the menaces and remonstrances of Belisarius, induced them to retire. Italy had long presented the appearance of a wilderness, waste and uncultivated in consequence of the war, and famine was decimating the Goths. Witigis began to look for foreign assistance. He not only entered into communication with Wacis, king of the Lombards, but sent two Ligurians to Chosroes Nushirvan to induce him to vex the eastern frontier of the Empire; for the Goths saw that the effectiveness of Justinian's operations in the West was conditioned by the maintenance of peaceful relations in the East, as arranged by the treaty of 532. This attempt to negotiate with Persia, and the menace of hostility in that quarter, had the effect of disposing Justinian to conclude the war in Italy as speedily as possible.

The surrender of Faesulae and Auximum at the close of 539 prepared the way for the fall of Ravenna, which Belisarius immediately invested. At this juncture the situation at Ravenna was complicated, though not really determined, by various other interests in distant places. The first problem was whether Italy should be divided between Franks and Goths or between Goths and Romans. An embassy of the Franks waited on Witigis, making the former proposal; but this was counteracted by an embassy from Belisarius, to whose offer Witigis inclined. In the second place, the attitude of Chosroes, who was preparing to invade Syria, and the dangers of the Haemus peninsula, which was threatened by Hunnic inroads, affected the disposition of the Emperor, who proposed to Witigis the very moderate terms that he should reign as king in trans-Padane Italy, that the rest of the peninsula should be Roman, and that the royal treasure of the Goths should be equally divided. But Belisarius was dissatisfied with these terms, which seemed disproportionate to his success. A remarkable proposal of the Goths themselves made it possible for him to set them aside and convert the entire land of Italy into an imperial prefecture. This proposal was that Belisarius should himself assume the dignity of Emperor, and govern both the Goths and Romans. He did not reject the proposal, and the Goths surrendered on that understanding (spring 540). But the general's acquiescence was only a ruse to obtain unconditional mastery of the king and the capital of the Goths, and the idea of a revival of a separate dynasty in western Europe was not carried out. Witigis, the second king who had been vanquished by Belisarius, was conducted in triumph to Constantinople, and the treasures of the Ostrogothic palace were laid at the feet of Justinian.

We have seen that the attitude of the Franks was an element in Italian politics, and it seems desirable to say something in this place of the relations of the Franks and their Merovingian kings to the Empire. Though Gaul was really independent of the Empire in all respects, there were still theoretical ties which bound her to New Rome, and these theoretical ties influenced to some extent practical politics. Chlodwig, as we saw, was created honorary consul, and probably Patrician[1]; he thus held a place in the hierarchy of the Empire, and one might almost look on him as the Catholic champion of Anastasius in the West against Arian Theodoric.[2] The Merovingian sovereigns placed the word *Vir inluster* after their names,[3] thus acknowledging that they belonged to the Roman system. Theudebert, the grandson of Chlodwig, was adopted by Justinian, and addresses him as father in two extant letters,[4] just as Childebert in later days was the *son* of Maurice. In a contemporary Life of a certain Saint Trevirius we read of Gaul as "under the legal sway of the Empire" (*sub imperii jure*) in the consulship of Justin (519 or 524)[5]; the theory of imperial Gaul was not yet a thing of the past.

From the consulate of Chlodwig until the year 539 the relations of the Empire with Gaul were friendly, but in that year Theudebert, the lord of Austrasia,[6] and "son" of the Emperor, assumed a hostile attitude. He seems to have formed the idea of a confederacy of Teutonic nations against the Empire, but the execution of his plans was cut short by his death in 547. But neither the action of Theudebert nor that of his son Theudebald some years later (*see* below, cap. vii.) dissolved the ties of theoretical connection which bound the Frankish kingdoms of Gaul with the Roman Empire.

SAINT BENEDICT.[7]—It is appropriate to mention here that while Justinian and Belisarius were carrying on a war in Italy which was to affect profoundly the future of that country, Saint Benedict was founding his monastery at Monte Cassino,

---

[1] Bouquet, ii. 538 : "Patricius magno sublimis fulsit honore."

[2] Gasquet, *L'empire byzantin*, p. 133 : "Il était en Occident le soldat d' Anastase."

[3] *Ib.* pp. 135-140. On the subject of this title there is great difference of opinion among French scholars.

[4] Bouquet, iv. epp. 14, 15.

[5] Gasquet, *L'empire byzantin*, p. 168. For Vita S. Trevirii, *see* Bouquet, iii. 411.

[6] On Chlodwig's death, 511 A.D., his kingdom was divided among his four sons. The eldest, Theuderic, received the eastern lands on the Rhine and Meuse, which became subsequently known as Austrasia, and a considerable region in Aquitaine, including Auvergne. The western provinces (which were to receive the conjugate name of Neustria or Neustrasia) fell to the share of Childebert. Chlodomer received the provinces south of the Loire (chief towns, Orleans, Tours, Poitiers), while to the youngest, Chlothachar, were assigned the districts of the Salian Franks in the north-east (capital Soissons). Theudebert succeeded his father Theuderic.

[7] A picturesque chapter on St. Benedict has been written by Mr. Hodgkin, vol. iv. cap. 16. I have consulted the article of A. Vogel in Herzog and Pflitt, *Encyclopädie für protestantische Theologie*. The life and teaching of St. Benedict do not strictly come within the province of my work; he did not perceptibly affect the Roman Empire.

which in the Middle Ages was to be an important factor in medieval civilisation. Benedict was born at Nursia, in the province of Valeria. Sent as a boy to study at Rome, he found his school companions sunk in corruption, and was so deeply disgusted at the presence and prevalence of vice that he fled from the world, at the age of fourteen. He went eastward, accompanied by his nurse, to the lakes at the sources of the Anio. Near Subiaco, having obtained a monk's garment from a holy man, he set up his abode in a cave at the foot of a mountain. The temptations which he underwent, the perils which he escaped, his conflicts with the Ancient Enemy, *antiquus hostis*, and the legends which in the course of a few years had encompassed his name, may be read in the biography which was written of him by his admirer Pope Gregory the Great. In 510 he was made abbot of Vicovano, but the monks could not endure his severe principle of obedience; in other matters he was not over strict. In 528 he went southwards to Campania, and founded the cloister of Monte Cassino, midway between Rome and Naples. He died on 21st March 543. His monastic *regula*, supported by the authority of Pope Gregory the Great, ultimately became the recognised rule of all monastic institutions. This, however, did not immediately come to pass. It appears that it was in the pontificate of Gregory II, in the beginning of the eighth century, that it decidedly obtained the ascendency over the rules of other monastic reformers. For there were other monastic reformers even in the time of Benedict himself, for example, Aurelian and Caesarius at Arelate. The movement which Benedict represented in Italy was general and widespread, but the rules which he prescribed were more reasonable, mild, and moderate, notwithstanding his excessive personal austerity, than those of others.

CHAPTER VI

THE GREAT PLAGUE

AT various periods of the world's history mankind has been visited by plagues on a great scale. It is noteworthy that they generally attend some moral change in the races which they visit,—that they generally mark roughly a historical period. Thus the pestilence in the reign of Marcus Aurelius may be said to have accompanied the inauguration of a new epoch of the Roman Empire. The continuity of history is not broken, but in the last years of the second as in the third century we feel that we have passed into an atmosphere totally different from that of the earlier Empire. The Black Death of 1346 accompanied the inauguration of the Renaissance, and if a single date is desirable to mark the close of the Middle Ages, perhaps 1346 is the most suitable. The great pestilence of 747 A.D. was the concomitant of an important transition from the early semi-antique medievalism to medievalism proper in the Roman Empire, as I hope to show in its due place. The plague at Athens in the fifth century B.C. likewise accompanied the change from an old to a new spirit, from the old spirit which Aristophanes praises to the new spirit which he ridicules and breathes, from the old spirit of Herodotus, Aeschylus, and Pindar to the new spirit of Thucydides, Euripides, and Agathon.

The great plague of 542 A.D. similarly defines the beginning of a new period. If we may speak of watersheds in history, this plague marks the watershed of what we call the ancient and what we call the medieval age. The whole period from Constantine to Justinian was a preparation for the Middle Ages, but its character was more ancient than medieval; the period from Justinian to Constantine V was also a preparation for the Middle Ages, but it was far more medieval than ancient. The four centuries elapsing between Constantine I. and Constantine V might be well considered a separate period, neither the ancient nor the medieval, and yet partaking of both characters, the twilight between the day and the night. But it is more convenient to divide it, and assign part of it to ancient history and part of it to medieval history. The question being at what point we are to divide it, I venture to say that the most natural point of division is the great plague in the sixth century.

For really nothing is more striking than the difference between the first half and the latter half of Justinian's reign. We feel in 550 that we are moving in a completely other world than that of 540. The hope and cheerfulness with which his reign opened have vanished, and though the tasks willed in hours of insight are not surrendered, it is veritably in hours of gloom that they are fulfilled, and the Emperor himself, quite a changed man, seems to have forgotten his interest in them. Contemporaries noticed this change that had come upon Justinian, and it has been mentioned in a previous chapter.

The peculiarity of great plagues—that they are concomitants of moral or psychical changes—naturally suggests a problem, the data necessary for whose solution are veiled in obscurity. Are these pestilences to be placed in the same category as earthquakes, for example, which may destroy a city and thereby modify history, although there is no conceivable intrinsic connection between their own causes and the societies which they affect? In this case two alternatives are possible. Either the moral and spiritual change is in the first instance quite independent of the plague, and the synchronism is a pure accident, though when the plague has set in it may facilitate the changes by removing the old generation and transforming the population; or else the plague is the cause of the moral and spiritual revolution. The second alternative must be rejected, because in all cases we see the change at work before the appearance of the disease; and perhaps the first theory will recommend itself as reasonable.

Yet we must not ignore another possibility, which cannot be proved, but does not seem improbable, the possibility that the rise and spread of the plague may be intrinsically connected with the moral and spiritual changes which it so often accompanies. In the present century it is not necessary to remind the reader that, though we reject the unreasonable formula that mind is a mere function of matter, we cannot reject the physiological fact that all processes of the individual consciousness are accompanied by corresponding physical processes of cerebration, and that there is a continual action and reaction between the psychical and physical operations. We can hardly help concluding from this that great psychological—moral and spiritual—changes which transmute societies must be accompanied by biological changes, modifications in the adjustments of the functions of the various parts of the brain, and morphological changes in its configuration. Such cerebral modifications would be naturally and necessarily attended by changes of an imperceptible but actual kind in the whole organism. Now, as the spread of a disease must depend on the state of each patient's organism as well as on the germs which are propagated in the atmosphere, it is quite conceivable that the circumstance that the organisms of a people were undergoing a process of transformation might condition and determine the diffusion, if not the appearance, of a pestilence.

The great plague ravaged the Empire for four years. It began at Pelusium, whence it spread in two directions, throughout Egypt and into Palestine. Its presence in Persia caused Chosroes to retire prematurely from his campaign in 542, and in the spring of the same year it reached Constantinople, where it raged for four months. Procopius, the historian, an eye-witness of its course, has left us an account of it, which one sets beside the description of the plague at Athens by Thucydides, or that of the Black Death by Boccaccio. Procopius does not hesitate to reject all attempts to account for it by natural causes and to attribute its origin directly to the Deity. His reason for this scepticism or faith was that the visitation was universal, and therefore excluded a special cause. This circumstance especially impressed Procopius; the plague did not assail any particular race or class of men,[1] nor prevail in any particular region, nor at any particular season of the year. Summer or winter, north or south, Greek or Arabian, washed or unwashed —of these distinctions the plague took no account; it pervaded the whole world. A man might climb to the top of a hill, it was there; or retire to the depth of a cavern, it was there also. If it passed by a spot, it was sure to return there again; and one condition at least it seemed to obey in the line of its route, for Procopius tells us that it spread from the coast inlandwards. The chief symptom of the disease was the swelling of the groin, whence it is called by Gregory of Tours *lues inguinaria*. Some of those who were attacked were warned by the sight of demon spectres in human forms and by a feeling as if they were struck by an invisible hand. This feature was also characteristic of the plague of 747; it is a medieval trait. The plague of the age of Pericles was not accompanied by spectral apparitions, or at least the rational Thucydides does not condescend to record such puerilities. When the plague reached its height, 5000, it is said, perished daily, sometimes even 10,000. Justinian himself caught the infection, but recovered. Constantinople was in a pitiable condition. In many houses none remained to bury the dead, and Justinian appointed Theodorus, a referendarius, to provide for the interment of the neglected corpses. The feuds of the Blues and Greens were quenched in the common woe. The attitude of the light and dissolute to religion deserves mention. With the prospect of death before them, they cleansed their ways and piously frequented churches; but when they recovered and felt secure, they plunged headlong into their old amusements, and their last state was worse than the first. Procopius made the generalisation that "this pestilence, whether by chance or providential design, strictly spared the most wicked."

The plague aggravated the disastrous condition of the population, which had suffered from the pressure of taxation. It produced a stagnation of trade and a cessation of work. All customary occupations were broken off, and the market-places were empty save of corpse-bearers. The consequence was that

[1] Females, however, were said to be less susceptible than males. Procopius' description will be found in *Bell. Pers.* ii. 22, 23, 30.

Constantinople, always richly supplied, was in a state of famine, and bread was a great luxury.

In 558 there was another outbreak of this pestilential scourge in the East; it lurked and lingered in Europe long after the first grand visitation. In the last years of Justinian it produced a desolation in Liguria which was graphically described by Paul, the historian of the Lombards. "Videres," he writes,[1] "saeculum in antiquum redactum silentium"; the country seemed plunged in a "primeval silence."

[1] Paul Diac. *Hist. Lang.* ii. 4.

CHAPTER VII

THE FINAL CONQUEST OF ITALY AND THE CONQUEST OF SOUTH-EASTERN SPAIN

By the fall of Witigis and the capture of Ravenna the conquest of Italy was not completed. There were still germs of patriotism among the Ostrogoths, which the hasty departure of Belisarius left unstifled, to revive and cause many more years of labour to the Roman armies.

The town of Ticinum (Pavia) was still in the possession of the Goths, being held by Ildibad,[1] whom they elected as their new king. The Roman command was divided among several generals, whom Belisarius, destined himself to conduct the Persian war, had left behind. A third factor in the situation was the introduction of the stringent financial system of the Empire, under the direction of a *logothete*. It cannot be said that annexation to the Empire was a blessing to the inhabitants of Italy; it entailed the desolations and miseries of five years of war, followed by the imposition of grinding taxes.[2] These two circumstances, the divided command and the financial system, combined with the dissatisfaction of the Roman soldiers at not receiving the promotions and higher pay to which they were entitled, rendered a revival of Gothic hopes far from

---

[1] I suspect that Ildibad is for Ildibald (on the principle that one of two l's in the same word has a tendency to drop out), and that thus the termination is the same as in Ethelbald, Theudibald, Willibald. For the first part of the word, compare Ildiger (= Hildi-gern, "eager for battle," compare Frithigern); it is the same as Childi, or Hildi, in Frankish and Vandalic names. Hildi-bald = "bold in battle."

[2] The most unseasonable and imprudent claim was the requisition of accounts for moneys paid under Gothic kings. Compare Hodgkin, *Italy and her Invaders*, iv. 431.

impossible. Alexander, the first logothete, who was called "Scissors" from his practice of clipping coins, "alienated the minds of the Italians from Justinian Augustus; and none of the soldiers were willing to undergo the hazard of war, but they advanced the cause of the enemy by intentional laziness."[1] The attitude of the soldiers led to the inactivity of the generals; and in the meantime the power of Ildibad, who had been collecting the relics of the Goths and enlisting many dissatisfied Italians, was extending over Liguria and Venetia. The only general who tried to oppose him suffered a severe defeat.

In the following year Ildibad was murdered on account of a private quarrel, and after the short reign of a Rugian, named Eraric, who entered into negotiations with Justinian and dissatisfied his subjects, the hero of the second part of the Gothic war, Baduila or Totila,[2] a nephew of Ildibad, was elected king of the Goths. In the history of this war the names of Witigis and Totila stand out, while that of Ildibad remains in obscurity —is read, and forgotten; but it should be remembered that at a critical juncture he sustained the life of the Ostrogothic nationality and energetically took advantage of the circumstances which favoured such a hope, to revive the cause of his people.

Within a year of Totila's accession the position of Romans and Goths in Italy was reversed. An unsuccessful attempt to take Verona, made by the Roman generals, whom the rebukes of Justinian had stimulated to action, was followed by a Roman defeat in the battle of Faenza, in which a remarkable single combat is said to have taken place between a gigantic Goth and Artabazes, a Persian conspicuous for bravery. Another victory, achieved at Mugillo over John the nephew of Vitalian, laid the centre and south of Italy open to Totila's attack. By the middle of 542 A.D. he had reduced and imposed taxes on Bruttii, Calabria, Apulia, Lucania, and he had begun the siege of Naples. That city surrendered in 543, and was treated with a spirit of humanity which Totila adopted as a principle of warfare. He put to death one of his prae-

---

[1] Procopius, *B. G.* iii. 1.
[2] Totila, and afterwards his successor Teias, minted coins with the image and legends of the Emperor Anastasius. We may compare the coins of the Suevians which continued in the sixth century to bear the types of Avitus and Honorius. The coinage of Totila, as M. Gasquet neatly puts it (*L'empire byzantin*, p. 176), represented at once fidelity to the Empire and revolt against the Emperor.

torian guards (for the Goths had "praetorians") who had violated the daughter of a Calabrian. The criminal was a brave and popular man, and a number of distinguished Goths pleaded with Totila to save his life; but the king answered the deputation in a speech in which he laid down that the general policy and principles whereon the Gothic cause depended were involved in this particular case.[1] The behaviour of Totila was all the more conspicuous, as it contrasted with the rapacity and incontinence in which the Roman leaders were at this time indulging.

After his success at Naples Totila undertook the siege of Hydruntum, or Otranto, and prepared also to besiege John, who had shut himself up in Rome. He addressed a sort of manifesto to the Roman senate, in which he appealed to the actual contrast between the government of Theodoric and Amalasuntha and that of the Greek logothetes; copies of this were posted up in Rome, and in consequence thereof John expelled the Arian clergy from the city.

The hold of the Empire on Italy had thus become extremely precarious. Totila's star was in the ascendant. There was no ability, no energy, no unity on the side of the imperialists. Constantine, the commander at Ravenna, wrote to the Emperor a letter representing the situation, and it was resolved to permit Belisarius to return to the scene of his successes. But Belisarius had changed as well as the situation in Italy. It seems that he had fallen into disgrace at court, and had been saved from punishment by the influence of his wife Antonina with the Empress; but for these transactions we have only the dubious authority of the *Secret History*. A cloud at all events had fallen over him; he was not allowed to command in the Persian war, as he would have chosen.[2] This personal experience had probably a considerable effect on his spirits; but we must chiefly notice that Justinian did not support him when he set out. The army, including his own special troops, were in Asia, and not permitted to accompany him; he was obliged to scour Thrace to collect, at his own expense, soldiers, whom he afterwards described as a "miserable squad."

---

[1] Proc. *B. G.* iii. 8. He attributed the ill success of the Goths, who were really well equipped, at the beginning of the war to their failure in these respects. Compare Hodgkin, iv. 523.

[2] Ranke accepts the main features of this story as genuine history, *Weltgeschichte*, iv. 2, 85.

When we start with Belisarius on his second expedition to the West, the brightness of his day seems to have gone; in fact, after his departure from Ravenna in 540 we feel that the darkness is upon us, and that the Middle Ages have begun. Belisarius, in the period of his glory, as the champion of the Roman Empire, threw a light as of the ancient world on the scene; but the gloom of his return to Italy, the appearance of Totila, who was a sort of "knight," that king's visit to Benedict, bringing us into contact with the saint whose shadow dominates the medieval centuries—all this gives the impression that the dim ages are beginning.

Belisarius was not invested with the highest rank; he was only *comes stabuli*, count of the stable. He arrived in Italy in the middle of 544, along with Vitalian, the master of soldiers in Illyricum, and took up his quarters at Ravenna. This was a mistake. Everything was adverse to him, and he did not possess his old energy. In May 545—during the whole intervening year all that had been done was to relieve the besieged garrisons of Hydruntum and Auximum, and to fortify Pisaurum (Pesaro)—he was obliged to write to Justinian. His letter is a model of conciseness and directness, with a certain tinge of irony.[1] He asked for three things, if the Emperor wished to affirm Roman dominion in Italy, (1) his own mounted lancers and foot-guards; (2) a large body of Huns and other barbarians; (3) money to pay the troops.

He sent John, the nephew of Vitalian, with this letter, binding him by solemn oath to hasten his return. It will be remembered that John had disobeyed Belisarius in the affair of Ariminum, and had acted on the side of Narses; he is a man who cannot be neglected in the history of the time, for he played a considerable though subordinate part. On this occasion his visit to Byzantium brought him again into close connection with a party politically opposed to Belisarius. He married the daughter of the Emperor's nephew Germanus, and thus allied himself to the interests of the kin of Justinian. Belisarius, on the other hand, had attached himself to the directly opposed interests of Theodora and her relations by the arrangement of a marriage between his daughter Joannina and Anastasius, the grandson of the Empress.

[1] Proc. *B. G.* iii. 12.

Towards the end of the year, Totila, having taken several important towns in central Italy, including Spoletium, invested Rome, where Bessas was in command, and in the course of a few months reduced it to such extremities of hunger that the chief food of the inhabitants was cooked nettles. At last Bessas, after much importunity, allowed those inhabitants who were useless for fighting to depart.

Meanwhile John had returned from his nuptial festivities with a considerable army and joined Belisarius at Dyrrhachium. The new marriage connection emphasised the opposition of the generals, which was immediately displayed in diverging plans of warfare. The question at issue was the relief of Rome, Belisarius urging immediate action, and John insisting on the preliminary reduction of Calabria and Lucania. A compromise was made; each was to execute his own plan. John recovered the southern provinces without much difficulty, but the undertaking of Belisarius was more difficult, and proved unsuccessful.

The town of Portus, at the mouth of the Tiber, situated on the right bank and facing the fort of Ostia, was occupied by Belisarius, who was accompanied by his wife Antonina. It was all-important to supply the distressed garrison with food as soon as possible, and for this purpose it was necessary to break the boom which Totila had thrown across the Tiber. This boom consisted of long beams connecting, like a bridge, the two banks of the river at a narrow part of the stream. On each bank a wooden tower, manned with brave warriors, was erected to defend the boom. To overcome this obstacle Belisarius invented the following device. Two wide boats were firmly joined together and surmounted by a wooden tower considerably higher than those which dominated Totila's fortification. On the top of the tower was placed a boat filled with pitch, sulphur, rosin, and other combustible substances. Two hundred fast vessels (*dromones*), protected by plank-walls pierced with holes for the discharge of missiles, were laden with corn and manned with brave men. Belisarius embarked himself in one of the vessels, having committed the care of Portus and his wife Antonina to his captain Isaac of Ameria, whom he enjoined not to stir from the place on any pretext. Portus was the only friendly position, on which, in case of need, he could fall back. The Roman ships, tugging the tower with them, sailed up the Tiber without opposition, until, not far from the bridge, they were met by an iron chain, which spanned the river, and some Goths set there to defend it. The Goths were easily scattered and the chain was removed. A firmer resistance was offered at the bridge, but the boat of inflammable materials was dexterously dropped on the tower of the right bank; the structure was enveloped in flames and almost 200 Goths were burnt alive. The arrows of the Romans completed the discomfiture of the enemy.

But the envy of fortune did not permit to Belisarius the success which seemed within his grasp. As he prepared to break the boom, the alarming news arrived that Isaac was taken. It appears that Isaac, hearing a rumour of the success of Belisarius, and desirous of emulating his glory, had disobeyed his orders, attacked Ostia, and been taken prisoner. Belisarius "thinking that all was over with Portus, his wife, and his cause, and that no place of refuge was left to fall back on, lost his presence of mind, a thing which had never befallen him before."[1] He issued orders for a hasty retreat, and when he reached Portus was relieved and exasperated to find that it was a false alarm. The excitement led to a fever which proved almost fatal to the disappointed general.

The blame of the capture of the city, which was achieved through the treachery of some Isaurian soldiers, seems partly to rest with the commandant Bessas, who was so avaricious as to enrich himself by trading in corn with the famished garrison and, engrossed in these practices, forgot his duty.[2] Totila took Rome in the last month of 546 A.D.

The behaviour of the Gothic soldiers in the captured city is a curious illustration of the nascent medieval feelings of the time. They were allowed by their king to plunder property and massacre men, but they were strictly prohibited from ravishing women. This prohibition did not rest on feelings of humanity, which would have prevented the worse evil of butchery, it rested on a religious feeling which regarded the interests of the Goths themselves and not those of the possible victims.

[1] Procopius, *B. G.* iii. 19.
[2] Bessas afterwards displayed the same tendencies in Lazica and Armenia.

The speeches attributed to Totila on the occasion are also noteworthy. In his address to the Goths he repeats a point which he had insisted on before, the contrast between their present position and their position at the beginning of the war; then the Ostrogoths were numerous and rich, now they are few and poor; but then they suffered disaster on disaster, now they gain success after success. The cause of this contrast is that then they had acted unrighteously, while now their conduct is void of reproach; hence a change has taken place in the regard of the Deity. In his address to the Roman senators Totila contrasted in the usual manner the oppression of the "Greeks" with the mild government of the Goths, and doomed them to slavery in return for their deafness to his appeals.

Another notable feature in connection with this capture of Rome was Totila's intention to destroy it, and the argument by which Belisarius, who was then lying ill at Portus, dissuaded him from his design. Belisarius appealed to the judgment that posterity and mankind would pass on the destruction of the Eternal City. He also urged the alternative: if you conquer, Rome preserved will be your best possession; if you are conquered, by the destruction of Rome your claims to clemency will be forfeited.

Totila and all his troops went southward to Lucania, and for forty days Rome was uninhabited. Then the Roman general re-occupied it and repaired the walls and fortifications, which Totila had partially dismantled. Totila had not anticipated this movement, and when he heard the news returned to retake the city. His attack, however, was unsuccessful, and he was obliged to withdraw to the citadel of Tibur.

But the position of Belisarius became untenable, and he was unable to cope with the Goths in the open field. He sailed to Tarentum, and made one last attempt to unite his forces with those of John in order to make a joint attack on the foe, but the attempt miscarried, and Belisarius desired nothing better than to be recalled to Constantinople. He had sent thither his wife, Antonina, to beg for further assistance in men and money; but on the 1st July 548 she lost an advocate by the death of Theodora, and then she requested that her husband should be recalled. Although Belisarius had not been able to conquer Totila, he was, nevertheless, a check on the Gothic operations; and after his recall the power of the Goths began to rise to its highest point. Totila besieged Rome again, and it was again delivered to him by Isaurian treachery; this was the third siege during the war. He occupied and ravaged Sicily, and built a large fleet with which he pillaged the coasts of Sardinia and Epirus. Thus he was now undisputed king of Italy, and possessed a naval power.

During the preceding years Justinian's heart had not been centred on the conquest of Italy; all his thoughts and attention were engrossed in the theological controversy of the "three articles." Nothing was done in 549 and 550, but in 550 an idea was conceived which, if it had been carried out, might have altered to some extent Italian history. Justinian surrendered the design, which Belisarius had momentarily accomplished, of making Italy a province or prefecture governed from New Rome, and formed a new plan—a sort of compromise—to unite the house of Theodoric with his own, so that Gotho-Roman Italy should be governed by a Gotho-Roman line. He appointed his nephew Germanus, who, now that Theodora was no longer alive, was in higher favour, general commander of the Italian armies, with full powers; and Germanus married Matasuntha, the widow of Witigis, and granddaughter of Theodoric. Great enthusiasm prevailed for the expedition of Germanus. The news thereof made the Goths waver in their allegiance to Totila, and the Italians were prepared to welcome him cordially. Numbers of recruits flocked to his standard.

But Germanus was not destined to rule in Italy as a colleague of Justinian. Efficient action in the Italian war was at this time seriously impeded by the ruinous invasions of Slaves and Huns, who depopulated the provinces of Illyricum and threatened the capital. In the early part of 550, while Germanus was making preparations for his Italian expedition, one of these incursions took place, and he received orders to turn aside to protect Thessalonica. He caught fever, and died; and with him perished the prospects of a restoration of the Amal line. After his death a son was born to Matasuntha, Germanus Posthumus, on whom Romanising Goths seem to have built hopes for the future; at least the Gothic history of

Jordanes must be placed in the year 551, and it has been most plausibly argued by Schirren that it is a work with a tendency, written to induce Justinian to recognise the infant Germanus as Emperor and ruler of Italy.

In the same year Justinian decided to make a great final effort to reduce Italy and exterminate the Goths, whose very name, we are told, he hated. The problem was to find a general whom all would obey, and Justinian solved it well by the strange choice of a eunuch, seventy-five years old, his grand-chamberlain Narses, the same whose presence in Italy had sown dissensions among Belisarius' officers in 538. By his high position at court and his influence with the Emperor he had immense authority, whereby he could secure united action in the warfare, and he was not stinted, as Belisarius had been, in the matter of funds.

Before Narses arrived two blows had been dealt to Totila, which so damped his spirits that he treated for peace. The Romans held only four places on the eastern coast of Italy, Ravenna, Ancona, Hydruntum, and Crotona. The Goths were besieging Ancona, but when it was already hard pressed, John, the son of Vitalian, and Valerian forced them to raise the siege by completely defeating the Gothic fleet off Sinigaglia. This was a severe blow to the naval power of the Goths, the deficiencies of whose sea craft were evident in the battle. The second misfortune was the loss of Sicily, from which they were driven by the Persarmenian Artabanes, and this was followed by the relief of Crotona early in the following year (552). Justinian would not listen to the Gothic proposals for peace. The situation was further perplexed by the attitude of the Franks, who held nearly all northern Italy, and invariably considered the difficulty of the Goths their own opportunity.

Narses' army was chiefly composed of barbarians—Heruls, Lombards, Gepids, Huns, and Persians.[1] His march into Italy, along the coast of Venetia, was opposed by both the Franks, who hated Lombards, and a band of Gothic troops under Teias; but it was successfully accomplished with the

[1] Dagisthaeus and other Persian captives were sent to fight in Italy. Kobad, the nephew of King Chosroes, who had fled to the Empire to avoid his uncle's hate, commanded Persian deserters. The Romans of Narses' army were led by John the Glutton.

help of the ships which coasted slowly round, attending the progress of the army. Narses marched southward without delay, and Totila marched northward to meet him. The scene of the final battle (July or August 552) which decided the fate of Italy is disputed, some placing it near Sassoferrato, on the east side of the Via Flaminia, others near Scheggia, on the west side. Procopius, who was not present, is not sufficiently precise. Two circumstances may be noticed which helped to determine the result. The Romans anticipated the Goths in occupying a small hill which commanded the battlefield, and Totila, who trusted to his cavalry chiefly, made the mistake of enjoining on them to use no weapons but spears. Narses' tactics consisted in strengthening his wings, on which he relied for the victory. The Gothic army was routed, and Totila received a mortal wound, from which he expired at about thirteen miles from the field. In the month of August the bloodstained garments of Totila arrived at New Rome, as a trophy of Narses' success.[1]

After the victory the Lombard auxiliaries displayed their nature by acts of barbarous violence and licence, and it was found necessary to pay them their hire and conduct them out of Italy.

This victory decided the war, but Narses' position was not yet firm. The imperialists in the meantime had taken Rome, and almost all the fortresses had been surrendered by the Gothic commandants. But the remnant of those who were defeated in the battle reunited under the general Teias. Him they elected king, and Narses was forced to fight once more near the Draco, in south Italy. Teias was slain (553),[2] but the battle did not end with his death; it was renewed on the following day. Finally, however, the Goths proposed to conclude the war on condition that they should be allowed to leave Italy, and the proposal was agreed to. A thousand of the vanquished escaped to Pavia.

At this point the Ostrogothic war and the history of Pro-

---

[1] Theoph. 6044 A.M. The date (August) is important, for Procopius gives no date for the battle, and I can find no indication in Mr. Hodgkin's work more precise than the *implication* that it was fought after the early part of spring and before the winter months of 552. We are justified in determining the date as July or August.

[2] The battlefield was determined by the siege of Cumae, and the siege of Cumae was pressed because a large treasure had been hoarded there by Totila.

copius come to an end; but opposition was raised to the establishment of the imperial authority in Italy from another quarter.

Teias had in vain begged the king of the Franks, Theudebald, for assistance in the death-conflict, and had tried to bribe him by presenting him with a large part of the Gothic treasures; but Theudebald had given no succour. Now, however, he intervened, though not directly, by countenancing the Italian expedition of Leutharis and Bucelin, two Alemanni who were at his court. They entered Italy with 75,000 men to oppose the arms of Narses, and many Goths throughout Italy regarded them as deliverers. But others deemed the Romans preferable, as masters, to the Franks, and among those who held this view was Aligern, Teias' brother, who was commander of the still uncaptured fortress of Cumae. He presented the keys of that town to Narses, who had withdrawn to Ravenna. Leutharis and his army were destroyed by a disease due to the climate, and Bucelin was completely defeated near Capua in an engagement, remarkable for a curious incident which threatened Narses with defeat, and, as it turned out, led to his victory. The eunuch punished with death a noble Herul for killing one of his own servants, and the act inflamed all the Heruls with indignation, as they claimed the right of dealing with their servants as they thought fit, without interference. They announced that they would take no part in the battle. This report induced the enemy, feeling assured of an easy victory, to attack their opponents with a careless and imprudent haste. But when Narses, who was quite prepared, called his troops to battle, the Heruls could not bring themselves to persist in executing their threat, and the strong-minded independence of Narses signally triumphed.

Thus the whole land of Italy,[1] including the islands and the Istrian and Illyrian regions, which were connected with it under the old imperial administration, became once more part of the Roman Empire; and Narses was the first *exarch* or governor of the reconquered peninsula.

[1] Verona and Brixia were not taken till 562, Theoph. Βηρωίαν καὶ Βρίγκας. The "names were corrupted by the ignorance or vanity of the Greeks" (Gibbon). Narses' restoration of the Salarian bridge, which Totila had destroyed, is commemorated in an inscription of eight Latin verses (*C. I. L.* vi. tit. 1199, p. 250).

qui potuit rigidas Gothorum subdere mentes,
hic docuit durum flumina ferri jugum.

CONQUEST OF SOUTH - EASTERN SPAIN. — When he had conquered the Ostrogoths, Justinian proceeded to undertake hostilities against the Visigoths, and attempt to win back Spain as he had won back Italy. Theodoric, the king of the Visigoths, had held aloof from the struggle in the neighbouring peninsula, and lent no aid to the East Goths, but Theudis, his successor, supported his nephew Ildibad, the Ostrogothic king, and fomented a rising against the Romans in Africa. He saw that the Teutonic kingdoms of the West were threatened by the reviving power of the Empire.

Of the operations of the Romans in Spain we have unluckily no consecutive account; we have only the scattered notices in the Chronicles of Isidore of Seville and John of Biclaro. It seems that, as in the case of the war in Africa and as in the case of the war in Italy, internal dissensions afforded a pretext for Roman interference. Athanagild headed a party which was opposed to King Agila, and this party called in the aid of the Patrician Liberius from Africa.[1] Liberius crossed the straits and subdued the coast of Spain, as the Carthaginians had done in ancient times, and as the Saracens were to do at a later period. Corduba, Spanish Carthage —New Carthage, Carthagena, or Carthago Spartaria, as it was variously called,—Malaga, and Assidonia, with many places on the coast, passed once more into the hands of the Romans.

But the Goths were alarmed at the advance of the Romans in the south; the adherents of Agila patriotically slew him and joined the abler Athanagild, to make common cause against the invader.[2] It was a somewhat parallel case to that of the Romans themselves in Africa in the year 429: there were then two parties in Africa, the party of Boniface and the party of Sigisvult, the general of Placidia; one or both of them called in the Vandal, and then they joined together to make common cause against the stranger. But the stand of the Goths against the Romans was more effectual than that of the Romans against the Vandals. After their first successes the imperialists do not seem to have acquired much more territory; they never

---

[1] Jordanes, *Get.* 58.
[2] Isidorus, *de regibus Gothorum*, 46 (ed. Migne, p. 1070): "ne Hispaniam milites Romani auxilii occasione invaderent."

penetrated really into the centre of Spain; and the reason was that the Roman Spaniards found the yoke of the Teuton king lighter than the yoke of the Roman Emperor had formerly been. The heavy taxation, which was always imposed by New Rome, had given her a bad name among the provincials who had passed from under imperial domination and become subjects of Teutonic rulers.

When sixteen years, during which we lose the Spanish provinces from sight, had passed away, and when Justinian no longer reigned, there arose a great king among the Visigoths, by name Leovigild. He set it before him to drive the Romans from the Iberian peninsula, and, though he did not entirely succeed, he materially weakened their power. He recovered Malaga, Assidonia, and even Corduba.

The struggles of the Arian with the Catholic party in the Visigothic kingdom, the discord of Arian Leovigild with his Catholic son Hermenigild, the husband of the Frankish princess Ingundis, led to new hostilities with the Romans; for, even as Athanagild had called in the help of Liberius, Hermenigild called in the help of "the Greeks," as the historian of the Franks calls them.[1] Leovigild, however, paralysed this combination; Hermenigild surrendered, and was sent in exile to Valentia. This happened in 584; and in the same year the arms of the Visigoths were successful against the third power in the Peninsula, that of the Suevians, whose kingdom embraced Lusitania and Galicia. Suevia was made a province of the Gothic kingdom.

I am here anticipating the chronological order of events; but our knowledge of this chapter of Roman or Spanish history —for it has the two sides—is so small, and the events in this corner are so far removed from the general current of the history of the Empire, that I think it will be more convenient for

---

[1] Gregory of Tours, v. 38: "Herminigildis vero vocatis Grecis contra patrem egreditur, relicta in urbe conjuge sua. Cumque Leuvichildus ex adverso veniret, relictus a solatio, cum viderit nihil se praevalere posse, eclesiam qui erat propinquam [quae erat propinqua] expetiit," etc. The natural conclusion from the words *relictus a solatio* is that no battle was fought but that the "Greeks" did not venture to face the army of the king. An excellent account of the reign of Leovigild by Mrs. Humphry Ward will be found (*sub voce*) in the *Dict. of Christ. Biography*. The same writer has contributed to the same work a useful summary of the results of Dr. H. Hertzberg's important monograph on the writings and sources of Isidore of Seville. For the history of the Visigoths, the fifth volume of Dahn's *Kön. der Germ.* may be considered the standard work.

the reader to have this episode of Baetica presented to him in continuity than in disconnected parcels.

At the beginning of the seventh century King Witterich,[1] " a man strenuous in the art of arms, but nevertheless generally unsuccessful," renewed the policy of Leovigild and the war against the Romans, with whom his predecessor, Reccared, famous in ecclesiastical history, had for the most part preserved peace.[2] Witterich recovered Segontia, a town a little to the west of Gades; and Sisibut[3] fought successfully against the Patrician Caesarius. All the towns which the Romans held to the east of the straits were recovered by the Goths, and the fact was recognised by Heraclius (615). Svinthila completed the work of Leovigild, Witterich, and Sisibut; all the other cities which were still imperial were taken (623), and thus the whole peninsula for the first time became Visigothic, for before Baetica was lost the existence of the Suevian kingdom curtailed the dominion of the Goths in Spain.

[1] Isidore, *de regibus Gothorum*, 58. Gundemar was Witterich's immediate successor, 59.
[2] *Ib.* 52: *hic fide pius et pace praeclarus;* 54, *saepe etiam contra Romanorum insolentias et irruptiones Vascorum movit.*
[3] *Sisebut de Romanis bis feliciter triumphavit.*

CHAPTER VIII

SECOND PERSIAN WAR (540-545 A.D.)

WHEN Chosroes Nushirvan, after his accession to the Persian throne, contracted the "endless peace" with Justinian, he had little idea what manner of man the Emperor was soon to prove himself to be. Within seven years from that time (532-539) Justinian had overthrown the Vandal kingdom of Africa, he had reduced the Moors, the subjection of the Ostrogothic lords of Italy was in prospect, Bosporus and the Crimean Goths were included in the circle of Roman sway, while the Homerites of southern Arabia acknowledged the supremacy of New Rome. Both his friends and his enemies said, with hate or admiration, "The whole earth cannot contain him; he is already scrutinising the aether and the retreats beyond the ocean, if he may win some new world." The eastern potentate might well apprehend danger to his own kingdom in the expansion of the Roman Empire by the reconquest of its lost provinces; and the interests of the German kings in the west and the Persian king in the east coincided, in so far as the aggrandisement of the Empire was inexpedient for both. We can consider it only natural that Chosroes should have seized or invented a pretext to renew hostilities, when it seemed but too possible that if Justinian were allowed to continue his career of conquest undisturbed the Romans might come with larger armies and increased might to extend their dominions in the East at the expense of the Sassanid empire.

Hostilities between the Persian Saracens of Hirah and the Roman Saracens of Ghassan supplied the desired pretext; it may be that Chosroes himself instigated the hostilities. The cause of contention between the Saracen tribes was a tract of land called Strata, to the south of Palmyra, a region barren of trees and fruit, scorched dry by the sun, and used as a pasture for sheep. Arethas[1] the Ghassanide could appeal to the fact that the name *Strata* was Latin, and could adduce the testimony of the most venerable elders that the sheep-walk belonged to his tribe. Alamundar, the rival sheikh, contented himself with the more practical argument that for years back the shepherds had paid him tribute. Two arbitrators were sent by the Emperor, Strategius, minister of finances, and Summus, the duke of Palestine. This arbitration supplied Chosroes with a pretext, true or false, for breaking the peace. He alleged that Summus made treasonable offers to Alamundar, attempting to shake his allegiance to Persia; and he also professed to have in his possession a letter of Justinian to the Huns, urging them to invade his dominions.[2]

About the same time pressure from without confirmed the thoughts of Chosroes in the direction which they had already taken. An embassy arrived from Witigis, king of the Goths, now hard pressed by Belisarius, and pleaded with Chosroes to act against the common enemy. The embassy consisted not of Goths, but of two Ligurians, one of whom pretended to be a bishop; they obtained an interpreter in Thrace, and succeeded in eluding the vigilance of the Romans on the frontiers.[3] Another embassy arrived from Armenia making similar representations, deploring and execrating the Endless Peace, and denouncing the tyranny and exactions of Justinian, against whom they had revolted. The history of Armenia had been certainly unfortunate during the years that followed the peace. The first governor, Amazaspes, was accused by one Acacius of treachery, and, with the Emperor's consent, was slain by the accuser, who was himself appointed to succeed his victim.

---

[1] The proper form of the name is Harith. This king reigned from 530 to 572. Justinian conferred on him the title of Patrician, and the Arabs called him the "Magnificent."

[2] Procopius says that he does not know whether these allegations were true or false (*B. P.* ii. 1). The second Book of the *de Bello Persico* of Procopius is our main source for this Persian war until the end of 549 A.D.

[3] The reader may ask how the details of this embassy were known. Procopius tells us in another place (*B. P.* ii. 14) that the interpreter, returning from Persia, was captured near Constantina by John, duke of Mesopotamia, and gave an account of the embassy. The pseudo-bishop and his attendant remained in Persia.

Acacius was relentless in exacting a tribute of unprecedented magnitude (£18,000); and some Armenians, intolerant of his cruelty, slew him, and fled, when they had committed the deed, to a fortress called Pharangion. The Emperor immediately despatched Sittas, the master of soldiers *per Armeniam*, to recall the Armenians to a sense of obedience, and, when Sittas showed himself inclined to use the softer methods of persuasion, insisted that he should act with sterner vigour. A numerous tribe of the Armenians, called Apetiani, professed themselves ready to submit, if the safety of their property were guaranteed, and Sittas sent them a promise to that effect in writing. But unluckily the letter-carrier, not knowing the exact position of the territory of the Apetiani, lost his way in the intricate Armenian highlands; and while Sittas advanced with his troops to receive their submission, the Apetiani were ignorant that their proposal had been accepted, and looked with suspicion on the approaching army. Some of their number fell in by chance with Roman soldiers and were treated as enemies. Sittas, unaware that his communication had miscarried, was indignant that the promised submission was delayed; the Apetiani were put to the sword and their wives and children were slain in a cave. This severity, which might seem almost a breach of faith, exasperated the other tribes and confirmed them in their recalcitrant temper. But though Sittas was accidentally killed in an engagement soon afterwards, they found themselves unequal to cope with the Roman forces, which were then placed under the command of Buzes, and they decided to appeal to the Persian monarch. The servitude of their neighbours the Tzani and the imposition of a Roman duke over the Lazi of Colchis seemed to stamp the policy of Justinian as one of odious enormity.

Accordingly Chosroes, in the autumn of 539, decided to begin hostilities in the following spring, and did not deign to answer a pacific letter from the Roman Emperor, conveyed by the hand of a certain Anastasius, whom he retained an unwilling guest at the Persian court. The war which thus began lasted five years (540-545), and in each year the king himself took the field. He invaded Syria in 540, Colchis in 541, Commagene in 542; in 543 he began but did not carry out an expedition against the northern provinces; in

544 he invaded Mesopotamia; in 545 a peace for five years was concluded.

I. *Chosroes' Invasion of Syria*, 540 A.D.

Avoiding Mesopotamia, Chosroes advanced northwards with a large army along the left bank of the Euphrates. He passed the triangle-shaped city of Circesium, but did not care to assault it, because it was too strong; while he disdained to delay at the town of Zenobia, named after the queen of Palmyra, because it was too insignificant. But when he approached Sura or Suron, situated on the Euphrates in that part of its course which flows from west to east, his horse neighed and stamped the ground; and the magi, who attended the credulous king, seized the incident as an omen that the city would be taken. On the first day of the siege the governor was slain, and on the second the bishop of the place visited the Persian camp in the name of the dispirited inhabitants, and implored Chosroes with tears to spare the town. He tried to appease the implacable foe with an offering of birds, wine, and bread, and engaged that the men of Sura would pay a sufficient ransom. Chosroes dissimulated the wrath he felt against the Surenes because they had not submitted immediately; he received the gifts and said that he would consult with the Persian nobles regarding the ransom; and he dismissed the bishop, who was well pleased with the interview, under the honourable escort of Persian notables, to whom the monarch had given secret instructions.[1]

"Having given his directions to the escort, Chosroes ordered his army to stand in readiness, and to run at full speed to the city when he gave the signal. When they reached the walls the Persians saluted the bishop and stood outside; but the men of Sura, seeing him in high spirits and observing how he was escorted with great honour by the Persians, put aside all thoughts of suspicion, and, opening the gate wide, received their priest with clapping of hands and acclamation. And when all had passed within, the porters pushed the gate to shut it, but the Persians placed a stone, which they had provided, between the threshold and the gate. The porters pushed

---

[1] *See* Proc. *B. P.* ii. 5.

harder, but for all their violent exertions they could not succeed in forcing the gate into the threshold-groove. And they did not venture to throw it open again, as they apprehended that it was held by the enemy. Some say that it was a log of wood, not a stone, that was inserted by the Persians. The men of Sura had hardly discovered the guile, ere Chosroes had come with all his army and the Persians had forced open the gate. In a few moments the city was in the power of the enemy." The houses were plundered; many of the inhabitants were slain, the rest were carried into slavery, and the city was burnt down to the ground. Then the Persian king dismissed Anastasius, bidding him inform the Emperor in what place he had left Chosroes the son of Kobad.

Perhaps it was merely avarice, perhaps it was the prayers of a captive named Euphemia, whose beauty attracted the desires of the conqueror, that induced Chosroes to treat with unexpected leniency the prisoners of Sura. He sent a message to Candidus, the bishop of Sergiopolis, suggesting that he should ransom the 12,000 captives for 200 lbs. of gold (15s. a head). As Candidus had not, and could not immediately obtain, the sum, he was allowed to stipulate in writing that he would pay it within a year's time, under penalty of paying double and resigning his bishopric. Few of the redeemed prisoners survived long the agitations and tortures they had undergone.

Meanwhile the Roman general Buzes was at Hierapolis. Nominally the command in the East was divided between Buzes and Belisarius; the Roman provinces beyond the Euphrates being assigned to the former, Syria and Asia Minor to the latter. But as Belisarius had not yet returned from Italy, the entire army was at the disposal of Buzes, the *magister militum per Armeniam*.[1]

If we are to believe the account of a writer who was probably prejudiced,[2] this general behaved in the most extraordinary manner. He collected the chief citizens of Hierapolis and

---

[1] The fact that Theophanes calls Buzes "general of the East" (*ad* 6033 A.M.) does not count for much; he probably made a wrong inference from Procopius' language. We learn from Malalas and Theophanes that in 528 Justinian created a new office, that of a *magister militum in Armenia*, and conferred it upon Tzitas (Mal. Ztittas), presumably Sittas, who married Theodora's sister Komito. Buzes was the successor of Sittas.

[2] Procopius, *B. P.* ii. 6.

pointed out to them that in case of a siege, which seemed imminent, the city would be less efficiently protected if all the forces remained within the walls, than if a small garrison defended it, and the main body of the troops, posted on the neighbouring heights, harassed the besiegers. Following up this plausible counsel, Buzes took the larger part of the army with him and vanished; and neither the inhabitants of Hierapolis nor the enemy could divine where he had hidden himself.

Informed of the presence of Chosroes in the Roman provinces, Justinian despatched Germanus to Antioch, at the head of a small body of three hundred soldiers. The fortifications of the "Queen of the East" did not satisfy the careful inspection of Germanus, for although the lower parts of the city were adequately protected by the Orontes, which washed the bases of the houses, and the higher regions seemed secure on impregnable heights, there rose outside the walls adjacent to the citadel a broad rock, almost as lofty as the wall, which would inevitably present to the besiegers a fatal point of vantage. Competent engineers said that there would not be sufficient time before Chosroes' arrival to remedy this defect by removing the rock or enclosing it within the walls. Accordingly Germanus, despairing of resistance, sent Megas, the bishop of Beroea, to divert the advance of Chosroes from Antioch by the influence of money or entreaties. Megas reached the Persian army as it was approaching Hierapolis, the city abandoned by Buzes, and was informed by the great king that it was his unalterable intention to subdue Syria and Cilicia. The bishop was constrained or induced to accompany the army to Hierapolis, which was strong enough to defy a siege, and was content to purchase immunity from the attempt by a payment equivalent to £90,000. Chosroes then consented to retire without assaulting Antioch on the receipt of 1000 lbs. of gold (£45,000), and Megas returned speedily with the good news, while the enemy proceeded more leisurely to Beroea. From this city the avarice of the Sassanid demanded double the amount he had exacted at Hierapolis; the Beroeans gave him half the sum, affirming that it was all they had; but the extortioner refused to be satisfied, and proceeded to demolish the city.

From Beroea he advanced to Antioch, and demanded the

1000 lbs. with which Megas had undertaken to redeem that city; and it is said that he would have been contented to receive a smaller sum. All the Antiochenes would probably have followed the example of a few prudent or timid persons, who left the city in good time, taking their belongings with them, had not the arrival of six thousand soldiers from Lebanon, led by Theoctistus and Molatzes, infused into their hearts a rash and unfortunate confidence. Julian, the private secretary of the Emperor, who had arrived at Antioch, bade the inhabitants resist the extortion; and Paul, the interpreter of Chosroes, who with friendly intentions counselled them to pay the money, was almost slain. Not content with defying the enemy by a refusal, the men of Antioch stood on their walls and loaded Chosroes with torrents of scurrilous abuse, which would have inflamed less intolerant monarchs than he.

The siege which ensued was short, but the defence at first was brave. Between the towers, which crowned the walls at intervals, platforms of wooden beams were suspended by ropes attached to the towers, that a greater number of defenders might man the walls at once. But during the fighting the ropes gave way and the suspended soldiers were precipitated, some without, some within the walls; the men in the towers were seized with panic and left their posts; and the defence of the city was abandoned except by a few young men, whom an honourable rivalry in the hippodrome had trained in vigour and bravery. The confusion was increased by a rush made to the gates, occasioned by a false report that Buzes was coming to the rescue; and a multitude of women and children were crushed or trampled to death. But the gate leading to the remote suburb of Daphne was purposely left unblocked by the Persians; it was Chosroes' prudent desire that the Roman soldiers and their officers should be allowed to leave the city unmolested; and some of the inhabitants escaped with the departing army. But the young men of the Circus factions made a valiant and hopeless stand against superior numbers; and the city was not entered without a considerable loss of life, which Chosroes pretended to deplore. It is said that two illustrious ladies cast themselves into the Orontes, to escape the cruelties of oriental licentiousness.

It was nearly three hundred years since Antioch had experienced the presence of a human foe, though it suffered frequently and grievously from the malignity of nature. The Sassanid Sapor had taken the city in the ill-starred reign of Valerian, but it was kindly dealt with then in comparison with its treatment by Chosroes. The cathedral was stripped of its wealth in gold and silver and its splendid marbles; all the other churches, many richly endowed, met the same fate, except that of St. Julian, which was exempted owing to the accident that it was honoured by the proximity of the ambassadors' residences. Orders were given that the whole town should be burnt, and the sentence of the relentless conqueror was executed as far as was practicable.

While the work of demolition was being carried out, Chosroes was treating with the ambassadors of Justinian, and expressed himself ready to make peace, on condition that he received 5000 lbs. of gold, paid immediately, and an annual sum of 500 lbs. for the defence of the Caspian gates. While the ambassadors returned with this answer to Byzantium, Chosroes advanced to Seleucia, the port of Antioch, and looked upon the waters of the Mediterranean; it is related that he took a solitary bath in the sea and sacrificed to the sun. In returning he visited Daphne, which was not included in the fate of Antioch, and thence proceeded to Apamea, whose gates he was invited to enter with a guard of 200 soldiers. All the gold and silver in the town was collected to satisfy his greed, even to the jewelled case in which a piece of the true cross was reverently preserved. He was clement enough to spare the precious relic itself, which for him was devoid of value. The city of Chalcis purchased its safety by a sum of 200 lbs. of gold; and having exhausted the provinces to the west of the Euphrates, Chosroes decided to continue his campaign of extortion in Mesopotamia, and crossed the river at Obbane by a bridge of boats. Edessa, the great stronghold of western Mesopotamia, was too secure itself to fear a siege, but paid 200 lbs. of gold for the immunity of the surrounding territory from devastation.[1] At Edessa, ambassadors arrived from Justinian, bearing his con-

---

[1] The people of Edessa were generous enough to subscribe to ransom the Antiochene captives; farmers who had no money gave a sheep or an ass, prostitutes stripped off their ornaments. But, according to Procopius, Buzes, who happened to be there, seized the money that was collected and allowed the captives to be carried off to Persia.

sent to the terms proposed by Chosroes; but, in spite of this, according to the Roman historian, the unscrupulous Persian did not shrink from making an attempt to take Daras on his homeward march.

The fortress of Daras, which Anastasius had erected to replace the long-lost Nisibis as an outpost in eastern Mesopotamia, was girt with two walls, between which stretched a space of fifty feet, devoted by the inhabitants to the pasture of domestic animals. The inner wall reached the marvellous [1] elevation of sixty feet, while the towers superimposed at intervals were forty feet higher. A river, descending in a winding and rocky bed, and exempted by nature from all danger of diversion, flowed into the city; and not long before the arrival of Chosroes some physical disturbance of the ground had concealed its point of egress in a newly-formed whirlpool and buried its waters in the mazes of a subterranean passage. Thus, in case of a siege, while the beleaguered were well supplied, the beleaguerers stood in sore need of water.

Chosroes attacked the city on the western side, and burned the gates of the outer wall, but no Persian was bold enough to enter the interspace. He then began operations on the eastern side, the only side of the rock-bound city where digging was possible, and ran a mine under the outer wall. The vigilance of the besiegers was baffled until the subterranean passage had reached the foundations of the outer wall; but then, according to the story—which we must relegate to that region of history to which the visions of Alaric at Athens belong—a human or superhuman form in the guise of a Persian soldier advanced near the wall under the pretext of collecting discharged missiles, and while to the besiegers he seemed to be mocking the men on the battlements, he was really informing the besieged of the danger that was creeping upon them unawares. The Romans then, by the counsel of Theodorus, a clever engineer,[2] dug a deep transverse trench between the two walls so as to intersect the line of the enemy's excavation; the Persian burrowers suddenly ran or fell into the Roman pit; those in front were slain, and the rest fled back unpur-

---

[1] Procopius calls it ἀξιοθέατον.

[2] ἐπὶ σοφίᾳ τῇ καλουμένῃ μηχανικῇ λογίου ἀνδρός. The mode of expression suggests that the word μηχανική was popularly (though not in very strict prose) used in the modern sense.

sued through the dark passage. Disgusted at this failure, Chosroes raised the siege on receiving from the men of Daras 1000 lbs. of silver.

When he returned to Ctesiphon the victorious monarch erected a new city near his capital, on the model of Antioch, with whose spoils it was beautified, and settled therein the captive inhabitants of the original city, the remainder of whose days was perhaps more happily spent than if the generosity of the Edessenes had achieved its intention. The name of the new town, according to Persian authorities,[1] was Rumia (Rome); according to Procopius it was called by the joint names of Chosroes and Antioch (Chosro-Antiocheia).

II. *Chosroes' invasion of Colchis, and Belisarius' campaign in Mesopotamia*, 541 A.D.

From this time forth the kingdom of Lazica or Colchis was destined to play an important and tedious part in the wars between the Romans and Persians. This country seems to have been in those days far poorer than it is at present; the Lazi depended for corn, salt, and other necessary articles of consumption on Roman merchants, and gave in exchange skins and slaves; while "at present Mingrelia, though wretchedly cultivated, produces maize, millet, and barley in abundance; the trees are everywhere festooned with vines, which grow naturally, and yield a very tolerable wine; while salt is one of the main products of the neighbouring Georgia."[2] The Lazi were dependent on the Roman Empire, but the dependence consisted not in paying tribute but in committing the choice of their kings to the wisdom of the Roman Emperor. The nobles were in the habit of choosing wives among the Romans; Gobazes, the sovereign who invited Chosroes to enter his country, was the son of a Roman lady, and had served as a

---

[1] Mirkhond and Tabari; see Rawlinson, *Seventh Oriental Monarchy*, p. 395. The new Antioch had one remarkable privilege; slaves who fled thither, if acknowledged by its citizens as kinsmen, were exempted from the pursuit of their masters.

[2] Rawlinson, *op. cit.* p. 406, where the facts are quoted from Haxthausen's *Transcaucasia*. Procopius himself mentions (*B. G.* iv. 14) that the district of Muchiresis in Colchis was very fertile, producing wine and various kinds of corn. For the languages spoken by the various Caucasian peoples, see an article by Mr. R. N. Cust, in the *Journal of the Royal Asiat. Soc.* vol. xvii. p. 154 *sqq.* (1885).

silentiary in the Byzantine palace. The Lazic kingdom was a useful barrier against the trans-Caucasian Scythian races, and the inhabitants defended the mountain passes without causing any outlay of men or money to the Empire.

But when the Persians seized Iberia it was considered necessary to secure the country which barred them from the sea by the protection of Roman soldiers, and the unpopular general Peter, originally a Persian slave, was not one to make the natives rejoice at the presence of their defenders. Peter's successor was Johannes Tzibos, a man of obscure station, whose unprincipled skill in raising money made him a useful tool to the Emperor. He was certainly an able man, for it was by his advice that Justinian built the maritime town of Petra, at a point of the Colchian coast considerably to the south of the mouth of the Phasis. Here he established a monopoly and oppressed the natives. It was no longer possible for the Lazi to deal directly with the traders and buy their corn and salt at a reasonable price; John Tzibos, perched in the fortress of Petra, acted as a sort of retail dealer, to whom both buyers and sellers were obliged to resort, and pay the highest or receive the lowest prices. In justification of this monopoly it may be remarked that it was the only practicable way of imposing a tax on the Lazi; and the imposition of a tax might have been deemed a necessary and just compensation for the defence of the country, notwithstanding the facts that it was garrisoned solely in Roman interests, and that the garrison itself was unwelcome to the natives.

Exasperated by these grievances, Gobazes, the king of Lazica, sent an embassy to Chosroes, inviting him to recover a venerable kingdom, and pointing out that if he expelled the Romans from Lazica he would have access to the Euxine, whose waters could convey his forces against the palace at Byzantium, while he would have an opportunity of establishing a connection with those other enemies of Rome, the Huns of Europe.[1] Chosroes consented to the proposals of the ambassadors; and keeping his real intention secret, pretended that pressing affairs required his presence in Iberia.

---

[1] Another element in Chosroes' Colchian policy was the circumstance that the Iberians did not obey the Persians with a good will. If Lazica were Persian, they would have no power in the rear to support them if they revolted. Compare Procopius, *B. P.* ii. 28.

Under the guidance of the envoys, Chosroes and his army passed into the devious woods and difficult hill-passes of Colchis, cutting down as they went lofty and leafy trees, which hung in dense array on the steep acclivities, and using the trunks to smooth or render passable rugged or dangerous places. When they had penetrated to the middle of the country, they were met by Gobazes, who paid oriental homage to the great king. The chief object was to capture Petra, the stronghold of Roman power, and dislodge the retail dealer, as Chosroes contemptuously termed the monopolist, Johannes Tzibos. A detachment of the army under Aniabedes was sent on in advance to attack the fortress; and when this officer arrived before the walls he found indeed the gates shut, but the place seemed totally deserted, and not a trace of an inhabitant was visible. A messenger was sent to inform Chosroes of this surprise; the rest of the army hastened to the spot; a battering-ram was applied to the gate, while the monarch watched the proceedings from the top of an adjacent hill. Suddenly the gate flew open, and a multitude of Roman soldiers rushing forth overwhelmed those Persians who were applying the engine, and, having killed many others who were drawn up hard by, speedily retreated and closed the gate. The unfortunate Aniabedes (according to others, the officer who was charged with the operation of the battering-ram) was crucified for the crime of being vanquished by a retail dealer.

A regular siege now began. It was inevitable that Petra should be captured, says our historian Procopius, displaying a curious idea of causes and effects,[1] and therefore Johannes, the governor, was slain by an accidental missile, and the garrison, deprived of their commander, became careless and lax. On one side Petra is protected by the sea, landwards inaccessible cliffs defy the skill or bravery of an assailant, save only where one narrow entrance divides the line of steep cliffs and admits of access from the plain. This gap between the rocks was filled by a long wall, the ends of which were dominated by towers constructed in an unusual manner, for instead of being hollow all the way up, they were made of solid stone to a considerable height, so that they could not be shaken by the most

[1] καὶ γὰρ ἔδει Πέτραν Χόσρωι ἁλῶναι.

powerful engine. But oriental inventiveness undermined these wonders of solidity. A mine was bored under the base of one of the towers, the lower stones were removed and replaced by wood, the demolishing force of fire loosened the upper layers of stones, and the tower fell, the Romans stationed in it escaping just in time. This success was decisive, as the besieged recognised; they readily capitulated, and the victors did not lay hands on any property in the fortress save the possessions of the defunct governor. Having placed a Persian garrison in Petra, Chosroes remained no longer in Lazica, for the news had reached him that Belisarius was about to invade Assyria, and he hurried back to defend his dominions.

Belisarius, accompanied by all the Goths whom he had led in triumph from Italy, except the Gothic king himself, had proceeded in the spring to take command of the eastern army in Mesopotamia.[1] Having found out by spies that no invasion was meditated by Chosroes, whose presence was demanded in Iberia—the design on Lazica was kept effectually concealed—the Roman general determined to lead the whole army, along with the auxiliary Saracens of Arethas, into the confines of Persian territory. What strikes us about the campaign is that although Belisarius was chief in command he never seems to have ventured or cared to execute his strategic plans without consulting the advice of the other officers. It is difficult to say whether this was due to distrust of his own judgment and the reflection that many of the subordinate generals were more experienced in Mesopotamian geography and Persian warfare than himself,[2] or to a fear that some of the leaders in an army composed of soldiers of many races might prove refractory and impatient of too peremptory orders. At Daras a council of war was held; all the officers declared for an immediate invasion except Theoctistus and Rhecithancus, the captains of contingents from Lebanon, who apprehended that the Saracen Alamundar might take advantage of their absence to invade Syria and Phoenicia; but when Belisarius reminded them that it was now the summer solstice, and that it was the

---

[1] The Italian generals accompanied Belisarius. One of them, Valerian, succeeded Martin as general in Armenia; Martin had been transferred to Mesopotamia.

[2] This is dwelt on in one of the speeches which Procopius places in Belisarius' mouth.

Saracen custom to spend sixty days from that date in religious devotion, they withdrew their objection on condition that they were to return to Syria two months thence.

The army marched towards Nisibis, and some murmurs arose when Belisarius, instead of advancing to the walls, halted at a distance of about five miles away. Having justified his action in a speech, he sent forward Peter, and John the duke of Mesopotamia, ordering them to approach within about a mile of the city. He reminded them that the Persian garrison, commanded by the able general Nabedes, would be more likely to attack them at noonday than at any other hour, as the Romans were wont to dine then, and the Persians in the evening. But under the heat of the meridian sun, the soldiers of Peter, yielding to a natural lassitude, laid aside their arms and carelessly employed themselves in eating the cucumbers which grew around. The watchful garrison sallied forth from the city, but as there was more than a mile's distance to traverse, the Romans had time to assume their arms, though not to form in an orderly array. The Persian onslaught was successful, the standard of John was taken, and fifty Romans were slain. But all was not yet lost. Belisarius was hastening to the scene before Peter's messenger had time to reach him; the long lances of the Goths retrieved the slender loss, and 150 Persians strewed the ground. But Nisibis was too strong to be attacked, and the army moved forward to the fortress of Sisaurani, where its assault was at first repulsed with loss. Belisarius decided to invest the place, but as the Saracens were useless for siege warfare, he sent Arethas and his troops, accompanied by 1200 guardsmen, to invade and harry Assyria, intending to cross the Tigris himself when he had taken the fort. The siege was of short duration, for the garrison was not supplied with provisions, and soon consented to surrender; all the Christians were dismissed free, the fire-worshippers were sent to Byzantium [1] to await the Emperor's pleasure, and the fort was levelled to the ground.

Meanwhile the plundering expedition of Arethas was successful, but he played his allies false. Desiring to retain

---

[1] These Persians, with their leader Bleschanes, were afterwards sent to Italy against the Goths. It was Roman policy to employ Persian captives against the Goths, Gothic captives against the Persians.

all the spoils for himself, he invented a story to rid himself of the Roman guardsmen who accompanied him,[1] and he sent no information to Belisarius. This was not the only cause of anxiety that vexed that general's mind. The Roman, especially the Thracian, soldiers were not inured to and could not endure the intense heat of the dry Mesopotamian climate in midsummer, and disease broke out in the army, demoralised by physical exhaustion. All the soldiers were anxious to return to more clement districts, and as it was already August, the captains of the troops of Lebanon were uneasy, fancying that Alamundar might be advancing to plunder their homes. There was nothing to be done but yield to the prevailing wish, which was shared by all the generals. It cannot be said that the campaign of Belisarius accomplished much to set off against the acquisition of Petra by the Persians.

III. *Chosroes' Invasion of Commagene*, 542 A.D.

The first act of Chosroes when he crossed the Euphrates in spring was to send 6000 soldiers to besiege the town of Sergiopolis because the bishop Candidus, who had undertaken to pay the ransom of the Surene captives two years before, was unable to collect the amount, and found Justinian deaf to his appeals for aid. But the town lay in a desert, and the besiegers were soon obliged to abandon the attempt in consequence of the drought. It was not the Persian's intention to waste his time in despoiling the province Euphratensis or Commagene; he purposed to invade Palestine, and plunder the treasures of Jerusalem. But this exploit was reserved for his grandson of the same name, and the invader returned to his kingdom having accomplished almost nothing. This speedy retreat was probably due to the outbreak of the plague in Persia, though the Roman historian attributes it to the address of Belisarius.[2]

Belisarius travelled by post-horses (*veredi*) from Constantinople to the Euphratesian province, and taking up his quarters at Europus on the Euphrates, close to Carchemish, the ancient

---

[1] Trajan and John the Glutton were in command of these 1200 ὑπασπισταί. When they separated from Arethas they proceeded to Theodosiopolis, in order to avoid a hostile army which did not exist. [2] *See* above, p. 401.

capital of the Hittites, he collected there the bulk of the troops who were dispersed throughout the province in its various cities. Chosroes was curious about the personality of Belisarius, of whom he had heard so much,—the conqueror of the Vandals, the conqueror of the Goths, who had led two fallen monarchs in triumph to the feet of Justinian. Accordingly he sent Abandanes[1] as an envoy to the Roman general, on the pretext of learning why Justinian had not sent ambassadors to negotiate a peace.

Belisarius did not mistake the true nature of Abandanes' mission, and determined to make an impression. Having sent a body of one thousand cavalry to the left bank of the river, to harass the enemy if they attempted to cross, he selected six thousand tall and comely men from his army and proceeded with them to a place at some distance from his camp, as if on a hunting expedition. He had constructed for himself a pavilion[2] of thick canvas, which he set up, as in a desert spot, and when he knew that the ambassador was approaching, he arranged his soldiers with careful negligence. On either side of him stood Thracians and Illyrians, a little farther off the Goths, then Heruls, Vandals, and Moors; all were arrayed in close-fitting linen tunics and drawers, without a cloak or ἐπωμίς to disguise the symmetry of their forms, and, like hunters, each carried a whip as well as some weapon, a sword, an axe, or a bow. They did not stand still, as men on duty, but moved carelessly about, glancing idly and indifferently at the Persian envoy, who soon arrived and marvelled.

To Abandanes' complaint that "the Caesar" had not sent an embassy to his master, Belisarius answered, as one amused, "It is not the habit of men to transact their affairs as Chosroes has transacted his. Others, when aggrieved, send an embassy first, and if they fail in obtaining satisfaction, resort to war; but he attacks and then talks of peace." The presence and bearing of the Roman general, and the appearance of his followers, hunting indifferently at a short distance from the Persian camp without any precautions, made a profound impression on Abandanes, and he persuaded his master to abandon

[1] Theophanes calls him Abandazes, but his account tallies so closely (even in expression) with that of Procopius that he does not seem to have had a second authority before him.

[2] παπυλεών, which Procopius introduces with his usual apologetic formula. See below, Bk. iv. pt. ii. cap. viii.

the proposed expedition. Chosroes may have reflected that the triumph of a king over a general would be no humiliation for the general, while the triumph of a mere general over a king would be very humiliating for the king; such at least is the colouring that the general's historian put on the king's retreat. According to the same authority, Chosroes hesitated to risk the passage of the Euphrates while the enemy were so near, but Belisarius, with his smaller numbers, did not entertain the intention of obstructing him, and a truce was made, Johannes, son of Basil, being delivered, an unwilling hostage, to Chosroes. Having reached the other bank, the Persians turned aside to take and demolish Callinicum, the Coblenz of the Euphrates, which fell an easy prey to their assault, as the walls were in process of renovation at the time. This retreat of Chosroes, according to Procopius, procured for Belisarius greater glory than he had won by his victories in Africa and Italy.

But the account of Procopius, which coming from a less illustrious historian would be rejected on account of internal improbability, cannot be accepted with confidence. It displays such a marked tendency to glorify his favourite and friend Belisarius, that it can hardly be received as a candid unvarnished account of the actual transactions. Besides, there is a certain inconsistency. If Chosroes retired *for fear of* Belisarius, as Procopius would have us believe, why was it he who received the hostage, and how did he venture to take Callinicum ? It might be said that these were devices, connived at by Belisarius, to keep up the dignity of a king; but as there actually existed a potent cause, unconnected with the Romans, to induce his return to Persia, namely the outbreak of the plague, we can hardly hesitate to assume that this was its true motive.[1]

IV. *The Roman Invasion of Persarmenia*, 543 A.D.

In spite of the plague Chosroes set forth in the following spring to invade Roman Armenia. He advanced into the district of Azerbiyan (Atropatene), and halted at the great shrine of Persian fire-worship, where the *magi* kept alive an eternal

---

[1] So Rawlinson (*op. cit.* p. 401), who perhaps is more generous to Procopius than he deserves. The plague broke out in Persia in the summer of 542.

flame, which Procopius wishes to identify with the fire of Roman Vesta. Here the Persian monarch waited for some time, having received a message that two ambassadors[1] were on their way to him, with instructions from "the Caesar." But the ambassadors did not arrive, because one of them fell ill by the road; and Chosroes did not pursue his northward journey, because a plague broke out in his army. The Persian general Nabedes sent a christian bishop named Eudubius to Valerian, the Roman general in Armenia, with complaints that the expected embassy had not appeared. Eudubius was accompanied by his brother, who secretly communicated to Valerian the valuable information that Chosroes was just then encompassed by perplexities, the spread of the plague, and the revolt of one of his sons. It was a favourable opportunity for the Romans, and Justinian gave command that all the generals stationed in the East should combine to invade Persarmenia.

Martin was the master of soldiers in the East; he does not appear, however, to have possessed much actual authority over the other commanders. They at first encamped in the same district, but did not unite their forces, which in all amounted to about thirty thousand men. Martin himself, with Ildiger and Theoctistus, encamped at Kitharizon, about four days' march from Theodosiopolis; the troops of Peter and Adolios took up their quarters in the vicinity; while Valerian, the general of Armenia, stationed himself close to Theodosiopolis and was joined there by Narses and a regiment of Heruls and Armenians. The Emperor's nephew Justus and some other commanders remained during the campaign far to the south in the neighbourhood of Martyropolis, where they made incursions of no great importance.

At first the various generals made separate inroads, but they ultimately united their regiments in the spacious plain of Dubis, eight days from Theodosiopolis. This plain, well suited for equestrian exercise, and richly populated, was a famous rendezvous for traders of all nations, Indian, Iberian, Persian, and Roman.[2] About fifteen miles from Dubis there was a

---

[1] Constantianus, an Illyrian, and Sergius of Edessa, both rhetors and men of intellect.

[2] The Christians of these parts were subject to the spiritual government of a bishop called the *Catholicus*, a term which has survived to the present day.

steep mountain, on whose side was perched a village called Anglon, protected by a strong fortress. Here the Persian general Nabedes, with four thousand soldiers, had taken up an almost impregnable position, blocking the precipitous streets of the village with stones and waggons. The ranks of the Roman army, as it marched to Anglon, fell into disorder; the want of union among the generals, who acknowledged no supreme leader, led to confusion in the line of march; mixed bodies of soldiers and sutlers turned aside to plunder; and the security which they displayed might have warranted a spectator in prophesying a speedy reverse. As they drew near to the fortress, an attempt was made to marshal the somewhat demoralised troops in the form of two wings and a centre. The centre was commanded by the Master of Soldiers, the right wing by Peter, the left by Valerian; and all advanced in irregular and wavering line, on account of the roughness of the ground.[1] The best course for the Persians was obviously to act on the defensive. Narses and his Heruls, who were probably on the left wing with Valerian, were the first to attack the foes and to press them back into the fort. Drawn on by the retreating enemy through the narrow village streets, they were suddenly attacked on the flank and in the rear by an ambush of Persians who had concealed themselves in the houses. The valiant Narses was wounded in the temple; his brother succeeded in carrying him from the fray, but the wound proved mortal. This repulse of the foremost spread the alarm to the regiments that were coming up behind; Nabedes comprehended that the moment had arrived to take the offensive and let loose his soldiers on the panic-stricken ranks of the assailants; and all the Heruls, who fought according to their wont without helmets or breastplates,[2] fell before the charge of the Persians. The Romans did not tarry; they cast their arms away and fled in wild confusion, and the mounted soldiers galloped so fast that few horses survived the flight; but the Persians, apprehensive of an ambush, did not pursue.

Never, says Procopius, did the Romans experience such a great disaster. This exaggeration makes us seriously inclined

[1] Procopius assigns as an additional cause the want of discipline or previous marshalling of the troops; but I feel some suspicions of the whole account of this campaign.

[2] The Herul's only armour was a shield and a cloak of thick stuff.

to suspect the accuracy of Procopius' account of this campaign. We can hardly avoid detecting in his narrative a desire to place the generals in as bad a light as possible, just as in his description of the hostilities of the preceding year he manifested a marked tendency to place the behaviour of his hero Belisarius in as fair a light as possible. In fact he seems to wish to draw a strong and striking contrast between a brilliant campaign in 542 and a miserable failure in 543. We have seen reason to doubt the exceptional brilliancy of Belisarius' achievement; and we may be disposed to question the statement that the defeat at Anglon was overwhelming, and the insinuation that the generals were incompetent.

V. *Chosroes' Invasion of Mesopotamia ; Siege of Edessa—544 A.D.*

His failure at Edessa in 540 rankled in the mind of the Sassanid monarch; he determined to retrieve it in 544. The siege of this important fortress, the key to Roman Mesopotamia, is one of the most interesting in the siege warfare of the sixth century. The place was so strong that Chosroes would have been glad to avoid the risk of a second failure, and he proposed to the inhabitants that they should pay him an immense sum or allow him to take all the riches in the city. His proposal was refused, though if he had made a reasonable demand it would have been agreed to; and the Persian army encamped at somewhat less than a mile from the walls. Three experienced generals, Peter, Martin, and Peranius, were stationed in Edessa at this time.

On the eighth day from the beginning of the siege, Chosroes caused a large number of hewn trees to be strewn on the ground in the shape of an immense square, at about a stone's throw from the city; earth was heaped over the trees, so as to form a flat mound, and stones, not cut smooth and regular as for building, but rough hewn, were piled on the top, additional strength being secured by a layer of wooden beams placed between the stones and the earth. It required many days to raise this mound to a height sufficient to overtop the walls. At first the workmen were harassed by a sally of Huns, one of whom, named Argek, slew twenty-seven with his own hand. This could not be repeated, as henceforward a guard of Persians stood by to protect the builders. As the work went on, the mound seems to have been extended in breadth as well as in height, and to have approached closer to the walls, so that the workmen came within range of the archers who manned the battlements, but they protected themselves by thick and long strips of canvas, woven of goat hair, which were hung on poles, and proved an adequate shield. Foiled in their attempts to obstruct the progress of the threatening pile, which they saw rising daily higher and higher, the besieged sent an embassy to Chosroes. The spokesman of the ambassadors was the physician Stephen, a native of Edessa, who had enjoyed the friendship and favour of Kobad, whom he had healed of a disease, and had superintended the education of Chosroes himself. But even he, influential though he was, could not obtain more than the choice of three alternatives—the surrender of Peter and Peranius, who, originally Persian subjects, had presumed to make war against their master's son; the payment of 50,000 lbs. of gold (two million and a quarter pounds sterling); or the reception of Persian deputies, who should ransack the city for treasures and bring all to the Persian camp. All these proposals were too extravagant to be entertained for an instant; the ambassadors returned in dejection, and the erection of the mound advanced. A new embassy was sent, but was not even admitted to an audience; and when the plan of raising the city wall was tried, the besiegers found no difficulty in elevating their construction also.

At length the Romans resorted to the plan of undermining the mound, but when their excavation had reached the middle of the pile the noise of the subterranean digging was heard by the Persian builders, who immediately dug or hewed a hole in their own structure in order to discover the miners. These, knowing that they were detected, filled up the remotest part of the excavated passage and adopted a new device. Beneath the end of the mound nearest to the city they formed a small subterranean chamber with stones, boards, and earth. Into this room they threw piles of wood of the most inflammable kind, which had been smeared over with sulphur, bitumen, and oil of cedar. As soon as the mound was completed, they kindled the logs, and kept the fire replenished with fresh fuel. A considerable time was required for the fire to penetrate the entire extent of the mound, and smoke began to issue prematurely from that part where the foundations were first inflamed. The besieged adopted a cunning device to mislead the besiegers. They cast burning arrows and hurled vessels filled with burning embers on various parts of the mound; the Persian soldiers ran to and fro to extinguish them, believing that the smoke, which really came from beneath, was caused by the flaming missiles; and some thus employed were pierced by arrows from the walls. Next morning Chosroes himself visited the mound and was the first to discover the true cause of the smoke, which now issued in denser volume. The whole army was summoned to the scene amid the jeers of the Romans, who surveyed from the walls the consternation of their foe. The torrents of water with which the stones were flooded increased the vapour instead of quenching it and caused the sulphurous flames to operate more violently. In the evening the volume of smoke was so immense that it could be seen as far away to the south as at the city of Carrhae [1]; and the fire, which had been gradually working upwards as well as spreading beneath, at length gained the air and overtopped the surface. Then the Persians desisted from their futile endeavours.

Six days later an attack was made on the walls at early dawn, and but for a farmer who chanced to be awake and gave the alarm, the garrison might have been surprised. The assailants were repulsed; and another assault on the great gate at mid-day was likewise unsuccessful. One final effort was made by the baffled beleaguerers. The ruins of the half-demolished mound were covered with a floor of bricks, and from this elevation a grand attack was made. At first the Persians seemed to be superior, but the enthusiasm which prevailed in the city was ultimately crowned with victory. The peasants, even the women and the children, ascended the walls and took a part in the combat; cauldrons of oil were kept continually boiling, that the burning liquid might be poured on the heads of the assailants; and the Persians, unable to endure the fury of their enemies, fell back and confessed to Chosroes that they

---

[1] The distance of Carrhae from Edessa was about thirty miles.

were vanquished. The enraged despot drove them back to the encounter; they made yet one supreme effort, and were yet once more discomfited. Edessa was saved, and the siege unwillingly abandoned by the disappointed king, who, however, had the satisfaction of receiving 5000 lbs. of gold from the weary though victorious Edessenes.

In the following year, 545 A.D., a peace or truce[1] was concluded for five years, Justinian consenting to pay 2000 lbs. of gold and to permit a certain Greek physician, named Tribunus, to remain at the Persian court for a year. Tribunus of Palestine, the best medical doctor of the age, was, we are told, a man of distinguished virtue and piety, and highly valued by Chosroes, whose constitution was delicate and constantly required the services of a physician. At the end of the year the king permitted him to ask a boon, and instead of proposing remuneration for himself he begged for the freedom of some Roman prisoners. Chosroes not only liberated those whom he named, but others also to the number of three thousand, and Tribunus won the blessings of those whom his word had ransomed and great glory among men.

[1] No distinct mention of this truce is made by Gibbon, who passes over these campaigns with a vague sentence.

CHAPTER IX

THE LAZIC WAR (549-556 A.D.)

THE Lazi soon found that the despotism of the Persian fire-worshipper was less tolerable than the oppression of the christian monopolists, and repented that they had taught the armies of the great king to penetrate the defiles of Colchis. It was not long before the magi attempted to convert the new province to a faith which was odious to the christianised natives, and it became known that Chosroes entertained the intention of removing the inhabitants and colonising the land with Persians. Gobazes, who learned that Chosroes was plotting against his life, hastened to ask for the pardon and seek for the protection of Justinian, whose name seemed appropriate to his character when compared with a tyrant whose title, "the Just" (like that of Haroun *Al Raschid*), seemed the expression of a prudent irony. In 549 A.D. 7000 Romans were sent to Lazica, under the command of Dagisthaeus, to recover the fortress of Petra, which was the most important position in that country. Their forces were strengthened by the addition of a thousand Tzanic auxiliaries. Procopius has warned us against identifying the Tzani with the Colchians, apparently a common mistake in his time. The Tzani were an inland people living on the borders of Pontus and Armenia, and separated from the sea by precipitous mountains and vast solitudes, impassable torrent-beds and yawning chasms.[1]

---

[1] Proc. *B. G.* iv. 1. At the beginning of 558 A.D. we find the Tzani plundering Armenia and Pontus. Theodorus subdued and rendered them tributary—a success of which Justinian did not disdain to boast in one of his Novels (Agathias, v. 2). A good map of Colchis is much wanted. I have not found that in Spruner's *Historischer Atlas* satisfactory.

The acquisition of Colchis pleased Chosroes so highly, and the province appeared to him of such eminent importance, that he took every precaution to secure its retention.[1] A highway was constructed from the Iberian confines through the country's hilly and woody passes, so that not only cavalry but elephants could traverse it. The fortress of Petra was supplied with sufficient stores of provisions, consisting of salted meat and corn, to last for five years; no wine was provided, but vinegar and a sort of grain from which a spirituous liquor could be distilled. The armour and weapons which were stored in the magazines would, as was afterwards found, have accoutred five times the number of the besiegers; and a cunning device was adopted to supply the city with water, while the enemy should delude themselves with the idea that they had cut off the supply.[2]

When Dagisthaeus laid siege to the town the garrison consisted of 1500 Persians. The besieging party numbered 7000 Roman soldiers and 1000 Tzani, who were assisted by the Colchians under Gobazes. Dagisthaeus committed the mistake of not occupying the clisurae or passes from Iberia into Colchis, and thereby preventing the arrival of Persian reinforcements. The siege was protracted for a long time, and the small garrison was ultimately reduced to 150 men capable of fighting and 350 wounded or disabled. The Romans had dug a mine under the wall and loosened the foundations; a part of the wall actually collapsed, and John the Armenian with fifty men rushed through the breach, but when their leader received a wound they retired. It appears that nothing would have been easier than to enter the city and overpower the miserably small number of defenders, but Dagisthaeus purposely delayed, waiting for letters from Justinian. The commander of the garrison protracted the delay by promising to surrender in a few days, for he knew that Mermeroes was approaching to relieve him. Mermeroes, allowed to enter Colchis unopposed with large forces of cavalry and infantry, soon arrived at the pass which commands the plain of Petra. Here his progress was withstood by a hundred

---

[1] He tried to build a fleet in the Euxine, but the material was destroyed by lightning.

[2] The way in which this was effected will be described below, p. 449.

Romans, but after a long and bloody battle the weary guards gave way, and the Persians reached the summit. When Dagisthaeus learned this he raised the siege, and marched northwards to the Phasis.

Mermeroes left 3000 men in Petra and provisioned it for a short time. Directing the garrison to repair the walls, he departed himself with the rest of the army on a plundering expedition in order to obtain more supplies. He finally left 5000 men under Phabrigus in Colchis, instructing them to keep Petra supplied with food, and withdrew to Persarmenia. Disaster soon befell these 5000; they were surprised in their camp by Dagisthaeus and Gobazes in the early morning, and but few escaped. All the provisions brought from Iberia for the use of Petra were destroyed, and the passes which admitted the stranger to Colchis were garrisoned.[1]

In the spring of 550 Chorianes entered Colchis with a Persian army, and encamped by the river Hippis, where a battle was fought in which the Romans, under Dagisthaeus, were triumphantly victorious, and Chorianes lost his life. The engagement was notable for the curious behaviour of the Lazi and the bravery of a Persarmenian who fought under the Roman standard. The Lazi protested against associating themselves with their allies in the battle, and insisted on facing the foe foremost and alone, on the ground that they had a greater stake in the event than their protectors, and perhaps thinking that the stress of a graver danger would increase their defective courage. They were allowed to have their way in so far that the Lazic cavalry led the van, but at the very sight of the enemy they turned and fled for refuge to those with whom they had disdained to march in company. The Persarmenian Artabanes, a deserter who had proved his fidelity to the Romans by slaying twenty Persians, exhibited his courage in a conspicuous place between the adverse armies by dismounting and despatching a mighty Persian. These single combats were perhaps a feature in many of the battles of the sixth century; they are certainly a feature in the pages of the historians.

---

[1] At this point the two books of Procopius known as *de Bello Persico* come to an end, but the thread of the narrative is resumed in the *de Bello Gothico*, Bk. iv., which was written after the other books had been given to the world. Procopius apologises for the necessity which compels him to abandon his method of *geographical* divisions (*B. G.* iv. 1).

Meanwhile Dagisthaeus was accused of misconducting the siege of Petra, through disloyalty or culpable negligence. Justinian ordered that he should be arrested, and appointed Bessas, who had recently returned from Italy, in his stead. Men wondered at this appointment, and thought that the Emperor was foolish to entrust the command to a general who was far advanced in years, and whose career in the West had been inglorious; but the choice, as we shall see, was justified by the result. The subordinate commanders were Wilgang[1] a Herul, Benilus the brother of Buzes, Babas a Thracian, and Odonachus (all of whom preceded Bessas to Lazica); and John the Armenian, who had shown his valour at the battle of the Hippis.

The first labour that devolved on Bessas was to suppress the revolt of the Abasgi. The territory of this nation extended along the lunated eastern coast of the Euxine, and was separated from Colchis by the country of the Apsilians, who inhabited that ambiguous district between the western spurs of Caucasus and the sea, a district which belongs to Asia, and might be claimed by Europe. The Apsilians had long been Christians, and submitted to the lordship of their Lazic neighbours, who had at one time also held sway over the Abasgi. Like the Roman Empire in the fourth and fifth centuries, Abasgia was governed by two princes, of whom one ruled in the west and the other in the east. These potentates increased their revenue by the sale of beautiful boys, whom they tore in early childhood from the arms of their reluctant parents and made eunuchs; for in the Roman Empire these comely and useful slaves were in constant demand, and secured a high price from the opulent and luxurious nobles. It was the glory of Justinian to compass the abolition of this unnatural practice; the subjects supported the remonstrances which the Emperor's envoy, himself an Abasgian eunuch, made to their kings; the monarchy, or tyranny, was abolished, and a people which had worshipped trees embraced Christianity, to enjoy, as they thought, a long period of freedom under the protection of the Roman Augustus. But the mildest pro-

---

[1] Uligagus (Procopius), but Agathias calls the same man Οὐλίγαγγος. The name is evidently Wilgang: for the first part compare *Wil*-helm, for the second Wolf-*gang*.

tectorate tends insensibly to become domination. Roman soldiers entered the country, and taxes were imposed on the new friends of the Emperor. The Abasgi preferred being tyrannised over by men of their own blood to being the slaves of a foreign master, and accordingly they elected two new kings, Opsites in the east and Sceparnas in the west. But it would have been rash to brave the jealous anger of Justinian without the support of some stronger power, and when Nabedes, after the great defeat of the Persians at Hippis, visited Lazica, he received sixty noble hostages from the Abasgi, who craved the protection of Chosroes. They had not taken warning from the repentance of the Lazi, that it was a hazardous measure to invoke the Persian. The king, Sceparnas, was soon afterwards summoned to the Sassanid court, and his colleague Opsites prepared to resist the Roman forces which Bessas despatched against him under the command of Wilgang and John the Armenian.

In the southern borders of Abasgia, close to the Apsilian frontier, an extreme mountain of the Caucasian chain descends in the form of a staircase to the waters of the Euxine. Here, on one of the lower spurs, the Abasgi had built a strong and roomy fastness in which they hoped to defy the pursuit of an invader. A rough and difficult glen separated it from the sea, while the ingress was so narrow that two persons could not enter abreast, and so low that it was necessary to crawl. The Romans, who had sailed from the Phasis, or perhaps from Trapezus, landed on the Apsilian borders, and proceeded by land to Trachea, as the glen was appropriately called, where they found the whole Abasgic nation arrayed to defend a pass which it would have been easy to hold against far larger numbers. Wilgang remained with half the army at the foot of the glen, while John and the other half embarked in the boats which had accompanied the coast march of the soldiers. They landed at no great distance, and by a circuitous route were able to approach the unsuspecting foe in the rear. The Abasgi fled in consternation towards their fortress; fugitives and pursuers, mingled together, strove to penetrate the narrow aperture, and those inside could not prevent enemies from entering with friends. But the Romans when they were within the walls found a new labour awaiting them. The Abasgi fortified themselves in their houses, and vexed their adversaries by showering missiles from above. At length the Romans conceived the idea of employing the aid of fire, and the dwellings were soon reduced to ashes. Some of the people were burnt, others, including the wives of the kings, were taken alive, while Opsites escaped to the Huns. But it must not be thought that the nation was exterminated, as the words of Procopius might lead us to infer. We shall meet the Abasgi again, one hundred and fifty years later, in the days of another Justinian.

Shortly before or shortly after this episode in Abasgia, another episode was enacted in the neighbouring country of Apsilia. Terdetes, a Lazic noble, quarrelled with King Gobazes, and entered into correspondence with the Persians to betray a strong fort called Tzibilon, in Apsilia. When the garrison saw foreign troops approaching under a Lazic convoy they admitted them unhesitatingly, and for a moment it seemed that Apsilia was a Persian dependency. But the Persian leader, seized with a passion for the beautiful wife of the governor, compelled her by force to his embraces. The enraged husband slew the violator and all his soldiers; the Apsilians were fain to reject the supremacy of the Colchians, who had not protected them against the risk of slavery; but the bland words of John the Armenian restored them to their old allegiance.

The truce of five years had now elapsed (April 550), and while new negotiations began between the courts of Byzantium and Ctesiphon, the Romans in Lazica, under the command of Bessas, made another attempt to recover Petra.[1] A new garrison, three thousand strong, had been placed in the fort; the breaches which had been made by Dagisthaeus in the foundations of the wall were filled up with bags of sand, over which thick planed beams were placed to form the basis of a new wall. Bessas bored a mine, as Dagisthaeus had done, under the wall, which was shaken by the removal of the earth beneath; but the layers of the stones were not disarranged, the

---

[1] While Bessas was at Petra, Odenachus and Babas held Archaeopolis (on the right bank of the Phasis) with 3000 men, and Benilus and Wilgang were encamped at the mouth of the Phasis.

whole mass supported by the smooth beams sank regularly as if it were purposely lowered by a machine, and the only effect was that the height was reduced. The sinking of the wall overwhelmed the mine; and as the approach to this, the only expugnable, part of the city was an inclined plane, it was impossible to apply the battering-rams, whose heavy frames could only be impelled along a horizontal surface.

It happened that at this time three nobles of the Sabiric Huns [1] visited the Roman camp, in order to receive a sum of money from an envoy of Justinian, who feared to continue his journey to their homes in the Caucasus through a country beset with foes. The cunning of the barbarians profited the Romans in their perplexity and surpassed the skill of civilised engineers. " They constructed such a machine," says the marvelling Procopius, " as within the memory of man never entered into the mind of a Roman or Persian, though in both realms there has never been, nor is now, lacking a plentiful number of engineers, and though in all ages a machine of the kind has been wanted by both peoples for battering fortifications in steep places." The simplicity of the Hunnic invention might have put the engineers to shame. Instead of the perpendicular and transverse beams, which made the regular machine so heavy, a light frame was constructed of woven osier twigs, and covered with skins, so that in appearance it did not differ from the ordinary ram, while its lightness was such that forty men, placed inside, could advance supporting it on their shoulders without inconvenience. The battering beam itself, hung in loose chains and pointed with iron, was of normal construction; in fact the old machines supplied the new frames with their beams.

At each side of these engines, when they were applied to the walls, stood men protected with helmets and cuirasses, and provided with long poles, whose iron hooks removed the stones which the rams had loosened. The besieged hurled from a wooden tower, which they placed on the wall, vessels of sulphur, pitch, and naphtha (" oil of Medea ") upon the roofs of the machines, and it required all the agility of the men with

---

[1] These Huns did not form a united nation. Some of their princes Medised, others Romanised; and those of both classes received from their respective patrons occasional grants of money. (Proc. *B. G.* iv. 11.)

the poles to remove the flaming missiles before the frames caught fire.

When an appreciable breach had been made in the wall, Bessas, with all his forces, advanced to scale it. The general himself, in spite of his seventy years, was the first to place his foot on the ladder, and in the combat that ensued, of the 2300 Persians who resisted and the 6000 Romans who attacked, there were many slain and very few unwounded. Suddenly a shout was raised, and both sides rushed to the spot, where Bessas lay prostrate on the ground. The Persians attempted to pierce him with their darts, but the guardsmen formed a dense array around their general in the form of a testudo, and protected him from hurt. The Romans had paused for a moment and held their breath when they witnessed the fall of Bessas, but soon comprehending that he was not injured they renewed the fray and redoubled their efforts. The master of soldiers, who found himself unable to raise his obese and aged body, weighed down by armour, was dragged slowly to a safe place, and the incident so little affected him that, once more erect, he again essayed to scale the wall. At length the Persians declared themselves ready to surrender, and begged for a short space of time to pack up their belongings; but Bessas, suspecting their intentions, refused to check the assault, and indicated another place under the walls where he would entertain the proposals of those who desired to capitulate. His caution was justified by the fact that the Persians continued to fight.

The situation was changed when another portion of the wall, which had been previously undermined by the besiegers, collapsed. Both the Persians and Romans were obliged to divide their forces, and the superiority of the latter in point of numbers began to tell. At this point John the Armenian, with a few of his countrymen, succeeded in climbing up a precipitous ascent of rock, where the beleaguerers could not have hoped and the beleaguered could not have feared that it would prove possible to gain the battlements. The Persian guards were killed, and the venturous Armenians entered the fort. Meanwhile the battering-rams had continued to play on the walls, and the defenders in their wooden tower had continued to shower inflammable substances from above; but a violent south wind suddenly began to blow, and the tower caught fire from the dangerous materials which were handled by its inmates. These, along with the structure, were consumed in the flames, and their burning corpses fell among their comrades or their adversaries. The Persians were fast giving way; at length the Romans penetrated the breaches, and Petra was taken. Five hundred of the garrison fled to the citadel, seven hundred and thirty were captured alive. Among the Romans who fell in the final assault was John the Armenian, who, as it seems, when he had scaled the wall, attacked the enemy in the rear.

Attempts were made to induce the soldiers who had shut themselves up in the citadel to surrender, but they proved deaf to arguments and menaces. In the pages of Procopius a military orator persuades the reader that it was foolish and culpable in these inflexible men to court an unnecessary death; but the 500 fire-worshippers, if they heard these christian remonstrances, were not convinced of their cogency. The citadel was fired by the order of Bessas, who expected that at the eleventh hour, with a painful death imminent, the headstrong Persians would yield. He was disappointed; they did not hesitate, before the wondering gaze of the Roman victors, to perish in the flames. "Then," says the historian, "it appeared how dear Lazica was to Chosroes, in that he had sent the most excellent of all his soldiers to garrison Petra."

One of the first acts of the Romans had been to destroy the aqueduct, but in the course of the siege a Persian prisoner informed them that there was a second pipe invisible to the eye, because it was concealed by stones and earth. This duct was also destroyed, and yet to their astonishment the Romans found when they entered the fortress that it was supplied with water. Chosroes had dug a deep ditch, in which he placed two pipes, one above the other, separated by a layer of clay and stones, and above them a third pipe, which he made no attempt to conceal. The two superior ducts were cut off by the besiegers, to whom the thought never occurred that there might be yet a third channel.

The news of the capture of Petra, which took place in the early spring of 551 A.D., reached Mermeroes as he was approaching with a Persian army to relieve it. As there was no other important place south of the Phasis, he retraced his steps in order to cross the river by a ford, and attack Archaeopolis and other fortresses on the right bank, which were occupied by the Romans or the Lazi. The total number of Roman soldiers in Lazica amounted to 12,000. Of these, 3000 were stationed at Archaeopolis, under the command of Babas and Odonachus; the remaining 9000 were entrenched in a camp at the mouth of the Phasis, with the generals Benilus and Wilgang, and an auxiliary corps of 800 Tzani. The commander-in-chief, Bessas, thinking that he had done enough by capturing Petra, occupied himself in Armenia and Pontus with collecting tribute, instead of following up his success and securing the Iberian frontier.

Of Mermeroes' troops the greater part were cavalry. Eight elephants accompanied the march, and of 12,000 Caucasian Huns who proffered their services, the general, fearing that such a large number might prove unmanageable, accepted the aid of 4000. Having halted on the borders of Iberia to re-erect the fort of Scanda, which the Lazi had demolished, Mermeroes marched towards Archaeopolis; but when he learned that a large division of the enemy was encamped at the mouth of the Phasis, he decided to attack it first, and afterwards storm the city. His way led him past the city walls, and he jeeringly informed the inhabitants that when he had paid a visit to their friends in the camp he would return to them. "If you meet those Romans," they replied, "you will never return to us." But those Romans did not await his approach. Having packed up all the provisions they could take with them, and destroyed the rest, they rowed across to the left bank of the river; the Persians, unable to follow, destroyed their camp, and returned to besiege Archaeopolis.

The chief city of Lazica is situated on a steep hill; mountains impend above it, and the river that descends from their heights flows near its gates. Protected by a wall on either side of a narrow path which runs down to the river-bank, the inhabitants could draw water securely in time of siege. The approaches to the gates in the higher parts of the town were precipitous and obstructed with wood and bramble; but the wall at the base of the hill was easily accessible, though the ground sloped. Mermeroes' plan of action was to attack both the higher and lower places at the same time, and divide the attention of the defenders. There was a corps of auxiliary soldiers in his army called Dilimnites,[1] men who dwelt in the interior parts of Persia, but had never been forced to be the thralls of a Persian monarch. The steep and pathless mountains, which were their homes since remote antiquity, secured them their liberty, but they deigned to serve for pay in the army of the great king. They fought on foot, armed each with a sword, a shield, and three javelins; and they could run as nimbly on the rugged acclivities of a mountain as on a level plain. These mercenaries were told off to harass the besieged on the steep sides of the hill; while the Sabiric Huns were employed to construct light battering-rams, such as their tribesmen had provided for the Romans at Petra. With these engines and the eight elephants, the Persians and Huns exerted all their strength to make an impression on the lower gate, and a thick cloud of arrows almost expelled the Roman defenders from the battlements; while in another place the javelins of the Dilimnites, who fought from behind the bushes, increased the discomfiture of the garrison.

But by a happy inspiration the commanders apprehended in what their sole chance of safety lay, and decided to make a sudden sally on the enemy with all their forces. Just as they were on the point of executing this design, to which they had stimulated the soldiers by an oration, the cry was raised that the corn magazine was on fire. Some of the garrison hastened to the spot and succeeded with difficulty in extinguishing the flames, while the rest, undisturbed by the alarm, poured forth through the opened gate upon their unprepared and astonished antagonists. The Persians had been building on the hope that when a Lazic traitor, who had communicated with Mermeroes, should have set fire to the stores, the Romans would either desert the defence in order to save their corn or submit to the loss of their corn in order to continue the defence. Never imagining that such a small number would have the heart to leave the protection of their walls in the face of an army so superior, the besiegers were scattered in small groups here and there in front of the city; some had only

[1] So called by Agathias. Procopius calls them Dolomites.

bows, which were useless in hand-to-hand fight, others totally unarmed were carrying battering engines; so that the sudden onslaught of the Romans met with almost no resistance. The confusion was increased when one of the elephants, perhaps wounded, broke into the Persian ranks. The front rows retreated, and the soldiers in the rear, ignorant of the cause, caught the alarm; while the Dilimnites, beholding from above the consternation that prevailed below, fled in panic. In all, four thousand of the enemy fell, including three captains, and four Persian standards were sent to the Emperor. It was said that not less than twenty thousand horses perished in the flight, not from wounds, but from the effects of mere fatigue and want of adequate food.

Having thus failed at Archaeopolis, Mermeroes and his army proceeded to Muchiresis, the most fertile district of Colchis, watered by the river Rheon. Winter was now approaching, and the Persians took up their quarters in the ruins of an old fort called Cutatisium (originally Cotiaeum), which they roughly restored; here they commanded the roads to Suania and Scymnia, and could prevent the Lazi from supplying with provisions the neighbouring fort of Uchimerium. But this stronghold was soon delivered into the hands of Mermeroes by the treachery and guile of a Colchian named Theophobius, and having left both in this place and in Cutatisium sufficient garrisons, the general of Chosroes established himself in another fort on the Lazic frontier called Serapanin. During the winter the Persians dominated the land; the Romans skulked in Archaeopolis and near the mouths of the Phasis, while Gobazes and many of the Lazi endured the untold hardships of a Colchian winter's severity in the recesses of inaccessible mountains, where they were scantily supplied with food. Mermeroes tried to seduce the Lazic king to desert the Romans, but Gobazes had not forgotten that Chosroes had plotted against his life.

Meanwhile, ambassadors had gone to and fro between the Roman and Persian courts; the negotiations had been protracted for eighteen months, and Chosroes' delegate, the arrogant Isdigunas,[1] had enjoyed the generosity of Justinian's court

---

[1] Menander gives the name as Jesdegusnaf (fr. 11). He was accompanied by his wife and two daughters.

and excited the disgust of his courtiers. At length a new truce of five years was concluded, the terms being that the Romans were to pay two thousand six hundred pounds of gold[1]; but this peace was not to necessitate the cessation of hostilities in Colchis. A contemporary states that there was considerable popular indignation that Chosroes should have exacted from the Empire no less than four thousand six hundred pounds of gold in the space of eleven years; and the Byzantines murmured at the unprecedented respect shown to Isdigunas and his retinue, who were permitted to move about in the city, without a Roman escort, as if it belonged to them.

Nothing of striking importance took place in the campaign of 552. The Persians were successful. Mermeroes expelled Martin and his troops from the strong fort of Telephis[2] by a ruse; the dissemination of a false rumour of his own death, which even the Persian army believed, caused the Romans to relax their vigilance. Both Martin, and Justin (the son of Germanus) who was encamped at Ollaria, about a mile from Telephis, were forced to flee in the confusion of a nocturnal surprise and take up their quarters in the "Island," where the prudence of Mermeroes permitted them to remain in peace. The Island was a tract of ground formed by two rivers and an artificial canal. The Phasis and the less famous Doconus, flowing from widely different quarters of the mountains, gradually approximate their courses, and at length unite their waters about twenty miles from the Euxine. At some distance to the east of their point of union, the Romans had dug a channel connecting them, and thus formed an island, which would have been a triangle but for the irregular curves and twists of the streams.

Mermeroes retired to Iberia to winter, but died in the autumn

---

[1] 2000 lbs. for the five years' truce, and 600 lbs. (at the same rate) for the negotiation of a year and a half. The *Emperor* wished to pay the 2000 lbs. in annual portions; but Isdigunas pressed for the lump sum. At length the *Romans* decided to pay it all at once, so that it should not seem a tribute, "according to the habit men have of blushing at names, and not at the things themselves" (Procop. *B. G.* iv. 15). Procopius' wary mode of expression here is noteworthy; he changes from the *Emperor* to the *Romans*, because he wishes to introduce an unfavourable reflection.

[2] Telephis seems to have been about forty miles inland from the sea; it was five parasangs (150 stadia) from the "Island," which was six parasangs from the mouth of the Phasis.

of disease.[1] His death was a serious loss to Chosroes, for though old and lame, and unable even to ride, he was not only a prudent and brave general, but as unwearying in activity as a youth. Nachoragan was sent to succeed him.

Meanwhile Gobazes, the Lazic king, who had been involved in constant quarrels and recriminations with the Roman commanders, sent a complaint of their conduct to Justinian, giving an account of their recent defeat, and attributing it to their negligence; Bessas, Martin, and Rusticus were specially named. The Emperor deposed Bessas from his command, and banished him temporarily to Abasgia, but he consigned the chief command to Martin, and did not recall Rusticus. This Rusticus was not a general, but an imperial finance official, who had been sent to bestow rewards on soldiers who distinguished themselves in battle. The complaints which the Lazic king had lodged made him more obnoxious to the persons whom he had ventured to accuse; and Martin and Rusticus resolved to remove an inconvenient and jealous critic. To secure themselves from blame, they despatched John, Rusticus' brother, to Byzantium, with the false message that Gobazes was "Medising,"—was this ancient term really used in the sixth century outside the pages of the historians? Justinian was surprised and alarmed, but reserved his judgment, and commanded that Gobazes should come to Constantinople. "What," asked John, "is to be done if he refuses?" "Compel him to come," replied the Emperor; "he is our subject." "But if he resist our compulsion," urged the conspirator. "Then treat him as a *tyrant*." "And will he who slays him have nought to fear?" "Nought, if he act disobediently and be slain as an enemy." Justinian signed a letter to the same effect, armed with which John returned to Lazica, and the conspirators carried out their

---

[1] I have departed from the usually received chronology for the Lazic campaign recorded by Agathias (see Clinton, *F. R.*) Agathias begins in Bk. ii. cap. 19, at the point where Procopius leaves off in Bk. iv. cap. 17 of the *Gothic War*. The last events related by Procopius fall in the year 552, and as Agathias continues his narrative, without mentioning an intervening winter, we must conclude that the events which he describes up to the end of the 4th chapter of Bk. iii. also fall in 552, and that the first words of the 15th chapter, ἅμα γὰρ τῷ ἦρι ἀρξαμένῳ, mean the spring of 553. Thus the last Lazic events described by Agathias belong, not to 557, but to 555. The chronology of Bk. v. cannot be determined with certainty, as it is connected with preceding events by nothing more precise than ἐν τούτῳ. If this means in 555, the invasion of the Huns of Zabergan took place in 556-7, not in 558-9.

intention. Gobazes was invited to assist in an attack on the Persian fortress of Onoguris; and with a few attendants he met the Roman army at the river Chobus. An altercation arose between the king and Rusticus, and on the pretext that the gainsayer of a Roman general must necessarily be a friend of the Persians, John drew his dagger and stabbed Gobazes in the breast. The wound was not mortal, but it was dealt so unexpectedly that it unhorsed the king, who was sitting with his legs round the neck of his steed, and when he attempted to rise from the ground, a blow from the squire of Rusticus killed him outright.

The unfortunate Lazi, not strong enough to revenge the death of their monarch, silently buried him according to their customs, and turned away in mute reproach from their Roman protectors. They no longer took part in the military operations, but hid themselves away as men who had lost their hereditary glory. The indignation which Justin and Buzes felt at the outrage was prudently concealed, as they thought it had been commanded by the Emperor's wisdom. Some months later, when winter had commenced, the Lazi assembled a secret council in some remote and wild Caucasian ravine, and considered the question whether they should abandon their Roman allies and seek once more the protection and oppression of Chosroes.[1] They fortunately decided not to take the fatal step, and it is worthy of note that the chief motive which induced them to adhere to the Romans was their attachment to the christian religion. They determined to appeal for justice and satisfaction to the fountain of justice in the Roman Empire, the Emperor himself; and at the same time supplicate him to nominate Tzathes, the younger brother of Gobazes, as the new king of the Lazi. Justinian promptly complied with their demands. Athanasius, one of the most illustrious senators, was immediately sent to Lazica to investigate the circumstances of Gobazes' assassination; and when he arrived he incarcerated both Rusticus and John in the city of Apsarus,

---

[1] Agathias pleases himself and wearies the reader by making two Colchians, Aietes and Phartazes, deliver harangues, respectively for and against Medism. The name Aietes is probably fictitious (as the index of Niebuhr asserts), the name of the opponent of the Romaioi being borrowed from that of the mythical enemy of the Argonauts. Hereby a suspicion is also thrown on the identity of Phartazes.

pending a trial. In the beginning of spring (553) Tzathes arrived with all the state of a Lazic monarch; and when the Colchians saw the Roman army saluting him as he rode in the splendour of his royal apparel, a tunic embroidered with gold reaching to the feet, a plain white mantle with a gold stripe, purple shoes, a turban adorned with gold and gems, and a golden crown set with precious stones, they forgot their sorrow and escorted him in a gay and brilliant procession. It was not till the ensuing winter that the authors of the death of the late king were brought to justice and the natives witnessed the solemn procedure of a Roman trial. John and Rusticus were executed, but the implication of Martin in the affair was not quite so clear, and his case was referred to the Emperor, who in 555 deposed him from the command in favour of his own nephew Justin. The secret of Martin's acquittal probably was that he was highly popular with the army and a very skilful general.

Meanwhile the hostilities between the Romans and Persians had continued without a pause. The few months that intervened between the death of Gobazes and the inactivity of winter (552 A.D.) were occupied with the siege of Onoguris, or Stephanopolis[1]—apparently its new name, from a church erected there in honour of the first martyr—which had been fortified by Mermeroes about the time of his unsuccessful siege of the neighbouring Archaeopolis. The Romans were preparing their *spalions*[2] to shake the foundations of the towers, when a Persian was captured, who disclosed, under the compulsion of the lash, the design of his compatriots. Nachoragan, he said, had already arrived in Iberia, and the troops stationed in Muchiresis and Cotaisis were on their way to relieve Onoguris. Buzes and Wilgang the Herul were in favour of proceeding with all the forces (about 50,000) against the advancing Persians before they attempted to besiege the fort: "First frighten away the bees," said Wilgang, "and then

---

[1] τῷ ἐκείνου ὀνόματι (Στεφάνου τοῦ θεσπεσίου) καλεῖσθαι τὸν τόπον νενόμισται (Agathias, iii. 5).

[2] These machines were in construction very like the machines constructed by the Sabiric Huns at the siege of Petra; but they were not batteringrams. The men inside were provided with implements to lay bare the foundations of towers, and hammers to loosen the stones.

gather the honey." But the opposite opinion of Rusticus carried the day; the siege operations began, and a small body of six hundred horse was sent to obstruct the march of the party of relief.

The commanders of the corps of cavalry were Dabragezas, a Wend, and Wiscard or Wisgard, whose name[1] shows that he was a Teuton. It is one of the curious things of history to meet in the sixth century by the banks of the Phasis a general bearing the celebrated name which was borne in the eleventh century by the great Norman, Robert of Apulia; and we are reminded that the mission of the great duke and the task of the obscure captain were essentially of the same kind, to repel the enemies of Christianity and of occidental development from the limits of European Christendom. Robert's chief work was to organise a power, which waged war against the Mohammedan in the Mediterranean; Wisgard helped in his degree to beat back the Fire-worshipper from the coasts of the Euxine.

The horsemen with Wisgard and Dabragezas fell suddenly on the three thousand Persians who had ridden to relieve the fortress and were already near at hand. At first the larger number were confused by the surprise and fled; the announcement of their flight reached the besiegers, who were encouraged to assail the walls with greater boldness and less order; but when the Persians comprehended that a very small division of the whole army of their opponents had advanced against them, they turned suddenly and reversed the position. The Romans fled and the Persians pursued; pursuers and fugitives rushed together into the Roman entrenchments; the besiegers, overwhelmed with astonishment and terror, thought no more of the fortress, and, hardly waiting to discover what had happened, abandoned their camp in haste and disorder. Thus fifty thousand were routed by three thousand.

In the following spring Nachoragan (553) advanced with sixty thousand men to the Island, where Martin and Justin

---

[1] Οὐσίγαρδος. For the meaning of the name, compare the lines of William the Apulian about Count Robert—

cognomen Guiscardus erat, quia calliditatis,
non Cicero tantae fuit aut versutus Ulysses.

As to the Slavonic name Dabragezas, Dabra means "good" (Russian *dobry*). With -gezas compare *Belegezitae*, the name of a Slavonic tribe near Salonica in the seventh century.

were stationed with their forces. The Romans had placed two thousand federate Sabiric Huns in the neighbourhood of Archaeopolis to harass the enemy; and by a fortunate stratagem they succeeded in slaughtering an immense number of Dilimnites who were sent to surprise them. When he arrived at the Island, the Persian commander, after a short and futile conference with Martin, determined not to remain there, but to march westward and besiege the city of Phasis, the great seaport of Colchis, situated at the mouth of the like-named river. Before the Romans were aware, he had crossed the stream by a bridge of boats, for he purposed to march along the left bank and attack Phasis on the southern side. The Romans, having been thwarted in an attempt to send some vessels down the river to the city, left in the Island a small garrison under the charge of Buzes and marched to the defence of Phasis by a different route from that which the enemy had taken.

The walls of Phasis, which were wooden and in some places dilapidated through age, were protected by a palisade and a foss, which was filled with water to the brim. The garrison was thus arranged: at the extreme west, close to the river, Justin, the son of Germanus, was in command; the battlements at the south-western point were occupied by the regiments of Martin; Angilas with Moorish peltasts and lancers, Theodore with his Tzanic infantry, Philomathius with his Isaurian slingers and javelin-men were placed due south; Lombard and Herul troops under Gibros were posted south-east; and in the extreme east, where the river washes the walls, were stationed the forces of the oriental prefecture under Valerian. At both extremities, in close proximity to the stations of Justin and Valerian, were moored large ships, from whose masts huge boats were securely swung; these boats supported large towers manned with soldiers and some bold sailors, who were equipped with bows, with divers sorts of missiles and engines to hurl them. Dabragezas the Wend, and Elmingir, a Hun, sailed to and fro in small double-sterned boats to prevent the ships from receiving any hurt.

The operations began with volleys of arrows, discharged by the Persian archers. Martin had given strict orders that the defenders should not leave their posts; but Angilas and Philomathius, in spite of the protests of Theodore, were provoked into making a sally on the enemy. The Dilimnites, who happened to be posted opposite to the southern point of the wall, quietly awaited the approach of the Isaurians and Moors, whom Theodore with his Tzani reluctantly accompanied; the small number of the rash defenders was easily surrounded; and it only remained for them to retrieve their temerity and win an ambiguous glory by cutting their way, valiantly and hardly, back to the gates.

Meanwhile men had been busily engaged in filling up the foss, so that the battering-ram and the assailants might advance against the walls over level ground. The process was a slow one, although numberless hands were busy, for they had not sufficient earth and stones to fill the ditch completely, and the Romans had previously destroyed all the wood for miles around, so that they could only obtain that material by cutting it in a distant glen. It was not till the fall of evening that the foss had disappeared.

On the ensuing day Martin adopted a felicitous stratagem, by which he succeeded both in confirming the spirits of his soldiers and in spreading apprehensions among the enemy. He convoked the army for the purpose of consulting on measures for the defence of the city. When all were assembled, an unknown person, covered with dust and having the marks of travel about him, burst into the midst, and stating that he had come from Constantinople with an imperial message presented a letter to the general. Martin received it eagerly, but instead of reserving it for private perusal, and without even glancing over it, he read aloud so that all could hear. Perhaps, says the historian, the contents of the document were really different, but at all events the words recited were as follows:—

"We send you yet another army, not smaller than that which you have. It is true that if the enemy are more numerous, they do not surpass you in numbers so much as you surpass them in valour; so that the disproportion does not render you unequal. Nevertheless, that they may not be able to boast of superiority even in this one respect, we send you another army, for the sake of honour and display, not because it is necessary. Be of good courage and continue in your work with zeal; for we will not neglect any requisite measures."

Being asked where the army was, the messenger said that

he had left it at the river Neocnus, about ten miles away. Martin feigned indignation, and said that he would never receive the new forces, nor permit that soldiers who had come at the last moment should share the glory and spoil with those who had borne the burden and heat. These sentiments were received with acclamation, and the garrison was animated to exertions more strenuous than ever. The report of the presence of Roman troops at the Neocnus reached the Persian camp, and the besiegers trembled at the thought of facing a fresh and unwearied army. A large reconnoitring detachment was sent in that direction on the futile errand of watching for hostile forces that were never destined to come, because they did not exist.

Meanwhile Nachoragan, desiring to anticipate the arrival of the fictitious reinforcements, organised without delay a general attack on the walls, boasting that he would burn the city with all its inmates. The servants and workmen who attended the camp were despatched to the wood to cut timber, and were ordered, when they saw a smoke ascending to heaven in the distance, to learn that Phasis was in flames, and to return without delay that they might assist in hastening the progress of the conflagration. While the Persians were making these preparations, Justin, ignorant of the intended attack, was prompted by a pious inspiration—which, as it happened, proved fortunate in the event—to visit a holy church in the neighbourhood. Thither he rode to worship with 5000 soldiers, and his departure was unperceived by the besiegers, even as their operations were unperceived by him.

The attack began, and the air was soon obscured with arrows and darts, that rained like hail or snow. The wooden walls were hewn with axes wielded by the men in the *spalions* ; but the defenders cast from the battlements huge blocks of stone, which broke the sutures of those slender engines, while stones, less immense, hurled from slings, shattered the helmets of the soldiers; and the missiles discharged by the men, who were suspended aloft in the towers attached to the ship-masts, descended with tremendous effect. When the excitement of battle had reached its intensest point, the troops of Justin returned from their pious errand. Perceiving the situation, and convinced that his excursion to the church had been the direct inspiration of God, the general formed his cavalry in order, and raised aloft the standards. The Persians were absorbed in fighting in close proximity to the wall, and Justin's forces, attacking them on the west side, close to the sea, broke their line, and wrought great havoc among them. Filled with alarm, and supposing that their new assailants were the expected army from Neocnus, the enemy began to fall back from their position, and the Dilimnites, who were attacking (as on the previous day) the southern portion of the wall, seeing the confusion from afar off, rushed to the spot, leaving a few of their number behind. Angilas and Theodorus, who on the preceding day had made the unsuccessful excursion, seized the occasion to rush out and put to flight the small remnant of the Dilimnites; but on observing this their companions, who had run westward to assist the hard-pressed Persians, returned to support their fugitive countrymen. The spectacle of the Dilimnites rushing to and fro in this uncertain and disorderly manner communicated alarm to the Persians who were stationed near (in the south-west). Deeming that the behaviour of the bellicose Dilimnites presupposed a real and present danger, they bethought themselves of flight, and their panic reacted on the Dilimnites, unaware that their own conduct was its cause. When all these troops were seen fleeing over the plain, the Romans opened the gates, rushed in pursuit, and harassed the rear of the fugitives. Some of the enemy turned and formed a line, and an irregular battle was fought, in which the left wing of the Persians was completely routed, while the right wing forced the Romans at first to retreat; but the accident of an infuriated elephant turning against the ranks of its masters and maddening their horses, secured for the defenders of Phasis a full victory, and the Persian army was scattered. Nachoragan, stupefied by the unexpected course of events, gave the unnecessary command that all should flee. The loss incurred by his army was estimated at 10,000 men.

Returning from the pursuit, the victors burned the engines of the Persians and all the relics of their leaguer. The unfortunate woodcutters (about two thousand in number), ignorant of all that had passed, when they saw the smoke of the conflagration, returned in haste, as they thought, to share the triumph, and, as they found, to be butchered by the Romans. The corpses of the fallen soldiers yielded a considerable spoil, not only of arms, but of golden necklets and earrings.

The discomfited Nachoragan retreated to Muchiresis, where he left the greater part of his army, and wintered himself in Iberia. All the western districts of Colchis now remained, undisputed, in the hands of the Romans.

The chief event of the following year (554 A.D.) was the expedition against the Misimiani, a people who lived to the north-east of the Apsilians. They had committed an outrage, which had excited the indignation of the Romans, in the previous spring, but the advance of Nachoragan had necessitated the postponement of revenge. Soterichus, accompanied by his two sons, had travelled from Byzantium with the new Lazic king, Tzathes, in order to distribute sums of money to allied tribes in the vicinity of Mount Caucasus. The Misimiani conceived the idea that the envoy intended to "betray to the Alans" one of their forts, and make it a centre for receiving the ambassadors of the more distant nations, so that he might not have to undergo the trouble and risk of traversing the Caucasian passes himself. They consequently sent two delegates to complain of the intention which they imputed to him, as he was bivouacking near the fort in question. Soterichus, who looked upon the barbarians with all the disdain of a ruling race, would not tolerate their impertinent remonstrances, and ordered his attendants to chastise them. Beaten with staves, they returned in a half-dead condition to their countrymen, while the Roman lord, thinking no more of the matter, composed himself carelessly to rest, and his sons and all his servants slept without posting a sentry or taking any precautions. The Misimiani, infuriated by the treatment of their representatives, stole to the tents in the middle of the night and slew Soterichus, his children, and almost all the rest; for even after the first alarm had spread, very few of them, heavy as they were with slumber and impeded with blankets, succeeded in escaping.

After this outrage—it can hardly be called anything but an outrage, as it so far exceeded its provocation—the Misimiani felt that they had taken an irretrievable step, and saw that nothing was left but to seek the protection of the great enemy of the Empire. Nachoragan honoured their emissaries with a gratifying reception when they repaired to him in Iberia after his signal defeat at Phasis.

In spring the Romans determined to avenge the death of Soterichus and those who shared his fate. Buzes and Justin were left in the Island to protect Lazica, while four thousand soldiers were sent to the land of the Misimiani. Martin himself was soon to follow them. But when they reached the friendly country of Apsilia, through which their way lay, they found that the Persians had anticipated them, and sent troops to defend the land of their new allies. Not wishing to face the combined forces of the Misimiani and the Persians, the Romans spent the summer in the Apsilian fortresses, waiting until the Persians should retire. They retired on the approach of winter to Iberia and Cotaisis, and as Martin was hindered by illness from assuming the command, the Romans entered the borders of the Misimiani under two leaders of less note. Before proceeding to hostilities they sent an embassy of Apsilians, if perchance the renegade people would consent to submit themselves and restore the money they had taken from the tent of Soterichus. The reply of the Misimiani was the commission of a new outrage; they slaughtered the ambassadors. It might have been thought that after the departure of their allies they would have been glad to avoid the risks of waging war with a superior enemy; but the secret of their confidence lay in the wildness and difficulty of their territory, whose approach was protected by a mountain, which, though not high, was almost perpendicular and provided with only one narrow pass. The Romans, however, crossed it and entered the wide plains, before the dilatory barbarians had taken precautions to defend it. The Misimiani then retreated into a strong fort called Tzachar, or, from its impregnable strength, the "iron" fort.

About forty of the Roman cavalry, who happened to be riding apart from the main body, were suddenly attacked by six hundred of the enemy. The few horse soldiers, all of whom were picked men, ascended a small hill, and performed wonderful deeds of valour, suddenly rushing down on the barbarians and reascending as swiftly to their position on the summit. On the appearance of the rest of the Roman troops on the top of a neighbouring hill, the Misimiani, supposing that the apparent accident was a concerted plan, took flight. The whole army pursued, and only eighty of the six hundred reached the secure refuge of Tzachar.

The Roman commanders, however, were neither harmonious nor energetic; they encamped in the vicinity of the fort, but not near enough to beleaguer it. Martin, on receiving tidings of the state of affairs, sent John Dacnas (who succeeded Rusticus as the distributer of imperial rewards to brave soldiers) to take the supreme command, and he, on his arrival, immediately instituted a strict blockade of the fortress.

Outside the actual walls of Tzachar, on a neighbouring rock perched amid precipitous ravines, were some dwellings, accessible only by a secret path. The inhabitants used to descend at night to draw water from a spring at the foot of the hill; and a certain Illus, who, it is hardly necessary to add, was an Isaurian, concealed himself close to the spot, and when the water-drawers ascended followed in their tracks. He noted carefully the direction of the path, and observed that only eight men were set to guard it. The general was informed of the discovery, and on the ensuing night a body of one hundred men made the steep ascent. Illus led the way, and was followed by Ziper, the squire of Marcellinus, after whom came Leontius the son of Dabragezas, and Theodore the captain of the Tzani :—

"When they had advanced more than half-way, the foremost saw distinctly the watch-fire burning, and the guards themselves reclining very close to it; seven of them were clearly asleep, and snored as they lay. Only one, leaning on his arm, had the attitude of one awake, and he too was overcome by sleepiness, and his head was heavy; nor was it yet evident what the result would be, as he was constantly nodding and then shaking himself up. At this juncture Leontius slipped in a miry place and fell; the fall broke his shield. At the loud clatter caused thereby all the watch leaped up in a state of terror and sat on their pallets; having drawn their swords they looked about everywhere, craning their necks, but they could not conjecture what it was that had happened. Illuminated themselves by the fire, they could not see the men who were standing in the gloom, and the noise, having fallen on their ears in sleep, was not quite clear or distinct enough to betray its cause, the fall of arms. The Romans, on the other hand, could see every detail of the scene. They halted, and stood as noiseless as if they were rooted to the earth; not the sound of a whisper passed their lips, not the slightest motion agitated their feet; they stood firm and fixed on whatever spot, whether a sharp stone or a bramble, they had chanced to step. Had they not done so, and had the sentinels received the least intimation of their presence, a huge stone would certainly have been dislodged and rolled down the steep to crush the advancing party. So they stood without motion of voice or body, even holding in and husbanding their breath. . . . The barbarians, perceiving no sign of danger, soon returned again to the pleasant occupation of slumber.

"Then the Romans advanced on them in their sleep and slew all, including the 'half-waking' man, as one might call him in jest. Then they proceeded fearlessly and scattered themselves about the streets of the village, and the trumpet sounded the battle-call. When the Misimiani heard this they were dumbfounded, and, not comprehending the situation, they arose and prepared to go into their neighbours' houses and assemble together. The Romans met them at the doors of their houses and received them with the salutation of the sword; the slaughter was enormous. Some had already emerged and been despatched, others were just on the thresholds, and others yet were to follow and meet the same doom. The horror had no pause, for all pressed on to reach the street. Even the women, who had risen from their beds and rushed shrieking to the doors, were not spared by the Romans in their anger, but were ruthlessly slaughtered in retribution for the outrage committed by the men. Conspicuous among them was one comely woman, who came with a lighted torch, but even she was pierced in the stomach with a lance and perished pitiably, while one of the Romans seized the brand and set fire to the dwellings, which, built of straw and wood, were soon consumed. The flames mounted so high that the Apsilian nation, and tribes still further off, saw it and learned what had happened" (Agathias, iv. 18, 19).

We need not follow the distressing scene further. It is enough to remark that the historian expresses strong indignation at the massacre of the infants, who had no participation in the iniquities of their parents, and regards the reverse which a few hours later befell the invaders as a retribution of this cruelty.

About dawn the victorious party, stained with the blood of their enemies, rested amid the smouldering ruins of the village, thinking it superfluous to set a watch. Five hundred well-armed Misimiani issued from the fort and surprised them in their security; some Romans were slain, and all the rest, rushing in wild consternation down the steep and stony ascent, reached the camp with wounds and bruises. After this all thought of holding the rock was abandoned, and the forces of the army were concentrated against the wall of the fort. The foss was filled up, siege machines were set in operation, and the garrison was hard pressed. A diversion was caused by an attack on the palisades of the Roman camp; the enemy moved a *spalion* against it, but a javelin cast by a Slavonic soldier, Svarunes, inflicted a mortal wound on the foremost assailant, and caused the collapse of the engine.

Despairing of receiving any assistance from the Persians, and unable to cope with the superior skill and power of the Romans, the Misimiani decided to yield. Their ambassadors implored John Daenas not to exterminate their race, reminding him that they were Christians, and confessing in accents of repentance their "uncivilised folly"; they had now been punished with more than adequate severity for their transgression. John gladly acceded to their supplication, their hostages were accepted, the money of which the tent of Soterichus had been rifled was restored,[1] and the penitent nation was pardoned. Only thirty men of the Roman army, which immediately returned to Colchis, were killed in this campaign.

Soon after this, apparently in the spring of 555, Martin was superseded in his command in Armenia and Colchis, and Justin appointed in his stead. The term of Justin's command was marked by no hostilities, for Chosroes, who, in consequence of the defeat at Phasis, had flayed alive the general Nachoragan, decided that it would be inexpedient to continue the war in a distant country which the enemy, being masters of the sea, could reach without difficulty, while his own armies were obliged to accomplish a long journey through desert regions. Isdigunas, also called Zich, was sent to Constantinople, and a provisional treaty was concluded on the terms that things were to remain *in statu quo*, the two parties retaining their respective possessions, cities or forts, in Lazica.

I have dwelt on the details of these wars at some length, partly because Gibbon has passed over them lightly as undeserving of the attention of posterity. But the idea of writing history for its own sake was strange to Gibbon, and in any case the operations in Lazica concerned serious interests. The question was at stake whether the great Asiatic power was to have access to the Euxine, and these operations decided that on the waters of that sea the Romans were to remain without rivals.

The conclusion of a fifty years' peace in 562 between

---

[1] 28,800 nomismata or solidi; about £18,000.

Rome and Persia forms the natural termination of this chapter. Peter the Patrician, as the delegate of Justinian, and Isdigunas, as the delegate of Chosroes, met on the frontiers of the realm to arrange conditions of peace.[1] The Persian monarch desired that the term of its duration should be long, and that the Romans should pay at once a sum of money equivalent to the total amount of large annual payments for thirty or forty years; the Romans, on the other hand, wished to fix a shorter term. The result of the negotiations was a compromise. A treaty was made for fifty years, the Roman government undertaking to pay the Persians at the rate of 30,000 aurei (£18,750) annually. The total amount due during the first seven years was to be paid at once, and at the beginning of the eighth year the Persian claim for the three ensuing years was to be satisfied. From the tenth year forward the payments were to be annual. The inscription of the Persian document, which ratified the compact, was as follows:—

"The divine, good, pacific, ancient Chosroes, king of kings, fortunate, pious, beneficent, to whom the gods have given great fortune and great empire, the giant of giants, who is formed in the image of the gods, to Justinian Caesar our brother."

The style of this address, compared with the most imposing list of Justinian's titles, illustrates the difference between the oriental insanity of an Asiatic despot and the vanity of a Roman Emperor, which, even when it becomes intemperate, remains sane.

It will be instructive to enumerate the articles of the treaty, as they show the sort of questions that arose between the two powers:—

(1.) The Persians were bound to prevent Huns, Alans, and other barbarians from traversing the pass of Chorutzon (or Tzur) or that of the Caspian gates with a view to depredation in Roman territory; while the Romans were bound not to send an army to those regions or to any other parts of the Persian territory. (2.) The Saracen allies of both States were included in this peace. (3.) Roman and Persian merchants, whatever their wares, were to carry on their traffic by certain prescribed routes, where custom-houses were stationed, and by no others. (4.) Ambassadors between the two States were to have the privilege of making use of the public posts, and their baggage was not to be subjected to custom duties.

---

[1] Our source for these transactions is Menander Protector, fr. 11, ed. Müller (*F. H. G.* iv.)

(5.) Provision was made that Saracen or other traders should not smuggle goods into either Empire by out-of-the-way roads ; Daras and Nisibis were named as the two great emporia where these barbarians were to sell their wares.[1] (6.) Henceforward the migration of individuals from the territory of one State into that of the other was not to be permitted ; but such as had deserted during the war were allowed to return if they wished. (7.) Disputes between Romans and Persians were to be settled—if the accused failed to satisfy the claim of the plaintiff—by a committee of men who were to meet on the frontiers in the presence of both a Roman and a Persian governor. (8.) To prevent dissension, both States bound themselves to refrain from fortifying towns in proximity to the frontier. (9.) Neither State was to harry or attack any of the subject tribes or nations of its neighbour. (10.) The Romans engaged not to place a large garrison in Daras, and also that the *magister militum* of the East[2] should not be stationed there ; if any injury in the neighbourhood of that city were inflicted on Persian soil, the governor of Daras was to pay the costs. (11.) In the case of any treacherous dealing, as distinct from open violence, which threatened to disturb the peace, the judges on the frontier were to investigate the matter, and if their decision was insufficient, it was to be referred to the master of soldiers in the East ; the final appeal was to be made to the sovereign of the injured person. (12.) Curses were imprecated on the party that should violate the peace. (13.) The term of the peace was fixed for fifty years.

A codicil to the treaty provided for the toleration of the Christians and their rites of burial in the Persian kingdom. They were to enjoy immunity from the persecution of the magi, and, on the other hand, they were to refrain from proselytising. One small question remained still undecided, the question of Suania, which both Persians and Romans claimed as a dependency ; but, although it continued to form the subject of tedious negotiations, it was not allowed to interfere with the concluding of the peace.

---

[1] The word for smuggling is κλεπτοτελωνεῖν.

[2] In both these cases the same expression is used, τὸν τῆς ἕω στρατηγόν, and must refer to the same officer. The Latin translation in Müller's edition is misleading, if not positively erroneous ; in the first place the words are rendered *dux orientis*, in the second place *praefectum orientis*, which would naturally mean the praetorian prefect of the East. The reference of legal disputes to the master of soldiers is noteworthy.

CHAPTER X

THE LATER YEARS OF JUSTINIAN'S REIGN

JUSTINIAN'S policy aimed not only at extending the limits of the Empire in the West at the cost of German nations, but also at diffusing his influence among minor peoples and tribes on other frontiers. In fact he pursued an *imperial* policy, in the modern sense of the term. Lazica became dependent on the Empire, and the appointment of a Lazic king rested with his suzerain the Emperor. The Tzani and the Apsilians occupied a similar position. Conversion to Christianity usually attended the establishment of such relations. Justinian had the glory of superintending the baptism of Gretes, king of the Heruls, and Gordas, king of the Huns, who lived near Bosporus [1]; he had the privilege of converting the Abasgians and the Nobadae to the true religion, and of sending a bishop and clergy to the king of the Axumites. It is recorded that Zamanarzus, the king of the Iberians, came to Constantinople and was admitted to Justinian's friendship, and Theodora presented his wife with pearl ornaments.[2]

An event occurred which increased Roman influence in southern Arabia. Roman merchants bound for the land of Abyssinia were obliged to pass through the kingdom of the Homerites or Himyarites, which was ruled by Damian in the early part of Justinian's reign. Damian adopted the imprudent policy of plundering and slaying the traders who passed

---

[1] Theophanes, *Chron. ad* 6020 A.M. (527, 528 A.D.) As to the Tzani, cf. Nov. xxxi. (ed. Zachariä) 535 A.D., ἡ Τζάνων χώρα νῦν πρῶτον ἐφ' ἡμῶν ὑπὸ 'Ρωμαίων κατακτηθεῖσα.

[2] *Ib.* 6027 A.M. (534, 535 A.D.) This gift reminds us that Theodora herself is represented as adorned with pearls in the well-known mosaic in San Vitale at Ravenna.

through his dominions, and the consequence was that the commerce between the Empire and Abyssinia ceased. Then Adad, the king of Axum (as Abyssinia was called), said to Damian, "You have injured my kingdom"; and they made war. And Adad said, "If I defeat the Homerites, I will become a Christian." He took Damian alive, and subdued the land of Yemen. True to his promise, he besought Justinian to send him a bishop and clergy, and an Abyssinian church was founded.[1]

Less promising converts to Christianity were the Heruls, proverbially notorious for brutish habits and stupidity,[2] who had first sought an asylum with the Gepids, but were soon driven away on account of their intolerable manners. Then admitted into the Empire by Anastasius, they incurred his resentment and chastisement. Justinian made corps of Heruls a standing part of his army.

In the year 548 four envoys arrived at Constantinople from the Goths of Crimea, who are known as the Tetraxite Goths, to request Justinian to send them a new bishop, as their bishop had died. These Goths were presumably converted in the fourth century, and not joining in the westward movement of the other tribes of their nationality, lived quietly in a secluded nook in the peninsula of Bosporus and Cherson. Their religion no longer possessed the distinctive marks of Arianism, though originally they were Arians. Procopius says that their religion was simple and pious.[3] Thus in the Crimea, where Justinian had already made the city of Bosporus an imperial dependency, the Tetraxite Goths acknowledged his supremacy.

There was some reason for the fears of Chosroes, and for the words which Procopius puts into the mouth of the Armenian ambassadors concerning Justinian, "The whole world does not contain him,"—and that was in 539. At that time, as the ambassadors said, besides having subdued Africa and Sicily and almost subdued Italy, he had imposed the yoke of servitude on

---

[1] Theophanes, *Chron. ad* 6035 A.M. (542, 543 A.D.) Theophanes calls the realm of Axum ἡ ἐνδοτέρα Ἰνδία. Coins show that Greek was known in the country for some time after the introduction of Christianity, and disappeared only about the seventh century. Aurelian conquered the Axumites (Vopiscus. 33, 4). On the "Axumitic Kingdom," see an essay by Dillmann in the *Abhandlungen der Berliner Akademie*, 1878.

[2] *See* Procopius, *B. G.* ii. 14.

[3] *Ib.* iv. 4.

the Tzani and the yoke of tribute on the Armenians; he had set a Roman *dux* over "the king of the wretched Lazi"; he had sent military governors to the Bosporites, who were formerly subject to the Huns, and had added a city to his sway; he had made an alliance with the Ethiopians; the Homerites and the Red Sea were included in his rule, and the land of palms (ὁ Φοινικῶν). Before he died he had completely reduced Italy, as well as the islands of Corsica and Sardinia, and he had recovered a portion of Spain for the Roman Empire. The Franks, however, ceased to revere the Empire as they had been wont, and began to coin their own gold money without the Emperor's image, although no other barbarian king, not even the Sassanid, was permitted, according to Procopius, by the conditions of commerce, to impress his own effigy on gold coins.[1]

It has already been noticed that a medieval gloom pervades the second period of this reign, and affects the Emperor, who applies himself more and more to the ecclesiastical side of his policy. The observations of Agathias on this later character, with special reference to military affairs, are instructive[2]:—

"When the Emperor conquered all Italy and Libya, and waged successfully those mighty wars, and of the princes who reigned at Constantinople was the first to show himself an absolute sovereign in fact as well as in name—after these things had been achieved by him in his youth and vigour, and when he entered on the last stage of life, he seemed to be weary of labours,[3] and preferred to create discord among his foes or to mollify them with gifts, and so keep off their hostilities, instead of trusting in his own forces and shrinking from no danger. He consequently allowed the troops to decline in strength, because he expected that he would not require their services. And those who were second to himself in authority, on whom it was incumbent to collect the taxes and supply the army with necessary provisions, were infected with the same indifference, and either openly kept back the rations altogether or paid them long after they were due; and when the debt was paid at last, persons skilled in the rascally science of arithmetic demanded back from the soldiers what had been given them. It was their privilege to bring various

---

[1] Proc. *B. G.* iii. 33.
[2] Bk. v. 14. Complaints of Justinian's treatment of the army, substantially agreeing with this passage of Agathias, will be found in the *Secret History*, cap. 24, where it is mentioned that the logothetae stopped promotion.
[3] Compare what Menander says in fr. 4, but it is probable that his statement of Justinian's ῥᾳθυμία rests on this passage of Agathias.

charges against the soldiers, and deprive them of their food. . . . Thus the army was neglected, and the soldiers, pressed by hunger, left their profession to embrace other modes of life."

Thus the decay of the army was one of the chief characteristics of this period. The Asiatic provinces were slowly recovering after the plague; the Balkan provinces were subject to the constant irruptions of barbarians; and all were oppressed by the severe fiscal system, which the execution of Justinian's designs in the West did not permit him to relax. The establishment of monopolies, which was a feature of his policy, aimed at increasing his revenues, without regard to their effects on trade; nevertheless he encouraged commerce, and the wars which were carried on in Persia probably concerned mercantile interests a great deal more than historians indicate. Although John of Cappadocia partially did away with the *cursus publicus*, the Emperor was active in improving roads and constructing bridges in the provinces, thereby facilitating commerce; but he seems to have made the custom duties at Abydos and at the entrance to the Euxine heavier, and perhaps even farmed this source of revenue.

Justinian's reign is notable in the history of industry for the introduction of silk manufacture into Europe.[1] Certain monks arrived from India and sought an interview with the Emperor. They informed him that, having lived long in Serinda (China), they had learned a method by which silk could be made in the Roman Empire, so that the Romans would no longer be obliged to obtain the precious material through their enemies the Persians. The liberal promises of Justinian induced them to return to "India," and they succeeded in bringing back safely eggs of silkworms. Some years later, when the Turks came to the court of Justinian's successor, they were surprised when they were shown the silk manufactories, "for at that time they possessed all the markets and harbours of the Chinese."[2]

There has probably never been a period in which more public works were executed than the reign of Justinian. New towns were founded, innumerable churches were erected, aque-

---

[1] See Procopius, *B. G.* iv. 17. Theophanes of Byzantium tells a different story (fr. 3). According to him, a Persian from China brought the "sperm of the worms in a hollow wand" (narthex) to Byzantium.

[2] Theophanes Byz. *ib.* I do not attempt to discuss the relation of the Turks and the Seres.

ducts were constructed,[1] bridges were built; cities were fortified, extended, or restored and enriched with new baths and palaces; the mere enumeration of these results of Justinian's activity would fill pages.[2] It may be doubted whether the expenses which he thus incurred would be justified by the rules of a prudent economy; his "mania" for building certainly furnished a ground of complaint for the party of opposition to use against him. Yet his works, both secular and sacred, were useful, and under ordinary conditions should have contributed to the prosperity of the Empire. New roads and secure bridges facilitated commerce, aqueducts and fortifications provided for the health and the safety of the inhabitants, while the erection of churches by the Emperor tended to strengthen the ties between the provinces and the central government. The enormous outlay on the building of St. Sophia, the creation of Anthemius, needs no justification.

Earthquakes were frequent in the days of Justinian, who did his utmost to alleviate their effects. Antioch suffered in 526, Pompeiopolis in 536, Cyzicus in 543. In 551 there were great physical disturbances in Greece; 4000 inhabitants were engulfed at Patrae. Three years later an earthquake destroyed many cities both in the islands and on the mainland, causing great loss of life. Among the rest, it reduced to ruin Berytus, then "the pride (ἐγκαλλώπισμα) of Phoenicia," and hardly a trace of that city's splendid buildings was left. Berytus was the seat of a law school, and many educated strangers who had gone thither to study law perished, so that the misfortune was unusually tragic. While the city was being rebuilt, the professors of law (ὑφηγηταί) lectured in Sidon. This earthquake was so severe that a slight shock was felt even at Alexandria, where the historian Agathias was sojourning at the time.[3] All the inhabitants were terrified at the unwonted sensation, and none

---

[1] At Trapezus, Nicaea, Perinthus, Libyan Ptolemais, and Alexandria. The aqueduct at Alexandria is mentioned by Malalas. Justinian strengthened the corn magazine at Alexandria; a strong building was necessary, as in times of scarcity the populace tried to storm it. Caesarea in Cappadocia was improved by a change in the fortifications. Nicomedia and Nicaea were enriched with new buildings. Next to St. Sophia, the most important church which Justinian erected in the East was that of the Virgin at Jerusalem (Proc. de Aed. v. 6).

[2] See the work of Procopius in Six Books περὶ κτισμάτων (de Aedificiis).

[3] Agath. ii. 15.

remained in the houses. Although the shock was slight, there was some reason for their terror, as the houses at Alexandria were of very unsubstantial structure. The island of Cos suffered more than any other tract of land. Agathias visited it in returning from Alexandria to Constantinople, and found it in a state of utter desolation. Three years later another earthquake visited the region of Byzantium and threatened to destroy the whole city. It was peculiarly severe both in violence and duration, and Agathias gives us a vivid account of its horrors and moral effects. The only victim of distinction was the curator of the palace, Anatolius, who perished by the fall of a marble slab fixed in the wall close to his bed. I mention this for the sake of Agathias' comment. Many people said that it was a providential punishment of Anatolius for acts of injustice and oppression. "I doubt it," said Agathias,[1] "for an earthquake would be a most desirable and excellent thing if it knew how to discriminate the bad from the good, slaying those and passing these by. But, even granting that he was unjust, there were many more like him, and worse, who escaped unharmed. And besides," he adds, " if Plato is right, the man who is punished in this life is more fortunate than he who is allowed to live in his sins."

As Justinian grew old and weak and had no issue, an element which affected political life in Constantinople was the question of the succession to the throne. It led to a sort of party rivalry between the relations of Theodora and the relations of Justinian; and the difficulty was ultimately solved by the marriage of Sophia, Theodora's niece, with Justin, Justinian's nephew. While she was alive Theodora had looked with disfavour on Justinian's kin.[2] She died in 548 (27th June), and perhaps it was the loss of her that clouded the spirits and depressed the energy of the Emperor in his later years.

The conspiracy which was formed against the life of the Emperor in 548 was of no serious political importance; it was organised by a pair of dissatisfied Armenians, who owed

---

[1] v. 3.
[2] The statement of the *Secret History* that she hated Germanus and prevented his sons from marrying is quite credible (cap. 5).

Justinian a personal grudge.[1] Artabanes, the commander in Africa, had overthrown the usurper Gontharis and delivered from his hands the Emperor's niece Praejecta, whose husband Areobindus had been put to death by the tyrant. From gratitude, not from love, Praejecta consented to become the wife of Artabanes, who aspired to an alliance with the imperial house; and the count of Africa hastened to surrender the newly conferred dignity and obtain his recall from Justinian, that he might return to Constantinople, whither Praejecta had preceded him, and celebrate the marriage. He was received with open arms in the capital; he became *magister militum in praesenti* and captain of the *foederati*; his tall and dignified stature, his concise speech, and his generosity won the admiration of all. But an unexpected obstacle to the proposed marriage occurred in the person of a previous wife, whom he had put away many years before. As long as Artabanes was an obscure individual, the lady was contented to leave him in peace and give no sign of her existence; but when he suddenly rose to fame, she determined to assert her conjugal rights, and, as a wronged woman, she implored the aid of Theodora. The Empress, "whose nature it was to undertake the cause of injured women," compelled the unwilling master of soldiers to take his wife once more to his bosom, and Praejecta became the bride of John, the son of Pompeius and grandson of the Emperor Anastasius. Shortly after this the Empress died, and Artabanes immediately put away for the second time his unwelcome wife, but Praejecta was lost to him, and he nourished a grudge against the Emperor.

Had it depended only on himself, Artabanes would never have undertaken any sinister design, but a countryman of his, named Arsaces, a descendant of the Parthian Arsacidae, was animated with a bitter desire of revenge upon Justinian, who had inflicted a comparatively light punishment on him for treacherous correspondence with Chosroes; and he diligently fanned into flame the less eager feelings of Artabanes. He reminded him that he had lost the bride he desired and been obliged to submit to the presence of the wife he hated; he urged the facility of despatching Justinian, "who is accustomed to sit without guards in the Museum, in the company

---

[1] Our source for this conspiracy is Procopius, *B. G.* iii. 31, 32.

of old priests, till late hours of the night, deep in the study of the holy books of the Christians." Above all, he expressed his conviction that Germanus would readily take part in such a conspiracy. For Boraides, the brother of Germanus, had on his death left almost all his property to his brother, allowing his wife and daughter to receive only as much as was legally necessary. But Justinian had altered the will so as to favour the daughter, and this was felt by Germanus, her uncle, as a grievance.

When he had won Artabanes to his plan, Arsaces opened communications with Justin, the eldest son of Germanus. Having bound him by oath not to reveal the conversation to any person except his father, he enlarged on the manner in which the Emperor ill treated and passed over his relations, and expressed his conviction that it would go still harder with them when Belisarius arrived. He did not hesitate to reveal the plan of assassination which he had formed in conjunction with Artabanes and Chanaranges, a young and frivolous Armenian who had been admitted to their counsels.

Justin, terrified at this revelation, laid it before his father, who immediately consulted with Marcellus, the prefect of the palatine guards, as to whether it would be wise to inform the Emperor immediately. Marcellus, an honourable, austere, and wary man, dissuaded Germanus from taking that course, on the ground that such a communication, necessitating a private interview with the Emperor, would inevitably become known to the conspirators and lead to Arsaces' escape. He proposed to investigate the matter himself beforehand, and it was arranged that Arsaces should be lured to speak in the presence of a concealed witness. Justin appointed a day and hour for an interview between Germanus and Arsaces, and the compromising revelations were overheard by Leontius, a friend of Marcellus, who was hidden behind a cloth screen. The programme of the matured plot was to wait for the arrival of Belisarius and slay the Emperor and his general at the same time; for if Justinian were slain beforehand, the revolutionists might not be able to contend against the military forces of Belisarius. When the deed was done, Germanus was to be proclaimed Emperor.

Marcellus still hesitated to reveal the plot to the Emperor, out of friendship or pity for Artabanes. But when Belisarius was drawing nigh to the capital, he could hesitate no longer, and Justinian ordered the conspirators to be arrested. Germanus and Justin were at first not exempted from suspicion, but when the senate inquired into the case, the testimony of Marcellus and Leontius, and two other officers to whom Germanus had prudently disclosed the affair, completely cleared them. Even then Justinian was still indignant that they had concealed the treason so long, and was not mollified until the candid Marcellus took all the blame of the delay upon himself. The conspirators were treated with clemency, being confined in the palace and not in the public prison. It is to be concluded from the words of Procopius, which are not express, that they were ultimately pardoned.

The policy of Justinian in playing off one barbarian people against another is well exemplified in his dealings with the Cotrigur and Utrigur Huns,[1] who dwelt on the northern shores of the Euxine. It appears that the Gepids called in the help of the former against their neighbours and rivals the Lombards. Twelve thousand Cotrigurs, under the warrior Chinialus, answered the call, and arrived a year before the truce which existed between the Gepids and their foes had expired. The Gepids persuaded their guests to occupy the interval by invading the provinces of the Empire. Justinian, who was in the habit of allowing large donations both to the Cotriguri and Utriguri, sent a message to Sandichl, the chief of the latter, and chid him for his supineness in allowing his neighbours to advance against the Empire. New gifts induced the Utriguri to march against the land of the invaders, and the Roman allies were reinforced by two thousand Tetraxite Goths. The Cotrigur Huns were defeated with great slaughter in their own territory; their wives and children were led captive beyond the river Tanais, which separated the two countries, and many thousand prisoners, who languished in slavery, were enabled to escape. The invaders then withdrew beyond the Roman borders, having received a sum of money from the Roman captain Aratius; but two thousand Huns,[2] who had fled before the Utrigurs, threw

---

[1] Also written Coturguri and Uturguri. See Procopius, B. G. iv. cap. 18, 19.

[2] One of their leaders was Sinnio, who had served with Belisarius in the Vandalic war.

themselves on the mercy of the Emperor and were graciously allowed to settle in a district of Thrace. The news of this clemency exasperated the Utrigurs; Sandichl sent envoys to remonstrate, but the gifts and soft words of Justinian appeased their resentment.

A great invasion of the Cotrigur Huns, under Zabergan, took place in the last months of 558.[1] The real motive, as Agathias remarks, was the greed of an uncivilised barbarian, though Zabergan cloaked it with the complaint that the Emperor had been friendly with Sandichl, the king of the Utrigur Huns. The invader crossed the frozen Danube, and, passing unopposed through Scythia and Moesia, entered Thrace, where he divided his hordes into three armies. One was sent westward to Greece, to ravage the unprotected country, the second was sent into the Thracian Chersonese to capture the towns of Aphrodisias, Thescus, Ciberis, Sestos, and the ugly little Kallipolis, which belied its name, and to seize ships and cross to Abydos; the third army, consisting of seven thousand cavalry, marched under Zabergan himself to Constantinople.

The terrible ravages and cruelties committed by the third and main body are thus described by the contemporary writer Agathias:—

"As no resistance was offered to their course, they overran and plundered everything mercilessly, obtaining a great booty and large numbers of captives. Among the rest, well-born women of chaste life were most cruelly carried off to undergo the worst of all misfortunes, and minister to the unbridled lust of the barbarians; some who in early youth had renounced marriage and the cares and pleasures of this life, and had immured themselves in some religious retreat, deeming it of the highest importance to be free from cohabitation with men, were dragged from the chambers of their virginity and violated. Many married women who happened to be pregnant were dragged away, and when their hour was come brought forth children on the march, unable to conceal their throes, or to take up and swaddle the new-born babes; they were hauled along, in spite of all, hardly allowed even time to suffer, and the wretched infants were left where they fell, a prey for dogs and birds, as though this were the purpose of their appearance in the world.

"To such a pass had the Roman Empire come that, even within the

---

[1] The Huns were almost a whole year in Roman territory (Agath. v. ii. *sqq.*) See Clinton, *F. R. ad* 559 A.D.; but the date is doubtful, *see* above, note, p. 454.

precincts of the districts surrounding the imperial city, a *very small* number of barbarians committed such enormities. Their audacity went so far as to pass the long walls and approach the inner fortifications. For time and neglect had in many places dilapidated the great wall, and other parts were easily thrown down by the barbarians, as there was nought to repel them—no military garrison, no engines of defence, nor persons to employ such. Not even the bark of a dog was to be heard ; the wall was less efficiently protected than a pig-sty or sheep-cot. For the Roman armies had not continued so numerous as in the days of ancient Emperors, but had dwindled to a small number, and no longer were sufficient for the size of the State. The whole force should have been six hundred and forty-five thousand fighting men, but actually it hardly amounted to one hundred and fifty thousand. And of these, some were in Italy, others in Africa, others in Spain, others in Colchis, others at Alexandria and in the Thebaid, a few on the Persian frontier (where only a few were needed on account of the peace)."

The Huns encamped at Melantias, a village on the small river Athyras, which flows into the Propontis. Their proximity created a panic in Constantinople, whose inhabitants saw imminent the horrors of sieges, conflagrations, and famine. The terror was not confined to the lower classes ; the nobles trembled in their palaces, the Emperor was alarmed on his throne. All the treasures of the churches, which were scattered in the tract of country included between the Euxine and the Golden Horn, were either carted into the city or shipped to the Asiatic side of the Bosphorus. The undisciplined corps of the Scholarian guards, ignorant of real warfare, who were supposed to defend the gates, did not inspire the citizens with much confidence.

On this critical occasion Justinian appealed to his veteran general Belisarius to save the seat of empire. In spite of his years and feebleness Belisarius put on his helmet and cuirass once more, and he won greater glory among the men of his time by saving New Rome on the Bosphorus than he had won by recovering Old Rome on the Tiber. He relied chiefly on a small body of three hundred men who had fought with him in Italy ; the other troops that he mustered knew nothing of war, and they were more for appearance than for action. The peasants who had fled before the barbarians from their ravaged homesteads in Thrace accompanied the little army. He encamped at the village of Chettus, and employed the peasants in the congenial work of digging a wide trench round the camp. Spies were sent out to discover the numbers of the enemy, and at night a large number of beacons were kindled in the plain with the purpose of misleading the Huns as to the number of the forces sent out against them. For a while they were misled, but it was soon known that the Roman army was small, and two thousand cavalry selected by Zabergan rode forth to annihilate it. The spies informed Belisarius of the enemy's approach, and he made a skilful disposition of his troops. He concealed two hundred peltasts and javelin-men in the woods on either side of the plain, close to the place where he expected the attack of the barbarians; the ambuscaders, at a given signal, were to shower their missiles on the hostile ranks. The object of this was to compel the lines of the enemy to close in, in order to avoid the javelins on the flank, and thus to render their superior numbers useless through inability to deploy. Belisarius himself headed the rest of the army; in the rear followed the rustics, who were not to engage in the battle, but were to accompany it with loud shouts and cause a clatter with wooden beams, which they carried for that purpose.

All fell out as Belisarius had planned. The Huns, pressed by the peltasts, thronged together, and were hindered both from using their bows and arrows with effect, and from circumventing the Roman wings. The noise of the rustics in the rear, combined with the attack on the flanks, gave the foe the impression that the Roman army was immense, and that they were being surrounded; clouds of dust obscured the real situation, and the barbarians turned and fled. Four hundred perished before they reached their camp at Melantias, while not a single Roman was mortally wounded. The camp was immediately abandoned, and all the Huns hurried away, imagining that the victors were still on their track. But by the Emperor's orders Belisarius did not pursue them.

We must now follow the fortunes of the Hunnic troops who were sent against the Chersonese. Germanus, the son of Dorotheus, a native of Prima Justiniana, had been appointed some time previously commandant in that peninsula, and he now proved himself a capable officer. As the Huns could make no breach in the great wall, which shut in the peninsula, and was skilfully defended by the dispositions of Germanus, they resorted to the expedient of manufacturing boats of reeds fastened together in sheaves; each boat was large enough to hold four men; one hundred and fifty were constructed, and six hundred fully armed soldiers embarked secretly in the bay of Aenus (near the mouth of the Hebrus), in order to land on the south-western coast of the Chersonese. Germanus learned the news of their enterprise with delight, and immediately manned twenty galleys with armed men.

The armament of reed-built boats was easily annihilated, not a single barbarian escaping. This success was followed up by an excursion of the Romans from the wall against the army of the dispirited besiegers; the latter abandoned their enterprise and joined Zabergan, who was also retreating after the defeat at Chettus.

Soon after this the other division of the Huns, which had been sent in the direction of Greece, returned without having achieved any signal success. They had not penetrated farther than Thermopylae, where the garrison of the fort that commanded the pass prevented their advance.

Thus, although Thrace, and presumably also Macedonia and Thessaly, suffered terribly from this invasion, Zabergan was unsuccessful in all three points of attack, owing to the ability of Belisarius, Germanus, and the garrison of Thermopylae. Justinian redeemed the captives for a considerable sum of money, and the Cotrigurs retreated beyond the Danube. But the wily Emperor laid a trap for their destruction. He despatched a characteristic letter to Sandichl, the friendly king of the Utrigurs, whose friendship he had cultivated by periodical presents of money. He informed Sandichl that the Cotrigurs had invaded Thrace and carried off all the gold that was destined to enrich the treasury of the Utriguric monarch. "It would have been easy for us," ran the imperial letter, "to have destroyed them utterly, or at least to have sent them empty away. But we did neither one thing nor the other, because we wished to test your sentiments. For if you are really valiant and wise, and not disposed to tolerate the appropriation by others of what belongs to you, you are not losers; for you have nothing to do but punish the enemy and receive from them your money at the sword's point, as though we had sent it to you by their hands." The Emperor further threatened that, if Sandichl proved himself craven enough to let the insult pass, he would transfer his amity to the Cotrigurs. The letter had the desired effect; the seeds of discord were sown; the Utrigurs were stirred up against their neighbours, and a series of ceaseless hostilities wasted the strength of the two nations.[1]

After the repulse of the Huns, Belisarius lived in high honour at Constantinople, but was perhaps an object of suspicion to Justinian. A conspiracy to murder the Emperor was discovered in November 562, and one of the names mentioned by a culprit who confessed was that of the general, now nearly seventy years old. His age did not serve to acquit him of treasonable designs, and he remained in disgrace for eight months, until July 563, when he was restored to favour. The great Patrician died in March 565,[2] his wife, Antonina, who had already passed the age of eighty, surviving him; but his riches passed to Justinian, who died in the following November.[3]

---

[1] A short account of this transaction will be found in a fragment, probably of the Chronicle of Malalas, but included by Müller (*F. H. G.* iv.) in the fragments of John of Antioch,— evidently taken from Agathias. Menander (fr. 3) states that Sandichl promised to deprive the Cotrigurs of their horses, and thereby disable them for the invasion of Roman territory. In 562 there was another invasion of Huns (Theoph. 6054 A.M.) Anastasiopolis was taken by them (April).

[2] For the conspiracy in which Belisarius was said to be implicated, *see* Malalas and Theophanes. The legend that Belisarius ended his days as a blind beggar in the streets of Byzantium is, as has been suggested, possibly due to a confusion with John of Cappadocia, of whom it is related that he begged for pence (Proc. *B. P.* i., ἄρτον ἢ ὀβολὸν ἐκ τῶν προσπιπτόντων). The authorities for the story are lines of Joannes Tzetzes and a passage in the *Antiquitates Constantinopolitanae*, whose author is not known, but perhaps flourished at the beginning of the twelfth century. *See* the second Appendix in Finlay's *History of Greece*, vol. i., where the evidence for, and origin of, the story are discussed. A similar story is told of Symbatius the Armenian, son-in-law of Michael III, in the ninth century; one of his eyes was put out, his right hand cut off, and he was set in a public place with a vessel in his lap to receive the pence of the charitable.

Another legend prevailed in the West as to the end of Belisarius. According to Fredegarius (*Hist. Franc. Epit.* cap. 50), he was slain by the Franks in Italy, and this tale was adopted by Aimoin.

[3] 14th November, *Chron. Pasch.* (and Clinton); 11th November, Theophanes.

END OF VOL. I

Printed by R. & R. CLARK, *Edinburgh*

MESSRS. MACMILLAN AND CO.'S PUBLICATIONS.

Library Edition. Uniform with "The American Commonwealth."
The Holy Roman Empire. By JAMES BRYCE, M.P., D.C.L. Eighth Edition. Library Edition. Demy 8vo. 14s.—Popular Edition. Cr. 8vo. 7s. 6d.

By Rev. A. H. SAYCE, M.A., Hon. LL.D. Dublin, Deputy-Professor of Comparative Philology in the University of Oxford.
The Ancient Empires of the East. Crown 8vo. 6s.
Herodotos.—BOOKS I.-III. **The Ancient Empires of the East.** Edited, with Notes, Introduction, and Appendices, by Professor SAYCE, LL.D. 8vo. 16s.

Livy.—BOOKS I.-IV. Translated by Rev. H. M. STEPHENSON, M.A., late Head-Master of St. Peter's School, York. [*In preparation.*
BOOKS XXI.-XXV. Translated by ALFRED JOHN CHURCH, M.A., of Lincoln College, Oxford, Professor of Latin, University College, London, and WILLIAM JACKSON BRODRIBB, M.A., late Fellow of St. John's College, Cambridge. Crown 8vo. 7s. 6d.

Pliny.—Correspondence with Trajan. C. Plinii Caecilii Secundi Epistulae ad Traianum Imperatorem cum Eiusdem Responsis. Edited, with Notes and Introductory Essays, by E. G. HARDY, M.A., Fellow of Jesus College, Oxford, and formerly Head-Master of Grantham School. 8vo. 10s. 6d.

Polybius.—The Histories of Polybius. Translated from the Text of F. HULTSCH by E. S. SHUCKBURGH, M.A., late Fellow of Emmanuel College, Cambridge. Two vols. Crown 8vo. 24s.

Tacitus.—The Annals. Edited, with Introductions and Notes, by G. O. HOLBROOKE, M.A., Professor of Latin in Trinity College, Hartford, U.S.A. With Maps. 8vo. 16s.
The Histories. Edited, with Introduction and Notes, by Rev. W. A. SPOONER, M.A., Fellow of New College, and H. M. SPOONER, M.A., formerly Fellow of Magdalen College, Oxford. 8vo. [*In the press.*
The Works of Tacitus. Translated by A. J. CHURCH, M.A., and W. J. BRODRIBB. Crown 8vo. The Annals, 7s. 6d. The History, 6s. The Agricola and Germany, with the Dialogue on Oratory, 4s. 6d.

Works by W. T. ARNOLD, M.A.
A Handbook of Latin Epigraphy. [*In preparation.*
The Roman System of Provincial Administration to the Accession of Constantine the Great. Crown 8vo. 6s.
The Second Punic War: being Chapters on the History of Rome. By the late THOMAS ARNOLD, D.D., formerly Head-Master of Rugby School, and Regius Professor of Modern History in the University of Oxford. Edited, with Notes, by W. T. ARNOLD, M.A. With 8 Maps. Crown 8vo. 8s. 6d.

Cults and Monuments of Ancient Athens. By Miss J. E. HARRISON and Mrs. A. W. VERRALL. Illustrated. Crown 8vo. [*Just ready.*
The Attic Orators from Antiphon to Isaeos. By R. C. JEBB, Litt.D., LL.D., Professor of Greek in the University of Cambridge. Two vols. 8vo. 25s.
Ancient Rome in the Light of Recent Discoveries. By RODOLFO LANCIANI, LL.D. (Harv.), Professor of Archaeology in the University of Rome, Director of Excavations for the National Government and the Municipality of Rome, etc. With 100 Illustrations. Small 4to. 24s.
Roman Literature in Relation to Roman Art. By Rev. ROBERT BURN, M.A., Fellow of Trinity College, Cambridge. With numerous Illustrations. Extra Crown 8vo. 14s.

MACMILLAN AND CO., LONDON.

MESSRS. MACMILLAN AND CO.'S PUBLICATIONS

By J. P. MAHAFFY, M.A., D.D., Fellow and Professor of Ancient History in Trinity College, Dublin, and Hon. Fellow of Queen's College, Oxford.

Social Life in Greece; from Homer to Menander. Fifth Edition, Revised and Enlarged. Crown 8vo. 9s.

Greek Life and Thought; from the Age of Alexander to the Roman Conquest. Crown 8vo. 12s. 6d.

Rambles and Studies in Greece. With Illustrations. Third Edition, Revised and Enlarged. With Map. Crown 8vo. 10s. 6d.

Essays in Art and Archaeology. By Sir CHARLES NEWTON, K.C.B., D.C.L., formerly Professor of Archaeology in University College, London, and Keeper of Greek and Roman Antiquities at the British Museum. 8vo. 12s. 6d.

FITZWILLIAM MUSEUM.

Catalogue of Casts in the Museum of Classical Archaeology. By CHARLES WALDSTEIN, Litt.D., Ph.D., LL.D., University Reader in Classical Archaeology, and Director of the Fitzwilliam Museum. Crown 8vo. 1s. 6d.
  *** Also an Edition on Large Paper. Small 4to. 5s.

By EDWARD A. FREEMAN, D.C.L., LL.D., Regius Professor of Modern History in the University of Oxford, etc.

Historical Essays. First Series. Fourth Edition. 8vo. 10s. 6d.
Contents:—The Mythical and Romantic Elements in Early English History—Tl Continuity of English History—The Relations between the Crown of England an Scotland—St. Thomas of Canterbury and his Biographers, etc.

Historical Essays. Second Series. Third Edition, with additional Essay. 8vo. 10s. 6d.
Contents:—Ancient Greece and Mediaeval Italy—Mr. Gladstone's Homer and the Homeri Ages—The Historians of Athens—The Athenian Democracy—Alexander the Great-Greece during the Macedonian Period—Mommsen's History of Rome—Lucius Cornelit Sulla—The Flavian Caesars, etc. etc.

Historical Essays. Third Series. 8vo. 12s.
Contents:—First Impressions of Rome—The Illyrian Emperors and their Land—Augusta Treverorum—The Goths at Ravenna—Race and Language—The Byzantine Empire—First Impressions of Athens—Mediaeval and Modern Greece—The Southern Slaves—Sicilian Cycles—The Normans at Palermo.

Historical and Architectural Sketches; chiefly Italian. Illustrated by the Author. Crown 8vo. 10s. 6d.

Subject and Neighbour Lands of Venice. Being a companion volume to "Historical and Architectural Sketches." With Illustrations. Crown 8vo. 10s. 6d.

English Towns and Districts. A Series of Addresses and Essays. With Illustrations and a Map. 8vo. 14s.

The Methods of Historical Study. Eight Lectures read in the University of Oxford in Michaelmas Term, 1884, with the Inaugural Lecture on "The Office of the Historical Professor." 8vo. 10s. 6d.

The Chief Periods of European History. Six Lectures read in the University of Oxford in Trinity Term, 1885, with an Essay on "Greek Cities under Roman Rule." 8vo. 10s. 6d.

By JOHN RICHARD GREEN, M.A., LL.D., late Honorary Fellow of Jesus College, Oxford.

History of the English People. In four vols. With Maps. 8vo. 16s. each.

The Making of England. With Maps. 8vo. 16s.

The Conquest of England. With Maps and Portrait. 8vo. 18s.

A Short History of the English People. New and Thoroughly Revised Edition. With Coloured Maps, Genealogical Tables, and Chronological Annals. Crown 8vo. 8s. 6d. 148th Thousand.

The American Commonwealth. By JAMES BRYCE, M.P., D.C.L., Regius Professor of Civil Law in the University of Oxford, Author of "The Holy Roman Empire." Three vols. Demy 8vo. 54s.

PART I. The National Government.	PART IV. Public Opinion.
PART II. The State Governments.	PART V. Illustrations and Reflections.
PART III. The Party System.	PART VI. Social Institutions.

By JOHN FISKE, formerly Lecturer on Philosophy at Harvard University.

The Critical Period in American History, 1783-1789. Extra Cr. 8vo. 10s. 6d.

The Beginnings of New England; or, The Puritan Theocracy in its Relations to Civil and Religious Liberty. Crown 8vo. 7s. 6d.

American Political Ideas viewed from the Standpoint of Universal History. Three Lectures delivered at the Royal Institution of Great Britain. Crown 8vo. 4s.

MACMILLAN AND CO., LONDON.

Milton Keynes UK
Ingram Content Group UK Ltd.
UKHW042116220324
439862UK00005B/486